Representing Renaissance art, *c.*1500–*c.*1600

MANCHESTER
1824

Manchester University Press

Representing Renaissance art, *c.*1500–*c.*1600

Catherine E. King

Manchester University Press
Manchester and New York
distributed exclusively in the USA by Palgrave

Published by Manchester University Press
Oxford Road, Manchester M13 9NR, UK
and Room 400, 175 Fifth Avenue, New York, NY 10010, USA
www.manchesteruniversitypress.co.uk

Distributed exclusively in the USA by
Palgrave, 175 Fifth Avenue, New York,
NY 10010, USA

Distributed exclusively in Canada by
UBC Press, University of British Columbia, 2029 West Mall,
Vancouver, BC, Canada V6T 1Z2

British Library Cataloguing-in-Publication Data
A catalogue record for this book is available from the British Library

Library of Congress Cataloging-in-Publication Data applied for

ISBN 978 0 7190 7556 8 *hardback*
ISBN 978 0 7190 7557 5 *paperback*

First published 2007

16 15 14 13 12 11 10 09 08 07 10 9 8 7 6 5 4 3 2 1

Typeset in 10/12pt Ehrhardt
by Graphicraft Limited, Hong Kong

Printed in Great Britain
by Biddles, King's Lynn

Dedicated to Kitty, Louis and Gracie

Contents

List of plates *page* ix
Acknowledgements xix

Introduction 1

1 Painting, sculpture and architecture – Liberal or Practical Arts? 20

2 *Disegno*/design 61

3 New types of commemorative portrayals 103

4 Patron saints as exemplars 146

5 Mercury as protector of artists: from astrology to mythology 191

6 Allegories 236

7 Programmes of decoration for artists' houses 279

Conclusion 317

Bibliography 327
Index 346

Plates

1 Attributed to Andrea Previtali, *Painting as a Practical Art*, 1512, formerly Villa La Zogna, now Villa di Trescore, Bergamo. Copyright Photo Studio Fotografico da Re *page* 22

2 Gerard de Jode, *Temporis utendi*, *c.*1551. Copyright The Trustees of the British Museum 24

3 Barthélémy de Chasseneux, *Catalogus gloriae mundi*, Lyons, 1546, fol. 212 verso. Copyright The British Library 25

4 Jost Amman, Barthélémy de Chasseneux, *Catalogus gloriae mundi*, Frankfurt, 1571. Copyright The British Library 26

5 Michelangelo, *Captive Art*, 1505–42, for tomb of Julius II, Louvre, Paris. Photo RMN Copyright René-Gabriel Ojéda 29

6 Attributed to Giorgione, *Giovanni Borgherini and his Tutor*, *c.*1509, canvas, 47 × 60 cm, National Gallery of Art, Washington. Copyright National Gallery of Art, Washington 30

7 Giulio Romano and Giovanni Francesco Penni, *Painting, Poetry and Sculpture Celebrate the Impresa of Clement VII*, 1524, soffit of a window, Sala di Constantino, Vatican, Rome. Copyright Photo Musei Vaticani 31

8 Attributed to Raffaellino dal Colle, *Fame and Victory of Duke Francesco Maria della Rovere and the Emperor Charles V*, *c.*1530, Villa Imperiale, Pesaro. Copyright Fratelli Alinari 2006 33

9 Giorgio Vasari, vault of the Sala della Fama, 1542, Casa del Vasari, Arezzo. Copyright Index Tavanti 35

10 Giorgio Vasari, *Painting, Sculpture and Architecture present the plans for Saint Peter's to Paul III*, Sala dei Cento Giorni, Palazzo della Cancelleria, 1546, Rome. Copyright Fratelli Alinari 2006 36

11 Giorgio Vasari, final page of *Vite*, 1550. Copyright The British Library 37

12 Philibert de L'Orme and Pierre de Bontemps, *Funerary Urn of François I*, 1550–56, formerly

Notre Dame des Hautes-Bruyères near Rambouillet, now Saint Denis. Copyright Pascal Lemaître 39
13 Frans Floris, *The Awakening of the Arts*, 1559–60, Museo de Arte, Ponce, Puerto Rico. Copyright Museo de Arte, Ponce 40
14 After Frans Floris, *Painting, Sculpture and? Geometry*, over door for the artist's house, painted *c.*1563, engraving signed 'T.G.', Antwerp, 1576, Graphische Sammlung Albertina, Vienna. Copyright Albertina, Wien 41
15 L. van Opstal, the house of Cornelis van Dalem dated 1563, Antwerp, catalogue number A.LXXXV 34 Inv. no. 1915, Museum Plantin-Moretus, Stedelijk Prentenkabinet. Photo Peter Maes 42
16 Drawing for the catafalque of Michelangelo, attributed to Vincenzo Borghini, 1564, Graphische Sammlung, Munich. Copyright Staatliche Graphische Sammlung, Munich 43
17 Giorgio Vasari, *Sculpture, Painting, Architecture, Poetry and Music*, 1574, Casa del Vasari, Florence. Copyright Index Tosi 45
18 Giorgio Vasari, *Painting, Sculpture, Architecture and Music with Geometry, Poetry and Philosophy*, 1555–65, Scrittoio, Palazzo Vecchio, Florence. Copyright Fratelli Alinari 2006 47
19 Giovanni de'Vecchi, *Painting*, 1574–75, Sala del Mappamondo, Caprarola. Copyright Ministero Beni Culturali e Ambientali, Rome 48
20 a and b After Frans Floris, *Poetry and Architecture*, engraving inscribed 'T.G.', Antwerp, 1576, Graphische Sammlung Albertina, Vienna. Copyright Albertina, Wien 50
21 Federico Zuccari, engraved by Cornelis Cort, *The Lament of the Arts*, 1579, Fitzwilliam Museum, Cambridge. Copyright The Fitzwilliam Museum, Cambridge 51
22 Style of Giuseppe Arcimboldo, *'Art man' ennobled in the service of the Emperor*, *c.*1580, The Royal Library, Windsor. Copyright The Royal Collection *c.*2006 Her Majesty Queen Elizabeth II 53
23 Anton Claeissens, *Jupiter (or Mars) and Hercules protect the Seven Liberal Arts and Painting*, 1605, 197.5 × 279 cm, panel, Groeninge Museum, Bruges. Copyright Brugge, Groeninge Museum. Photo Reproductiefonds Vlaamse Musea NV 54

24 Pierre de Bontemps, Drawing after ancient statuary *en plein air*, 1550–56, Funerary urn of François I, Saint Denis, Centre des Monuments Nationaux Basilique. Photo CMN Paris, Copyright Pascal Lemaître 74
25 Benvenuto Cellini, Apollo for the seal of the Accademia del Disegno, 1564–69, pen and wash on paper, 300 × 218 mm, Graphische Sammlung, Munich 78
26 Benvenuto Cellini, Diana for the seal of the Accademia del Disegno, 1564–69, pen and wash on paper, 330 × 218 mm, British Museum, London. Copyright The Trustees of the British Museum 79
27 Giorgio Vasari or his circle, Design as a three headed 'woman', *c.*1565, Collection Anthony Blunt. Copyright Courtauld Art Gallery, London 83
28 Giorgio Vasari, Giotto, *Vite*, 1568. Copyright The British Library 84
29 Giorgio Vasari, *The story of Zeuxis and the Five Maidens of Croton*, *c.*1573, Gabinetto Disegni e Stampe 1180E. Copyright Foto Quattrone 85
30 Federico Zuccari, vault of the Sala del Disegno, 1599, Palazzo Zuccari, Rome. Photo Fototeca Max Planck Institut e Bibliotheca Hertziana 89
31 Andrea Cavalcanti il Buggiano, commemorative portrait of Filippo Brunelleschi, 1447, cathedral, Florence. Fratelli Alinari 2006 106
32 Erhard Schön, portrait of Albrecht Dürer, 1528, woodcut. Copyright Warburg Institute 111
33 Melchior Lorch, portrait of Albrecht Dürer, 1550, engraving. Copyright Warburg Institute 112
34 Giulio Bonasone, portrait of Michelangelo, 1546, engraving. Copyright Warburg Institute 115
35 Giorgio Ghisi portrait of Michelangelo, *c.*1556, engraving. Copyright The Warburg Institute. 116
36 Giorgio Ghisi, portrait of Raphael, *c.*1545, engraving. Copyright The Warburg Institute. 117
37 Attributed to Willem van den Brouck, portraits of Albrecht Dürer and Jan van Eyck, 1563, Museum Vleeshuis, Antwerp. Copyright Museum Vleeishuis Antwerp. 119
38 Lambert Lombard, self-portrait, title page from Dominique Lampsonius, *Lamberti Lombardi apud Eburones pictoris celeberrimi vita*, Bruges, 1565, National Art Library London. Copyright V&A Images/Victoria and Albert Museum 121

39 Giorgio Vasari, *Cosimo de'Medici il Vecchio with his artists*, 1555–56, Sala del Cosimo il Vecchio, Palazzo Vecchio, Florence. Copyright Archivi Alinari Firenze 123
40 Giorgio Vasari, Painting and Sculpture in the pendentives with portrait lunettes below, Sala della Fama, 1542–68, Casa del Vasari, Arezzo. Copyright Index Tavanti 126
41 Anonymous, practitioners of Florentine art, Giotto, Uccello, Donatello, Manetti and Brunelleschi, late fifteenth- or early sixteenth-century, Louvre, Paris. Photo RMN Copyright Daniel Arnaudet 126
42 Hieronymous Cock, commemorative portrait of Jan van Eyck, from *Pictorum aliquot celebrium*, Antwerp, 1572. Copyright The British Library 128
43 Lavinia Fontana, self-portrait, 1579, copper, 15 cm diameter, Uffizi, Florence. Copyright Fratelli Alinari 2006 130
44 Jan van der Straet, *The invention of oil painting by Van Eyck*, engraving, 1590–95. Copyright The Warburg Institute 131
45 Nicoletto da Modena, *Apeles poeta tacentes*, 1507, engraving. Copyright The Warburg Institute 135
46 The house of Stephan Ziegler, 1545, Sélestat, Alsace. Copyright Photo Hubert Meyer, Bibliothèque Humaniste, Sélestat 136
47 Giorgio Vasari, *Protogenes throws his sponge*, 1548, Casa del Vasari, Arezzo. Copyright Index Tavanti 138
48 Frans Floris, Saint Luke the Evangelist as artist and physician, 1556, 214 × 197 cm, Koninklijk Museum voor Schone Kunsten, Antwerp. Copyright Koninklijk Museum voor Schone Kunsten 152
49 Lanceloot Blondeel, Saints Luke and Eligius with the Virgin and Child, 1545, 136 × 95 cm, canvas, Sint Salvatorskerk, Bruges. Copyright IRPA-KIK Brussels 155
50 Jan Gossaert, Saint Luke draws the Virgin and child, 1515, originally in the Chapel of Saint Luke and Saint John, Sint Rombouts, Mechelen, panel, 230 × 205 cm, Narodni Gallery, Prague. Copyright The Metropolitan Chapter of Saint Vitus 157
51 Niklaus Manuel Deutsch, Saint Luke, 1515, for the Confraternity of Saints Luke and Eligius, Bern, 118 × 81 cm, Kunst Museum, Bern. Copyright Kunst Museum, Bern 160

52 Marten van Heemskerck, Saint Luke painting the Virgin and Child, 1532, Frans Hals Museum, Haarlem. Copyright Frans Hals Museum, Haarlem 161

53 Marten van Heemskerck, Saint Luke the Evangelist as painter and doctor 1550, 158 × 144 cm, Musée des Beaux Arts, Rennes. Copyright Musée des Beaux Arts, Rennes 164

54 Marten de Vos, *Saint Luke the Evangelist painter and doctor*, oil on panel, 1602, Musée Royale des Beaux Arts, Antwerp. Copyright A.C.L. Brussel 167

55 Giorgio Vasari, *Saint Luke Painting the Virgin and Child in a vision*, 1571, Chapel of the Confraternity of Saint Luke attached to the Academy, Santissima Annunziata, Florence. Copyright Conway Library, Courtauld Institute 169

56 Monument for the Master of Work, Wolfgang Tenck, 1513, red marble, Stadtpfarrkirche, Steyr. Copyright Bildarchiv Foto Marburg 174

57 Attributed to Niccolò Pisano, funerary altar for the sculptor Giovanni Andrea dei Giraldoni from Como at San Niccolò, Ferrara, 1520, 227 × 170 cm, Worcester Art Gallery, Massachusetts Accession number 1940–64. Copyright Worcester Art Museum 176

58 French illuminator, *Four Crowned Martyrs*, Book of Hours commissioned by Lodewijk van Boghem, 1526, 170 × 114 mm, Grootseminarie, Bruges, MS66/35, front end paper and fol. 1 recto. Copyright H. Maertens 177

59 Giannicola di Paolo di Giovanni Manni, altarpiece for the Università dei Lombardi, Santa Maria Nuova in Perugia, 1512, Louvre, Art Galleria Nazionale Perugia, Paris. Fratelli Alinari 2006 178

60 Brussels, second half of the sixteenth century, an anonymous altarpiece for the Guild of Four Crowned Martyrs at Sainte Catherine, Brussels, Musée Communal. Copyright Brussels, A.C.L. Brussel 180

61 Attributed to Raffaellino da Reggio, the four Roman martyrs refuse to obey the seated Emperor Diocletian, chapel at San Silvestro, Rome, 1570, for the Corporation of Statuary makers and Stone cutters. Copyright Soprintendenza per i Beni Ambientali e Architettonici del Lazio 182

62 *Children of Mercury*, attributed to Maso Finiguerra, *c.*1470, engraving, 324 × 22 mm, British Museum, London. Copyright The Trustees of the British Museum London 196

63 *Children of Mercury*, *c.*1490, *De sphaera* Latin 209, fol. 9, Reale Biblioteca Estense, Modena. Copyright Foto Roncaglia 197
64 *Children of Mercury*, attributed to Georg Pencz, *c.*1530, woodcut, 298 × 206 mm, British Museum. Copyright The Warburg Institute 200
65 *Children of Mercury*, attributed to Georg Breu the Elder, pen and ink, 23 cm in diameter, Kupferstichkabinett Staatliche Museen, Berlin. Copyright Kupferstichkabinett Staatliche Museen zu Berlin. Photo Jörg P. Anders 202
66 Marten van Heemskerck, *Children of Mercury*, 1568, engraving, 211 × 246 mm, Rijksmuseum Stichting, Amsterdam. Copyright Rijksmuseum Stichting, Amsterdam 203
67 *Children of Mercury*, *c.*1550, panel, 30 × 41 inches, Collection Kenneth Clark. Copyright The Warburg Institute 204
68 Hendrik Goltzius, *Children of Jupiter*, 1596, engraved by Jan Saenredam. Copyright The Warburg Institute 206
69 Hendrik Goltzius, *Children of Mercury*, 1596, drawing, 235 × 175 cm, Prentenkabinett, Leiden. Copyright Leiden University Library 207
70 Cesare Cesariano, *Mercury watches over the learned architect escaping Poverty*, 1521. Copyright The Trustees of the British Museum. 210
71 Mercury on the façade of Giulio Romano's house, Mantua, 1540–44. Fratelli Alinari 2006 212
72 a and b Giulio Romano, *Mercury and Minerva*, Sala grande, House of Giulio Romano, Mantua, 1540–44. Copyright Photo Foto Giovetti per gentile concessione Archivio di Stato Mantova 214
73 Annibale Fontana, Portrait medal of Giovanni Paolo Lomazzo, ?1562, bronze, 50 mm diameter, British Museum, George III illustrious persons 551. Copyright The Warburg Institute 215
74 Marcus Gheeraerts, *Mercury attempts to help the painter in poverty*, 1577, ink and wash on paper, 239 × 376 mm, Bibliothèque Nationale de France, Paris. Copyright Photo Bibliothèque Nationale de France, Paris 218
75 Bartholomaeus Spranger, *Mercury leads the learned and hardworking artist to Minerva*, 1592, engraved 1628 by Jan Muller. Copyright The Warburg Institute 221

76 Federico Zuccari, *The young Taddeo with Spirito and Disegno*, *c.*1590, Galleria degli Uffizi, Gabinetto Disegni e Stampe, 11018F, Florence. Copyright Galleria degli Uffizi 223
77 Frontispiece to *Pictorum aliquot celebrium*, The Hague, 1610, published by Hendrik Hondius. Copyright The British Library 224
78 Anonymous, *Mercury and Minerva assist Painting and Sculpture to attain Virtue*, 1613, Musée Fabre, Number 82088, Montpellier. Copyright Photo Claude O'Sughrue 225
79 Rubens's house to left and studio to right, Antwerp, 1618, engraved by Jacob Harrewijn, 1684. Copyright The Warburg Institute 226
80 Hendrik Goltzius, *Eer boven Golt* ('Honour before wealth'), 1600, drawing, 150 × 100 mm, Graphische Sammlung, Albertina, Vienna. Copyright Albertina Wien 228
81 Jacob Matham, funerary portrait of Hendrik Goltzius, 1620, engraving. Copyright The Warburg Institute 229
82 Lorenzo Leonbruno, *Calumny of Apelles and Fortune*, *c.*1530, oil on wood, 76 × 100 cm, Pinacoteca di Brera, Milan. Copyright Fratelli Alinari 2006 238
83 Federico Zuccari, *Calumny of Apelles*, engraved by Cornelis Cort, Rome, 1572, 518 × 557 mm, Prints and Drawings, British Museum. Copyright the Trustees of The British Museum 239
84 Leonardo da Vinci, *Pleasure is inseparable from Pain*, *c.*1485, drawing, Christchurch Art Gallery, Oxford. Copyright The Governing Body of Christchurch, Oxford 247
85 Giorgio Vasari, *Virtue grasps Opportunity by the forelock and vanquishes Envy*, 1548, fresco, Sala della Virtù, oil on wood, ceiling, Casa del Vasari, Arezzo. Fratelli Alinari 2006 248
86 After Frans Floris, *Diligence*, engraved by 'T.G.', 1576, Antwerp, Albertina Vienna. Copyright Albertina Wien 249
87 Raffaellino da Reggio, The house of Francesco da Volterra and Diana Scultori, drawing, *c.*1575, British Museum. Copyright The British Museum 252
88 Federico Zuccari, *The Choice of Hercules*, *c.*1595, vestibule, fresco, Palazzo Zuccari, Rome. Copyright Fototeca Max Planck Institut e Bibliotheca Hertziana 254
89 Federico Zuccari, virtuous artists reach the summit of the mountain of virtue, *c.*1590, Pierpont Morgan

Library, New York. Copyright The Pierpont Morgan Library New York 256
90 Jan van der Straet, self-portrait, engraved by Jan Wiericx, *c.*1587, Prints and Drawings, The Trustees of the British Museum 257
91 Anonymous, *The progress of the young artist*, *c.*1590, drawing, Graphische Sammlung Albertina, Vienna, Inventory number 2763. Copyright Albertina Wien 258
92 Pieter Isaacsz, portrait of Hans van Aachen, 1601, 401 × 324 mm, engraving by Jan Saenredam. Copyright The Warburg Institute 261
93 Alonso Chacon, drawing, *c.*1585, of the stucco by Daniele da Volterra showing satyrs weighing up his abilities, Bibliotheca Angelica, Rome, MS. 1564, fol. 288 recto. Copyright Bibliotheca Angelica, Rome 262
94 Antonio Abbondio, façade of the house of Leone Leoni, 1567, Milan. Copyright author 265
95 Federico Zuccari, *Porta virtutis*, 1581, drawing, Number JBS 544, Christchurch Gallery, Oxford. Copyright The Governing Body of Christchurch, Oxford 266
96 Federico Zuccari, *Time reveals Truth*, Casa del Federico Zuccari, 1578, Florence. Copyright Kunsthistorisches Institut Florenz 269
97 Federico Zuccari, *Aesop is made to cook pigs' trotters*, Casa del Federico Zuccari, 1578, Florence. Copyright Kunsthistorisches Institut Florenz 270
98 Federico Zuccari, *Time below Minerva and Apollo, with Perseverance (left) and Wisdom (right)*, hall vault, *c.*1595, Palazzo Zuccari, Rome. Copyright Archivio Vasari Roma 271
99 The house of Francesco and Bartolomeo Grazioli, before 1536, Asolo. Copyright Fratelli Alinari 2006 284
100 Giorgio Vasari, Sala della Virtù, with copy of Ammanati's Venus over the mantle, 1548, Casa del Vasari, Arezzo, Copyright Fratelli Alinari 2006 288
101 Giorgio Vasari, *Abraham, with Virtue, Peace, Concord and Modesty*, 1548, Casa del Vasari, Arezzo. Copyright 1990 Foto Scala Firenze su concessione del Ministero per i Beni e Attività Culturali 290
102 Giorgio Vasari, *Apollo and the Muses*, 1548, Casa del Vasari, Arezzo. Copyright Index Tavanti 291
103 Luigi Trezza, drawing of the portal of the house of Giovanni Battista Bertano (1556, Mantua) Biblioteca

Civica, Verona, MS1010 *c.*100. Copyright Biblioteca Civica, Verona 292

104 Anonymous, the house of Lelio Orsi, Novellara, mid sixteenth-century, ink and brown wash on paper, 270 × 340 mm, Devonshire Collection Chatsworth, number 351. Copyright: reproduced by permission of the Duke of Devonshire, and the Chatsworth Settlement; photo The Photographic Survey, Courtauld Institute of Art 293

105 After Bartholomeus Spranger, *Rome triumphant*, *c.*1585, Rensi Collection, Museum der Bildenden Künste, Leipzig. Copyright Museum der Bildenden Künste, Leipzig; photo Ursula Gerstenberger 304

106 The house of Andries de Valckenaere, 1590, Middelburg (destroyed 1940). Copyright Zeeuwse Bibliotheek, Middelburg, Koninklijk Zeeuwsch Genootschap der Wetenschappen Zeeland. 305

107 Federico Zuccari, portraits of Federico Zuccari and Francesca Genga, *c.*1595, hall, Palazzo Zuccari, Rome. Copyright Fototeca Max Planck Institut e Bibliotheca Hertziana 308

108 Federico Zuccari, Federico and Francesca Genga with Chastity, Concord, Felicity and Continence, *c.*1595, Palazzo Zuccari, Rome. Copyright Fototeca Max Planck Institut e Bibliotheca Hertziana 309

Acknowledgements

I am grateful to the Research Committee of the Arts Faculty and also to the Pro Vice-chancellor (Research) of the Open University for their generous help in obtaining the photographs for this book. I thank all the friends and relations who have encouraged me during the lengthy period of research which contributed to this book, and especially Aileen Cousins who generously commented in detail on the penultimate version of the manuscript. I would like to acknowledge the importance to this study of the guiding hand of the late Professor Andrew Martindale, formerly at the University of East Anglia, who was the best of supervisors for my PhD: 'Representations of Art and Artists in Western Europe, *c.*1300–*c.*1570' (1991). My thanks go also to the organisers of conferences at the Musée du Louvre, Paris, and the Universities of Bonn and Lille, who assisted me to clarify my arguments by kindly inviting me to deliver papers on the area covered by this study. I thank Jonathan Bevan, Sara Peacock and Alison Welsby for their assistance in making the book possible. Finally, I would like to thank the Warburg Institute and especially the staff of the Photographic Collection for their assistance throughout my investigation.

Introduction

During the sixteenth century changes took place which meant that artists (that is, figurative artists and architects) could draw on a wider range of visual traditions for representing the nature of art and artists than had previously been available. Artists sustained earlier traditions, for presenting the visual arts and architecture as Practical Arts (Chapter 1), for displaying the devout examples of their patron saints (Chapter 4), and for illustrating artistic dispositions as subject to astrological influence (Chapter 5). They also maintained established traditions of signing their works with inscribed portraits, and of providing 'bystander portraits' of artists in narratives, as well as maintaining the more recent convention of making funerary effigies and producing portraits of significance for their families and workshops (Chapter 3). Alongside these strands of continuity there were however many iconographic innovations.

Artists explored new conventions for showing painting, sculpture and architecture as scholarly Liberal Arts or the arts suited to the education of gentlemen (Chapter 1), and produced imagery for signifying the value of the concept of *disegno* (that is to say, planning as well as drawing) for the first time (Chapter 2). New types of portraiture appeared in print to publish the achievements of recent artists, and collections were made for the first time of recent artists' portraits. Artists were portrayed in the earliest pictorial tributes to great art patrons, and pictorial narratives were planned to celebrate artists' careers. Furthermore, artists began to make visual celebrations of the histories of ancient Greek artists, so as to represent contemporary artistic concerns (Chapter 3). Artists adopted mythological figures associated with learning and inventiveness, as protectors of the visual arts (Chapter 5). In addition they appropriated themes which had previously been used only to celebrate the achievements of rulers, writers and thinkers to demonstrate the virtuous pursuit of fame and honour, and the defence of artistic worthiness (Chapter 6). Finally, from the sixteenth century derives a large increase in evidence concerning the way artists were decorating their houses with programmes exploring the dignity of art and artists (Chapter 7).

The question of nomenclature remains problematic. It would be more accurate not to use the term 'artist' to designate both the craftsmen who were figurative specialists in any medium and the architects whose representation is the subject of this study. The term was used infrequently in the root word *artista* to denote such a person from the second half of the century onwards;[1] originally, it was applied solely to scholars. The use of such an anachronistic word is therefore overtly retrospective, and excusable only as shorthand for indicating the kinds of specialists whose dignity was being celebrated in representations of painting, sculpture and architecture as Liberal Arts for the first time, and for considering how figurative specialists and architects were being portrayed in other contemporary iconographic traditions.

To some extent new traditions of visual imagery were employed to assert that the best artists were individuals with outstanding innate talent. Commemorative portraits of artists could suggest that the personal flair and style of artists were as recognisable as their appearance. In taking over various genres of commemorative portraiture for their own use, artists were laying claim to art forms which had previously been associated only with leaders in spirituality, state, literature and thought.

To a considerable degree these visual representations were employed to advertise new ideas concerning the cerebral nature of painting, sculpture and architecture. This was true of the imagery which showed these disciplines in the company of Liberal Arts from around 1509 onwards, and as unified under the conceptual umbrella of *disegno* from about 1542 onwards. This held good for the innovating adaptations of the traditional idea of depicting Saint Luke the Evangelist as artist, which emphasised that he had been a physician, from the 1520s onwards, and of the interpretation of the lives of the Four Crowned Martyrs (or sculptors' patron saints), which showed them handling tools of measurement and calculation more than hammers, at about the same time. It might also be found in astrological representations of artists in the traditional manner as the Children of Mercury, which had pointed to the affinities of painters and sculptors with physicians, astronomers and geometricians. The new ambitions of artists to be treated as members of an elevated profession were also served by showing them as being protected by the mythological god of the Liberal Art of Rhetoric, Mercury, and by Minerva, goddess of wisdom, in the manner associated with scholarly and philosophical academies, from the 1540s onwards. Artists were making strong claims to cerebral powers when, following the example of the *Calumny* of Apelles, they adapted the allegorical mode to their own concerns, and took over the prestigious themes of the pursuit of fame through virtue, and the defence of virtue against detractors, from rulers, scholars and philosophers.

While the new visual tropes invented during the sixteenth century highlighted the intellectual dignity, inventiveness and personal inborn talents of artists, it is important to stress that throughout the period some visual traditions carried on supporting the view that painting, sculpture and architecture were Practical Arts to do with repetitive manual skills. Furthermore, commissioners of most representations of the patron saints of sculptors and builders went on representing them undertaking both mental and manual work. In addition, viewers of some astrological illustrations could note the way artists kept company with craftsmen such as armourers, and served in their shops at the marketplace, amongst the Children of Mercury, in what were relatively fluid images capable of a variety of interpretations. Rather than prioritising those traditions of visual representation which appear to have furthered what Andrew Martindale termed the 'rise of the artist', it seems important also to examine ways in which continuities in attitudes were reproduced during the sixteenth century. The fact that such a diverse body of imagery was sustained during this period, as well as being invented, means that it is a viable time frame for studying the changing identities of artists.

Iconographies of art during this period were produced mostly by artists working in Italy; in addition, many worked in the Netherlands and in German-speaking areas, and a few worked in French-speaking areas. It has been customary to trace change and continuity occurring in discrete geographical areas. This has the advantage of examining traditions broadly unified by similar political and social frameworks, by language and by shared visual experiences and references. It is an important principle to retain, in grouping discussion of imagery. However, the approach needs to be handled with care. Italian artists and patrons often led in the discussion of new ambitions concerning the status of art and artists. However, their lead was not completely overwhelming in the fields of visual representation. By examining developments to some extent across linguistic, stylistic and geographical barriers, the initiatives of non-Italian artists (for example the invention by German-speaking artists of single-leaf printed portraits of the artist during the first half of the sixteenth century) become apparent. Equally, the speed with which forms and ideas of Italian origin were taken over and adapted (for example in the house decorations of Frans Floris (1519–70) and Cornelis van Dalem (before 1534–73) in the 1560s in Antwerp) may be better appreciated. The topographical distinctiveness of artistic traditions must be acknowledged. Nevertheless, developments in print culture meant that motifs and ideas could be exchanged with increasing rapidity. Patterns of publication also meant that illustrated books might be issued in one city (for example, Barthélémy de Chasseneux, the *Catalogus gloriae mundi*, in French-speaking Lyons, 1546) and re-issued with the same imagery in another (Barthélémy de Chasseneux, the *Catalogus gloriae mundi*, in Italian-speaking Venice, 1571). In addition, prints might be made in more than one centre. By the end of the period, for example, designs commissioned and made in Florence by the Antwerp painter Jan van der Straet (1523–1605) were being sent north to Antwerp, for Jan Wiericx (1549–*c.*1618) to engrave them. During the sixteenth century more and more transalpine artists made the journey south to Italy for study purposes. At the same time Italians (such as Jacopo de'Barbari (*c.*1465–before 1516) at the beginning of the century and Federico

Zuccari (*c*.1541–1609) towards the end) went on travelling north in search of work. Some artists' success was measured by the extent of their journeys: for instance, the Netherlandish painter Bartholomaeus Spranger (1546–1611) moved south from Antwerp, to work and study in Rome, and then took up a post at court in Prague.

In these circumstances it is helpful to be alert to the processes of appropriation which were occurring when artists set out to take over motifs and ideas from one local tradition and to make them their own.[2] Such borrowings tended to be selective and to involve transformation when the artist added new ideas and forms. Several of the new iconographies of art entailed reference to classical literature and classicising styles. Italian artistic traditions – of drawing on Latin and Greek texts, and studying the art and architecture of ancient Rome – were relatively long ones and, in addition, Italian makers and viewers were likely to know some antique art in the original. By contrast, some artists working beyond the Alps had become interested in employing classicising subject-matter and styles rather more recently, spectators were less likely to have seen examples of ancient Roman art and architecture, and, in addition, there were many artists who did not emulate the antique. Consequently, the ways in which, for example, a classicising personification of Painting displayed in association with the Liberal Arts might be interpreted differed considerably, depending on whether it was placed in Rome or in Antwerp. Such appropriations were not all in one direction, as shown for instance in the case of the anonymous draughtsman in the circle of Federico Zuccari, who translated elements from a drawing and a poem by the Amsterdam artist Cornelis Ketel (1548–1616), at the very end of the century, for his own purposes (Plate 91). What was untranslatable is sometimes as interesting as what was: a case in point is the way the Haarlem engraver Jacob Matham (1571–1631), in 1620, used the Italian inscriptions *disegno* and *spirito* to denote personifications which had no Netherlandish nor even Latin equivalents (Plate 81). While the diversities between artistic traditions north and south of the Alps are most obvious, the cities of the Italian peninsula were also distinctive. When, for example, the Venetian painters invented a personification for a figure they labelled *disegno* it is likely that the personification denoted local understanding of the importance of handling hue and tone, rather than line, in designing paintings. By contrast, Florentine personifications of *disegno* were made in different contexts with regard to local Tuscan approaches to 'designing'.

Institutions

In contrast with some of the visual rhetoric putting forwards ambitious claims for art, the social status, education and training of a majority of artists throughout the period were those of skilled artisans. Painters, goldsmiths and sculptors rarely obtained schooling beyond the age of eleven, and at this point were set to an apprenticeship until the age of about eighteen, when they might fulfil their guild's masterpiece regulations and gain the right to operate a workshop of their own. (In 1611, for example, records show that one painter in Delft was unable to sign his name.[3]) If they lacked funds or parental backing to establish their own shop, they might bind themselves to work for another master for short periods, or be paid at a daily rate. The numbers of apprentices one master could take on were usually limited, for example to two pupils. Architects did not undergo a formal apprenticeship as such but were painters, sculptors or goldsmiths who employed skills in drawing, modelling and building acquired after apprenticeship. Workshops might be placed directly under the jurisdiction of the city council, as in Nuremberg, or, in other cities, they might be organised in guilds which were, in their turn, regulated by civic authorities.[4] In some German-speaking areas, masons and stone carvers belonged to guilds which were attached to long-term building enterprises, such as the cathedral in Vienna, rather than located in a particular city.[5] Civic authorities or guilds regulated the quality of production and adjudicated disputes. They also vetted the credentials of those seeking work in their city. In locations which remained Catholic, guilds were linked with religious confraternities, which encouraged ceremonies of group piety and ensured that members had dignified burial.[6] Civic guilds tended to gather together a variety of skills. In Delft, the Guild of Saint Luke comprised glaziers, painters, tapestry and embroidery makers, sculptors in wood and stone, printers, booksellers, scabbard makers, and engravers.[7] In Cologne the guild system grouped painters, glaziers and sculptors in wood.[8] The Venetian guild comprised painters of chests, illuminators, playing-card makers, embroiderers and the *figureri* or picture makers.[9]

Guilds could provide artists with respected, if median, social positions. In some cities – such as Antwerp, but not Venice – guilds had some political representation. They could display prosperity, as in 1520 when the Guild of Saint Luke in Antwerp entertained Albrecht Dürer (1471–1528) at a dinner in which he reported 'all their service was of silver and they had other splendid ornaments'.[10] The protective powers of guilds could promote claims to being well paid, as when the Antwerp guild supported the Ghent painter Lucas de Heere (1534–84) in a dispute in 1588.[11] Guilds also provided charitable support for their members. However, artists were not necessarily well off, and only a few artists might command consistently large fees, such as the painter Frans Floris and his brother, the architect Cornelis Floris (*c.*1513–75), in Antwerp.[12] For instance, in 1575, according to tax records, painters in Delft were less comfortably off than glaziers within their guild. In Antwerp in the 1580s, across occupations in the city, painters and sculptors were poorer than doctors, printers, metal workers and wood workers, but richer than makers of musical instruments, textile workers and builders.[13]

Throughout the period artists earning in courts could be exempt from the control of local guilds. Rulers might wish to hire and treat artists as they pleased, without civic vetting. Martin Warnke dated the exclusion of some court artists from civic controls from the late thirteenth century onwards.[14] Yet while the mounting importance of court patronage meant that the numbers of artists beyond guild control increased, all were trained in workshop systems.

In the second half of the period, the treatment of the figurative arts and architecture as manual trades began to be contested. Criticism of some aspects of the guild system was published. For instance, Karel van Mander (1548–1606) in his *Het Schilderboek* (*Book on Painting*; Alkmaar, 1604) objected to any form of such organisation because it treated art as a trade:

> Almost everywhere a guild is made of the noble art of painting, as is done with all the coarse handicrafts and trades such as weaving, furriery, carpentry, smithing and suchlike. In Bruges in Flanders painting is not just in a guild on its own but the guild also includes harness making. In Haarlem, where there have always been many noble spirits in our art, there are tinkers, tinsmiths and old clothes traders included in the guild.[15]

Artists might negotiate within the guild system in small ways for proper acknowledgement that it was their skill in making figurative images – rather than the physical materials with which they worked, such as stone, colours, wood or metals – which should determine their affiliation. In 1593, for example, the figurative sculptors in stone at Antwerp petitioned the civic authorities to allow them to belong to the Guild of Saint Luke, and thus join other figurative specialists in paint and wood carving, who already belonged to that guild. Finally, they achieved their aim, and were exempt from having to enter the masons' guild in 1607.[16] Guild workers might reform the terminology used to describe their activities. Thus, in the 1590s those writing the records belonging to the Guild of Saint Luke in Antwerp ceased to use the term *ambacht* or 'trade' to describe their activities, although the civic authorities ignored the change.[17] With sufficient authority the scope of a guild might be redefined. Thus in 1585 the Emperor Rudolph II, whose castle was at Prague, decreed that the Guild of Saint Luke in the city at his gates should describe painting, glazing and embroidery as 'arts', rather than 'trades', and that his court painters should henceforth become guildsmen, on these new terms.[18]

The most substantial challenges both to the traditional system of training artists in separate workshops and also to conventions as to issues which masters should take joint responsibility for, in a city, were represented by the three academies which were initiated in Italy. These were the Accademia del Disegno, founded in Florence by Duke Cosimo I in 1563; the Accademia di San Luca, also known as the Accademia del Disegno, instituted with the encouragement of a succession of popes following Gregory XIII in Rome in 1593; and the Accademia degli Incamminati (meaning 'those who have been put on the right road') which was run unofficially in Bologna from 1582 onwards, by Ludovico Carracci (1555–1619) and his cousins Agostino (1557–1602) and Annibale (1560–1609). All three groups challenged the trade association of guilds, in naming themselves 'academies': a term linked with scholarly gatherings in ancient Greece and Rome and recent Italian literary and philosophical societies. All three academies set out to provide improved teaching concerning those areas of theoretical knowledge which the figurative arts and architecture were considered to share with scholarly professions – such as mathematics, geometry and anatomy – and laid emphasis on skills in drawing.[19] With the Florentine and Roman academies the aim of the masters was to provide some teaching to which all apprentices would have access. However, it seems that it was the unofficial Bolognese academy which provided regular teaching during three decades, while the two official academies were stronger on plans than on delivering a regular curriculum.[20] The Bolognese academy, which mainly served painters, was distinctive in its emphasis on drawing from life as well as from the antique. The Florentine and Roman academies emphasised expertise in planning or *disegno*, which was considered the factor unifying the study of the figurative arts and architecture. While the Roman academy replaced the guild of painters in Rome, and then in 1596 allowed sculptors to become members, its responsibility, as a regulatory body, was to the papacy rather than the civic government of Rome.[21] In contrast, the Florentine academy developed from the Confraternity of Saint Luke, in which painters and sculptors had united since they were separated in the Florentine guild structures. From 1572 onwards this academy was also instituted with the powers of a guild and placed under the control of the Mercanzia or commercial court of Florence.[22] The trade context ensured, as Anthony Hughes pointed out, that the Florentine academy represented an area of practice 'straddling intellectual and manual labour'.[23] Nevertheless, the publication in 1604 of the first series of lectures on art given by members of the Roman academy was a milestone: discussion of theoretical issues was now endorsed as the proper concern of a regulatory body.[24]

The critique of workshop and guild systems represented by the official academies was perhaps more about ambitions and new terminology than pedagogic fact. Nevertheless academic rhetoric made some impression, as is evident in van Mander's diatribe of 1604 cited earlier. Natives of cities in Italy which did not have academies were also likely to voice discontent, as when the Genoese painter of noble family Giovanni Battista Paggi (1554–1627) wrote to his brother from Florence in 1591, scorning the art education available in Genoa. What, he asked, could a poor boy learn about the most noble knowledge (*nobilissima scienza*) of painting by staying seven years to be taught by a gilder who just understood how to paint little stools (*sgabelli*)?[25]

Treatises

In gauging the changing status of art and artists, reference may be made to the great increase in the production of theoretical publications concerning art and architecture during the sixteenth century. These treatises emphasised that painting, sculpture and architecture drew on knowledge of arithmetic and geometry to calculate correct proportions and produce linear perspectival constructions. It was argued that the figurative arts required understanding of anatomy and physiognomy to represent figures and their emotions convincingly, while the architects needed expertise in astronomy, geography and even meteorology to position buildings and cities appropriately. These branches of knowledge were regarded as Liberal Arts worthy of the education of gentlemen rather than of traders. In addition the Liberal Arts were defined as requiring theory, as well as practice, so that the very publications of such theorising, many of which were written by artists themselves, offered proofs that artist were not just manual, practical craftsmen. Moreover, figurative artists tended to argue that their arts were similar to that of poetry, since they used imagination to carve and paint scenes which conveyed stories and ideas vividly. In doing so, artists quoted the dictum of the Roman poet Horace (first century BCE), who had conceded in his treatise on poetry that 'as for painting so for poetry'. Since poetry was treated as a branch of the Liberal Art of Rhetoric, this was, yet again, a claim to genteel status.[26]

The circulation of treatises on art was dominated by Italian artists during the fifteenth century, beginning with the treatise by the Florentine painter Cennino Cennini (*c.*1370–*c.*1440) in his *Libro dell'arte* (*c.*1390). He had argued in his introduction that painting deserved a position only a little below that of poetry, quoting Horace. He had been followed by Leon Battista Alberti (*c.*1404–72), in his treatise *De pictura* or *On Painting* in 1435. The Florentine sculptor Lorenzo Ghiberti (1378–1455) had contributed a discussion of optics to his autobiography about 1450, while the Florentine Antonio Averlino il Filarete (*c.*1400–*c.*1465) had composed a treatise on architecture about 1461–64. Alberti's own treatise on architecture (*De re aedificatoria*) was circulating by 1457 and published in 1485.[27] A trawl though the authors examined by Julius von Schlosser in his *La letteratura artistica* (1956) reveals that Italian painters, sculptors and architects, as well as scholars, continued to produce a rich array of treatises during the late fifteenth and sixteenth centuries, especially during and after the 1540s. From the learned treatise on sculpture by the Neapolitan scholar Pomponio Gaurico (*c.*1481–*c.*1529) published in 1504 to the treatises on painting printed by the Milanese painter Giovanni Paolo Lomazzo (1538–1600), in 1584 and in 1590, Italian treatises were being produced at the rate of almost two every decade. Such a succession meant that artists, mostly in Italy, were developing a practice in which debates about strategies and values were no longer solely oral, but recorded.[28]

While some publications on art were issued north of the Alps, these tended to demonstrate techniques rather than theorise or debate. For example, in 1505 a cleric from Toul, Canon Jean Pélerin (*c.*1445–1524), published the first printed account of the single-point perspectival construction. The treatises Dürer published between 1525 and 1528 conformed to this pattern in some respects, for example his *Unterweisung der Messung mit dem Zirkel und Richtscheyt im Linien, Ebenen und gantzen Corporen*, translated as a *Course in the Art of Measurements with Compasses and Rule* (Nuremberg, 1525). Nevertheless, his survey of fortifications and his book on human proportions *Vier Bücher von Menschlicher Proportion* (*Four Books on Human Proportions*; Nuremberg, 1528) more closely resembled the theoretical focus of Italian counterparts.[29] It may be noted, however, that treatises, whether concentrating on techniques or on theoretical positions, entailed the sharing of advice once confined to single workshops. The idea of pooling wisdom, especially to educate the young, was paralleled in the policies of the first academies.

Italians were also prominent in the production of sixteenth-century treatises on architecture, with Jacopo Barozzi detto il Vignola (1507–73) publishing the *Regole delle cinque ordine d'architettura* (*Rules for the Five Orders of Architecture*; Rome, 1562) and Andrea Palladio (1508–80) producing the *I quattri libri dell'architettura* (*Four Books on Architecture*; Venice, 1570). It is of some interest, however, that only two of the seven parts into which the treatises by Sebastiano Serlio (1475–1554) were divided were first published in Italy (Venice, 1537, 1540). The successive volumes were written in France while he was working for François I at Fontainebleau from 1540 onwards, and were published in Paris, Antwerp and Frankfurt. All were published in Italian, but one was also issued in Latin, four were translated into French, and one was translated into Netherlandish and into German too. Serlio's theoretical activities at the French court presumably encouraged two French architects to follow suit: in the *Livres d'architecture* (*Books on Architecture*) by Jacques Androuet du Cerceau (1559–61) and the *Premier tome d'architecture* (*First Volume on Architecture*; 1568) as well as the *Nouvelles inventions pour bien bastir* (*New Inventions for Building Well*; 1561) by Philibert de L'Orme (1514–70).[30]

Histories

One important factor denoting shifts in the status of some artists was the increasing interest shown during the second half of the sixteenth century in publishing histories of art. The existence of a written history was prestigious in itself, since otherwise only leaders in thought, spirituality and in church and state were accorded literary commemorations of this type. In addition, writers tended to describe their heroes or themselves as behaving in ways which were worthy of respect. The sixteenth-century histories of art drew on Tuscan precedents, the earliest of which dated from the late fourteenth century, when the Florentine scholar Filippo Villani (1325–*c.*1408) had made the landmark decision to write a series of thirty-five brief biographies of famous Florentines around 1380 which included Florentine painters, *De viris illlustribus* (*On the Illustrious City of Florence and its Famous Men*). In this text Villani claimed ancient Roman precedent in recording artists amongst illustrious citizens, and praised them along with statesmen, doctors of medicine, jurists, orators, astronomers and musicians. Villani set the trend by representing Cimabue (1240–before 1302) and his pupil Giotto (*c.*1270–1337) as reviving the standards of ancient Roman and Greek painting. In the mid-fifteenth century another Florentine – this time a sculptor, Lorenzo Ghiberti – in his *Commentari* wrote the first surviving autobiography of an artist in the European tradition. He also included an account to date of the rise and fall of ancient art and the recent Tuscan revival. Ghiberti argued that the early fourteenth-century Tuscan sculptor Nicola Pisano (*c.*1220–before 1284) had initiated a revival of ancient quality in sculpture similar to that achieved by Giotto for painting. In the 1480s the first lengthy biography of an artist in the European tradition was written concerning the Florentine architect Filippo Brunelleschi (1377–1446). The life has been attributed to the amateur architect and mathematician Antonio di Tuccio Manetti (1423–1497) and has been dated to the 1480s. Manetti's biography argued that Brunelleschi had led a revival of the styles of ancient architecture. In the late fifteenth century the Florentine scholar Cristoforo Landino (*c.*1424–98) compiled the first printed edition of the *Historia naturalis* by Pliny the Elder in Italian (Venice, 1476). Although the Latin text of the *Natural History* was relatively well known in manuscript – and, from 1469, in print – artists could now read the sole surviving substantial account by a classical writer of ancient Greek and Roman art.[31]

These pioneer treatments were followed by a stream of texts issuing mostly from Tuscany, but also from other Italian cities, which provided short summaries of works of recent artists whether in manuscripts or printed form. A few of these records were manuscripts devoted to the praise of art such as that by the Florentine Giovanni Battista Gelli (1498–1563), or were parts of a treatise on art as for instance the treatise on sculpture by Pomponio Gaurico (Florence, 1504). Yet the praise of recent artists and mention of some of their works were more often inserted in passing, by authors who were writing books which were not focused on art, for instance in a guidebook to Rome or the encomium of a ruler.[32] The landmark history devoted entirely to art and architecture was that written by Giorgio Vasari (1511–74), *Le vite de' più eccellenti architetti, pittori, e scultori* (Florence, 1550). Vasari was a painter and architect who had taken service with the Medici, leaving his native Arezzo for the court in Florence. This history of art was expanded and revised for a second edition (Florence, 1568). Here was a text which made wide-ranging claims for the high status of artists, with an emphasis on the superiority of all things Tuscan and, to a lesser extent, Italian. Vasari took over the imagery of revival, which was a key element in the traditions begun by Villani, Ghiberti and Manetti, as well as their emphasis on the notion of individual talent as the agent of progress. However his book represented even bolder claims for the dignity of art than those of his predecessors. Vasari was the first artist to assert the right to take on the scholarly job of representing the story of recent art in print. Vasari's accounts in both editions were also the longest narratives to that date, entirely devoted to the histories of art. In their very bulkiness the *Lives* claimed the importance of recording the attainments of artists. Vasari now offered a grand narrative of triumph, decline and rebirth, covering two millennia, in which modern artists could be portrayed as heroes, who imitated the achievements of the ancient artists acclaimed by scholars. He presented the, by then, traditional idea of revival with a wealth of detail, charting the development of ancient art in stages from beginnings to perfection, followed by the decline of art after the period of Constantine. He innovated by suggesting that recent changes had mirrored the very phases of ancient development outlined by Pliny the Elder. Vasari described the beginnings of success in Tuscany in the late thirteenth century, its improvement in the early fifteenth century, and its summation from the late fifteenth century onwards, culminating in the achievement of Michelangelo (1475–1564). Vasari's hyperbole extended to dubbing Michelangelo *divino* with reference to his God-given talent.[33] Furthermore, Vasari included many anecdotes in his biographies which promoted the status of artists. Thus, for instance, his stories of Leonardo (1452–1519) being attended at his deathbed by the King of France, or of Raphael (1483–1520) living 'like a prince' emphasised the social dignity accorded the most talented men. Other reports stressed the capacity of artists to put their own values on a work, as when Donatello (1386–1466), supposedly, smashed a sculpture after a patron set too low a price on it. Vasari also put forwards the ideal of artists devoting themselves to intellectual attainments rather than their own comforts, as in the tale of Paolo Uccello researching the rules of perspective far into the night. Art was as much about thinking things out, he argued, as it was about manual execution, as he illustrated in the tale of the Prior of the monastery where Leonardo was painting the *Last Supper*, chiding the painter for spending half a day just examining what he had done. These touching and amusing incidents with their ambitious claims were laid out as part of a grand pattern of progress in which artists were shown as significant agents in the cultural revival of their times.

Following Vasari's first edition, interest in the life of Michelangelo was sufficient to enable a lengthy rival account of the life of Michelangelo to be published (Rome, 1553). The author Ascanio Condivi (1525–74) was an artist, by origin from Ripatronsone in the Marche. Like Vasari, Condivi singled out Michelangelo as someone able to inspire awe in spectators through his work. Whereas Vasari had remarked on Michelangelo's *terribiltà* or 'terror-striking power', Condivi used the term *formidabile* or 'fearful' to describe the Sistine ceiling. Such descriptors were far from praising the work of a mere craftsman. These were the first rival printed biographies in the western European tradition, and Michelangelo was still living when they were issued. The sense that keeping records of artists' lives was increasingly valued is suggested in the survival of quite numerous manuscript autobiographical accounts by Italian artists, written during the second half of the sixteenth century. However, only the autobiography which Vasari added to the second edition of the *Lives* and the poetic accounts of his painting by Lomazzo (*Grottesche*, Milan 1587) were actually published.[34]

From around 1500 onwards writers from France and Germany also started to publish their views on ancient and recent art history. French-speaking writers praised artists from Italy, France, the Netherlands and Germany. The German-speaking writers tended to laud German artists. Both praised ancient Greek artists. However, the number of histories produced north of the Alps was slight by comparison with those from Italian-speaking areas. Most of the texts were composed by scholars and tended to be brief addenda to works celebrating a famous patron, or building, or listing the cultural achievements of a city or region. Writers transposed concepts from Italian texts, for example in complimenting Dürer for reviving the standards of art to those of the ancient Greeks. The lengthiest transalpine text devoted to an artist was the Latin life printed in 1528, immediately following Dürer's death in that year, by his loyal friend Joachim Camerarius (1500–74). This man, who was Professor of Greek in Nuremberg, wrote a tribute to the author that dwelled further on the appearance of his subject. His appreciation of what he called Dürer's 'skill and talent' was published as the preface to his own translation of the *Four Books on Human Proportion* into Latin as *De symmetria partium humanorum corporum* (Nuremberg, 1528). Camerarius stated that he wanted to retail something of 'the life and habits of a remarkable man'.[35]

The lengthiest text devoted to an artist to be issued in the Netherlands was the *Life of Lambert Lombard* by the scholar Dominic Lampsonius (Bruges, 1565), published one year before the subject's death. This was perhaps something of a Netherlandish riposte to Condivi's publication of the life of Michelangelo in 1553, and it is documented as having been produced with advice, by letter, from Vasari. Typically, the title stressed patriotic motives: the 'Life of Lambert Lombard the most celebrated painter of French-speaking Belgians' (*Lamberti Lombardi apud Eburones pictoris celeberrimi vita*). Unlike that of Condivi, this biography was written in Latin. However, it is indicative of the social mobility of some artists that Lampsonius was a former pupil of Lombard (1505–66). Lambert Lombard, painter of Liège, had travelled to Rome in 1537 and Lampsonius underlined his learning comparing him to ancient Greek painters and to the Italian architect and theorist Leon Battista Alberti (1404–72). Lampsonius pointedly bewailed the low status of painting in practice, when Lombard had shown by his skills and knowledge how refined it could be.[36]

In general there was less interest in the production of histories of artist in transalpine areas, a fact marked by the scantier survival of autobiographical manuscripts. That histories were being produced is suggested by the report by van Mander that a poetic celebration of the achievements of Netherlandish artists was composed by the Ghent painter Lucas de Heere around the middle of the sixteenth century. However, it was not until the end of the period that van Mander published his *Het schilderboek*. What is indicative of the powerful attraction of Italian models is that van Mander imitated Vasari by beginning with a history of ancient artists, and following with an account of Italian artists. Only after treating the ancients and the Italians did he devote himself to the lives of artists working in *Germania*, that is in the Netherlands and parts of present-day Germany. Van Mander had trained in the South Netherlands but emigrated to Haarlem, and wrote his 'Painter's Book' from there. He adapted the views on periodisation publicised by Vasari for his local conditions, and termed *oude moderne* or 'early modern' those artists working at the time of Jan van Eyck (?1395–1441), and *moderne* those who had learned something of the styles of ancient Roman and Greek art, techniques of classicising proportions, linear perspectival constructions and anatomy, largely from Italian sources.[37] In this way van Mander, like Vasari thirty years earlier, presented his readers with the vision of contemporary artists as heirs to a rich and valuable group of traditions.

Funerary tributes

It is indicative of the increasing status of some artists during the sixteenth century that accounts of tributes paid to three German-speaking and two Italian-speaking artists in ceremonies at their funerals were published. The funeral of Dürer in 1528 was celebrated with scholarly tributes, amongst those being an elegy by Wilibald Pirckheimer

(1470–1530), scholar and friend of the artist. This was published in Dürer's posthumously printed *Four Books on Human Proportion* (Nuremberg, 1528).[38] The funeral oration of Michelangelo was delivered by Benedetto Varchi, Rector of Florence (1503–65), in 1564, and an account of the obsequies was issued by Vasari in his *Lives* (Florence, 1568). In 1586 the funeral of the painter Lucas Cranach the Younger, Bürgermeister of Wittenberg (1515–86), was marked by a printed *Leichenpredigt* or funeral sermon delivered by Georg Mylius in the Stadtkirche at Wittenberg. The custom of funding such vernacular sermons began in the 1550s and was accorded to members of the aristocracy and citizens of high standing. Cranach's example was followed by the funeral sermon delivered in respect for the painter Johann Rauscher in Leipzig in 1601, by the archdeacon of the Nikolaikirche.[39] Finally, the funerary tributes for the Bolognese painter Agostino Caracci in 1603 were recorded by Guido Reni (1575–1642) and immediately published.[40] Whether in Catholic or Protestant contexts, such tributes honoured artists.

Ennoblement and court culture

During the sixteenth century there was a considerable increase in the number of artists who were ennobled or knighted. Warnke registered eighteen artists as having been so honoured between the first recorded instance in 1289 and 1500 – that is during two centuries. During the next century though there were nearly sixty such instances and two-thirds of these were granted after 1550, so the process was accelerating.[41] A social elite of artists were therefore enjoying the noble status that the treatise writers were claiming for the noble arts of painting, sculpture and architecture. As analysed by Warnke, all the artists ennobled or knighted in the fifteenth century were Italian: seven out of twelve of them being granted by non-Italian courts.[42] Italians were rather less in demand during the sixteenth century, when only half of the artists honoured in the period were Italians, but again, two-thirds of those Italians were being ennobled by rulers from outside Italy. Warnke argued that the availability of court patronage for some artists (whether or not they were awarded the highest honours) could provide superior financial rewards.[43] Artists who enjoyed court appointments and access to court commissions, but who conducted business independently from the home base of city houses, were perhaps the best placed (such as Raphael, Michelangelo, Titian (*c.*1485–1576), Anthonis Mor (*c.*1516–?1576), Frans Floris, Bartholomaeus Spranger, Hans van Aachen (1552–1615) and Peter Paul Rubens (1577–1640)).[44] Court culture, in Warnke's view, promoted the trend of making fine houses so that courtiers could visit artists in comfort. For instance, King Christian II of Denmark stayed with Lucas Cranach the Elder (1472–1553) at Wittenberg in 1523.[45] According to van Mander, in Antwerp the Prince of Orange and the Counts of Egmont and Horn dined at the house of Frans Floris.[46] Court culture could also provide other models for representing the relationship between artist and commissioner. Rather than the tradesman offering good-quality goods through his shop, the imagery could be that favoured by scholars working for courts, whereby the artist was thought of as serving his lord with expertise.[47] In this atmosphere there was some increase in the number of nobles and scholars practising the visual arts in a dilettante manner.[48]

Contacts with scholars

The intellectual status, and perhaps the social regard, of some artists was also enhanced by the relationships between them and scholars. Examples are quite numerous throughout the period, such as the links between the mathematician Luca Pacioli (1445–1514), Leonardo and Piero della Francesca (1415–92), as well as the friendship between Dürer and Pirckheimer. Artists were likely to be advised by scholars on the subject matter to be represented, as for instance when the Mantuan courtier Conte Teodoro Sangiorgio sent a description of narratives required for the Venetian painter Tintoretto (1519–94).[49] Scholars were brought together with engravers in the making of illustrated books, as seems to be the case with the scholar Lampsonius and the publishing house of Hieronymous Cock (*c.*1510–70) in Antwerp. Lampsonius was close to the painter Lombard because he had initially trained in his workshop. The writer Antonio Francesco Doni (1513–74) was close to the sculptor Giovanni Angelo Montorsoli (?1507–63) since they had trained together in Florence as young sculptors. The Aretine sculptor Leone Leoni (*c.*1509–90) was kinsman of the Venetian writer Pietro Aretino (1492–1556). The interests of some patrons in having erudite, especially classicising, subject matter represented in sculptural and pictorial schemes encouraged scholar and artist relationships. The interest of the members of the elite in reconstructing the admired art and architecture of ancient Greece and Rome meant that artists with the skills to assist scholars in antiquarian research were respected.

The consideration of the visual evidence for change and continuity in the image of the artists has attracted considerable scholarly attention, although no single study has been devoted to the sixteenth century.[50] As Francis Ames-Lewis has pointed out, 'visual evidence is by definition "soft" and needs to be interpreted with great tact'.[51] Interpretations need to be discussed with reference to the textual traditions related to each strand of visual imagery, and to comparative visual representations, especially those bearing inscriptions. However, where newly invented images are being examined, data for comparison will be scanty. Texts, unless they bear close documented relationships to the production of the images being interpreted, can only indicate a range of possible connotations.

It is convenient to describe the conventions of visual representations which were developed to denote the varied identities of artists and the concerns of art as iconographical traditions. It is important to dissociate this study from the kinds of Panofskian iconographical studies which have been linked by critics associated with 'the new art history' to the search for singular meanings as consciously intended by one initiator, or the tabulation of dictionaries of meanings.[52] However, the value of iconographical study may be asserted in the sense that it can, instead, be used to investigate the range of meanings which might be imputed to some visual image or object, at a particular place and time, by different kinds of viewers, depending on their cultural and educational capital. Iconographical studies may take account of diversities of interpretations, for makers, first users and later audiences and therefore enable consideration of those very subtleties and complexities which the 'new art history' set out to study. This study adopts, on occasion, the term 'visual discourse', taken from the theories of cultural representation, which were responsible for the critiques of Panofskian iconographical approaches. The phrase has the advantage of highlighting the importance of power in enabling sets of ideas to receive acceptance, and it also draws attention to the ways different visual traditions did or did not share common ground. Out of this complex pattern of traditions, new and old, emerged a situation in which Italian artists were still leading the field when it came to claiming higher status, but also one in which many artists and viewers north of the Alps were discussing the issue of the dignity of art, with some focus on workshops and audiences in the Netherlands, especially Antwerp.

Part of the value of the 'soft' visual evidence lies in the ways it differs from the 'hard' evidence of the treatises and the histories. Books were published in small editions, in hundreds rather than thousands of copies, and could reach a small number of readers. While some visual images were displayed in relatively exclusive locations, such as a prince's study, a book of hours, or a guild chamber, many were on public show on guild altarpieces or processional banners, on the façades of artists' houses, or on civic festival decorations. The public locations of some visual representations meant that many different sorts of viewers could consider their import. Arguably such visual representations played an important role in publicising debates about the status and nature of art and artists.

Over and above their value for understanding the to and fro of debates about the status of art and architecture, the fact that so many of these objects were made by artists for themselves, and for other artists as primary users, means that they have a special interest in indicating the tastes and standards of artists. This applies to items made for specialists as commissioners (for instance guild and confraternity pieces), who could be expected to be the most rigorous critics in town. It also applies to the decorative schemes designed by artists, say, for the funerals of other artists and for the decoration they made for their own houses. What if anything was special about art for artists? I suggest, for example, that the allusive and learned characters of the altarpieces by Jan Gossaerts (*c.*1478–1532) and Marten van Heemskerck (1498–1574) for the guilds at Mechelen and Delft may be explained by the fact that both guilds comprised figurative specialists only (Plates 50, 52). Artists might appreciate narrative ploys that others would find puzzling. Thus the Tuscan architect Francesco da Volterra (1535–94) and the Mantuan engraver Diana Scultori (*c.*1547–1612) chose a scene for the façade of their house in Rome in which all the figures are represented as turning their backs on the viewer, and as if walking away (Plate 87). Artists had learned to imagine what painted people looked like in the round during their training in drawing. When Bartholomaeus Spranger made an engraved version of the same composition for ordinary sale he swung the figures round, so that the spectator got the expected front view. Artists often seem to have wanted suitably modest versions of the genres for which their clients paid good money, yet sometimes they selected for themselves subject matter which patrons were unlikely ever to have accepted. In this manner Federico Zuccari painted in his own house, as a role model, the trials of the disabled, humiliated and enslaved philosopher Aesop (Plate 97). It seems therefore important to be alert to the ways in which comparison between artists' work for themselves and their work for non-artists may sometimes denote artists' ways of looking.

These visual discourses were employed by some artists who were also writing on art, and who took major roles in the new academies which were foci for change in artistic status. This may be found for instance in the case of Federico Zuccari and Giorgio Vasari, who both contributed to most of the different representational traditions analysed in this study. It is also true to a slightly lesser extent in the cases of Lomazzo and Benvenuto Cellini (1500–71), who wrote treatises, and to Ketel, who wrote poetry as well as painting new ideas about the role of the visual arts. However the iconographies of art were also produced by artists who did not otherwise record their ideas. Painters such as van Heemskerck, Frans Floris, Cornelis van Dalem, Raffaellino da Reggio (*c.*1512–77) and designers like van der Straet and Hendrik Goltzius (1558–1617), amongst others, emerge as artists making significant interventions in the debates about the status and nature of the visual arts and architecture. Studying the visual data underlines the importance of certain key artists whose contributions have been amply documented in studies of the literary evidence, and at the same time brings into play many practitioners whose views and positions have been otherwise muted. Above all, visual imagery provided the means which artists knew best, and presumably valued highly, for conveying their views on their arts.

Notes

1 Francis Ames-Lewis, *The Intellectual Life of the Early Renaissance Artist*, New Haven, CT, 2000, p. 3.
2 Robert S. Nelson and Richard Shiff, *Critical Terms for Art History*, Chicago, 1992, pp. 116–27, especially p. 117.
3 J.M. Montias, *Artists and Artisans of Delft*, Princeton, NJ, 1982, p. 114.
4 Hans Huth, *Künstler und Werkstatt der Spätgotik*, Darmstadt, 1967, pp. 5–10.
5 Franz von Rhiza, 'Die Siegel der ehemaligen Bauhutte von St Stefan in Wien', *Mitteilungen der kaiserliche, königliche Central-Commission zur Erforschung und Erhaltung der Kunst und historischen Denkmale*, 16, New Series, 1890, pp. 151–6.
6 Montias, *Artists and Artisans of Delft*, p. 33. The Delft guild was secularised in 1572.
7 Montias, *Artists and Artisans of Delft*, p. 44.
8 Huth, *Künstler und Werkstatt der Spätgotik*, p. 89.
9 Michael Hochmann, *Peintres et commanditaires à Venise 1540–1628*, Rome, 1992, pp. 40–2.
10 Albrecht Dürer, *The Writings of Albrecht Dürer*, ed. and trans. W.M. Conway, London, 1958, p. 96.
11 Zirka Zaremba Filipczak, *Picturing Art in Antwerp, 1550–1700*, Princeton, NJ, 1987, p. 43.
12 Zaremba Filipczak, *Picturing Art in Antwerp*, pp. 42–5.
13 Montias, *Artists and Artisans of Delft*, pp. 33–7. Zaremba Filipczak, *Picturing Art in Antwerp*, pp. 40–1.
14 Martin Warnke, *Hofkünstler, Zur Vorgeschichte des modernen Künstlers*, Cologne, 1985, p. 328, translated by David McLintock as *The Court Artist: On the Ancestry of the Modern Artist*, Cambridge, 1993, pp. 5–33.
15 Karel van Mander, *The Lives of the Illustrious Netherlandish and German Painters Het Schilderboek*, ed. Hessel Miedema, trans. Derry Cook Radmore, 6 vols, Doornspijk, 1994–99, I, p. 265.
16 Zaremba Filipczak, *Picturing Art in Antwerp*, pp. 15–16.
17 Zaremba Filipczak, *Picturing Art in Antwerp*, p. 13.
18 Michal Šroněk, 'Rudolf II and the Guild of Saint Luke', pp. 216–21, in R. Konecny, ed., *Rudolf II, Prague and the World*, Prague, 1998, pp. 216–19.
19 Bram Kempers, *Painting, Power and Patronage: The Rise of the Professional Artist in Renaissance Italy*, Harmondsworth, 1992, p. 290.
20 Karen Edis-Barzman, *The Florentine Academy and the Early Modern State: The Discipline of Disegno*, Cambridge, 2000, pp. 152–73.
21 Anthony Hughes, 'An Academy for doing', *Oxford Art Journal*, IX, 1986, p. 5.
22 Edis-Barzman, *The Florentine Academy*, p. 207.
23 Hughes, 'An Academy for doing', p. 9.

24 Romano Alberti, *Accademia del Dissegno de' Pittori, Scultori e Architetti di Roma*, Pavia, 1604.
25 Giovanni Bottari and Stefano Ticozzi, *Raccolta di lettere sulla pittura, scultura, ed architettura*, 8 vols, Milan, 1822, VI, pp. 85–6.
26 Catherine King, 'Making Histories, Publishing Theories', pp. 251–80, in Kim Woods, ed., *Making Renaissance Art*, New Haven and London, 2007, p. 256.
27 King, 'Making Histories, Publishing Theories', pp. 272–6.
28 Julius von Schlosser, *La letteratura artistica*, Florence, 1956, pp. 235–49, 349–403.
29 King, 'Making Histories, Publishing Theories', pp. 276–8.
30 Von Schlosser, *La letteratura artistica*, pp. 405–24.
31 King, 'Making Histories, Publishing Theories', pp. 257–60.
32 King, 'Making Histories, Publishing Theories', pp. 263, 267–71; Von Schlosser, *La letteratura artistica*, pp. 193–5.
33 Martin Kemp, 'The super-artist as genius: the sixteenth-century view', pp. 32–53 in Penelope Murray, ed., *Genius*, Oxford, 1989.
34 Von Schlosser, *La letteratura artistica*, pp. 358–64.
35 King, 'Making Histories, Publishing Theories', pp. 263–7.
36 J. Hubaux and J. Puraye, 'Dominique Lampson Lamberti Lombardi vita: traduction et notes, *Revue belge d'archeologie et d'histoire de l'art*, XVIII, 1949, pp. 53–77.
37 W.S. Melion, *Shaping the Nethelandish Canon: Karel van Mander's Schilder-boek*, Chicago and London, 1991.
38 Jan Bialstocki, *Dürer and his Critics: 1500–1971*, Baden-Baden, 1986. p. 23.
39 Marina Arnold, 'Der Tod des Künstlers. Die Leichenpredigt auf Lucas Cranach d.J.', pp. 145–74, in Gunther Schweikhart, ed., *Autobiographie und Selbst Portrait in der Renaissance*, Cologne, 1998.
40 Benedetto Morrello, *Il funerale d'Agostin Carracci*, Bologna, 1603.
41 Warnke, *Hofkünstler*, pp. 168–71.
42 Warnke, *Hofkünstler*, p. 156.
43 Warnke, *Hofkünstler*, p. 41.
44 Warnke, *Hofkünstler*, p. 71.
45 Warnke, *Hofkünstler*, pp. 127–30.
46 Zaremba Filipczak, *Picturing Art in Antwerp*, p. 29.
47 Warnke, *Hofkünstler*, pp. 144–55.
48 Ulrich Middeldorf, 'On the Dilettante sculptor', *Apollo*, CVII, 1978, pp. 310–12.
49 Hochmann, *Peintres et commanditaires*, pp. 147–62.
50 A.M. Lecoq and P. Georgel, *La Peinture dans la peinture*, Dijon, 1983; Andrew Martindale, *The Rise of the Artist in the Middle Ages and the Early Renaissance*, London, 1972; Ames-Lewis, *Intellectual Life of the Renaissance Artist*.
51 Ames-Lewis, *Intellectual Life of the Renaissance Artist*, p. 13.
52 Frances Borzello and Alan Rees, eds, *The New Art History*, London, 1986.

Painting, sculpture and architecture – Liberal or Practical Arts?

I

During the sixteenth century significant changes took place in the visual representation of painting, sculpture and architecture in the abstract. While in some cases they were shown in the traditional manner as manual crafts, in other, innovating, images they appeared as intellectual skills. These occupations were sometimes represented as men working at their arts, sometimes by means of female personifications holding the tools of their trades and occasionally by showing just the tools themselves. The conventional displays of painting, sculpture and architecture as Practical Arts stressed their importance for the well-being of society and tended to appear in the broad context of allegories of good government. However, the experimental iconographies undertaken from the first decade or so of the sixteenth century onwards invented ways of representing painting, sculpture and architecture as companions of the intellectual and imaginative Liberal Arts. These challenging new visual discourses were launched in a sequence of commissions for patrons connected with courts in Italy and France during the first half of the century. Then, as if they felt licensed by such prestigious precedents, from just before the mid-century onwards, artists themselves began to present the new imagery in designs, both in Italy and the Netherlands, which they made for their own use and which included decorations for their own houses as well as the funerary commemoration of talented artists. Finally, towards the end of the century, engravers started to issue prints, so as to circulate even more widely the idea that the figurative arts and architecture could be honoured with new respect. In this way, a body of imagery was produced which contested the notion that painting, sculpture and architecture were merely Practical Arts. The importance of leadership by courts in this account helps to confirm Warnke's contention in 1985 that 'it was through the courts that the arts discovered their higher destiny'.[1] Nevertheless, the evidence also underlines the role played by artists themselves, when designs for their dwellings were involved, in publicising new identities for their professions.

Parts of this story have been thoroughly researched, for example in the analysis of the tomb of Julius II and the funerary commemoration of Michelangelo, in studies of specific commissions such as the funerary urn of François I, and in accounts of the house decorations of Giorgio Vasari and Frans Floris in Tuscany and Antwerp.[2] Nevertheless, some significant pieces of evidence – for example, murals by followers of Raphael for the Villa Imperiale at Pesaro, and a painting attributed to Giorgione (*c.*1477–1510) – have not yet been woven into the narrative. What began in the early sixteenth century as the panegyric of princes was soon joined by the praise of artists and art, effecting something of a visual revolution in the representation of the figurative arts and architecture in the abstract in many parts of Europe.

During this period some commissioners continued to require artists to show the figurative arts and architecture as Practical Arts (such as agriculture, hunting, textile manufacture, metalworking, navigation, medicine and commerce) which were important to the running of human society in what may broadly be termed allegories of good government. This convention was a respectable way of regarding art, with emphasis on its utility, whether decorative or functional, for a well-ordered community. It drew on a long scholarly tradition of defining the Mechanical Arts stretching from the twelfth to the sixteenth century, whose continuity is epitomised in the statements made in the Latin encyclopaedia by Barthélémy de Chasseneux, the *Catalogus gloriae mundi*, which was published in six editions between 1546 and 1603. While he praised the Practical Arts – such as printing, wagon building and painting – as necessary to human society, he termed them 'plebian' and treated them as 'adulterated' or applied sciences rather than pure sciences like the Liberal Arts.[3] He quoted the fifteenth-century scholar Saint Antoninus of Florence as stating that

> the mechanical arts are seven in number that is to say weaving, armature, navigation, agriculture, hunting, medicine and theatre. It is said that a mechanical art is an adulterated form of science rather than a liberal one.[4]

'Armature' was defined as including on the one hand the beating and melting of metal to make objects and on the other the shaping of wood, cement and stone to form buildings – that is 'architectura'. Painting and sculpture were very much humble adjuncts to architecture in this system, which had first been laid out by Hugh of Saint Victor in the twelfth century.[5]

The iconographic tradition of the Practical Arts included well-known examples such as the Florentine campanile decoration attributed to Giotto and Andrea Pisano and completed about 1340.[6] This programme had shown painting and sculpture together on adjacent reliefs for the first time on a monumental scale amongst other Practical Arts such as weaving and medicine. The idea that sculpture is a manual art had been represented in choir-stall carvings during the fifteenth century showing sculptors carving images in wood and stone alongside other tradesmen

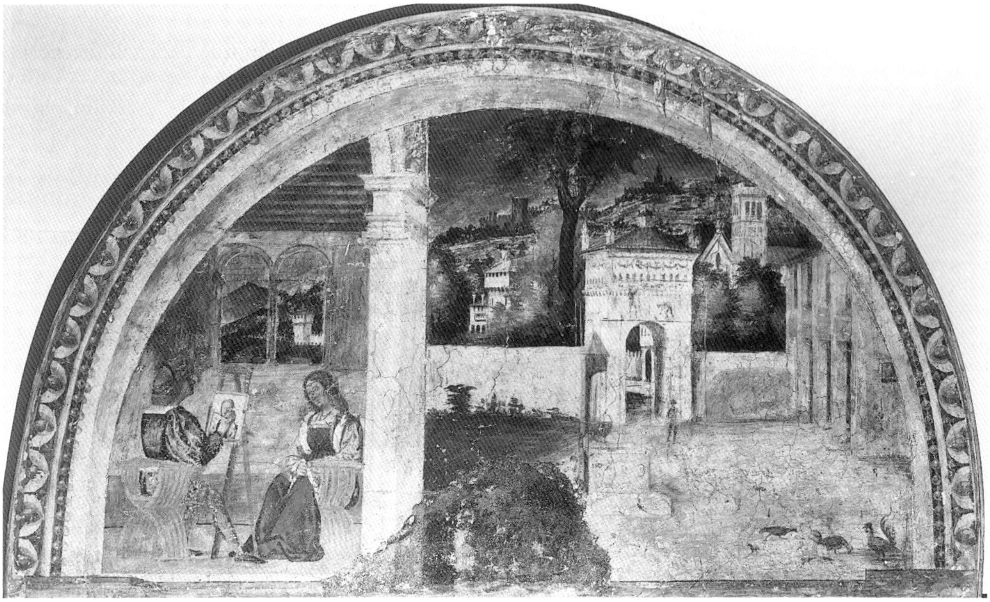

1 Attributed to Andrea Previtali, *Painting as a Practical Art*, 1512, formerly Villa La Zogna, now Villa di Trescore, Bergamo.

and women: for example, at Bruges (1425), Rouen (1470) and Beauvais (1500).[7] Amongst the reliefs adorning the choir stalls at Rouen were also a carpenter and a mason. In all cases the arts of sculpting and building were represented by male exponents busy at their work.

Painting, sculpture and architecture as Practical Arts: Bergamo, Amiens, Antwerp, Lyons, Frankfurt, Nuremberg

The relatively lowly position of painting and building was sustained in some quarters in Italy as one can see in the series of Practical Arts originally adorning the lunettes below the vault of a reception room in the Villa La Zogna at Bergamo, which were inscribed by Andrea Previtali (*c.* 1480–1528) and seem to have been painted in 1512.[8] In this scheme painting, woodworking and building are depicted as contributing – along with commerce, navigation, blacksmithing, dyeing cloth, farming sheep, ploughing the land, and the trade of the barber – to the efficient running of society (Plate 1). This villa belonged to the wealthy local family Casotti de Mazzolenis, who may have chosen the theme to affirm their ideals of well-ordered government. Two of the lunettes which suggest the allegiance of the family to Venetian control of Bergamo were placed on either side of the chimney flue, which was decorated with the arms of the family. They showed to the left the Doge seated, to give justice as overall ruler, while in the right-hand lunette the local representative of the Republic is seated with the ten citizens making up the civic council. Below the central seat is the date '1512' and the inscription 'Bartholomeus Mostus et decem deputati' (Bartolomeo da

Mosto and ten deputies). In another lunette a view of the Piazza San Marco from the lagoon has been depicted. Andrea Previtali placed his initials 'A.P.' on one of the bales of merchandise in the lunette showing merchants at a harbour exchanging goods. To signify painting he depicted a male painter portraying a woman. Both are sitting under a loggia. The activities of building are represented by masons cutting stone and measuring it with a compass. The work of carpentry is depicted as entailing sawing, the use of the plane and measuring. The emphasis in all these is on the way different occupations serve the rulers of the city.

The figurative arts and architecture were also represented as Practical Arts in ecclesiastical settings during the sixteenth century, as, for example, in the choir stalls for Amiens cathedral commissioned by the Chapter and carved between 1508 and 1519 by Arnould Boulin and his assistants Linard le Clerc, Guillaume Quentin and Pierre Meurisse. Other wood carvers included Jehan Turpin, Antoine Avernier, Alexandre Huet and a carver named Breton. Here, different trades were carved at the ends of the arm rests of the richly historiated seats, literally and perhaps figuratively under the hands of the canons of the cathedral. The wood carver is represented carving a statue. The builder works at a table composing a plan with a set square. These skills were portrayed alongside many other mechanical occupations such as that of the scribe, the baker, the butcher, the beggar, the schoolmaster, and women selling vegetables and carrying water.[9]

The currency of these attitudes towards painting and sculpture is evident in such moralising engravings as that representing the proper use of 'Time' for the benefit of society by Gerard de Jode (*c.*1509–91), which he printed in Antwerp soon after 1551.[10] Here a tall personification of Time – perhaps intended to represent a civic statue – presides over busy artisans, and the painter and sculptor are shown along with farmers, shopkeepers, cobblers, tailors and blacksmiths (Plate 2). Latin inscriptions explain that, 'It is a profitable way of using time to see to the needs of the body' and 'The hand of the master and expertise in inventing things praiseworthily gladdens cities and kingdoms with riches' (*Temporis utendi commoda ratio ad corporis necessitatem. Artificum manus et solers inventio rerum divitiis urbes, regnaque laude beant*). Art, then, is about wealth and physical well-being. The engraving was issued as one of a suite of four displaying the use and abuse of Time.

In all these cases the skills were represented by artisans demonstrating their techniques. However, in the engravings illustrating the discussion of the Practical Arts by Barthélémy de Chasseneux, Lyons, 1546, more abstract female personifications were chosen to represent painting, sculpture and architecture. Architecture is seated in a workshop surrounded by the tools of painters and sculptors which are placed on her table or hanging on the wall (Plate 3). She is associated with other female personifications numbered in sequence on the illustration: 1 Agriculture, 2 Goldsmithing, 3 Commerce, 4 Architecture, 5 Hunting, 6 Surgery and

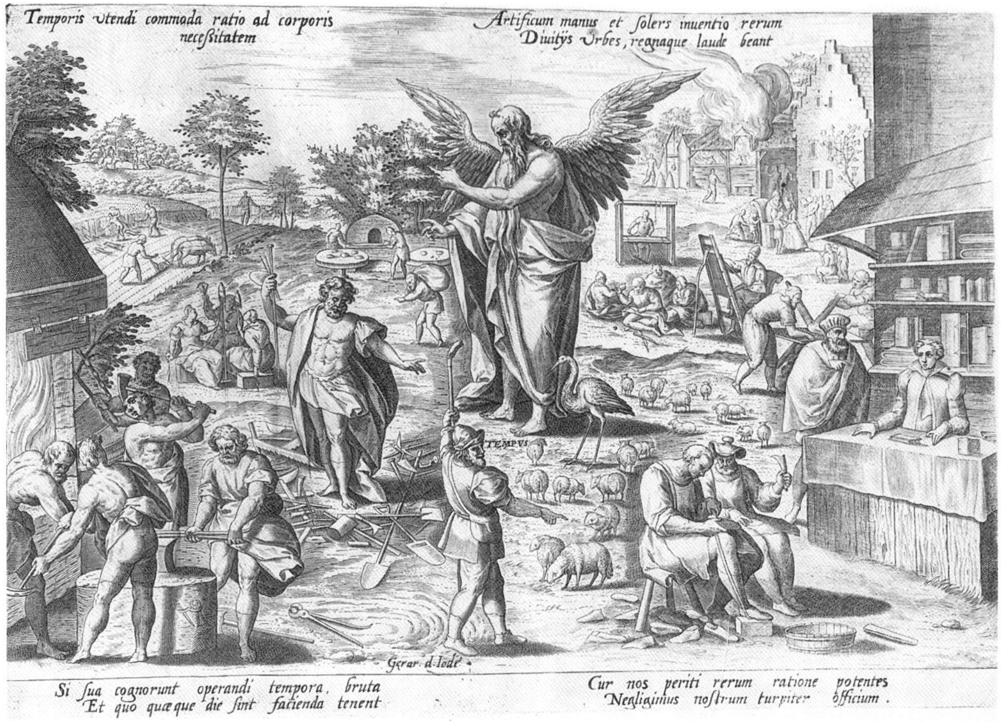

2 Gerard de Jode, *Temporis utendi*, *c.*1551. British Museum.

7 the making of armour and musical instruments (labelled in Latin *Agricultura*, *Aurifabra*, *Mercatoria*, *Architectura*, *Venatoria*, *Cururgia* [*Chirurgia*] and *Tympanistria*). Although Barthélémy quoted Lorenzo Valla's assertion in his *De elegantia linguae latinae* (*Concerning the Elegance of the Latin Language*; 1444) of the near liberal status of the figurative arts and architecture, he and the illustrator still categorised them as manual.[11]

It is indicative that these illustrations continued to represent the notion that architecture is the leading art, to which painting and sculpture are subordinates because they are assumed to decorate buildings. The 1571 Venice edition employed a simplified version of this illustration.[12] In the 1579 edition of this encyclopaedia, which was published in Frankfurt, new illustrations were made by Jost Amman, and he represented the same sequence of Practical Arts, though this time with standing female personifications (Plate 4). Architectura was represented with a small painting and a sculpture at her feet.[13] The fact that Jost Amman, like Andrea Previtali, signed his name on the representation of commerce (*mercatoria*), may suggest how both artists were interested in merchant status.

A little earlier in 1568, also at Frankfurt, Jost Amman (1539–91) had designed two graphic surveys of trades, one in German and the other in Latin: Hans Sachs' *Eygentliche Beschreibung aller Stände auf Erden* (*Truthful Description of all Occupations*) and Hartmann Schopper's *Panoplia illiberalium mechanicarum aut sedentariarum artium genera* (*Survey of Illiberal, Manual and Sedentary Arts*). These publications each provided over a hundred engravings of Practical Arts, which represented them in the traditional way – that of artisans working. Here he had shown the painter, the stained-glass maker, the embroiderer, and the carver of statuary, along with the range of skills recalling the occupations

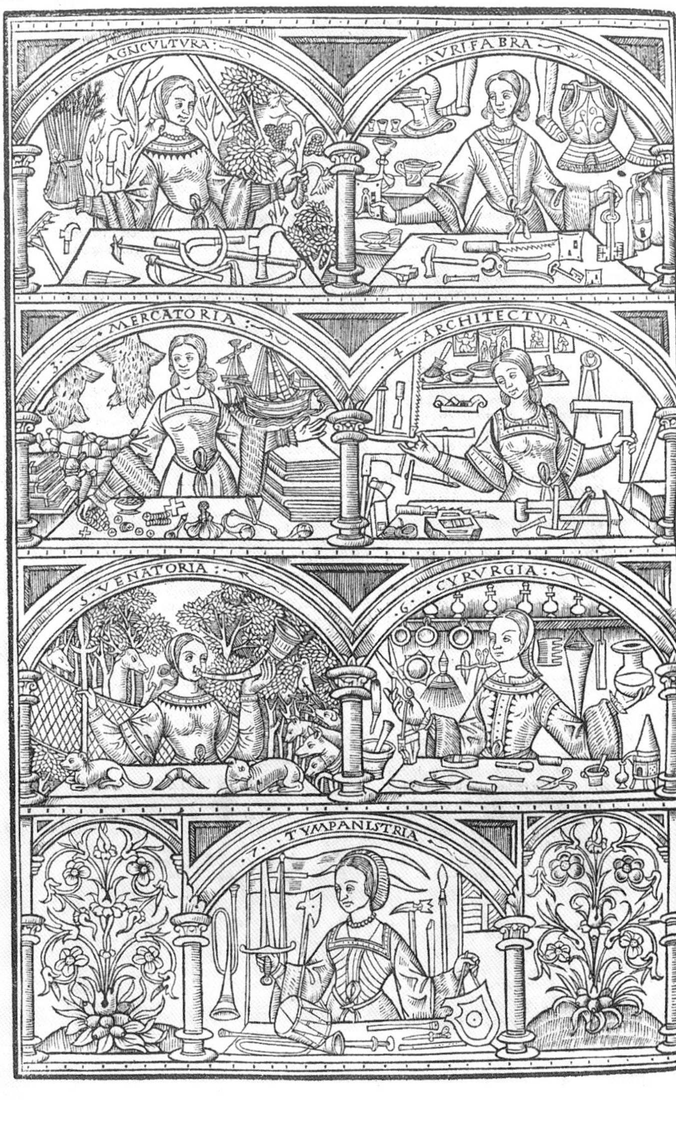

3 Barthélémy de Chasseneux, *Catalogus gloriae mundi*, Lyons, 1546, fol. 212 verso. British Library.

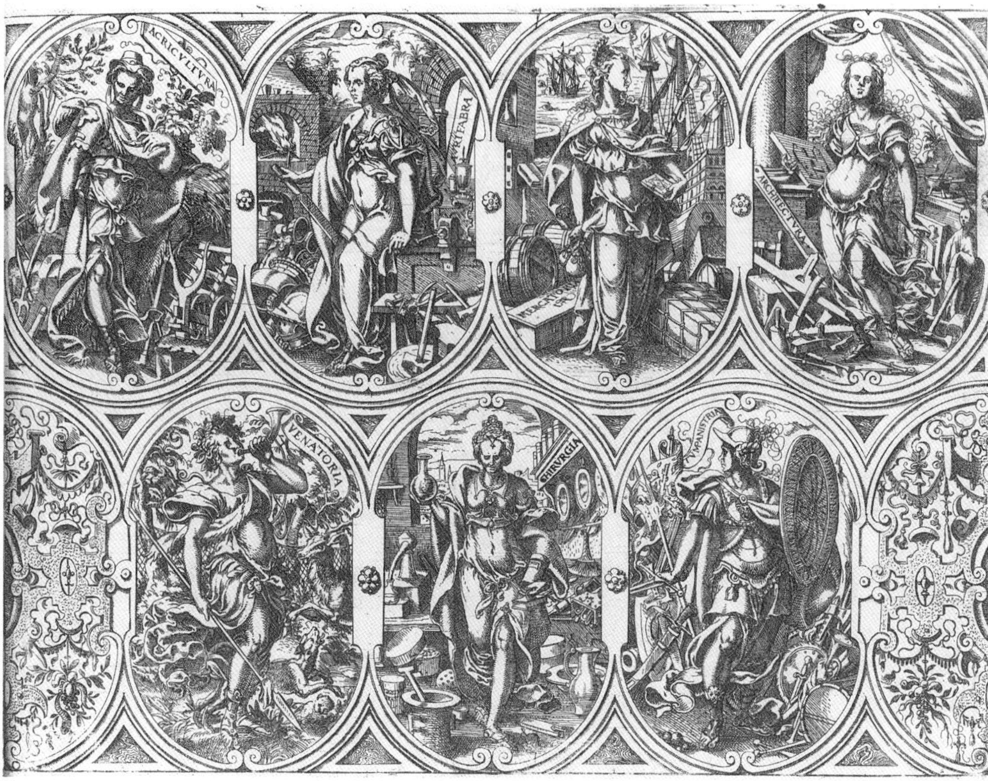

4 Jost Amman, Barthélémy de Chasseneux, *Catalogus gloriae mundi*, Frankfurt, 1571, British Library.

placed on the choir stalls such as the miller, the printer, the soldier and the baker.[14] There was therefore a persistent tradition of representing the activities of figurative arts and building as Practical Arts.

Nevertheless, this does not seem to have been a rigid system and there is some evidence that Painting at least might be treated as a special case and given genteel status even where arts entailed in carving and building had been shown as Practical Arts. An etched series of the Seven Liberal Arts also by Jost Amman published in Nuremberg in 1577, for example, begins with an etching showing a woman crowned and with wings seated on clouds, while on earth men hold up the tools representing their skills to her. Possibly she represents Glory. On the left are grouped the Practical Arts, including men holding the chisels and hammers of masons and sculptors, while on the right are Music, Geometry, a scholar with a book, a doctor of medicine and a painter.[15]

Introducing painting, sculpture and architecture as Liberal Arts: Rome, Venice, Pesaro, Arezzo, Florence

Such visual debate had been made possible by the arrival from the first decades of the sixteenth century of a visual tradition employing new types of personification for painting, sculpture and architecture and showing them in the company of the Liberal Arts such as music and poetry. These personifications and devices initially appear in the context of the panegyric of princes in their grand palaces, in advice to young rulers or on the funerary commemorations of rulers. Whereas the iconography of the Practical Arts presented architecture as the dominant overarching skill, the new iconography of the Liberal Arts treated sculpture, painting and architecture on an equal footing with one another. This visual rhetoric drew on a literary tradition which had gathered strength during the fifteenth century. Already in 1380, Filippo Villani's praise of famous Florentines had included painters: 'In the estimation of many, and not indeed foolishly, painters are not regarded as of inferior talent with respect to those whom the Liberal Arts make Masters.'[16] Assertions of the genteel associations of sculpture and architecture together with painting came a little later when for example Leon Battista Alberti in *Della pittura* in 1436 placed them in the company of the Liberal Arts when he lamented on the dearth of 'painters, sculptors, architects, musicians, geometricians, rhetoricians, augurs, and similar most noble and most marvellous intellects which nowadays are found most rarely and little to be praised'.[17] Likewise Lorenzo Valla wrote in his treatise on the elegance of the Latin language in 1444 of 'those arts, that is to say the arts of painting, sculpture, modelling and architecture which approach most closely to the liberal ones'.[18] The noble status of painting was quite frequently claimed as, for example, when Jacopo de'Barbari (*c.*1460/70–1516) in 1501 called it 'the eighth Liberal Art'.[19] Supporters of sculpture were less vociferous, although in 1504 Pomponio Gaurico (in *De sculptura*, published in Florence) had one of his speakers pronounce that sculpture 'stands amongst the others of noble status and seems to me to be worthy of a free man'.[20] Alberti in the *De re aedificatoria* published in Florence in 1485 had carefully differentiated the profession of the architect from the manual art of the carpenter. The architect could be compared to 'the highest of the other disciplines . . . I define the architect quite differently as one who completes work by means of reliable and admirable reason and also via the powers of the mind and soul'.[21] The visual representation of the three arts as Liberal Arts in the panegyric of princes advertised these ideas prominently and in a new and particularly prestigious way. They began with experiments by an artist in the circle of Giorgione as well as by members of the workshop of Raphael, and possibly by Michelangelo, before any set formulae had been accepted for the iconography of painting, sculpture and architecture as Liberal Arts.

The experiment may have commenced with the figures of Liberal Arts along with painting, sculpture and architecture which, the biographer of Michelangelo Ascanio Condivi claimed, were planned for the tomb of Julius II during the period 1505–42. Condivi described the original scheme in 1553:

> there were other bound statues representing liberal arts like Painting, Sculpture and Architecture each with their attributes, so that one might easily identify them by these means which denoted that together with Pope Julius these worthy arts were imprisoned by death.[22]

Horst Janson argued that elements of this scheme survived in the two prisoners – one with the attribute of a monkey and the other with the attribute of a capital – which were eventually given in 1546 by Michelangelo to Roberto Strozzi, who transported them to Lyons in 1550 (Plate 5). Janson suggested that the ape signified painting since it was described as an ape of nature while the capital could be an attribute for sculpture.[23] More recently, Mary Garrard has argued that – given the less precise identification by Vasari as to the figures signifying the arts on this tomb and given the later use of winged Victories taken from Roman Imperial sculpture as models for personifications of Painting, Sculpture and Architecture – it is more likely that painting, sculpture and architecture were represented by the winged Victories standing between the prisoners which were part of the original tomb programme, according to early drawings.[24] Since the first personifications of Painting and Sculpture as Liberal Arts actually completed by Raphael's pupils around 1524 did indeed derive from winged Victories, her argument is plausible. On the other hand, it is also true that the long tradition of showing the figurative arts and architecture as men working could have led Michelangelo to envisage masculine arts at this early stage. One prestigious scheme which did a little later show sculpture, architecture and drawing as Liberal Arts, and as masculine was completed at the French court for Henri II between 1550 and 1556.

Two precedents for the funerary commemoration of a ruler as a patron of the Liberal Arts have been noted: the tomb of King Robert of Anjou commissioned by Queen Joanna in 1343 for Santa Chiara in Naples, and the tomb of the uncle of Julius II, Pope Sixtus IV, in Saint Peter's completed between 1484 and 1493. There was in addition another one – that is to say the celebrated chapel of the Liberal Arts and Muses with Apollo and Mnemosyne at San Francesco in Rimini, completed around 1460 for Sigismondo Malatesta.[25] However, none of these had included allusions to the figurative arts and architecture, although the tomb of Sixtus IV which Julius himself had been responsible for commissioning had significantly selected the art of perspective, a skill associated with the latter arts, which he had had placed along with the conventional trivium, quadrivium, theology and philosophy on the floor tomb.[26] However, no truly contemporary sources confirm Condivi's report, and it seems possible that it was more a token of the regard with which the three arts were held in the 1550s than of what had been planned in 1505.

It is from the Veneto that secure evidence survives for the invention of an iconography showing painting as a Liberal Art. Here the context

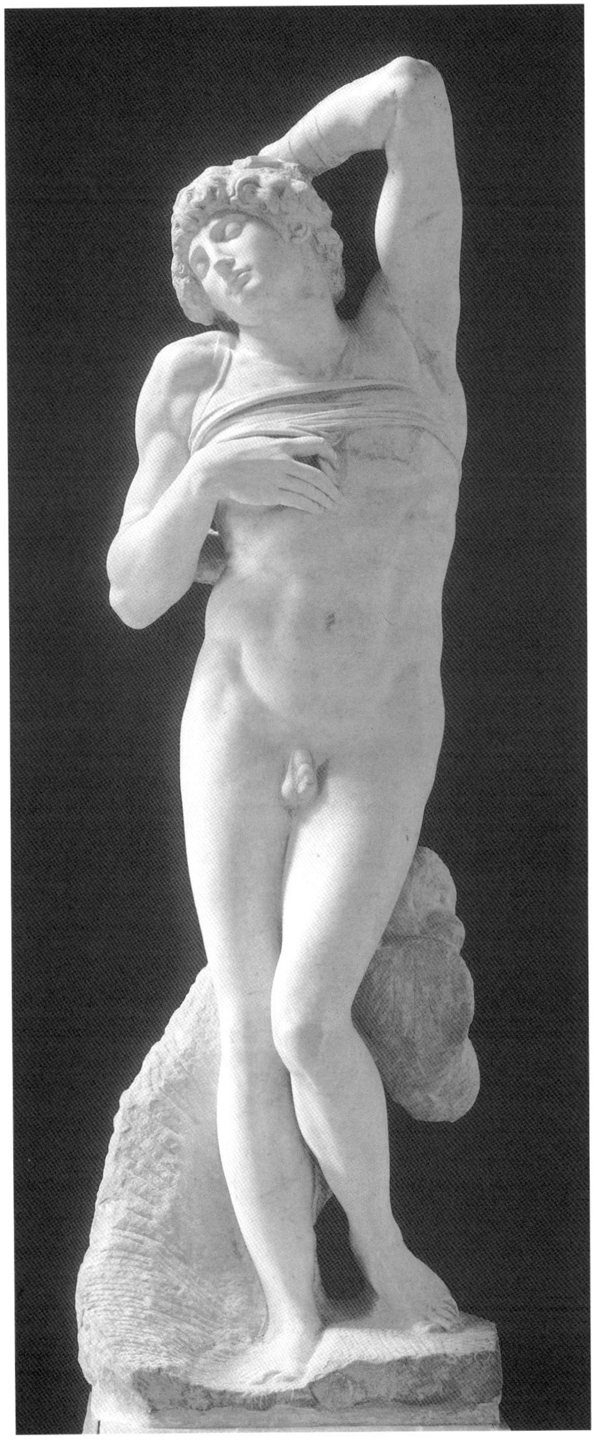

5 Michelangelo, *Captive Art*, 1505–42, for tomb of Julius II, Louvre, Paris.

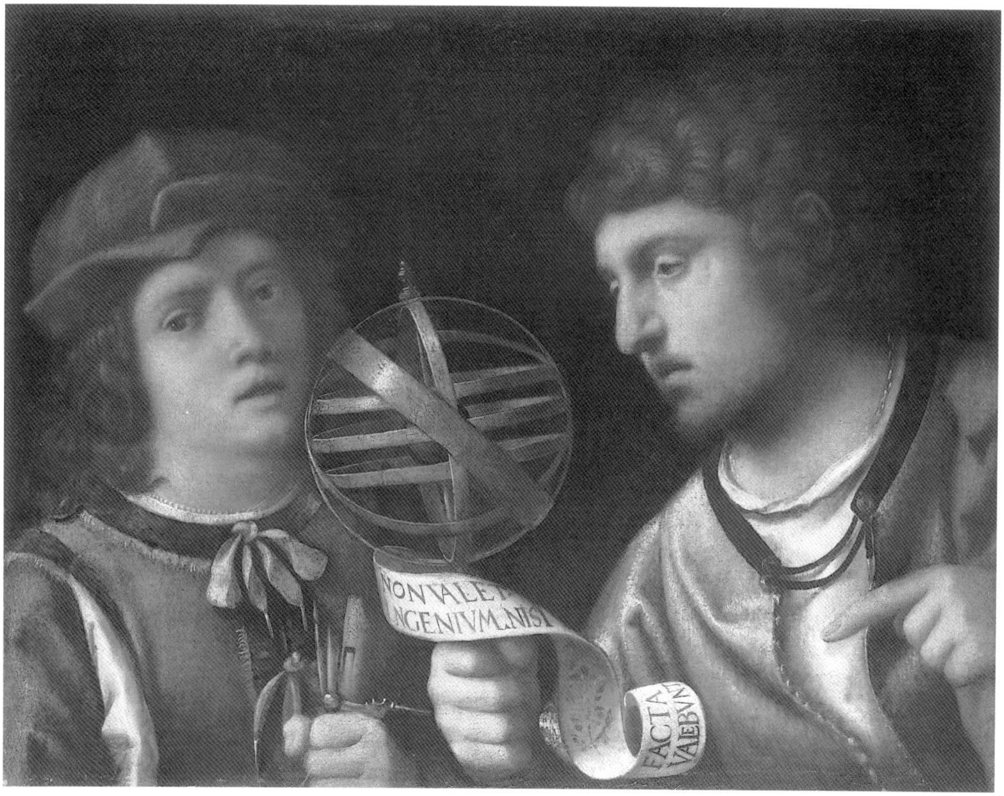

6 Attributed to Giorgione, *Giovanni Borgherini and his Tutor*, *c.*1509, canvas, 47 × 60 cm, National Gallery of Art, Washington.

was that of displaying the education and career goals of ruling men. Dated about 1509, the portrait shows a boy being taught Liberal Arts (including the art of painting) by a tutor, and is attributed to Giorgione or his circle[27] (Plate 6). The tutor holds a celestial globe signifying astronomy and the boy holds the compasses associated with geometry, a flute for music, a pen linked with the trivium and a brush for painting.[28] An inscription on a banderole asserts that 'Personal talent is of no use unless one's deeds bear it out' (*Non valet ingenium nisi facta valebunt*). The use of the term *ingenium* in relation to painting made important claims since only the Liberal Arts were considered to require both *ars* (skill) and *ingenium* (unique personal aptitude). It has been suggested that the boy was the Florentine Giovanni Borgherini, then resident with his family in Venice (as described by Vasari).[29] It is of interest that Luca Pacioli in the *De divina proportione* published in Venice in 1509 had argued that painting should be allied to the Liberal Arts, because of its use of perspective, and should be placed beside music.[30] Scholars could refer to texts such as the accounts of Pliny the Elder to argue that ancient Greek and Roman societies had regarded painting as a dignified profession and as a suitable element in the curriculum for a well-born boy.[31] Indeed, this was the time when Baldesarre Castiglione (1478–1529) was completing the writing of *Il libro del cortegiano* with its advice to gentlemen to learn the art of drawing and painting, considering that in Greek and Roman societies painting 'had been received in the first class of the liberal arts'.[32]

Around 1524 Raphael's pupils Guilio Romano (?1599–1546) and Giovanni Francesco Penni (?1496–1528) made a further important intervention, when they depicted painting and sculpture along with poetry, recording the virtue of their patron Clement VII (Plate 7).[33] They took as their models the winged female Victories which were visible on reliefs carved on the Arch of Constantine, and the column of Trajan, and had been shown as writing the deeds of these Roman emperors on oval shields.[34] They painted their small scene somewhat hidden away on the intrados of one the window embrasures. The scene was probably more of a tribute to the Pope who had paid for the decoration than to his artists and poets. The room, now called the Sala di Constantino, was dedicated to narrating the achievements of the Emperor Constantine, so that the adoption of imagery from Constantine's arch in Rome would have

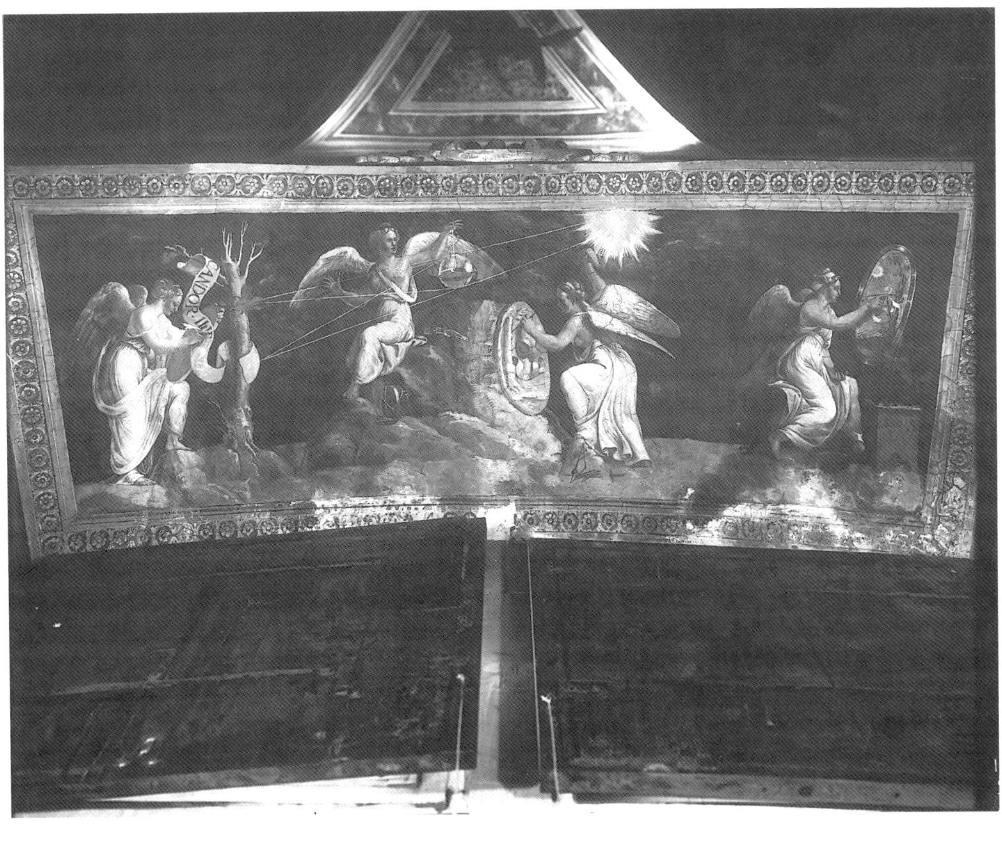

7 Giulio Romano and Giovanni Francesco Penni, *Painting, Poetry and Sculpture Celebrate the Impresa of Clement VII*, 1524, soffit of a window, Sala di Constantino, Vatican, Rome.

seemed appropriate. In the Sala di Constantino, Painting, Sculpture and Poetry are shown recording the *impresa* of Clement VII, *Candor illaesus* ('Purity unsullied'). Poetry inscribes these words on a scroll, but the figurative arts represent, in painting and sculpture on oval shields, how the rays of the sun pass harmlessly through a crystal ball (which signified the purity or transparency of Clement VII) but set on fire any 'impure' object (in this case a tree) straight away. Paolo Giovio (1483–1552) explained the import of this *impresa*. In this representation, painting and sculpture were being firmly dissociated from the image of the worker in the workshop employed in the Practical Arts series, and given more conceptual status.

As early as 1400 or so Cennino Cennini had compared poetry and painting following the Horatian dictum 'ut pictura poesis' in the *Libro dell'arte*.[35] However, he had conceded that, whereas poetry belonged to the first class of Liberal Arts, painting could only hold the second rank. In his Italian translation of *De pictura* in 1436 Leon Battista Alberti had advised painters to be learned in the Liberal Arts: 'It will be an advantage if they take pleasure in poets and orators, for these have many ornaments in common with them.'[36] Leonardo's drafts for a *paragone*, probably written from 1490s onwards, between painting and poetry made more explicit claims for the status of the painter, asserting for example that 'the many sidedness which painting commands is incomparably greater than can be attained by words'.[37] However, it was not until 1504 that sculpture was drawn into the comparison with literary production by Gaurico, when he argued that 'writers work with words and sculptors work with things: the former narrate while the latter portray and exhibit'. He went on to demonstrate that ancient Greeks employed the one term *graphein* to denote both the writing of words and the carving and painting of images. To underline their propinquity he cited the use of hieroglyphs as picture writing.[38]

The Sala di Constantino experiment was transposed to a much larger size and given a prominent role by artists close to the Raphael workshop a decade later at Pesaro. In fact, the introduction of victorious personifications of Painting and Sculpture along with Liberal Arts praising the deeds of a prince was advertised influentially in the decorations of the Villa Imperiale soon after 1530 as part of the panegyric of Duke Francesco Maria della Rovere. The mural painting team included Agnolo Bronzino (1503–72), the Dossi brothers (Dosso, *c.*1486–*c.*1541, and Battesta, ?–1548), Camillo Mantovano and Raffaellino dal Colle (*c.*1490–1566), all under the direction of Girolamo Genga (1476–1551).[39] Girolamo Genga and Raffaellino had had close connections with the workshop of Raphael, while Duke Francesco Maria was the nephew and heir of Julius II, who had first planned some such programme for his tomb. In the pendentives of the vault of the Sala dei Semibusti, Painting and Sculpture were again accompanied by Poetry, but for the

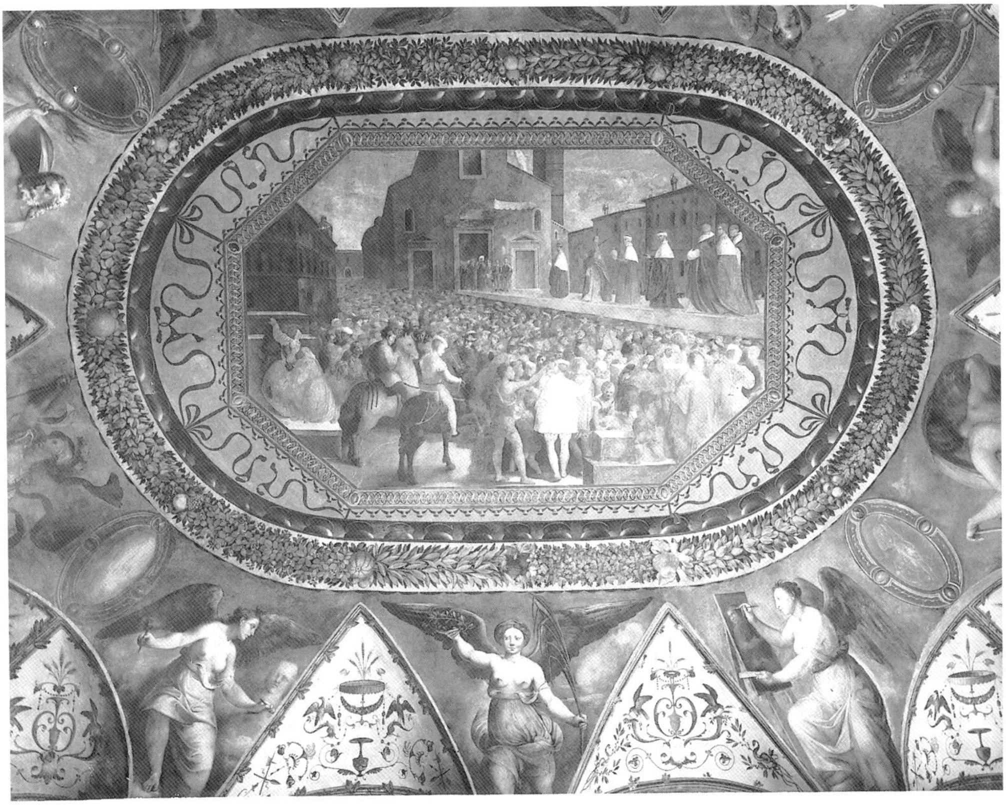

8 Attributed to Raffaellino dal Colle, *Fame and Victory of Duke Francesco Maria della Rovere and the Emperor Charles V*, *c.*1530, Villa Imperiale, Pesaro.

first time they were joined by a personification of Music (Plate 8). All are depicted as winged women working at their arts. Painting stands at her easel and Sculpture carves a figure. Poetry holds a pen to write on a tablet while Music plays a viol. The motif of the oval shields is retained but is used here for the four spandrels at the corners of the vault. The central scene at the apex of the vault commemorates Duke Francesco Maria's attendance as witness to the coronation of the Holy Roman Emperor Charles V at Bologna in 1530. As in the Sala di Constantino the idea seems to be that the figurative arts, along with poetry and music, all celebrate the patron's achievements and indeed those of Charles V. Below the coronation scene Victory offers a crown of laurel and the palm of eternity and she is flanked by Painting and Sculpture. On the other side of the vault Fame blows a trumpet and is flanked by Poetry and Music. All six personifications are depicted as female and as having wings. The pendentives on the shorter sides of the vault represent Jupiter paired with Mars and Mercury beside Amor.

The imagery seems to draw on the traditions of the *trionfi* of Petrarch with the idea of the triumph of Fame being followed by even more lasting Victory. A comparable encomium had been portrayed when Piero della Francesca had represented Francesco Maria's predecessor as Duke of Urbino, Federigo da Montefeltro, crowned by Fame.[40] The presence of Jupiter as king of the gods and Mars as soldier could suggest the celestial company to which Charles V and Francesco Maria aspired as Emperor and as military leader respectively. Mercury could be present in his role as the guide and messenger of the gods, in order to introduce the Emperor and the Duke to the heavenly realm. Amor, as a *putto* carrying a bow and arrow, could indicate love of virtue here. This seems likely to place the programme in the *via virtutis* tradition of the Dream of Scipio employed for the encomium of rulers as told by Silius Italicus (first century CE). In his poem describing the Punic wars – *Punica* – Silius Italicus had related the dream experienced by the soldier Scipio, in which Virtue instructed him to turn from the easy life of pleasure, to protect his people, in war and had described her companions: 'My attendants are Honour and Praise, Renown and Glory with joyful countenance, and Victory with snow-white wings like mine. And Triumph crowned with laurel raises me at last to heaven.'[41] Fired by love of virtue 'calet amor virtutis', Scipio vows to place the laurel wreath of victory in the temple of Jupiter.[42] The scheme at Pesaro provided noble acceptance to the new iconography by giving it a prominent position on the vault of what may have been the Duke's bedroom, and promoted the idea of Music joining the company of Poetry, Painting and Sculpture. The personifications of the arts are depicted as inhabiting the heavens so that again their activities are being far removed from the actuality of manual labour in the workshop.

Not surprisingly, it was only after the most powerful patrons had employed the new iconography that artists began to use it for their own purposes. This important shift was made by Giorgio Vasari when, in 1542, he appropriated the new imagery for the decoration of his own house at Arezzo.[43] From this point onwards, artists began to develop the visual rhetoric of the dignity of the figurative arts and architecture in schemes for themselves, augmenting the continuing trend for rulers to enjoy being praised as patrons of the figurative arts, architecture and the other Liberal Arts. At Vasari's house Painting, Sculpture and Poetry were shown on the pendentives of the vault of one of his reception rooms and here he innovated significantly by adding Architecture (Plate 9). Painting depicts the image of a man, Sculpture similarly carves the statue of a man, while Architecture holds compasses and the plan of a building. In the centre of the vault Vasari depicted the figure of Fame, winged and blowing a golden trumpet. However, the figurative arts and Architecture are depicted as without wings – so that they seem to represent a salient move towards the conventions adopted for the majority of personifications of the Liberal Arts. Poetry did, however, retain her wings, perhaps following her depiction in this way by Raphael in the Stanza della Segnatura.[44]

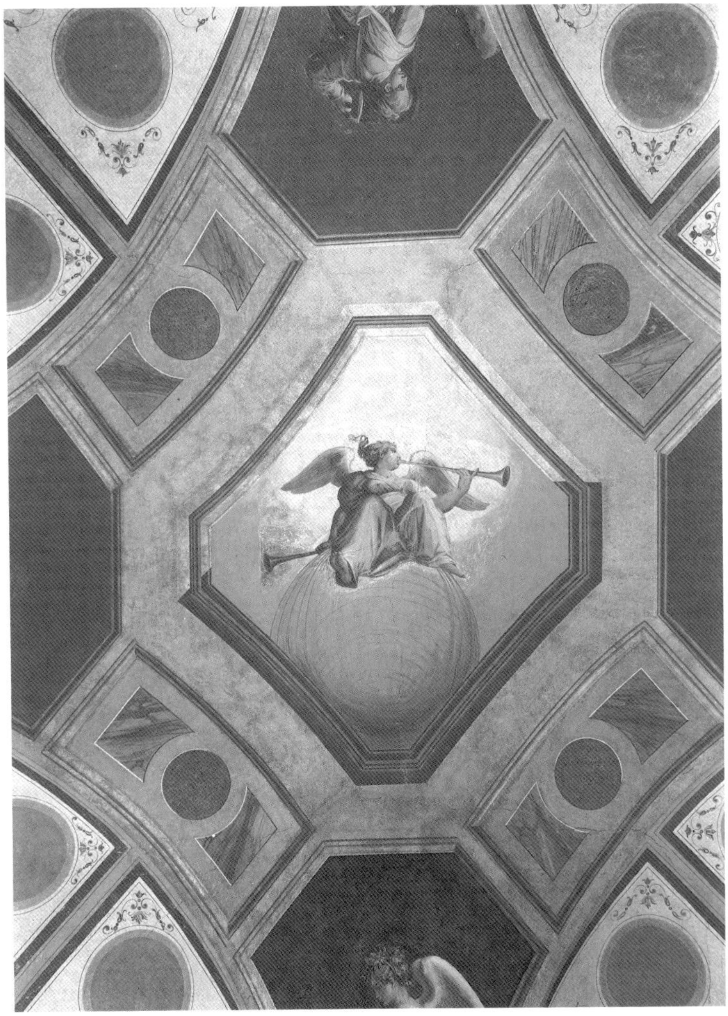

9 Giorgio Vasari, vault of the Sala della Fama, 1542, Casa del Vasari, Arezzo.

In 1546 Vasari was able to exhibit the three personifications of Painting, Sculpture and Architecture for the first time on a grand scale, and in a prestigious location, in Rome. As he related, he depicted them kneeling before Pope Paul III to present the plans for the new Saint Peter's. Their various tools are placed on the ground in front of the table upon which they have spread their plans.[45] This mural was commissioned by Cardinal Alessandro Farnese in the Sala dei Cento Giorni at the Palazzo della Cancelleria, in Rome (Plate 10). The figures are female and are dressed in classicising robes, and, as at Arezzo, they have no wings. The context of the whole mural is again panegyric. Each of the four walls in the room celebrated the qualities of the Pope as head of Christendom, and this scene seems to have represented his Magnificence since the word 'Magnificentia' is inscribed on the base of the

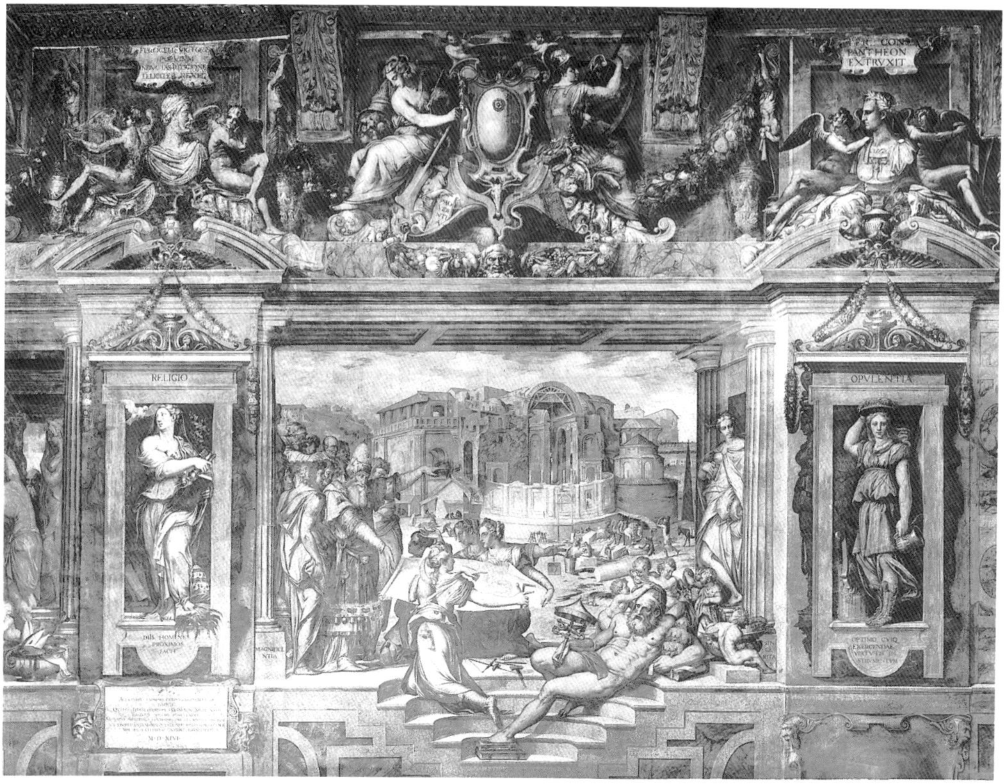

10 Giorgio Vasari, *Painting, Sculpture and Architecture present the plans for Saint Peter's to Paul III*, Sala dei Cento Giorni, Palazzo della Cancelleria, 1546, Rome.

column behind the Pope. Following Vasari's description, the other three walls show the liberality of the Pope in granting honours (notably to Michelangelo as well as numerous scholarly churchmen such as Pietro Bembo (1470–1547) and Paolo Giovio), as well as his role as peacemaker and his eloquence as a diplomat. Three women denoting Painting, Sculpture and Architecture cluster behind the table while Geometry kneels in the foreground with a set square and compasses in her hand.[46] A project designed by Vasari around 1546 for Don Pedro di Toledo Viceroy of Naples placed Painting, Sculpture and Architecture explicitly in the presence of the Liberal Arts. The drawing for the decoration of a vault, which was not however executed, offered the viewer the path to Truth, Fame and Eternity if they avoided Ignorance. Instead they were to follow a virtuous path guided by personifications of Theology, Philosophy, the Seven Virtues, the Seven Liberal Arts, Painting, Sculpture and Architecture. All the personifications were labelled in Italian.[47]

Vasari also advertised this imagery to a wide range of viewers in the engraving which he published on the last page of his *Lives of the Artists* issued in 1550 (Plate 11). Since these personifications illustrated a text which accorded art and architecture unprecedented status, it seems likely that they furthered the visual campaign for the recognition of the figurative arts and architecture as worthy of a liberal education. On the final page Vasari presented Fame holding a trumpet and a torch, flying overhead. Her torch illuminates three seated personifications. Sculpture carries a chisel and a statuette, Painting has a brush and a palette in her hand while Architecture has compasses and a set square. Below them are naked figures of men and women shown as if being awakened in a secular version of resurrection – possibly indicating the revival of the arts. Later Raffaele Borghini (*c.*1537–88) in 1584 interpreted it to indicate that Vasari's history would always keep the memory of the artists alive, appending this motto: 'Hac sospite numquam hos perisse viros, victos aut morte fatebor' (With this protection never shall it be shown that these men perished through death). Vasari's initiative was positively backed

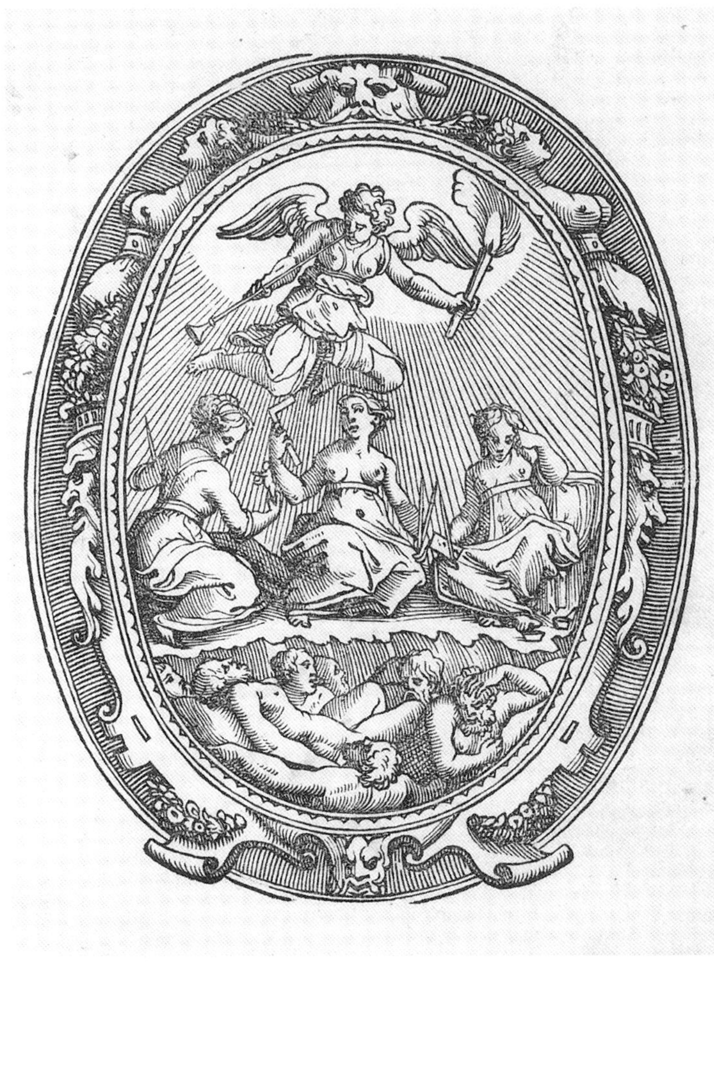

11 Giorgio Vasari, final page of *Vite*, 1550. British Library.

by his patrons since the publication of the *Lives* was supported by the Medici to whom he dedicated his book.[48]

To sum up it seems then that it was in the circle of Giorgione, about 1509, that painting was first visually placed with the Liberal Arts, to be followed by images made by the pupils of Raphael, who put painting and sculpture with poetry about 1524 and with music soon after 1530. It was Vasari, in his own house, who first added Architecture in 1542.

Translating painting, sculpture and architecture as Liberal Arts to France and the Netherlands 1540s–1560s

The three decades from the 1540s to the 1560s were another decisive period for publicising new ambitions for the dignity of art and architecture in visual terms. This was the time when the pictorial and plastic ideas of those in the circle of Giorgione, of Raphael's pupils and of Vasari, were transposed to France and the Netherlands and given significant new interpretations.

One influential scheme comprised the white marble funerary urn of François I (Plate 12). This represented Drawing, Sculpture and Architecture along with Geometry, Astronomy and the Muses on a monument which was contracted in 1550 and completed in 1556. The funerary urn was designed to contain the heart, brain and entrails of the king on the commission of his son Henri II, and related to the interest shown by the dead monarch in the ideas of Italian artists, encouraged by his marriage to Catherine de' Medici. It was designed by the royal architect (and former sculptor) Philibert de l'Orme and placed in the convent church of Notre Dame des Hautes-Bruyères near Rambouillet.[49] It was carved by Pierre de Bontemps (*c.*1512–*c.*1570) and consisted of a base adorned with reliefs showing Apollo and the Muses with Astronomy. This supported an urn decorated with scenes showing Geometry, Architecture and Sculpture. Architecture is represented as a man seated beside a building which is being erected and as holding a set square and compasses. Sculpture is illustrated by three men (one of whom is holding compasses) working on statuettes of nude women. In addition, there is a relief of a man drawing with a quill on a tablet *en plein air*, before an antique statue in what look like Roman ruins. Although this has been identified as Painting, it seems more likely to denote Drawing instead. Philibert, who had trained in Lyons, had also spent a study period in Rome 1533–36 when he had a chance to draw after the antique.[50]

Following his return from a visit to Italy in 1545, Frans Floris of Antwerp also transported and transformed this visual rhetoric, for a commission by a Netherlandish patron, when in around 1559–60 he made a large canvas which has been associated with the commission of a tax farmer of Philip II, Nicolaas Jongelinck of Zeeuwse (Plate 13).[51]

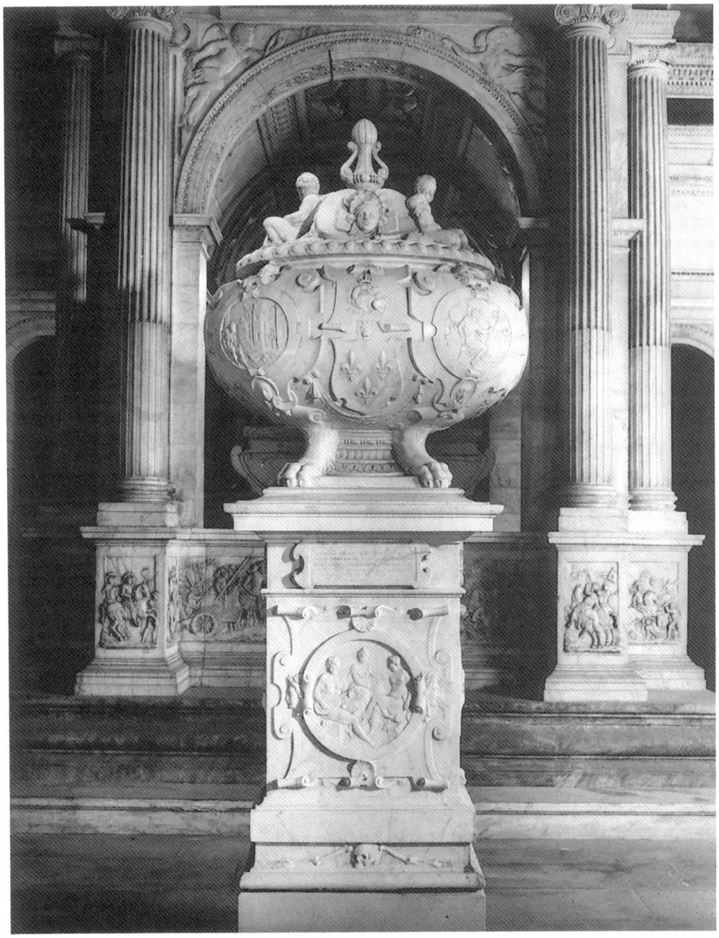

12 Philibert de L'Orme and Pierre de Bontemps, *Funerary Urn of François I*, 1550–56, formerly Notre Dame des Hautes-Bruyères near Rambouillet, now Saint Denis.

This depicted female personifications of Painting, Sculpture and Architecture, and these were shown for the very first time, in a completed work, along with all seven of the Liberal Arts. The scene, which has been identified as *The Awakening of the Arts*, depicted the arts being protected against the ravages of war. The ten female personifications are shown asleep, except for one who is writing. A bearded man, who may perhaps be interpreted as Apollo, is waking them. To the left Sculpture has the attribute of a statuette, while Architecture has a carved column base, and Painting is accompanied by a panel painting. The other figures have attributes of the Liberal Arts: music books, a viol, a ruler, a terrestrial and a celestial globe as well as some compasses. The ruins of buildings and a wild landscape suggest the ravages of war, but Mars is being led away by four women, one of whom is carrying his sword and battle trophies. Carl van de Velde

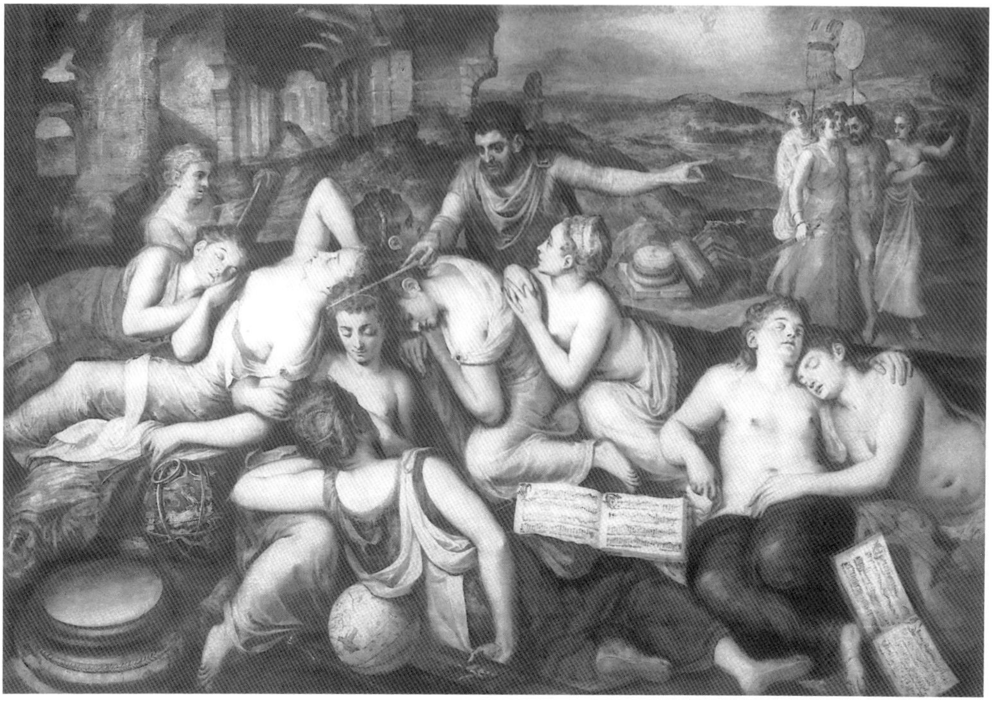

13 Frans Floris, *The Awakening of the Arts*, 1559–60, Museo de Arte, Ponce, Puerto Rico.

suggested that this was commissioned in thanksgiving for the conclusion of peace by Henri II in 1559.

A further decisive shift occurred in the 1560s when personifications of these arts accompanied by signifiers of liberal status were placed on public show in the streets of Antwerp on two artists' house façades.[52] Frans Floris placed Painting, Sculpture and Architecture along with Poetry in a pictorial scheme on his house façade in Antwerp in about 1563 (Plate 14). His design was sufficiently acclaimed to be considered worth engraving in 1576, and was still being talked about approvingly by the sculptors of Antwerp in the early seventeenth century. In the central scene over the door, Painting was represented as a woman at her easel, painting a nude woman, while Sculpture was carving a statuette. Between them it seems possible that Geometry was also portrayed. To left and right were fictive statues of Poetry and Architecture, portrayed as if standing in niches. Architecture held a set square, a plumb line and compasses, and was crowned with trowels. At her feet were placed hammer and chisels. Poetry was portrayed with a laurel wreath on her head, holding a book and a scroll and with the swan sacred to Apollo at her feet. He laid out these personifications with figures signifying Labour, Diligence, Experience and Practice in such a way as to suggest the kinds of qualities and attainments which were necessary for success in the figurative arts and architecture.

At the same time in Antwerp, in a scheme dated 1563, the painter Cornelis van Dalem had a relief made representing Painting, as a woman reclining with her easel and brushes, and labelled *Pictura* over the doorway to his house (Plate 15). She was flanked, in the spandrels of the doorway, by sculptures of Minerva and Mercury. The whole ensemble was placed above portraits of Dürer and van Eyck, and these are the only two elements to have survived. They have been attributed to the work of the local sculptor Willem van den Brouck (*c.*1520–79). The pairing of Minerva and Mercury was connected with philosophical and literary academies in antiquity, especially with the academy of Cicero (first century BCE) and as *Hermathena* (that is, Mercury-with-Minerva) placed as frontispieces on scholarly works in the sixteenth century.[53] These academic and scholarly associations were therefore now placed on view to a mass audience of citizens in one of the most populous and cosmopolitan cities in northern Europe. As with Vasari's house at Arezzo, artists were taking decisive actions on behalf of their arts.

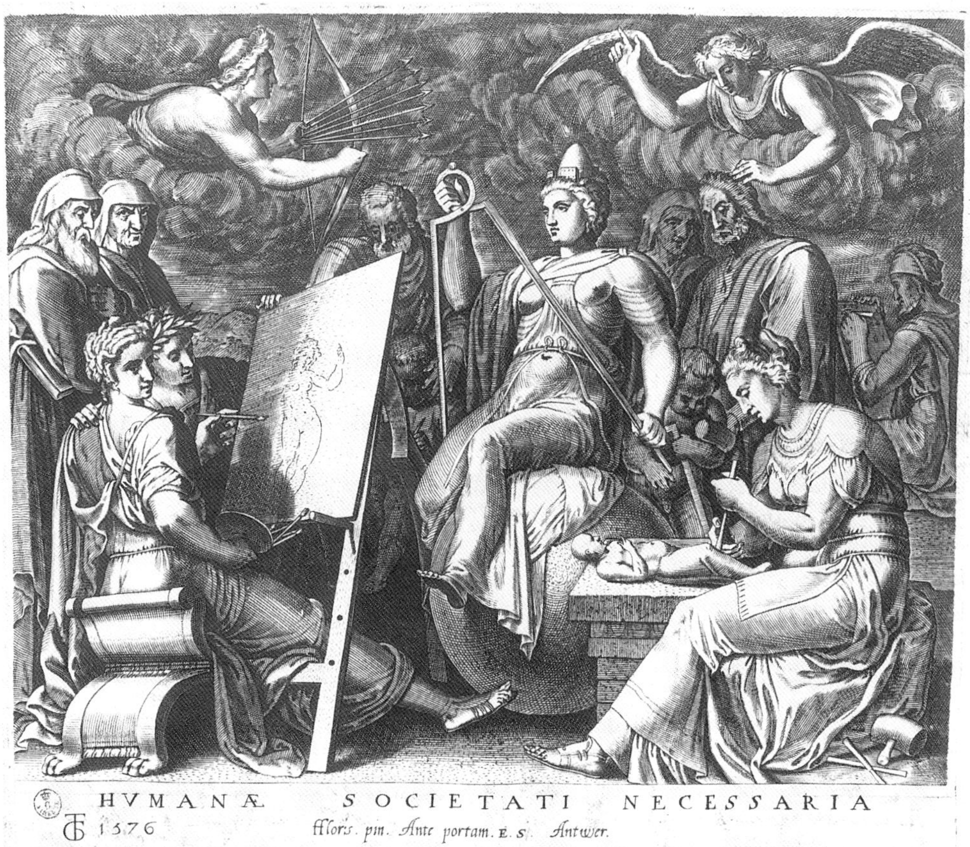

14 After Frans Floris, *Painting, Sculpture and? Geometry*, over door for the artist's house, painted *c.*1563, engraving signed 'T.G.', Antwerp, 1576. Graphische Sammlung Albertina Vienna.

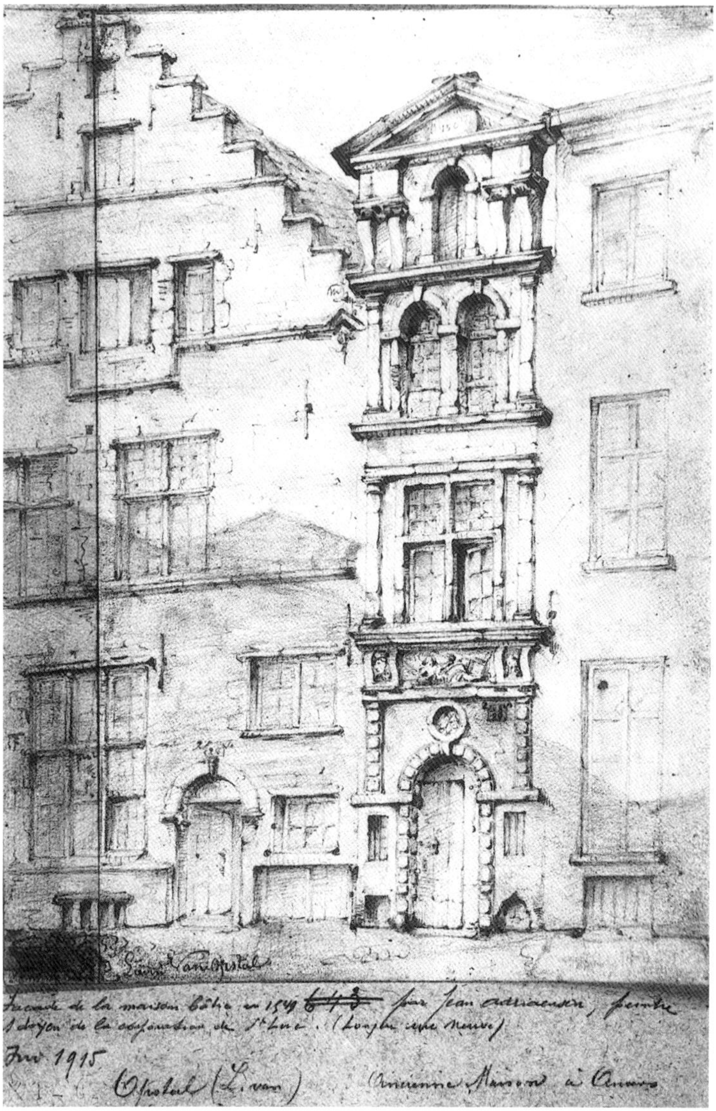

15 L. van Opstal, the house of Cornelis van Dalem dated 1563, Antwerp, catalogue number A. LXXXV 34 Inv. no. 1915, Museum Plantin-Moretus, Stedelijk Prentenkabinet.

Confirming the new iconography in Italy from the 1560s: schemes acclaiming artists

At the same time, in the Italian peninsula, the new claims for the genteel status of the figurative arts and architecture were being confirmed in a series of commissions for artists, and for ruling families. The most significant spectacle putting forward these ideas was the scheme devised for the temporary catafalque made by the new Accademia del Disegno for the lying in state of their first president Michelangelo at San Lorenzo in Florence in 1564 (Plate 16).[54] This impressive display was seen by many viewers. The Academicians elected Benvenuto Cellini, Bronzino, Bartolommeo Ammanati (1511–92) and Vasari as designers. In practice, the organiser seems to have been Vasari with the advice of Vincenzo Borghini. Personifications of Painting, Sculpture, Architecture and Poetry were seated at the four corners of the catafalque each holding their instruments as attributes. Fame was positioned at the apex.[55] Because of his skill in poetry, Michelangelo was able to stand for the links claimed between the Liberal Arts and architecture, painting and sculpture. In using San Lorenzo as the location for the obsequies, the academicians were tying Michelangelo's triumphs to the Medici family, whose parish church this was. Equally Duke Cosimo de' Medici was

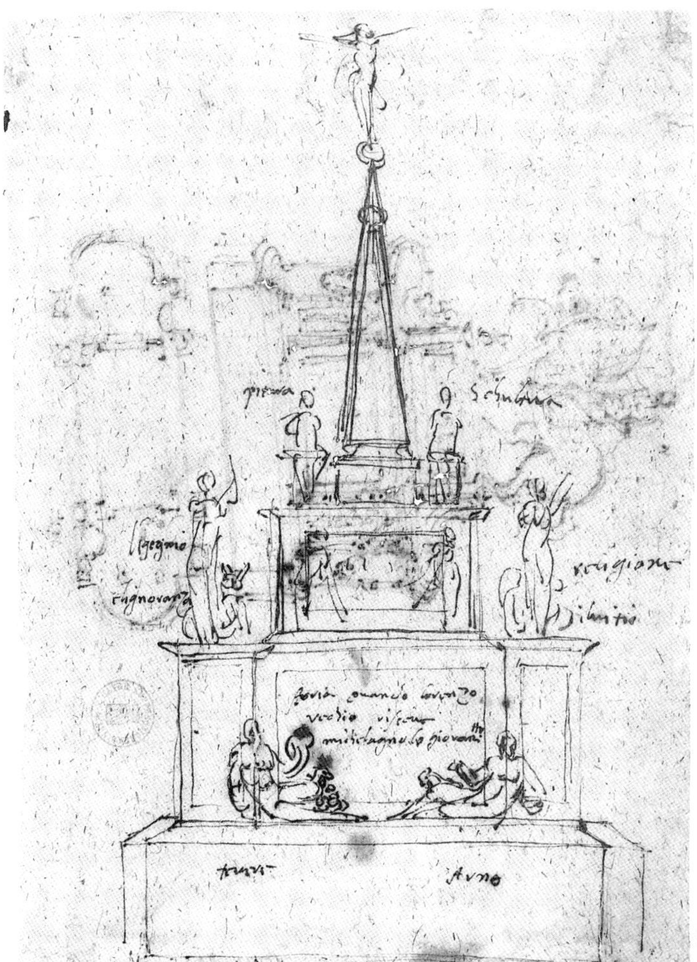

16 Drawing for the catafalque of Michelangelo, attributed to Vincenzo Borghini, 1564, Graphische Sammlung, Munich.

the head of the Academy, so this was a display relating, if indirectly, to the panegyric of rulers.[56]

The widening currency of these ideas is also indicated by their appearance on small items made by artists for artists. This is illustrated in the medal made for the Milanese painter Girolamo Figino (1548–1608), probably in the early 1560s, for his personal use.[57] In the medal, which has been attributed to Pietro Paolo Galeotti (1520–84), Girolamo had himself represented nude, wearing antiquising drapery. This form of representation may have expressed admiration for ancient Greek and Roman artists and had begun in the mid-fifteenth century with the medal of Giovanni Boldù (flourished 1454–*c.*1477).[58] Girolamo chose as his obverse a figure of Minerva, seated with emblems of the Liberal Arts at her feet (there is a viol and a book of music for the musician, the compasses and set square of the geometrician or architect, and a torso appropriate to a sculptor) with the motto *Omnis in hoc sum* ('In all this I am'). As medals were made in small editions, Girolamo may have used it to introduce himself to clients or other artists. Girolamo was described by his younger colleague, the artist and writer Giovanni Paolo Lomazzo, as a poet and sculptor, while Antonio Maria Venusti (1562) praised his expertise in anatomy and painting. It may be supposed that Girolamo was well informed as to ambitions for high status, since he was the pupil of Francesco Melzi (*c.*1491–*c.*1570), who was the heir to Leonardo's literary estate.[59]

The spread of the personifications of the three arts in a prestigious context was achieved in the 1568 edition of Vasari's *Lives*, which for the first time provided 150 portraits of artists – one to preface each biography. These were framed using personifications of Painting, Sculpture and Architecture, depending on the arts in which an artist had been skilled. This edition also repeated the graphic format for the final page used first in the 1550 edition, but making it even more vigorous, with Fame blowing a triple trumpet, and the 'dead' responding even more enthusiastically to the three arts seated below.[60] It too was dedicated to Cosimo I, and this underlines the reflected glory shone by the praise of artists on the prestige of the prince.

Vasari was also able to display this message again, this time in his house in Florence. There, during the period 1573–74, he designed an elaborate mural for his main reception room, depicting the three arts along with Music and Poetry (Plate 17). Small ovals in the frieze contained portraits of artists who were important to Vasari's career, including his self-portrait.[61] The personifications are large scale and placed in the main zone of the mural. Painting represents a human figure on an oval panel. Sculpture energetically carves a River God. Architecture holds compasses and a set square. They have been given victorious wings, as if recalling the original iconographic models invented for the Sala di Constantino. The personifications flank three large narratives

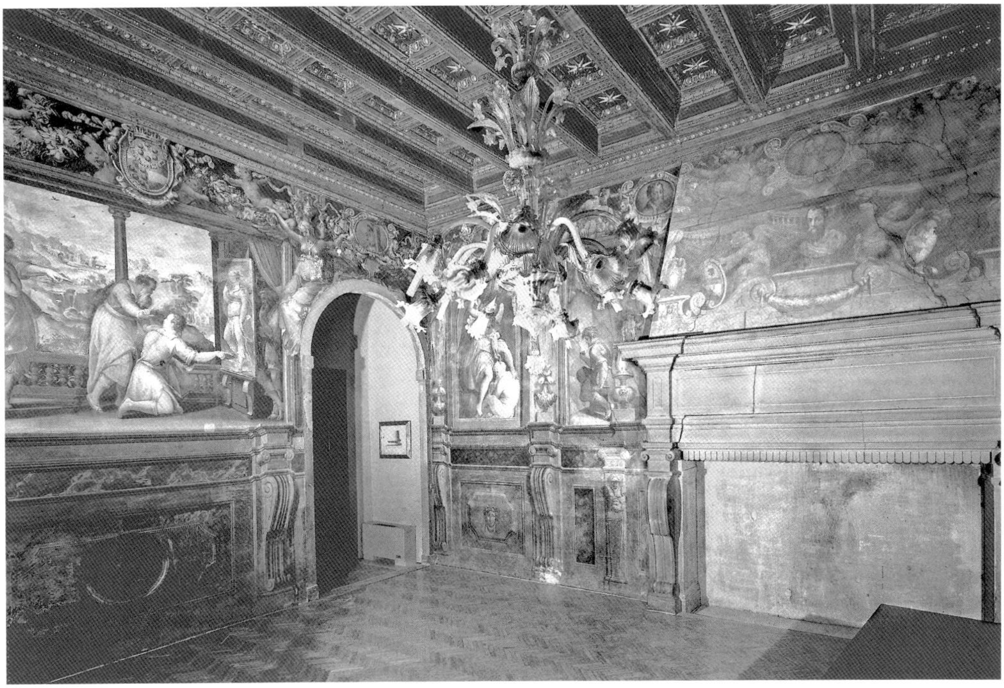

17 Giorgio Vasari, *Sculpture, Painting, Architecture, Poetry and Music*, 1574, Casa del Vasari, Florence.

celebrating events in the lives of ancient Greek artists. Music and Poetry are also portrayed with wings.

Following the lead of the Accademia del Disegno in its funeral apparatus for Michelangelo, a programme entailing personification of the figurative arts and architecture and associating them with lofty status was planned for the funeral of Titian in 1576. This was devised by the Fraglia de' Pittori and the obsequies were to be staged in the painters' church of San Luca in Venice. The elaborate scheme was never fully effected because of plague, but the preparations reached a mature stage, and art historian Carlo Ridolfi (1594–1658) transcribed documents concerning the proposals. These plans suggest the consensus amongst Venetian artists as to the liberal status of painting, sculpture and architecture. The spectacle was intended to centre on the full-length effigy of the painter himself dressed with all the dignity of a Knight and Count Palatine, who had been honoured by the Emperor and Pope. The stress on Titian's noble social status was matched with the emphasis on the idea that painting was the companion of poetry and history. At the apex of the apparatus for the lying in state would have appeared a personification of a mourning Painting, 'and from her neck shall hang a mask and two boys will hold up her mantle and at her feet will be written the motto "Imitation"', Beneath Painting there were to have been eight other statues surrounding the body. Ridolfi transcribed them in the following order. First came the figure of Apollo who, Ridolfi related, stood for poetry, with the inscription 'It soothes souls' (*Mulcet animos*). Next came a female personification of History with the inscription 'It concerns the past' (*Praeterita refert*). Then came a figure of Design (*Disegno*) and one of Sculpture, who was to be shown as a woman, 'with a hammer and chisels making the form of a head and bodies in relief' which was to be inscribed 'From marble come men' (*De marmore viros*).[62] Beside her would be Architecture, 'with the grave face of a matron holding a plumb line for levelling, and a compass in her hand' and at her feet the model of a rich palace. She would be given the inscription 'For ornament and use' (*Ornamento et usui*).[63] These five figures were to be flanked by Symmetry (*Simmetria*), Hard work (*Fatica*) and Honour, demonstrating that the programme was planned to represent the virtuous way in which Titian had achieved his success.[64]

Confirming the new iconography in Italy in the 1560s: schemes acclaiming rulers

The confirmation of the intellectual status of the figurative arts and architecture was also publicised by a new generation of ruling families, in schemes commissioned in Tuscany, Liguria, the Veneto and Caprarola. Between 1555 and 1565, Vasari was able to underscore the princely prestige of the three arts by placing them on the vault of the *scrittoio* or writing room of Duke Cosimo in the Palazzo Vecchio (Plate 18). The room has also been called a little treasury or *tesoretto* and the paintings have been attributed to the assistance of the Antwerp painter Jan van der Straet. In the centre of the ducal study were painted the symbols of the Four Evangelists. Four narratives were placed on the cross vault illustrating the activities of Poetry (with Minerva and the Muses), Philosophy (with ancient philosophers disputing), Geometry (with scholars using compasses, books and globes), and a scene which has not been identified because of damage. Personifications of Painting, Sculpture, Architecture and Music were placed between these narratives: Painting works at an easel, Music is represented by three women musicians, Architecture holds a compass and set square, and Sculpture carves a bust. Here the arts of design were being represented as worthy of the attention of a learned ruler.[65]

Painting, sculpture and architecture were placed with the seven Liberal Arts even more overtly in a grand programme of decoration in a room on the second floor of the Palazzo Lamba Doria in Savona, Liguria. The painting has been attributed to Ottavio Semino dal Soprani (?1527–1604) or his workshop and has been dated to about 1566.[66] The scheme was completed for Bernardo Ferrero, who belonged to one of the patrician families in the town. The apex of the vault told the stories of Jason and the Argonauts while the pendentives of the vault were adorned

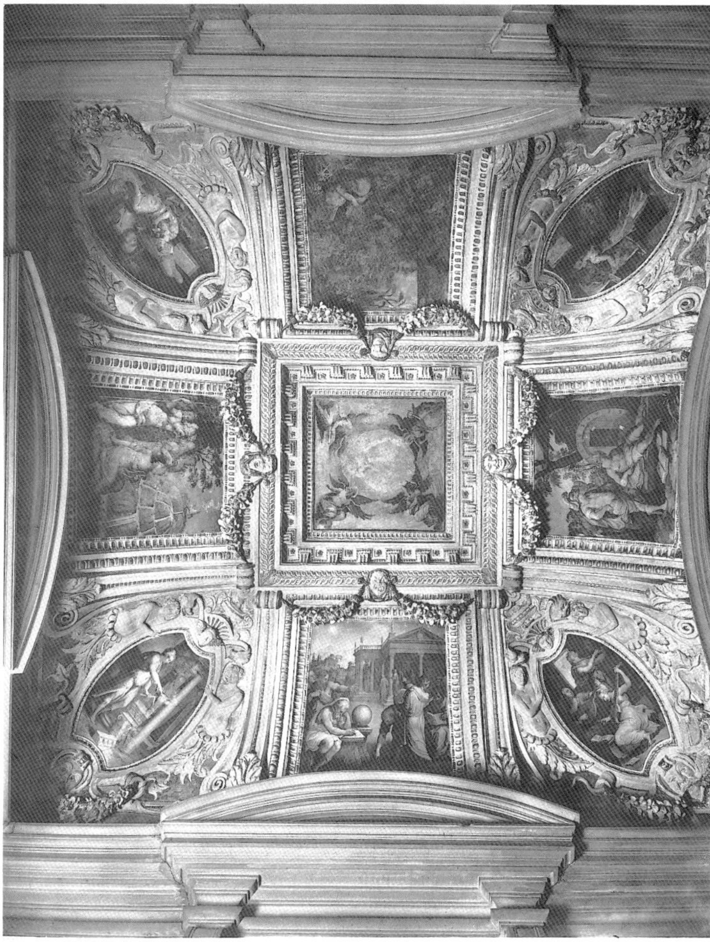

18 Giorgio Vasari, *Painting, Sculpture, Architecture and Music with Geometry, Poetry and Philosophy*, 1555–65, Scrittoio, Palazzo Vecchio, Florence.

with personifications of the seven Liberal Arts, along with Painting, Sculpture and Architecture. All the figures are labelled in Italian. Painting is represented in the act of depicting a nude, Sculpture holds a statuette while Architecture carries a small gothic chapel. All three are shown as perched on clouds and dressed *all'antica*. On the long walls Painting, Grammar and Rhetoric faced Arithmetic, Music and Geometry. On the short walls Architecture and Sculpture were represented opposite Philosophy and Astronomy. While there is little information on Ottavio's views when in Savona, we know that he entered aspirant intellectual circles once he arrived in Milan in 1568 since he is recorded as having been put forward as a member of the literary Academy of the 'val de Blerio' by Giovanni Paolo Lomazzo in that year.

In 1566 the currency of this new visual rhetoric was underlined in the Veneto in the scheme painted by Giovanni Battista Zelotti (*c.*1526–78) at the Villa Emo near Asolo. This villa was designed by Andrea Palladio in 1550 for the Venetian patrician Leonardo Emo. The *camera delle arti*, on the piano nobile, depicts female figures personifying Architecture, Astronomy and Poetry on one wall with Music, Sculpture and Painting opposite them. These were presented as women working. Painting is seated at her easel portraying an ancient philosopher leaning on a tree. Sculpture is working on a life-size statue of a woman dressed in antique clothing. Architecture is seated by an incomplete building, holding a treatise in which she points out a ground plan. Such associations would have been dear to the heart of the painter, since Palladio assisted Zelotti to apply for membership of the Florentine Accademia del Disegno in 1566.[67]

The extent of elite interest in the new iconographical theme is indicated by its appearance in the Sala del Mappamondo at Caprarola, painted by Giovanni de' Vecchi (*c.*1536–1615) in 1574–75 for Cardinal Alessandro Farnese.[68] Here Painting is paired with Music, and they are flanked by Sculpture and Architecture – all presented as female personifications at work (Plate 19). These representations are depicted above three windows, on one side of the room, beneath portraits of the

19 Giovanni de'Vecchi, *Painting*, 1574–75, Sala del Mappamondo, Caprarola.

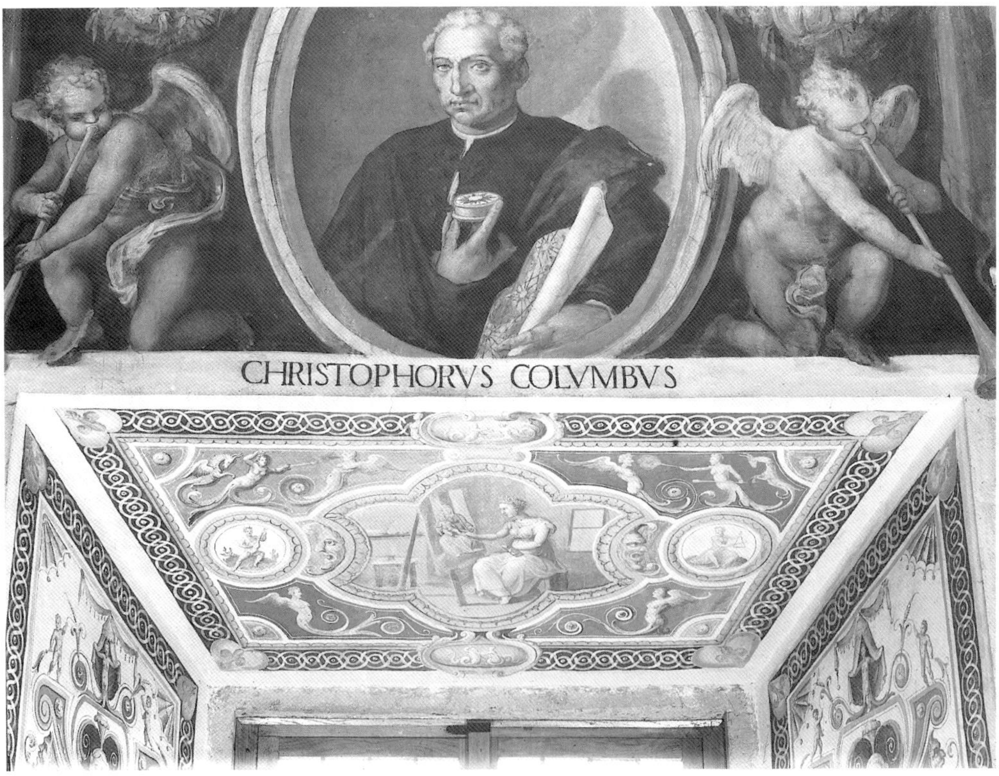

explorers Marco Polo, Christopher Columbus and Hernando Cortez. Their portraits are wreathed and flanked by angels blowing trumpets, and so we might expect that the conceit might be that the three arts, and Music below, celebrate their fame. However, Painting is actually making a picture of the Virgin and Child on her easel, so that the emphasis seems to be on the equivalence of the arts in their devout roles here – which was after all appropriate for the cardinal patron of the decoration.

Printing 1570s onwards

From the 1570s onwards the ambitions of figurative artists and architecture began to be quite widely advertised in printed form as well as in other media. Given the assumption that they would sell well, such graphic images, in sizeable editions, are evidence that the notion of high status for painting, sculpture and architecture was gaining further salient ground.

The two earliest examples of personifications of the three arts being used in engravings in this way are the series of eight leaves recording the façade murals on the house of Frans Floris in Antwerp signed by the monogram 'T.G.' and dated 1576, and the large engraving dated 1579, printed in Florence, which was invented by Federico Zuccari and incised by Cornelis Cort (1533–78), a Netherlandish engraver working in Rome. This is sometimes called the 'Lament of Painting', though it should perhaps be referred to as the 'Lament of the Arts'.

The engravings of 'T.G.' have already been mentioned, as they are part of the surviving evidence of the programme invented by Frans Floris for his house around 1563 (Plates 20a, b). The engravings printed in Antwerp suggest the value placed in this mural, thirteen years after their completion. 'T.G.' displayed Latin inscriptions explaining the import of the fictive statues and reliefs adorning the house.[69] Beneath the central scene of Painting, Sculpture and Geometry over the doorway were the words *Humanae societati necessaria* ('Necessities for human societies'). The other figures were inscribed with their names. At the feet of Architecture were the words 'Architecture ornament of cities' (*Architectura urbium ornamentum*). Beneath Poetry were the words 'Let the worthy man be prevented from dying by the praise of the Muses' (*Dignum laude virum musae vetat mori*).

These ideas were selling well in Rome during the same decade. For his large engraving, printed on two leaves and dated 1579, Federico Zuccari invented a scenario where 'Virtue and the good arts' (*La virtù et le buone arti*), meaning the Liberal Arts, choose Painting to take their case, concerning their ill treatment in the world, to the high court of heaven (Plate 21). Federico Zuccari shrewdly inserted a topos from the *paragone* here, when he explained that she had been chosen, because of 'how well she could demonstrate things as if they were alive, whereas

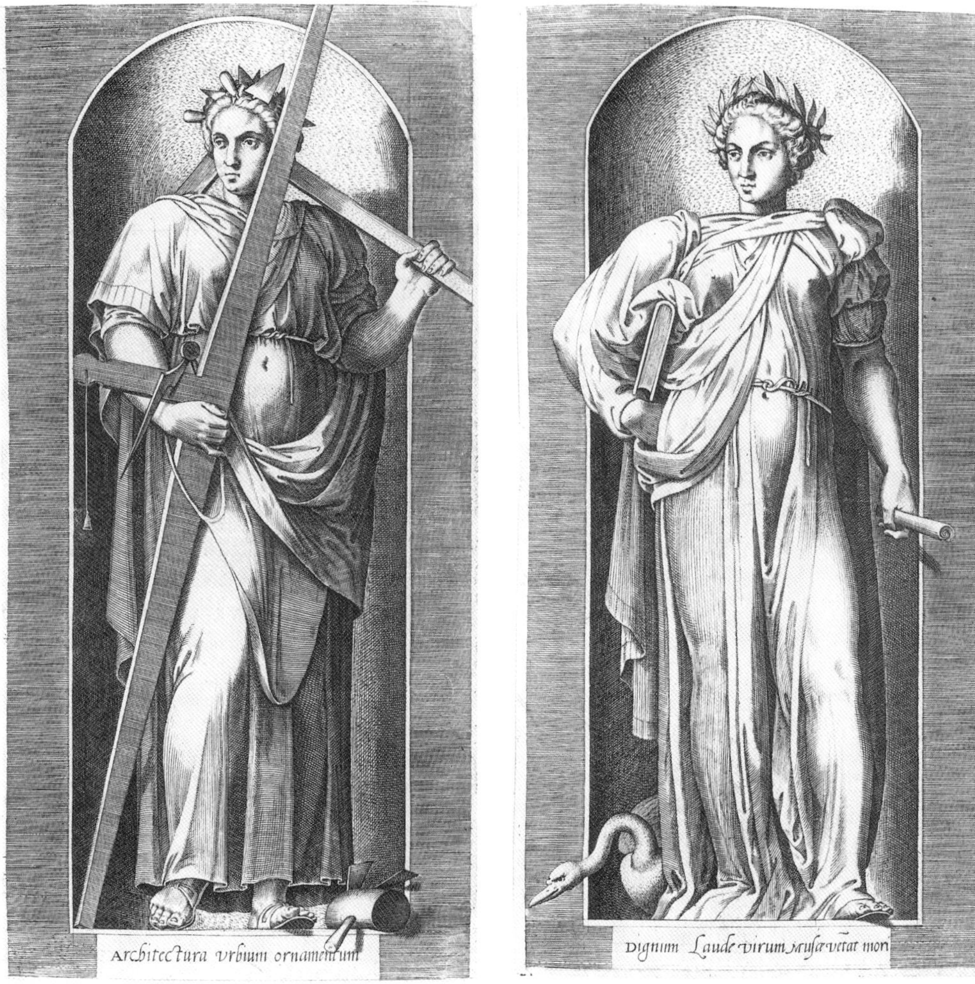

20 a and b After Frans Floris, *Poetry and Architecture*, engraving inscribed 'T.G.', Antwerp, 1576. Graphische Sammlung Albertina, Vienna.

words would never be able to express the cause of their sorrow so effectively'.[70] Painting personified is shown gaining the help of Jupiter to force those on earth to treat the arts better. While Painting is given the lead role, Zuccari took care to display the tools of architecture in her hands and those of sculpture and painting, along with those of the Liberal Arts, at her feet,on the ground, beside the Muses. According to Zuccari's accompanying text, the Muses have just flung these instruments at Jupiter's feet in anger. Painting is plainly dressed and her hair is disarranged. She stands by the picture she has made, to show the woes of all the Liberal Arts, holding a box, a set square and compasses. The visual statement that sculpture and architecture require the protection of the Muses along with the Liberal Arts, and the ambitious assertion that the eloquent Liberal Arts need Painting to put their case in the highest court, underlines the progress of the idea that painting, sculpture and architecture deserved lofty status. Federico Zuccari shows a painter in the lower section of the print, who is making the painting displayed in the upper half of the composition. Within this upper scene, the personification of Painting points to her own small picture. The whole sophisticated design is dominated by a figure of Intelligence, who has vanquished Envy. While the import is that of defending all the arts, painting is here associated with the loftiest qualities. Since it was published with Zuccari's explanation in an Italian and also a Latin version, it was geared for a variety of audiences. Zuccari was later to be elected first president of the Accademia di San Luca, and published his ideas on the dignity of the arts both in his lectures to academicians in the 1590s and eventually in his treatise entitled *Idea* (1607). He and Vasari are the exceptions in representing their ideas on the liberal status of their arts in literary publications as well as in visual imagery.

Significantly, less than a decade later, in 1587, Wolf Drechsel (1550–1602) published a woodcut broadsheet at Nuremberg which seems to be inspired by Zuccari's and Cort's engraving. The medium of the woodcut suggests that the consumers envisaged were somewhat humbler, though the design still used the sophisticated genre of a mythological allegory to urge the need for enlightened protection for the arts

21 Federico Zuccari, engraved by Cornelis Cort, *The Lament of the Arts*, 1579, Fitzwilliam Museum, Cambridge.

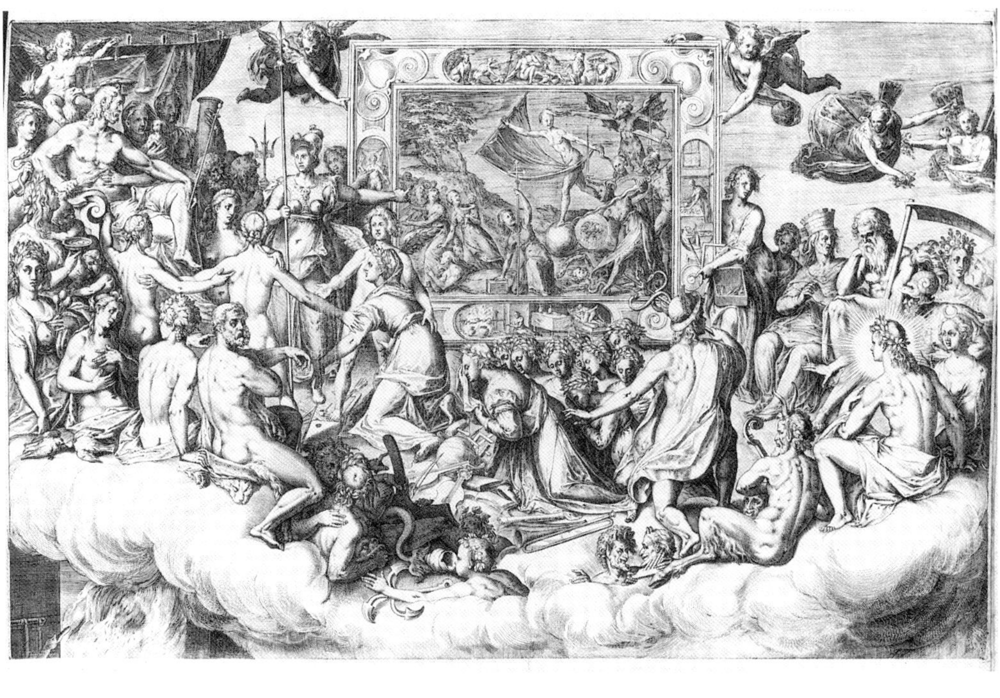

by government. Drechsel entitled his scene 'The Lament of the Seven Liberal Arts'.[71] Despite this title, however, he represented Painting and Sculpture to the left, while the seven Liberal Arts are to the right. All are begging help from Jupiter, as king of the gods as well as other male deities: Apollo, Mercury, Neptune, Saturn and Mars. He appended an explanatory poem in German, asking for Jupiter's assistance. By the end of the sixteenth century therefore, the representation of painting, sculpture and architecture as genteel scholarly art forms had gained some acceptance and could be expected to play roles in a variety of new allegories invented by artists to glorify the powers, and explore the problems, of these arts.

The allegiance of the three arts with one another and their noble aspirations were encapsulated in an engraving by, or after, Giuseppe Arcimboldo (?1527–93), the Milanese painter, perhaps dating from the 1580s (Plate 22). The courtly acceptance of the three arts as lofty in status in Hapsburg domains, is indicated in this image of a noble man, wearing the portrait medal of his lord hung round his neck, and composed of the instruments used by artists.[72] The fact that the plinth on which the bust of the composite 'Art Man' rests displays a shield including the double eagle of the Emperor, as well as a griffin, suggests that it pays tribute to Rudolph II. Arcimboldo had been painter at the Hapsburg court from about 1560 to 1587 and was himself made Count Palatine in 1580: an office signalled by the wearing of just such a chain carrying the medal of his liege lord.

Finally, the notion that government sought to protect the Liberal Arts, including painting, was affirmed in the large panel signed and dated by the Bruges painter Antoon Claeissens (1536–1613) in 1605 (Plate 23).[73] The allegorical scene, presenting near-life-size figures, has been plausibly related to 'a panel of Hercules' listed in an inventory of 1654, as in the *Stadthuis* at Bruges. This depicts the Liberal Arts with Painting, protected by a soldier – perhaps Mars or possibly Jupiter – while Hercules subdues Ignorance, who is represented with long ears, suggesting that Hercules stands for Virtue. A *putto* awards Jupiter or Mars a palm for victory and a crown of laurel. The scene is set against a carefully observed contemporary panorama of the city of Bruges and seems to have been a civic commission expressing the commitment of its rulers to protecting the arts.

These are a hotch potch of sources upon which to rely: a series of engravings from Antwerp, prints made in Rome and Nuremberg; an engraving relating to a Milanese artist working in Vienna and Prague, as well as a civic decoration from Bruges. Each of these art works were made in different artistic traditions for varied contexts. Yet they do suggest that traditions for representing the figurative arts and architecture as Liberal Arts had achieved some currency by the end of the sixteenth century in their milieux, and, in the case of the prints, that they were saleable elsewhere.

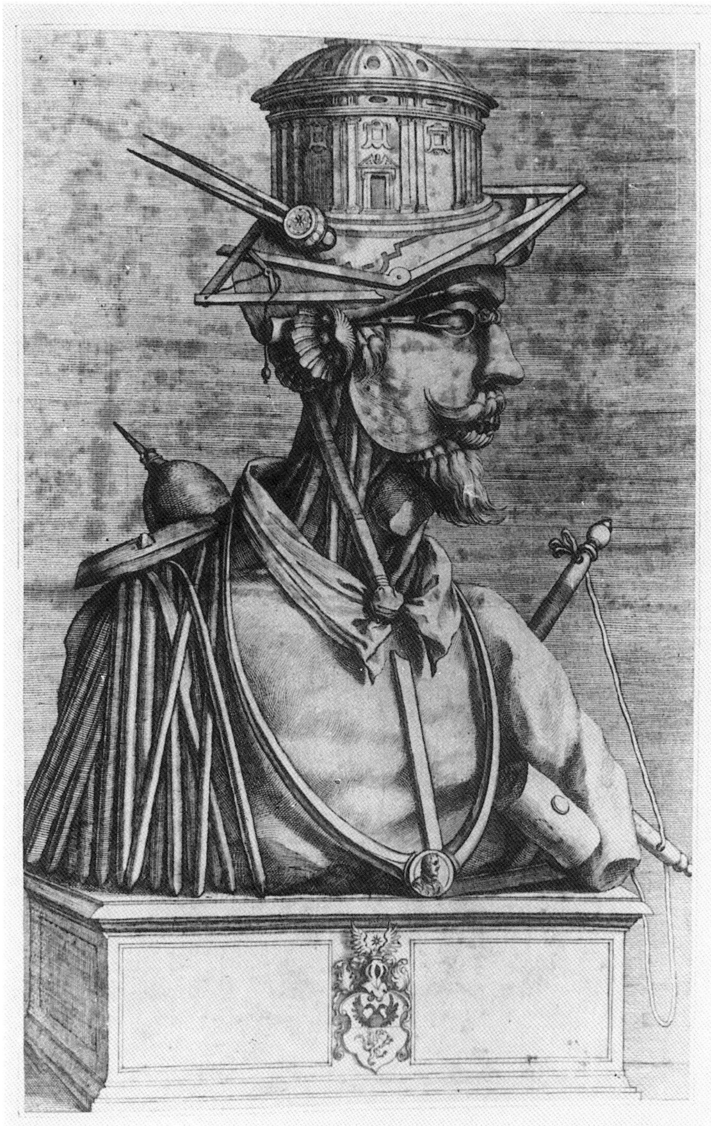

22 Style of Giuseppe Arcimboldo, *'Art man' ennobled in the service of the Emperor*, *c.*1580, Windsor Royal Collection.

During the first half of the sixteenth century two different sets of conventions for representing painting, sculpture and architecture were in contention for the first time in the western European tradition: one established older convention and one new convention. Representations of art as 'mechanical' did appear in prestigious contexts (choir stalls, moralising engravings, a villa decoration, a scholarly encyclopaedia). However, they were gradually being overtaken in numbers by images contesting such menial status. The efforts by some artists to promote their arts on the books they wrote about art, on their houses, as well as

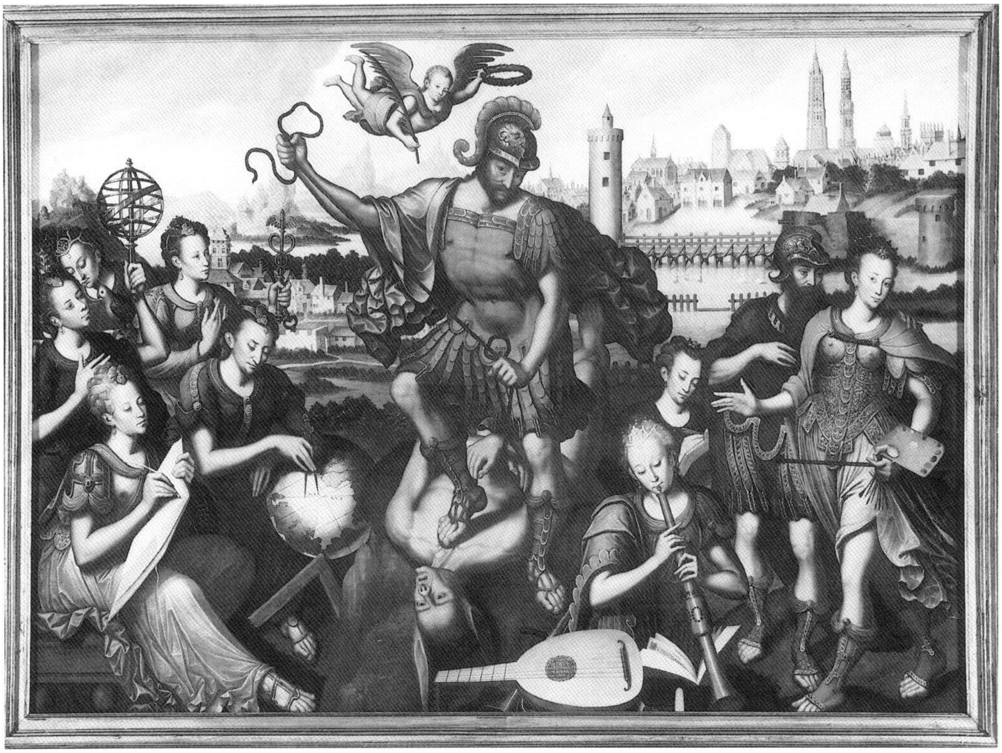

23 Anton Claeissens, *Jupiter (or Mars) and Hercules protect the Seven Liberal Arts and Painting*, 1605, 197.5 × 279 cm, panel, Groeninge Museum, Bruges.

on their funerary and other personal commemorations, would presumably have had limited effect in the face of longstanding assumptions. What seems likely to have been more decisive in shifting attitudes was the insertion of imagery promoting artistic status in commissions for powerful patrons. After all, the schemes which initially promoted the liberal status of figurative arts and architecture, began with commissions praising ruling men (Clement VII, Francesco Maria della Rovere, François I). Only then, did artists begin to represent such ideas on objects made for members of their own profession, starting with his house decoration by Vasari, at Arezzo, in 1542. It seems then that new attitudes to the high status of painting, sculpture and architecture were first promoted by princes of church and state, who took pride in their patronage of acclaimed artists, and were then joined by visual rhetoric initiated by artists themselves. The relationship of patron and artist in these developments could be mutually reinforcing. Where artists worked for a court, the splendid decorative schemes in, say, an artist's house might reflect well on his patron. Following an early phase of experiment, the new theme was translated to France and the Netherlands, and was also firmly entrenched in schemes both for artists and for rulers in Italy during the period *c.*1540–*c.*1570. A further decisive stage can be identified when, from the 1570s onwards, Italian, German-speaking and Netherlandish artists began circulating these ideas in prints, as well as in other media.

The proposition that painting, sculpture and architecture might be treated as Liberal Arts had been justified in a sequence of Italian literary texts written from the mid-fifteenth century onwards, which had developed the argument that they all relied on the theoretical foundation of mental planning, or designing, denoted by the term *disegno*. Not surprisingly, during the sixteenth century, artists produced a variety of visual images which set out to represent the new concept of *disegno* as the shared root of the figurative arts and architecture. By comparison with the representations of painting, sculpture and architecture as Liberal Arts, the iconographies of *disegno* were produced relatively late, and employed relatively infrequently. Nevertheless, the esotericism of the concept and its lofty philosophical connotations meant that its visualisation held an attraction and importance all of its own.

Notes

1 Warnke, *Hofkünstler*, p. 259.

2 For the Julius II tomb see Mary D. Garrard, 'The Liberal Arts and Michelangelo's first project for the tomb of Julius II (with a Coda on Raphael's "School of Athens")', *Viator*, XV, 1984, pp. 335–404; and for the obsequies and tomb of Michelangelo see M. and R. Wittkower, *The Divine Michelangelo*, London, 1964. For the urn of François I see Victoria Goldberg, 'Graces, Muses and Arts: the urns of Henri II and François I', *Journal of the Warburg and Courtauld Institutes*, XXIX, 1966, pp. 206–18. For Vasari see Alessandro Cecchi, 'Le case di Giorgio Vasari ad Arezzo e Firenze', pp. 30–56 and 56–77 in R.P. Ciardi, ed., *Case di artisti in Toscana*, Florence, 1998. For representations and theories of *disegno* see W. Kemp, 'Beiträge zur Geschichte des Begriffs zwischen 1547 und 1607', *Marburger Jahrbuch für Kunstwissenschaft*, XIX, 1974, pp. 214–40. For the house of Floris see Catherine King, 'Artists' houses: mass-advertising artistic status in Antwerp *c.* 1565', pp. 173–89 in Michèle Caroline Heck, Frédérique Lemerle and Yves Pauwels, eds, *Théorie des arts et création artistique dans l'Europe du Nord du XVIe au début du XVIIIe siècle*, Lille, 2002.

3 Barthélémy de Chasseneux, *Catalogus gloriae mundi*, Lyons, 1546, fol. 212 verso–232 verso. It was reprinted in 1569 and 1571 at Venice, then in 1579, 1586 and 1603 at Frankfurt.

4 Barthélémy de Chasseneux, *Catalogus gloriae mundi*, fol. 213 verso, 'Quod mechanica ars septem habet species, Lanificium, Armaturam, Navigationem, Agriculturam, Venationem, Medicinam, et Theatricam. Et dicitur Mechanica scientia adulterina sive non liberalis.'

5 Barthélémy de Chasseneux, *Catalogus gloriae mundi*, fols 231 verso–232 verso and Hugh of Saint Victor, *Didascalicon Opera Omnia*, III, Rouen, 1648, p. 62. For the textual tradition see Elspeth Whitney, 'Paradise restored: the mechanical arts from antiquity through the thirteenth

century', *Transactions of the American Philosophical Society*, 80: 1, 1990, pp. 1–169.

6 For the Campanile see Luisa Becherucci and Giulia Brunetti, *Il Museo dell' Opera del Duomo a Firenze*, 2 vols, Milan, 1969–71, I, pp. 232–7. For the medieval visual tradition see Michael Evans, 'The iconography of the artes reconsidered', pp. 305–29, in Derek Baker, ed., *Medieval Women*, Oxford, 1978.

7 For Bruges see Nadine Debergh, *Koorgestoelten in West-Vlanderen*, Lannoo, 1982, pp. 18–21, Plate 15 for the sculptor working on a statue. For Rouen see C. Enlart, *Rouen*, Paris, 1928, pp. 53–4. For Beauvais see E. Maillard, F. de Montremy and E. Harancourt, *Catalogue des bois sculptés et meubles: Museé des Thermes et de l'Hôtel de Cluny*, Paris, 1925, p. 87, catalogue number 412, inventory number 19. 627.

8 Jürg Meyer zur Capellen, *Andrea Previtali*, Lüneburg, 1972, pp. 156–7. The frescoes were removed in 1885 to the Villa di Trescore Bergamo when Villa La Zogna was converted into a hospital. Drawings record the position of some of them. 'Filocolo' [sic pseudonym], 'Una villa bergamasca, la Zogna' in *Emporium*, XXXIII, 1911, pp. 465–78; P. Zampetti and I. Chiappini, 'Andrea Previtali', pp. 87–167 in G.A. dell'Acqua and P. Zampetti, eds, *Il cinquecento*, Bergamo, 1975, especially pp. 151–3 (part 1, of volume 3, in the series *I pittori bergameschi dal XIII al XIX secolo*, in 5 volumes).

9 Georges Durand, *Monographie de l'église Notre-Dame cathédrale d'Amiens*, 2 vols, 1901–03, II, pp. 148–50, 250–61. Durand contested a previous description of an embroideress sewing a picture and identified it as a painter working on a diptych (p. 261).

10 F.W.H. Hollstein, *Dutch and Flemish Etchings, Engravings and Woodcuts c. 1450–1700, IX*, ed. Menno Herzberger, Amsterdam 1953, p. 202, numbers 296–9: one of four sheets. De Jode arrived in Antwerp from Amsterdam in 1547 and obtained a licence to publish prints there in 1551.

11 Barthélémy de Chasseneux, fol. 232 recto, 'Hinc dicit Lorentius Valla in proemio suarum elegantiarum quod artes liberales proximae sunt ars pingendi, sculpendi, fingendi, architectandi.'

12 Barthélémy de Chasseneux, *Catalogus gloriae mundi*, Venice, 1571, fol. 212 recto.

13 Giulia Bartrum and Marjolein Leesberg, eds, *The New Hollstein: German Engravings, Etchings and Woodcuts, Jost Amman 1539–91*, compiled by Gero Seelig, 11 vols, Rotterdam, 2003, *Book Illustrations*, Part VI, pp. 84–7.

14 Giulia Bartrum and Marjolein Lessing, eds, *The New Hollstein: German Engravings, Etchings and Woodcuts, Jost Amman 1539–91*, compiled by Gero Seelig, 11 vols, Rotterdam 2002, *Book Illustrations*, Part III, pp. 2–46.

15 Giulia Bartrum, ed., *The New Hollstein: German Engravings Etchings and Woodcuts 1400–1700: Jost Amman*, compiled by Gero Seelig, 11 vols, Rotterdam, 2001, Part I, pp. 66–7.

16 Julius von Schlosser, *Quellenbuch zur Kunstgeschichte des abendländischen Mittelalters*, Vienna, 1896, p. 371, 'Extimantibus multis, nec stulte quidem, pictores non inferioris ingenii his quos liberales artes fecere magistros.'

17 Leon Battista Alberti, *Della pittura*, ed. Luigi Mallè, Florence, 1950, p. 53, 'pictori, sculptori, architecti, musici, geometri, rethorici, auguri e simili

nobilissii e meravigliosi intellecti oggi si truovano rarissimi pocho da lodarli.'

18 Lorenzo Valla, *Libri sex elegantiarum latinae linguae*, Lyons 1544, p. 9, 'illae artes, quae proxime ad liberales accedunt, pingendi, scalpendi, fingendi, architectandi'.

19 Pomponio Gaurico, *De sculptura*, Florence, 1504, ed. and trans. André Chastel and Robert Klein, Geneva, 1969, p. 41.

20 Gaurico *De sculptura*, p. 40, 'ars est et inter caeteras nobilis et libero mihi ut videtur homine digna'.

21 Leon Battista Alberti, *L'architettura, de re aedificatoria*, ed. and trans. Giovanni Orlandi, 2 vols, Milan, 1966, I, pp. 1–2: 'summis caeterarum disciplinarum viris . . . Architectum ego hunc fore constituam, qui certa admirabilique ratione et via tum mente animoque diffinire tum et opere absolvere didicerit'; P. Sternagel, *Die Artes Mechanicae im Mittelalter*, Munich, 1966, p. 20.

22 Condivi, quoted in Giorgio Vasari, *La vita di Michelangelo*, ed. Paola Barocchi, Milan, 5 vols, 1962, II, p. 292: 'erano altre statue legate come prigioni: le quali rappresentavano l'arti liberali similmente Pittura, Scultura et Architettura ognuna con le sue note, sì che facilmente potesse esser conosciuta per quel che era, denotando per queste insieme con Papa Giulio esser prigioni della morte tutte le virtù.'

23 H.W. Janson, *Apes and Ape-lore in the Middle Ages and Renaissance*, London, 1952, pp. 285, 290–5 and Vasari, *La vita di Michelangelo*, II, pp. 309–14.

24 Garrard, 'The Liberal Arts'.

25 Catherine King, 'Mnemosyne and Calliope in the chapel of the Muses, San Francesco, Rimini', *Journal of the Warburg and Courtauld Institutes*, LI, 1988, pp. 187–8.

26 Catherine Wilkinson, 'Renaissance treatises on military architecture', pp. 467–74 in J. Guillaume, ed., *Les Traités d'architecture de la Renaissance*, Paris, 1988, draws attention to the way Gundisalvo and Alfarabi argued that practical arts entailing geometrical and optical knowledge should be placed in a special category aligned to the theoretical Liberal Arts.

27 Teresio Pignatti, *Giorgione*, Venice, 1969, p. 140, catalogue number A67, Plate 133, canvas, 49 × 59 cm. Fern Rusk Shapley, *Catalogue of the Italian Paintings, National Gallery of Art, Washington*, 2 vols, Washington, 1979, I, p. 217. Under drawings in radiographic examination display a different pose for the young boy, looking down and turned away from the tutor, which has been interpreted as indicating that Giorgione painted the portrait which was then worked on by another artist.

28 The motif of the sphere being held along with the banderole could refer to illustrations in the astronomical text book by Johannes de Sacrobosco, *Sphaera mundi*, Venice, 1488, fol. A7 verso and fol. A4 verso. Pignatti, *Giorgione*, pp. 103–4 related this text to the scheme for the frieze of the Casa Marta Pelizzari at Castelfranco di sopra attributed to Giorgione or his circle at about the same time, without making the connection with this double portrait.

29 Giorgio Vasari, *Le opere di Giorgio Vasari con nuove annotazioni e commenti*, ed. Gaetano Milanesi, 9 vols, Florence, 1906 (reprint 1973) IV, p. 94, 'In

Firenze é di man sua in casa de'figliuoli di Giovan Borgherini il ritratto d'esso Giovanni quando era giovane in Venezia, e nel medesimo quadro il maestro che lo guidava'.

30 Luca Pacioli, *De divina proportione*, Venice, 1509, ed. G. Masolti Biggiogero, Milan, 1956, pp. 16–18.

31 Pliny the Elder, *Chapters on the History of Art*, ed. Eugenie Sellars and trans. Katharine Jex-Blake, London, 1968, pp. 89–91 and 119 provide statements of the high regard in which ancient Greek and Roman society supposedly held painting.

32 William H. Woodward, *Studies in Education during the Renaissance 1400–1600*, New York, 1965, p. 258; Baldessare Castiglione, *Il libro del cortegiano*, ed. Vitttorio Cian, Florence, 1947, p. 122, 'voleano che i fanciulli nobili nelle scole alla pittura dessero opera, come a cosa onesta e necessaria, e fu questa ricevuta nel primo grado dell'arti liberali'.

33 R. Quednau, *Die Sala di Constantino im Vatikanischen Palast*, Hildesheim, 1979, pp. 165–6.

34 For the Column of Trajan, see Diane E. Kleiner, *Roman Sculpture*, New Haven, CT, 1992, Figure 184, p. 220; for the Arch of Constantine, see Hans P.C. Orange, *Die spätantike Bildschmuck des Konstantinsbogens*, Berlin, 1939, Figure 29.

35 Cennino Cennini, *Il libro dell'arte*, ed. Franco Brunello, Vicenza, 1971, pp. 3–4.

36 Alberti, *Della pittura*, pp. 103–4, ' Et farassi per loro [pittori] dilettarsi de' poeti et delli horatori: questi anno molti ornamenti comuni col pittore'.

37 Leonardo da Vinci, *The Literary Works of Leonardo da Vinci*, ed. Jean Paul Richter, 2 vols, New York, 1970, I, pp. 21, 41–51 especially p. 54.

38 Gaurico, *De sculptura*, p. 43, 'illi [scriptores] quidem agunt verbis, at vero hi [sculptores] rebus, illi narrant, hi vero exprimunt explicant'.

39 Paolo dal Poggetto, 'La Villa Imperiale; l'attività di Rafaellino dal Colle', in *Pesaro nell'età dei Della Rovere*, ed. Guido Arbizzoni, Antonio Brancati, Maria Rosaria Valazzi and Maria Letizia Brancati, Venice, 2001, pp. 218–21 (dal Poggetto identified the winged personifications as angels).

40 Thomas Martone, 'Piero della Francesca's "Triumphs of the Duke and Duchess of Urbino"', pp. 211–22 in Konrad Eisenbichler and Amilcare Iannucci, eds, *Petrarch's Triumphs: Allegory and Spectacle*, Toronto, 1990.

41 Silius Italicus, *Punica*, ed. and trans. J.D. Duff, London and New York, 1934, II, Book XV, 332–3.

42 Silius Italicus, *Punica*, 327–35, especially p. 334 for the phrase 'calet amor virtutis'. See also Catherine King, 'Late sixteenth-century career's advice: a new allegory of artists' training: Albertina inventory number 2763', *Wiener Jahrbuch für Kunstgeschichte*, XLI, 1988, p. 82 for the general theme of the *via virtutis*.

43 Cecchi, 'Le case di Giorgio Vasari', pp. 30–56.

44 Garrard, 'The Liberal Arts', p. 345.

45 Vasari, *Le opere di Giorgio Vasari*, VII, p. 679, 'sono innanzi al papa ginocchioni la Pittura, la Scultura e l'Architettura'.

46 Vasari, *Le opere di Giorgio Vasari*, p. 679.

47 Paola Barocchi, *Mostra di disegni del Vasari e della sua cerchia*, Florence, 1964, pp. 19–20.

48 Laura Corti, Margaret Daly-Davis, Charles Davis and Julian Kliemann, eds, *Giorgio Vasari, La Toscana nel'500: principi, letterati e artisti nelle carte di Giorgio Vasari*, Florence, 1981, p. 239.
49 The urn is now at Saint Denis. Victoria Goldberg, 'Graces, Muses and Arts: the urns of Henri II and François I', *Journal of the Warburg and Courtauld Institutes*, XXIX, 1966, pp. 206–18; P. Wingert, 'The funerary urn of Francis I', *Art Bulletin*, XXI, 1939, pp. 383–96.
50 Anthony Blunt, *Philibert de l'Orme*, London, 1958, pp. 1–14.
51 Carl van de Velde, *Frans Floris 1519/20–1570, Leven en Werken*, Brussels, 1975, 2 vols, I, pp. 262–5 (canvas 157 × 238 cm).
52 For both houses see King, 'Artists' houses', pp. 182–9.
53 King, 'Artists' houses', pp. 173–82.
54 Margaret and Rudolf Wittkower, *The Divine Michelangelo*, London, 1964, pp. 9–25.
55 Wittkower and Wittkower, *The Divine Michelangelo*, pp. 101–33.
56 Anthony Hughes, 'An Academy for doing', *Oxford Art Journal*, IX, 1986, pp. 3–10.
57 G.F. Hill, *Portrait Medals of Italian Artists in the Renaissance*, London, 1912, pp. 63–4.
58 Hill, *Portrait Medals*, for Giovanni Boldù, 34, and Lomazzo, pp. 62–3.
59 Francesco Frangi and Alessandro Morandotti, *Il ritratto in Lombardia da Moroni a Ceruti*, Milan, 2002, pp. 80–1.
60 Corti et al., *Giorgio Vasari, La Toscana nel'500*, pp. 236–42.
61 Cecchi, 'Le case di Giorgio Vasari', pp. 56–77.
62 Carlo Ridolfi, *Le meraviglie dell'arte*, ed. D.F. von Hadeln, 2 vols, Berlin, 1914, p. 212, 'martelli e scalpelli et à canto forme di corpo e teste di rilievo con questo scritto'.
63 Ridolfi, *Le meraviglie dell'arte*, I, p. 213, 'con volto di grave Matrona con l'archipendolo e'l compasso in mano'.
64 For the whole account see Ridolfi, *Le meraviglie dell'arte*, I, pp. 211–18. For Pittura see pp. 211–12, 'dal collo gli penderà una catena con maschera, e due fanciulli le sostentaranno il manto e à piedi registrato in un breve Imitatio'. (This is the earliest mention of the use of the attribute of the mask later explained by Cesare Ripa as signifying the ability of Painting to feign any emotion in paint.) We might note that the mask recalls the attribute of some of the Muses. Warnke, *Hofkünstler*, p. 197 highlighted the knightly prestige of the interment.
65 Alessandro Cecchi and Ettore Allegri, *Guida storica: Palazzo Vecchio e i Medici*, Florence, 1980, pp. 191–3.
66 Elena Parma, *Il cinquecento: la pittura in Liguria*, Genoa 2000, pp. 73–5, 187–92; Figs 59–61, 167.
67 Katia Brugnolo Meloncelli, *Battista Zelotti*, Milan, 1992, pp. 107–11, Figures 160–3, Plates XXV–XXVI.
68 Loren Partridge, 'The Room of the Maps at Caprarola 1573–75', *Art Bulletin*, LXXVII, no. 3, 1995, pp. 413–44.
69 King, 'Artists' houses', pp. 182–7.
70 Manfred Sellink and Huigen Leeflang, *The New Hollstein: Dutch and Flemish Etchings, Engravings and Woodcuts 1450–1700, Cornelis Cort*, 3 vols, Rotterdam, 2000, III, pp. 130–341, upper plate 343 mm × 543 mm, 'La

Virtù et le buone arti . . . elessero la Pittura come quella che ben dimostra le cose al vivo, che non parole quanto più poteva esprimere la cagione d[e]lla mestitia loro'.

71 Wolf Drechsel (1550–1602) made woodcuts and prints and was active in Nuremberg in 1576–1602: see W.L Strauss, *The German Single Leaf Woodcut 1550–1600*, New York, 1975, I, pp. 175–80, p. 175, 'Die sieben Freyen Kunst Klagen auff Erdt' (The seven Liberal Arts lament on Earth).

72 For comparable examples see the scholar and the cook in Francine C. Legrand and Felix Sluys, *Arcimboldo et les Arcimboldesques*, Aalter, 1955, Plates 1, 14.

73 Dirk de Vos, *Groeninge Museum, Catalogus Schilderijen 15 de en 16de Eeuw*, Bruges, 1979, pp. 115–17, 197.5 × 279 cm, panel.

2 *Disegno*/design

From the mid-sixteenth century onwards a variety of visual images were invented to signify the concept of *disegno* or 'design' as the cerebral element of the figurative arts and architecture, and therefore as the factor unifying the arts of painting, sculpting and architecture and standing for them as a whole. The concept of design entailed the idea that painting, sculpture and architecture had a common foundation: that of planning in two and three dimensions to produce drawings and models. Like the term 'design' in modern English, *disegno* in Italian could indicate both mental planning, and also making marks with brush, pen or stylus to record or explore ideas graphically. More specifically, starting in the fifteenth century, writers on art had linked skills in designing with expertise in perspectival construction, in painting and sculpture, and in the study of proportions in the figurative arts and architecture. These were elements which could be allied to expertise in the Liberal Arts of geometry, arithmetic and music in a way which was prestigious for artists. In the case of proportional studies, design might also have lofty spiritual associations associated with the idea of matching terrestrial, or microcosmic, to divine, or macrocosmic, ratios and structures. Consequently, good design might be related to the notion of discerning and producing ideal, divine beauties. In addition, in the practice of these arts, drawings were increasingly being used to record antique buildings and statuary in ways which were valued by scholars. These ideas were institutionalised in the first academy of art – that is the Accademia del Disegno founded in Florence in 1563 and also in the alternative title for the Accademia di San Luca in Rome (1593) as the 'Accademia del Dissegno'.[1] The notion of 'design' as the key artistic activity has been analysed by Maurice Poirier and Wolfgang Kemp in terms of its intellectual genealogy from the mid-sixteenth century onwards.[2] However, the genealogy of the term needs to be traced from the early fifteenth century, taking into account the neglected sources dealing with sculpture and architecture. In the following discussion it seems appropriate to retain the Italian noun *disegno* rather than translating it, to avoid confusion with other modern usages of 'design' when translating Italian texts.

Design has theoretical and intellectual connotations

During the fifteenth century some texts recorded the high regard in which good *disegno* was held. Around 1400, Cennino Cennini in his *Libro dell'arte* had emphasised the cerebral side of painting, when he defined the kind of young apprentice who would succeed in the profession, by writing that in such a pupil, 'the intellect will take delight in *disegno* provided that their nature attracts them to it through natural enthusiasm'.[3] Here Cennini links *disegno* with the intellect and with the personal talent which was associated with training in the Liberal Arts, so that the prestigious connotations of *disegno* are highlighted.[4] As early as the 1450s, in the *Commentari* of Lorenzo Ghiberti, the theoretical elements in *disegno* were underlined. '*Disegno* is the foundation and theoretical basis of these two arts [sculpture and painting] and necessarily one must be highly expert in that theory'.[5] He had stressed that it required application and discipline to achieve.

> The theory of *disegno*, without which theory no one can become a good sculptor or a good painter for the good sculptor or painter is only as good as he is an expert in that theory – that is in the said *disegno* – and this is not acquired without great study and discipline.[6]

In the same passage Ghiberti had listed *disegno* (which he was careful to qualify with the adjective 'theoretical') among the 'liberal' requirements of the painter and the sculptor, that is: 'mastery of all the Liberal Arts: Grammar, Geometry, Philosophy, Medicine, Astrology, Perspective, History, Anatomy, *Theoretical Disegno*, and Arithmetic' [my italics].[7] Ghiberti derived this list from that made by Vitruvius in his discussion of the appropriate education of architects. This had covered letters, designing, geometry, optics, arithmetic, history, philosophy, music, medicine, jurisprudence and astrology.[8] Vitruvius had used the Latin phrase *peritus graphidos*, or 'graphic expertise', which some translations have, narrowly, rendered as 'drawing'.

In the *Decem libri de aedificatoria*, first recorded in manuscript in 1457, Alberti had devoted Book 1 to discussing the making of plans for buildings and delineating them or *lineamentum* – the Latin term favoured by him for designing – stating it to be the basis of architecture. Alberti defined architecture as resulting from 'the delineation of a precise and exact prescription conceived in the mind, executed with lines and angles, and conducted to completion by an erudite mind and talent'.[9] Only then did Alberti turn to considering techniques and materials for building.

It is clear from the treatise by Filarete written a little later (*Trattato di architettura*, 1460–64) that *disegno* was an important concept for architects keen to differentiate themselves from masons, by claiming that they planned buildings rather than simply erecting them. Filarete made clear that *disegno* entailed thinking, and shaping, in three dimensions as well as two. Following Alberti, he began by stressing the architect's ability to invent plans which suit his patrons' requirements, saying that he must, 'fantasise and think up and turn over in his memory in many ways and make various *disegni* in his mind . . . making one small *disegno* in relief using wood'.[10] According to Filarete, the architect is treated with respect in teaching designing to the young 'lord' to whom the treatise is addressed, and Filarete makes the grand if vague claim that '*disegno* is the foundation and method of all arts which are executed by the hand'.[11]

Drawings record ideas as writing inscribes poetry or diagrams demonstrate astronomy

In the late fifteenth century the argument that designing was an activity parallel to that of writing for poets, making diagrams for geometers and astronomers, and inscribing numbers for mathematicians, was explored by Francesco di Giorgio (1439–?1501), Leonardo da Vinci and Pomponio Gaurico.

In the introduction to his treatise on architecture (transcribed in the period 1489–92), the Sienese architect and sculptor Francesco di Giorgio explained the importance of the *arte del disegno*. In his view, all arts required arithmetic and geometry, and, equally, relied on the art of designing:

> Eupompus of Macedonia, a respected mathematician, wrote that no art could be perfected by humanity without arithmetic and geometry. Similarly, not only by him but by many other excellent men, the art of designing was esteemed to be no less necessary to all scientific operations, than were the forenamed [geometry and arithmetic].[12]

Francesco di Giorgio went on to relate that the ancient Greek painters Apelles and Melanthius had begun the tradition of teaching designing to well-born boys as a liberal art, because of its 'great usefulness and necessity in all human activities, whether in invention so as to explain one's concepts, or in activities such as military matters'.[13] Leonardo (who owned a copy of Francesco's treatise) employed the term *disegno* in his praise of the superiority of painting in his *paragone* or comparison of the arts in texts composed during the period *c.*1490–*c.*1510. He affirmed the importance of *disegno* in the sense of drawing because, in terms of recording pictorial ideas, it could be seen as the equivalent to writing down the thoughts of poets or scholars. Leonardo argued that painting was the equal of poetry, since

> all the arts that pass though the hands of scribes are in the same position, for they are a kind of designing which is a branch of painting; and astrology and other arts pass through manual operations but are primarily mental, just as is painting, which is first in the mind of the one who speculates and cannot reach perfection without manual operation.[14]

Leonardo's argument that the painter is one who speculates was a powerful one, and was echoed by the Venetian painter Jacopo de'Barbari in 1509, when he wrote to Friedrich der Weise concerning the high status that painting deserved. He argued that painting is the equal of all the Liberal Arts, theology and philosophy, 'with their divine speculations'.[15]

Leonardo turned the tables on the Liberal Arts which employ writing, by terming their inscription 'designing with the pen' (*dissegnando con la penna*). 'If you call it [Painting] mechanical because it is primarily manual since the hands represent what they find in the fantasy – you writers draw with the pen by manual work what you find in your personal talent'.[16] Designing could be related to other graphic forms, and this allowed Leonardo to show that it had a key role to play in different activities in society:

> But the deity [*la deità*] of the science of painting extends over works human as well as divine in so far as they are bound by surfaces, namely, the outlines of figures. With these she prescribes to the sculptor the perfection of his statues. By designing, which is her beginning, she teaches the architect to make his edifices agreeable to the eye, she guides the potters in the making of various vases, the goldsmiths, weavers and embroiderers. She [the deity of Painting] has invented the characters in which the different languages are written, she has given the ciphers to the mathematicians, and has described the figures of geometry, she teaches opticians, astronomers, mechanics and engineers.[17]

Through designing, the 'goddess' of Painting has the role of guide to the figurative and decorative arts and architecture, and is linked here with perfection and agreeableness. Whereas Alberti and Ghiberti had argued that painters, architects and sculptors needed to be well informed about the Liberal Arts, Francesco di Giorgio and Leonardo now argued also that the Liberal Arts were dependent on designing.

While Francesco di Giorgio's and Leonardo's ideas were circulated only in manuscript, the printed Latin treatise by Pomponio Gaurico, entitled *De sculptura* and published in Florence in 1504, suggests that comparison of poetry, painting, architecture and sculpture had gained considerable currency.

Disegno is especially associated with the perspectival and proportional skills needed for painting, sculpture and architecture and is the equivalent of writing

In *De sculptura* Gaurico proposed that sculpture was worthy of liberal status, and as part of his argument emphasised the comparability of sculptors, poets and orators in their common reliance on an ability to imagine the diversities of humanity, so as to evoke reality in their narrations. He also stressed that the ancient Greeks at the time of Demosthenes employed the same verb *graphein* to mean writing, painting and sculpting, while for the ancient Egyptians, communicating with hieroglyphs entailed painting and carving.[18] Gaurico also overtly compared current terms employed by writers, painters, sculptors and architects for different kinds of designing and writing:

> *Graphicen*, that in reference to writing we call description [*descriptio*], in painting and in sculpture is called designing [*designatio*] (while we reserve to the architect delineation [*lineatio*] that is *grammike*). Donatello judged this to be so necessary to sculpture that it is related that he used to tell his many disciples that there was only one word which summed up the whole art of sculpture and that was the imperative 'design' [*designate*]. Certainly it comprises the head and the foundation of sculpture and in its turn consists of two elements: symmetry [*symmetria*], which has not received a Latin name yet, unless perhaps we accept the coinage of Cicero in 'commensurateness' [*commensuratio*], and *optike* – which we call perspective.[19]

'Proportionality' might provide a translation of commensurateness. It seems likely that Gaurico thought of Donatello's imperative as including the idea of designing in three dimensions by modelling. Gaurico's text, which was printed in two more editions during the sixteenth century (Antwerp, 1528; Nuremberg, 1542), emphasised the associations between designing and writing, the graphic common ground between architecture, painting and sculpture and the use of designing for studying proportionality and perspective.[20]

Gaurico's ideas were developed by Cesare Cesariano (*c*.1476–1543), in the first translation of Vitruvius into the vernacular, which he printed in 1521 in Como. In his Italian commentary Cesare explained why Vitriuvius required architects to be skilled in 'designing' (*perito di la graphida*):

> This word γραφω [*grapho*] signifies in Latin not only the act of writing, but also that of painting, and other times, of sculpting. Therefore the architect needs to know how to read, write and design or represent as one does for painting.[21]

Cesare Cesariano stated that if we are to believe Valerius Maximus (first century BCE–first century CE) and Pliny the Elder (first century CE), designing was taught to freeborn boys in Ancient Greece and not to 'libertines or slaves': 'And this was so that they might have better understanding of universal things and know how to express them, and even to the end that those freeborn might always be the better in spirit and bodily purity.'[22] In this way he linked designing with lofty social position and learning as well as elevated behaviour.

The translation of Vitruvius by Francesco Lucio of Castel Durante printed in Venice (1524) publicised this idea further. He explained what Vitruvius had meant, by stipulating 'graphic knowledge' (*graphida scientia*) as essential for the architect: 'that is knowledge of designing, which is produced with a certain stylus of metal which some also call *graphio* because γραφιά means painting, designing, description and indeed sculpture.'[23] Cesariano's statement on the multifaceted powers of *disegno* was repeated by Gianbattista Caporali in his translation of Vitruvius, published in Perugia in 1536.[24]

The translation by Daniele Barbaro (1513–70) of Vitruvius (Venice, 1556) which became the definitive one in Italian, sustained the high dignity of designing, in his commentary on the passage in which Vitruvius had recommended skills in design (*habbia disegno*) to the architect so that he could render his mental conception (*concetta nella mente*) affirming that *disegno*, 'which serves painters, sculptors, engravers and the like, stands to these arts in the manner in which mathematics services philosophy'.[25] So, for Barbaro, who held high office in the Veneto as Patriarch of Aquileia, designing was the equivalent of mathematics, while painting, sculpture and architecture were the equals of philosophy. Such lofty associations made sense because of the notion that the figurative arts and architecture imitated the underlying, as well as the surface, beauties of the entire universe.

Achieving correct proportions artistically meant harmonising microcosmic with macrocosmic ratios

In the sense that *disegno* entailed understanding the Liberal Arts of arithmetic and geometry, it might also be regarded as having the task of attempting to represent the underlying order of the cosmos, as structured by God, through the proportions and forms chosen for buildings and figures. These ideas could be related to contemporary beliefs about the structure of the universe, according to which the earth was spherical and the motion of the seven planets was circular. This system was considered to be enclosed by the sphere of the fixed stars, making eight intervals between earth and the threshold of heaven, beyond which the Prime Mover dwelt. All motion on earth was considered imperfect, being up and down, rather than circular. Motion was thought to become more perfect, the closer one approached the fixed stars. Ultimately one reached God and perfect rest. On earth the most perfect shapes were considered to be those displaying features of equivalence, such as the circular, spherical and equilateral.

Other proportional theories related to the belief that human figures reflected divine order. According to Vitruvius, 'the human body was composed by nature':[26] an idea which could be supported with reference to the biblical statement that humanity was made in God's image. Vitruvius advised that temples should be regulated 'after the fashion of the members of a finely shaped human body' following simple ratios, such as the head equalling one eighth of a person's height, or the proposal that the measurement from the middle of the breast to the crown of the head equalled a quarter of the total height.[27] He also favoured the circle and the square, asserting that the human body could be inscribed within those two figures. Francesco di Giorgio in a manuscript dated 1482–86 sought to demonstrate his dictum, as did Leonardo around 1485 – in both cases by means of drawings accompanying the description by Vitruvius.[28] Vitruvius had gone on to argue that the number ten (derived from the digits of hands and feet) was the perfect module for calibrating buildings and human bodies.

Theories of proportion were also related to the Pythagorean tradition, which had shown that the consonant notes made on a stringed instrument in the Greek octave (the octave, fifth and fourth) could be expressed in terms of the proportional ratios 1:2:3:4, adding up to ten. In the Vatican in 1512, Raphael showed this formula being demonstrated by Pythagoras in the 'School of Athens' completed in the Stanza della Segnatura. Given belief in an ordered universe created by a deity, it is no surprise to find that there was a long tradition of believing that the cosmos, with its eight intervals between earth and God, made the 'music of the spheres'. These ideas were connected with theories of ideal human and architectural proportion. For example, in *De architectura* Alberti wrote that 'the numbers by means of which the agreement of sounds affects our ears with delight, are the very same which please our eyes and minds.'[29] The dependence on proportion in the visual arts and music allowed Leonardo to claim that painting was superior to music, because

> it keeps alive that harmony of proportion which Nature with all its force could not keep. How many paintings have preserved the image of divine beauty of which time or sudden death have destroyed Nature's original, so that the work of the painter has survived in nobler form than that of Nature, his mistress?[30]

Consequently, 'such a science is in the same relation to divine Nature as its works are to the works of Nature, and for this is to be adored'.[31] According to Leonardo, then, good proportions could not only record 'divine beauty', but also produce a spiritual response in beholders: 'Do you not know that our soul is composed of harmony, and that harmony is only produced when proportions of things are seen or heard simultaneously?'[32] In 1509 Fra Luca Pacioli (*c.*1445–1517) dedicated *De divina proportione* ('On divine proportion') to Lodovico Maria Sforza, Duke of Milan. Pacioli was a Franciscan, who reported demonstrating his ideas to fellow Franciscans at the Frari in Venice. Pacioli had worked in the courts of Milan and Urbino. Printed in Venice, his illustrated text demonstrated the cosmic and spiritual significance of certain proportions, with reference to music, geometry and neo-Platonic ideas about relationships between terrestrial and divine beauty. He recommended ideal proportions for human figures, the letters of the alphabet and columns.[33] Pacioli proposed that 'from the human body derive all measures and their denominations, and in it is to be found all and every ratio and proportion by which God reveals the innermost secrets of nature'.[34]

In the mid-sixteenth century, the analogies between music and painting on grounds of proportion permitted the Portuguese painter Francisco de Holanda (1517–84) to put into the mouth of Michelangelo the aspiration of painters: to achieve union with the divine through imitating cosmic harmonies. In his *Da pintura antiga* published in Lisbon in 1548, he had Michelangelo say that the best painting does not imitate surface appearance, but seeks to render underlying structural qualities such as 'symmetry' and 'proportion':

at its best nothing is more noble and devout, since with discreet persons nothing so calls forth and fosters devotion as the difficulty of a perfection which is bound up in union with God. For good painting is nothing but a copy of the perfections of God and a recollection of his painting; it is a music and a melody which only the intellect can understand, and that with great difficulty. And that is why painting of this kind is so rare that no man may attain it.[35]

The idea of relating human, architectural and cosmic structures was sustained throughout the sixteenth century. For example, in 1535 the Franciscan friar and scholar Francesco Giorgi advised on the building of a church:

When God wished to instruct Moses concerning the form and proportion of the tabernacle which he had to build, He gave him as model the fabric of the world and said (as is written in *Exodus* 25) 'And look that thou make them after their pattern, which was shewed thee in the mount.' By this pattern was meant, according to all the interpreters, the fabric of the world. And rightly so, because it was necessary that the particular place should resemble His universe, not in size, of which He has no need, nor in delight, but in proportion, which He wills should be not only in the material places, in which He dwells, but particularly in us of whom Paul says, writing to the Corinthians: 'Ye are the Temple of God.' Pondering on this mystery, Solomon the wise gave the same proportions as those of the Mosaic tabernacle to the famous Temple which he erected.[36]

In the *Idea del tempio della pittura* (1590) the Milanese painter Lomazzo continued to affirm the relationships of terrestrial and divine worlds, in terms of proportional studies:

Man's body is perfect and beautiful and was made by God in his own image. Very judiciously it has been called a lesser world, for the body contains within itself the most perfect harmony and composition of all numbers, measures, weights, movements and elements of the world. For this reason the human body, rather than anything else constructed by God's hand, and its members, is taken as the norm and model for making churches, theatres – indeed all buildings and their parts such as columns, capitals, even canals, and such things as boats, machines and all sorts of constructions. This same God got Noah to make an ark following the measurements of the human body.[37]

Lomazzo also elaborated on the idea, which had been recounted by Leonardo, that the soul is structured harmonically:

> Each one [artist] concentrated their study and industry on understanding perfectly this beautiful harmony, especially Leonardo, Michelangelo and Gaudenzio [Ferrari, *c.*1470–1546]. These came to an understanding of harmonic proportion by means of music, and through considering the structure of our body, which, is also constructed according to musical harmony, as I have explained in the following chapter and in other places in this book. Besides, men of talent and great learning think that the consonance of the soul is made according to the temperament and proportions of its powers and operations. These are concupiscent, angry and intellectual ones. They are related in the following proportions: reason and concupiscence has the proportion of the octave, reason and anger the proportion of the fourth and anger and concupiscence the proportion of the fifth.[38]

Publicising the value of *disegno*

The texts stating the importance of *disegno* were largely specialist ones, dedicated to the visual arts and architecture. However, Erasmus (*c.* 1466–1536) and Baldassarre Castiglione (1479–1529), both publishing in 1528, advertised the value of designing to a wider audience. Erasmus put forward the value of drawing and painting for a liberal education, in a dialogue entitled *De recta latini graecique sermonis pronuntiatione* (Basel, 1528). This work, which was dedicated to the Emperor Maximilian and discussed the best teaching methods for Latin and Greek, stressed the usefulness of all forms of designing: 'People whose fingers are practised in drawing all sorts of lines [*ducendis in omnem formam lineis*] write the letters of the alphabet with greater flexibility and grace.'[39] Erasmus commended Dürer's book on drawing – the *Unterweysung der Messung* (1525) – and compared him to the learned Greek artist Pamphilos. Erasmus was referring to the praise of the Greek artist Pamphilos in the *Historia naturalis* by Pliny the Elder as 'the first painter who was thoroughly trained in every branch of learning, more particularly in geometry and arithmetic'. Pliny the Elder had gone on to claim that 'It was owing to his influence that drawing [*graphicen*] on tablets of box wood was the earliest subject taught to freeborn boys and accepted as the first step to a liberal education'.[40] Scholars could therefore refer to the account of Pliny the Elder to argue that ancient Greek and Roman societies had regarded drawing (and painting) as a suitable element in the curriculum for a well-born boy.[41]

In *Il libro del cortegiano* (Venice, 1528), Castiglione advised that the courtier should have knowledge of drawing (*il saper disegnare*),

> and the art of painting itself. And do not be surprised that I demand this ability, even if nowadays it might appear mechanical and hardly suited to a gentleman. For I recall having read that in the ancient world, and in Greece especially, children of gentle birth were required to learn painting at school,

as a worthy and necessary accomplishment, and it was ranked the foremost of the liberal arts.[42]

Here Castiglione was thinking of 'drawing'. However, he also used *disegno* in the more cerebral sense, since he went on to argue that although ancient painting had not survived, its quality could be deduced from looking at the excellence of the surviving ancient statuary for, 'although painting and sculpture differ, both the one and the other derive from the same source: that is, good *disegno*'.[43] Here he seems to mean qualities of proportionality and good planning, common to sculpture and painting, rather than manual techniques of designing. By the mid-sixteenth century the importance of *disegno* was relatively well known. For example, we find de Holanda in his *Da pintura antigua* (1548) having Michelangelo pronounce to a Portuguese audience, 'Designing, that is otherwise termed tracing, is the key constituent, fountain and body of painting, sculpture, and architecture and of all the other kinds of art and the root of all the sciences'.[44] By this time too the discourses of *disegno* had become sufficiently familiar for them to be treated in a playful way. In a letter written to the Florentine Servite sculptor Fra Giovanni Angelo Montorsoli in 1546, Antonio Francesco Doni stated that he was amused by those who claim that *disegno* is father to the figurative arts.

I am amused by those who say that God first made man of clay, then that he coloured him, and before He made him, that He would have worked in that form that the artificer does, who first imagines a palace in fantasy (the *disegno*) and then makes a model; consequently they say that *disegno* is the father of painting and sculpture.[45]

Doni was a Florentine who had trained as a sculptor with Montorsoli, when he had entered the Servite order at Santissima Annunziata for a short time, and had been in contact with the family of Baccio Bandinelli (1488–1560) in his youth. Here he poked fun at the arguments which had been advanced since the time of Leonardo, that design belongs to all the operations of the hand. Doni's examples included a maidservant painting her face, a manservant playing musical instruments, and poets. Rather than acting sequentially like humans, Doni argued, God acts instantaneously:

I believe that one cannot be a painter or a sculptor without *disegno*. Just as the Prime Mover caused the making of them all at one stroke, so I believe that each one is as noble as the other. And long live my *disegno*.[46]

This view was published in Doni's collected letters in 1547. In a more solemn mood Doni went on to place *disegno* at the heart of painting and sculpture in a lengthy dialogue entitled *Disegno* (Venice, 1549). In a conversation between Nature and Art, Doni had Nature assert that

'Painting and sculpture cannot execute anything without *disegno*, which, if ill handled, gives art her verdict whatever that may be.'

Art. 'I would say that *disegno* should be the industry of the intellect, in the act of putting to work its power.'

Nature. 'Indeed you may not, as Art, speak otherwise, nor call it by any other name, but listen and hold in your mind for another time. *Disegno* is none other than a divine speculation, which produces an excellent art. So you cannot execute anything in sculpture or painting without the guide of this speculation and design.'[47]

While Art sees *disegno* as the careful labour entailed in expressing thought, Nature interprets it as a more contemplative activity, taking the imagery of celestial speculation, which Leonardo and Jacopo de'Barbari had both used when comparing painting to poetry. In this elevated mode Doni allows Nature to elaborate on the idea that *disegno* is indeed a human version of the originating activities of the Creator:[48] 'The first *disegno* was the invention of the whole universe imagined perfectly in the mind of the Prime Cause, before it came to be made in relief and colour, which relief we call in common parlance sculpture.'[49] It was only late in this debate, in the mid-sixteenth century, that some schemes began to represent *disegno* in visual form. As with personifications of Painting, Sculpture and Architecture (see Chapter 1), the primary context was that of the panegyric of the prince.

Cellini and the Fountain for François I, 1541–42

The introduction of the iconography of design occurred, according to Benvenuto Cellini, in the model he made for François I at Fontainebleau for a colossal fountain displaying the King's power as the God of War in protecting the arts.[50] Cellini arrived at the French court in 1540, and in his autobiography he described making the model after he had designed the famous salt cellar, so he probably presented the project during the period 1541–42. The autobiography describes how he showed the King his model, and pointed out all its features:

This figure in the middle is to be fifty-four feet (at these words the King gave a huge gesture of astonishment) which represents the God Mars. These other four figures are made to show the Virtue in which Your Majesty takes delight and favours so greatly. This, on the right hand, represents the science of Letters; and you see that it has its attributes which demonstrate philosophy accompanied by all its virtues. This other shows itself to be all the arts of *disegno*, that is, sculpture, painting and architecture. This other represents music, who is so appropriately the companion of all these sciences. This other, that appears so gracious and benign, represents liberality, without which one cannot show forth any of these wonderful virtues that God has given us. This large statue in the middle represents Your Majesty Himself, as the God Mars, who is the bravest in the world.[51]

The model was '2 cubits' high (about a metre) and comprised a square basin raised up on flights of steps with four personifications at the corners. Mars was placed in the centre on a square podium. No visual record so far has emerged of the form of the fountain, although a full-size clay model was made of the centrepiece and was documented as still extant in 1546 at Fontainebleau.

Given the history of the concept of *disegno*, the citation of letters, philosophy and music as the companions of 'the arts of *disegno*' were well calculated to ensure that the connotations of *disegno* were of the most elevated sort. Traditionally, personifications of Philosophy had been placed at the very head of the seven Liberal Arts.[52] The comparison of music and *disegno* emphasised not only the mathematical and geometric skills of painting, sculpture and architecture, but also their capacity to mirror cosmic harmonies. The comparison with 'Letters' related to the parallels between *disegno* and writing which had been made since the time of Leonardo and Gaurico. Cellini's description in the autobiography suggested that the arts of *disegno* were the equivalents of 'science' (that is to say, 'theoretical knowledge') and 'virtues' (meaning not only 'goodness' but also 'being good at something').

The autobiography was written in 1557–61, more than a decade after the events. In his treatise on goldsmithing, published in 1568, Cellini repeated the account, except that he termed Mars the personification of the art of war.[53] Given the lateness of Cellini's claim, it seems sensible to treat it with caution, possibly more as a testimony of the high regard in which the concept of *disegno* was held in the 1550s at the date of writing, than of what Cellini actually modelled in the 1540s. However, some factors do support the idea that he might have invented the earliest representation of *disegno* for the French monarch. He had been trained in Florence, and had worked in Rome for the papacy, where he admired the ideas of Raphael and of Michelangelo. He was sufficiently well regarded to be included by Benedetto Varchi (on Cellini's return to Florence in 1546) in the debate on the relative merits of painting and sculpture. Significantly, Cellini recorded that he owned 'a manuscript copy of the treatise on sculpture, painting and architecture by Leonardo'.[54]

François I had invited other Italians to work at his court, including Rosso Fiorentino (1494–1540) and Francesco Primaticcio (*c.*1504–70). Like his predecessors, he seems to have been keen to adopt Italianate ideas as well as styles. The annotated edition of Vitruvius published by Guillaume Philandrier (1505–65), at Strasburg in 1543, was dedicated to François I. It complimented the King as another Emperor Augustus and affirmed interest in the new status of *disegno* at the French court, during the period when the fountain was being made. Philandrier (who was a classical scholar also called Philander) repeated the arguments of Gaurico, with reference to the common dependence of architects, writers, painters and sculptors on graphic skills to render their ideas. Here he glossed Vitruvius's statement that architects should have knowledge of graphics. *Graphis* means the formation of lines or designing. Nor is this lacking to what pertains to the architect which they call *grammike* or as you may say making lineaments, *graphice* indeed relates both to the writer and to the painter and the sculptor, when the term 'description' is used for the first [writing], while 'design' is used for the two latter [painting and sculpture].[55]

Cellini stressed the dignity of the arts of *disegno* in emphasising that it was he, and not some scholar, who had invented the scheme, and that the *bella fantasia* had to be explained by him to the King. The fountain is presented as an allegory of an ideal artistic commonwealth, in which a warrior monarch protects the arts and funds them liberally. It proposed to a patron enamoured of all things Italian, the latest ideas about the equivalence of painting, sculpture and architecture under the aegis of *disegno*. As with the panegyrics in honour of Clement VII or Francesco Maria della Rovere, the visual representation of the importance of *disegno* arguably impressed this ruler, because art and architecture were indeed understood to enhance his powers. The anecdote of the commission even mirrors its allegory in a sense, since the King was described as being impressed by Cellini's 'great creative ideas – *gran virtuosi concetti*'[56] and as ordering his treasurers to release the funding with liberality.

Although written in 1546, four years after Cellini claimed he had devised the fountain, Cellini's views about *disegno* are recorded. Varchi had asked his opinion on the question of the *paragone*, and Cellini replied: 'Amongst all the arts that *disegno* is involved in, I say that sculpture is seven times the greatest.'[57] In his description of the personification of *disegno* for the fountain, Cellini placed sculpture first. He explained to Varchi:

> Sculpture is the mother of all the arts which employ *disegno*, and one who is a worthy sculptor and has a good manner will be able to be good at perspective and architecture and be a greater painter, more easily than those who do not fully possess the skills of the sculptor.[58]

If Cellini's account of his programme for the fountain is to be believed, it may be regarded as having paved the way for a representation of 'design' completed by Philibert de L'Orme, on the funerary urn of François I, which was begun eight years after the conversation which Cellini claimed to have had with that same monarch (Plate 24).

The funerary urn for François I by Philibert de l'Orme 1550–56

Following the death of François I, his son Henri II ordered a marble funerary urn to be designed by the royal architect (and former sculptor) Philibert de l'Orme (1514–70) and placed in the convent church of Notre Dame des Hautes-Bruyères near Rambouillet.[59] This was planned to

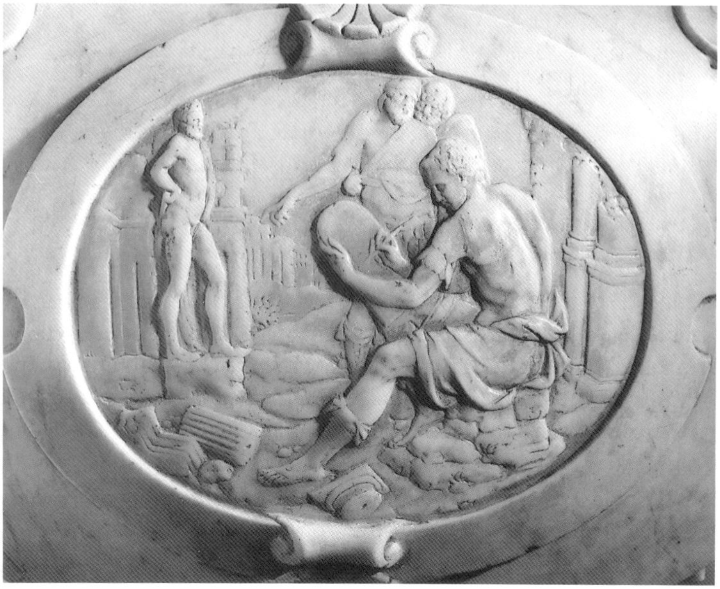

24 Pierre de Bontemps, Drawing after ancient statuary *en plein air*, 1550–56, Funerary urn of François I, Saint Denis, Centre des Monuments Nationaux Basilique.

hold the heart, brain and entrails of the dead king following the will of François I, who had wished them to be cared for by the nuns at Notre Dame. In 1550 Philibert contracted Pierre de Bontemps, specifying

> a pedestal adorned with histories in bas-relief on the four sides and wherein he will sculpt the Muses and inscriptions which he has agreed to do, and above this is to be a vase which shall be hollow, adorned all around with the devices and heraldry of the said dead King carved in medium relief of the arts and other appropriate things.[60]

The resulting base is adorned with scenes showing Apollo and the Muses with Astronomy. This supports an urn decorated with scenes showing Geometry, Architecture, Sculpture and Drawing. *Disegno* (if the personification is to be thought of as Italianate) is signified by means of a man who is seated before an antique statue, amongst what look like Roman ruins. He seems to be drawing the statue, and holds a quill pen. As with Cellini's account of the fountain, the companions of Architecture, Sculpture and Drawing were prestigious intellectually. Apollo and the Muses were associated with the Liberal Arts and here the Muses are playing musical instruments. The selection of Astronomy and Geometry perhaps drew attention to the roles of architecture and sculpture in emulating cosmic harmonies. Instruments for measuring are represented in the majority of the reliefs. The urn, which bears dedicatory inscriptions by Henri II, was completed in 1556. The allegory could also have had further cultural and spiritual connotations. As suggested by Geneviève Bresc-Bautier, the urn could express the commitment by

François I, who had founded the Collège de France, to the arts and letters and also neo-Platonic ideas concerning the harmony of the universe and the role of the ruler:

> Beauty, order and structure are born from this universal harmony in which the human soul also participates. The musician Muses, the Arts, the sciences of numbers (Geometry and Astronomy) form also the different facets of one harmony of which the King is the guarantor on earth, just as he is a mediator between human beings and the divinity.[61]

The appearance of Liberal Arts with Apollo and the Muses in a funerary context had at least one forerunner – that of the chapel of Sant'Agostino in San Francesco at Rimini made for the dynastic church of Sigismondo Malatesta by Agostino di Duccio.[62] Philibert had been made *architecte ordinaire du roi* in 1547, in charge of all the King's works. Trained in Lyons as a sculptor, he had spent the years 1533–36 in Rome, studying ancient art and architecture. When he came to compose his own treatises on architecture, in the period 1561–68, he affirmed the importance of *dessin* for the architect, following Vitruvius.[63]

Major developments in the iconography of *disegno* took place next, in Florence during the 1560s, in the context of the founding of the first academy of *disegno*, and the premium placed by the new ruler of Florence, Cosimo de' Medici, on these arts in bolstering his regime. A variety of forms were tried out: for the official seal of the new academy (1563–69); for the decorations put up for the Medici wedding (1565); and, finally, for the woodcuts decorating Giorgio Vasari's *Lives* (1568), whose publication was assisted by the Medici. Only the latter had permanent and wide currency. The visual data gives a sense of the debate about a concept, which had the dynamic to unite the figurative arts and architecture in a new way.

A seal for the Accademia del Disegno, Florence, 1563–69

In Florence, the licence to explore this new iconography was granted by Duke Cosimo, who supported new associations, such as the academy, which set up professional structures at one remove from the guild groupings, with their republican associations. Cosimo's political strategies also made good sense in terms of cultural politics for the group of Florentine artists (Vasari, Agnolo Bronzino, Montorsoli, Bartolomeo Ammanati (1511–92), and Cellini) who founded the first Accademia del Disegno.[64] In 1560 Montorsoli, the friend of Doni who had written the first book wholly devoted to *disegno*, used his influence as a Servite to obtain the Chapterhouse of the Servite convent of Santissima Annunziata in Florence to inter members of the Compagnia di San Luca. In that year, Montorsoli and forty-eight members of the confraternity reburied the painter Jacopo da Pontormo (1494–1556) on their new chapel. It was out of the reconstituted Compagnia di San Luca (Confraternity of Saint Luke) that the Accademia was formed in 1563, uniting those who had been split into a variety of guilds according to the materials they handled into the one association – of *Disegno* – which indicated what they shared. The seventy members chose as joint presidents Cosimo de' Medici and, *in absentia*, Michelangelo. At its first meeting, in 1563, the Academy resolved that it needed a seal to stamp on its official documents as a replacement for the seal of the Compagnia di San Luca, which it was using for the time being and which consisted of a winged bull lying down with the gospel at its front hooves. Vasari wrote to Cosimo on 1 February 1563, giving an account of the proceedings, and asking him, as president, to be ready to choose the best submission for the new seal.[65]

A variety of designs were put forward between 1563 and 1569, all referring to Cosimo as Duca rather than Granduca – the title he took in 1569.[66] These proposals did not reach a large audience. However, they do register the kind of visual imagery which circulated inside the new academy, allowing artists to test out shared ground. The book containing the seal designs seems to have been used later by Federico Zuccari, the first President of the Roman Academy, with reference to his own representation of *disegno*.

The suggested seals stressed the unity of the arts, their high – even celestial – status and their dependence on Duke Cosimo. Descriptions of the proposals of Domenico Poggini (1520–90) and Stefano Pieri Rossi (1542–1629) remain. Poggini offered a representation of what he described as 'Minerva Goddess of Science' embracing the three arts of painting, sculpture and architecture: 'And because all three grow from the one stem and from one branch of knowledge I represent her as resting and seated upon the Capricorn which symbolises the strength of Your Most Illustrious Majesty.'[67] Capricorn was the Zodiac sign of the Duke, so the sycophantic conceit was that the arts gained their power from Cosimo. The seal design then belongs in part to the familiar tradition of the panegyric of the prince, even as it claimed high status in regarding the figurative arts and architecture as stemming from one plant – the science of *disegno*. Since Poggini had been appointed die engraver to the Florentine Mint in 1556, he may well have felt on his professional mettle to provide a design.

The Florentine painter Rossi presented another emblem, which was also part encomium of Cosimo, and part apotheosis of the three arts. It displayed a temple of the arts within which was a statue of Cosimo I. Flying down to him from the heavens were personifications of Painting, Sculpture and Architecture:

> all three in agreement, and accompanied with Zeal and Love, crown him with a crown of laurel, with a motto around the seal which reads 'Tu das epulis accumbere divum', that is 'You enable us to be seated at our ease at the tables of the Gods'. The food of the Gods is interpreted as that of

> immortality, which is to say ambrosia and nectar, whence it is possible to say that through the good offices of Your Most Illustrious Excellency these three arts are in heaven and immortal.[68]

Here the emphasis is on the concord of the three arts, provided by defining all three as arts of design. Stefano had assisted Vasari in painting a chapel in the duomo and was a pupil of Bronzino.

Cellini also provided suggestions for the seal.[69] Although he had gained prestige from setting up his *Perseus* in the Piazza della Signoria for the Duke in 1553, Cellini's influence at court was on the wane, as Vasari and the Duke's scholarly representative in the Academy, Vincenzo Borghini (1515–80), the Prior of the Ospedale degli Innocenti, increasingly dominated artistic politics. However, as die maker to Clement VII and Paul III, and by his account, having devised ways for showing the concept already for François I, he was pre-eminently qualified to design the new seal. His submissions draw elevated parallels between the creation of the physical world through the forces of Nature, the creation of mankind by God, and the creations of mankind through *disegno*.

One of his proposals showed Apollo, who, he explained, was the symbol of both the Duke and of *disegno* (Plate 25). The God is presented nude with his cloak curling around him, carrying his bow and with the dead python at his feet. He is accompanied with a motto which compares Duke Cosimo to 'cosmic' power: 'Apollo is the sunlight. Cosimo is the source and leader for the great school.'[70] Cellini explained in his accompanying notes that just as the Sun (Apollo) makes all growth of plants and animals in the universe possible, so the Duke provides prosperity for all his subjects in Florence, especially the new Academicians. Just so, Cellini claimed, *disegno* enables men to create civilisation in general by building cities, adorning them with figures of marble, metal and paint and ornamenting their bodies with jewels and gold. Such an interpretation recalls that of De Holanda: that *disegno* is the basis of all the arts and sciences. Cellini explained:

> The great planet Sun is the sole light of the universe and the ancients and our forebears showed and represented it in the form of Apollo. They did so because after the great Flood, which covered all the earth, there remained, when all the water had returned to its place, a very thick mist which prevented the earth from germinating her seeds. Yet the sun struck the mist with its rays so forcibly that it dispersed. Therefore the ancients represented Apollo with the bow and arrows with which he struck the serpent Python which gave its name to that thick mist. For this reason I have put them in the drawing, for it seems to me that our Accademia del Disegno is worthy of this lovely *impresa*, since *disegno* is the true light of all the activities men participate in, in all the professions. *Disegno* is of two sorts: the first kind is that which is created in the imagination. The second derives from the first, and expresses it in lines, and *disegno* has made man so ambitious that he has set himself to rival this great father Apollo.[71]

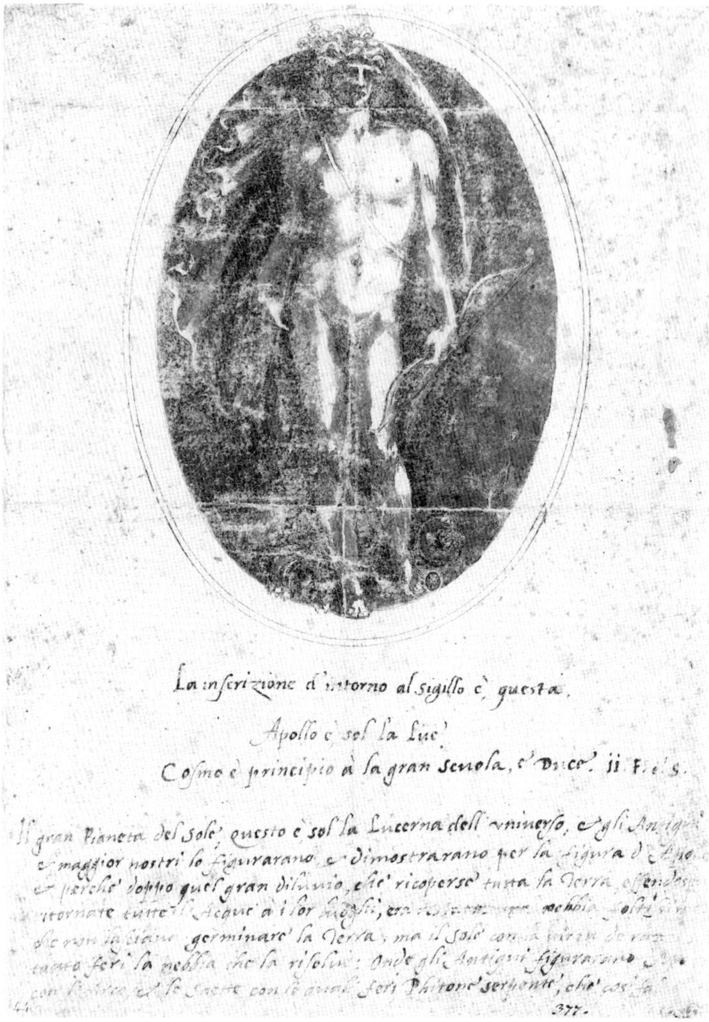

25 Benvenuto Cellini, Apollo for the seal of the Accademia del Disegno, 1564–69, pen and wash on paper, 300 × 218 mm, Graphische Sammlung, Munich.

Interestingly, Cellini's choice of Apollo as *disegno* recalls the association between *disegno* and Apollo with the Muses found on the urn of François I. This *disegno* is masculine, dynamic enough to escape his framing, and conceived as a beautiful, victorious, deity *all'antica*.

Cellini's other suggestion also combined flattery of Cosimo with lofty ambitions for the concept of *disegno*. This time *disegno* was represented by the goddess Diana (Plate 26). Just as Diana in her role as Nature is the mother of all things, Cellini argued, so 'the art of *disegno* is the true mother of all the actions of man'[72] (as the noun *arte* was feminine he could figure the art of *disegno* as Diana). Cellini placed a snake and a lion at her feet. The snake, he explained, signified the prudence of Cosimo's leadership, while the lion represented the strength of Academicians.[73] This time Cellini chose a four-sided frame, which Piero Calamandrei persuasively connected with the Cellini's campaign for the Accademia to recognise the art of modelling as a well as the art of carving, and therefore to think in terms of four arts – not three. The seal designs show Diana as symbol of Nature in the form of the many-breasted cult image originating at Ephesus. Cellini gave her a nimbus and trumpets in her arms, or in some versions of this composition with trumpets instead

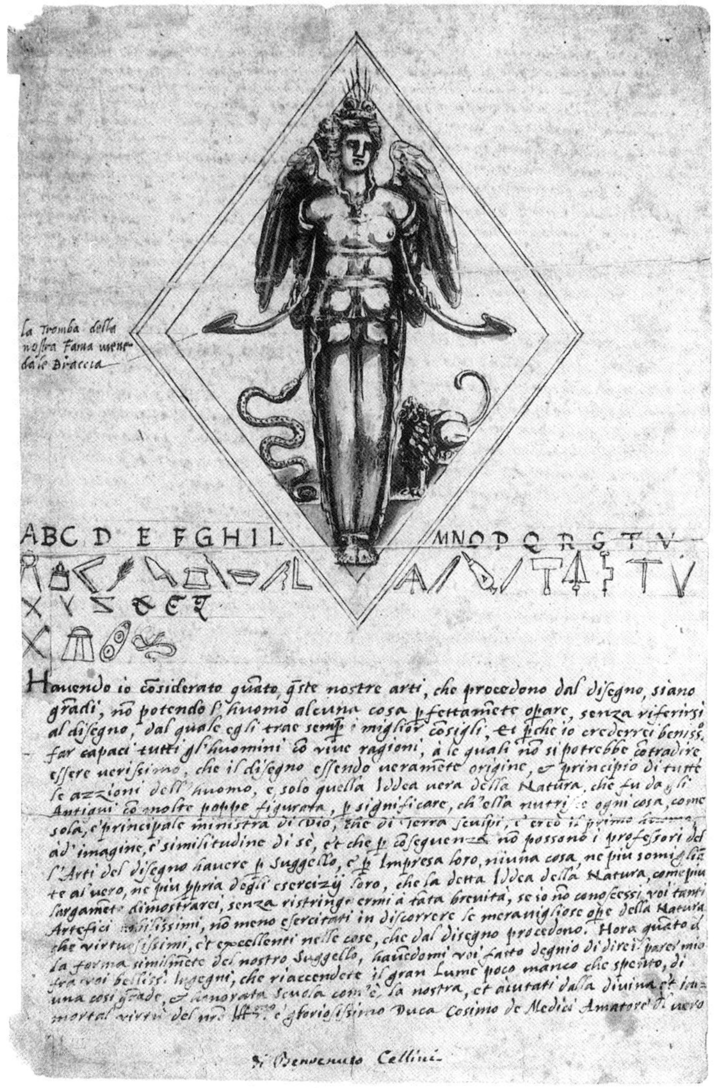

26 Benvenuto Cellini, Diana for the seal of the Accademia del Disegno, 1564–69, pen and wash on paper, 330 × 218 mm, British Museum.

of arms. Cellini had chosen the motto 'The trumpet of our Fame comes from the arms'.[74]

Beneath two of these versions Cellini drew a new pictographic alphabet made of the tools of artists, showing, for instance, the compass placed first, for 'A'. Such artistic letters may recall Gaurico's allusion to the graphic skills needed for making Egyptian hieroglyphs, or even Leonardo's idea that painting 'invented the characters in which the different languages are written'.[75] In his own explanation Cellini suggested that artists could have their own script just as had the Egyptians, Hebrews, Greeks, Romans and Etruscans. Cellini began the gloss on the version of Diana that is currently held by the British Museum, by stating that nothing perfect can be made without *disegno*, 'since it always shows the best solution' and that '*disegno* is truly the origin and beginning of all the actions of man'. For these reasons he had decided to signify it by the image of Diana-Natura,

> that true Goddess of Nature, which was represented with many breasts by the ancients, to symbolise that she suckled all things as the only and chief handmaid of God, Who sculpted and created the first man from the earth in the image and similitude of Himself.[76]

Cellini therefore proposed the grandest significance for *disegno*: relating to the creation of mankind by God; and by Him of the world, through the mediation of Nature; and finally in the role of all the things, which mankind contributed to civilisation through *disegno*.

On the drawing owned by Calamandrei, Cellini explained that the seal had four sides to stand for the four elements making up the world, and the corresponding four arts of sculpture ('the first because God made the first man from sculpting the earth with his divine and immortal hands') painting, architecture and modelling.[77] His polemic on behalf of a wider interpretation of *disegno* highlights the way the seal designs of Poggini and Pieri Rossi had assumed without question the idea that *disegno* comprised just three arts.

The sketches which survive by Fra Montorsoli for the new seal suggest that he supported the tripartite definitions of Poggini and Pieri Rossi. As the founder of the renovated Confraternity of Saint Luke, friend of Doni and supervisor of the redecoration of the chapterhouse at Santissima Annunziata as the chapel of the new Academy (Plate 55), Montorsoli played an important role in the new Accademia del Disegno. One of his drawings represents a single male figure – probably as a personification of *disegno* – who stands on a globe holding the instruments of painting, sculpture and architecture. The inscription reads 'I am the basis of the three arts of sculpture, painting and architecture' (*Basis ego sum triarium artium sculpt.* [*urae*], *pict.* [*urae*] *et arch.* [*itecturae*]).[78]

The presence of the globe perhaps suggested the worldwide aegis of *disegno*. Montorsoli also experimented with a seal which showed a hand holding a stylus surrounded with the instruments of the arts and also with triangular shapes decorated with three personifications of sculpture, painting and architecture. In addition, Fra Montorsoli tried out a composition entailing three interlocking circles, adorned with the instruments of the three arts. However, no decision was made in 1569, or in 1571 when the matter was raised again by the Academicians, as to the form of the new seal. As pointed out by David Summers, this last symbol was, however, employed in the ornament of the academy chapel completed in 1575.[79]

Only in 1597 was it confirmed that a seal which used the three interlocking circles was the right one for the new academy. This *impresa* was reported as having been invented by Michelangelo in the *Lives* (1568). According to Vasari, Michelangelo's design of three circlets signified that 'the three professions of sculpture, painting and architecture are interwoven one with another and so bound together, that each of them receives assistance and decoration from the others, and they neither can nor should be separated'.[80] This device had been adapted by the Academicians for the funeral of Michelangelo in the decoration of the walls of the church of San Lorenzo in Florence in 1564; then the circlets had been turned into crowns. When the Academicians came to make his marble tomb in Santa Croce they had changed it again to form three interlocking laurel wreaths (1564–73): the form finally taken in 1597. The seal submissions suggest that the idea of *disegno* comprising just the three arts was the dominant view from early on.

Vasari, Borghini and the decorations put up for the Medici wedding: 1565

Vasari was able to publicise – if briefly – another symbol for *disegno* on one of the triumphal arches for the marriage of Joanna of Austria to Francesco de' Medici, in December 1565, at the Porta del Prato in Florence. Vasari and Borghini had been planning this festival since August 1565. Borghini's notebook, recording his ideas for the triumphal arch, has survived.[81] The Princess was greeted on the outer face of the arch with paintings showing Florentine feats of arms, theology and philosophy. As she passed under the arch she saw depictions of Florentine poetry and *disegno*. The wall facing the city pictured commerce and agriculture. The account published at the end of the *Lives* (1568) described how Alessandro Allori (1535–1607) painted Vasari's image of *disegno* in the form of a fictive statue:

> the statue of *disegno*, the father of painting, sculpture and architecture, who if not born in Florence, as may be seen in past writings, may be said to have been born again there, and nourished and grown as in his own nest. He was figured as a statue wholly nude, with three similar heads for the three arts

that he embraces, each holding in the hand some instrument, but without any distinction.[82]

The fictive statue presided over a canvas showing the teaching activities of the Academy and the famous Florentine artists of the past (see Chapter 3).[83] At the base was a frieze of children learning the precepts of successful artists. A drawing survives which may have been for the 1568 edition of the *Lives*, representing a related emblem of *disegno*, whose three heads are adorned with a crown consisting of a set square, while three different plants sprout from her hair. In her hands are a hammer and a palette (Plate 27). That the imagery of painting, sculpture and architecture belonging to the 'one body' of design was current in thought is confirmed by the fact that it had been employed by de Holanda two decades earlier in 1548.[84]

The determination to show *disegno* as three-fold was also present in Borghini's composition for the medallion, which decorated the triumphal arch in the fashion of Roman Imperial architecture. This medallion showed *disegno* as three female personifications, posed like the Three Graces, and holding painters', sculptors' and architects' tools. They were standing on a base on which the zodiacal emblem of Capricorn for the Duke appeared, in a triangular field, flanked by further artistic tools. The medallion recalled the statement which Borghini had made a year earlier, in a lecture to the Academicians, urging them to imitate the unity of the Three Graces, and to cease quarrelling about their relative status.[85] The Graces in these poses, with linked arms, were interpreted as emblems of *Amicitia*, or mutual friendship, in contemporary emblem books.[86] Clearly the concept of *disegno* was perceived as signalling professional solidarity.

During the decade in which the Academy was founded, Vasari made a further contribution to the budding iconography of *disegno* in some of the woodcuts decorating the frames on the portraits in his *Lives* (1568), which were being designed from 1560 onwards. Vasari placed a woman seated and designing on a tablet at the apex of the frame used for the portraits of artists, such as Leonardo, Michelangelo, Andrea del Verrocchio (1435–88) and Giotto, who had achieved equally in more than one art (Plate 28). By this means he was able to display their 'chief' skill as that of *disegno*. This frame type is sketched on the same sheet as the unused composition for the three-headed design (Plate 27). The idea seems to have provided a precedent for Vasari's Netherlandish colleague working in Florence Jan van der Straet when he composed an allegorical frame for his self-portrait about 1580. Van der Straet placed a woman drawing inscribed *disegno* at the apex of his composition and personifications of *Architectura*, *perspectiva* and *Pittura* on either side. The composition was engraved by Hendrik Goltzius in 1583 when van der Straet was sixty (see also Plate 90). In this way, Vasari's approaches were

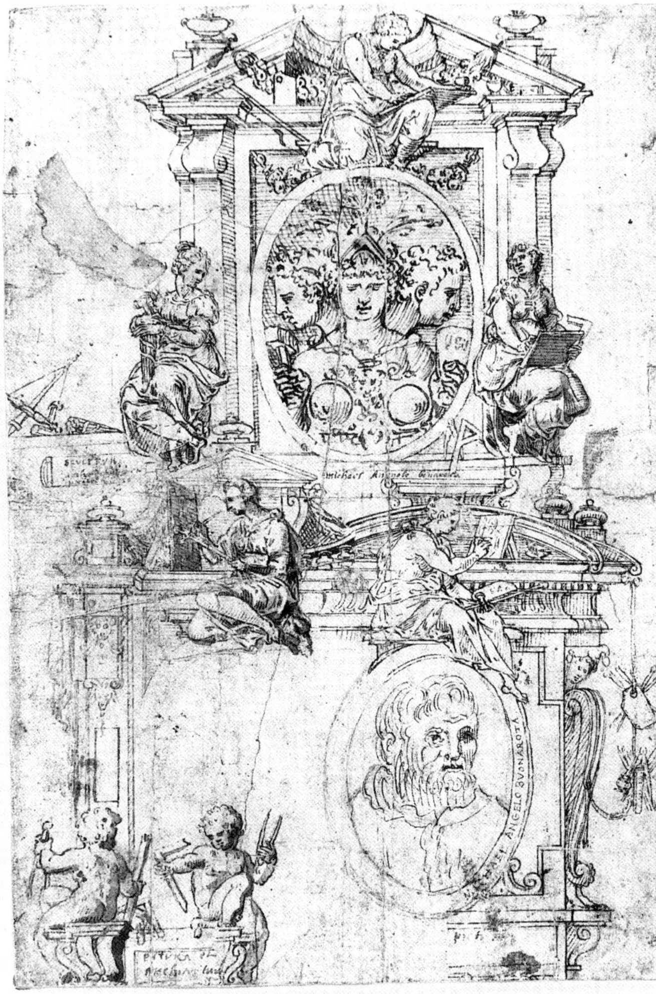

27 Giorgio Vasari or his circle, Design as a three headed 'woman', *c.*1565, Collection Anthony Blunt.

appropriated by artists trained in the traditions of Antwerp and Haarlem.[87]

Vasari's house, 1573

Vasari's final contribution to the visualisation of *disegno* was his most personal one, since it was painted as part of the decoration of his Florentine house. Vasari had entered the employment of Cosimo de' Medici in 1554 and had been lodged in a house on the Borgo Santa Croce from 1557 onwards but the Grand Duke did not give him the house until 1570. Here in 1573 Vasari set about decorating his reception room on the *piano nobile* with three windows opening onto the Borgo.[88]

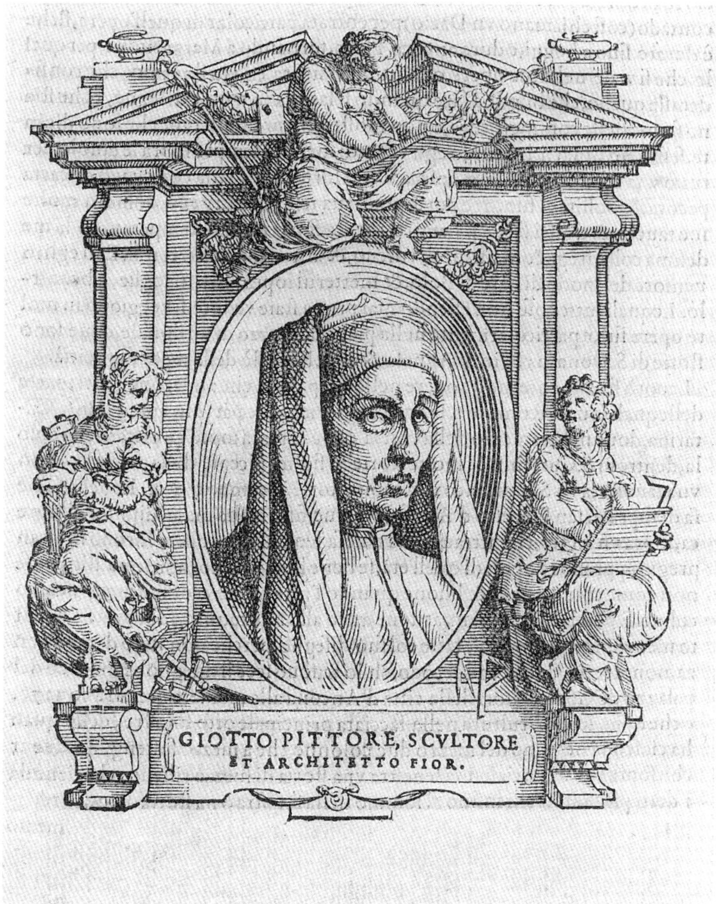

28 Giorgio Vasari, Giotto, *Vite*, 1568.

For one wall of this most public space in his house, Vasari thought out a complex pictorial allegory of the powers of *disegno*, which employed the personification he had made for the wedding celebrations in 1565, along with a narrative of Zeuxis taking the best features from the five young women of Croton so as to make a perfect image of a goddess. Vasari presented the story as an allegory of the transformation by an excellent painter of the imperfect creatures to be observed in 'reality', into ideal beauty, through the skills of *disegno*. On the right he showed young women each with some feature of beauty coming to the entrance to Zeuxis' studio as models. A statue of many-breasted Diana Natura here reminds the viewer that these women are the flawed products of Nature's creations. But on the left-hand side Vasari represents the artist selecting from the imperfect women, so as to depict what he is able to judge as an ideally beautiful goddess, through the knowledge given him by *disegno*. As pointed out by Alessandro Cecchi, the passage between the imperfect world of nature and the studio at the centre of the composition is decorated with a fictive statue of *disegno*, personified as a naked man with three heads, whose attributes are discernible in one of Vasari's drawings (Plate 29).

Vasari had meditated long and hard on the process of artistic idealisation as his section *On Painting* in the *Lives* (1568) demonstrated, and the allegory is very much a painted exploration of his theories.

> *Disegno*, father of our three arts, Architecture, Painting and Sculpture, proceeding from the intellect, draws forth a universal judgement from many things, like a form or an idea of all the things in nature, which is most singular in its measurements – that is, he [*disegno*] understands, not only in human bodies and animal ones, but also in plants as well and in buildings, sculptures and paintings, the proportion of the whole in relation to its parts as well as the proportion of the parts to one another and to the whole. And since this understanding gives birth to a sure concept and judgement, which forms in the mind the thing that later, expressed by the hands, is called *disegno*, one may conclude that this *disegno* is nothing but an apparent expression and declaration of that concept which one has in the soul, and that which is imagined in the mind and fabricated in the idea. And from this capacity, perhaps, derives the Greek proverb 'from the claw of a lion' relating to a talented man who, seeing solely the claw of a lion carved in a lump of stone, comprehended with his intellect sufficiently from that measure to form the parts of the whole animal and then put them together as if he had had them present before his eyes. Some people consider that the father of *disegno* and the arts came into being by chance, and that practice and experience, like nurse and the tutor, nurtured him with the help of understanding and discourse.[89]

Vasari defined *disegno*, following a similar argument to that of Gaurico, as the intellectual power of understanding the generic laws of symmetry or proportionality to be found in the entire natural world, as well as

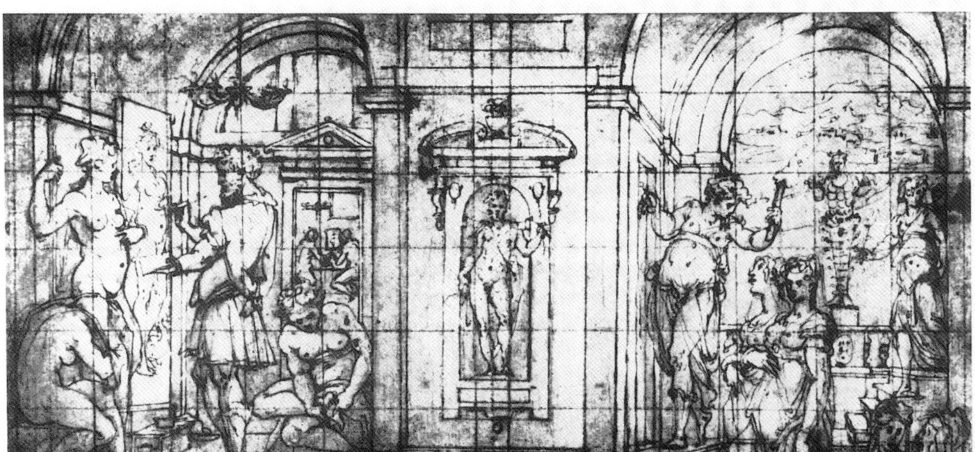

29 Giorgio Vasari, *The story of Zeuxis and the Five Maidens of Croton*, *c.*1573, Gabinetto Disegni e Stampe 1180E.

in the products of architects, painters and sculptors. Through studying the visual world the artist acquires reliable discrimination, which allows him to sift sense data and choose elements from Nature, so as to achieve an ideally beautiful representation. As all the writers on the issue had emphasised since the fifteenth century, *disegno* (or its Latin and Portuguese equivalent) was seen firstly as a mental operation and only secondly as physical execution. Vasari stated that *disegno* is fabricated in the 'idea'. This was a term transposed from Platonic philosophy, where it had referred to the doctrine that the soul remembers ideas of perfect beauty, from its existence before birth, when it was part of the world soul, and therefore is able to recognise dim reflections of beauty, during its sojourn on earth, as beautiful. In this passage Vasari seems to be using the term 'idea' in a distinctive way, as the power of generalising about sense data possessed by the intellect. Manipulating the prestigious language of Platonism, Vasari therefore represented *disegno* as the capacity to employ correct judgement based on analysis of the proportional structures underlying the visible world.

The various ways in which Vasari presented *disegno* were profoundly implicated in proposals for the new status of the figurative arts and architecture as theoretical, cerebral, Liberal Arts. It is telling that when the personification of *disegno* was first described, in Cesare Ripa's *Iconologia* in 1603 (and again in 1611), Ripa (*c.*1560–*c.*1620) followed Vasari's invention of the three-headed man with the tools of a draughtsman: 'One may depict *disegno* as being the father of sculpture, painting and architecture with three equal and similar heads, who holds in his hands various instruments used in the above mentioned arts.'[90] The fact that personifications or devices signifying *disegno* were illustrated in the *Lives*, and were associated with the new academy, as well as decorating Vasari's house suggests that the new iconography was moving from the panegyric of rulers to the panegyric of artists themselves. During the 1570s, significantly, it was transposed to a Venetian context, when it was chosen for display in Titian's funerary commemoration.

Titian's funerary apparatus, 1576

The apparatus planned by the confraternity of painters in Venice for Titian's funeral in 1576 offered a somewhat different view of the value of *disegno*. As one might expect, a statue of Painting was given priority in the planned ensemble of personifications gracing the lying-in-state of the artist. However, Ridolfi listed a further eight statues as being designed to encircle the corpse. Firstly, he listed two figures: one of Apollo who stood for Poetry, and one of History. These two were followed by *Disegno*, who was shown as

> an old man with a long beard, wearing a simple robe, because one must have long experience in a skill to understand it well, and he shall demonstrate

designing on a sheet of paper and there shall be the inscription 'No beauty without me.'[91]

Next came Sculpture and Architecture, who were accompanied by Hard Work, Symmetry and Honour.[92] It seems then that the Venetian *Fraglia* was claiming that Titian was highly experienced in *disegno*. The funeral apparatus is likely to have been planned in some measure to defend Titian's reputation in relation to the debate which had developed during the mid-sixteenth century as to the rival merits of painters (especially Titian and Michelangelo), depending on whether they were claimed to be more proficient in drawing or in colouring. Whereas Lodovico Dolce (1508–68) in his dialogue *Aretino* (1557), for example, had defended Titian warmly ('in invention and *disegno* none ever exceeded him'), Vasari had argued that Titian was inferior because of his lack of interest in drawing in the *Lives* (1568).[93] The debate depended on rival definitions of good *disegno* in painting. The protagonists of Romano-Florentine studio routines associated good *disegno* in painting, with the extensive use of studies and preparatory drawing. Conversely, the defendants of Venetian pictorial practices related good *disegno* to the production of an illusion of pictorial reality, by designing through tone, colour and texture on the painted surface itself. Because of the dual meaning of *disegno*, Venetian painters might be placed in a relatively weak position in the textual debate. But here the identification of 'beauty' with *disegno* in the inscription ensured that the broader cerebral meanings of *disegno* were registered, rather than the narrow one of 'drawing'. (It is of some interest to note that Apollo was to have been present as in the scheme of De L'Orme.)

The motto chosen for *disegno* ('No beauty without me') might relate to the notion that beauty derives from understanding proportions, which had been stated as early as the 1450s in Ghiberti's *Commentari*: 'But only proportionality makes beauty.'[94] The identification of beauty with *disegno* was elaborated by Lomazzo in the *Idea del tempio della pittura* (1590): 'The foundation of everything . . . and whence derives all beauty, is that which the Greeks call *euritmia*, and which we call *disegno*.'[95] It was repeated by Romano Alberti (1555–1604; the scholarly secretary to the Roman academy) in 1604, who stated that painters regarded '*disegno* as the principal sustenance they possess for forming the figure perfectly'.[96] The link between experience and *disegno* was also a commonplace, as demonstrated in Vasari's definition in the *Lives*.

During the late sixteenth century, Italian texts continued to discuss *disegno*. For instance, the Florentine scholar Raffaello Borghini in *Il Riposo* (Florence, 1584) stated that *disegno* is 'an apparent demonstration with lines of what has first been conceived in the human soul and imagined in the idea'.[97] At greater length the painter Giovanni Battista Armenini (*c.*1525–1609) in *De veri precetti della pittura* (1587) quoted

Doni and summarised Vasari. He explained that *disegno* is 'the light, the foundation and the support' of painting, sculpture and architecture:

> Some have said that it [*disegno*] must be a speculation born in the mind, and an endeavour [*industria*] full of the artifice of the intellect, with the putting to work of its forces according to the beautiful idea. While others then say, rather, that it must be a science of beautiful and regulated proportion of all that one sees, with ordered components, through which one discerns the fineness of their due measurements, and which develops through study, through divine grace and through good discourse . . . only this we say, that it is enough for us that *disegno* may be like a living light of beautiful talent, and that it may be of such great force and so necessary to all, that one who is entirely deprived of it may be likened to a blind person.[98]

The statement that *disegno* is the science of beautiful proportions, developed through study, suggests the attitudes which helped to produce the plans for Titian's funeral a decade earlier.

Federico Zuccari, Sala del Disegno, Palazzo Zuccari, Rome, *c*.1599

The most spectacular apotheosis of *disegno* was provided by Federico Zuccari in his role as the first President of the Roman Academy, which had been founded in 1593. Zuccari had been trained in Rome, and had worked in Venice, Orvieto and Loreto as well as having travelling to Spain, England and the Netherlands. Significantly, as a young man, he had helped to make the festival decorations in Florence for the entry of Joanna of Austria in 1565 alongside Vasari. His commitment to theorising about the intellectual standing of the three arts is demonstrated by his lectures on the topic of *disegno* to the new academy in 1593–94 and his treatise entitled *L'idea de' pittori, scultori ed architetti* (Turin, 1607), which set out a scheme of human knowledge and activity according to the governing principle of *disegno*. In 1599 he painted the vault of a large room in his palace in Rome with a visual exploration of his proposals as to the importance of *disegno* in intellectual and social life (Plate 30).[99]

The decoration presents Zuccari's view of the executive place of *disegno* in the scheme of human knowledge and action. Rather than a mere adjunct of Practical Arts, he placed it as a universal principle, from which stemmed the intellectual skills enabling the smooth running of human society. He represented *disegno* as a venerable patriarch with a beard and cloak, who holds a sceptre and the tools of painting, sculpture and architecture, in the centre of the vault. It is worth noting that the *Fraglia dei Pittori* in Venice in 1576 had already represented *disegno* as an old experienced man, and that Vasari had shown *disegno* as holding the attributes of the arts. Seated with him are three female personifications of architecture, sculpture and painting, and at their feet are young children being taught their arts. This educative motif had

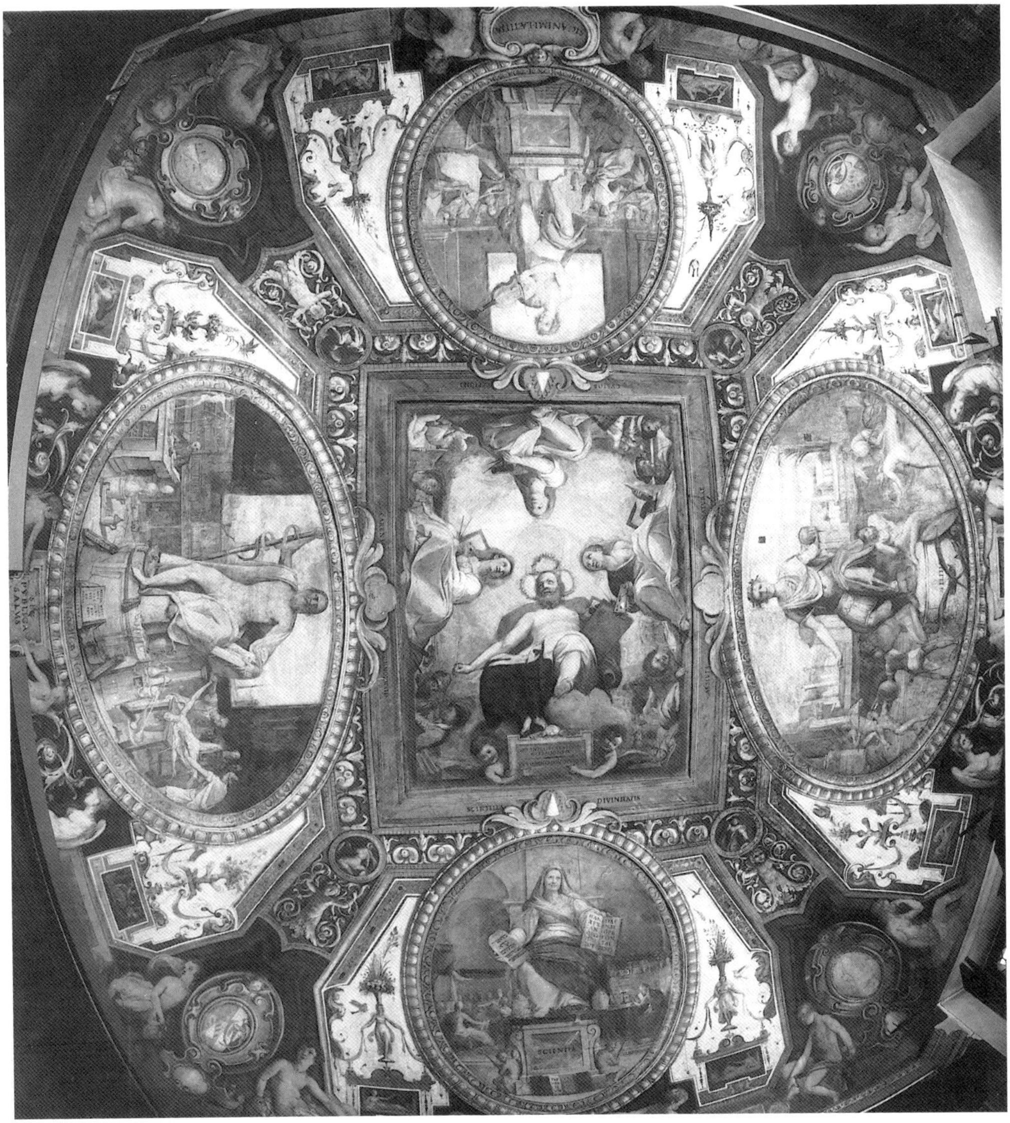

30 Federico Zuccari, vault of the Sala del Disegno, 1599, Palazzo Zuccari, Rome.

been used in association with *disegno* by Vasari for the Medici wedding. *Disegno*, over whose head are the three joined circles which the Florentine academy had taken as their seal in 1597, stands over a tablet inscribed with Trinitarian claims for the importance of *disegno*: 'One light in three, glowing light of the intellect and life of operations' (*Una lux in tribus refulgens, lux intellectus et vita operationum*). On the frame of the scene below *disegno* was inscribed the phrase 'Spark of divinity' (*Scintilla divinitatis*). Also on this frame are phrases explaining the roles of painting (*Aemula naturae*: 'emulatrix of nature'), sculpture (*Custos effigiei*: 'guardian of effigies') and architecture (*Parens commoditatis*: 'provider of convenience') which Zuccari explained or quoted in *L'idea*.[100]

The four scenes on the lower parts of the vault seem to represent the way human *disegno* benefits society, according to the scheme of knowledge he described in his treatise. In *L'idea* Zuccari subdivided *disegno* into divine, angelic and human sorts, and categorised human *disegno* into two kinds: that is internal and external *disegno*, defining the 'internal *disegno*' as conceptual, whereas the 'external *disegno*' entailed physically making objects. The conceptual kinds of *disegno* could, in his view, be more practically orientated, such as the arts of painting, sculpture, architecture, medicine, war and government. However, 'internal *disegno*' could also be of a more speculative sort such as metaphysics, mathematics or geometry.[101]

The vault represents some of these conceptual sorts of 'internal *disegno*'. In the centre of the vault he showed *disegno* presiding over painting, sculpture and architecture. On the lower facets of the vault he depicted the arts of war and medicine along with the more speculative arts of metaphysics. There too are depicted the arts of poetry and music. Zuccari's scheme was a clever way of bypassing the traditional system of the system of 'Liberal' versus 'Practical' Arts, since it allowed for a continuum of intellectual *disegno* with the more speculative at one end, and more practical at the other. In his 1594 lecture to the Academicians Zuccari had explained that, 'the external designs made by us painters, sculptors and architects are caused and formed by virtue of our speculative and practical *disegno*'.[102]

One scene is labelled *sic salus publica* ('thus the health of the public'). It shows the knowledge of *Medicina* in a statue of Aesculapius, holding his snake staff and a herbal. Scenes on either side display the distillation of medicines, the dissection of the human body, and the practices of surgery. Books labelled as by Avicenna, Hippocrates and Galen are propped up at the base of the statue, along with the book of *Ecclesiasticus* (38, 16) open at the words *Altissimus creavit de terra medicamenta et vir prudens* ('The most high created medicines from earth and a prudent man will not despise them'). A second allegory represents a seated Roman ruler, crowned with a laurel wreath, and holding the sceptre and baton of power. His plinth is inscribed *Militia*. Below the frame are the words *sic potentia et imperium* ('thus power and sovereignty'). A more speculative type of *disegno* described by Zuccari included metaphysics. A third allegory depicts a crowned woman holding Aristotle's *Metaphysics* and the book of *Genesis* (presumably denoting theology). She is seated on a plinth inscribed *Scientia*. A further book entitled *Ius gentium et ius civile* ('the law of the people and the law of civil society') suggests the sphere of jurisprudence. In the background scholars are disputing with one another, and one is reading in a library. The whole scene is inscribed *sic vera nobilitas* ('thus true nobility'). The fourth allegory depicts a statue of Apollo with his lyre, as patron of poetry and music, surrounded by the nine Muses playing and singing. His plinth is inscribed *Harmonia*, with the explanatory label below stressing the way humanity needed the ordering of music to be happy: 'thus the joy of the soul' (*sic animi laetitia*). Although Zuccari did not discuss the role of music, he referred to poetry as a species of *disegno* which moves our soul to follow the truth.[103] Health, good government, noble conduct, and happiness for society are therefore presented as being dependent on different species of 'internal *disegno*'.

The vault shows *disegno* as a godlike figure probably with reference to the idea that God was the ultimate designer. As Zuccari wrote in *L'idea*: 'God then is the true *Disegno*, and true author, and perfect and divine Painter, Sculptor and Architect.'[104] Zuccari explained in *L'idea* that God had endowed man with a little of his own divine power: 'This internal human *disegno* is called . . . Spark of Divinity; because man in forming this internal *disegno* . . . is Spark of Divinity, which is part of the substance Divine':[105] hence the inscription *Scintilla divinitatis* on the vault. Academicians who attended Zuccari's lecture in 1594 had heard how humans had been given the ability to employ *disegno*:

> because our soul is made in the image and similitude of God, almost like a spark of that divinity which illuminates the soul and our intelligence, and which makes us rise from the earth and speculate on lofty and divine matters.[106]

In this lecture he stated that whereas God's *disegno* was comprehensive, instantaneous and infinite, human *disegno* was focused on particulars, happened in sequence, and was finite in scope. Zuccari compared human *disegno* to forms of light – to the spark from God's fire and to the sun:

> So this *disegno* is almost like another sun in the human soul and intellect, which moves, gives life to, and illuminates all our activities and is as necessary to us as is the sun to the earth.[107]

The inscriptions which Zuccari used for the vault – 'light of the intellect and life of activities' – were therefore Latin versions of phrases he had used in his lecture to the Academicians in 1594, when he declaimed: 'Our intelligence and activities all derive from the light, from this fount and from this great *disegno*.'[108]

According to Kemp, these light metaphors may relate to the ideas of Cellini, for the Florentine Academy seal. They also echo the view of Armenini that *disegno* is 'a living light of beautiful invention'. Erwin Panofsky connected Zuccari's description of *disegno* as 'the spark of divinity' to a passage in the commentary by Marsilio Ficino (1433–90) on Plato's *Phaedrus* ('By sparks He designates the Ideas . . . and He also designates the impressions of these Ideas innate in us'). Panofsky's suggestion is plausible given that this text was available in Italian at the time (Rome, 1544).[109] Zuccari's Latin inscription for *disegno* as 'one light shining in three' had latent Trinitarian resonances, equally perhaps significant, but unspoken, in the tripartite seal designs for the Florentine Academy and in Michelangelo's three interlocking circles.[110]

In emulation of the Florentines, the Roman Academy had discussed the choice of an *impresa* at their February and October meetings, in 1594. Romano Alberti related the proposals by Antonio da Faenza and Zuccari. Antonio da Faenza suggested three styluses for drawing, with their tips together pointing upwards to 'gather light' alluding to the three professions. Zuccari proposed a lantern with three apertures and the motto *sic operatur* ('thus it operates'), claiming that *disegno* 'is like light which illuminates everything hidden'. He also suggested the image of a 'luminous sun' (recalling Cellini's Apollo) which shines on part of the earth having the same effect as our intelligences and activities in 'revivifying and feeding everything'. In October 1594 he returned to the competition, and he put forward the motto *Scintilla divinitatis*. None of these ideas seems to have been accepted.[111] Arguably then, the vault of the Sala del Disegno allowed Zuccari to give permanent form to these proposals on his own terms.

By the end of the sixteenth century, therefore, a largely Italian succession of artists had devised a variety of ways of representing *disegno*. Some of them showed a man or woman drawing, as on the funerary urn commissioned by Henri II, the illustrations of the *Lives* by Vasari, and the plans for Titian's funeral. Otherwise, *disegno* was represented as an old man with a sceptre (Zuccari), or as a man or woman having three heads (Vasari). In the latter cases, the figures were accompanied by the tools of painting, sculpture and architecture. Some artists chose mythological personages to signify the powers of *disegno*: Diana as Nature itself (Cellini); Apollo as the Sun shedding light and warmth on the universe (Cellini); or the Three Graces emphasising the unity of the arts (Borghini). Others were more low key and chose female personifications of painting, sculpture and architecture (Poggini) or three circles (Michelangelo) to stand for the three arts of *disegno*.

As with the representations of painting, sculpture and architecture as Liberal Arts, the visual experiments took place in terms of the context of: the panegyric of princes (François I, Henri II, Duke Cosimo); the debates about the seal and *imprese* for the academies of *disegno*; the decoration of houses belonging to leading members of academies; and the celebration of the careers of individual artists (Vasari's *Lives*, the funeral of Titian, the commemoration of van der Straet). Perhaps even more obviously than the representation of painting, sculpture and architecture as equivalents of the Liberal Arts, the visual imagery invented for *disegno* encouraged highly ambitious claims for the status of art, to the level, in some cases, of cosmic significance, and was linked with artists undertaking philosophical discussions which related to categorising all the arts. Although the systems of the Practical Arts had grouped architecture, painting and sculpture together, this had been in terms of architecture as the leading art. In contrast the new theories and iconographies of *disegno* showed the three arts as equals.

Reviewing the literary discussion of the liberal status of painting, sculpture and architecture, and writings on *disegno*, it becomes apparent that (with some exceptions, such as Gaurico) the debate was initially conducted by writers with some, or a lot of, artistic experience. Whereas artists were usually put in the position of being the visualisers of texts produced by scholars, here they were inventing visual images in relation to a body of texts which had been produced by a succession of artists. Whether or not artists were relying on scholarly advice to help them produce their new ideas for personifications and devices (for example the relationship between Borghini and Vasari) these new iconographies of art occasioned some shifting in the traditional boundaries demarcating the artistic from the scholarly.

One way to show that the figurative arts and architecture were worthy of high status was to display their theoretical nature, in literary texts and visual images. However, another important route to this goal was to stress that these arts were worthy of being recorded in histories. Perhaps the most obvious ways of celebrating the lives of artists were provided in books. However, commemorative portraits of artists produced during the fifteenth and sixteenth centuries may also be regarded as forms of history which could help to document the personal qualities of especially talented artists for posterity.

Notes

1 Romano Alberti, *Accademia del Dissegno de' Pittori, Scultori e Architetti di Roma*, Pavia, 1604.

2 Wolfgang Kemp, 'Beiträge zur Geschichte des Begriffs zwischen 1547 und 1607', *Marburger Jahrbuch für Kunstwissenschaft*, XIX, 1974, pp. 219–40; and Maurice Poirier, 'The role and concept of *disegno* in mid sixteenth-century Florence', pp. 53–68, in *The Age of Vasari*, New York, 1970.

3 Cennino Cennini, *The Craftsman's Handbook: The Italian Il libro dell'arte*, trans. D.V. Thompson, New York, 1960, p. 2.

4 Alberti had preferred the term 'circumscription' in discussing graphic operations connected with painting in *De pictura* (1435) and in *Della pittura* (1436): 'la circumscrittione, cioè il modo del disegniare', in Alberti, *Della pittura*, p. 87. In 1483 Mantegna was praised for possessing 'el gran disegno, vero fondamento de la pittura': see Giovanni Santi, *La vita e le gesta di Federico di Montefeltro*, ed. Luigi Michelini Tocci, 2 vols, 1985, Vatican, Rome, II, p. 669.

5 Lorenzo Ghiberti, *Ghibertis Denkwürdigkeiten (I commentari)*, ed. Julius von Schlosser, Berlin, 1912, p. 5: 'el disegno è il fondamento et teorica di queste due arti, conviene sia molto perito in detta teorica'.

6 Ghiberti, *Ghibertis Denkwürdigkeiten*, p. 8: 'la teorica del disegno, sança essa teorica non si può essere buono statuario nè buon pittore, tanto buono lo scultore o veramente el pittore quanto perito in detta teorica cioè in detto disegno el quale non s'aquista sança grande studio nè sança grande disciplina.'

7 Ghiberti, *Ghibertis Denkwürdigkeiten*, pp. 4–5: 'conviene che'llo scultore etiamdio el pictore sia amaestrato in tutte queste arti liberali: Grammatica, Geometria, Phylosophia, Medicina, Astrologia, Prospectiva, Istori[osri]coi [sic], Notomia, Teorica Disegno, Arismetrica.'

8 Vitruvius Pollio, *De architectura*, ed. Laura Cherubini, Pisa, 1975, pp. 14–19. Vitruvius uses (p. 15) the term 'graphidos' – 'peritus graphidos' – not 'designatio'.

9 Leon Battista Alberti, *L'architettura: de re aedificatoria*, ed. and trans. Giovanni Orlandi, Milan, 1966, pp. 19–21, 'erit ergo lineamentum certa constansque perscriptio, concepta animo, facta lineis et angulis perfectaque animo et ingenio erudito.'

10 Antonio Averlino, il Filarete, *Trattato di architettura*, 2 vols, ed. Anna Maria Finoli and Liliana Grassi, Milan, 1972, I, p. 40: 'fantasticare e pensare e rivoltarselo per la memoria in più modi, e fare varii disegni nella sua mente . . . farne uno disegno piccolo rilevato di legname.'

11 Il Filarete, *Trattato di architettura*, I, pp. 10–11: 'disegno è il quale fondamento e via d'ogni arte che di mano si faccia.'

12 Francesco di Giorgio Martini, *Trattati di architettura, ingegnieria e arte militare*, ed. C. Maltese Corrado, 2 vols, Milan, 1967, pp. 293–4: 'Scrive Eupompo di Macedonia, egregio matematico, nissuna arte perfettamente nelli omini essere senza aritmetica e geometria. Similmente non solo da lui ma da molti altri eccellenti non meno necessaria era stimata l'arte del disegno a qualunque operativa scienzia che le prenominate.' Francesco seems to have confused Eupompus with Melanthius.

13 Francesco di Giorgio Martini, *Trattati di architettura*, pp. 293–4: 'Quanto sia utile e necessaria in ogni opera umana, sì nella invenzione, sì in possere esplicare li concetti, sì nell'operare, sì all'arte militare.'

14 Italian in Leonardo, *Literary Works of Leonardo*, I, p. 34: 'io dirò il medesimo di tutte l'arti, che passano per le mani delli scrittori, le quale è di spetie di dissegno, membro della pittura; e l'astrologia e l'altre passano per le manuali operationi; ma prima sono mentali, com'è la pittura, la quale è prima nella mente del suo speculatore e non puo pervenire alla sua perfettione senza la manuale operatione.'

15 Paola Barrocchi, *Scritti d'arte del Cinquecento*, 3 vols, Milan, 1971–77, I, p. 65: 'con sue divine speculatione'.

16 Leonardo, *Literary Works of Leonardo*, I, p. 57: 'se voi la chiamate mechanica, perche è prima manuale, che le mani figurano quello, che trovano nella fantasia, voi scrittori, dissegnando con la penna manualmente quello, che nello ingegno vostro si trova.'

17 Leonardo, *Literary Works of Leonardo*, I, p. 63.

18 Pomponio Gaurico, *De sculptura*, ed. Paolo Cutolo, Naples, 1999, pp. 126–7.

19 Gaurico, *De sculptura*, pp. 148–50: 'Graphicen vero, quam nostri in scriptore descriptionem, in pictore et sculptore designationem vocaverunt

– nam lineationem quae γράμμικη (grammike) dicitur, architecto damus, usque adeo necessariam sculptori iudicavit Donatellus – sive enim accepimus – ut plerunque discipulis dicere solitus fuerit uno se verbo sculptoriam artem eis omnem traditurum, quem dicebat 'Designate'. Et profecto id est totius sculpturae caput ac fundamentum. Ea vero duabus etiam hisce rebus maxime constat ςυμμετρία (symmetria), quae nondum sibi Romanum nomen invenit – nisi fortasse Latinam linguam augentes, ut Cicero ait, commensurationem dixerint, et όπτίκκη (optike), quam perspectivam appellant.'

20 Julius von Schlosser, *La letteratura artistica*, ed. Otto Kurz, Florence, 1954, p. 248 (Antwerp, 1528; Nuremberg, 1542).

21 Cesare Cesariano, *Cesare Cesariano e il classicismo di primo Cinquecento*, ed. Alessandro Rovetta, Milan, 1996, p. 362: 'Questo vocabulo γραφω latinamente significa non solum scribere, ma etiam pingere e altre volte, sculpire. Adiunca, lo architecto convene sapia legere e scribere e designare seu affigurare, como si usa a depingere.'

22 Cesariano, *Cesare Cesariano*, p. 363: 'E questo aciò meglio avesseno la cognitione de le cose universale a saperle exprimere et etiam aciò loro ingenui semper potesseno essere più buoni di anima e di onestate corporea.' Rovetta cited Valerius Maximus, *Factorum* VIII, 11–12 and Pliny, *Historia naturalis*, 35, 77.

23 Vitruvius Pollio, *De architectura*, trans. and ed. Francesco Lucio Durantino, Venice, 1524, fol. BBi verso: 'graphida scientia: cioe sapere designare, come si usa con un certo stillo de metallo, quale anchora alcuni chiamano graphio. Perche γραφιά significa pictura, designatione, descriptione, o vero sculptura.'

24 Vitruvius Pollio, *De architettura*, trans. and ed. Gianbattista Caporali, Perugia, 1536, fol. Avii.

25 Vitruvius Pollio, *I dieci libri dell'architettura*, trans. and ed. Daniele Barbaro, Venice, 1556, p. 10: 'che serve à pittori, à scultori, intagliatori, e simiglianti, la quale alle arti predette in quel modo serve, che le mathematice servono alla filosofia'.

26 Vitruvius, *On Architecture*, ed. Frank Granger, 2 vols, London, 1931, I, pp. 158–9.

27 Vitruvius, *On Architecture*, I, pp. 158–9.

28 A.E. Popham, *The Drawings of Leonardo da Vinci*, London, 1971, pp. 61–2; F.P. Fiore and M. Tafuri, eds, *Francesco di Giorgio architetto*, Siena, 1993, pp. 362–5.

29 Rudolf Wittkower, *Architectural Principles in the Age of Humanism*, London, 1949, pp. 97–110, especially p. 97.

30 Leonardo, *Literary Works of Leonardo*, I, p. 77.

31 Leonardo, *Literary Works of Leonardo*, I, p. 77.

32 Leonardo, *Literary Works of Leonardo*, I, p. 66.

33 Luca Pacioli, *De divina proportione*, ed. G. Masolti Biggiogero, Milan, 1956, pp. 16–18.

34 Wittkower, *Architectural Principles*, p. 14.

35 Francisco de Holanda, *Four Dialogues on Painting*, trans. A.E.G. Bell, London, 1928, pp. 16–17.

36 Wittkower, *Architectural Principles*, p. 136.

37 Giovanni Paolo Lomazzo, *Idea del tempio della pittura* (1590), ed. Robert Klein, 2 vols, Florence, 1974, I, p. 331: 'Il corpo umano, il quale è un'opera perfetta e bellissima, fatta dal grande Iddio a simiglianza della sua imagine, con grandissima ragione è stato chiamato mondo minore: perché contiene in sé, con più perfetta composizione e con più sicura armonia, tutti numeri, le misure, i pesi, i moti et elementi. Onde da lui principalmente, e non da altra fabrica che uscisse dalla mano d'Iddio a dalle sue menbra, fu tolta la norma et il modello di formar i tempii, i teatri e tutti gli edificii con tutte le sue parti, come colonne capitelli canali e simili, naviglii machine et ogni sorte d'artificio. E così l'istesso Iddio insegnò a Nòe fabricar l'arca secondo la misura del corpo umano.'

38 Lomazzo, *Idea del tempio della pittura*, p. 321: 'E però ciascuno di loro pose ogni suo studio et industria per comprehender perfettamente questa armonica beltade, e principalmente Leonardo, Michelangelo e Gaudenzio, il quali pervennero alla cognizione della proporzione armonica per via della musica e con la considerazione della fabrica del corpo nostro, il quale anch'egli con musico concento è fabricato; sì come nel seguente capitolo et in altri lochi di questo libro si discorre. Imperoché, sì come uomini d'ingegno et erudizione grandissima, considerarono che la consonanza dell'anima è fatta del debito temperamento e proporzione delle sue virtù et operazione. Le quali sono concupiscibili, irascibili e ragionevoli, che in questo modo si proporzionano, percioché la ragione con la concupiscenza ha la proporzione diapason, con l'iracondia ha la proporzione diatesseron, e l'irascibile con concupiscibile ha la proporzion diapente.'

39 Desiderius Erasmus, *Collected Works*, volume 26, ed. J.K. Sowards, *Literary and Educational Writings*, 4, *De recta pronuntiatione*, trans. Maurice Pope, Toronto, 1985, pp. 398–9.

40 Pliny the Elder, *Chapters on the History of Art*, p. 119. The editor, Sellars, related that, according to Diogenes Laertius, Melanthius the pupil of Apelles had written a treatise on designing entitled *Peri graphikes*.

41 Pliny the Elder, *Chapters on the History of Art*, pp. 89–91, 119.

42 Baldassare Castiglione, *The Book of the Courtier*, trans. George Bull, Harmondsworth, 1967, p. 96; and Baldassare Castiglione, *Il libro del cortegiano*, ed. Vittorio Cian, Florence, 1947, p. 122: 'e questo è il saper disegnare, ed aver voleano che i fanciulli nobili nelle scole alla pittura dessero opera, come a cosa onesta e necessaria, e fu questa ricevuta nel primo grado dell'arti liberali'.

43 Castiglione, *Il libro del cortegiano*, p. 123: 'E benché diversa sia la pittura dalla statuaria, pur l'una e l'altra da un medesimo fonte, che è il bon disegno, nasce.'

44 Francisco de Holanda, *Da pintura antigua*, ed. Joaquim de Vasconcellos, Porto, 1918, p. 328: 'O desenho, a que po outro nome chamam debuxo, nelle consiste e elle é a fonte e o corpo da pintura e da escultura e da arquitetura et de todo outro genoro de pintar e a raiz de todas as sciencias.'

45 Paola Barocchi, *Scritti d'arte del cinquecento*, 3 vols, Milan and Naples, 1971–77, II, p. 1906: 'Ridomi di loro che dichino Domenedio fece prima l'uomo di terra, poi gli dette colore, et inanzi che lo facesse, e' fece in quella forma che fa l'artefice, il qual prima si imagina un palazzo nella

fantasia (il disegno) e poi fa il modello; così dicono che il disegno è padre della pittura e della scultura.'

46 Barocchi, *Scritti d'arte*, II, p. 1910: 'Credo che non si possa essere pittore o scultore senza disegno. Così come la prima causa le fece tutte a un tratto, così credo che sia nobile l'una quanto l'altra. E viva il mio disegno.'

47 Barocchi, *Scritti d'arte*, I, p. 558: 'la pittura e la scoltura non si possono mettere in opera senza il disegno, del quale pùo malamente dar l'arte la sua sentenza, che cosa egli sia. Arte. Io direi che fusse industria dell'intelletto, con atto di mettere in opere il suo potere. Natura. Veramente tu non potevi (come arte) favellare altrimenti, né chiamarlo per altro nome; ma ascolta e tieni a mente per un'altra volta. Il disegno non altro che speculazion divina, che produce un'arte eccellentissima, talmente che tu non puoi operare cosa nessuna nella scoltura e nella pittura senza la guida di questa speculazione e disegno'.

48 Kemp 'Beiträge zur Geschichte des Begriffs', pp. 225–6; Poirier, 'The role and concept of *disegno*', pp. 53–68.

49 Barocchi, *Scritti d'arte*, I, p. 559: 'Il primo disegno è un'invenzione di tutto l'universo, imaginato perfettamente nella mente della prima causa, inanzi che venisse all'atto del relievo e del colore, il qual rilievo volgarmente si chiama scoltura.'

50 S. Barbaglia, ed., *Benvenuto Cellini, L'opera completa*, Milan, 1981, pp. 90–1; John Pope-Hennessy, *Cellini*, London, 1985, pp. 141–2.

51 Benvenuto Cellini, *Vita di Benvenuto Cellini*, ed. Orazio Bacci, Florence, 1901, p. 282: 'Quella figura di mezo si è cinquantaquattro piedi. Questa parola il Re fe'grandissima segnio di maravigliarsi; appresso, è fatta figurando lo Iddio Marte. Quest'altre quattro figure son fatte per la virtù, di che si diletta e favorisce tanto vostra maestà. Questa a man destra è figurata per la scienza di tutte le Lettere: vedete chel'ha i sua contra segni, qual dimostra la filosofia con tutte le sue virtù compagnie. Quest'altra dimostra essere tutta l'arte del disegno, cioè scultura, pittura, e architettura. Quest'altra è figurata per la musica qual si conviene per compagnia a tutte queste iscientie. Quest'altra che si dimostra tanto grata e benigna è figurata per la liberalità: che sanza lei non si può dimostrare nessuna di queste mirabil virtù che Iddio ci mostra. Questa istatua di mezo grande è figurata per vostra maestà istessa, qual è un dio Marte, che voi siete sol bravo al mondo.'

52 Michael Evans, 'Allegorical women and practical men: the medieval *artes* reconsidered', pp. 305–30 in Derek Baker, ed., *Medieval Women*, Oxford, 1978, Plate 1.

53 Benvenuto Cellini, *The Treatises of Benvenuto Cellini on Goldsmithing and Sculpture*, trans. C.R. Ashbee, New York, 1967, p. 139.

54 Benvenuto Cellini, *Opere di Benvenuto Cellini*, ed. Giuseppe Guido Ferrero, Turin, 1971, p. 819.

55 Vitruvius Pollio, *De architectura*, ed. Guillaume Philandrier, Strasburg, 1543, p. 1: 'Graphidos scientiam habere. Graphis est linearis deformatio, sive designatio. Non desunt tamen qui eam quae ad Architectum pertinent, γράμμικη quasi lineationem dicas, vocent: γράφὶκη vero, et ad scriptorem, et ad pictorem Sculptorem[q]ue referant, cum ad illum descriptionem, cum ad hos designationem transferentes'.

Philandrier's Vitruvius was reprinted frequently during the sixteenth century.

56 Cellini, *Vita*, p. 282.

57 Barocchi, *Scritti d'arte*, I, p. 519: 'infra tutte l'arte che s'interviene disegno è maggiore sette volte'. Varchi published his survey in 1547.

58 Cellini in Barocchi, *Scritti d'arte*, I, p. 522: 'la scultura è madre di tutte l'arte dove si interviene disegno, e quello che sarà valente scultore e di buona maniera, gli sarà facilissimo l'esser buon prospettivo e architetto e maggior pittor, che quegli che bene non poseggono la scultura'.

59 The urn is now at Saint Denis. Victoria Goldberg, 'Graces, Muses and Arts: the urns of Henri II and François I', *Journal of the Warburg and Courtauld Institutes*, XXIX, 1966, pp. 206–18; P. Wingert, 'The funerary urn of Francis I', *Art Bulletin*, XXI, 1939, pp. 383–96. The urn is 2.10 metres high. For the inscriptions which do not refer to the allegory see R.F.F. Guillhermy, *Inscriptions de la France du Ve au XVIIIe siècle*, 5 vols, Paris, 1873–83, II, p. 168.

60 M. Roy, *Artistes et monuments de la renaissance en France*, Paris, 1929, p. 173, 19 February 1550: 'ung Sillobastre a[d]orné de quatre faces des histoires à basse taille, et où sera insculpé les muses et escriptures qui lui seront baillées et au-dessus d'icelluy ung vase qui sera creux, a[d]orné tout autour des devises et armoyries dud[it] feu Roy, histoires à demoye des tailles des Arts et autres covemens comme il sera dit et ordonné.'

61 Geneviéve Bresc-Bautier, 'L'Urne du coeur de François I', pp. 398–401 in *Primatice, maître de Fontainebleau*, Paris, 2004.

62 Catherine King, 'Late sixteenth-century careers' advice: a new allegory of artists' training – Albertina, inv. No. 2763', *Wiener Jahrbuch für Kunstgeschichte*, XLI, 1988, pp. 77–96.

63 Philibert de l'Orme, *Traités d'architectures*, ed. Jean-Marie Pérouse de Montclos, Paris, 1988, *Le Premier Tome de l'architecture*, Paris, 1567, fol. Biiii recto.

64 Anthony Hughes, 'An Academy for doing', *Oxford Art Journal*, IX, 1986, pp. 3–10.

65 Piero Calamandrei, *Scritti e inediti celliniani*, Florence, 1971, pp. 128–9; Kemp 'Beiträge zur Geschichte des Begriffs', pp. 219–24; Vasari, *Le opere di Giorgio Vasari*, VIII, p. 359.

66 Calamandrei, *Scritti e inediti celliniani*, p. 145; and Kemp, 'Beiträge zur Geschichte des Begriffs', pp. 220–1.

67 Giovanni Bottari and Stefano Ticozzi, *Raccolta di lettere sulla pittura, scultura, ed architettura*, 8 vols, Milan, 1822, I, p. 265, number LXXVII, Domenico Poggini ai molto magnifici Consoli [of the Accademia]: 'E perchè tutte e tre si partono da un solo gambo e da una sola scienza, figuro ch'ella si riposi e regga sul Capricorno, come virtù di S[ua]. E[xcellentia]. Ill[ustrissima].'

68 Bottari and Ticozzi, *Raccolta di lettere*, I, pp. 266–7, number LXXVIII: 'Stefano Pieri a M. Baccio Valori: tutte tre d'accordo, e unite insieme di Zelo et Amore, lo coronino con una corona di lauro con un motto intorno al Sigillo, che dica: "tu das epulis accumbere divum". Tu fài che noi segghiamo alle mense degli Dei. Le vivande degli Dei sono interpretate per l'immortalità, cioè l'ambrosia e nettare; onde si viene a dire che

mediante Sua Eccellenzia Illustrissima queste tre arti sono in cielo, ed immortali.'

69 Pope-Hennessy, *Cellini*, pp. 311–12, and Barbaglia, *Benvenuto Cellini*, pp. 99–100 list drawings linked to seal designs. Calamandrei, *Scritti e inediti celliniani*, pp. 129–46, discusses them.

70 Calamandrei, *Scritti e inediti celliniani*, p. 131: 'Apollo è sol la luce. Cosmo [meaning 'the world'] è principio alla gran scuola e Duce.'

71 Calamandrei, *Scritti e inediti celliniani*, p. 145, 'Il gran Pianeta del Sole, questo é sol la Lucerna dell'Universo e gli Antiqui e maggior nostri lo figurarano e dimonstrarano per la figura d'Apollo e perché dopo quel gran diluvio, che ricoperse tutta la terra, essendosene ritornate tutte le Acque a i loro luoghi, era restata una nebbia foltissima che non lasciava geminare la terra, ma il sole con la virtù de razzi sì tanto ferì la nebbia che la risolvé: onde gli Antiqui figuravano Apollo con l'Arco et le Saette con le quali ferì Phitone serpente che cosi [illegible in the original] puosero nome a quella folta nebbia: e cosí io l'ho messo in disegno parendomi che la nostra Academia del Disegno sia degna di questa bella Impresa, perché siccome questo é, la vera Lucerna di tutte le azzione che fanno gli Uomini in ogni Professione; perché il disegno è di due sorte, il primo è quello che si fa nell'Immaginativa e il secondo tratto da quello si dimostra con linee, e questo ha fatto l'huomo tanto ardito che egli si è messo a ghareggiare con questo gran padre Apollo.'

72 Calamandrei, *Scritti e inediti celliniani*, p. 133: 'l'arte del disegnio si è la vera madre di tutte le azioni de l'huomo.'

73 Calamandrei, *Scritti e inediti celliniani*, p. 134.

74 Calamandrei, *Scritti e inediti celliniani*, p. 137, and Plate XVI: 'La tromba della nostra Fama viene da le braccia.'

75 Leonardo, *Literary Works of Leonardo*, I, p. 63.

76 Calamandrei, *Scritti e inediti celliniani*, p. 145: 'e solo quella Iddea vera della Natura, che fu dagli Antiqui con molte poppe figurata, per significare, che ella nutrisce ogni cosa, come sola, e principale ministra di Dio, che di Terra sculpì e creò il primo huomo ad imagine e similitudine di sé.'

77 Calamandrei, *Scritti e inediti celliniani*, pp. 133–4, 'Tutte le cose che sono ristrette in mezzo a questi cieli sono composte di quattro cose, né piú né di manco, di modo che ogni cosa che fa l'huomo si viene a essere composta di queste quattro cose. Io truovo l'arte della schultura la prima, perché il nostro Iddio fecie il primo huomo di schultura di terra colle sue proprie divine et immortali mani. Di poi da questa naqque la maravigliosa et lasciva pittura. Appresso si trasse da queste la utilissima architettura.'

78 Vasari, *Le opere di Giorgio Vasari*, VII, p. 313; and Birgit Laschke, 'Montorsolis Entwürfe für das Siegel der Accademia del Disegno in Florenz', *Mitteilungen des Kunsthistorischen Institutes in Florenz*, XXXI, 1987, pp. 392–402.

79 David Summers, 'The sculptural programme of the Cappella di San Luca', *Mitteilungen des Kunsthistorischen Instituts in Florenz*, XIV, 1969, pp. 67–90.

80 Vasari, *Le opere di Giorgio Vasari*, VII, p. 313: 'le tre professioni di scultura, pittura ed architettura fussero intrecciate ed in modo legate

insieme, che l'una dà e riceve dall'altra comodo ed ornamento, e ch'elle non si possono nè deono spiccar d'insieme.'

81 R.A. Scorza, 'Vincenzo Borghini and *invenzione*: the Florentine Apparato of 1565', *Journal of the Warburg and Courtauld Institutes*, XLIV, 1981, pp. 57–75.

82 Giorgio Vasari, *Lives of the most Eminent Painters, Sculptors and Architects*, trans. Gaston du C. de Vere, 10 vols, London, 1910–15, X, p. 46; Vasari, *Le opere di Giorgio Vasari*, VIII, p. 528.

83 Vasari, *Le opere di Giorgio Vasari*, VIII, pp. 521–5; see *Giorgio Vasari*, ed. Laura Corti et al., pp. 236–42.

84 De Holanda, *Da pintura antigua*, p. 328.

85 A. Lorenzoni, *Carteggio artistico inedito di Vincenzo Borghini*, 2 vols, Florence, 1912, I, p. 10.

86 Georg Pictorius, *Theologia mythologica*, Antwerp, 1532, fol. 48 verso.

87 Karel G. Boon, *The Netherlandish and German Drawings of the XV and XVI th centuries in the Frits Lugt Collection*, 3 vols, Paris, 1992, I, pp. 345–7; III, Plate 85.

88 Cecchi, 'Le case di Giorgio Vasari', pp. 56–77.

89 Vasari, *Le opere di Giorgio Vasari*, I, pp. 168–9:'Perchè il disegno, padre delle tre arti nostre, Architettura, Scultura e Pittura, procedendo dall'intelletto, cava di molte cose un giudizio universale; simile a una forma ovvero idea di tutte le cose della natura, la quale è singolarissima nelle sue misure; di qui è che non solo nei corpi umani e degli animali, ma nelle piante ancora, e nelle fabbriche e sculture e pitture, conosce la proporzione che ha il tutto con le parti, e che hanno le parti fra loro e col tutto insieme. E perchè da questa cognizione nasce un certo concetto e giudizio, che si forma nella mente quella tal cosa che poi espressa con le mani si chiama disegno; si può conchiudero che esso disegno altro non sia che una apparente espressione e dichiarazione del concetto che si ha nell'animo, e di quello che altri si è nella mente immaginato e fabbricato nell'idea. E da questo, per avventura, nacque il proverbio dei Greci "Dall'ugna un leone"; quando quel valente uomo, vedendo scolpita in un masso l'ugna sola d'un leone, comprese con l'intelletto da quella misura e forma le parti di tutto l'animale, e dopo il tutto insieme, come se l'avesse avuto presente e dinanzi agli occhi. Credono alcuni che il padre del disegno e dell'arti fusse il caso, e che l'uso e la sperienza, come balia e pedagogo, lo nutrissero con l'aiuto della cognizione e del discorso.' See Erwin Panofsky, *Idea: A Concept in Art Theory*, New York, 1968, pp. 61–2 for further readings.

90 Cesare Ripa, *Iconologia*, Rome, 1603, p. 108: 'Si potrà dipingere il disegno per essere padre della scoltura, pittura, e architettura, con tre teste uguali, e simili, e che con le mani tenghi diversi istromenti convenevoli alle sopradette arti'; repeated in Paduan edition (1611), p. 123.

91 Ridolfi, *Le meraviglie dell'arte*, I, p. 212: 'vecchio con barba lunga, da semplice panno ricoperto, poichè fa di mestieri, per arrivare all'apprensione di quello, lunga esperienza. Mostrerà disegnare sopra una cartella, e sarà inscrizione, "Nil sine me pulcrum."'

92 Ridolfi, *Le meraviglie dell'arte*, I, pp. 211–18.

93 Lodovico Dolce, *Aretino: A Dialogue on Painting*, trans. W. Brown, London, 1770, p. 227; and Vasari, *Le opere di Giorgio Vasari*, VII, pp. 427–8, 447–8.

94 Ghiberti, *Ghibertis Denkwürdigkeiten*, p. 105: 'Ma la proportionalità solamente fa pulchritudine.'

95 Barocchi, *Scritti d'arte*, II, p. 2031: 'Il fondamento di tutto . . . et onde deriva tutta la bellezza, è quello che i Greci chiamano euritmia, e noi nominiamo disegno.'

96 Barocchi, *Scritti d'arte*, II, p. 2035: 'il molto utile e principale alimento che hanno dal dissegno, per formare perfettamente la figura.'

97 Barocchi, *Scritti d'arte*, II, p. 1983: 'un apparente dimostratzione con linee di quello che prima nell'animo l'uomo si avea concetto e nell' idea imaginato.'

98 Barocchi, *Scritti d'arte*, II, p. 2001: 'onde alcuni hanno detto dover essere quello una speculazion nata nella mente et un' artificiosa industria dell'intelletto col mettere in atto le sue forze secondo la bella idea. Altri poi dicono più tosto dover esser una scienza di bella e regolata proporzione di tutto quello che si vede, con ordinato componimento, dal quale si discerne il garbo per sue debite misure, al che si proviene pe lo studio e per la divina grazia d'un buon discorso, primamente nato e nodrito in quello . . . solamente questo vogliamo noi che ci basti, che il dissegno sia come un vivo lume di bello ingegno e che egli sia di tanta forza e così necessario all'universale, che colui, che n'è intieramente privo, sia quasi che un cieco.' He went on to cite the leadership of Phamphilos and Apelles in teaching children design.

99 Kristina Hermann Fiore, 'Die Fresken Federico Zuccaris in seinem römischen Künstlerhaus', *Römisches Jahrbuch der Bibliotheca Hertziana*, 18, 1979, pp. 35–112.

100 Federico Zuccari, *Scritti d'arte di Federico Zuccaro*, ed. Detlef Heikamp, Florence, 1961, pp. 253, 255, 265.

101 Zuccari, *Scritti d'arte*, pp. 163–4, 166, 188, 251.

102 Barocchi, *Scritti d'arte*, II, p. 2045: 'I disegni esterni fatti di noi pittori, scultori et architetti, sono cagionati e formati per virtù del disegno nostro speculativo e prattico.'

103 Zuccari, *Scritti d'arte*, p. 188.

104 Zuccari, *Scritti d'arte*, p. 277: 'Iddio adunque è il vero Disegno, e vero autore, e perfetto, e divin Pittore, Scultore et Architetto'.

105 Zuccari, *Scritti d'arte*, p. 162: 'Questo Dissegno interno humano si chiama . . . Scintilla della Divinità; perchè l'huomo nel formare questo interno Dissegno . . . esser Scintilla della Divinità, cioè parte della sostanza Divina.'

106 Barocchi, *Scritti d'arte*, II, p. 2043: 'perché l'anima nostra è fatta ad imagine e similitudine di Dio, come quasi una scintilla di quella divinità che ne alluma l'anima e l'intelligenze nostre, e ne fa alzare da terra e speculare le cose alte e divine.'

107 Barocchi, *Scritti d'arte*, II, p. 2040: 'Si che questo disegno è quasi un altro sole nell'anima e nell'intelletto umano, che muove, vivifica et alluma tutte le nostre operazioni, e necessario in noi come il sole nel mondo.'

108 Barocchi, *Scritti d'arte*, II, p. 2048: 'Intelligenze et operazioni nostre tutte derivano da questa luce, da questo fonte e da questo gran disegno.'

109 Erwin Panofsky, *Renaissance and Renascences in Western Art*, London, 1960, p. 56: 'Per scintillas designat ideas . . . designat et formulas idearum nobis ingenitas.'

110 Barocchi, *Scritti d'arte*, II, Doni quoted a sermon in 1546, p. 1909: '"La fiamma ha tre parti in sé: luce, fuoco, e fiamma e perché voi intendiate meglio" disse il predicatore "pittura, scoltura e disegno, che son tutte in Michelangelo equali."' ('The flame consists of three elements: light, heat and flame and thus you may understand better' said the preacher 'how painting, sculpture and design are all equal in Michelangelo.')
111 Barocchi, *Scritti d'arte*, II, pp. 2049–60.

3 New types of commemorative portrayals

Several new types of commemorative portraiture were initiated during the sixteenth century. They joined what was already quite a wide range of well-established portrait genres devoted to the commemoration of artists. The commemoration of artists in portraits of all types, new and older, could reinforce the assertion, which had been established in the literary traditions, that the best art required outstanding innate personal talent. Visual images were able to suggest that this *ingenium* was as distinctive as was the individual appearance of a person. Such portrayals meant that artists were joining other persons of talent such as statesmen, poets, philosophers and rulers, whose appearance had been recorded to mark their historical significance. Both the new genres of portraiture launched in the sixteenth century and the earlier traditions for portraying artists in a commemorative manner, which were also maintained throughout the period, seem to have sustained such claims. However, in the cases in which the new genres used print, commemorative portraiture was reaching out to wider audiences than ever before. The interest in celebrating individual prowess could therefore be seen as promoting the dignity of the profession.

The new types of commemorative portraiture appeared in a variety of contexts. Some, from 1553 onwards, were attached to printed histories of art. Some, from 1552 onwards (or earlier if one counts Paolo Giovio's collection) were made to be part of actual or printed museums of famous leaders in letters, church and state. Others, from 1546 onwards, celebrated the history of enlightened patronage, in palatial settings. A few from 1568 onwards were made by one artist of a series, to whose examples he felt especially indebted, in personal, autobiographical, tributes. Portrayals of eminent artists were also used for the first time to accompany state occasions and the ceremonies of civic institutions. These include, for example, the triumphal arch featuring Giotto and Michelangelo ordered by the Florentine merchants of Antwerp for the entry of Charles V into the city in 1549, and the drinking cup adorned with the portraits of Raphael, the Greek painters Zeuxis and Apelles, van Eyck and Dürer which a group of wealthy merchants in Antwerp gave to the Guild of Saint Luke in the same year. For the first time, artists were to be honoured with narrative cycles illustrating important events in their lives, at the obsequies organised for Michelangelo by the new academy in Florence in 1564, as planned by the Venetian confraternity of painters for Titian in 1576, and as painted by Federico Zuccari for his dead brother Taddeo (1529–66) in the 1590s. The period was characterised in some respects by the way artists exploited the relatively new medium of print to reach many spectators with commemorative portraiture. Engraved portraits of artists illustrated printed histories of art and culture. In addition separate prints were issued, from the late fifteenth century onwards, commemorating the attainments and appearance of artists. Some may have been intended to be sold along with engravings of other subjects by the artists concerned; others presumably served a new market comprising those interested in collecting their own galleries of artists' portraits. The portrayal of named ancient Greek artists in an art-historical context was also initiated, in about 1507, and was a somewhat more rarefied activity, since it was confined to three artists' houses, two artist's funerals, the adornment of a guild chamber and an engraved print. For the first time, from 1549, visual images of artists were juxtaposed to claim the equivalence of ancient and modern, as well as Italian and transalpine, art.

The portrayal of named ancient artists as part of art history linked modern artists to the art forms which held the highest intellectual prestige in this period and which tended to be associated with notions of political power and cultural success. They were related to the claims made since the fourteenth century, that recent art could be compared with that of the ancient world, and indeed, in a few cases in the sixteenth century, portrayals of ancient and modern artists were placed in parity. Portrayals of ancient forebears could allow artists to advertise their own artistic values and beliefs, through their selection of scenes to portray. Seeing recent art histories in the context of ancient art histories could not only lend authority to present practices, but also represent recent art history as part of a grand scheme covering two millennia, in which standards had been raised, lost and, recently, retrieved. These representations appear to have begun in the early sixteenth century, and related both to the tradition of illustrating some scholarly and popular books and also to the literary celebration of named ancient artists in texts which had survived during the medieval period.[1] These new sorts of portraits joined what was already a rich tradition for representing artists.

Older traditions of commemorative portraiture and their maintenance

The largest body of artists' portraits comprised those which acted as 'portrait signatures' and entailed a self-portrait of the artist inscribed on some larger work with his or her name. These were executed throughout Christendom from at least the ninth century CE.[2] While such portraits were produced for posterity, many possessed a devout element, too, in showing the artist at prayer. They were attached to objects such as buildings, wooden choir stalls, murals or altarpieces, bronze doors and books. Recent Italian examples existed, such as the author portrayal made by the Florentine sculptor Filarete in 1445 on the bronze doors which he had completed at Saint Peter's for Eugenius IV. This relief represented Filarete leading his assistants in a dance to celebrate their success.[3] Italian artists continued to make portrait signatures, as, for example, did Baccio Bandinelli, in inscribing the statue of God the Father for the cathedral in Florence, which he completed in 1556.[4]

Other portraits of artists might be seen in the 'bystander portraits' which painters and sometimes sculptors had included in crowd scenes, as if witnessing a pictured or sculpted event. For instance in his life of Giotto of around 1380, Filippo Villani recorded the tradition that Giotto had painted himself with Dante (1265–1321) in a mural for the Palazzo del Podestà in Florence.[5] Such portraits were not inscribed, but relied on word of mouth to sustain the fame of the persons portrayed. Italian artists continued the traditions of commemorating themselves in this way as, for instance, when Vasari depicted himself as witness to his scene of *The Triumph of the Sienese War* in 1565 in the Sala Grande at the Palazzo Vecchio in Florence.[6] If bystander portraits represented a commemorative gamble, the invention in artists' portraiture from the early 1440s onwards in Italy, of inscribed bronze portrait medals, such as that of Alberti, placed the celebration of artists on a sounder footing (see Chapter 5).[7] Portrait medals of Italian artists were numerous in the sixteenth century, as for instance in the bronze medal celebrating the Mantuan engraver Diana Scultori about 1575.[8] Some of them were probably made to advertise one's prowess in hope of commissions, as much as to record one's attainment, for posterity.

The earliest funerary portrait for an Italian artist was identified by Gesa Schütz Rautenberg as that placed for the architect Brunelleschi in 1447 in the cathedral at Florence, by the committee of works for the cathedral. It included an inscription which referred to his 'heavenly talent' (*divino ingenio*) – an epithet later adapted by Vasari for Michelangelo (Plate 31).[9] As pointed out by Francis Ames-Lewis, this monument had links with the medieval transalpine tradition of allowing architects to be buried and commemorated in the edifices which they had helped to build, including portraits and inscriptions explaining their role.[10] Schütz Rautenberg demonstrated that the design by Brunelleschi's heir, Andrea Cavalcanti, il Buggiano (1412–*c.*1462), consisting of a bust placed in a circular frame, had been used previously only in ancient Roman portraiture and in the series of popes depicted in Old Saint Peters.[11] As traced by Schütz Rautenberg, there followed a succession of portraits on funerary monuments for Italian artists, the most famous of which is, perhaps, that of Michelangelo.[12]

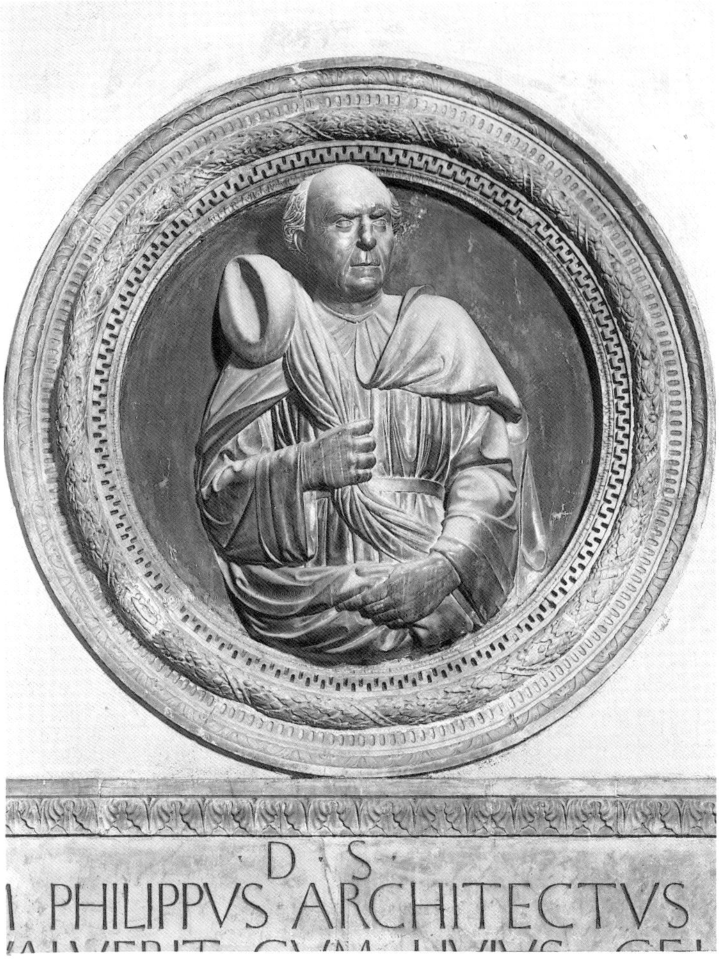

31 Andrea Cavalcanti il Buggiano, commemorative portrait of Filippo Brunelleschi, 1447, cathedral, Florence.

Independent portable portraits were also made by Italian artists commemorating the appearance of artists, for family and colleagues. An early example, which is known to have been retained for family use, is the portrait in a small tondo of the gem cutter Valerio Belli (*c.*1468–1546), dated 1517 and attributed to Raphael.[13] This genre for display in domestic locations soon became quite widespread, with, for instance, the wistful self-portrait made by Andrea del Sarto (1486–1531) about 1529, for his wife, painted on a small tile.[14]

Commemorative portrait traditions for artists north of the Alps

The tradition of the author portrait had flourished north of the Alps The author portrait of the Netherlandish architect Johannes of Liège completed in 1387, for instance, signed the choir stalls at Saint François in Lausanne and shows his own figure kneeling at the feet of the Count of Savoy, in whose service he was court architect.[15] The relief was placed on a bench end and accompanied by a verse in Latin, which can be translated as 'Johannes of Liège, architect of Savoy, sculpted with special care this multifarious work in the year of our Lord one thousand three hundred and eighty seven. Here may prayer be offered with a full heart.'[16] While artists continued to place portrait signatures in traditional locations, they also put them on books which they had illustrated, as for instance did the Haarlem painter van Heemskerck on his series of plates representing the history of Israel in classical times (*Clades* or *Inventiones Heemskerckianae ex utroque testamento*, 1568–69). On the title page van Heemskerck created the effect of a sculpted self-portrait, in relief, adorning the base of a classical column.[17]

Bystander portraits are documented north of the Alps in 1452 with the account given by Cardinal Nicholas of Cusa of a panel which had recently been made by Rogier van der Weyden (*c.*1399–1464) for the Town Hall at Brussels. This apparently displayed a portrait of the artist in one of the scenes of the wise judgement of Trajan and Herkinbald.[18] Bystander portraits continued to be produced during the sixteenth century. For instance, the Utrecht painter Jan van Scorel (1495–1562) introduced his own portrait background centre amongst the bystanders pictured in an altarpiece he signed and dated 1520. This depicted the Holy Kin, for the chapel at Obervellach in Carinthia (present-day Austria), belonging to the family of Apollonia Lang von Wellenberg.[19] Medallic portraits were adopted too, although there seems to have been relatively little interest in them amongst Netherlandish artists. The earliest appears to have been that for the bronze sculptor Hermann Vischer of Nuremberg (*c.*1486–1517) in 1507 (Chapter 5).[20] Later examples are quite numerous, such as the signed bronze medal made by Matthes Gebel (*c.*1500–74) for the Nuremberg engraver Augustin Hirschvogel (*c.*1503–53) in 1543 when the sitter declared himself to be thirty-nine years old. The motto on the reverse displayed a sphere with the optimistic motto *Spero fortunae regressum* ('I hope for the return of good fortune').[21]

Artists had also experimented with various forms of funerary portraiture. There were inscribed tomb portraits for architects such as that dated 1263 for Hugues Libergier (flourished 1231–63) in the nave of the church he had built at Reims, in Saint Nicaise. He held his ruler, and the compasses and set square were at his feet. The inscription in French sought the prayers of the beholder for him.[22] There were also funerary altarpieces, the earliest of which seems to be that of the painter Friedrich Herlin (*c.*1425–1500), who made a funerary altarpiece for his family chapel in Nördlingen in 1488. In it he represented himself and his four sons to the left and his wife and their five daughters on the right, all kneeling to honour the Virgin and Child, while their patron saints of painting and childbirth (Luke and Margaret) offer protection.[23] Artists continued to be accorded funerary portraits north of the Alps during the sixteenth century, as for instance with the tomb designed for van Scorel in the Mariakerk in Utrecht by his pupil Anthonis Mor in 1562.[24]

Those with access to an artist's home or work place might see self-portraits and portraits of colleagues or family members. Netherlandish artists had shown interest in painting independent portraits for family commemoration from early in the fifteenth century. This was shown, for example, in the portrait by Jan van Eyck of his wife Margaret dated 1439 and by the marriage portrait of the Master of Frankfurt dated 1496. German-speaking artists had started to produce drawings and paintings as visual family records in the late fifteenth century. Thus the Augsburg painter Hans Burgkmair (1473–1531) recorded in drawings and words how he looked at his betrothal in 1497 and his wedding in 1498.[25] They had also begun to portray colleagues, as in the case of the drawing from about 1490 attributed to Hans Holbein the Elder (1465–1534) and inscribed as showing the architect and writer Matthes Roriczer of Regensberg (?1430–1495).[26] Family and collegial portraits continued to be produced as for example in the family portrait painted by Dirck Cornelisz. van Oostsanen of Amsterdam (*c.*1497–1567), which he made of his father and mother in the 1550s, or the double portrait dated 1529 which Lucas Furtenagel (1505–*c.*1546) painted of his teacher Hans Burgkmair and his wife, in Augsbourg.[27]

These traditional sorts of portrait represented social status to some extent since wealthy patrons liked having versions of every one of them, from author and bystander portraits, to medals, to funerary portraits and family portraits. Nevertheless the artists' versions of these genres were usually differentiated from those of loftier commissioners, through, for example, adopting smaller dimensions, showing merely the head or head and shoulders, and taking marginal positions where part of larger designs. Artists might wish for some improved status, but most were mindful of social decorum.

Collecting portraits of famous artists

Family and collegial portraits were probably made for domestic or workshop viewing in the fifteenth century. However, one German-speaking engraver, at least, in the case of Israel van Meckenem (*c.*1440–1503), from Meckenheim, engaged a potentially wider audience by printing his marriage portrait with the inscription 'figuracio facierum Israhelis et Ida suis uxoris' or, 'the image of the faces of Israhel and of Ida his wife'. This has been dated about 1490–95 or a little later,[28] which suggests that there was some market for portraits of well-known artists by this time. The collection of painted portraits of famous artists is confirmed by written sources during the first decades of the sixteenth century, when buyers began to preserve them, whatever their original purpose, in the historicising context of their collections of celebrated masters. Thus Marcantonio Michiel (*c.*1484–1552) recorded the existence in Venice of a portrait of Hans Memling (*c.*1430–94) in the collection of Cardinal Grimani in 1521 and one of Rogier van der Weyden dated 1462 in the house of Giovanni Ram in 1531.[29] A similar trend is found in the Netherlands with the Governess of the Netherlands Margaret of Austria displaying the marriage portrait of the Master of Frankfurt (active 1480–1520) in her collection before 1516.[30] At about the same time, between 1514 and 1521, Paolo Giovio, Bishop of Nocera (1483–1552), began the collection of portraits of rulers, soldiers and writers which, at some point, came to include modern artists. He eventually placed it in what he called the 'museum' at his house on Lake Como, which he built during the period 1538–41.[31] This contained portraits of the architects Antonio da Sangallo (*c.*1460–1534) and Guillaume Philandrier (1505–65), the painters Titian and Andrea del Sarto, the sculptors Baccio Bandinelli and Valerio Belli, as well as Leonardo and Michelangelo.[32] It is not recorded when most of these artists' portraits entered Giovio's collection, although the portraits of Titian and Michelangelo were sent to Como from Rome in 1549.[33] As befitted a museum, Giovio placed brief notes under each portrait explaining their subject's claim to fame.[34] While some were, perhaps, originals, others were copies.

Evidence that the visual celebration of recent artists might be accepted on quite a popular level at this time is documented in the presence of labelled portrayals of contemporary artists employed by Sigismondo Fanti of Ferrara in his astrological publication the *Triompho* [sic] *di fortuna*, printed in Venice in 1527. This woodcut picture book offered diagrams of various wheels of fortune, some of them relating to the dispositions of painters, architects, sculptors and scholars. One type of portrayal showed the painter at his easel, and the other illustrated him holding his panel. These images were not given idiosyncratic features but were labelled haphazardly, with the names of modern artists (such as Mantegna, Raphael, Peruzzi, Dossi), or on other pages, with the names of ancient artists (for instance Zeusis, Policles, Parasio).[35]

The sense that the appearance of an artist might be noteworthy was also displayed for the first time in two brief life stories written in the period 1523–28 in Rome and Nuremberg. One was of the recently dead Leonardo by Giovio and formed part of his unfinished opus on the lives of artists. Giovio began by admiring Leonardo's learning in the Liberal Arts, detailing his university-level understanding of 'optical theories' and 'his dissection of bodies in the schools of medicine'.[36] Giovio then considered Leonardo's character in representing him as a perfectionist, who does not finish things because of the 'changeability of his nature and his innate fastidiousness'. He ended by recalling that Leonardo had a pleasing personality, an attractive appearance and fine accomplishments:

He had a character which was very amiable, impressive and generous and the most beautiful appearance [*vultu venustissimo*]. He was a splendid critic and inventor of all things elegant and delightful especially in theatrical displays. He sang to his own accompaniment on the lyre and he was on an excellent footing with all the princes of his time.[37]

In 1528, Camerarius also paid attention to the appearance of Dürer in the tribute he placed to him in the preface to his own translation of Dürer's *Four Books on Human Proportion* (Nuremberg, 1528). Camerarius began by describing the personal appearance of the recently deceased artist, adding that his conversation was witty and amiable:[38]

His head was intelligent, his eyes flashing, his nose nobly formed and, as the Greeks say, τέτράγωνον [tetragonon, that is, 'square']. His neck was rather long, his chest broad, his body not too stout, his thighs muscular, his legs firm and steady. But his fingers – you would vow that you had never seen anything more elegant.[39]

Camerarius averred that, in general, handsome faces and figures partnered fine minds and dispositions, suggesting that such qualities were equally expressed in one's products:

The nature of a man is never more certainly and definitely shown than in the works he produces as the fruit of his art. What single painter has there ever been who did not reveal his character in his works?[40]

Camerarius therefore set up the expectation that there were links between artists' looks, character and art. Such views arguably relate to the value beginning to be placed by collectors upon the portraiture of artists.

Early printed portraits in German-speaking areas: Dürer, Gassel, Hoecsster, Aldegrever, Lautensack, Cranach

The interest of artists in commemorating members of their profession, and the market for their efforts, is evident in the many posthumous printed portraits of Dürer. It seems likely that interest in his appearance was partly fuelled by a policy of self-promotion which had produced four portrait signatures on altarpieces between 1506 and 1511, several self-portrait drawings, and a number of painted self-portraits.[41] Two bronze medals had been made in his lifetime, one of which was commissioned by him from Hans Schwarz (1492–after 1521) in 1520. This portrayed him with a fur coat and long ringlets and the inscription 'Albertus Dürer pictor germanicus', but which had no reverse.[42] Another medal was made by Matthes Gebel (*c.*1500–74) in 1527 showing him with short hair accompanied by his heraldry and the motto *inclita virtus* (that is, 'renowned virtue') on the reverse. It is not clear whether this was commissioned by the painter himself. In 1528, following Dürer's death,

Gebel reissued the 1527 medal, but this time inscribed the date of his death on the reverse.[43] According to the contemporary account by Christoph Scheurl (1481–1542), a death mask was taken.[44] Copies of the medal by Schwarz were made in the following years,[45] and the Gebel medal was also reproduced.[46] Printed portraits were much in demand, as demonstrated by the way the woodcut printed by Erhard Schön in 1528 was reprinted eight more times during the sixteenth century. In 1550, for instance, the portrait appeared with laudatory verses in Nuremberg, whilst in 1588 it was published by Andrea Andreani (1540–1623) in Siena (Plate 32).[47] The Schwarz portrayal was translated into an

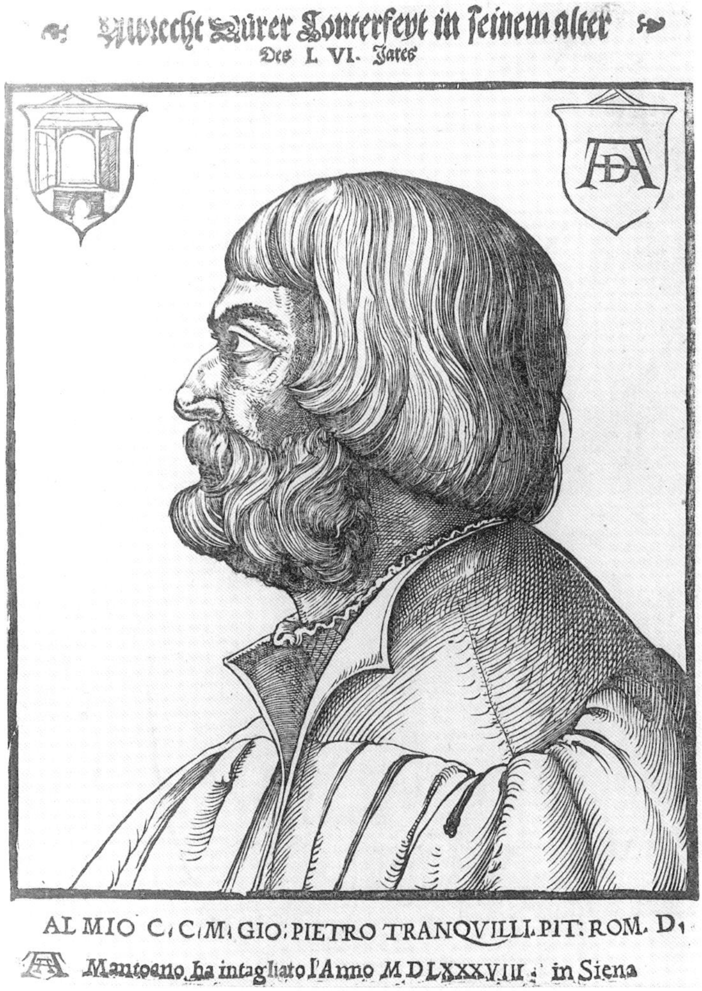

32 Erhard Schön, portrait of Albrecht Dürer, 1528, woodcut.

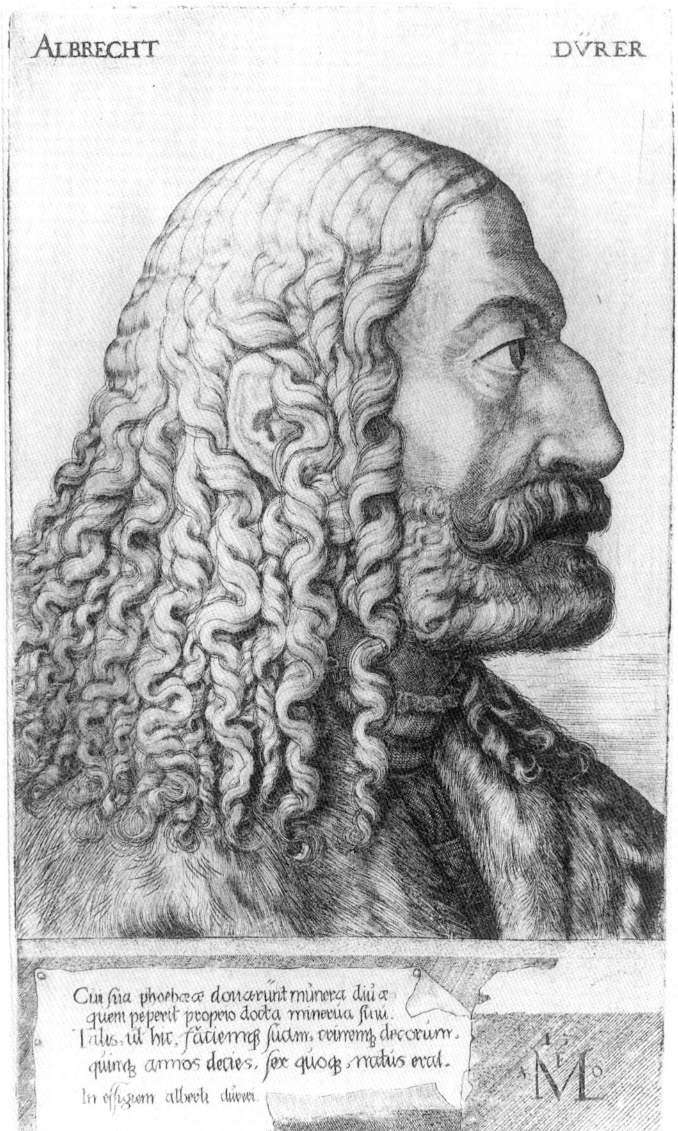

33 Melchior Lorch, portrait of Albrecht Dürer, 1550, engraving.

engraving by the Danish draughtsman Melchior Lorch (*c.*1526–*c.*1585) dated 1550 (Plate 33). This portrait was accompanied by a fulsome Latin verse praising Dürer in allegorical terms as helped by Apollo and Minerva: 'This was the face and the divine decorum of the man who was given the godlike gifts of Phoebus Apollo and whom Learned Minerva nursed at her very own bosom.'[48] The continuing interest in the portrayal of Dürer beyond Nuremberg is shown by the fact that in 1601 the inventory of the Antwerp publisher Volcxken Diercx (flourished 1572–1600), widow of Hieronymus Cock, contained a silver medal of Dürer 'in een ront lystken'.[49]

The posthumous portrayal of Dürer had arguably been encouraged by the way a series of historians had praised him as the equal to ancient painters. These writers included Jakob Wimpfeling (1450–1528), who had entitled his account of the history of German speaking peoples *The Epitome of Things Germanic up to Our Times* (*Epithoma rerum Germanicarum usque ad nostra tempora*; Strasburg, 1505). He reported that his work was valued as on the level of the paintings of the ancient Greek painters Parrhasius and Apelles.[50] In 1508 Christoph Scheurl even stated that Dürer was 'of divine talent' (*divini ingenii*).[51] By the year of the artist's death the Netherlandish scholar Desiderius Erasmus (*c.*1466–1536) was recommending his book on measurement to teachers as a school text (Erasmus *De recta latini graecique sermonis pronuntiatione* or *Concerning the Correct Pronunciation of Greek and Latin Speech*, Basel, 1528).[52] Elegies were produced for his funeral and through the many editions of the *Four Books* his reputation was maintained.[53] That his name was associated with the ideal of the learned artist is suggested in the way Walther Rivius compared him to the ancient Greek painter Pamphilus, who had taught all his pupils geometry, in the first German translation of Vitruvius, which was published in 1548 and thence reprinted in 1575 and 1614 (Nuremberg, 1548; Basel, 1575, 1614).[54]

The publication of single leaf prints of artists' portraits by van Meckenem and Schön was followed by a cluster of artists between 1529 and 1553, most of whom worked in Nuremberg. Jacob Bink (*c.*1500–*c.*1569) portrayed the Netherlandish artist Lucas Gassel (*c.*1495–*c.*1570) in a print dated 1529; and then the Augsbourg painter Joachim Hoecsster in a print dated 1532. Bink had trained initially in Cologne but then worked in Nuremberg copying prints by Dürer. Both Gassel and Hoecsster were shown bust length, leaning on parapets containing carved inscriptions, and richly dressed. The inscriptions stressed Bink's skills as a *Germanus Apelles* ('German Apelles') below the portrait of Hoecsster, and averred that 'Honour feeds the arts' on the portrait of Gassel.[55] This phrase had appeared in the Latin edition of Pliny the Elder's *Natural History* (Basel, 1526), edited by the historian and philologist of Strasburg and Basel, Bildius Beatus Rhenanus (1485–1547). He had explained his praise of Dürer, Cranach, Hans Baldung (*c.*1485–1545) and Hans Holbein by affirming that 'Honour feeds the arts'.[56] At the same time, in 1530, Heinrich Aldegrever, a painter at Soest in Westphalia (1502–*c.*1561), printed his self-portrait, taking the same format as those by Bink, but simply stating his identity and age.[57] These were followed by a cluster of printed portraits made by Nuremberg artists. One dated 1552 was by Paul Lautensack, and commemorated his father Hans (*c.*1520–66); it again took the form of bust over a parapet.[58] Two more works, this time self-portraits, were printed in 1548 and 1553, to honour Augustin Hirschvogel, cartographer to the Emperor, who had published a work in geometry in 1543. In both prints, which seem to be posthumous as they state his age at death, his affiliations were displayed in the heraldry of his Guild, of Saint Luke, of the Emperor Charles V, for whom he worked, and of his own family shield.[59] The high status of Lucas Cranach the Elder as court painter and his period of office as *Bürgermeister* at Wittenberg (1537–40) has been linked in date with the issue of a woodcut portrayal of Cranach wearing fur robes and resting his palette and brushes on the parapet before him.[60]

The earliest printed artist's portraits in Italy: Michelangelo, Raphael, Titian, Bandinelli, Floris

Post-dating the onset of these Germanic examples are a cluster of single-leaf printed portraits produced in Italy. The only artist south of the Alps who was celebrated with as many printed portraits as Dürer was Michelangelo, although prints were also made to honour Raphael, Titian, Bandinelli and Frans Floris. The earliest dated example derives from 1545 and is attributed to the Bolognese engraver Giulio Bonasone (*c.*1510–after 1576), who worked briefly in Rome in 1544–47. It displayed Michelangelo in profile, as if in a bare room, while an inscription below, as if carved on a ledge, stated his age as seventy-one and opined that 'those who have not heard of Michelangelo must have neither brain nor eyes'.[61] An engraving dated 1546, and this time inscribed by Giulio Bonasone, represented a portrait bust of Michelangelo framed in a tondo, recalling the funerary form invented for the earliest funerary monuments to Florentine artists (Plate 34). It recorded Michelangelo's age as seventy-two and praised him as possessing, equally, the talent he had been born with and the skill he had acquired: 'How much natural ability can affect skill and how much skill can influence innate talent, this man, whose skill is equal to his talent, teaches us.'[62] This design was selected by Condivi for his title page to the biography of Michelangelo (Rome, 1553), which was the earliest account of any artist's career to be issued with an accompanying portrait. In his very first sentence, Condivi had praised Michelangelo as a unique talent (*pittore e scultore singhulare*).[63] Bonasone brought out a further variant himself with a modified frame.[64]

An engraving signed by the Mantuan engraver Giorgio Ghisi (1520–82), who also worked in Rome, between 1534 and 1549, represented the portrait bust of Michelangelo placed as if in an oval niche, framed by an elaborate border and containing a bold inscription, claiming that Michelangelo was 'another inventor of painting and sculpture' (Plate 35). While it still seems to have been being issued as late as 1563,

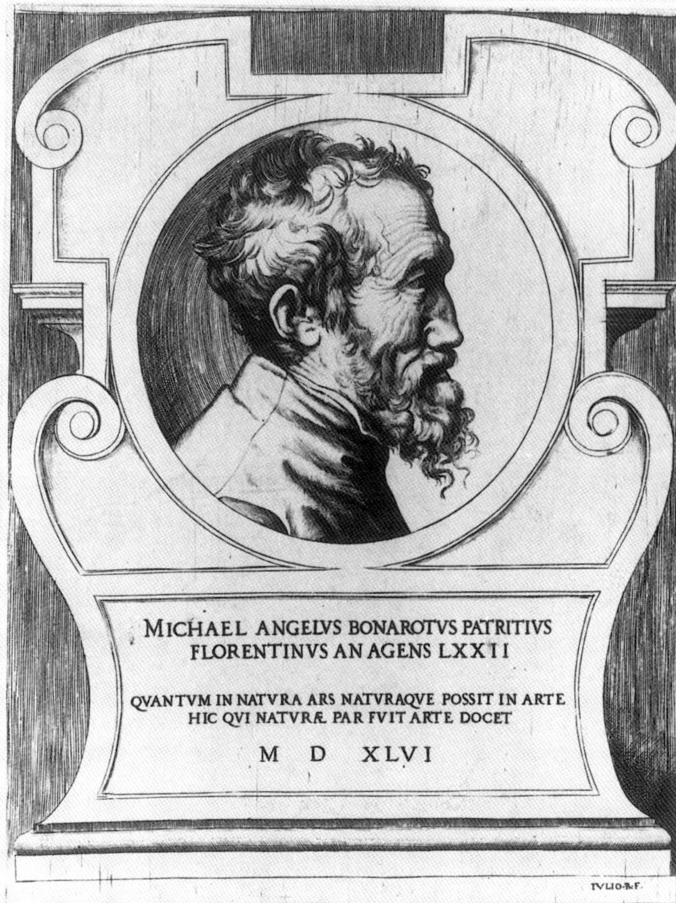

34 Giulio Bonasone, portrait of Michelangelo, 1546, engraving.

when it was labelled as showing the artist aged eighty-eight, it was sold in 1556 with a series of engravings by Giorgio Ghisi reproducing Michelangelo's *Last Judgement*.[65] Other unsigned prints, of similar design, were published which record Michelangelo's celebrity and purported to show him at the ages of seventy-three, seventy-four, seventy five and eighty-one years old, presumably being issued between 1548 and 1556.[66]

As in the case of Dürer, Michelangelo had already been celebrated in a succession of literary texts. Writers had included Cesariano, who praised him in his commentary on Vitruvius in 1521, and Giovio, in the biographies he composed in the period 1523–27.[67] Michelangelo had also been accorded the loftiest compliments by the poet Lodovico Ariosto (1474–1533), in his *Orlando furioso* in 1535, as 'Him, more than mortal (as his name implies), an angel given by propitious skies'.[68] This

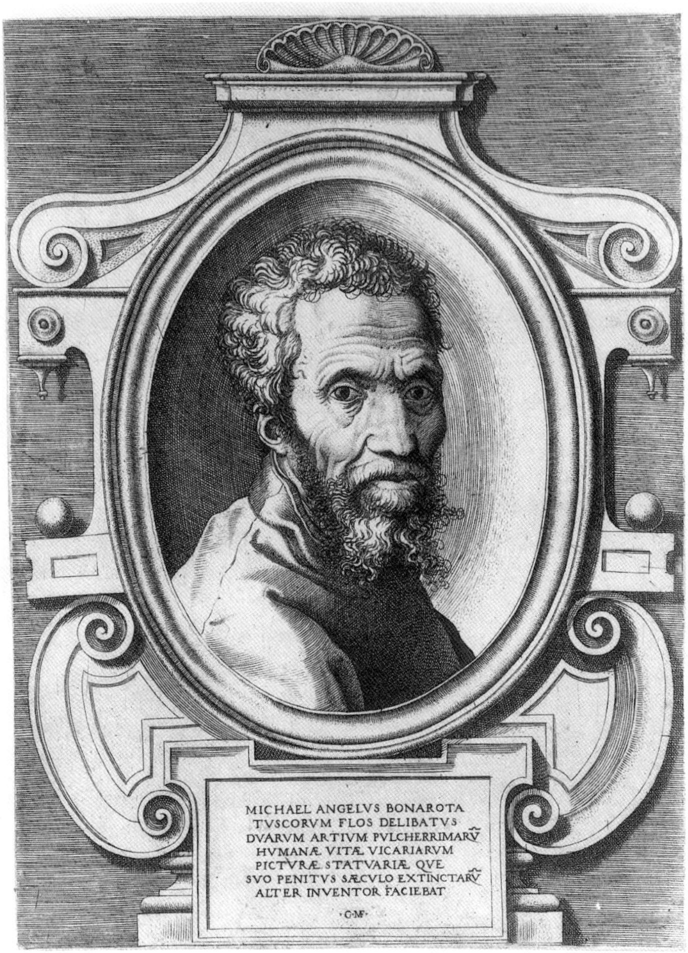

35 Giorgio Ghisi, portrait of Michelangelo, *c.*1556, engraving.

literature of encomium accelerated with the publication of dialogues which included him as an interlocutor by Francisco de Holanda (Lisbon, 1548).[69] It was rapidly followed by the biography which concluded the first edition of Vasari's *Lives* in 1550, and the publication of the account of Michelangelo's career, by Condivi, in 1553.

No other Italian artist received quite this level of treatment during the first half of the sixteenth century although there was sufficient interest in the appearance of Raphael for Bonasone to issue one portrait purporting to record a sculpted original. The print, probably made around 1545, was signed by Bonasone and inscribed as 'the effigy of Rafaello Santi most eminent painter of Urbino taken from a carved exemplar' (Plate 36).[70] In 1550, in Venice, Giovanni Britto (alias Johannes

Breit; *c.*1500–after 1550) published a woodcut after a self-portrait of Titian which commemorated his achievement as Count Palatine in 1533; Luba Freedman has argued that this was commissioned by Titian himself to promote his prospects.[71] Self-promotional, also, appears to have been the printed self-portrait holding a statuette of Hercules, inscribed as representing the Florentine sculptor Baccio Bandinelli. The print is likely to post-date the sculptor's completion of the statue of *Hercules and Cacus* for the Piazza della Signoria in Florence in 1534.[72] Just before his return from Italy, in 1545, Frans Floris of Antwerp was celebrated in a print, signed by Bonasone, which praised him as one 'who holds a not

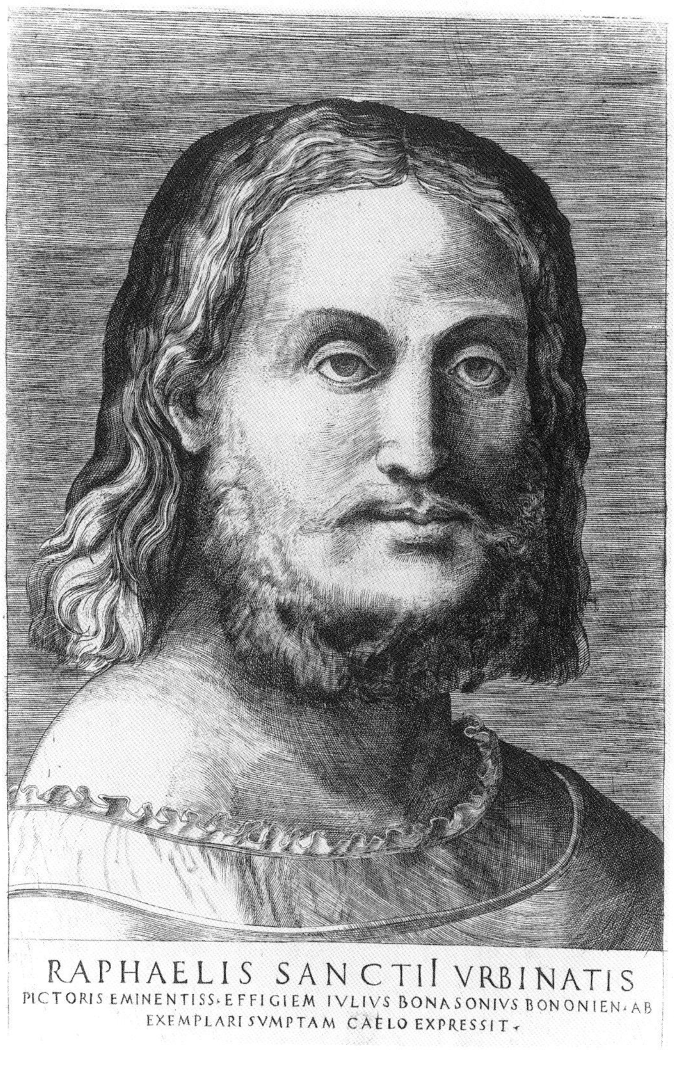

36 Giorgio Ghisi, portrait of Raphael, *c.*1545, engraving.

inferior place amongst Belgian painters'.[73] Printed single-leaf portraits of artists were therefore produced in Italy, though at a somewhat later date than that of the first examples deriving from German-speaking engravers.

Civic display: Antwerp and Bruges 1549–63

Accounts of the prowess of artists had been linked with civic pride from the inception of forms of modern written art history in the late fourteenth century in Florence. However, it was during the middle decades of the sixteenth century that artists working in Antwerp made the innovation of using portraits of famous artists, each associated with different geographical 'schools' of art, to decorate artefacts employed in civic celebrations. The artists honoured in this way were Giotto, Michelangelo, Raphael, van Eyck, Dürer, Zeuxis and Apelles. As with the printed portraits such objects were viewed by quite large audiences.

The year 1549 seems to have been significant since this was when the Florentines advertised the prowess of their artists to the Netherlands – as is clear from the description of the Triumphal Arch made for the entry of Charles V into Antwerp in that year, which was erected by Florentine merchants. It showed portraits of Giotto and Michelangelo to represent the prowess of Florentines in art.[74] Perhaps not to be outdone, in the same year a group of Antwerp worthies gave their Guild of Saint Luke a silver gilt drinking cup, adorned with portraits of van Eyck and Dürer. These were presumably intended to stand for Netherlandish and Germanic painting, since the other three painters featured on the cup were Raphael, for Italian painting, and Zeuxis and Apelles, for ancient Greek painting. Called the *poculum hilaritatis* or 'cup of laughter' it became a centrepiece at guild festivities.[75]

The precedent for the accolade of van Eyck was provided in a genealogy of literary texts which had praised his powers since the mid-fifteenth century. Van Eyck had been acclaimed by scholars since Bartolomeo Facio (*c.*1400–57) in his treatise *On Famous Men* written in the period 1453–59.[76] Raphael's father Giovanni Santi (*c.*1435–94) had also sung his praises in 1483, as had French poems by Jean Lemaire (*c.*1473–*c.*1525), the court poet to Margaret of Austria. He had printed a poem in which van Eyck was complimented entitled *La Plainte du desiré* (*The Complaint of One Desirous*; Lyons, 1509).[77] He had also written a poem entitled *Couronne Margaritique* or *Crown of Pearls* as a pun on the name of the Governess (since *Margarita* means 'pearl') during 1503–11, which included praise of van Eyck and which was eventually printed in 1549.[78]

Records of the house front which the painter Cornelis van Dalem had made in 1563, in Antwerp, show that the idea expressed on the 'cup of hilarity' was soon given public airing. Cornelis commissioned sculpted

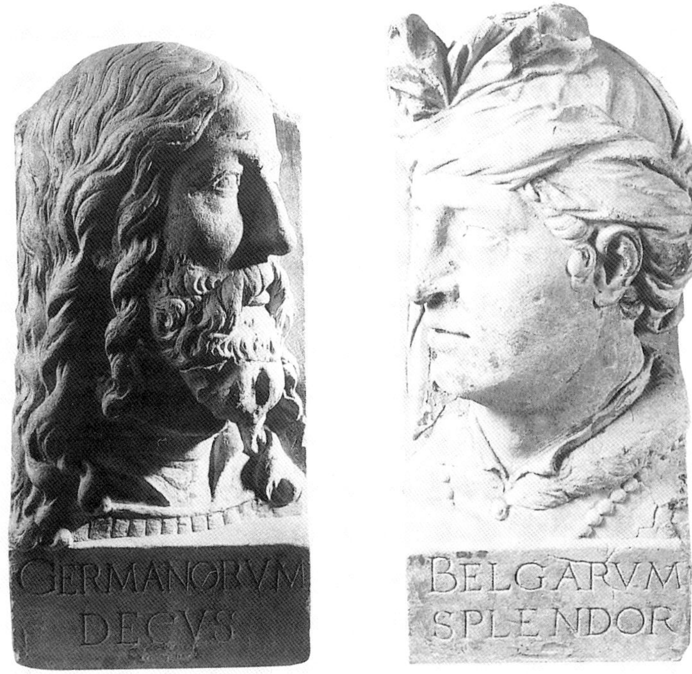

37 Attributed to Willem van den Broucke, portraits of Albrecht Dürer and Jan van Eyck, 1563, Museum Vleeshuis, Antwerp.

busts of van Eyck and Dürer to adorn his house in one of the most populous areas in the city, the Lange Nieeustraat (Plate 37). The Latin inscriptions confirm that the busts stood for 'national' schools, since the former was inscribed as the pre-eminent painter of the Belgians, 'Belgarum splendor' and the latter as the best painter of the Germans 'Germanorum decus' (the terms 'Belgians' and 'Germans' refer to the Latin names given to the tribes inhabiting areas much later called Belgium and Germany). The portraits decorated the frieze above the door and were the only part of the façade rescued when the house was pulled down in the nineteenth century (see Chapters 1, 5 and 7). These busts announced that painting was a dignified profession whose great inventors were a credit to their respective nations. Significantly, the cup of hilarity had been acquired when Cornelis' teacher, Jan Adriaensen, was the leader or Doyen of the Guild.

The term *splendor* had not apparently been associated with van Eyck. Primarily it signified pre-eminence, but it also had a specific meaning in relation to effects of 'glowing colour' created by the ancient painters, which would make it appropriate for the supposed inventor of the oil medium. In his account of ancient painting Pliny the Elder only used *splendor* once and then only in this latter sense. The term *decus* was in contrast already strongly associated with Dürer through its use in his funerary oration by Wilibald Pirckheimer, which had been widely circulated via its appearance in the Preface to the *Four Books* (1528). Pirckheimer had written *I decus, I nostrae non ultima gloria gentis* ('Do not go worthy and finest glory of our people').[79]

The model for the portrait of van Eyck derived from the Ghent altarpiece, made by the painter in 1432. The idea that a turbaned man among those labelled the Just Judges was a self-portrait of Jan van Eyck was first asserted in a poem celebrating the van Eycks by the Ghent painter Lucas de Heere in 1559. This poem was placed beside the altarpiece and affirmed that the man in black with rosary beads round his neck was Jan van Eyck. A small sixteenth-century panel (20 × 26 cm) excerpting the heads of the brothers Hubert and Jan from the crowd scene on the altarpiece suggests the oral traditions surrounding bystander portraits on which the de Heere poem and van Dalem's façade relied.[80] The model for the portrait of Dürer was either the medal which Hans Schwarz of Augsburg made when Dürer in about 1520 when he was still alive, or the engraving derived from it by Lorch, which used the phrase 'divine worthiness' (*divinemque decorum*) in its inscription.

Condivi and Lampsonius 1553–65: portraits preface a biography

It seems possible that the publication of the *Life of Lambert Lombard* by Dominic Lampsonius, in 1565, in Bruges, with an engraved portrait of the artist on the title page was something of a Netherlandish riposte to Condivi's publication of the life of Michelangelo (Rome, 1553), with its prefatory engraved portrait of Michelangelo. Following the convention for artists' funerary portraits, initiated in the early fifteenth century, it too showed a bust of Lombard in a circular frame. This was inscribed with the painter's age (forty-five) and the date 1551 (Plate 38). The Greek couplet beneath announced that while the self-portrait showed what Lombard looked like, the biography would describe his behaviour and his character.[81] Typically the title stressed patriotic motives: the 'Life of Lambert Lombard the most celebrated painter of French-speaking Belgians' (*Lamberti Lombardi apud Eburones pictoris celeberrimi vita*). In his peroration Lampsonius (who had eventually trained as a scholar) placed Lombard in a great tradition of masters, from antiquity to his own times, who had shown that artists could not succeed unless: 'they united scholarly learning with study of art, following the precepts of Phamphilus teacher of the greatest painter, and of Leone Battista Alberti, the Florentine, of Albrecht Dürer and of Pomponius Gauricus'.[82] Phamphilus was the teacher of Apelles and, Pliny the Elder explained, had instructed young artists in all the branches of the

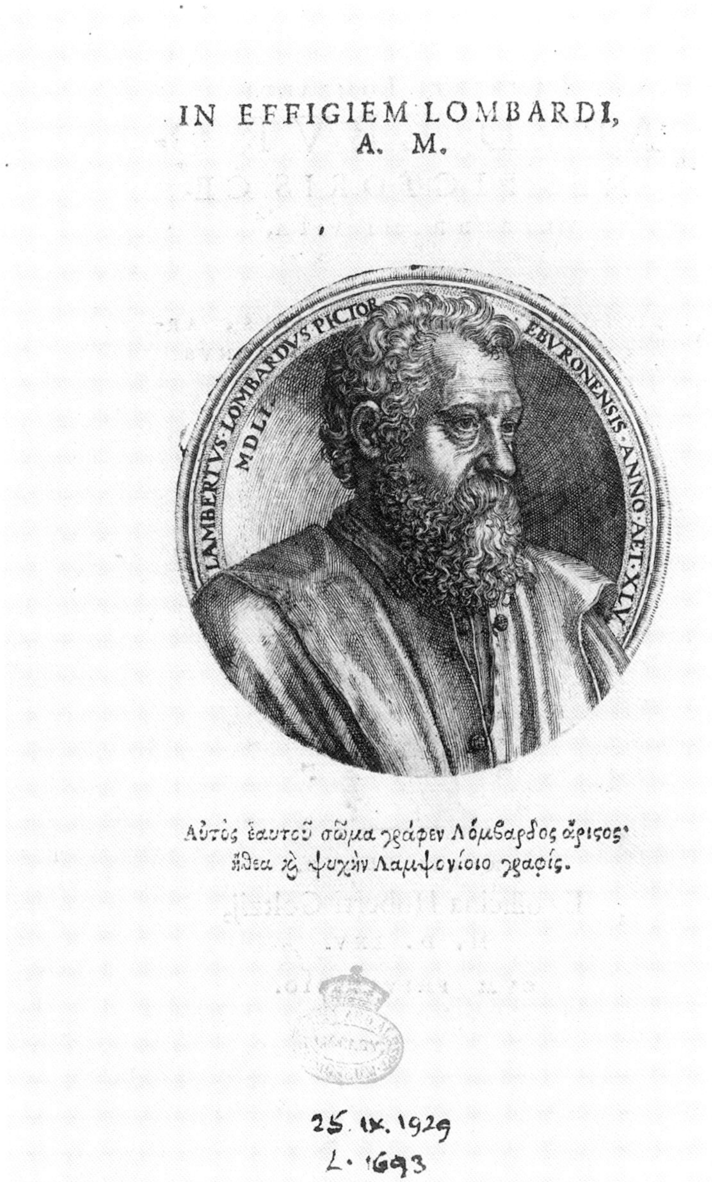
IN EFFIGIEM LOMBARDI, A. M.

Αὐτὸς ἑαυτοῦ σῶμα γράφεν Λόμβαρδος ἄριστος·
ἤθεα καὶ ψυχὴν Λαμψονίοιο γραφίς.

38 Lambert Lombard, self-portrait, title page from Dominique Lampsonius, *Lamberti Lombardi apud Eburones pictoris celeberrimi vita*, Bruges, 1565, National Art Library London.

Liberal Arts, especially geometry and arithmetic. Alberti, Dürer and Gaurico had all written treatises on art more recently.[83] Thus the first printed biographies devoted to artists, illustrated with a portrait of their subjects, were produced within a little more than a decade, north and south of the Alps.

Vasari's role and that of the Medici 1546–73

Literary histories of art had been part of the panegyric of princes since the late fifteenth century, when, for example, Giovanni Santi had praised Netherlandish and Italian artists whose work met the approval of his lord, Duke Federico da Montefeltro.[84] However, it was only in 1546 that Vasari began what was to be the first of a series of portraits of artists which charted the enlightened patronage of great rulers. In that year, Vasari portrayed Michelangelo as part of a princely panegyric in the mural narrative complimenting the Farnese pope, *Paul III Awarding Merit* in the Sala dei Cento Giorni at the Palazzo della Cancelleria in Rome. This scene, according to its author, represented the Pope bestowing rewards on cardinals such as Pole, and scholars such as Pietro Bembo and Bishop Giovio.[85] Michelangelo can be identified background left in a modest position. It seems significant that this genre of artists' portraits was invented in the context of a scheme which Giovio helped to plan for Cardinal Alessandro Farnese, and during the completion of which Giovio encouraged Vasari to compose the *Lives*. At this time Giovio was gathering the first collection of portraits to include those of artists.

The visual celebration of artists as part of the history of patronage was pursued by Vasari's most important patron, Cosimo de' Medici. In 1555, five years after publishing the first edition of the *Lives*, Vasari began a mural campaign for the Medici which lasted until 1562 in which he commemorated the artistic patronage of successive members of the Medici family in the Palazzo Vecchio. In the Sala named after him, Cosimo il Vecchio was depicted with 'his' artists: Fra Angelico, Luca della Robbia, Filippo Lippi, Pesello, Paolo Uccello and Andrea del Castagno, as well as Brunelleschi, Ghiberti and Donatello (Plate 39).[86] In the Sala di Cosimo I, painted between 1556 and 1559, Vasari depicted himself and his contemporaries Niccolò Tribolo, Cellini, Ammanati and Bandinelli as courtiers clustering round their ruler.[87] In the Sala di Leone X Vasari showed Giovanni de' Medici when he became Pope Leo X in the company of Leonardo and Michelangelo.[88] The painted histories became more universalising as Vasari moved onto the mural scheme for the Sala delle Carte Geografiche in the period 1563–65 when he represented famous persons in general, among them groups of statesmen, soldiers, scholars, poets, Christian and Muslim leaders, and four artists, three of whom were Italian: Leonardo, Titian, Michelangelo and Dürer.[89] The presence of Dürer was a significant acknowledgement of the fame of a transalpine talent. Between 1571 and 1573 the Antwerp artist Jan van der Straet was paid for tapestry designs for decorating the Sala di Lorenzo Il Magnifico. Amongst them was one which purported to show the said Lorenzo with the Accademia di San Marco, thus furthering the myth of the late fifteenth-century existence of an artistic academy encouraged in the *Lives* and by the Medici.[90]

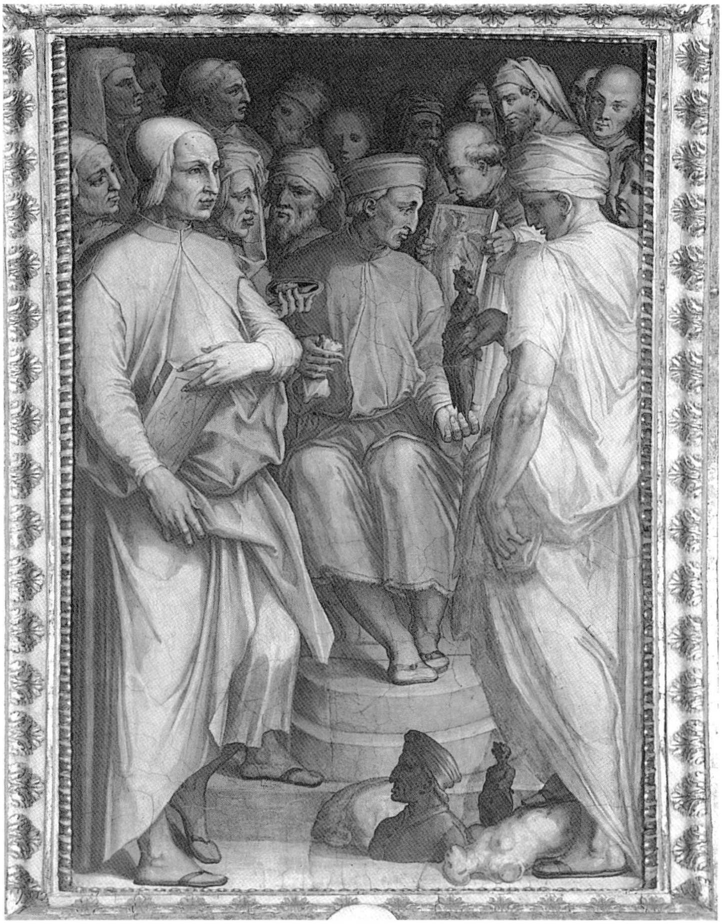

39 Giorgio Vasari, *Cosimo de' Medici il Vecchio with his artists*, 1555–56, Sala del Cosimo il Vecchio, Palazzo Vecchio, Florence.

Portraits of famous people

The portrayal of the Medici as great patrons proceeded hand in hand with the acquisition, by Cosimo, of the artists' – and others' – portraits collected by Giovio. In 1552, at Giovio's death, Cosimo dispatched the Florentine painter Cristofano Altissimo (flourished 1552–1605) north to Como to copy the entire gallery.[91] The portraits which Giovio had collected included some artists who had not worked for the Medici, and were not Florentines, so it appears that the dynasty wished to demonstrate cultural power, in terms of displaying information about art in general, as underlined in the programme for the Sala delle Carte Geografiche.

A pictorial biography

Medici patronage was to the fore in helping to fund a further milestone – in the portrayal of events in the life of a contemporary artist to form a pictorial biography of an artist for the first time. The occasion was the funeral of Michelangelo, when members of the newly founded Accademia del Disegno collaborated to provide a decorous funerary commemoration at San Lorenzo in 1564 for their first president. On the catafalque itself key events in his career were illustrated. Michelangelo was depicted as kneeling before Lorenzo de' Medici as a boy and obtaining his assistance, and then being commissioned to build the New Sacristy and Library of San Lorenzo by Giulio de' Medici. The series included a narrative which featured Michelangelo's republican sympathies in his fortification of San Miniato in defence of the Republic of Florence. In addition, he was represented as working for Paul III on the *Last Judgement* and the dome of Saint Peter's. In a further sequence of canvases that adorned the nave, other episodes in his long life were highlighted, including his services as ambassador to Julius II, as advisor on the design of a villa for Julius III and as consultant to the Doge of the Venetian republic. The message seems to have been that Michelangelo had worked for the most powerful rulers in the peninsula.[92]

Allegorising the history of art

Significantly, one allegory of the history of art as a whole was depicted for the first time at the funeral. It showed Michelangelo in the Elysian Fields with portraits of selected ancient and modern artists. The modern portraits were of the fourteenth-century heroes Giotto and Taddeo Gaddi (flourished 1320s–1366). Then there were the artists representing the 'second period' of the fifteenth century as outlined by Vasari in the *Lives*, that is to say Masaccio, Donatello, Brunelleschi, Filippo Lippi and Uccello. The academicians had selected for apotheosis, in the third, most recent period of modern art, the portraits of artists who had recently died – that is to say, Montorsoli, Francesco Salviati and Jacopo Pontormo. The allegory represented some artists carrying their most famous works: with Brunelleschi holding his dome and Donatello his *Zuccone*. This idea was able to reach quite a large readership since it was recorded in the *Lives* (1568).[93]

A year after the Florentine funerary apparatus was produced, another temporary but impressive scheme of decoration, this time secular, was invented for the Medici wedding festival of 1565, by the scholar Vincenzo Borghini and Vasari. This included another allegory of the history of Florentine art. It was made to adorn the archway at the Porta del Prato, where the bride Joanna of Austria entered Florence. The description by Vasari related that it displayed a composition comparable with that used for Michelangelo's funeral, featuring the tripartite periodisation he proposed in the *Lives*. Indeed, the allegory was divided into three groups of artists, each clustering about their leaders, who were identified as Cimabue, Donatello and Michelangelo. Nevertheless, the visual allegory demonstrated that notions of periodisation were still flexible, since Cimabue was here depicted as followed by Giotto, Gaddi, Bufalmacco (flourished 1315–36) and Benozzo Gozzoli. In contrast, the text of the *Lives* put Gozzoli (1420–98) in the second period. Yet here he had been relegated to the first epoch.[94] Such a complex allegory assumed some consensus amongst artists and viewers, as to the pattern of art-historical developments, and recognition of the appearance of a number of artists. The idea was to display to the new bride the skills of the domain she was entering: its prowess in fighting, scholarship, agriculture, poetry and commerce was shown alongside its powers in art.

Illustrating the *Lives* with portraits

Vasari had hoped to produce woodcut portraits for his first edition, according to a letter addressed to him by Giovio in 1548. The project did not get under way until 1560, however, when Vasari began having the first woodcuts made for the second edition (Plate 28).[95] In the event he presented 150 portraits framed with six different types of surround (see Chapters 1 and 2). As shown by Wulfram Prinz, Vasari usually had an original in mind, whether in some bystander portrait, or an independent portrait in the form of a painting, drawing or medal.[96] Charles Hope demonstrated that in four cases, pairs of artist shared the same woodcut, and the concern to produce an attractive book with a portrait for every life outweighed historical trustworthiness.[97] The fact that Vasari was otherwise able to produce 142 distinctive likenesses suggests that he had been planning the enterprise for many years, and that oral testimony concerning the identity of bystander portraits was prolific.

Portraying the artists who were most highly regarded by one artist

While these visual art histories were accessible to quite a broad public, schemes completed by Vasari for his two houses (in Arezzo and Florence) provided a more personalised slant.[98] In 1568 Vasari finished the Sala dell Fama in his Aretine house with portraits charting the artists who had trained him, and who were part of his artistic identity in his home town (Plate 40). They included his great-grandfather, Lazzaro, and his kinsman, Luca Signorelli (*c.*1450–1523), as well as del Sarto and Michelangelo, whose examples he had emulated. In addition, there were painters who had worked in Arezzo: Spinello Aretino (*c.*1350–1410) and Bartolomeo della Gatta (1448–1502). Soon after, in 1573, Vasari painted the decoration of his house in Florence and again included portraits of artists whom he had admired and who had encouraged him in his own career. There were the Tuscans whom he had termed pioneers –

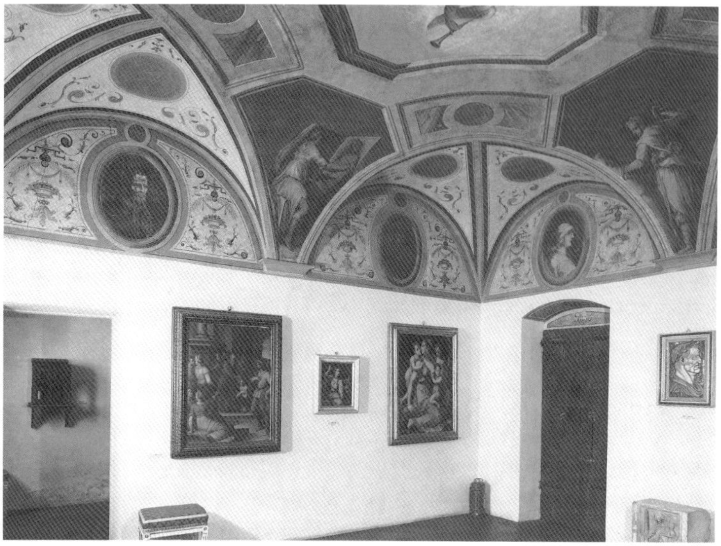

40 Giorgio Vasari, Painting, and Sculpture in the pendentives with portrait lunettes below, Sala della Fama, 1542–68, Casa del Vasari, Arezzo.

Cimabue and Giotto, and their followers Masaccio, Donatello and Brunelleschi. Then there were their heirs, Raphael, Michelangelo and Leonardo. Finally, there were artists relevant to Vasari's own life: Vasari's exemplar del Sarto; two pupils of Raphael, Perino del Vaga (1501–47) and Giulio Romano; Rosso Fiorentino, who had helped Vasari in his youth; and Vasari's friend, Salviati (Plate 17).

Although Vasari's houses provided the most spectacular examples, fragments of historicising friezes of famous artists on panel and canvas have survived from other room decorations as well. What may be an early example of a frieze celebrating famous artists depicted five of the Florentine artistic heroes of the fourteenth and fifteenth century. This showed, from left to right, Giotto, Uccello, Donatello, Manetti and Brunelleschi, with each artist's names inscribed beneath his portrait (Plate 41). In the *Lives* (1568), Vasari associated this panel with Uccello (who had died in 1475) and reported that it was preserved in the house of the architect Giuliano da Sangallo in Florence (who had died in 1516).[99] Vasari relied on this panel for portraits of Uccello, Donatello and Brunelleschi for his mural of Cosimo I, and also the *Lives*.[100] A later version, with a wider remit than Florentine art, showed Giotto, Donatello, Masaccio, Raphael and Michelangelo. This canvas placed the portraits, labelled, between fictive arches flanked by *putti*.[101] The idea that such portraits might form an appropriate decoration is confirmed in the fact that in 1563 the academicians in Florence planned to adorn the frieze of their meeting hall, had they obtained a permanent site at this stage, with portraits of 'the famous artists of Tuscany since Cimabue'.[102]

During the middle decades of the sixteenth century, when the artists of the Netherlands were starting to celebrate the prowess of trans-

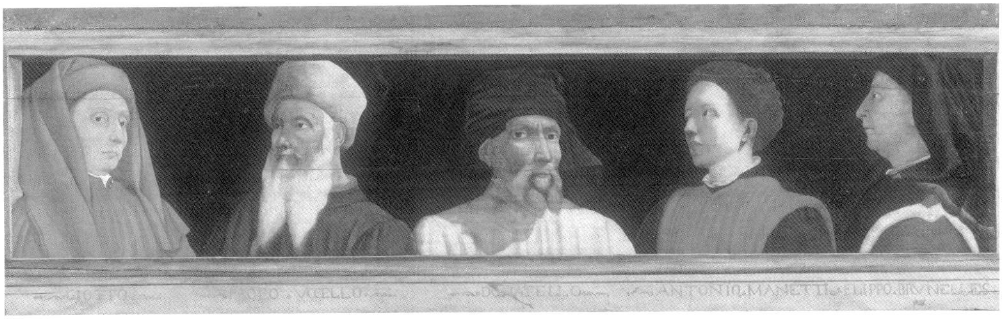

41 Anonymous, practitioners of Florentine art, Giotto, Uccello, Donatello, Manetti and Brunelleschi, late fifteenth- or early sixteenth-century, Louvre, Paris.

alpine painters, the Medici dynasty, in conjunction with members of the first Academy of Design, therefore explored the pictorial panegyric of the ruler as great patron, founded the second collection of artists' portraits, exhibited painted narratives of the life of an artist and displayed allegories of the course of the history of art for the first time. During the same period, Vasari, with the backing of the Medici, illustrated the most important history of art to date with a series of 150 portraits, and, in his own houses, depicted personalised visual histories, in groups of portraits which denoted the practitioners with whom he wished to be associated. This cluster of initiatives seems to have impressed contemporaries.

That Florentine initiatives made a considerable impact is evident in the elaborate plans for Titian's funeral designed in 1576 by the confraternity of painters at San Luca in Venice, which was to have included visual narratives of the great events in Titian's career.[103] These would have provided pictures associating him with his greatest patrons: Duke Alfonso of Ferrara, Charles V, Paul III and the Doge. In a further compliment to the Florentine scheme, there were to have been painted portraits, resembling bronze medals of the principal ancient and modern painters such as Apollodorus, Apelles, Zeuxis, Michelangelo, Raphael and Leonardo, to indicate the honour in which he was held.[104] The precedent of the pictorial narrative of Michelangelo's life was probably in the mind of Federico Zuccari when he composed his own pictorial account of the career of his dead brother Taddeo, in about 1590, in his own house in Rome (Plate 76).

Printed galleries including artists' portraits: Antwerp, Rome and Basel

The two experiments in making the visual history of art with the widest circulation were Vasari's *Lives* (1568) and Hieronymous Cock's (*c.*1510–70) series of portraits of Netherlandish artists published four years later in 1572 by his widow Volcxken Dircx. This important work was produced by a team of engravers that included Jan Wiericx and

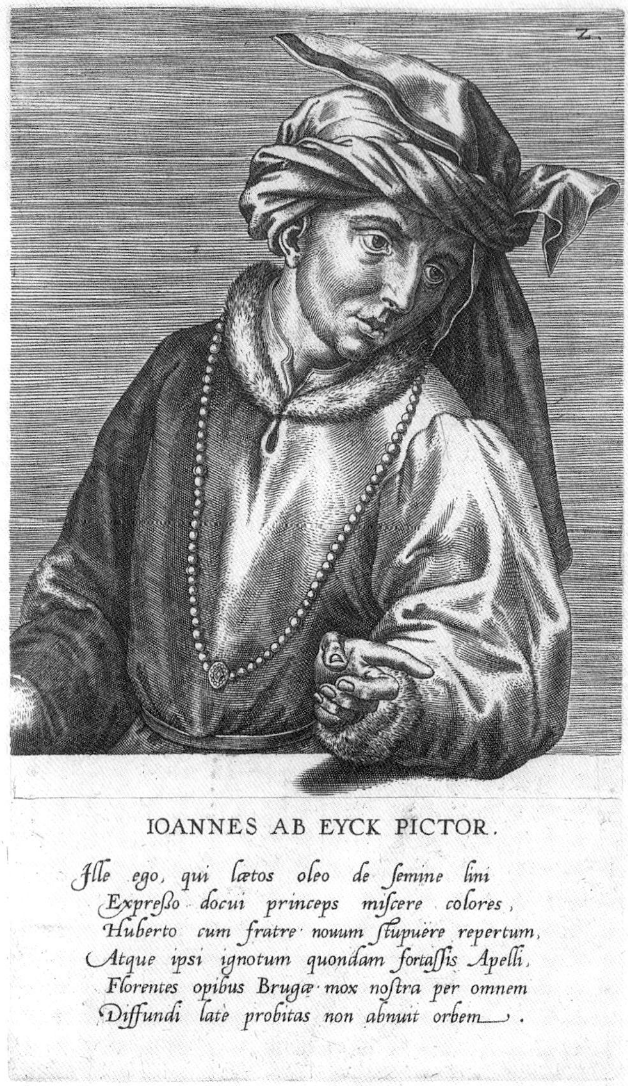

42 Hieronymous Cock, commemorative portrait of Jan van Eyck, from *Pictorum aliquot celebrium*, Antwerp, 1572.

Cornelius Cort. Whereas Vasari's visual history followed a large corpus of literary tributes, Cock's series, where each portrait was accompanied by a Latin verse, celebrated many artists for the first time in print, and did not rest on so rich a literary tradition. Indeed, van Mander's history of Netherlandish artists followed on from Cock's series of portraits (Plate 42). In 1572, in Antwerp, Dircx published her husband's collection of twenty-two engraved portraits of Netherlandish artists, with an introduction in Latin by Lampsonius and verses by him for each artist: *The Effigies of Some Celebrated Painters of the Low Countries* (*Pictorum aliquot celebrium Germaniae Inferioris effigies*). Beginning with the founding fathers of the van Eyck brothers, Hieronymus Bosch (*c.*1450–1516), Rogier van der Weyden and Thierry Bouts (*c.*1415–75), Dircx ended the book with the twenty-third portrait, which was that of her spouse.[105] The emphasis here was on painters, and on the image not the word, since the verses by Lampsonius were epigrammatic. For instance, the verses accompanying the portrayal of van Eyck simply claimed that he and his brother had invented painting using linseed oil, a technique unknown to Apelles.[106] As with the *Lives*, there is some evidence of research concerning the accuracy of the portrayals for the five artists who had died before Cock was born (1510). For example, following the oral history enshrined in the poem by de Heere and the house façade of van Dalem, Cock derived his portrait of the van Eycks from the Just Judges in the Ghent altarpiece. It seems likely that Cock had known many of the other artists who were his contemporaries. Cock was the oldest involved in the enterprise, dying aged sixty, and had travelled to Italy returning about 1550. Significantly, Giorgio Ghisi, who was responsible for one of the engraved portraits of Michelangelo, had come to Antwerp in 1550 and worked in Cock's printing house. Dircx was much younger, living on thirty years to direct The Four Winds until 1600. Lampsonius, who had been in correspondence with Vasari, was forty when the first edition came out. Cock's *Effigies* reached a wide audience since they were issued three more times up until 1600 and copied in 1610 at The Hague by Hendrik Hondius (1573–1650) (see Plate 77).

The precedent of the Giovio museum and the Medici collection of portraits was sufficiently admired for the Dominican scholar Alonso Chacon (see Chapter 5), based at Santa Trinità dei Monti in Rome, to plan a de luxe printed version, with the patronage of Ferdinand Archduke of Austria. Although the scheme remained unfulfilled, Chacon gathered together a number of the originals, which he intended to supply to the engravers of what he called his *museo*. The self-portrait requested from Lavinia Fontana (1552–1614) dated 1579, was one, and represents the manner in which the Bolognese painter felt it decorous to appear, as a woman famous in art history (Plate 43).[107] The portrayal of famous modern artists had assumed that personal talent was masculine, so that it is intriguing to examine the way Fontana appropriated *ingenium* for the feminine. Already maker of portraits of two Bolognese worthies for Chacon's publication, Fontana was asked by him in 1578 to send him her self-portrait:

> I beg you not to deprive me of my wish for this satisfaction and happiness, and for you, of this Glory that, granted you already have sufficient, still is not known by all, as I plan to celebrate and propagate it through the centuries, even for a kind of eternity.[108]

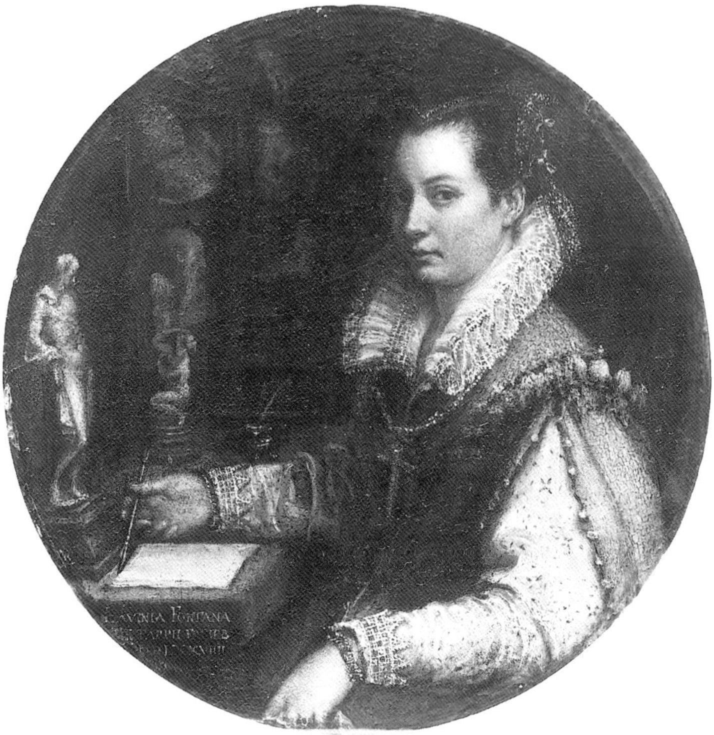

43 Lavinia Fontana, self-portrait, 1579, copper, 15 cm diameter, Uffizi, Florence.

For the museum, Fontana displayed herself as mistress of the nude and the antique gazing shrewdly out at viewers. Moreover, she was careful to stress feminine decorum by painting herself accessing these academic skills not through studying anatomy first hand or wandering the ruins of Rome but through drawing after antique statuettes and casts in her studio. She also emphasised her social position in the richness of her dress, her piety by means of the large jewelled cross hanging on her bosom and placed near the centre of the composition, and her position as a married woman via the inscription and her ringed left hand centre base.

Giovio's collection had been copied by several artists, including the German-Swiss artist Tobias Stimmer (1539–84) in about 1570.[109] His copies were eventually printed, accompanied by short explanatory verses in Latin in a small woodcut picture book issued by the publisher Waldkirch Perna in 1589 in Basel.[110] The print gallery was edited by Nikolaus Reusner (1545–1602), and entitled *Images or Representations of Illustrious Men of Letters* (*Icones sive imagines literis illustrium virorum*). It concentrated on portraits of illustrious men of letters and, perhaps significantly, isolated the artists at the end of the book, after the portrait of Giovio himself and the representations of two musicians. In this way

Giovio's portraits of Leonardo, Andrea del Sarto, Titian, Michelangelo, Bandinelli, Belli and Antonio da Sangallo reached a wider audience in quite a prestigious context.[111]

The sense that the histories of art belong to general cultural histories is also present in an impressive engraved tribute to the wonders of the modern world at the end of the century. In around 1588, Vasari's colleague at the Medici court, Jan van der Straet, made drawings in Florence which represented a variety of modern inventions, including that of oil painting supposedly by van Eyck and of book printing. These designs were engraved in the series entitled *Nova reperta* or *New Discoveries* by Philips de Galle (1537–1612) in Antwerp on the commission of the Florentine scholar Luigi Alamanni (Plate 44). Published in the period 1590–95, the series placed the invention of oil painting on an equal level with the discovery of America, silk weaving, the compass and gunpowder. Van der Straet pictured Jan van Eyck busy in a workshop, decorated with the heraldry of the Guild of Saint Luke, with the caption 'The distinguished Master Eyck invented oil colouring for the use of painters'.[112]

44 Jan van der Straet, *The invention of oil painting by Van Eyck*, engraving, 1590–95.

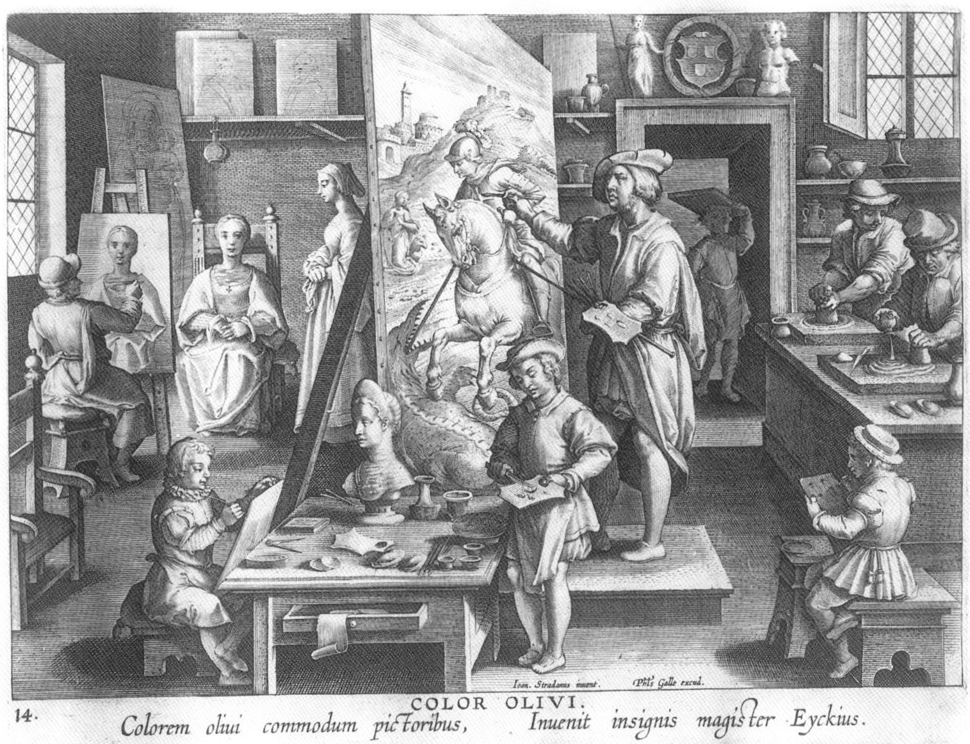

At the very end of the fifteenth and beginning of the sixteenth centuries, collectors in Italy and the Netherlands had begun valuing portraits of artists, whatever their original function, in ways which suggest new evaluations of the importance of individual artists' attainment. In conjunction with this trend appeared the production of single-leaf prints, which could reach consumers who were somewhat less well off than those able to purchase paintings. Many of these prints praised the fame of Dürer, posthumously, and Michelangelo during his lifetime. From the 1540s onwards, the display of portraits of artists, along with other great men, was furthered, in galleries actual and printed, and in narratives of princely patronage. During the second half of the century the first pictorial narratives centring on the career of an artist were made and planned, and allegories depicted the progress of Florentine art. During this period, again for the first time, sequences of printed portraits illustrated, or stood for, histories of Italian and Netherlandish art. In the houses of Vasari, personalised gatherings of artists' portraits were made to represent the artists that were most important to the owner. In many cases, the authors of the literature of art history (such as Condivi, Vasari, Lampsonius) promoted the new types of portraits which celebrated their heroes. On the other hand, this survey of new genres of portrayal suggests that the individual talent of artists was being prized, by many practitioners who did not publish their views in literary terms. To see the evidence of new sorts of portraiture as unequivocally suggesting that efforts were being employed to raise the dignity of artists would however be unwise. Although some of these new types of portrayal did celebrate artists as great personages in their own right, others highlighted their relative value in serving more powerful men. Furthermore, some portrayals (for example the Giovio collection and the Reusner version) kept artists separate from rulers and scholars. Others placed artists in ambiguous positions. Thus the *Nova reperta* associated oil painters with weavers and gunpowder makers, and the triumphal arch for the marriage of Joanna of Austria placed artists between the poets and farmers of Tuscany.

Portraying ancient artists

The portrayal of named ancient Greek and Roman artists in order to celebrate their role in the history of art arguably dates from about 1507. Such historically minded portrayals were employed for the decoration of three artists' houses and the adornment of one guild chamber, as well as being considered appropriate for the ceremony of two artists' funerals. This type of imagery was attractive to a certain clientele. Admiration of ancient art and architecture in general were key factors in the intellectual life of the sixteenth century, and representation of named ancient artists implied scholarly knowledge of a prestigious culture amongst present-day artists. More specifically, the artists and events that were picked for portrayal could display approval for particular facets of art practice. Thus Vasari might approve methods of idealisation through illustrating the story of Zeuxis and the maidens of Croton. In such designs modern artists might also display their sense of being the emulous heirs of the artists of ancient Greece and Rome.

Like many of the new genres of portrait employed to celebrate recent artists, the representation of ancient artists rested on literary traditions. The two most well-known texts were the chapters by Pliny the Elder on the history of art, and the manuscripts of Vitruvius' *Ten Books*, which contained references to ancient practitioners. The citation of the names of ancient artists with reference to recent ones had become commonplace from the fourteenth century onwards, when Boccaccio had described Giotto as another Apelles.[113] Alberti in *Della pittura* in 1436 had cited the techniques and approaches of some ancient artists with approval, while Ghiberti had summarised the deeds of ancient artists in his *Commentari*, in around 1450, drawing on the history of Pliny the Elder and Vitruvius.[114] Filarete had followed soon after, imagining that the architect's house should be adorned with portraits of ancient and modern artists.[115] A significant step was made by Cristoforo Landino (*c.*1424–98), who compiled the first printed edition of the *Historia naturalis* in Italian (Venice, 1476).[116]

By the late fifteenth century, audiences might have access to texts illustrated with portrayals of the deeds of some ancient named artists. These included the illustration of Cicero's *De inventione*, which was a handbook on rhetoric, of interest to contemporary scholars who wished to learn how to compose speeches.[117] Cicero had used the story of Zeuxis selecting what he thought the best features from five real women, to paint one ideal woman, as a simile for good oratory, when choosing the best arguments to compose a persuasive oration. More popularly, Zeuxis' idealisation had formed part of the illustration of the French poem the *Roman de la Rose* (Paris, 1494; Paris, 1500).[118] In addition, female artists had been illustrated in Giovanni Boccaccio's praise of famous women entitled *De mulieribus claris*, written between 1360 and 1374. This had included the Roman artists Cyrene, Thamar and Marcia mentioned by Pliny, and had circulated in manuscript in Latin, Italian and French.[119] For instance, the story of Marcia making her self-portraits was portrayed in woodcuts for the Ulm imprint of 1473 in both the Latin and the German versions.[120] From soon after the middle of the fifteenth century, in 1468, an event in the life of the Apelles in the allegorical form of his *Calumny* had been also represented in courtly contexts (see Chapter 6). Exemplary literature continued to employ such illustrations in the sixteenth century, for example in the edition of Cicero's *De officiis*, published in Augsburg in 1531 in Latin, and in the vernacular in Frankfurt am Main in 1550. Attributed to Hans Weiditz, this showed Zeuxis painting grapes so realistic that birds tried to eat them, surrounded by spectators, so as to explain the adage that one should learn from the advice of others.[121] In the sixteenth century the story of Apelles and Campaspe was also employed in courtly contexts when the patron could be compared with Alexander the Great. The story displayed the generosity of Alexander because he had admired Apelles' painting so much that he had given him not only money, but the model Campaspe herself, who was the royal concubine. In this manner, Francesco Primaticcio (*c.*1504–70) painted this subject for François I at Fontainebleau (1541–44) and Francesco Morandini (1544–97) depicted it for Grand Duke Francesco de' Medici in the *studiolo* of the Palazzo Vecchio in Florence (1570–75).[122]

Representing the history of ancient art

The portrayal of ancient artists as part of the history of art, however, should be distinguished from the illustration of good morals, rhetorical methods or liberality in patronage. Arguably the first representation which falls into this historical category is an engraving which portrays Apelles, dated about 1507, and probably made in Rome by Nicoletto da Modena (flourished 1500–20) (Plate 45).[123] The engraving is inscribed 'Apeles s. poeta tacentes [tacens] a tempo suo ciliberimus' which seems to mean 'Apelles, the mute poet celebrated by his own time' (the incorrect orthography argues for quite a popular audience). The Horatian assertion that painting is mute poetry, which had circulated amongst artists since the treatise written by Cennini in 1400, might have been considered relevant to the discussion of the *paragone*, which was active at this time. Apelles is shown wearing a toga-like garment and the poet's wreath on his head, contemplating a tablet on which are drawn four geometrical figures. The tablet is propped on the base of a column and this base is decorated with compasses and a paint pot. The linkage between poetry, painting and geometry in the print is telling. John Gage argued that the geometrical figures stood for the four colours reputedly used by Apelles.[124] The print of Apelles could have been calculated to sell to buyers of Nicoletto da Modena's other prints in Rome at this time, which displayed ancient mythological figures and ancient Roman statuary. His sense of the intellectual status of Apelles is nicely demonstrated by the fact that the figure is an adaptation of a philosopher in the *Triumph of Saint Thomas Aquinas* painted by Filippino Lippi (*c.*1457–1504) at the Caraffa chapel in Santa Maria sopra Minerva in Rome (completed in 1493).

A number of other designs employed portrayals of ancient artists for the benefit of artists and architects themselves. While one scheme showed all the architects mentioned by Vitruvius, the choice of painters represented suggests the somewhat limited number of events in Pliny

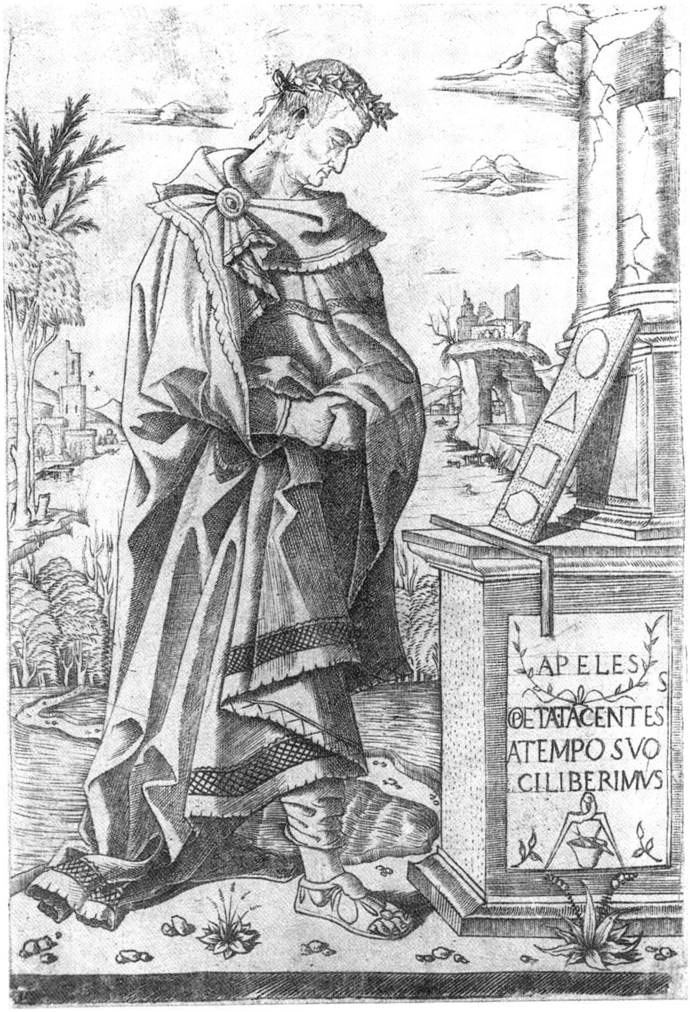

45 Nicoletto da Modena, *Apeles poeta tacentes*, 1507, engraving.

the Elder's account which were considered relevant to sixteenth-century practice. The scenes chosen could indeed give artists opportunities to make statements about the finer points in pictorial narration, to explain how artists could make images of ideal beauty and to assert the authority of artists themselves in matters of art. These celebrations were noticeably skewed in favour of painting.

The earliest large-scale scheme was designed for the city architect of Schlettstadt or Sélestat in Alsace and is dated 1545 (Plate 46). It represented the famous architects whom Vitruvius had listed in the *Ten Books*, as well as a bust portraying Vitruvius himself. Stephan Ziegler had added the decoration to the house – which is dated as being been

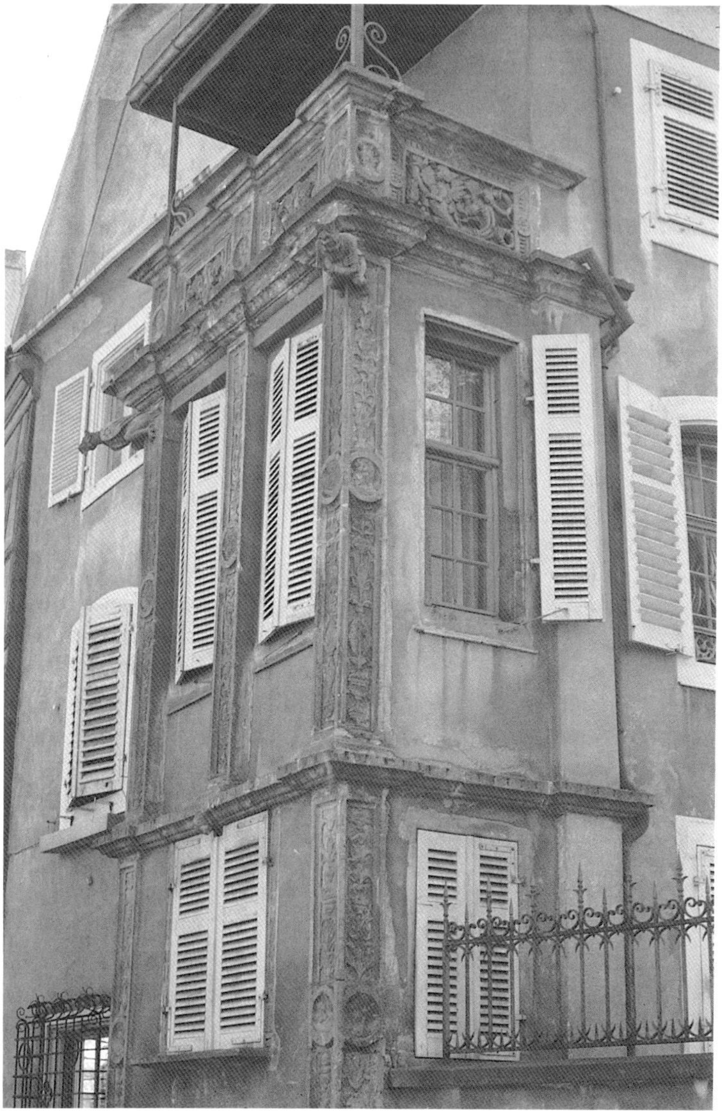

46 The house of Stephan Ziegler, 1545, Sélestat, Alsace.

built in 1538 – on the occasion of his marriage to Anna Romerin in 1545, as stated in the Latin inscription.[125] The ancient architects, each labelled with their name, were portrayed in the form of busts, carved in relief on roundels decorating the pilasters, which articulate the convex bay holding the portal, and windows above it. Ziegler used inscriptions which displayed his classical learning in a quotation from Cicero's *Tusculan Disputations* ('everyone considers their own work beautiful'; *suum cuique pulchrum*) and one from Erasmus'es *Adages* ('things which are excellent are difficult'; *difficilia quae pulchra*).[126] He inscribed the façade as dedicated to the ancient architects (*Architectis veteribus d[ed]icatum*). In most cases, the architect's political affiliation was located either in his native city ('Archimedes of Syracusa') or via his citizen status ('Cossutius citizen of Rome'). Ziegler named himself 'Architect and Public instructor of the city' on his house front, indicating that he took the role of city planner administering the execution of building works. This was because, in many German-speaking areas, masons qualified to build in the guilds attached to large buildings, and then they travelled from project to project, while cities appointed permanent civic architects who were members of the town council to manage the builds.[127] Ziegler had particular reason to be well informed on the work of Vitruvius, since a precious tenth-century manuscript of Vitruvius was then owned by his scholarly neighbour Beatus Rhenanus, and was given to the civic library in 1547 at the latter's death. It may be relevant that Philandrier had recently published an edition of Vitruvius in nearby Strasburg (1543) (see Chapter 2). Four years later, one further tribute was paid north of the Alps to ancient artists in the context of the history of art. As related earlier, this was the silver gilt cup which had been given to the Guild of Saint Luke in Antwerp in 1549. The choice of Apelles and Zeuxis on this vessel reiterated the prominence of these two ancient artists for this period.[128]

The second large-scale programme to display images of ancient artists was painted in the house of Vasari in Arezzo, in 1548, and showed scenes from the lives of Parrhasius, Timanthes, Apelles, Zeuxis and Protogenes drawn from the anecdotes in the *Natural History* by Pliny the Elder (Plate 47). The scenes selected explored a variety of techniques for producing convincing pictorial narratives (whether in the meticulous verism of Parrhasius' painted curtain, or in Timanthes' ploy of veiling the face of the father of Iphigenia to convey his grief, or in the story that Protogenes threw a sponge onto his painting to suggest the appearance of foaming spit on a dog's mouth). Such representations, placed around the walls in Vasari's main reception room, could be addressed both to painters and to people wanting to know about the finer points of painting. The scene showing Zeuxis selecting the most beautiful features from living women put a premium both on idealisation and on the discriminating masculine gaze. The portrayal of Apelles being given Campaspe accorded the artist power over the feminine in the act of painting superlatively, as well as paying profound respect to a masculine patron. Vasari completed this cycle with a scene of a man supposedly inventing painting by drawing along the outline of a shadow on a wall.[129]

Vasari also played a key role in the design by the Florentine academicians for the funeral apparatus of Michelangelo in 1564 which referred to the excellence of ancient artists. Vasari's own printed description related that Alessandro Allori painted a large scene showing Michelangelo in the Elysian fields flanked by great ancient artists, each

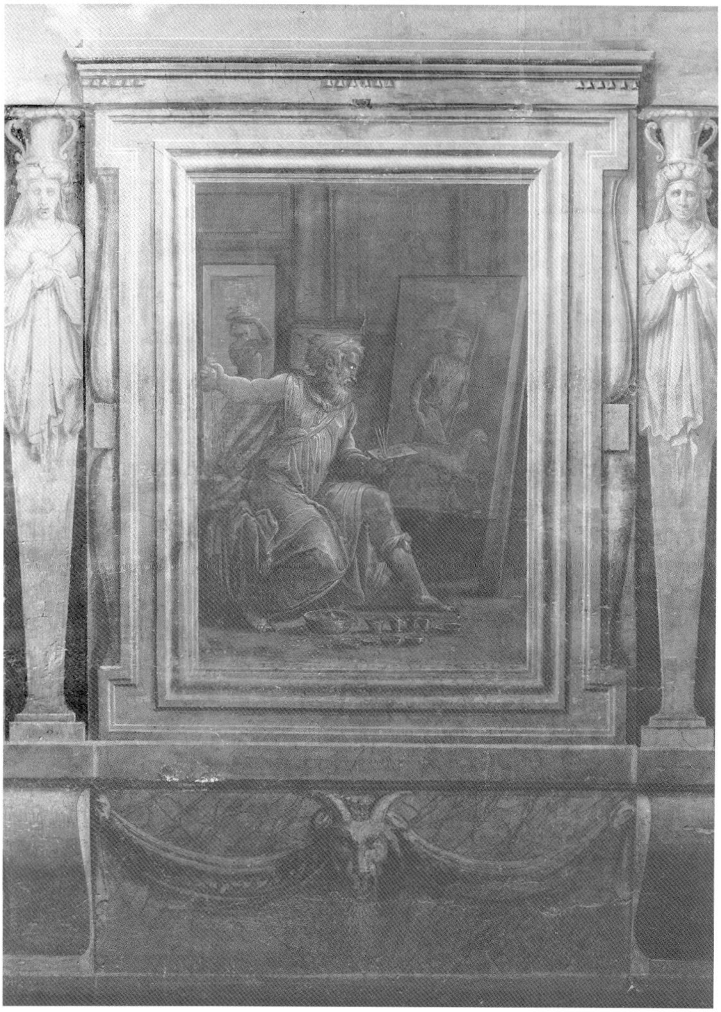

47 Giorgio Vasari, *Protogenes throws his sponge*, 1548, Casa del Vasari, Arezzo.

holding his work: Praxiteles with his satyr, Apelles with his portrait of Alexander the Great, Zeuxis with his picture of grapes, and Parrhasius with his curtain. The ancient masters were (see p. 124) accompanied by portraits of the modern ones – Masaccio, Giotto, Donatello, Brunelleschi, Filippo Lippi, Taddeo Gaddi, Paolo Uccello, Montorsoli, Pontormo and Salviati.[130]

Finally, in around 1573 Vasari painted three murals for his Florentine house showing ancient artists (Plates 17, 29).[131] His selection again represented Zeuxis idealising from the beauties of the five maidens of Croton. Vasari reworked the story to show how *Disegno* (see Chapter 2) helped artists to select and process the raw sense data of the visual world and turn it into a pictorially convincing and admirable illusion.

The second scene repeated the notion of the masculine invention of painting, which he had put forward at Arezzo. In the third scene he represented Apelles, but this time he showed him listening behind a curtain to the views of the Athenian people, including a cobbler, as to whether his painting was any good. In the story Apelles finally steps out and tells the cobbler to 'stick to his last'. Clearly, the painter knows best about his art. As described earlier, Vasari accompanied these scenes with portraits of thirteen modern artists. In his final representation of the ancient artists, therefore, Vasari was both more selective and more robust: the underlying message of his scheme seems to be that artists invented painting and have discovered how to employ it to produce superlative ideal beauty; concomitantly, they are the arbiters of artistic worth.

From the mid-sixteenth century onwards, therefore, a few artists began to deploy images of ancient pagan artists in ways which were relevant to their own careers and claims for the value of the figurative arts and architecture, on items for a guild, an academy and for the decoration of artists' houses. Artists could represent those regarded as the best ancient artists to demonstrate desirable aesthetic and technical values, and they sometimes displayed ancient artists together with modern artists, to emphasise the comparability of ancient prowess with modern achievements. Presumably, the representation of one's prestigious ancient predecessors laid claim to some learning and some cultural power.

The genres of commemorative portrayals of artists initiated in the sixteenth century did not all contribute to claims for greater dignity amongst the profession. However, to the extent that the new types adopted the media of print, they increased the likelihood that more viewers in more locations might have an idea of the appearance of some artists who had been distinguished for their attainment. In addition, the new genres included narrative forms previously exclusive to the representation of leaders in religion, in scholarship, in war and in peace. If contemporary artists had already adapted genres of portraiture for their own purposes by the end of the fifteenth century, it is significant that it was only in the sixteenth century that they took over what was considered the challenging mode of narrative. This situation may be contrasted with the long-standing traditions for representing the patron saints of artists, whose spiritual achievements had conventionally been accorded the narrative mode.

Notes

1 Vitruvius, *On Architecture*, ed. Granger, I, pp. xvi–xx; Pliny the Elder, *Historia naturalis*, ed. H. Rackham, 8 vols, London, 1938, I, pp. xii–xiii.

2 Ludwig Goldscheider, *Five Hundred Self Portraits*, Vienna and London, 1937, p. 15.

3 Catherine E. King, 'Italian artists in search of virtue, fame and honour', pp. 56–87 in Emma Barker, Nick Webb and Kim Woods, eds, *The*

Changing Status of the Artist, New Haven, CT, and London, 1999, Plate 63; Catherine E. King, 'Filarete's portrait-signature on the bronze doors of Saint Peter's and the dance of Bathykles and his Magnesian assistants', *Journal of the Warburg and Courtauld Institutes*, LIII, 1990, pp. 296–9.

4 Louisa Becherucci and Giulia Brunetti, *Il Museo del Opera del Duomo a Firenze*, 2 vols, Milan, 1969–71, I, p. 288, Catalogue number 176.

5 Wulfram Prinz, 'Vasari's Sammlung von Künstlerbildnissen', Beiheft zu Band XII der *Mitteilungen des Kunsthistorischen Instituts in Florenz*, Florence, 1966, p. 52.

6 Ettore Allegri and Alessandro Cecchi, *Guida storica: Palazzo Vecchio e I Medici*, Florence 1980, pp. 235–41.

7 Joanna Woods Marsden, *Renaissance Self-portraiture: The Visual Construction of Identity and the Social Status of the Artist*, New Haven, CT, and London, 1998, p. 72.

8 Catherine King, 'Portrait of the Artist as a Woman', pp. 37–60, in Gill Perry, ed., *Gender and Art*, New Haven, CT, 1999, p. 48.

9 Gesa Schütz Rautenberg, 'Künstlergrabmäler des 15 und 16 Jahrhunderts in Italien', PhD thesis, Cologne, 1978, pp. 12–37.

10 Francis Ames-Lewis, *The Intellectual Life of the Renaissance Artist*, New Haven, CT, and London, 2002, p. 96.

11 Schütz Rautenberg, 'Künstlergrabmäler des 15 und 16 Jahrhunderts', pp. 25–6.

12 Schütz Rautenberg, 'Künstlergrabmäler des 15 und 16 Jahrhunderts', passim.

13 Belli was from Vicenza and worked at the Papal Court. Prinz, 'Vasari's Sammlung', p. 132.

14 King, 'Portrait of the Artist', p. 68.

15 M. Grandjean, in *Die Kunstdenkmäler der Schweiz, Monuments d'art et d'histoire de la Suisse: du Canton de Vaud*, Ville de Lausanne, Basel, 1965, pp. 234–9. For numerous instances on buildings see Kurt Gerstenberg, *Die deutschen Baumeisterbildnisse des Mittelalters*, Berlin, 1966: for example, that of Peter Harperger at Saint Leonhard, Tamsweg, pp. 211–15.

16 Grandjean, *Kunstdenkmäler der Schweiz*, pp. 234–9: 'Johan[n]es de Leodio architect[u]s Sabaudi[a]e cultu sc[u]lpsit egr[e]gio opus h[o]c m[u]ltipharie . . . [1398] hic oretur cord[e] ple[n]o.'

17 Ilya M. Veldman, *Marten van Heemskerck and Dutch Humanism in the Sixteenth century*, trans. M. Hoyle, Maarsen, 1977, pp. 148–9 (engraved by Philips Galle).

18 Erwin Panofsky, *Early Netherlandish Painting*, 2 vols, New York, 1971, I, pp. 248, 264–5.

19 M.J. Friedländer, *Early Netherlandish Painting, XII, Jan van Scorel and Pieter Coeck van Aelst*, trans H. Norden, ed. H. Pauwels, G. Lemmers, Monique Gierts and Anne-Marie Hess, Leiden, 1975, Plate 160, p. 67.

20 G. Habich, *Die deutschen Medailleure des XVI Jahrhunderts*, Halle a. d. Saale, 1916, p. 3.

21 *Wenzel Jamnitzer und die Nürnberger Goldschmiedekunst 1500–1700*, Munich, 1985, p. 446.

22 Nicola Coldstream, *Medieval Craftsmen: Masons and Sculptors*, London, 1991, p. 15, Plate 14.

23 E. Buchner, 'Die Werke Friedrich Herlin', *Münchner Jahrbuch der bildenden Kunst*, XIII, 1923, Plates 22–5, pp. 1–51, now in the Stadtmuseum.

24 *Jan van Scorel d'Utrecht: retables et tableaux de son atelier vers 1540*, Utrecht 1977, pp. 72–3.

25 Heinrich Röttinger, 'Burgkmair in Hochzeitskleide', *Münchner Jahrbuch der bildenden Kunst*, II, 1908, pp. 48–52.

26 Coldstream, *Medieval Craftsmen*, Plate 32, p. 35; and for painted portraits of architects see Ingrid Severin, *Baumeister und Architekten: Studien zur Darstellung eines Berufstandes in Porträt und Bildnis*, Berlin, 1992, pp. 185–7.

27 Woods Marsden, *Renaissance Self-portraiture*, pp. 33, and 237.

28 F.W.H. Hollstein, *Hollstein's German Engravings, Etchings and Woodcuts 1400–1700, XXIV: Israhel van Meckenem*, 2 vols, ed. Tilman Falk and compiled by Fritz Koreny, Roosendaal, 1986, I, p. 1; II, Plate 1.

29 Marcantonio Michiel, *The Anonimo: Notes on Pictures and Works of Art in Italy*, trans. Paolo Mussi, London, 1903, pp. 117, 121.

30 Stephen H. Goddard, *The Master of Frankfurt and his Shop*, Brussels, 1984, p. 129.

31 Linda Susan Klinger, 'The Portrait Collection of Paolo Giovio', 2 vols, PhD thesis, Princeton University, 1991, I, pp. 66–8.

32 Klinger, 'Portrait Collection', II, p. 12, del Sarto; p. 22, Bandinelli; p. 28, Belli; p. 110, Leonardo; p. 129, Michelangelo; p. 143, Philandrier; p. 164, Sangallo; pp. 186–7, Titian.

33 Klinger, 'Portrait Collection', II, pp. 129, 186–7.

34 Klinger, 'Portrait Collection', II, p. 71.

35 Sigismondo Fanti, *Triompho* (sic) *della fortuna*, Venice, 1527, see the panel holding painter on fol. B8 recto for 'Raphael Urbinato', but fol. B5 verso for 'Mantegna', and see the easel painting figure on fol. C1 verso for 'Zeusis', but fol. D1 verso for 'Perusino'.

36 Barocchi, *Scritti d'arte*, I, pp. 7–23.

37 Barocchi, *Scritti d'arte*, pp. 7–8, 'Fuit ingenio valde comi, nitido, liberali, vultu autem longe venustissimo, et cum elegantiae omnis deliteaturumque maxime theatralium mirificus inventor et arbiter esset, ad lyramque scite caneret, cunctis per omnem aetatem principibus mire placuit.'

38 Albrecht Dürer, *The Writings of Albrecht Dürer*, ed. and trans. W.M. Conway, London, 1958, pp. 136–41.

39 Dürer, *Writings of Albrecht Dürer*, p. 137.

40 Dürer, *Writings of Albrecht Dürer*, p. 137.

41 F. Anzelewsky, *Albrecht Dürer: das malerische Werk*, Berlin, 1971, pp. 187–9, 212–18, 222–6, 228–30, Plates 95, 99–100, 133–4, Figs 82–4, Plates 141, 147, 148; and Joseph Leo Koerner, *The Moment of Self Portraiture in German Renaissance Art*, Chicago, 1993, in general and Plates 1, 2, 19, 20–2.

42 M. Mende, *Dürer Medaillen*, Nuremberg, 1983, Plate 1.

43 Habich, *Deutschen Medailleure*, p. 82.

44 P. Grotemeyer, *'Da ich het die gestalt': deutsche Bildnismedaillen des 16 Jahrhunderts*, Munich, 1957, p. 29.

45 Habich, *Deutschen Medailleure*, p. 63; Mende, *Dürer Medaillen*, pp. 191–200 catalogues several undated copies, including one dated 1561.
46 Mende, *Dürer Medaillen*, pp. 219–30.
47 Giulia Bartrum, *Albrecht Dürer and his Legacy: The Graphic Work of a Renaissance Artist*, London, 2002, pp. 86–7.
48 F.W.H. Hollstein, *German Engravings, Etchings and Woodcuts, XII*, ed. Fedja Anzelewsky, Amsterdam, 1965, p. 195: 'Cui sua phoeboeae donarunt[ur] munera divinae /quem peperit proprio docta Minerva sinu, /Talis ut hic faciemque suam divinemque decorum/quinque annos decies, sexquoque natus erat. In effigiem albreti durer M. L.'
49 E. Duverger, *Antwerpse Kunstinventorissen uit de Zeventiende eeuw*, Brussels, 1984, p. 19: 'in a round frame'.
50 H. Rupprich, ed., *Dürer schriftlicher Nachlass*, 3 vols, Berlin, 1956–69, I, p. 290: 'Albertus Türer [sic] et ipse Alemanus hac tempestate excellentissimus est et Nurenbergae imagines absolutissimas depingit, quae a mercatoribus in Italiam transportantur et illic a probatissimis pictoribus non minus probantur quam Parasii aut Apellis tabulae.'
51 Rupprich, *Dürer schriftlicher Nachlass*, III, p. 291.
52 Erasmus, *De recta pronuntiatione*, pp. 398–9.
53 Bialstocki, *Dürer and his Critics*, pp. 23–4; and Von Schlosser (1956) p. 274: for example, the Latin translation was reprinted in 1532, 1534, 1535, 1537 and 1557.
54 Rupprich, *Dürer schriftlicher Nachlass*, III, 1969, pp. 466–7.
55 Adam Bartsch, *The Illustrated Bartsch XVI: Early German Masters, Jacob Bink, Georg Pencz and Heinrich Aldegrever*, ed. Robert A. Koch, New York, 1980, p. 295, number 93; J.D. Passavant, *Le Peintre-Graveur*, 6 vols, Leipzig, 1860–64, IV, p. 96, number 139.
56 Rupprich, *Dürer schriftlicher Nachlass*, I, p. 296: 'Honos alit artes'.
57 W. Hoffmann, *Köpfe der Lutherzeit*, Munich, 1983, pp. 38–9, 42–3.
58 Adam Bartsch, *The Illustrated Bartsch XVIII: German Masters of the Sixteenth Centuries*, ed. Jane S. Peters, New York, 1982, p. 367.
59 Bartsch, *Illustrated Bartsch XVIII*, pp. 248–50.
60 T. Falk, *Lucas Cranach: Gemälde, Zeichnungen, Druchgraphik*, 2 vols, Basel, 1974, I, Plate 42, p. 103, Catalogue number 49.
61 Stefania Massari, *Giulio Bonasone*, Rome, 1983, 2 vols, I, Plates 85 d and c, pp. 73–4: 'Qui sim nomen habes satque est nam caetera cui non sunt nota aut mentem non habet aut oculos.'
62 Massari, *Giulio Bonasone*, Plates 85 a and b, pp. 73–4: 'Quantum in natura ars naturaque possit in arte. Hic qui naturae par fuit arte docet.'
63 Ascanio Condivi, *Vita di Michelangelo*, ed. Antonio Maraini, Florence 1927, p. 7.
64 Massari, *Giulio Bonasone*, Plate 87, p. 74.
65 Stefania Massari, *Incisori mantovani del '500 Giovan Battista, Adamo, Diana Scultori, e Giorgio Ghisi*, Rome, 1980, Plate 182, pp. 125–7: 'Michael Angelus Bonarota Tuscorum flos delibatus duarum artium pulcherrimarum humanae vitae vicariarum picturae statuariae que suo penitus saeculo extinctarum alter inventor faciebat.'
66 E. Steinmann, *Die Portraitdarstellungen des Michelangelo*, Leipzig, 1913, Plates 34–5, pp. 39–40.

67 Cesare Cesariano, *Cesare Cesariano*, p. 148; and Giovio in Barocchi, *Scritti d'arte*, I, pp. 7–23.
68 Ariosto quoted and translated in Lodovico Dolce, *Aretino: A Dialogue on Painting*, trans. W. Brown, London, 1770, p. 18.
69 De Holanda, *Four Dialogues on Painting*.
70 Massari, *Incisori mantovani del '500*, p. 75, dated in her view between 1545 and 1550: 'Raphaelis Sanctii Urbinatis pictoris eminentiss. Effigiem Julius Bonasonius Bononien. Ab exemplari sumptam caelo expressit.'
71 Luba Friedman, 'Britto's portrait after Titian's earliest self portrait', pp. 123–44 in Gunther Schweikhart, ed., *Autobiographie und Selbst Portrait in der Renaissance*, Cologne, 1998.
72 Passavant, *Le Peintre-Graveur*, VI, p. 124, catalogue number 4, attributed to Enea Vico or Niccolò della Casa.
73 Massari, *Incisori mantovani del '500*, I, Plate 89c, p. 76.
74 King, 'Artists' houses', pp. 178–9.
75 King, 'Artists' houses', pp. 178–9.
76 Michael D.K. Baxandall, *Painting and Social Experience in Fifteenth-century Italy*, Oxford, 1971, pp. 165–7.
77 Jean Lemaire, *La Plainte du Desiré*, Lyons, 1509, pp. 398–401.
78 Jean Lemaire, *Les Illustrations de Gaule*, Lyons, 1549, pp. 70–1.
79 Bialstocki, *Dürer and his Critics*, pp. 23–4.
80 Elisabeth Dhanens, *De Iconografie der Van Eycks*, Bruges, 1982, Plate 3, p. 67; Musée des Beaux Arts, Dijon.
81 Hubaux and Puraye, 'Dominique Lampson Lamberti Lombardi vita', p. 56.
82 Dominique Lampsonius, *Lamberti Lombardi apud Eburones pictoris celeberrimi vita*, Bruges, 1565, p. 37: 'nisi ex Pamphili illius, qui optimi pictoris magister fuit [Apelles], Leonis Baptistae Alberti Fiorentini, Alberti Dureri, et Pomponii Gaurici praeceptis litterarum studia cum his artibus coniunxerint.'
83 King, 'Artists' houses', pp. 184–5.
84 Giovanni Santi, *La vita e la gesta di Federico di Montefeltro*, ed. L. Michelini Tocci, Città di Vaticano, 1985.
85 Vasari, *Le opere di Giorgio Vasari*, VII, p. 679.
86 Vasari, *Le opere di Giorgio Vasari*, VIII, p. 100; Prinz, 'Vasari's Sammlung', Plate 3, p. 14.
87 Vasari, *Le opere di Giorgio Vasari*, VIII, pp. 159, 192; Prinz, 'Vasari's Sammlung', Plate 4, p. 15.
88 Allegri and Cecchi, *Guida storica: Palazzo Vecchio e I Medici*, pp. 131, 145, 120.
89 Allegri and Cecchi, *Guida storica: Palazzo Vecchio e I Medici*, pp. 303–14.
90 Alessandra Baroni Vannucci, ed., *Jan van der Straet detto Stradano*, Milan, 1997, p. 347. The tapestry is in deposit at the Museo di San Matteo, Pisa.
91 Klinger, 'Portrait Collection', I, pp. 78–9. Vasari, *Le opere di Giorgio Vasari*, VII, pp. 608–9.
92 Vasari, *Le opere di Giorgio Vasari*, VII, pp. 298–303.
93 Vasari, *Le opere di Giorgio Vasari*, VII, p. 307.

94 Vasari, *Le opere di Giorgio Vasari*, VII, pp. 528–9.
95 A. Cecchi, *Giorgio Vasari La Toscana nel '500, principi, letterati, e artisti nelle corte di Giorgio Vasari*, Florence, 1981, pp. 214, 239.
96 Prinz, 'Vasari's Sammlung', pp. 114, 136, 122–3, 134–5, 144, 151.
97 Charles Hope, 'Historical Portraits in the *Lives* and in the frescoes of Giorgio Vasari', pp. 321–8 in *Giorgio Vasari tra decorazione ambientale e storiografica artistica*, Florence, 1985.
98 Cecchi, 'Le case di Giorgio Vasari ad Arezzo e Firenze', pp. 30–56, 56–7. The El Greco group portrait in the *Expulsion from the Temple* may be related to this sort of tribute: see H. Wethey, *El Greco and his School*, 2 vols, Princeton, 1962, I, pp. 68–9.
99 Vasari, *Le opere di Giorgio Vasari*, II, 213–14; John Pope Hennessy, *Paolo Uccello*, London, 1969, pp. 157–8; Franco and Stefano Borsi, *Paolo Uccello*, Milan, 1992, pp. 349–51.
100 Prinz, 'Vasari's Sammlung', pp. 16–17.
101 Prinz, 'Vasari's Sammlung', pp. 18–19.
102 Wulfram Prinz, *Die Sammlung der Selbstbildnisse in den Uffizien: Geschichte der Sammlung*, Berlin, 1971, p. 25.
103 Ridolfi, *Le meraviglie dell'arte*, I, pp. 212, 214–16.
104 Even more ostentatiously they intended to provide an effigy of the painter dressed in his knightly robes. This placed him in the tradition of according wax effigies to persons of noble rank, according to Julius von Schlosser, 'Geschichte der Portraitbilderei in Wachs, ein Versuch', *Jahrbuch der Kunsthistorisches Sammlungen des allerhöchsten Kaiserhauses* XXIX, 1910–11, pp. 171–258.
105 Domenic Lampsonius, *Les Effigies des peintres célèbres des Pays-Bas*, 1572, ed. J. Puraye, Bruges, 1956, especially, pp. 17–19.
106 Lampsonius, *Effigies des peintres*, pp. 26–7.
107 Maria Teresa Cantaro, *Lavinia Fontana Bolognese 1552–1614*, Milan, 1989, pp. 86–7; Catherine King 'Looking a sight: sixteenth-century portraits of women artists', *Zeitschrift für Kunstgeschichte*, LVIII, 1995, pp. 381–406, especially pp. 401–2.
108 King, 'Looking a sight', p. 402.
109 Klinger, 'Portrait Collection', I, pp. 78–9.
110 Klinger, 'Portrait Collection', I, pp. 78–9.
111 Klinger, 'Portrait Collection', II, p. 12, del Sarto; p. 22, Bandinelli; p. 28, Belli; p. 110, Leonardo; p. 129, Michelangelo; p. 143, Philandrier; p. 164, Sangallo; pp. 186–7, Titian. Nicolaus Reusner, *Icones sive imagines*, Basel, 1589, fols R2 verso–R5 verso. The Latin verses were epigrammatic: for example, for Michelangelo it read 'Quid possit Natura arti societa, figuras sculpere Naturam qui docet arte, docet.'
112 Baroni Vannucci, *Jan van der Straet*, pp. 397–400: 'Colorem olivi commodum pictoribus invenit insignis magister Eykius.'
113 For this and many other citations see David Cast, *The Calumny of Apelles*, New Haven, CT, and London, 1981, p. 167.
114 King, 'Making Histories, Publishing Theories', pp. 258, 275.
115 Filarete, Antonio di Piero Averlino, called Filarete, *Filarete's Treatise on Architecture*, 2 vols ed. and trans. J.R. Spencer, New Haven, CT, and London, 1965, I, pp. 259–69.

116 Manuscripts of Pliny the Elder's encyclopaedia were quite numerous: see Lilian Armstrong, 'The illustration of Pliny's *Historia naturalis*: manuscripts before 1430', *Journal of the Warburg and Courtauld Institutes*, XLVI, 1983, pp. 19–39.
117 Andrew Martindale, *The Rise of the Artist*, London, 1972, p. 103, Plate 85; and for a late fifteenth-century manuscript see A. Derolez, *Inventaris van de Handschrift en de Universiteetsbibliothek te Ghent*, 1977, p. 1; Cicero *De inventione*, MS 10, fol. 69 verso, Bibliothek der Universiteet, Ghent. The owner was the Abbot of Saint Bavo in Ghent, 'Raphael de Mercatellis'.
118 G. de Lorris and J. de Meung, *Romance of the Rose*, ed. C. Dahlberg, Princeton, 1971, Plates 47–9; and for the printed example see G. de Lorris and J. de Meung, *Roman de la rose*, Paris, 1494, fol. 2 recto, 'le bon peintre Zeuxis'.
119 *Sotheby's Catalogue, London Lord Mostyn Sale: Manuscripts*, 13. 7. 1920, p. 5, Lot 9, Catalogue number 16, MS. dated about 1470.
120 Giovanni Boccaccio, *Von etlichen Frowen*, Ulm, 1473, fol. LXXXI recto.
121 Cicero, *Officia*, Augsburg 1531, fol. XXXV verso and Cicero, *Vonn Gebüre und Billicheit*, Frankfurt am Main, 1550, fol. XXXV verso.
122 *Primatice Maître de Fontainebleau*, pp. 226–40, especially pp. 230–1; Cecchi and Allegri, *Guida storica*, pp. 323–31, especially p. 331.
123 W.L. Strauss, *The Illustrated Bartsch: Early Italian Masters*, ed. Mark J. Zucker, New York, 1984, XXV, pp. 190–2.
124 John Gage, 'The *locus classicus* of colour theory: the fortunes of Apelles', *Journal of the Warburg and Courtauld Institutes*, XLIV, 1981, pp. 10–11.
125 D. Metzler, 'Renaissance Bildnisse antiker Architekten am Haus eines Stadtbaumeisters in Sélestat', *Antike und Abendland*, XIX, 1973, pp. 146–62; Han Peter Schwarz, *Das Künstlerhaus Anmerkungen zur Sozialgeschichte des Genies*, Braunschweig, 1990, pp. 150–60.
126 Marcus Tullius Cicero, *Tusculan Disputations*, trans. J.E. King, London, 1927, pp. 488–90; and Erasmus Desiderius, *The Collected Works of Erasmus*, 33, *Adages, II, i, 1 to II, vi 100*, trans. R.A.B. Mynors, Toronto, 1991, pp. 22–4 (II. i. 12).
127 Coldstream, *Medieval Craftsmen*, p. 10.
128 King, 'Artists' houses', pp. 178–9.
129 Cecchi, 'Le case di Giorgio Vasari ad Arezzo e Firenze', pp. 30–56.
130 Vasari, *Le opere di Giorgio Vasari*, VII, p. 307.
131 Cecchi, 'Le case di Giorgio Vasari ad Arezzo e Firenze', pp. 56–7.

Patron saints as exemplars

4

A variety of exemplars were available to figurative artists and architects during the sixteenth century. Of special importance were the saints who had been artists and who had been chosen as the patrons of the guilds which organised the lives of builders, carvers and painters from apprenticeship to grave. Guilds and confraternities serving builders and image specialists had honoured saints who were artists since the fourteenth century, and they included Saint Luke, the Four Crowned Martyrs and Saint Eligius. Saint Luke had, according to legend, been a painter, and the Four Crowned Martyrs were believed to have been Christian carvers working for the Emperor Diocletian. Saint Eligius had been a goldsmith before he became a bishop, when he had converted parts of the Netherlands in the seventh century. These devout exemplars were the subject of elaborate narratives, made to accompany the devotional and sometimes the administrative life of guilds and confraternities. Moreover, the new academies of Florence and Rome maintained devotion to Saint Luke and honoured him in their new chapels. Because of their status, artist-saints occasionally figured also on the funerary commemorations of artists, as for example in the vault decoration for the funerary chapel of Andrea Mantegna at Sant' Andrea in Mantua, painted in 1506–16, which shows Luke working at his easel with the other three evangelists.[1]

Saint Luke and the Four Crowned Martyrs were believed to have worked in Roman Imperial times and so they could be shown advantageously, given the passion for ancient art, as skilled ancient practitioners. During the sixteenth century, artists were also able to exploit those features of Saint Luke's biography which might enhance their own status. Luke was reported by Paul to have been a medical doctor, and, of course, he was also a gospel writer. This meant that some painters were able to present him as a painter of faith and of scholarship with literary gifts. Others emphasised his learning in the techniques and styles of ancient art, in anatomy and in astronomy, as a medical practitioner. The Four Crowned Martyrs could be represented as devout Imperial Roman artists too, but without Luke's scholarly refinement, for the legend described them as carving decorative masonry as well as free-standing statuary for the Emperor Diocletian. Eligius had high social status as a goldsmith who had risen to be a bishop, advising King Dagobert I.

Images of artist-saints provided spiritual exemplars for artists, and also for the populace, for, as well as decorating the chambers exclusive to guild members, they might also be carried in procession on the feast days of the saints and on civic occasions, and were used to decorate guild and academy chapels, to which the public often had some access. It seems likely that ordinary viewers, in cities which were not controlled by Protestant reformers, were more likely to know of representations of an artist-saint, than commemorative portraits of contemporary artists, or representations of painting, sculpture and architecture as Practical or Liberal Arts.

Saint Luke the Evangelist as artist and doctor

The representation of Saint Luke as artist appeared first in the western sector of Christendom in 1368 on a Gospel Book painted by Johannes of Troppau. This idea rested on a textual tradition dating from the twelfth century in the western church, when Johannes Diaconus described the image of Christ in the Sancta Sanctorum in Saint John Lateran in Rome: 'Miraculously painted on a certain panel, which Luke the Evangelist drew, but which the power of God completed by angelic means.'[2]

By the mid-thirteenth century this tradition was being cited in the works of leading theologians such as Saint Thomas Aquinas. For example, Saint Bonaventure considered that the fact that Luke had painted Christ and his Mother meant that religious images were ordained by 'divine traditions and apostolic sanctions' (*divinae traditiones et Apostolicae sanctiones*).[3] However, the story was usually treated as a legend, and had no place in the missal or the breviary. It is significant of its status that it was not referred to in the actual life of Saint Luke in the *Golden Legend*, written by Jacopo da Voragine, the Archbishop of Genoa, in the late thirteenth century, which was such a key source (being printed many times and translated into Flemish, German and English before 1600). Rather, Jacopo mentioned it in his life of Gregory the Great. Here, Jacopo recounted how Gregory, in the sixth century, led a successful procession in Rome against the plague carrying, 'the image of Saint Mary always Virgin, which is said to be still at Rome in the church of Santa Maria Maggiore; which image they say was formed by Saint Luke the medical doctor, who was a fine painter.'[4] Whether or not the story was a legend, guidebooks to Rome continued to list Luke's paintings. For example, the author of *Le cose maravigliose de l'alma città di Roma* (Venice, 1565) maintained the traditions of the medieval guidebooks to the marvels of Rome, in citing five pictures by Luke, including the one at the Lateran, 'designed by Saint Luke and completed by the angel'.[5] Leandro Alberti celebrated the painting by Luke in Bologna (Venice, 1579) and Ambrogio Landucci listed all the Roman paintings, as well as many others in Italy (Rome, 1646).[6] In addition, paintings attributed to Luke in locations outside Italy were still being documented by the Jesuit scholar Jacob Gretser in the early seventeenth century (*Syntagma de imaginibus manu non factis deque aliis a sancto Luca pictis*, Paris, 1625).

The legend of Luke as artist was therefore related to the panels which were honoured in churches in Rome, Venice, Padua, Bologna, Prague, Cambrai, Freising and Guadalupe. The high regard for these images stresses the power of the legend, and the aura of prestige surrounding Luke's activities as a painter. These images obtained a wider audience through copies. Twelve painted versions, for instance, were made of Luke's panel at Santa Maria del Popolo in Rome,[7] half of which were made by transalpine artists, for example by Hans Holbein der Älter (*c.*1465–1524).[8] Fifteen were authorised to be taken from the Luke panel at Cambrai soon after its arrival in 1450. Belief in the legend was furthered via woodcuts, as for example in one made at Pforzheim in 1500, which showed the Virgin Mary and in the inscription assured the viewer that 'she was painted also by Saint Luke which sacred image is in Rome'.[9]

Although the majority of paintings attributed to Luke were those showing the Virgin and Child, the Evangelist's oeuvre was more diverse. There were portraits of the Virgin alone as at the Aracoeli, and of Christ as an adult as at the Lateran, as well as Crucifixions.[10] As Cardinal Caesar Baronius reported in his list of pictures by Luke in 1610, 'we have seen images of the Apostles Peter and Paul and even Christ himself represented and preserved in pictures with various colours'.[11] In addition, some sculptures were attributed to Luke – the most famous example being in the Holy House at Loreto. There, by 1554, upon a tablet attached to one of the columns, was the information according to Pier Paolo Vergerio that 'Saint Luke the Evangelist made with his own hands that image in the likeness of the Virgin Mary, which has been within [the house] from that day to this'.[12] The earliest references to Luke as an artist, which originated in texts of the eastern church, had recorded simply that Luke made portraits of the Virgin and Christ.[13] It was only later, and in the western church, that the legend developed that he was assisted by angels when he had got no further than making a drawing.[14]

Reliance on the use of images to accompany worship, and the defence of this practice from the 1520s onwards against Protestant criticism, ensured that representations of Luke as artist were numerous throughout the sixteenth century. Because of the highly vocal and physical attack on the use of images in worship, in many parts of Europe the representation of Saint Luke as artist took on new assertive significance. The legend could be satirised, as for example in a drawing, apparently for a stained glass window, by the Swiss Protestant painter Daniel Lindtmayer (1552–*c.*1607), dated 1574 (when he was still living in Schaffhausen). Lindtmayer ridicules Luke portraying the vision of Mary and the Child, and scorns the legend by including a *putto* on the easel excreting into a pot, and also by suggesting the ignorance of artists who believe in it, by having 'Mark' crossed out and 'Luke' substituted on the artist's halo.[15]

Already, in 1505, one text by a Benedictine monk living near Bonn demonstrated that reverence for Luke as artist could be closely accompanied by admonitions as to the correct use of religious images by the devout. Johannes Butzbach (1478–1526) was Prior of the Benedictine monastery of Laach, and he wrote his manuscript account for the miniature painter Gertrud von Nonnenwurth and the writer Adelheid Rayscop, who were both nuns in the Benedictine convent close to Bonn dedicated to the Virgin Mary. Entitled *Libellus de praeclaris picturae professoribus* (or *Little Book Concerning the Eminent Professors of Painting*), the narrative referred to the work of ancient Roman and Greek artists derived from a reading of Pliny the Elder, including the three women whose fame Boccaccio had spread in his treatise on famous women. Butzbach then moved to Christian artists, praising the use of her veil by Veronica to record Christ's face, and also the painting of Saint Luke:

> Luke is awarded the most blessed status in the gospel as evangelist and medical doctor, and he was a distinguished painter who, one may read, represented, amongst other marvellous images, a painted portrait of the most saintly Virgin Mary Mother of God.[16]

Butzbach then cited paintings by Luke in Rome, and one in Prague which Brother Weit (Vittus) had seen, which were said to have enabled many miracles. Since the time of the apostles, other people who were worthy of commemoration, through occasioning miracles in their lifetime or after death, had been portrayed by painters: 'So as to excite souls to follow the virtues of the saints and so that those who were unlettered might know, as well through pictures as they might through reading, about matters of which they would otherwise be ignorant.'[17] Butzbach referred to the famous dictum of a member of his order, in Gregory the Great, that 'images of saints are the books of the unlettered: *imagines scilicet sanctorum esse libros laycorum*'. Butzbach's concept of Luke as artist is therefore bound up with his account of the central tenets of the church on the use of images. It ends with the warning that the images of the saints must not be adored: 'These images, however, whether painted or sculpted, are not to be adored, but rather it is the things which they designate that should be adored.'[18] Saint Luke and Saint Veronica were therefore seen as the founders of Christian art and associated with correct religious attitudes to paintings and sculptures of holy scenes.

The discussion by Johann von Eck 'on the use by apostles and Luke of images' in his treatise published in 1522 on 'not tolerating the images of Christ and the saints' gives a flavour of the criticism now levelled at images of saints being used in worship – a debate continuing throughout the period.[19] As Protestantism was embraced by many communities, whether permanently or intermittently, during the sixteenth century, the representation of Luke as artist gained new significance. Making and using religious images had been picked out as central tenets of faith. David Freedberg has charted the way in Antwerp, for example, Protestant reformers dismantled guild chapels as political and religious government changed hands during the second half of the century. When Catholic government was re-instated these chapels were rapidly re-decorated. These patterns were repeated in other cities.[20] Theologians raked through the evidence to defend their practices. For instance, the Flemish reformer and theologian Johannes Molanus, publishing in Louvain in 1570, presented the most recent historical evidence for believing that Luke had been an artist. He set great store by the discovery of a fourteenth-century history of the Byzantine Empire by Nicephores. This quoted the sixth-century historian Theodorus Lector, who described how, in the early fifth century, the Empress Eudoxia in Jerusalem had bought an image of the Virgin and Child made by Luke, and had sent it to Constantinople.[21]

The notion that Luke had portrayed the Virgin and Child, with angelic help, fitted well with the information in the New Testament concerning the career of the Evangelist. According to Eusebius's *Ecclesiastical History*, which had been written in the early fourth century, Luke had arrived from his native Antioch, in Syria, towards the end of Christ' ministry. The idea that he numbered among the seventy-two disciples appointed by Christ was expressed in the choice of the Gospel passage relating this episode for the Feast of Saint Luke in the *Missal*: *Luke* 10, 1–9. This passage described how Christ gathered the seventy-two and sent them out two by two to spread the gospel. Jacopo da Voragine's *Golden Legend* – which was available in Flemish, German, English and Latin in the sixteenth century – identified Luke as the unnamed companion of Cleophas, who had met Christ on the road to Emmaeus and shared supper with him after the resurrection.[22] All agreed that he had travelled with Paul in his ministry, and composed the *Acts of the Apostles*. To explain how Luke could write the early sections of his Gospel, Fra Jacopo da Bergamo related how:

> not only was he given evidence by the Apostle Paul, but by the other Apostles as he himself says at the beginning [of his gospel] . . . It is written that he was informed by Mary, the glorious and pure Mother of Jesus Christ, with whom he was on very familiar terms, of those matters which especially pertained to her and which she alone knew secretly, such as the Annunciation.[23]

Paul in the Epistle to the Colossians (*Colossians* IV, 14) had called him 'most beloved medical doctor' (*medicus charissimus*). This and the fact that he was thought to have had written in Greek meant that he was associated with learning. The *Golden Legend* related that he was childless and celibate and travelled in Greece, writing the *Acts* in Achaia.

The beast who symbolised the gospel of Saint Luke – which appears in the *Apocalypse* as *vitulus* ('bullock') (*Revelation*, IV, 4–6), but which was usually referred to as a bull, was often represented as the artist's companion. The creature had been associated with the man, the lion and the eagle since the fourth century CE, following Saint Jerome's discussion in his preface to the translation of Matthew. Jerome had interpreted Ezechial's four creatures (*Ezechial*, X) as forecasting the coming of the four gospels and interpreted the bull in the following way: 'The third [symbol is] that of a bullock, which prefigured that the gospel of Luke began with the priest Zacharias'[24] Luke had begun with the account of Zacharias coming to the temple to cense the altar when he was told of the birth of his son to come, as John the Baptist. Theologians could read the bull as referring to the role of people performing sacrifice, by association with pagan rites in which bulls had been sacrificed by priests. In this convoluted way, the bull could be linked with a gospel which was considered to stress the priesthood of Christ.[25] Others related the bull as sacrificial animal to the theme of Luke's gospel of the sacrifice made by Christ on the Cross.[26]

Luke for artists

The image of Luke as an artist was used in general by the devout because of the panels attributed to him, which were the objects of pilgrimage, and because of his status as one of the evangelists. However, this image had special significance for artists decorating their guild chambers, and chapels. Painters were only one of the groups of workers who belonged to the guilds of Saint Luke; others might include leather workers, glaziers, embroiderers, goldsmiths, clock makers, bookbinders, printers, or makers of organs. This body varied from city to city. Presumably the use of Luke as *the* religious figure standing for all these workers may have given painters some prestige within their institutions.

The guild chamber was the locus of the official acts of the guild: there its elected officers governed many aspects of painters', and sometimes sculptors', working lives. The guild was a small commonwealth demanding dues from every member, keeping its accounts and assisting the needy. Its officials were responsible for justice within the guild, ensuring for instance that workers and work duly contracted to one master were not filched by another. It might also arbitrate in disputes between a member and a patron. The guild controlled the quality of work being produced in its city by restricting the numbers of apprentices per master and setting the standards for achieving the status of master.

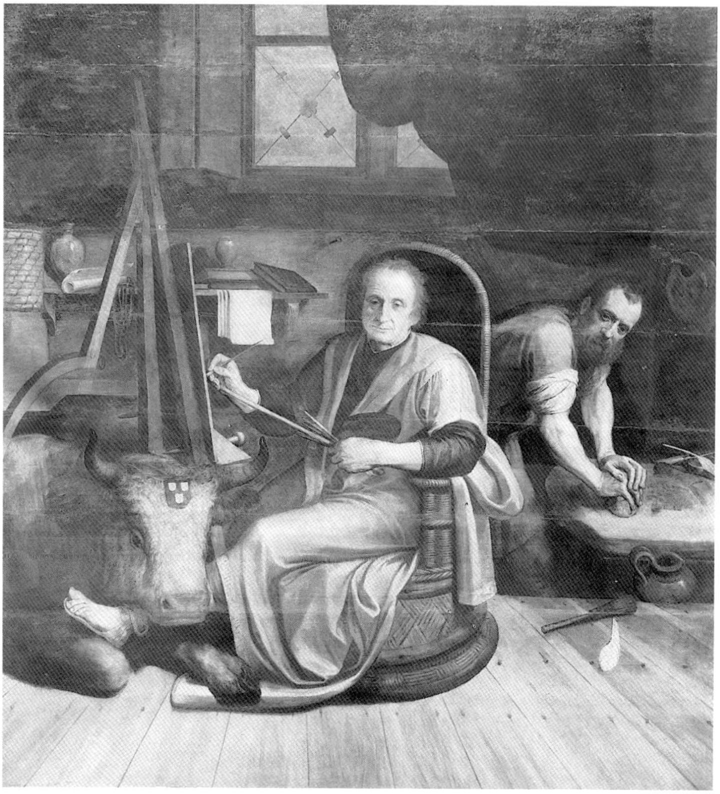

48 Frans Floris, Luke the Evangelist as artist and physician, 1556, 214 × 197 cm, Koninklijk Museum voor Schone Kunsten, Antwerp.

Masters from outside a town could not work without registering as guild members, and thus being vetted, unless they had very powerful patrons.

The guild chamber

One panel survives which was made for a guild chamber for the exclusive audience of guild members (Plate 48). In 1556 Frans Floris gave to his guild at Antwerp for their assembly rooms at the Kolveniershuis ('the house of the crossbowmen') a large panel showing Saint Luke at work with his colour grinder.[27] When Floris painted this picture the guild contained over three hundred workers, and numbers were on the increase throughout the sixteenth century. As with many other guilds, the membership was varied, including here painters, glass makers, mirror makers, harness gilders, engravers, gold- and silversmiths, scribes, illuminators, printers, bookbinders and organ makers.[28] Floris characterised Luke by means of the congenial bull (carrying the shield of the guild on his forehead), which provides the painter with a warm footrest and who places a possessive hoof on his robe. Floris identified Luke as medical doctor by depicting a urine flask basket woven from rush placed to the left of the easel.[29] There is a book and scrolls of paper on the shelves behind him to recall his work as a scholar. Most altarpieces for guilds gave the Virgin and Child an important role in the composition, presumably because of their liturgical significance and the role of the Virgin as intercessor on their behalf. But this panel was designed for the guild chamber so that it could concentrate on Luke himself. Indeed, the vanishing point for the perspectival construction lies behind Luke's hand holding his brushes and palette.

This is a matter-of-fact saint who has rolled up his sleeve to get down to work. Floris engages viewers intimately by having the saint turn towards us, as if we were in the position of the person or vision he is depicting. The colour grinder also gazes out, encouraging a sense of engagement. The saint is represented as a venerable old man in modest surroundings: seated on a wickerwork chair. He is placed on a plain wooden platform raised somewhat off the floor on which the colour grinder is standing. A white quill used as a pen (or even dropped by an angel) lies on this staging. The viewer is left to imagine what Luke is painting. There is minimal reference to classicising motifs; perhaps the sandal of the saint is one exception. Floris had travelled to Italy and filled his drawing books, but chose not to use his antiquising repertoire in this case. There is an oblique allusion to Luke's beatific distinction – in the lighted edge of his chair back, which gives him a version of a halo. Strength, wisdom, contemplativeness, candour: these are the qualities which this deceptively plain composition presents of the first Christian artist. Such qualities might well be admired in the chamber of the guild. Zirka Zaremba Filipczak pointed out that this is one of the first Netherlandish paintings to be signed not as executed by the painter (*fecit*) but as 'devised and executed' (*invenit et fecit*). A gift to one's guild could, in this way present new practices, styles and approaches to all the painters in a city.

A Flemish poem prefacing the Statutes of the Guild of Saint Luke at nearby Ghent in 1540 suggests the knowledge guildsmen had of Saint Luke. He is described as a Syrian, from Antioch, who was 'a young supporter of the twelve apostles' and 'very active in the arts'. He had neither wife nor children but gave himself up to preaching in Achaia (*Dats Grecenlant*, some one has added in the margin), wrote the Acts and his Gospel, and died at the age of seventy-four in Greece.[30]

The guild accounts at Antwerp show that there was continual expenditure on beautifying the chamber. For example, in 1506 a 'Last Judgement' was painted and money was spent on a painting or statue of Saint Luke and the brass candlestick to stand before it in the chamber. In 1526, a 'rich shield' (*rykelyck blasoen*) of the guild's heraldry was made to display at the chamber door.[31] The chamber was the setting for day-to-day administration, and also the scene of lavish celebration especially at the Feast of Saint Luke on 18 October each year. At Antwerp, for example, the account books for 1589 log payment for the vast quantities of food consumed at the Feast of Saint Luke (peas, pepper, saffron, butter, mutton, capons, fish, fruit, capers, sugar, olives, bread, herbs, cherry jam, beer and Rhine wine) as well as outlay on cooks, pastry makers and cauldrons.[32] Guild activity was geared to climax every year at this feast: a month before, the officers were elected, and the accounts audited; a week before, all guildsmen had to have paid their dues. So the image of Luke as artist might be seen as standing for the daily order of the guild and for its occasional plenitude.

Between chamber and chapel

Two processional banners survive which belonged to a guild of Saint Luke. These were carried by members of the guild on the route between their chapel to their chamber, and also on civic occasions, along with the other guilds of the town. These banners depicted the power and the piety of the guild to a large civic audience. In 1545 the Bruges painter Lanceloot Blondeel (1498–1561) signed and dated two large processional banners for his guild, one of which showed Saint Luke at work, while the other represented Saint Luke and Saint Eligius standing on either side of the Virgin enthroned with the Christ child (Plate 49).[33] The guild to which figurative artists belonged in Bruges was jointly dedicated to Luke and Eligius, the Bishop who was patron saint of many metalworkers because he had been a goldsmith. He was also associated with saddle makers, since he was said to have made a saddle for Dagobert I and he had made reliquaries for many saints. His feast day was celebrated on 1 December. According to the *Golden Legend* he wore rich clothing, but bore a hair shirt beneath it, and gave to the poor, as well as converting much of Flanders.[34] The banner is visually rich, the clothing of the saints is opulent, and the whole effect seems to be aimed at impressing outsiders with the wealth of the guild, in contrast to the panel given by Floris to the Antwerp chamber. Blondeel depicted a youthful and vigorous saint rather than the aged and contemplative Luke presented by Floris, again perhaps to stress the strength and activity of the guild. He holds his gospel in his right hand and his panel painting in his left. Blondeel inscribed his initials 'LAB' beside this panel, while the date is placed over the Virgin's head. The illusion is presented of a richly decorated architectural framing to carry the Virgin's throne, as if she were seated in the open air with a curved loggia behind her, and an arched opening below with an intriguing landscape view beneath. Eligius is gorgeously arrayed as a Bishop holding a mallet and a saddle as a smith. Luke is dressed in fur-lined robes of violet and green and arresting orange-yellow hose. The Virgin has a fine Turkish carpet at her feet. Blondeel showed off his knowledge of classicising ornament in the exquisite detailing pictured for the carving.

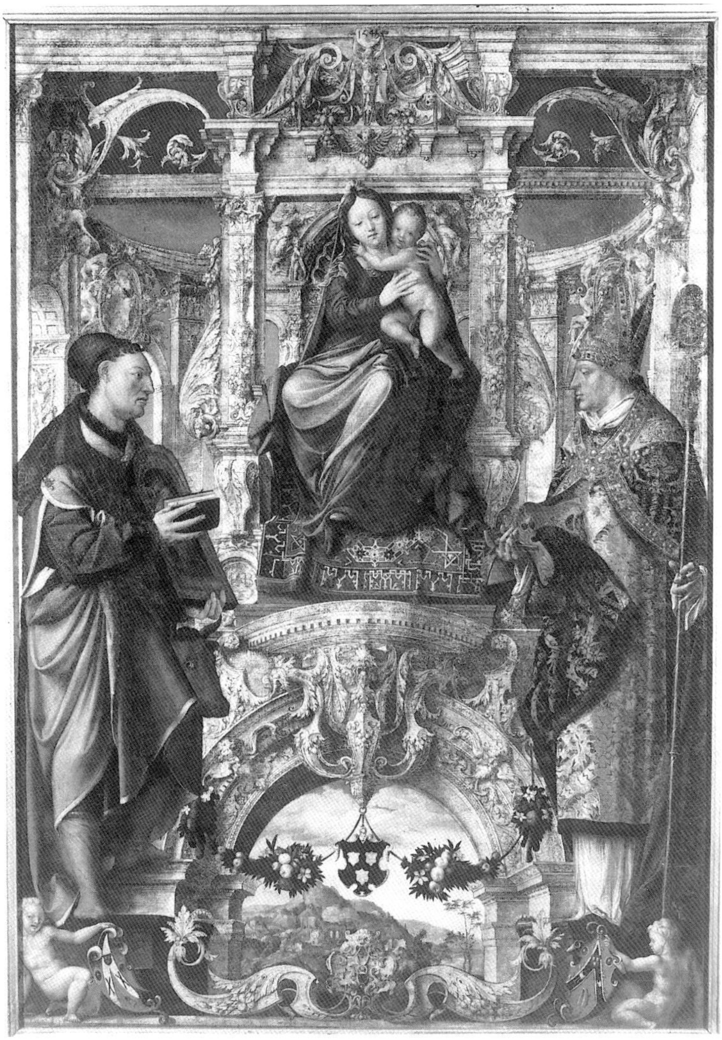

49 Lanceloot Blondeel, Saints Luke and Eligius with the Virgin and Child, 1545, 136 × 95 cm, canvas, Sint Salvatorskerk, Bruges.

The banner seems also to have been designed to satisfy the interests of the guild's varied skill base with the careful depiction of three different shields along the lower border. The guild comprised painters (of shields, panels and cloth) as well as mirror makers, glaziers, saddle makers and harness makers.[35] A central shield is suspended from festoons of flowers and displays the heraldry of three silver shields on a blue ground employed for guilds of Saint Luke all over German- and Flemish-speaking areas within the domain of the Holy Roman Empire. At the feet of Luke is another shield, this time displaying a smith's pincers, two mirrors and one paintbrush. Yet another shield at the feet of Eligius depicts two saddles, more mirrors and a horseshoe. There is evidence, at least from their records, that the Antwerp guild's chapel was decorated with festoons of greenery for the patronal festival, so the motif of garlands at the base of the banner could have echoed the fresh decoration in the chapel. The guild had been able to build its own separate chapel, next to its guild chamber, in Lange Zilverenstraete in Bruges and had instituted a daily mass there from 1455 onwards. This luxurious and flamboyant banner for public display contrasts strongly with the austere modesty of the panel which Floris made for his guild chamber a decade later. Blondeel was an active member of his guild, since he was elected as one of its seven *vinders* (councillors), three times, and in 1560 set up an annual personal subscription in its favour.

Chapels

The four surviving altarpieces – or parts of them – considered to have been made for the chapels of confraternities of Saint Luke between 1500 and 1600 stood, like the banners, for the prestige and piety of the guildsmen in the public eye. Whether donated or commissioned, they had been vetted by those who were, arguably, the most discriminating art critics in their town – fellow professionals. The chapel was the place for private devotion, for funerary commemorations of artists and their families, and for the celebration of the annual feast day, so that altarpieces needed to provide appropriate imagery for prayers on behalf of the dead, as well as a pious panegyric of an early Christian artist. The chapel usually provided a grand 'frame' for any new altarpiece. For instance, the guild records for Antwerp chart the payment in 1493 to Colijn de Coter for decorating the walls of the chapel with bull's heads and angels holding the guild heraldry, with more angels on the vault.[36] Guilds had their own funeral pall: thus in 1502 the Antwerp guild had made 'a new cross of red velvet for our funeral pall and a further four pieces belonging to it representing Our Lady and Saint Luke'.[37]

Records suggest the splendour of the occasions, including the feast day of Saint Luke, when the chapel was cleaned and decorated with greenery and the guild's own vestments and vessels were brought out. Payment was also made for musicians, bell ringers and the priest.[38] Members wore guild dress for such ceremonies and this underlines the way the imagery of Luke as artist called up common beliefs amongst its often variegated workers, and, amongst painters, confirmed notions of shared identity. Whereas the guild administration was masculine, and those registered as widows running workshops were a minority, the confraternity associated with the guild, which honoured the chapel, included the female relatives of masters. Thus, for example, the first mention of the Haarlem guild chapel in 1504 concerns the arrangements for three masses a week for the widow of Floris van Adrichem.[39] The users of the guild altarpieces were therefore diverse. The fact that all the guild altarpieces show Luke portraying the Virgin and Child meant that the compositions were appropriate to numerous feast days in the year, and the patronal festival, as well as catering for the trust in the Virgin as prime intercessor. As Molanus stressed in his influential treatise on the use of devotional images (Louvain, 1570), those of the Virgin, the first of which had been painted by Luke, were exalted second only to images of the Trinity.[40] All but one of these surviving known guild altarpieces, or parts of them, made in the sixteenth century show Luke in a Roman Imperial setting, as an artist skilled in the techniques and forms of ancient art. Consequently, it seems possible that viewers were being encouraged, in these guild pieces, to associate classicising styles with the earliest Christian art forms.

Jan Gossaert's large main panel for the altarpiece of the Mechelen guild chapel, dated 1515, was well calculated to accompany mourning and festivals as well as displaying much that he had learned in Rome (Plate 50).[41] Unusually, this guild chapel in Sint Rombouts was solely for painters, so Gossaert had an exclusive audience.[42] Gossaert

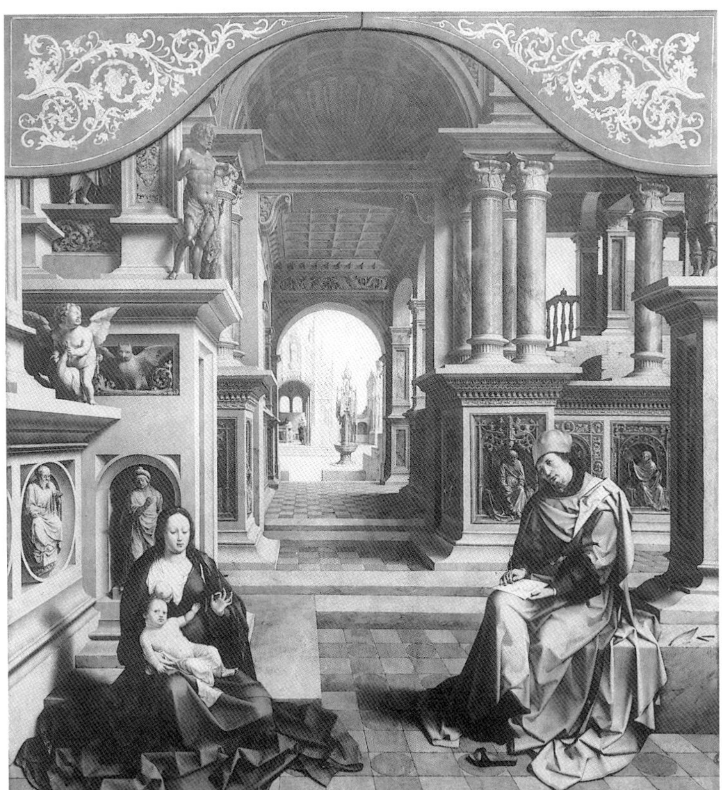

50 Jan Gossaert, Saint Luke draws the Virgin and child, 1515, originally in the Chapel of Saint Luke and Saint John, Sint Rombouts, Mechelen, panel, 230 × 205 cm, Narodni Gallery, Prague.

represented Saint Luke dressed expensively in a red gown and pink cloak with wide fur cuffs and fur collar, while Mary is robed in the traditional blue. Luke is depicted as making a silverpoint drawing of Mary and the Child. On the ledge beside him are chalks and a bird's wing, which viewers might imagine he will use to brush away the chalk sketch, once his silverpoint drawing is in place. Gossaert followed the convention, begun by van der Weyden in the 1430s, of depicting Luke making a drawing, which could be linked to the legend of Luke drawing, and then receiving angelic help to complete the painting. So far this was relatively conventional.

The innovation was to give over considerable compositional space to evoking an antique Roman building as setting for Luke's activities. There is a barrel vault of the sort associated with the contemporary buildings of Donato Bramante in Rome. There is a flat, gilded, coffered ceiling of the type visible, for example, in the fourth-century basilica of Santa Maria Maggiore in Rome. Paired columns are illustrated as the most opulent of supports: features which could be observed, for instance, at the fifth-century mausoleum of Santa Costanza in Rome. Gossaert arranged fictive statuary in this grand building, such as the Capitoline *putto* with a goose in marble, and the Hercules in gilded bronze, which show off his knowledge of antique sculpture.[43] Gossaert (1478–1532) worked in Antwerp and Middelburg, and had travelled to Rome with Philip of Burgundy, Admiral of Zeeland, between 1508 and 1509. As recorded by Gerard Geldenhauer called Noviomagus, 'Nothing delighted him [Philip of Burgundy] more in Rome than those sacred monuments of old which he took care to have painted for him by the most famous painter Jan Gossaert of Maubeuge'.[44] The Mechelen guild was therefore purchasing the very latest vision of what ancient art was like when they commissioned Gossaert, with his specialist expertise, to demonstrate that Luke was an artist working during the Roman Empire who could draw on the best ancient models.

Dramatic lighting from top right provides dark shadows to evoke a sense of deep space. As if in the distance, outside the building, Gossaert depicts a fountain signifying the Virgin's purity (*Song of Songs*, 4, 12). Beyond it Luke appears again, this time in a study, writing his gospel, with the Virgin standing beside him. The linear perspectival system has been arranged with the vanishing point behind the threshold of the study. This little scene recalls the description by Jacopo da Bergamo of the way the Virgin could have informed Luke of early events in her life. The foreground illustrates one of the things which she told him, for along the border of the Virgin's robe Gossaert painted the opening words of the Angel of the Annunciation: 'Ave Maria', which only he had reported in his Gospel. Here was an altarpiece which represented the skills, status and piety of the painters of Mechelen.[45]

Many figurative artists were unable to form a guild which catered for their special representational skills. However, they could establish their own confraternity and commission their own altarpiece, so that they could at least attend to one another's funerary needs and worship together. The figurative artists in Bern had been assigned to the Guild of the Tanners, but in 1503 they got together with the goldsmiths and coiners, and jointly founded the Confraternity of Saints Luke and Eligius, to which painters, goldsmiths, coiners, sculptors, glaziers and embroiderers in silk could all belong. In 1504 they set about commissioning an altarpiece in honour of 'God, His Mother, and especially Saint Anne, the Evangelist Luke and the saintly Bishop Eligius'.[46]

In 1518 the chapel (which was in the Dominican church) was documented as having received some relics of Saint Anne from Lyons, which were duly placed in the altar. However, the Confraternity had earlier commissioned a local painter, Niklaus Manuel Deutsch (*c.*1484–1530), to make their altarpiece, of which the wings survive inscribed with the date 1515 (Plate 51). The inner sides of these wings showed scenes from the life of Saint Anne as mother of the Virgin, and presumably the centre panel honoured Anne and her daughter further. The Confraternity confined their representation of their patrons to the outer sides of the wings. When closed, these displayed Eligius at work on the left, and Luke at work on the right. They seem to share the same work space: a wide loggia supported by classicising columns open to views of the mountains and lakes beyond. Whereas the Bruges guild chose to show him in his episcopal finery, Eligius is represented here seated in a long red robe surrounded by tools, with two other goldsmiths shaping chalices. Niklaus signed his initials as if incised on the pavement of Luke's workshop, and his name and the date on the stone table at which Eligius sits. Niklaus Manuel was a successful painter in his early thirties, with civic status, when he undertook this important commission, who had joined his guild in 1512 and had taken a role in city government as a member of the Great Council from 1510. He depicts Luke portraying the Virgin and Child, as if seen above him in a golden vision. He is painting on a panel with an integral frame and a gold ground reminiscent of the appearance of some of the panels attributed to Luke. No texts ever suggested that Luke had seen a vision, but ever since the 1430s artists had shown him experiencing one to achieve his painting.[47] His colour grinder is in the background, while tools are neatly laid out before him. The message seems to be that both patron saints worked to provide vessels and images for the service of Christian worship. It seems that it is in these terms they were honoured as exemplars at Bern. The allegiance of Eligius and Luke in the image and in the Confraternity itself stress how figurative artists working with textiles, paint, stone, glass and metal might see their work as similar, and also as allied with

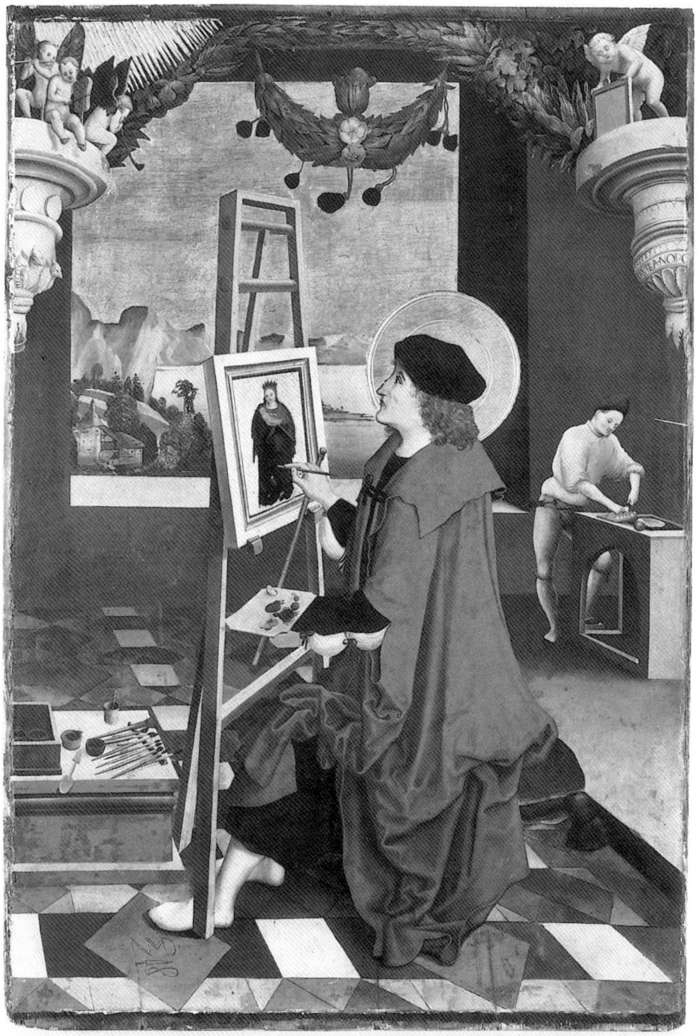

51 Niklaus Manuel Deutsch, Saint Luke, 1515, for the Confraternity of Saints Luke and Eligius, Bern, 118 × 81 cm, Kunst Museum, Bern.

those producing luxury vessels in gold and silver, despite being placed in separate guilds.

That painters might regard their patron saint very piously as their protector, as well as treating him as a moral and artistic exemplar, is suggested in the inscription placed on the altarpiece given by the Haarlem painter Marten van Heemskerck (1498–1574) to his own guild, as a votive gift in hope of safe return from Italy (Plate 52). His and his guild colleagues' trust in Luke's help is explained in the verse in Flemish, which he painted as if pinned below the enthroned Virgin and Child:

This panel is given as a remembrance of Marten van Heemskerck, the painter. He has created it in honour of Saint Luke and out of regard for his fellow guild members [*ghesellen*]. We should thank him, by day and by night, for his kind gift, here before us. Accordingly we pray, with all our strength, that God's grace attend him. Finished in the year 1532 May 23.[48]

The panel was completed just before his departure south to study ancient art and architecture first hand. The altar was in a prominent location at Sint Bavo on the north-west pillar, at the crossing, before the main altar, so the design could reach a general audience.[49] It was also aimed at a body of guild workers and their families which was wider than that at Mechelen, because the Haarlem confraternity drew its members from goldsmiths, iron founders, painters, sellers of colours and of paintings, engravers, glass painters, illuminators, sculptors, embroiderers, glaziers, clock makers, bookbinders, printers and organ makers.[50]

Like Gossaert, van Heemskerck advertised the classicism appropriate to images of the New Testament.[51] While Gossaert had illustrated what ancient architecture and sculpture looked like, however, van Heemskerck went one step further and presented the Virgin and Child with Luke almost as if they were themselves part of a coloured Roman

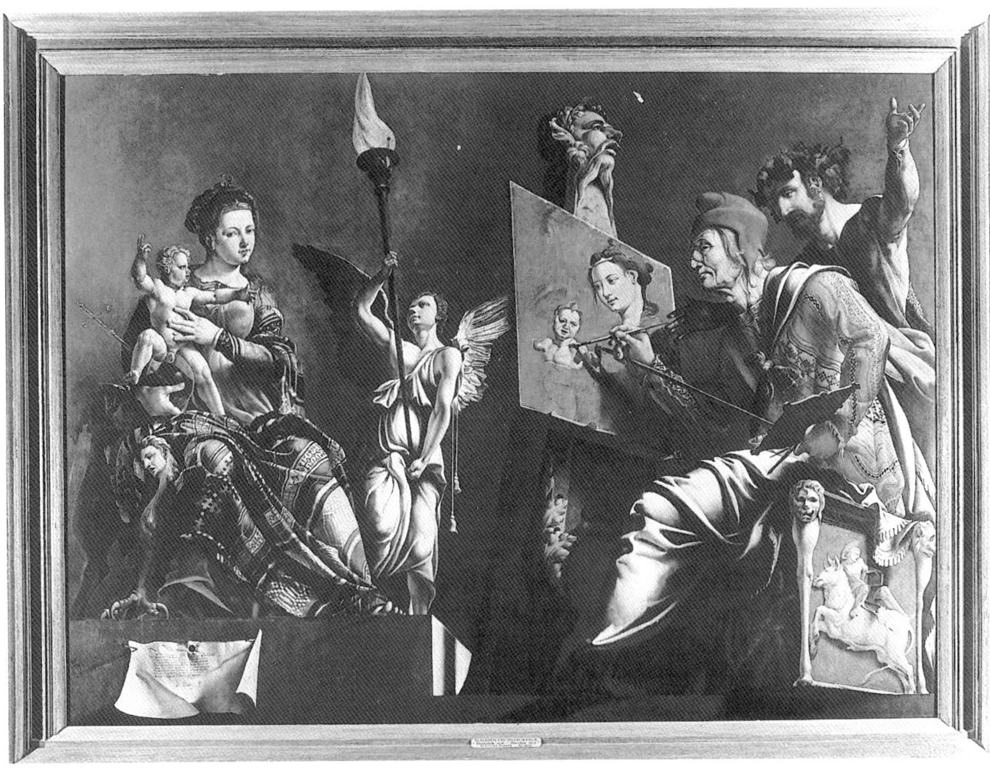

52 Marten van Heemskerck, Saint Luke painting the Virgin and Child, 1532, Frans Hals Museum, Haarlem.

relief. Van Heemskerck depicted his holy figures as if in classicising costume, with the easel stand resembling an ancient herm. The saint's seat is adorned with the classicising relief of the bull carrying away Saint Luke on its back, reminiscent of Jove carrying off Europa. Erwin Panofsky suggested:

> Since, we recall the *Ovide moralisé* interpreted Europa as a human soul, and the Bull as Christ, both these departures from tradition are not as strange as they may seem: as Luke the Evangelist obeys the dictates of the holy Spirit, so does Luke the painter, like every true artist, obey the dictates of Plato's divine frenzy.[52]

An angel, resembling a winged Victory from a Roman triumphal arch, holds a lighted torch. It is possible that as well as quoting classicising forms van Heemskerck also wished to allude to classicising ideas about art during Luke's times. The ivy-wreathed figure to the right might refer to the equivalence of painting and poetry. Van Mander in 1604 was the earliest writer to discuss the meaning of this figure:

> Behind Saint Luke stands a sort of poet with his head crowned with a wreath of leaves of the pea plant or of ivy, and it rather looks as if it could have been a portrait of Marten himself at that time. But whether he meant this to say that painting and poetry are related and painters need to have a poetic, inventive, spirit, or whether he wished to express that this scene was itself an invention I do not know.[53]

A reference to the affinity of painter and poet seems possible, since poets were shown with wreathes of ivy and laurel. The idea was current north of the Alps, as Johannes Butzbach had quoted the view put forwards by Horace in his *Art of Poetry*, in 1505: 'Obviously by study you may be as great in painting as in letters, and equal strength is usually required for these talents.'[54] Van Heemskerck could have set the scene at the time of Christ soon after Horace was writing.

Like Gossaert's altarpiece, van Heemskerck's design is a demonstration of pictorial virtuosity. We see this in the detail, such as the *trompe l'oeil* depiction of the transparent glass orb imagined for the universe held by Christ. It is also achieved in the challenge of presenting the scene as if in semi-darkness. Here van Heemskerck gave a new twist to the tradition that Luke had angelic assistance in painting the Virgin and Child, by showing an angel lighting the scene.

According to van Mander the panel originally had an apex which included a parrot in a cage; Rainuld Grosshans, with reference to near contemporary emblem books, has suggested that this might have referred to eloquence. Such interpretation might relate to any comparison of painting with poetry, since poetry – the ultimate decoration of words – was sometimes regarded as a branch of rhetoric. Luke, as painter and writer, was a good example of such claims. Grosshans also pointed out that the parrot could have represented an admonition to apprentices because it was associated with the adage 'Necessity forces the pupil to learn well'.[55] Others, however, have proposed in contrast that the parrot signified the immaculacy of the Virgin Mary.[56] Whatever the debate about such details, it is evident that van Heemskerck left behind him an altarpiece which demonstrated both how radical a shift might be expected concerning the way that the scenes of the New Testament were now to be imagined, and how rigorous and antiquarian the research might need to be for modern artists to realise the new vision of the pristine past in paint. Van Heemskerck continued to be a committed member of his guild. On his return to Haarlem, he was elected as *vinder* (councillor) of his guild in 1551 and 1552, and as *deken* (deacon) of it in 1554. He was church warden of Sint Bavo from 1552 to his death in 1574 and was buried in the church.[57]

On his return from Italy in 1536, van Heemskerck had created a sufficient reputation for the Guild of Saint Luke at Delft to commission him to paint the altarpiece for their guild chapel (Plate 53).[58] Again, van Heemskerck used this opportunity to emphasise that Luke was an artist of the Roman Empire, and could be an exemplar for producing Christian art in the latest classicising styles. However, he went further and made Luke's medical knowledge, as it related to modern artists' need to understand anatomy, a major feature of his composition. Emphasis on Luke as doctor, as well as painter and writer, opened up the possibility of associating him with new intellectual ambitions for artists, in studying anatomy and the sciences of the quadrivium. The earliest visual image to make this medical link had been the illuminated Gospel Book made by Johannes of Troppau in 1368, but the first large-scale example dates from about 1520 and is attributed to the Antwerp artist Quentin Metsys.[59] No artist had yet referred to Luke's supposed anatomical knowledge. It was van Heemskerck who exploited the idea to make Luke the exemplar for artists who wanted to respond to Italian calls for artistic expertise in human physiology.

The guild at Delft, unusually, concentrated on figurative specialists, such as the Mechelen guild which had commissioned Gossaert. It comprised painters, sculptors, stained-glass workers and embroiderers.[60] While the Delft guild had been founded in 1434, when a chapel dedicated to Saint Luke was founded in the New Church, the whole church had been damaged by fire in 1536, and the city council had decreed that each affected guild should devote half their income annually to replacing their chapels.[61] The guild moved quite slowly and it was not until 1550 that van Heemskerck arrived in person to supervise the installation of his commission.[62] He was no stranger to Delft, as he had spent part of his apprenticeship years there in the workshop of Jan Lucas.,[63] who had been head of the guild in 1540–41 as well as active in the general refurbishment of the New Church, and who was therefore perhaps in a position to recommend van Heemskerck.[64]

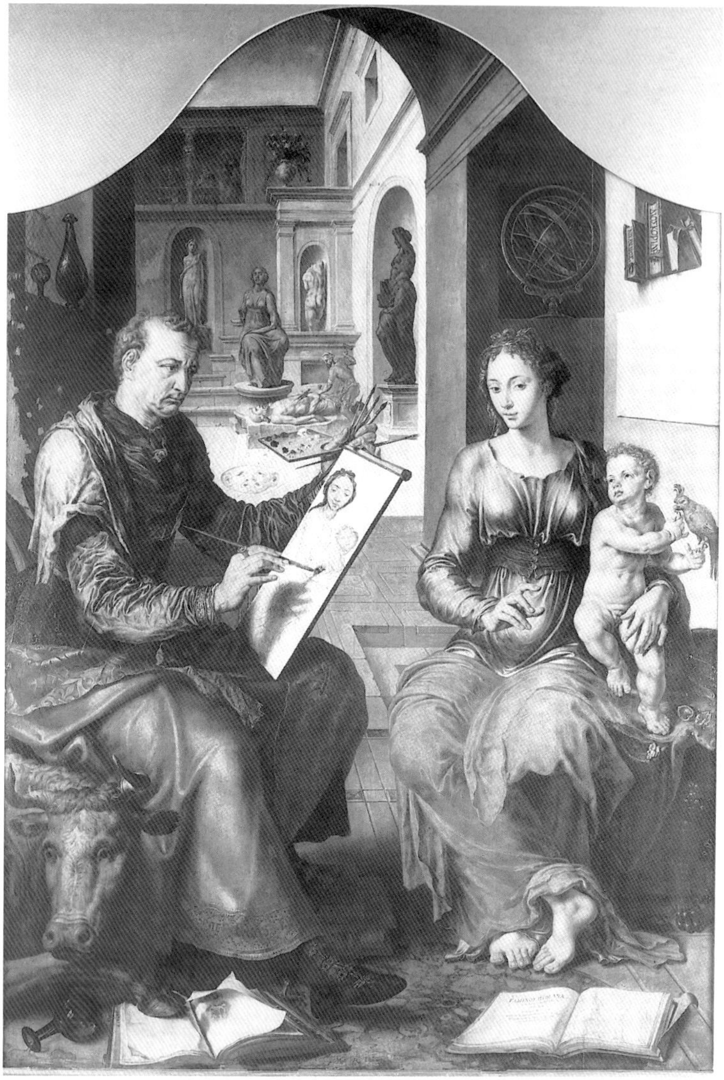

53 Marten van Heemskerck, Luke the Evangelist as painter and doctor, 1550, 158 × 144 cm, Musée des Beaux Arts, Rennes.

In the altar panel, van Heemskerck summed up for his fellow image specialists what he had learned in Italy, of the new 'academic' programme of studies, with its concern for the study of antique art and architecture, and human physiology. Van Heemskerck drew extensively on his Roman sketchbooks for the setting and props appropriate to depicting a Roman Christian workshop. For the courtyard in the background, he used the cortile of the Palazzo Sassi in Rome with its collection of antiques.[65] In the centre he painted a 'Triumphant Rome, seated and larger than life' as described by Ulisse Aldrovandi in his account of the Palazzo Sassi, printed in 1556. The statue has since been identified as a seated Apollo, but for van Heemskerck and his contemporaries it personified Rome herself, and was the centrepiece of the Sassi collection. Such a personification could suggest the artistic prowess of Rome in the time of Luke, as well as its status as the religious capital, for contemporaries in Delft.[66] He draws attention to this statue by having the vanishing point of the linear perspectival construction focus behind it. He added a grotesque drain taken from his drawing of the Palazzo della Valle in Rome.[67] He created a loggia whose columns are caryatids reminiscent of those in the latter drawing. In this loggia he placed men working at tables, from which hang drawings or engravings. As if in front of 'Rome Triumphant', van Heemskerck depicted a sculptor carving a supine statue, which recalls his drawing of the Jupiter at the Villa Madama.[68] It was in this way, with statuary laid down, that contemporary sculptors worked. Possibly this is included, like the figures in what seem contemporary sixteenth-century dress drawing in the loggia, to make the image relevant to the sculptors who belonged to the guild in Delft. Equally, van Heemskerck may have wanted to show that Luke was working with a large community of artists in a living tradition of (ancient) art. Possibly, the statuary in the *cortile* is intended to suggest a sculptor's workshop, with statuary at various stages of completion. As with Gossaert, the architectural style is reminiscent of the austere forms introduced by Bramante to Rome, and not the decorative and delicate motifs invented by Blondeel – who had not visited Rome.

Van Heemskerck also suggested the importance of anatomy and learning in general for the artist in this altarpiece. Ilja Veldman identified the scholarly books in Luke's study. At base right there are references to the ancient study of anatomy: van Heemskerck depicts a book open at the feet of Mary which shows female anatomy, and whose Greek inscription pronounces it to be Galen's treatise *On Anatomical Procedures*.[69] Van Heemskerck's drawings were derived from the anatomical illustrations of the works of Galen by the Brussels doctor Andreas Vesalius, printed in Venice in 1541–2.[70] He seems unaware that Galen post-dated Luke. Other details stress the scholarship of Luke. Above the Virgin and Child is a shelf on which are four books: one is the *Herbal* of Dioscurides and another is a treatise on poisons and antidotes by Nicandros, both of which could plausibly have been in Luke's library. On a nearby shelf van Heemskerck depicted an armillary sphere, which points to Luke's interest in astronomy, with special reference to its use in calculating the best times to give medicine.[71] In the foreground the bull has tipped over a glass urine flask. Saint Luke even rests his left foot on a pile of books. Van Heemskerck represents Luke and the Virgin in clothing, poses and proportions which compare well with the statuary he depicts in the courtyard. The Virgin is plainly dressed with some parallels with 'Rome Triumphant' in the high waist, the body visible beneath the clothing, and the pose with the ankles crossed and the knees apart. This conjunction could demonstrate the notion that ancient Greek and Roman sculpture represented ideals appropriate for indicating the divine beauties actually possessed by persons of spiritual distinction such as Mary and Christ.

Here is an altarpiece which is something of a treatise in paint. In selling 'academic' ideas it has some parallels with the didactic engraving labelled the 'Accademia of Baccio Bandinelli', which shows artists at night school in Rome at the Belvedere, drawing classical statuettes. This was issued around 1531 and is attributed to a follower of Marcantonio Raimondi.[72] The guild seems to have placed Paul's statement about Luke from the *Epistle to the Colossians* 4, 14, on the altarpiece frame, since the words *salutat vos Lucas medicus charissimus* ('Luke the beloved doctor of medicine salutes you') are recorded as being inscribed on the frame of the panel in 1705, when the picture is first documented. These words were read in front of the panel to the confraternity, as one of the lessons prescribed for the Feast of Saint Luke every year.[73]

There remain two puzzles. One is the significance of the second open book at the feet of Luke, whose pages are blank save for a blot. Perhaps this book is the one in which the Gospel will be written. The other puzzle is that the Christ child is holding a parrot which he is feeding with walnuts. Interpretations have ranged from eloquence, to learning well, to the immaculacy of the Virgin, including the role of Christ in the Passion.[74]

Van Heemskerck offered Luke as the exemplar of Christian artists, showing him replete with knowledge, which it was the modern artist's ambition to acquire. The appearance of the panels purporting to be by Luke, in the style of Byzantine icons, which we have seen were major carriers of belief in the legend, was completely ignored in order to prioritise this message. In his panel, of course, van Heemskerck took care to combine statements about the new agenda for Christian art education with the traditional functions of a confraternity altarpiece.

The final surviving Netherlandish altarpiece made in the sixteenth century for a guild was placed over the altar of the guild chapel at the cathedral in Antwerp in 1602. Since the earlier panel had been removed during the period of iconoclasm, the guild needed to re-decorate its chapel. The centre panel was painted by the seventy-one-year-old former pupil of Frans Floris, Marten de Vos (Plate 54). The wings were by Marten Pepijn (1575–*c*.1643) and Otto van Veen (1556–1629) and represented, when open, Luke preaching and Saint Paul accompanied by Luke before the ruler of Caesarea; when closed, they depicted all four evangelists. Marten was a committed guild member who had led his guild during the period 1571–2. The chapel of Saint Luke was in the cathedral at Antwerp and it was there that Marten was buried in 1603. He had travelled to Italy and visited Rome, Florence and Venice,

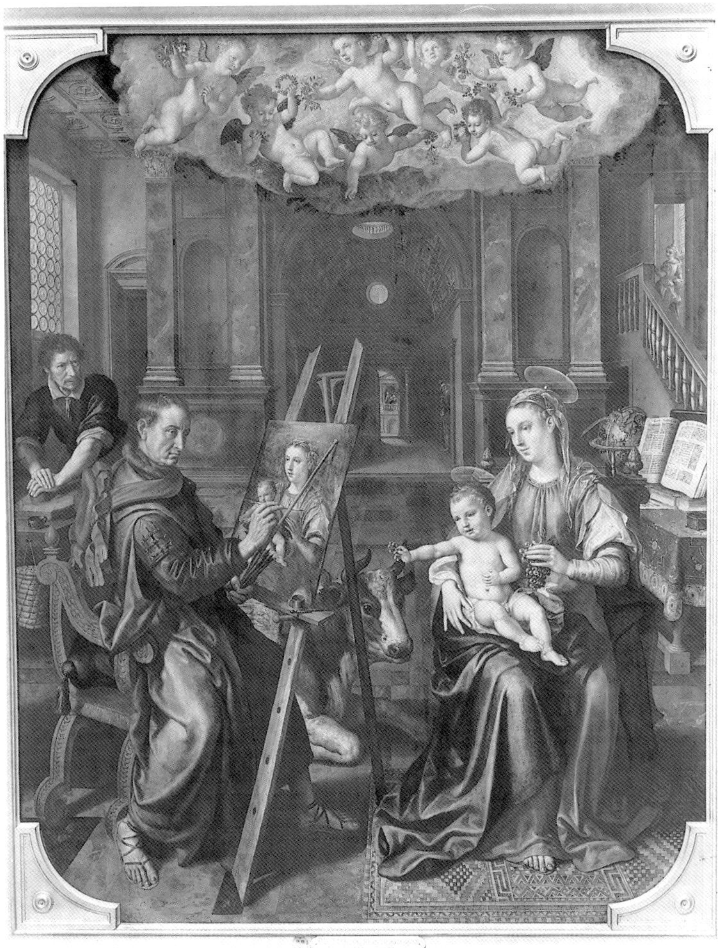

54 Marten de Vos, *Saint Luke the Evangelist painter and doctor*, oil on panel, 1602, Musée Royale des Beaux Arts, Antwerp.

between 1552 and 1558, so that he was able to evoke the opulent classical interior of Luke's palatial setting with its freckled marble walls with confidence. Marten picks up the theme of the learned Luke in the representation of the globe and books on the table to the right, while Luke's medical qualification is alluded to in the urine flask basket, which hangs from the colour grinder's table on the left.[75] There is some reference to classical Roman costume, for instance in Luke's sandals, but also a flavour of contemporary fashions, for example in the dress of the colour grinder, while the Virgin and Child are favoured with an expensive contemporary Turkish carpet. The presence of a bevy of angels, at the apex of the panel, suggests that Luke had angelic help in painting the Virgin and Child. Marten's panel gives evidence of continuity in the presentation of Luke as both as an intellectual and as a devout model for artists.

Throughout the sixteenth century in the Netherlands, Saint Luke was identified with the profession of painting. Thus, for example, the marriage portrait of the Master of Frankfurt, dated 1496, was labelled as that of a painter by means of the shield of the Guild of Saint Luke at its apex held by the bull of Saint Luke.[76] So at the end of the period the frontispiece for the first edition of van Mander's *Het Schilderboek* telling the stories of the painters of Germany and the Netherlands (Aalkmaar, 1604) featured Luke's bull at its centre.

In Italy, neither guilds nor confraternities honouring Saint Luke had quite the civic importance accorded them in the Netherlands, and expenditure of skill and money was not so lavished on representing Luke as artist, by organisations of artists. For instance, Florentine painters and sculptors had belonged to the Confraternity of Saint Luke since the late fourteenth century. The early Confraternity had served painters, goldsmiths, saddlers and sculptors, who wanted some statement of religious and social identity independent of the larger guilds under which they were severally subsumed (the painters, for instance, belonged to the guild of the Medici e Speziali). This Confraternity had its chapel in Santa Maria Nuova, which had been adorned with an altarpiece by Niccolò di Piero Gerini in 1383. This had shown the men and women of the Confraternity kneeling in the *predella* with Saint Luke painting the Virgin and Child above them.[77] When the first Accademia del Disegno was constituted in 1563, it grew as a professional and didactic association out of this Confraternity of Saint Luke. The Confraternity had lost membership during the early sixteenth century, and in order to revive it the sculptor and Servite brother Montorsoli obtained permission to convert the old chapterhouse of Santissima Annunziata into the Confraternity's chapel and burial place. As the only association which unified figurative specialists, otherwise separated in the guild system, it was the model for the secular institution of the Academy, which Montorsoli helped to set up soon afterwards. In the first decade of the existence of the Academy, a beginning was made on decorating this funerary chapel for all the members of the Academy. A large altarpiece depicting the Trinity was painted on the long wall of the chapel opposite the original entrance. This was related to the fact that it was on the Feast of the Trinity in 1562 that Montorsoli had instituted funerary commemorations, when Pontormo had been re-buried here. Possibly he was following the original dedication of the altar, whether that of the Servite chapter, or the Benizi family who preceded the artists in patronage of the chapel.[78] This was completed by 1571 and is attributed to Bronzino.[79] With the repositioning of the entrance in the nineteenth century, the role of the original altarpiece was obscured. On the short walls of the chapel the academy decided to place mural decorations. On the right as you face the altar was shown Solomon as builder, and on the left was depicted Luke as painter. These have been

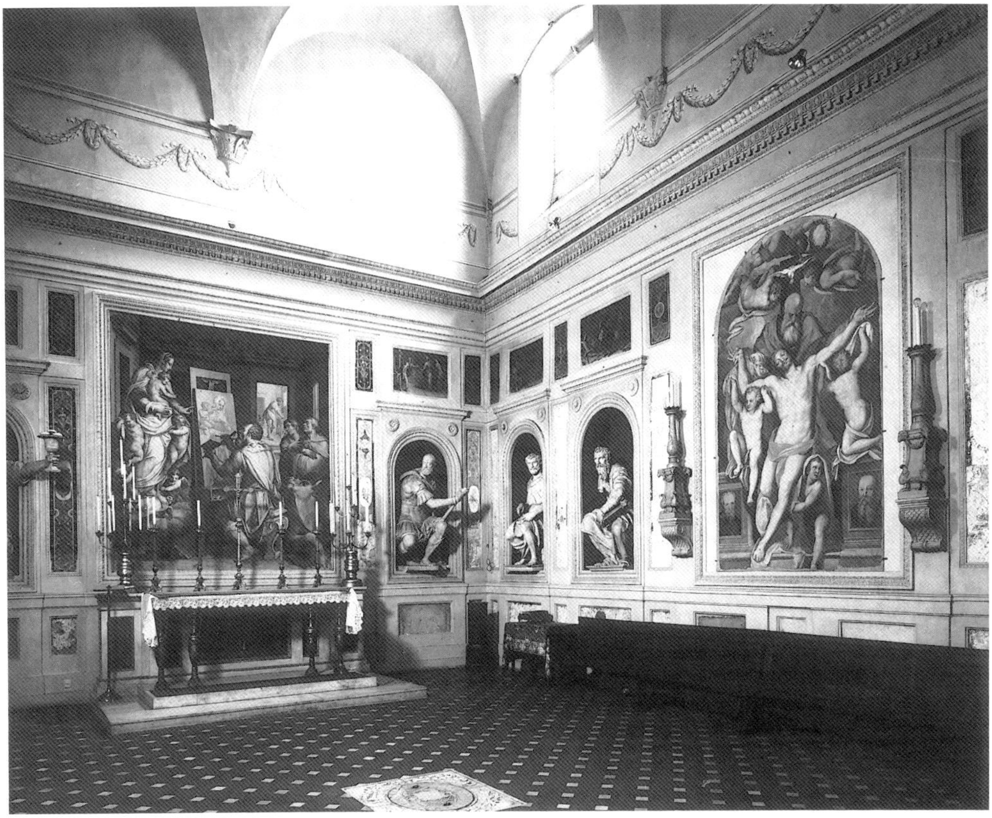

55 Giorgio Vasari, *Luke painting the Virgin and Child in a vision*, 1571, Chapel of the Confraternity of Saint Luke attached to the Academy, Santissima Annunziata, Florence.

attributed to Santi di Tito (1536–1602) and Alessandro Allori, on the design of Vasari (Plate 55).[80] Saint Luke is represented as seeing the Virgin and Child in a vision as he paints them, and as accompanied by his colour grinder. The setting is an austere classicising workshop. Uniquely, two male bystanders are portrayed behind the bull. They could perhaps signify two of the seventy-two disciples sent out in pairs, according to the Gospel reading for the Feast of Saint Luke, to proselytise. The fact that this is a mural and not the altarpiece helps to explain why, as in the Floris panel, Luke was placed centre as the focus of the design.[81] The academicians did not want Luke on their seal either, but rather, some symbol of the concept of the arts of 'design'. Presumably the Trinity, with its theological reference to 'three persons in one', was better suited to an Academy which unified the three arts of painting, sculpture and architecture than the (perhaps divisive) imagery of the Evangelist painter.

In contrast to the Florentine academy, the Roman academy, founded in 1593, did at least take the name of the Accademia di San Luca. The confraternity associated with the new academy had taken over the church of San Luca e Martina from the older Confraternity of Saint Luke, whose illuminated statutes as approved by Julius II in 1512 survive. (They had shown the confraternity members kneeling before Luke as he wrote his gospel.) This older confraternity had had its chapel at the tiny church of San Luca near Santa Maria Maggiore, until this had been demolished in 1587.[82] In 1588 the slow process of beautifying Santi Luca e Martina began for the original confraternity, but meantime, when the Roman academy finally got under way in 1593, the transformed academic confraternity still met in a modest room by the church, whose focus was an altarpiece of Saint Luke as painter, attributed to Raphael. This panel is documented in the earliest records of the academy. The altarpiece is surmised to have originally been placed in the earlier church of San Luca, and to have been made by a follower of Raphael. As well as representing Luke painting the Virgin and Child appearing to him as if in a vision, it also shows an onlooker to our right, wearing early sixteenth-century dress, and resembling posthumous portraits of Raphael. The panel was so highly prized as the work of Raphael that, in 1601, unsuccessful attempts were made to sell it. Despite such efforts, the new Roman academy maintained its devotion to the traditional focus of Christian artists. In other ways, however, the Roman academy resembled the Florentine academy in seeking new kinds of imagery for its official seal.

Representations of Luke as artist therefore decorated chapels for guilds and confraternities which included artists, and were employed for daily devotion, group celebrations and funerary rites. In some cities (such as Bern and Florence), where figurative and decorative specialists were allocated to separate guilds according to the media they worked on, artists and their families were able represent their sense of affiliation via confraternities dedicated to the patron saints of artists. Images of Luke as artist might also, in the case of the banners, show off the wealth and prestige of a guild or confraternity to a civic audience. In the cases of the altarpieces for Mechelen, Haarlem and Delft, the subject matter was exploited to advertise a new classicising and scholarly agenda for artists, both to the guildsmen and women, and also to the wider public who entered the church. In addition, following the protestant challenges of the 1520s, representations of Luke as artist were likely to be associated with the defence of the use of devotional images in rite and private prayer.

The Crowned Martyrs

The cult of the Crowned Martyrs was exclusive to sculptors, masons and builders, so that most surviving works probably did have some artistic connection whether or not this connection can be documented. Following confusion concerning their legend, which was clarified during the sixteenth century, guilds and confraternities had traditionally been dedicated in the name of the 'Four Crowned Martyrs'. As Luke was an evangelist he was represented in many contexts, and he was the more prestigious patron for artists to have. Representations of the Crowned Martyrs show the range of works they were thought to have produced and included building, as well as ornament and statuary. The emphasis is on the piety of the martyrs, who refused to make a cult statue to be worshipped of itself for Diocletian. They had been happy to build for the Emperor and make all types of decorative carving for his palace, before he had issued his final unacceptable command. The Martyrs were therefore important models for the Christian use of images, since it was considered allowable to make images of divine persons, as long as statues only reminded worshippers of the one God to whom they should pray. This was an important theological ruling, in didactic terms, for artists to understand. The legend of Saint Luke could also be attached to warnings about the misuse of religious images. With the Crowned Martyrs however, the correct usage of statuary of the deity and his saints was more central to their story. Nevertheless, their status as mason-sculptors, as well as statuary makers, in the legend, seems to have meant that they were not quite as attractive for socially ambitious artists as was Saint Luke the scholar and doctor. There is evidence, in one city at least, that sculptors of statuary, who had traditionally belonged to the Guild of the Four Crowned Martyrs, were keen to move into the Guild of Saint Luke. In 1593 the Antwerp statuary carvers began a lawsuit, which they eventually won in 1607, to be allowed to belong to the Guild of Saint Luke along with the painters, and to be saved from having to register with the Guild of the Four Crowned Martyrs.[83] The Martyrs may have been seen also as a conservative model of group-working, since they had operated as a team. All in all they were perhaps not necessarily such desirable models as Luke for any architects or statuary makers who wanted to stress their individual talent and their learned potential.

The Four Crowned Martyrs were first cited in the fifth-century Leonine Sacramentary *In Natalis Quattuor Coronatorum* as saints whose feast was celebrated in November. By the sixth century they had a church dedicated to them in Rome; the late sixth-century Gregorian Sacramentary gave their feast day as 8 November. During the next century their cult spread as far as Canterbury, where a church was dedicated to them.[84] In the seventh-century Roman guidebook *De locis sanctis*, the pilgrim learned that the Four Crowned Martyrs were buried at the via Labicana. It listed their names as Claudius, Nicostratus, Simpronianus, Castorius (adding a fifth in 'Simplicius'). In contrast, the seventh-century martyrologium attributed to Saint Jerome listed only the first four saints. The earliest manuscript of the legend dates from the eighth century and is narrated by a Greek land surveyor called Porphyrius, telling the story (supposedly in the fourth century) of the martyrdom of five sculptors under the Emperor Diocletian in 306 BCE. Porphyrius's quotations of pre-Vulgate versions of the Gospel of Saint Matthew support an early date.[85] He announces that he is telling the story of four sculptors – Claudius, Nicostratus, Simpronianus and Castorius – who were 'marvellous in the art of masonry' (*mirificos in arte quadratoria*).[86] The sculptors were Christians working in Pannonia for Diocletian, on the eastern Adriatic coast, who 'sculpted in the name of the Lord'. These sculptors delighted the Emperor by making out of a single block of marble 'a statue of the Sun with his chariot'. They were joined by a fifth sculptor called Simplicius and together they made columns with their capitals, vases and basins for Diocletian's new temple, from porphyry – that is the hardest and most valuable stone to work. At this point, Simplicius was baptised as a Christian by Bishop Cyrillus. All five sculptors were now ordered to make porphyry basins with ornament of little figures, 'fruits and foliage' (*cum malis et herbacantis*). The delighted Emperor now demanded 'Victories, Cupids, and more vases to be made, and especially a [figure of] Aesculapius' (*iussit Victurias et Cupidines et concas iterum fieri, maxime Asclepium*),[87] but the Christian sculptors refused to carve the cult statue of Aesculapius, as being a pagan idol, and were handed over to the jurisdiction of the tribune Lampadius, who attempted to beat them to death. Lampadius was struck dead by demons, and the five sculptors were goaded to worship a statue of Apollo. On their refusal, on 8 November 306 BCE, they were placed alive in lead coffins and thrown into a river.

The reason why these five sculptors were termed the 'Four Crowned Martyrs' was because they had been confused with four soldier martyrs who had been killed a year later, on 8 November, by Diocletian, for refusing to worship a pagan statue. Diocletian had returned to Rome and ordered another temple to Aesculapius to be built, at which Roman soldiers were to sacrifice. Four *cornicularii* (adjutants or trumpeters) refused to make sacrifice to Aesculapius, and were scourged to death on 8 November 307. Their bodies were thrown into a field where dogs could eat them, but Saint Sebastian and Pope Miltiades buried them on the via Labicana. Since they had been martyred on the anniversary of the death of the sculptor saints, the Pope decided to commemorate them as the *quattuor cornicularii* (four trumpeters) under the first four names of the five Pannonian sculptors.

These martyrdoms were referred to briefly in the *Golden Legend*. There, Jacopo da Voragine told how the Four Crowned Martyrs were soldiers called Severus, Severianus, Carpoforus and Victorinus and were beaten to death by Diocletian. Since Pope 'Melchiades' did not at this point know their names, he decided to honour them along with the five named Pannonian sculptors who had refused to make, or sacrifice to, a pagan cult statue. These sculptors had been placed in lead coffins and thrown into the sea. 'And though their names were afterward found and known, yet for the usage they be always called the Four Crowned Martyrs'.[88] Guilds, confraternities of builders and carvers and individual builders and sculptors therefore honoured their patrons as the 'Four Crowned Martyrs', sometimes unaware that the legend described five sculptors because the soldiers and sculptors were commemorated on the same feast day. The religious images they commissioned sometimes represented just four sculptors to match the title of their institution, and sometimes show five. During the late sixteenth century theologians made largely successful efforts to inform artists as to the status of the original five Pannonian martyrs, who were the correct patrons of stone workers in terms of ecclesiastical history.

Personal devotion

The Four Crowned Martyrs presumably appeared on quite numerous funerary commemorations of members of confraternities of the Four Crowned Martyrs, as well as on items associated with private devotion. Three such examples only can be documented.

For example, the Martyrs are carved in relief on the tomb slab of Wolfgang Tenck at the Stadtpfarrkirche at Steyr (Plate 56). At this church, Tenck was the Master of Work in charge of building and decoration from 1482, for thirty-one years until his death. Perhaps because of his status and long period of office, it was considered appropriate to include his own portrait in the position of honour to the left, and to carve it on a slab of expensive red marble. Tenck died in 1513 and the inscription in the vernacular reads 'Here lies buried the architect Wolfgang Tenc stone mason. As Master of Works he improved this church; and may God be merciful to him. He died on the Tuesday following the Feast of the Most Exalted Holy Cross [14 September] 1513.'[89]

Significantly, Tenck is dressed in a long-skirted and long-sleeved robe which indicated the status of one who directed rather than executed manufacture. The monument is located in the south aisle. The focus of the design is the Crucifix, labelled at its apex 'INRI' – that is, the mocking inscription placed by Christ's tormenters on his cross (*John*, 19, 19): 'Jesus of Nazareth King of the Jews' (*Iesus Nazarenus Rex Iudei*). Presumably this choice of subject related to the time of Tenck's death, close to the Feast of the Holy Cross. Tenck is represented as kneeling at the foot of the crucifixion. His shield with his personal mason's mark is at the base of the cross. A scroll issuing from his hands, which humbly hold his hat, may express his prayer to Christ crucified. It reads 'amo. mei. crucifi.', indicating perhaps 'for love of me he was crucified', followed by a mason's mark, presumably that of the carver who made the relief, and possibly 'o[pus]. f. [ecit]'. Opposite is a youth, perhaps an apprentice, wearing an apron and a hat, who holds the shield of the 'lodge' or *Brüderschaft* of masons and sculptors based at Kloster Admont to which Tenck belonged, and where he had been the head of the fraternity in

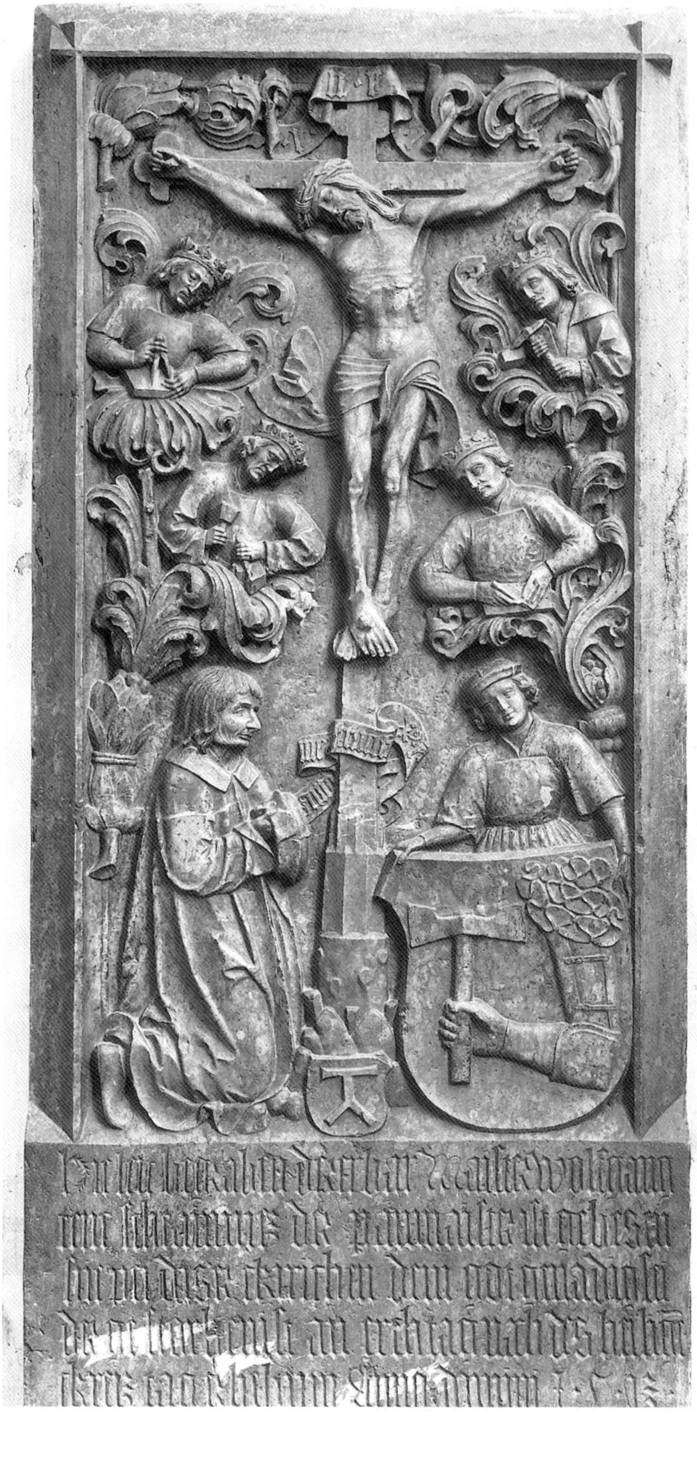

56 Monument for the Master of Work, Wolfgang Tenck, 1513, red marble, Stadtpfarrkirche, Steyr.

1480.[90] Masons, sculptors and builders in many German-speaking areas had formed societies which differed from guilds, in that they were independent of civic authorities and, rather, were located at large building projects. They resembled guilds, however, in so far as they regulated quality and education, registered a master's personal mark, ensured good and fair relations between masters, and defended its members. The grave slab of Tenck therefore pronounced his identity as member of the Kloster Admont fraternity. Surrounding the crucifix are the Four Crowned Martyrs, represented as if they were seated in foliage, who display the range of skills entailed in stone cutting and building. One holds compasses; another has a mallet and chisel; the next has a pointed hammer; while the fourth is working more delicately perhaps with a stylus on a tablet.[91] Presumably they are placed there as intercessors on behalf of one of their calling. The rule book which Tenck had followed as head of the Kloster Admont brotherhood had stated its dedication: 'In the name of the Father, of the Son and of the Holy Ghost and of the worthy Mother Mary and of our blessed patrons the Four Crowned Saints of eternal memory.'[92]

The church of Saints Aegidius and Kolomanus at Steyr had been made an independent parish in 1437, and the parishioners had embarked on a grand scheme of rebuilding as a *Pfarrkirche* or parish church forthwith, with a sequence of architects in which Tenck was the third. The grave slab signified his importance in directing such an enterprise by means of the portrait, his credentials as a professional in the coat of arms of the Kloster Admont brotherhood, and his pious hopes of reward in heaven through the intercession of the Four Crowned Martyrs.

Less than a decade later, in 1520, the stonecutter Giovanni Andrea dei Giraldoni from Tremico on Lake Como had a funerary altarpiece erected for himself and his family at San Niccolo in Ferrara (Plate 57).[93] This is attributed on stylistic grounds to Niccolò Pisano (1470–?1538), who worked as an artist to the court in the city. Giovanni Andrea had an inscription painted as if on two blocks of masonry in the foreground. In the inscription he dedicated the altar to the Four Crowned Martyrs, but was careful to name Simplicius as well, who had been converted by Bishop Cyrillus. This reads:

> These Saints were called the Four Crowned Martyrs who were the stonecutters Saints Castorius, Symphorianus, Claudius, Nicostratus and Simplicius. I, Master Giovanni Andrea stonecutter of the Giraldoni of Tremico on Lake Como had this made for me and my heirs 1520.

The painter depicted Saint Joseph, the carpenter, in the centre, kneeling to the Virgin, while the Christ child offers the lily of purity to his mother. The setting is austere with a simple stone canopy sheltering the holy family and revealing a mountainous landscape beyond. Light is quite low from the right as if at sunset or sunrise. The fourth-century

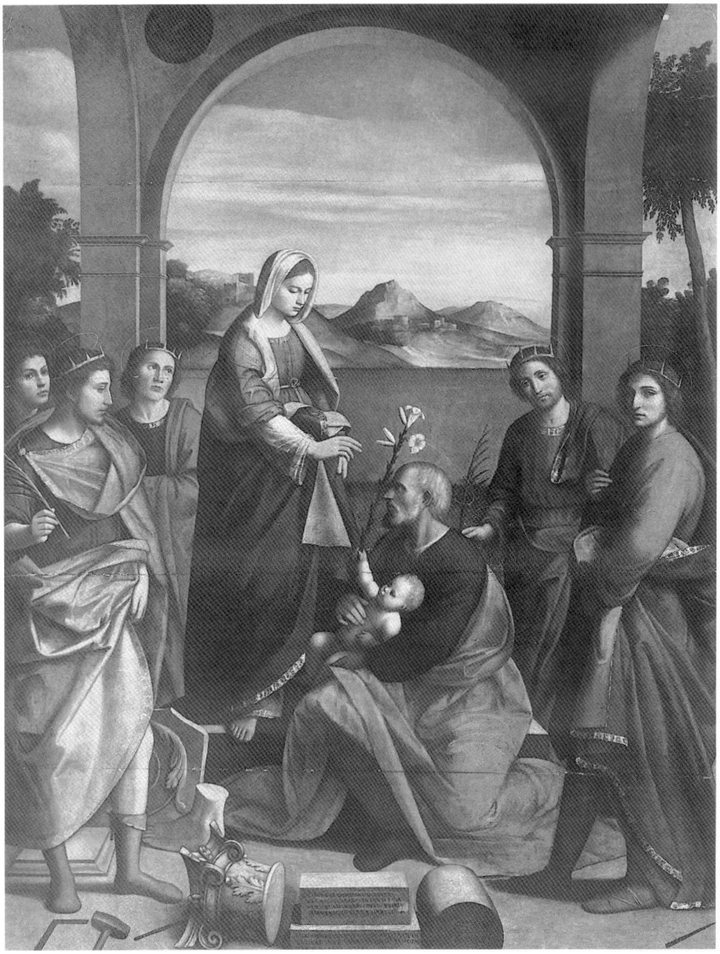

57 Attributed to Niccolò Pisano, funerary altar for the sculptor Giovanni Andrea dei Giraldoni from Como at San Niccolò at Ferrara, 1520, 227 × 170 cm, Worcester Art Gallery, Massachusetts Accession number 1940–64.

saints hold their martyrs' palms and Simplicius is shown back left, although he is distinguished by lacking a crown. The tools lie discarded on the ground along with a column, a capital, a base, a relief and a large stone foot, which may recall Diocletian's challenges to the sculptors. However, the gazes of the martyrs are on the holy family and on the viewer, while the linear perspectival construction places the vanishing point behind the body of Christ. The saints then seem to be offered as exemplars of heroic devotion, rather than models of carving virtuosity.

As with the dedication inscribed on the Haarlem altarpanel by van Heemskerck, there is a strong sense of the pious trust of artists in the Four Crowned Martyrs in the way the Brussels architect Lodewijk van Boghem (1470–1540) had his patrons placed on the very first page of his Book of Hours in 1526 (Plate 58).[94] Here was an intimate object for the private devotions of himself and his family, which contained pictorial references to his own patron, Saint Louis, and that of his wife (Anne for Anna) and son (Francis for Frans), as well as his own initials and family heraldry. Yet it is his professional patrons, of the Guild of the Four Crowned Martyrs at Brussels, which appear initially, beside the first page of the illuminated calendar for the year, which is bordered with depictions of the tools of his trade. Lodewijk was one of the most important practitioners in Brussels, being appointed as architect to the Governor of the Netherlands, Margaret of Austria, and working on her church at Brou in Savoy from 1512 onwards. He came from a family of stone cutters, masons and sculptors, but in the illumination he had the Four Crowned Martyrs depicted in a way which emphasised their mathematical and design skills. They hold, left to right, the measuring stick, the compasses and the set square, and only lastly the hammer for executing the builder's plans. They are dressed in contemporary clothing and sheltered by an elaborate canopy, which recalls the designs made by Lodewijk himself at Brou. Thus the architect prioritised his guild and confraternal identity. Interestingly enough, he chose depictions of his saintly heroes as planners and calculators more than as manual workers, suggesting that the Martyrs could, after all, be given roles which emphasised their theoretical skills. By having them placed in

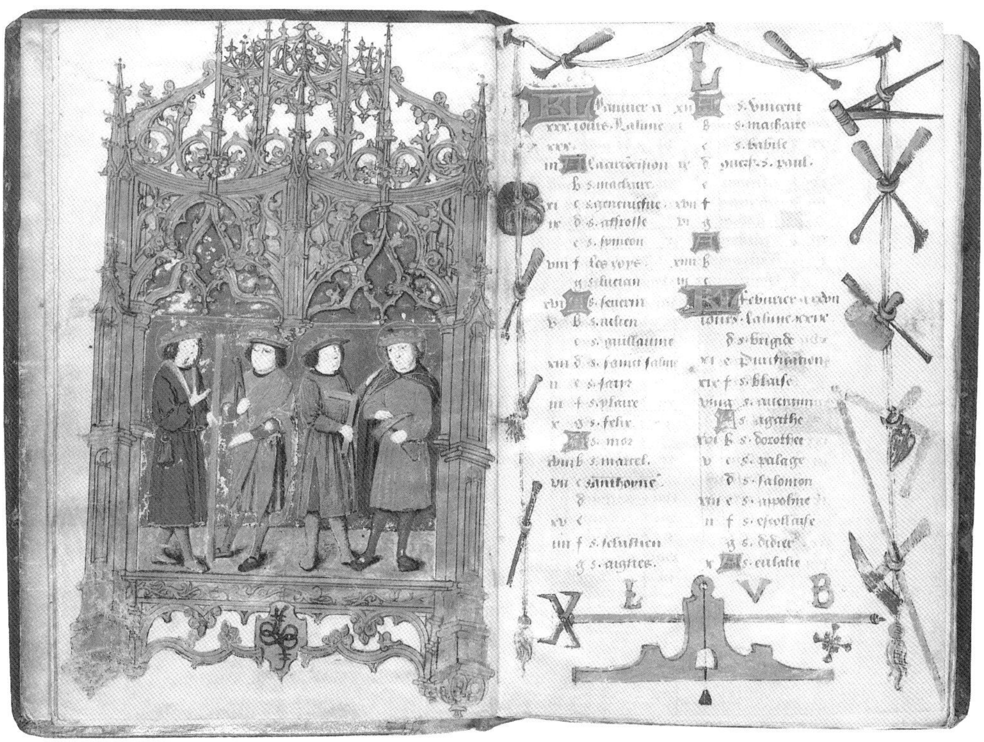

58 French illuminator, *Four Crowned Martyrs*, Book of Hours commissioned by Lodewijk van Boghem, 1526, 170 × 114 mm, Grootseminarie, Bruges, MS66/35, front end paper and fol. 1 recto.

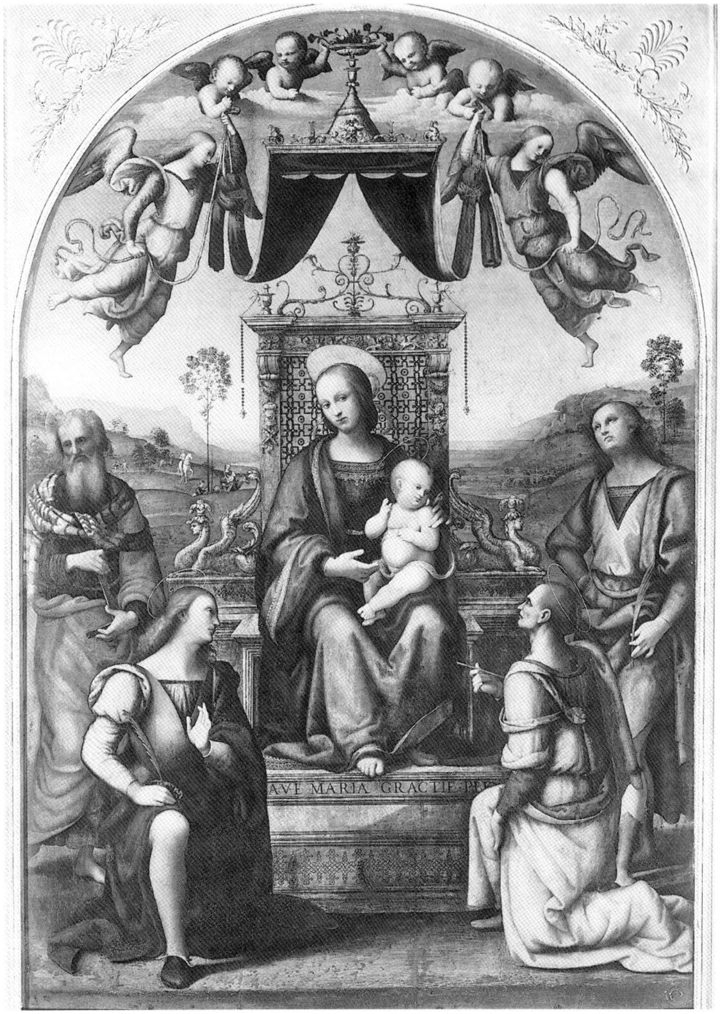

59 Giannicola di Paolo di Giovanni Manni, altarpiece for the Università dei Lombardi, Santa Maria Nuova in Perugia, 1512, Louvre, Paris.

contemporary settings and dress he seems to be making them the more accessible as exemplars. That the Martyr Saints might still be regarded highly in a domestic context, in some areas of the Netherlands, at the end of the century, is affirmed by their appearance on the house façade owned by the sculptor Andries de Valckenaere, at Middelburg, in the province of Zeeland (see Plate 106).

Decorating chapels

A few well-attested art works survive which were commissioned for guild chapels or to mark confraternity devotion. As with the guild pieces connected with Luke, these were objects denoting the power and the piety of groups of sculptors and builders. One altarpiece survives for Italian-speaking sculptors: the altarpiece contracted by the Università dei Lombardi, that is the Lombard masons, working in Perugia in 1512 (Plate 59).[95] It was painted by the local painter Giannicola di Paolo di Giovanni Manni, called Smicca, for the chapel in Santa Maria Nuova, the Servite church, and included three predella panels. As the contract stated, the main panel depicted the enthroned Madonna and Child, 'with fine colours and with gold' while the Four Crowned Martyrs surround them. References to the profession of the saints are sparse, with just a set square and chisel being held, as well martyrs' palms. On the throne base are the words *Ave Maria Gratia Plena* so the emphasis, as with the private funerary altarpiece for Giovanni Andrea dei Giraldoni, was on the hopes of the masons and their families for salvation. The three scenes below represent the four saints brought before the Emperor, their scourging by Lampadius and the taking of their coffins to be dropped into the water. The central predella panel contrasted the weakness of the Roman Tribune by comparison with the spiritual powers of Mary and her Child enthroned in the main panel, for it showed Lampadius enthroned and crowned himself, as he ordered the saints to be untied, after scourging has failed to kill them.[96] Gianninicola was an active member of his own Guild of Saint Luke in Perugia, being elected to office several times: a fact which underlines the way in which undertaking commissions for cognate guildsmen engaged artists in working for patrons whose interests they understood from their own experiences.

Whereas Gossaert and the young van Heemskerck were keen to show their knowledge of ancient sculpture in their work for guilds of Saint Luke, the painter who made the guild altarpiece for the guild of the Four Crowned Martyrs in Brussels in the second half of the sixteenth century showed little interest in the styles of antiquity, and concentrated rather on suggesting the expertise of the range of workers represented by his patrons (Plate 60). The Guild of the Four Crowned Martyrs in Brussels included the stone cutters, masons, sculptors and roofers.[97] They invested in an elaborate triptych for their guild chapel at the church of Sainte Catherine. On the centre panel their painter, who has not so far been identified, presented the narrative of the refusal by all five sculptor saints to carve a statue of Aesculapius, a model of which is being held up to them. The Martyrs work on carving elements of building and on a male statue. To inspire them, they are provided with a vision of Mary and the Child in the sky above. The Emperor Diocletian is dressed not in an ancient Roman style but in a Moorish turban.[98] Suitably, the orthogonals of the paving lead up to a point, as if beyond the vision. The scene is set in an open loggia, with some classicising columns and rounded arches, although gothicising architecture may be glimpsed in the distance. The open wings represented the guild members going about their business roofing, building walls,

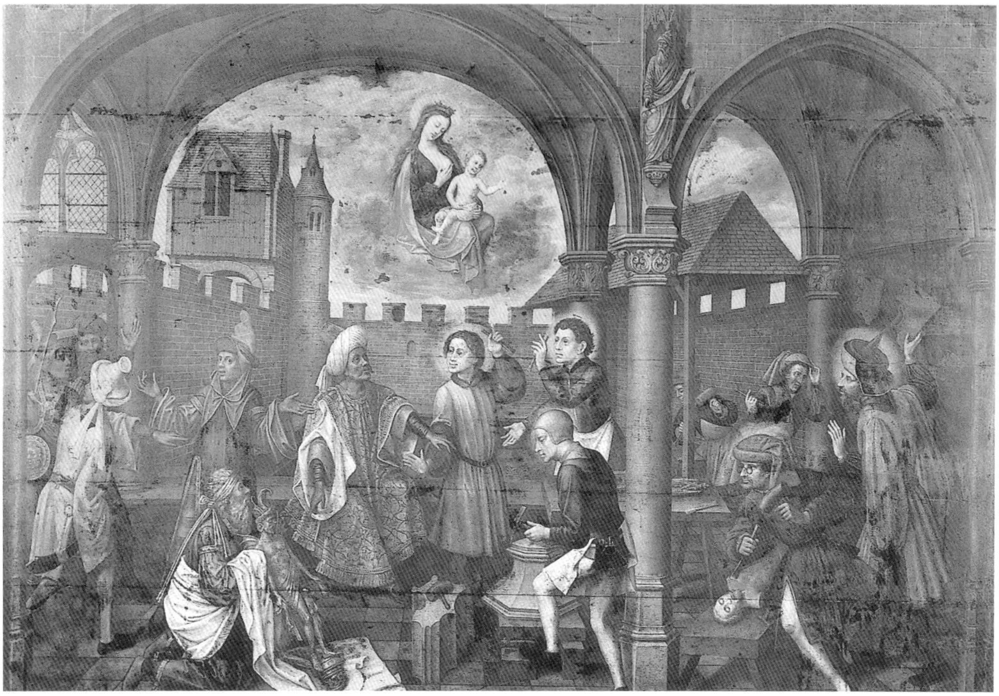

60 Brussels, second half of the sixteenth century, an anonymous altarpiece for the Guild of Four Crowned Martyrs at Sainte Catherine, Brussels, Musée Communal.

carrying stone by barge, and making figurative sculptures. The left wing concentrates on stone work and stone statuary being made for a church, and there is a castle in the background. Care has been taken to depict carvers of different ages and social status, from the humble cement mixer to the delicate work of filigree pinnacles. The right wing displays brick building and roof slating for what seem more domestic structures. Again, there is a range of age and rank from humble carriers of materials to well-dressed men directing work and carving low relief. Four men who are probably members of the guild are depicted as kneeling at the edges of these side wings, to contemplate the events depicted on the centre panel, with the attributes of their trades. It seems likely that these four were the four elected doyens or leaders who, according to civic rules, represented the four different branches of building work administered by this guild, on equal terms. In this sense, we might see the altarpiece as representing the equal rights, as well as the religious beliefs and status, of the guildsmen. When shut, the wings displayed four of the crowned martyrs painted in monochrome.

Images sometimes displayed the allegiance and piety of a body of workmen attached to the erection of one building rather than wider civic affiliations, as may be seen in the stained-glass window celebrating the five sculptor saints at Milan cathedral. The sculptors and masons who worked on the cathedral at Milan had founded a chapel on the site, dedicated to the Four Crowned Martyrs, during the fifteenth century. This was placed on the *camposanto* where the masons worked, although it was taken down in 1605.[99] The cathedral contains a magnificent stained-glass window on the north side of the nave designed by Pellegrino Tibaldi representing the legend of sculptor saints, which is considered to mark the interior altar of the confraternity of the Crowned Martyrs.[100] Tibaldi (1527–86) was Master of Works in the cathedral from 1567, and was contracted by the *fabbrica* (committee) in charge of the building of the cathedral to include designs for stained glass in his task as architect. His huge cartoons representing the passion of the Crowned Martyrs survive and were paid for in 1568. The window seems to have been the last project to be executed by the stained-glass specialist from Cologne Corrado (Konrad) de Mochis, who died in 1570. The presence at the base centre of the window of masons' tools arranged in an emblematic design led Gerolamo Biscaro to argue persuasively that the bay it adorned marked the internal chapel for the Confraternity. In this window, Tibaldi arranged the scenes so as to tell the story of the Martyrs, beginning with narratives displaying them at work for Diocletian at the base, and rising up to show Simplicius, the fifth sculptor saint, being baptised by Saint Cyrillus. On an equally grand scale, he showed the refusal to sculpt a cult statue for the Emperor, their imprisonment and finally, at the apex of the window, their death by drowning encased in coffins. The settings recalled the architecture of ancient Rome, while the pointed inclusion of the fifth Martyr underlined the fact that Tibaldi's design had to bear the scrutiny of Carlo Borromeo, the reforming Archbishop of Milan.

As well as representing Catholic convictions concerning the proper use of images, images of the sculptor saints were also the focus for displaying the fact that Catholic reformers were determined to untangle the confusions as to the historical identities of the Pannonian, as opposed to the Roman, martyrs, celebrated on 8 November. This latter project is most obvious in the mural decoration for the chapel of the 'corporation' of statuary makers and stone cutters in Rome, situated at San Silvestro, and completed in 1570 (Plate 61). This scheme makes every effort to provide clear information on the two groups of martyrs – the sculptors and the soldiers – who had been referred to by the one label as the Four Crowned Martyrs.[101] The determination to correct the record may relate to the fact that the chapel was next to the church of Santi Quattro Coronati, which was the original dedication of the Four Crowned Martyrs. It also responds to the Catholic Reformation determination to provide accurate scholarly evidence concerning the histories of the saints to be portrayed. As Johannes Molanus advised in 1570,

> For they paint four crowned men with the instruments of sculptors and cementers, when these instruments should have been attributed to the

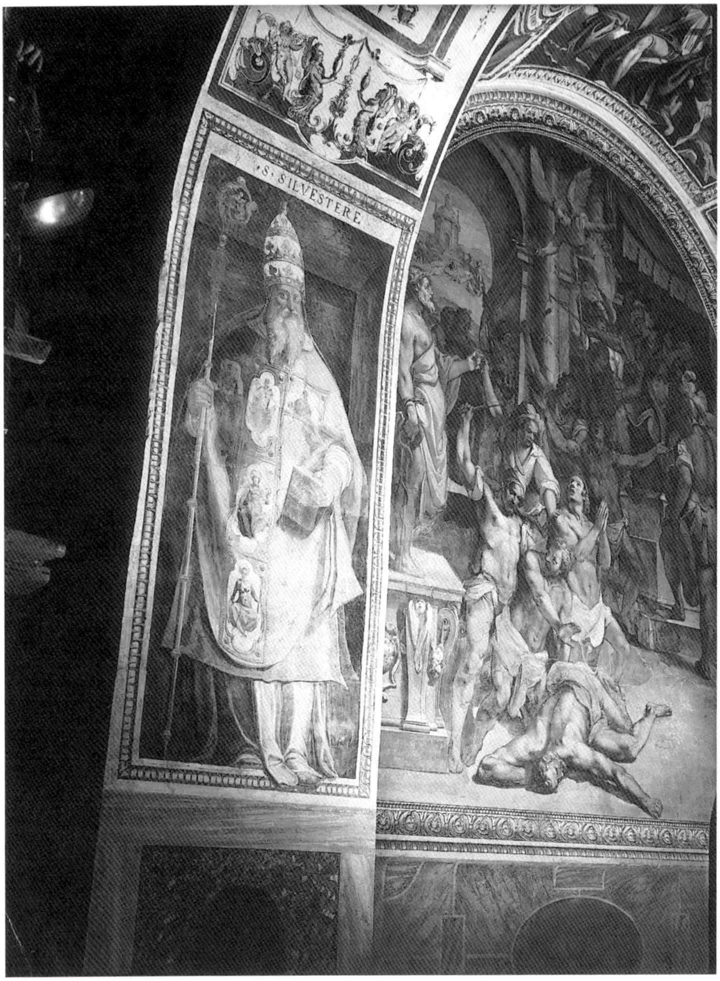

61 Attributed to Raffaellino da Reggio, the four Roman martyrs refuse to obey the seated Emperor Diocletian, chapel at San Silvestro, Rome, 1570, for the Corporation of Statuary makers and Stone cutters.

aforementioned five martyrs. And so those who are in error, need to recognise what is only too evident, and make correction.[102]

This mural was attributed to Raffaellino da Reggio by Giovanni Baglione (1571–1644) and was perhaps completed in 1570, since the inscription over the door of the chapel reads 'The corporation of statuary makers and stone cutters 1570' (*Statuariorum et lapicidorum corpus 1570*). On the right wall, the mural told the story of the Pannonian sculptors, while on the left it narrated that of the Roman soldiers. In the foreground the Roman soldiers were shown being beaten to death, after they refused to sacrifice to the statue of Aesculapius. In the background, a small scene showed their corpses put out for the dogs outside Rome. On the right-hand side are the five Pannonian sculptors refusing to worship a statue of Apollo, and, as if in the background, their martyrdom, when they were placed in coffins and thrown into the water, is represented. The guild comprised 'hewers and quarriers of stone, marble workers, carvers of ornament, fine chisellers, sculptors and statuary makers, and stone cutters'.[103]

In a review of all the images of artists available in the sixteenth century, the representations of artist saints should probably be judged the most ubiquitous and accessible, in those areas which were still obedient to the Catholic church. In this field there had been radical changes, beginning in the 1520s, as Protestant criticism had led to a situation in which images of artists' patron saints could be regarded with derision, or might be regarded anew, as affirming the orthodoxy of making devotional images for worship. Towards this latter goal, by the end of the period, Catholic theologians were seeking to ensure that representations of the Four Crowned Martyrs accorded with correctly documented hagiography. Because of the changes in belief, the ownership and making of representations of artist-saints could relate to new sorts of political affiliation, in the quite common situations in which cities passed back and forth, between Protestant and Catholic government. Shifts in religious beliefs therefore altered the contexts within which many images of artist-saints were viewed. The core function of the images of artist-saints in Catholic areas remained that of clarifying the pious use and production of religious images, in order to remind the worshipper of the persons to whom they prayed. However, it is interesting to find that in portraying these early Christian artists some artists suggested that the saints could be regarded as professional, as well as devout, exemplars. In this way, the fact that Saint Luke had been a writer and a doctor could be related to the recent ambitions of some artists to embrace scholarship and the sciences, or the geometric knowledge of the sculptor saints could be foregrounded. In general, the fact that the saints had worked in Imperial Roman times could be underlined, for audiences who admired the styles and techniques of ancient art. Changes in the representation of artist saints therefore related not only to wider religious changes, but also to new ambitions amongst some in the profession.

The images of the figurative arts as Practical or Liberal Arts, or as sharing *Disegno*, had related to the scholarly discussion of the hierarchy of different arts. The commemorative portrayals were linked with a sequence of written histories of art. The representations of artist-saints had referred to theological debates about the use of images in worship, and to hagiography. A fourth important grouping of images of artists, however, comprised those which showed artists as the Children of Mercury, within the context of widespread belief in astrology. As with the images of artist-saints, the mercurial representations of painters and sculptors were sometimes, subtly, exploited to enhance the social and intellectual status of the professions.

Notes

1 R. Lightbown, *Mantegna*, Oxford, 1986, Plates 153–64, pp. 452–4, Catalogue number 58.

2 Johannes Diaconus, *Liber de Ecclesia Lateranensis*, quoted in J. Mabillon and M. Germain, *Museum italicium*, 2 vols, Paris, 1689, II, pp. 572–3: 'et super hoc altare est imago Salvatoris mirabiliter depicta in quadem tabula, quam Lucas Evangelista designavit, sed virtus Domini angelico officio perfecit.'

3 Saint Thomas Aquinas, *Summa theologicae*, ed. J.F.B.M. de Rubeis and C.R. Billuart, Turin, 1922, p. 552; Saint Bonaventure in G.C. Trombelli, *De cultu sanctorum*, 2 vols, Bologna, 1743, II, pp. 256–9.

4 Jacopo da Voragine, *Leggenda aurea*, ed. A. Levasti, 3 vols, Florence, 1924–26, I, p. 377: 'la imagine de la beata Santa Maria sempre Vergine, la quale, come si dice, è ancora a Roma nella chiesa di Santa Maria Maggiore; la quale imagine si dice che la formasse Santo Luca, d'arte medico e uno bello dipintore.'

5 *Le cose maravigliose de l'alma città di Roma*, Venice, 1565, fol. 6 recto: 'fu diseg[nata] da Santo Luca e finita da l'Angelo'.

6 Leandro Alberti, *Cronichetta della Gloriosa Madonna di San Luca del Monte della Guardia di Bologna e de'suoi miracoli*, Venice, 1579; A. Landucci, *Origine dal tempio dedicato in Roma alla Vergine Madre di Dio Maria detto hoggi del popolo*, Rome, 1646.

7 C.J. Destombes, *Histoire de l'église de Cambrai*, Lille, 1890, II, pp. 244–9; D.C. Shorr, *The Christchild in Devotional Images*, New York, 1954, p. 53.

8 P. Strieder, 'Hans Holbein der Älter und die deutschen Wiederholungen des Gnadensbildes von Santa Maria del Popolo', *Zeitschrift für Kunstgeschichte*, 20, 1959, pp. 252–67.

9 W.L. Schreiber, *Manuel de l'amateur de la gravure sur bois et sur métal au XVe siècle*, 8 vols, Berlin, 1891–1900, II, pp. 2307–8, Catalogue number 1033: 'hat sie also gemalt der Ewangelist s. Lux welch heilig gemeld ist zu Rom.'

10 Roccho Pirro, *Notitiae Siciliensum ecclesiarum*, 2 vols, Palermo, 1733, I, p. 662; II, p. 874.

11 C. Baronius, *Annales ecclesiastici*, 12 vols, Antwerp, 1610, I, p. 663: 'Nos Petri et Pauli Apostolorum et Christi etiam ipsius imagines in picturis colorum varietate expressas conservatasque aspeximus.'

12 Pier Paolo Vergerio, *Della camera et statua della Madonna chiamata di Loretto*, Tübingen, 1554, fol. a 8: 'e lo beato Luca evangelista con le sue mani fece quella imagine à similitudine della beata Vergine Maria, la quale è in sino al dì' hoggi.'

13 E. von Dobschütz, *Christusbilder: Untersuchnungen zur christlichen Legende*, Leipzig, 1899; D. Klein, *Lukas als Maler der Maria*, Berlin, 1933. The earliest Greek references are by John Damascene, 'De sanctis venerandis imaginibus ad Theophilum Imperatorem', in J.P. Migne, ed., *Patrologiae graecae*, XCV, Paris, 1864, col. 350; and Andreas of Crete, 'De sanctarum imaginum veneratione', in J.P. Migne, ed., *Patrologiae graecae*, XCVII, Paris, 1865, col. 1303.

14 See n. 2 above.

15 F. Thöne, *Daniel Lindtmayer 1552–1606/07*, Zürich, 1975, p. 157, Catalogue number 55, Schweizerisches Landesmuseum, L.M. 25, 634, 350 × 247 mm.

16 Johannes Butzbach, 'Johannes Butzbach's "Libellus de praeclaris picture professoribus" aus der Bonnenser Handschrift veröffentlich', pp. 60–72 in Alwin Schultz, ed., *Jahrbücher für Kunstwissenschaft herausgegeben von A. von Zahn*, Leipzig, II, 1869, p. 71: 'Lucam etiam beatissimus ille evangelista cuius laus est in evangelio medicus et pictor insignis fuit, qui inter cetera beatissime virginis marie dei genetricis effigiem mirificis ymaginibus depictam expressisse legitur . . . Siquidem picturam laycorum seu ydeotorum scripturam fore censebant.'

17 Butzbach, 'Libellus de praeclaris picture professoribus', p. 71: 'Aliorum etiam postea apud nostrates qui dignum aliquid memoria in vita sive post mortem miraculose gesserant, nostri pictores cepere effigiare figuras, quibus sequatium animos ad eorum excitarent virtutes, ut qui eosdem ex litteris non cognovisset ex pictura veluti ex scriptura quarum? ignari essent cognoscerent' (Schultz's emendation).

18 Butzbach, 'Libellus de praeclaris picture professoribus', p. 71: 'Que tamen ymagines depicte sive exculte non sunt adorande, sed res per ipsas designate.'

19 J. Eck, *De non tollendis Christi et sanctorum imaginibus contra haeresim Faelicianum*, Ingolstadt, 1522, fols a3 verso–a4 recto.

20 D. Freedberg, *Iconoclasm and Painting in the Revolt of the Netherlands, 1566–1609*, New York and London, 1988, especially pp. 208–10 for the fate of the guild chapel of Saint Luke.

21 Johannes Molanus, *De historia sanctorum imaginum et picturam*, Louvain, 1570, and Ingolstadt, 1594, ed. and trans. François Boespflug, Olivier Christian and Benoît Tassel, 2 vols, Paris 1996, I, Book II, Chapter IX, pp. 55–6; D.M. Manni, *Dell'errore che persiste di attribuirsi le pitture al Santo Evangelista*, Florence, 1766.

22 Jacopo da Voragine, *The Golden Legend or Lives of the Saints*, trans. William Caxton, ed. F.S. Ellis, London, 1900, 7 vols, VI, pp. 46–59.

23 Jacopo da Bergamo, *Supplemento delle chroniche del Reverendo Padre Frate Jacopo Philippo da Bergamo*, Venice, 1539, fol. CXXXIII verso: 'et non solamente fu maestrato da Paulo apostolo, ma anchora da gli altri apostoli, come lui medesimo nel principio dice . . . Scrivesi anchora che fu maestrato dalla gloriosa e intemerata madre di Giesu Christo, Mara, della quale fu molto familiare, di quelle cose, massimamente che se appartenevano a lei, e che secretamente lei sola sapeva, come fu l'annunciatione fattagli della natività del figliuolo, fattagli da l'angelo e dalla natività di Giesu Christo, e simile cose.'

24 Jerome, 'Commentariorum in Evangelium Matthaei', in J.P. Migne, ed., *Patrologiae latinae*, LXXXVI, Paris, 1884, col. 19: 'Tertia vituli quae evangelistam Lucam a Zacharia sacerdote sumpsisse initium praefigurat.'

25 Voragine, *The Golden Legend*, VI, p. 47.

26 Isidore of Seville, 'Allegoriae quaedam scripturae sacrae', in J.P. Migne, ed., *Patrologiae latinae*, LXXXIII, Paris, 1862, col. 117: 'Lucas quoque per vituli mysticum vultum Christum pro nobis praedicat immolatum'

('Luke also through the mystic visage of the bull foretells the sacrifice of Christ for our sake').

27 Carl van de Velde, *Frans Floris 1519/20–1570 Leven en Werken*, 2 vols, Brussels, 1975, I, pp. 237–8. Signed 'F. F. i. [n]v. [enit] et fe. [cit]1556.' Floris had entered the guild in 1540–1: p. 437.

28 P. Rombouts and T. van Lerius, *De Liggeren en andere historische Archieven der Antwerpische Sint Lucasgilde*, 2 vols, 's Gravenhage, 1864–76, I, passim: throughout the sixteenth century the registrations cover many skills.

29 For the identification of these baskets, see Catherine King, 'National Gallery 3902 and the theme of Luke the Evangelist as artist and physician', *Zeitschrift für Kunstgeschichte*, 48, 1985, pp. 249–55.

30 V. van der Haeghen, *La Corporation des peintres et des sculpteurs de Gand*, Ghent, 1905, pp. 1–2: 'En es gheweest een jongher vailliant de twalef aposteln . . . In consten es hij ghewest zeer actijf'.

31 Rombouts and van Lerius, *Liggeren en andere historische Archieven*, p. 65 (1506); p. 108 (1526).

32 Rombouts and van Lerius, *Liggeren en andere historische Archieven*, pp. 348–50.

33 G.T. Faggin, 'Nuove opere di Lanceloot Blondeel', *Critica d'Arte*, XV, 1968, pp. 37–54.

34 Voragine, *The Golden Legend*, III, pp. 261–6.

35 D. van de Casteele, 'Documents divers de la société de s. Luc à Bruges', *Annales de la Société d'Emulation pour l'Etude de l'Histoire et des Antiquités de la Flandre*, Bruges, 1867, I, pp. 15–43.

36 Rombouts and van Lerius, *Liggeren en andere historische Archieven*, p. 47.

37 Rombouts and van Lerius, *Liggeren en andere historische Archieven*, p. 57: 'een nieu root fluweelen cruse doen maken aen ons pellen, ende oecke iiij lappen aen 't pellen behorende, met ons Lieve Vrouwe en St Lucas'.

38 Rombouts and van Lerius, *Liggeren en andere historische Archieven*, see for instance pp. 78, 308, 347.

39 A. van der Willigen, *Les Artistes de Harlem: notices historiques avec un préçis sur la gilde de St Luc*, Haarlem and The Hague, 1870, p. 1.

40 Molanus, *Historia sanctorum*, II, pp. 55–6: 'Trinitati proxima est deipara Virgo Maria, super omnes Angelos exaltata, cuius Imaginem a Luca depictam esse.'

41 For the Gossaert panel see H. Pauwels, *Jan Gossaert genaamd Mabuse*, Rotterdam and Bruges, 1965, pp. 86–9, 156. For dating, see E. Neefs, 'La peinture et la sculpture à Malines', *Messager des sciences historiques des archives des arts et de la bibliographie de Belgique*, Ghent, 1871, p. 357.

42 Neefs, 'La peinture et la sculpture', pp. 345–55.

43 For the antique prototypes see Phyllis Pray Bober and Ruth Rubenstein, *Renaissance Artists and Antique Sculpture*, Oxford, 1986, Plate 200, p. 200 and pp. 164–5. See also A. Montballieu, 'Bij de interpretatie en de datering van Jan Gossaerts Lucas en de Madonna vit Mechelen', I, pp. 125–38 in *Miscellanea Jozef Duverger: Bijdragen tot de Kunstgeschiedenis der Nederlanden*, 2 vols, Ghent, 1968.

44 Gerardus Geldenhaurius called Noviomagus Bishop of Utrecht, 'Vita et obitus clarissimum principis Philippi à Burgundia' in *Germanorum rerum scriptores varii*, 3 vols, Frankfurt am Main, 1602, III, p. 186: 'Nihil eum

Romae delectabat, quam sacra illa vetustatis monumenta, quae per clarissimum pictorem Joannem Gossardum Mabodium, dipingenda sibi curavit.'

45 Montballieu, p. 127: the confraternity had been assigned an altar dedicated to Saint John the Evangelist in 1479 so the side wings (attributed to Michel Coxcie and made in the second half of the sixteenth century) narrated the story of John boiled in oil and experiencing his Revelation on Patmos.

46 *Niklaus Manuel Deutsch: Maler, Dichter, Staatsmann, Katalog der Ausstellung*, Bern, 1979, Catalogue numbers 69 and 71, pp. 223–5.

47 *Walters Art Gallery Illuminated Books of the Middle Ages and Renaissance*, Baltimore, 1949, Catalogue number 99. The Hours are attributed to the Bedford atelier and have the arms of Thomas Malet de Berlettes and Jeanne de Lannoy, MS. 281. fol. 17.

48 Veldman, *Marten van Heemskerck*, p. 12, n. 11, gives the transcription of the Dutch verse and English translation. I emended her 'fellow painters' to 'fellow guild members'.

49 Van der Willigen, *Artistes de Harlem*, p. 7 and see also E.K.J. Reznicek, 'De reconstructie van t'Altaer van S. Lucas van Marten van Heemskerck', *Oud Holland*, LXX, 1955, pp. 233–46.

50 Van der Willigen, *Artistes de Harlem*, pp. 1–2.

51 R. Grosshans, *Marten van Heemskerck: die Gemälde*, Berlin, 1980, pp. 109–16.

52 E. Panofsky, *Renaissance and Renascences in Western Art*, London, 1960, p. 190.

53 Van Mander, *Lives*, I, pp. 238–41.

54 Butzbach, 'Libellus de praeclaris picture professoribus', p. 58: 'Magna quippe tam picturae quam litterarum studio sis et non impar ingeniis vis esse consuevit quibus.'

55 Grosshans, *Marten van Heemskerck*, pp. 114–16.

56 Van Mander, *Lives*, IV, p. 77.

57 Veldman, *Marten van Heemskerck*, p. 14.

58 Grosshans, *Marten van Heemskerck*, pp. 195–201.

59 King, 'National Gallery 3902', pp. 249–55.

60 J.M. Montias, *Artists and Artisans of Delft*, Princeton, 1982, p. 13.

61 Montias, *Artists and Artisans*, pp. 16–21.

62 Montias, *Artists and Artisans*, pp. 24–5: 'When Master Marten had been paid the guild coffers were empty.'

63 Veldman, *Marten van Heemskerck*, p. 12 analyses van Mander's account of Heemskerck's period in Delft.

64 Montias, *Artists and Artisans*, pp. 16–18 on his headship of the guild and his participation in rebuilding the church.

65 C. Hülsen and H. Egger, *Die römischen Skizzenbücher von Marten van Heemskerck*, 2 vols, Berlin, 1913–16, II, Plate 81, pp. 42–5.

66 A. Michaelis, 'Römische Skizzenbücher Marten van Heemskerck und anderer nördischen Künstler des XVI Jahrhunderts', *Jahrbuch des Deutschen Archaeologischen Instituts*, VI, 1891, pp. 125–72. Michaelis, pp. 171–2, analysed the sculpture in the Palazzo Sassi collection; he quoted Aldrovandi. See Bober and Rubenstein, *Renaissance Artists and Antique*

Sculpture, Plate 36, p. 36 for original identified as seated Apollo. The statue is of porphyry, which Heemskerck reproduces.

67 Bober and Rubenstein, *Renaissance Artists and Antique Sculpture*, Figure 75b, p. 110.

68 Bober and Rubenstein, *Renaissance Artists and Antique Sculpture*, Figure 2a, p. 50.

69 Veldman, *Marten van Heemskerck*, pp. 115–16.

70 Veldman, *Marten van Heemskerck*, p. 119.

71 Veldman, *Marten van Heemskerck*, p. 119.

72 Adam Bartsch, *The Illustrated Bartsch XXVII: The Works of Marcantonio Raimondi and his School*, ed. K. Oberhuber, New York, 1978, XXVI, p. 106, number 418 (314).

73 Grosshans, *Marten van Heemskerck*, pp. 196, 200.

74 Grosshans, *Marten van Heemskerck*, p. 200, referred to the thirteenth-century discussion by Konrad of Wurzburg of the parrot as signifying immaculacy and also to a patristic sermon by Saint Augustine explaining that a nut represented Christ as saviour of mankind: where the green outer covering of nut is the humanity of Christ, the hard shell beneath is the wood of the cross, while the kernel is his divinity which is the spiritual food of mankind.

75 A. Zweite, *Studien zu Marten de Vos*, Göttingen, 1974, number 8, p. 20; and also A.J.J. Delen, *Musée Royale des Beaux Arts Anvers*, Antwerp, 1948, number 88, p. 270.

76 S.G. Goddard, *The Master of Frankfurt and his Shop*, Brussels, 1982, Plate 2, pp. 129–30, Catalogue number 2.

77 Vasari, *Le opere di Giorgio Vasari*, I, pp. 673–5. Dorothy Klein, *Lukas als Maler der Maria*, Berlin 1933, p. 27 attributes the lost panel to Gerini.

78 For the dedication of the confraternity funerary masses to the Trinity, see J. Pope Hennessy, *Cellini*, London, 1985, pp. 278, 312, n. 18; Birgit Laschke, *Fra Giovanni Angelo da Montorsoli; ein Florentiner Bildhauer des 16 Jahrhunderts*, Berlin, 1993, p. 143.

79 E. and W. Paatz, *Die Kirchen von Florenz*, 6 vols, Frankfurt am Main, 1940–54, I, pp. 131–2.

80 Karen Edis Barzman, *The Florentine Academy and the Early Modern State: The Discipline of Disegno*, Cambridge, 2000, pp. 37–42; R. Siverio, *Accademia delle Arti del Disegno*, Florence, 1982, pp. 1–10.

81 Twelve stucco statues of Prophets and New Testament Saints were placed in niches flanking the mural decorations: see David Summers, 'The sculptural programme of the Cappella di San Luca', *Mitteilungen des Kunsthistorischen Instituts in Florenz*, XIV, 1969, pp. 67–90.

82 The Confraternity of Saint Luke in Rome included painters, gold leaf beaters, banner makers and embroiderers: see C. Pietrangeli, *L'Accademia Nazionale di San Luca*, Rome, 1974, pp. 6–12 and 82–5.

83 Zaremba Filipczak, *Picturing Art in Antwerp*, pp. 16–19.

84 R. Dionigi, *SS. Quattuor Coronati: Bibliography and Iconography, An Essay*, Milan, 1998; A. Amore, 'Quattro Coronati', *Bibliotheca sanctorum*, 10 vols, Rome, 1968, X, cols 1276–86; and J. Bollandus and G. Henschenius, eds, *Acta sanctorum novembris*, 5–8 November, Brussels, 1910, LXVI, pp. 748–84.

85 Amore, 'Quattro Coronati', col. 1286.

86 For the account see *Acta sanctorum novembris*, pp. 765–79.

87 *Acta sanctorum novembris*, p. 771.

88 Voragine, *The Golden Legend*, 6, pp. 139–40.

89 Franz von Rhiza, 'Die Siegel der ehemaligen Bauhutte von St Stefan in Wien', *Mitteilungen der Kaiserliche, Königliche Central-Commission zur Erforschung und Erhaltung der Kunst und Historischen Denkmale*, 16, New Series, 1890, pp. 151–6 (I have given right slashes to show the line breaks in the inscription): 'Hie leit begrabender erbar Master Volfgang/ Tenc schtanmetz des paumaister ist gebesen/ hie pei diser ckirche dem got gnadig sei /der gestorben ist an erchtag nach des heiligi[]/ ckreitz tag erhebnm Anno domini 1. 5. 1. 3.'

90 Arnold Luschin von Ebengreuth, 'Das Admonter Hüttenbuch und die Regensberger Steinmetz-ordnung vom jahre 1459', *Mitteilungen der Kaiserliche, Königliche Central-Commission zur Erforschung und Erhaltung der Kunst und Historischen Denkmale*, 19, New Series, 1893, pp. 227–41. See Fig. 3, p. 237, for Tenck's master mark.

91 P. du Colombier 'Les Quatre-Couronnées patrons des tailleurs de pierre', *La Revue des arts*, IV, 1952, pp. 216–17.

92 Luschin von Ebengreuth, p. 234: 'In dem Namen des Vater, des Suns [sic] und des heiligen Geists und der wirdigen Mueter Marie und auch ir feliger[sic] Diener der heiligen vier gekrönten zu ewiger gedachtnis.'

93 P.B. Cott, 'The Ellis Collection, Continental European Paintings', *Worcester Art Museum Annual*, Ghent, 1941, IV, pp. 7–33: 'Questi Santi se chiamanoli quattro coronati martiri che fu[ro]no taiaprede, S. Castorio, S. Sinfuriano, S. Nocostrato, S. Simplicio Magistro Giovanni Andrea Tagliapreda dei Giraldoni da Tremico de Lago di Como feci per mi et mia eredi, 1520'.

94 M. Smeyers and Jan van der Stock, eds, *French Illuminated Manuscripts 1475–1550*, 1996, pp. 200–1. The Book of Hours is attributed to a French illuminator and is in its original binding complete with a pouch for the architect's spectacles.

95 W. Bombe, *Urkunden zur Geschichte der Peruginer Malerei*, Leipzig, 1929, pp. 53–6, Louvre inventory number 1372.

96 Galleria Nazionale dell'Umbria houses the three predella panels: U. Gnoli, *Pittore e miniatori nell'Umbria*, Spoleto, 1923, pp. 135–40; G. Cecchini, *La Galleria Nazionale dell'Umbria in Perugia*, Rome, 1932 p. 160, Catalogue number 32, measuring 30 × 152 cm.

97 A. Henne and A. Wauters, *Histoire de la ville de Bruxelles*, Brussels, 1845, 3 vols, II, p. 590.

98 Du Colombier, 'Les Quatre-Couronnées', pp. 215–16; A. Pinchart, *Archives des arts, sciences et lettres*, I, Ghent, 1860, pp. 34–5; J. Casier and P. Bergmans, *L'Art ancient dans les Flandres*, Brussels and Paris, 1922, Plates CCXLI and CCXLII, pp. 54–5. The centre panel measures 144 × 211 cm.

99 *Acta sanctorum Novembris*, cols 1291–3.

100 U. Monneret de Villard, *Le vetrate del duomo di Milano*, Milan, 1918–20, I, pp. 153–5 and 209 records the designing of this window. Volume III illustrates the scenes in Plates CLXX–CLXXIV. The cartoons are in the Biblioteca Ambrosianana. See also G. Biscaro, 'La scuola dei Quattro

Martiri Coronati presso il duomo di Milano', *Archivio storico lombardo*, XX, 1913, pp. 214–27; Ernesto Brivio, *Le vetrate del Duomo*, Milan, 1998, pp. 86–9.

101 Italo Faldi, 'Contributi a Raffaellino da Reggio' *Bollettino d'arte*, XXXVI, 1951, pp. 324–33; A. Bessone Aureli, *I marmorari romani*, Rome, 1935, pp. 191–7; Dionigi, *SS. Quattuor Coronati*, p. 41.

102 Molanus, *Historia sanctorum*, Book III, Chapter XLVI, p. 363: 'Pingunt enim quatuor coronatos cum instrumentis sculptorum et caementiorum, cum ea forent quinque praedictis martyribus applicanda. Itaque qui in errore versantur, eundum ut nimis manifestum agnoscant et corrigant.'

103 M. Maroni Lumbroso and A. Martini, *Le confraternite romane nelle loro chiese*, Rome, 1963, p. 336; A. Martini, *Arti, mestieri e fede nella Roma dei papi*, Bologna, 1965, pp. 179–85: 'abbozzatori, lapicidari, marmisti, ornatisti, scalpellini, scultori, squadratori, statuari, tagliapietre.'

5 Mercury as protector of artists: from astrology to mythology

Throughout the sixteenth century painters and sculptors were portrayed as under the influence of the planet Mercury in the Netherlands, in German-speaking areas and in France. Although this visual discourse may seem to be in contrast to devout beliefs, astrology was regarded as part of a Christian world view in so far as the stars were considered to be the physical intermediaries of God's will. Just as with the belief in saints as patrons of the visual arts, astrological ideas enshrined popular beliefs about the sorts of people that painters, sculptors and architects might be. In these illustrations painters and sculptors appeared under the planetary influence of Mercury alongside merchants, accountants and money changers, those skilled as goldsmiths, makers of musical instruments and clock makers, as well as physicians, scribes, scholars and astrologers (a term interchangeable with astronomer at this period). These included those supposedly amongst the Practical Arts, as well as those amongst the Liberal, so that astrological beliefs provided malleable discourses. Astrology had the advantage of grouping painters and sculptors together as 'mercurial' occupations, whereas many guild systems divided them because they used different media. The visual representation of painters and sculptors as under the aegis of the planet rested on literary traditions dating back to the early fifteenth century, which derived from Ancient Greek and Roman cosmology, as well as Arabic and Judaic science, and had been continuously elaborated during the medieval period.[1]

On the strength of this familiar astrological association, some artists, beginning in 1540, began to represent the mythological god Mercury as their protector in new allegories which gave the achievements of art and artists the prestige that was linked with figures from the ancient Greek and Roman legend. Mercury had been associated in classical mythology with the invention of speech and writing, as well as of music, and he had been regarded as the guide of souls, helping people to achieve their aspirations. These legends meant that he was connected to the Liberal Art of Rhetoric, and to writing of all sorts, as well as presiding over inventiveness, and that he could take on the role of assistant in artistic endeavours. The astrological illustrations were made for general consumption. In contrast, the mythological allegories of Mercury as artists' helper were made specifically for artists and for people interested in art, even though they were all either published in print or on public show. These allegories could be seen on artists' houses in Rome, Antwerp and Prague, as well as in the decorations for Michelangelo's and Agostino Carracci's funerals, respectively, in Florence and Bologna, and also on the new guild insignia for artists at Prague. They were also produced for publications on art and architecture, and for engravings commemorating individual artists. Although the mythological images did not have the popularity of the astrological ones, they were still capable of taking their messages to sizeable audiences. Both the astrological and the mythological representations of Mercury display the tendency, in the sixteenth century, for makers of visual images to show their professions in the best possible light, in terms of social and intellectual standing. The former was a tradition which could be newly exploited; the latter was the innovation of sixteenth century. Arguably, the fact that the astrological association existed licensed the transposition from 1540 onwards to the more scholarly and elitist representations of Mercury, as inventive and erudite helper of artists. As if to distance him a little from the planetary reference and underline his intellectual standing, he was frequently placed with his sister Minerva, the goddess of wisdom, in these latter schemes.

Mercurial references were sufficiently attractive for Jacopo de' Barbari to take the caduceus or staff adorned with two serpents, which was an attribute for Mercury, as his engraver's mark, in prints produced around 1500 in Venice.[2] Jacopo was a painter and a theorist on proportion who showed his studies to Dürer, and who had a considerable reputation, since his drawing book was treasured by Margaret of Austria.[3] He argued that painting was the eighth Liberal Art, quoting Aristotle, Pliny and Cicero, in a letter he wrote to Friedrich der Weise of Saxony around 1500.[4] These activities suggest that he might well have seen his mark as having mythological associations with learning, rather than solely the conventional astrological connotations for artists. Contemporary mythological handbooks explained the caduceus as indicating the power of rhetoric. For example, the twelfth-century handbook by Albricus, still being used in the sixteenth century, entitled *Allegoriae poeticae* or *Allegories of Poetry* (Paris, 1520) referred to earlier texts, in stating that the caduceus stood for eloquence: 'the staff thus according to Remigius means the delivery of a speech which is eloquent, without hesitation, and logically argued'. Albricus stated that the two interwined serpents on the staff could indicate the reconciliation of disputes in civil life and in war, through well-calculated speech.[5] Rhetoric was one of the traditional seven Liberal Arts, and Horace in the *Carmina* had used the phrase 'mercurial men' (*Mercuriales viri*) to mean 'men drawn to poetry'.[6]

Astrological representations of painters and sculptors with the planet Mercury appeared on one painting, three engravings, a woodcut, one drawing and the illustration for an astrological handbook (which was still being reprinted at the end of the sixteenth century), as well as a book on architecture. Mercury as mythological assistant of artists appeared on a book about art, three houses of artists and one artist's commemorative medal, at two artists' funerals, on three allegories of the progress of artists, and on one guild insignia during the sixteenth century. In the early seventeenth century further instances occur: on an artist's house, on an artist's personal *impresa* and on an allegory of the progress of art.

Some scholars have discussed late fifteenth-century and early sixteenth-century texts which associated artists with the melancholy of the planet Saturn. Fritz Saxl and Erwin Panofsky showed the importance of these ideas in the development of Dürer's visual image of Melancholy; Margaret and Rudolf Wittkower charted references to artists as being melancholy during the sixteenth century.[7] However, these notions did not form part of a popular visual tradition for representing artists.

Artists as children of Mercury

Painting and sculpture had been illustrated as under the astrological domain of Mercury, along with other commercial and quick-witted professions, since the 1420s in western European astrological traditions. From Mercury's speedy and unpredictable physical behaviour and association with quicksilver as a planet derived beliefs that those under his dominion were changeable, inventive and temperamental in character. In Roman religion he had been god of merchants; in ancient literature he had been praised as inventor of musical instruments, and as teacher and inventor of speech and of writing, as well as being a traveller and a thief. Consequently, artists were shown alongside teachers, businessmen, those skilled as writers (scholars or scribes) and calculators (astrologers, physicians, money changers, accountants, clock makers) as well as those who used speech, such as actors and orators.

The theme of the Children of Mercury reached a wide audience in woodcuts, engravings and books in the vernacular and derived from traditional discourses of medicine and astrology. The idea of planetary influence on professions derived from Late Antique texts. According to this system, each of the seven planets presided over different activities. The planet disposed the abilities of those born under its star, who were termed its 'children', and when that planet was in the ascendant it was propitious also to undertake activities under its sway. In this system Luna or the Moon governed fishing and navigation, Mercury governed the arts and commerce, Venus presided over lovers and pleasure, Apollo presided over honours and dignities, Mars made men warlike and Jupiter was associated with sciences and government, while Saturn governed agricultural work. The planets also ruled different plants, minerals, animals and human capacities. For example, in the *Allegoriae*,

Albricus explained that the Moon was linked to the body, Venus to desires, Mars with blood, Apollo with spirit and Mercury with *ingenium* or personal talent.[8] The connection with *ingenium* was highly acceptable at a period when some artists were asserting possession of inborn inventiveness as well as learned skill, so as to compare themselves with the practitioners of the Liberal Arts.

It is important to emphasise that belief in astrological influence on the physical universe including the body were conventional in theological terms, considering biblical accounts, for example in the way a star had guided the Magi to Bethlehem. Theologians such as Saint Thomas Aquinas had explained that the notion that God used the planets as the means to effecting physical changes was acceptable as long as it did not risk belief in free will. Aquinas stated that 'the heavenly bodies cannot be the cause of the work of free will, but they are able to incline persons in so far as they may impress certain dispositions in the body of humans', although, 'a person may act against the inclination of the celestial bodies by means of reason'.[9] Astrological factors were likely to be consulted when administering medicine, founding buildings or planting trees. However, astrologers reminded readers that all took place according to God's will. Battista de' Ruberti explained in his *Osservazioni de astrologia, et altre appartenenze, circa la medecina, e mutazione de' tempi* (*Observations on Astrology and other Related Matters Concerning Medicine and the Alteration in the Weather*) (Florence, 1567):

> In the actions of man, one must give consideration to the hours that accompany the planets, when they are prosperous, and also adjust to the quality appropriate to the desired effect, but all depends on the will of the Blessed Lord God.[10]

The Sienese painter, sculptor and architect Francesco di Giorgio Martini (1439–1501), for example, made it clear that he understood the orthodox Christian position when he rejected the belief that design had declined after antiquity because of the waning influence of Mercury, in the introduction to his treatise on architecture. This was written in the period 1489–92, and entitled the *Trattato di architettura civile e militare*. Six copies made before about 1520 survive, including one belonging to Leonardo.[11] Francesco considered that lack of will had encouraged artistic decline, as artists bowed to greed. In his view, human reason could overcome the physical tendencies attributable to the planets:

> This causation has seemed to me for a long time to be dubious and suspicious – that is of the influence of Mercury, the Lord of those who strenuously seek excellence in the above mentioned arts [geometry, arithmetic, perspective, drawing]. This is because I myself have not been bound to do whatever nature has inclined me to do, but many times I have placed my trust in reason, rather than bending to corporeal inclinations.[12]

Astrology could be ridiculed, as in the short poem published in Siena in 1578 entitled *La piacevol astrologia di Ravanello nel qual si dichiara à tutti gli'uomini quello à che sono inclinati*. Here the invented hero Ravanello ('little radish root') quipped that those who were born on Mercury's day (Wednesday) will be chatterboxes, fraudsters and ruffians.[13] Yet books and visual images explaining the physical effects of the planets under God's aegis sold well throughout the sixteenth century. When the Bamberg scholar Lorenz Behaim cast Dürer's horoscope, he found that 'because Mercury is in the house, he gains from it his talent in painting'.[14] When Condivi came to write the introductory pages of his life of Michelangelo (Rome, 1553) he made sure to tell his readers that the artist had been born when Mercury and Venus were in the house of Jupiter, thus ensuring that the child would possess 'lofty talent: *alto ingegno*'.[15]

Two examples represent the way Italian audiences might be expected to regard artists at the beginning of the period astrologically. One is the woodcut series of seven separate sheets representing all the Children of the Planets made in Florence in the 1470s and attributed to Maso Finiguerra (Plate 62).[16] Here, under Mercury, are shown goldsmiths, sculptors and mural painters, with feasters, scribes, clock makers, organ makers and astrologers. The inscription explains what Mercury's child is like: 'Eloquent and most ingenious he loves and studies the sciences of mathematics and study in divination; and has a delicate figure, that is, slender, with thin lips and a stature which is well formed.'[17] To the left is represented a goldsmith's workshop, making vases, belt buckles and plates. The sculptor is working on the very latest Florentine genre, that is to say two portrait busts: one of a warrior and the other of a woman. The painters are executing a mural. Opposite them men are playing an organ and, below, scholars are consulting books, whilst one is making or setting a clock. In the centre are astrologers in orientalising costume, perhaps in token of the authorship by Arabic and Judaic scholars of astrological texts. In the forefront are two diners, one dressed in rich fashion, possibly with reference to fact that Mercury was said to preside over contracting business and other enterprises, as well as making friends. While the personnel show continuity with previous tradition, the way Mercury has been represented in a triumphal chariot is an innovation, and follows the Italian fashion of the Triumphs of Petrarch.[18] The engraving relates to contemporary practice by highlighting the latest fashion for portrait busts and classicising architecture. The inscription, however, is quoted from the medieval *Speculum naturale* by Vincent de Beauvais, composed in the thirteenth century.[19] The fact that Mercury was displayed wearing winged boots was sometimes related to the agility with which merchants were famed as traveling in contemporary texts.[20] The zodiacal signs with which the planet was associated were displayed on the wheels of the chariot.

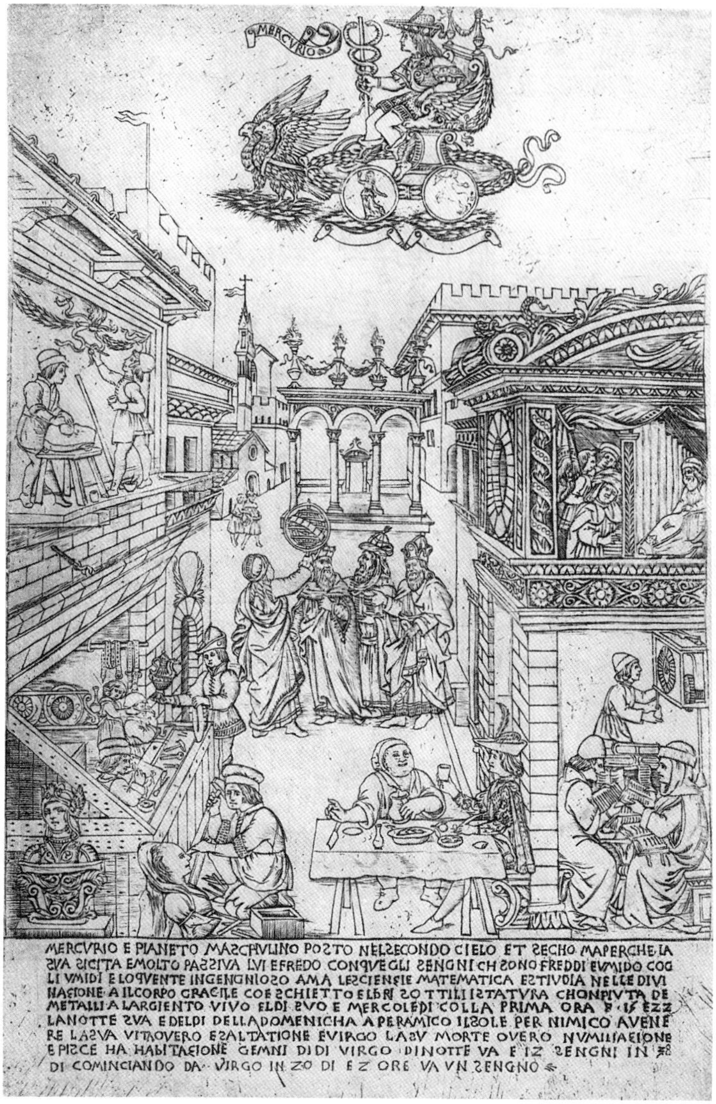

62 *Children of Mercury*, attributed to Maso Finiguerra, *c.*1470, engraving, 324 × 22 mm, British Museum.

A further example, this time for more of an elite audience, was made around 1490 and comprises the *De sphaera*, which is an illuminated manuscript for Duke Lodovico Sforza in Milan (Plate 63). This shows the same activities as the engraving, with the addition of an armourer.[21] The text states that 'Mercury is a shining star of reason, who produces a great fountain of eloquence, and subtle talents and every beautiful art, that is the enemy of all things vain'.[22] The book contains diagrams explaining the phenomena of the horizon, the eclipses of the sun and moon, the rotundity of the earth, the four elements and ether, as well as the movement of the planets, and their physical powers over terrestrial activities. Mercury is shown holding the money bag of a merchant and the twined serpents from his caduceus, while on the previous page are depicted a group of workshops. At the base is the shop of the armourer and the organ maker. In the centre are three feasters with their kitchen below them. On either side are scribes, a painter (painting an altarpiece depicting the Madonna and Child), a clock maker, and a sculptor (carving a life-size female nude).

The influences of the planets had been most thoroughly discussed by Ptolemy in his *Tetrabiblos* (that is *Three Books*) in the second century CE.[23] This text had sufficient longevity to explain the contents of fifteenth- and sixteenth-century illustrations of the Children of the Planets. It had been translated into Latin in 1138 by Plato of Tivoli and later handbooks on astrology had drawn on it.[24] For example, *Das gross Planetenbuch*, published in Strasburg in 1546, has the assurance on the

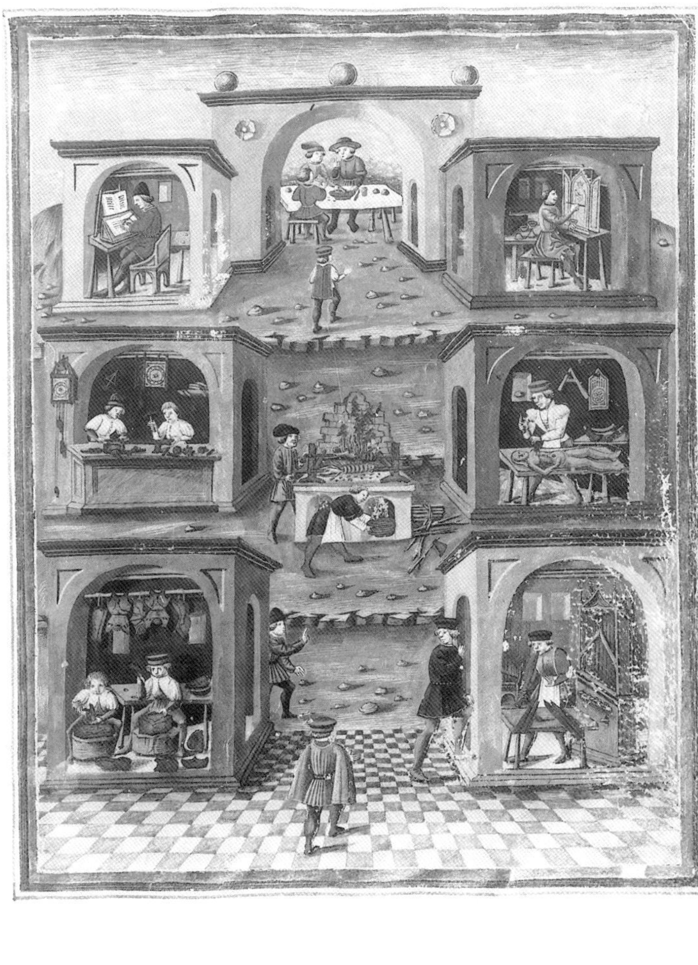

63 *Children of Mercury*, *c.*1490, *De sphaera* Latin 209, fol. 9, Reale Biblioteca Estense, Modena.

title page that all has been taken from Plato, Ptolemy and the Arabic philosopher Abu Ma'shar.[25] Ptolemy had written that Mercury makes people 'artistic, talented, poetic, lovers of beauty and the Muses, of worthy character, seekers after enjoyment, luxurious, happy, fond of friends, intellectual, quick to learn, eloquent, earnest'.[26] He then went on to assert that the influence of Mercury alone makes people, 'wise, shrewd, thoughtful, learned, inventive, experienced, good calculators, inquirers into nature, speculative, gifted, emulous and successful',[27] and that as a result Mercury governs, 'scribes, men of business, calculators, teachers, merchants, bankers, astrologers'.[28] He claimed that when Mercury is allied with Venus they 'bring out action expressed by the arts of the Muses – workers in the theatre, makers of musical instruments, painters, dancers, weavers',[29] and that if Mercury is allied with Mars, 'they produce sculptors, armourers, modellers and physicians'.[30] Here in the Greek text are the painters, sculptors, goldsmiths, organ makers, clock makers (as calculators) and party goers shown in the Florentine print and the Milanese illumination. Here is the astrologer and the scholar seen in the engraving, and the armourer depicted in *De sphaera*.

Arabic and Judaic scholars had provided commentaries on Ptolemy's work. For example, Hermann of Dalmatia, in the twelfth century, had translated the *Flores Abumazaris* or *Flowers of Abu Ma'shar*, a text written in Baghdad in the ninth century, and still considered worth printing in Augsburg in 1488. The *Flores* included architects or Masters of Works since Abu Ma'shar stated that Mercury is, 'the signifier of writers, of arithmetic, of merchants, and of the teachers of boys, and of the Masters of Works'.[31] The *Introductorium* or *Introduction to Astronomy* by Abu Ma'shar, published in Augsburg in 1489, expatiated on the patronage of Mercury to include 'the disciples of inventiveness, eloquence, complete wisdom, sane doctrine, the exhortation to healthy life, those wily in argument', adding those keen to study philosophy, poetry, mathematics, geometry, astronomy, expertise in divination, and skill in all trades.[32]

Abraham ben Ezra's Hebrew treatise entitled *The Beginning of Wisdom* had been composed in 1146 and had then been translated first into French by Hagan le Juif (1273) and then Latin (relying on the French translation) by Pietro d'Abano (1293).[33] The latter translation was regarded as sufficiently interesting to be printed in Venice in 1507 as *Abrahe[m] Avenaris judei astrologi peritissimi in re iudiciali opera* (*Abraham Avenezra, The Work of the most Skilled Hebrew Astrologer on Matters of Divination Pertaining to Making Decisions*).[34] According to Abraham ben Ezra, Mercury presides over:

> philosophers, the learned, doctors, scribes, mathematicians, geometricians, merchants and artisans of any profession related to carving and painting; in the metal kingdom to mercury, all coins and stones used as seals; and of places, to the markets, the educational institutions and all workshops.[35]

Pietro's translation ended with the advice that when Mercury is in the ascendant,

> it is good to buy all sorts of paintings, manuscripts, grain, millet, silk, cloth and all kinds of human clothes of every sort in various colours, it is good to buy bombazine, silk or satin and anything made of silk, and to begin to make a plea in court, to get married, to seal a partnership, to take medicine, to let blood, as well as to make a journey for business purposes.[36]

Sixteenth-century illustrations therefore represented concepts of painting, sculpture and goldsmithing which were part of a long tradition. Not surprisingly, there was a tendency in the texts to add new technologies. For instance, Leonhardt Thurneisser zum Thurn in 1569 included engravers, makers of letters for printing, and book printers as Children of Mercury in his treatise on the movement of the planets: *Archidoxa dorin der Recht war Motus Lauff und Gang der Planeten* (Munster, 1569).[37] However, these new technologies were never illustrated in cycles of the Children of the Planets.

The relative stability throughout the sixteenth century of the iconography of the Children of Mercury is suggested by the reprinting in 1569, and again in 1589, of *Le Calendrier des bergers* (Paris, 1499) all with the same text and woodcut for Mercury.[38] The rhymed calendar was named after the shepherds who had observed the Nativity star. The chapter heading for Mercury represented only the astrologer (gazing up at a star), a painter and a sculptor. Mercury was shown with his caduceus and his money bag, whilst the painter was a court painter portraying a king, and the sculptor was acquainted with classical models, since he was carving a nude. The emphasis was on status, learning and secular subject matter. The 1499 edition in the British Library contains end papers scribbled on in contemporary handwriting, which denotes its accessibility in a household.[39] The illustrations are supplemented by the text listing the Children of Mercury as being of *subtil engin* (that is to say, of subtle creativity or talent), who may be monks or other religious persons:

> He will not love to go to war but will pile up money with his prudence. He may be a good worker in some mechanical art. Or he may be a great preacher, orator, philosopher or geometrician. He will really love his writing, numbers and poetic verses, the art of music and measurement. He will know how to make fine cloth, or be steward to some great Lord or a receiver of his rents.[40]

Children of Mercury 1500–1600, visual images

German-speaking audiences seem to have enjoyed these ideas, as witnessed by the woodcut series of the Seven Planets that was issued in Augsburg in about 1530 and which has been attributed to Georg Pencz

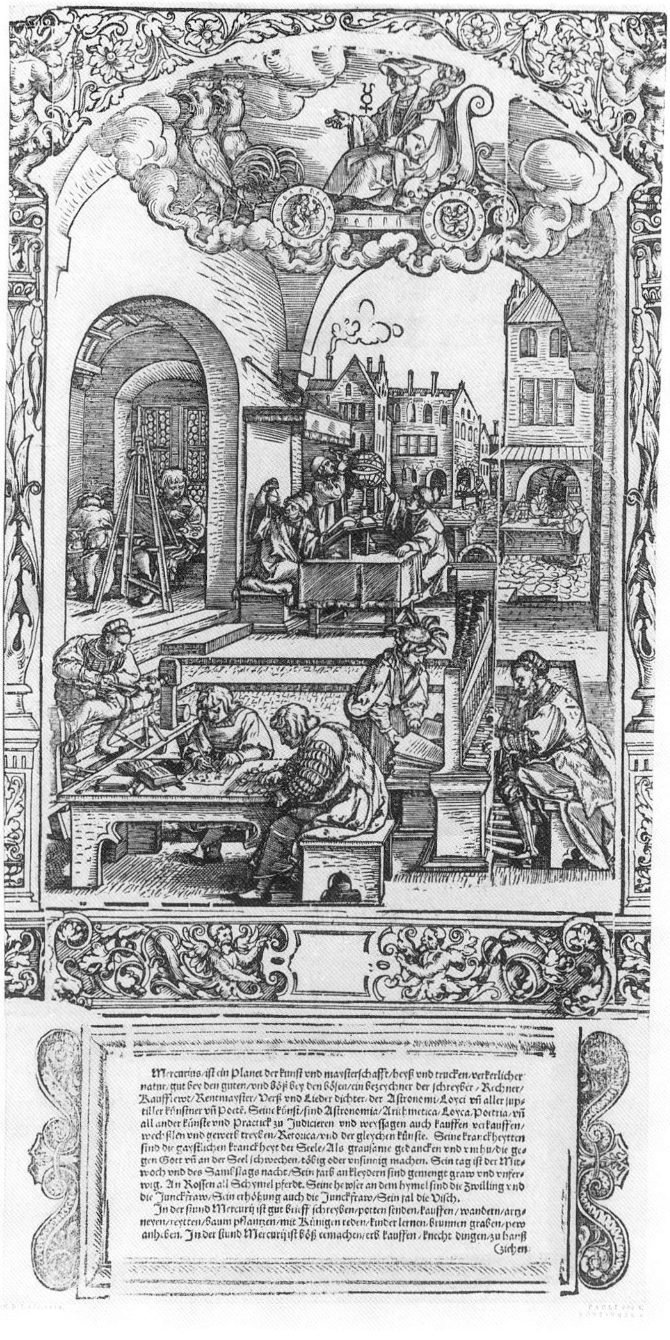

64 *Children of Mercury*, attributed to Georg Pencz, *c.*1530, woodcut, 298 × 206 mm, British Museum.

(*c.*1500–*c.*1550).[41] Pencz was a painter, engraver and woodcutter, born in Nuremberg and trained by Dürer; he is thought to have travelled to the Veneto in the period 1520–29 and he died in Leipzig. The series displayed the Children of Saturn as farming, of Jupiter as rulers, of Mars as soldiers, of Apollo as princes and gentry in their courts, of Venus as lovers, and of Luna as fishers (Plate 64). In this sequence, as in the Florentine engraving, the Children of Mercury were represented as artisans and members of the bourgeoisie, located in a town, below the social level of rulers and princes – indeed, in the market place as advised by Abraham ben Ezra. Mercury was shown in a chariot pulled by cocks after the Italian fashion, holding his caduceus but, unlike the Florentine engraving, wearing contemporary dress in a long-skirted robe and hat. Below him are the painter and the sculptor, while there is a goldsmith's shop background right. Beneath the goldsmith is an organ player, and in the centre background are astronomers, and a physician examining a urine flask. The presence of the physician points to the way the planetary discourse coincided with the representation by some painters from the 1520s onwards of Saint Luke as physician, scholar and painter. In the foreground, seated at a table, is someone with an open book, drawing, and another person, possibly casting accounts, who wears a fur-lined cloak. Following contemporary practice, the figure being sculpted is placed horizontally. All are well dressed, and the painter's studio has a grand barrel vault and glass windows. The verse inscription in the vernacular reads:

> Mercury is a planet of art and mastery entailing judgement and wisdom, and is changeable by nature being good with the good and bad with the bad. It is associated with one who draws, a writer, a calculator, a merchant, a master of rents, a composer of songs and verse, an astronomer, logician, a poet and all similar artists and poets. His arts are astronomy, arithmetic, logic, poetry . . . In the hour of Mercury it is good to write letters, send messengers, do business, travel, visit a doctor, ride, plant trees, petition kings, set children to school and dig wells.[42]

Although the inscription mentions neither the painter nor the sculptor in wood or the goldsmith, the printmaker has ensured their presence along with the draughtsman, astronomer and doctor, the two latter being occupation that *are* listed. While the inscription warns that Mercury is a bad sign in conjunction with some planets and constellations, it is his auspicious side that we are shown. This series was re-issued in woodcut form in 1587.[43]

Another series was at least planned in the same city at about the same time, possibly for stained glass. This is attributed to Georg Breu the Elder (1475/8–1537), with reference to surviving drawings of the Children of Mercury and of Saturn in circular fields (Plate 65).[44] Breu was a painter of Augsbourg, who wrote a chronicle of his city between

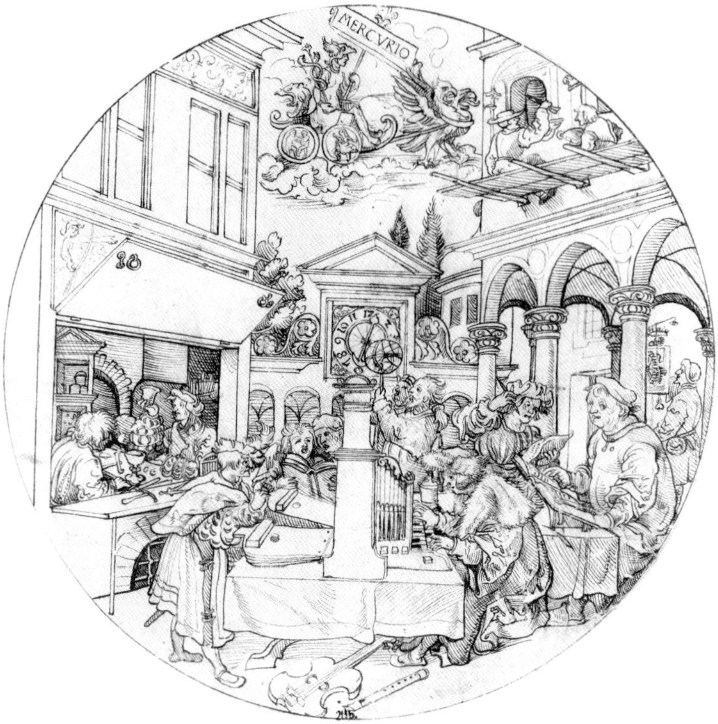

65 *Children of Mercury*, attributed to Georg Breu the Elder, pen and ink, 23 cm in diameter, Kupferstichkabinett Staatliche Museen, Berlin.

1512 and 1537.[45] This drawing of the Children of Mercury presented painters making a mural, and a goldsmith's shop, in a manner reminiscent of the Florentine engraving. Mercury rides in a chariot drawn by cocks, but this time he is shown in the antique fashion. The references to classical art are reinforced in the Italianate setting, with its arcade to the right and the triangular pediment adorning the central clock. There is no sculptor, but the goldsmith's shop is prominent to the left, where cups are being made. In the centre an organ is played. Two astronomers are holding up an armillary sphere beside the clock with Arabic numerals in the centre background. On the right two men are casting accounts at a ledger, with one scratching his head in puzzlement. Behind the organ a young man and an older one share a book, perhaps to sing, or possibly to indicate teaching. In the background to the right someone adjusts a wall clock.

In the Netherlands there was also an interest in such ideas. From 1568 derives the series invented by van Heemskerck, engraved by Cock and issued by Harman Jansz. Muller in Antwerp (*c.*1538–1617) (Plate 66). This was so successful that it was reissued in 1601, 1636 and 1638. Van Heemskerck had already been responsible for two important images of Saint Luke, exploring the way the roles of writer, painter and physician were joined in the Evangelist. Cock was the most important printmaker in northern Europe. Like van Heemskerck, he had appropriated Italianate classicising styles, and he had visited Italy in around 1550. Muller was from Amsterdam but ran his publishing house, called The Gilded Compasses, in Antwerp from 1555 to 1580.[46] Van Heemskerck imagines Mercury in a winged chariot, recalling the Florentine engraving (Plate 62), and presents him in a classicising manner; the setting is the marketplace appropriate to doing his sorts of business. Indeed, the *De imaginibus deorum*, by Caius Julius Hyginus the second-century CE Roman mythographer (issued in Basel in 1549), interpreted Mercury's wings as denoting his speed as a merchant: 'the winged boots allude to the feet of merchants who travel about as if they had wings'.[47] A large table, similar to that in the background of the print attributed to Pencz (Plate 64), has been brought forward, but again one finds astronomers pointing at a globe, and a physician analysing a urine flask. Close to the viewer, someone is writing, while another counts money. Two young men attend this company, possibly to suggest the teaching role for which Mercury was well known. The painter is at his easel back right, in a grand barrel vaulted studio with a top light, while the sculptor hammers vigorously at a male nude statue. Whereas the previous series had provided contemporary dress for their human participants, van Heemskerck registers the fashion for classicising narration which he had absorbed during his journey to Italy, and all are dressed in an antique manner. The fact that the organist is a woman with female

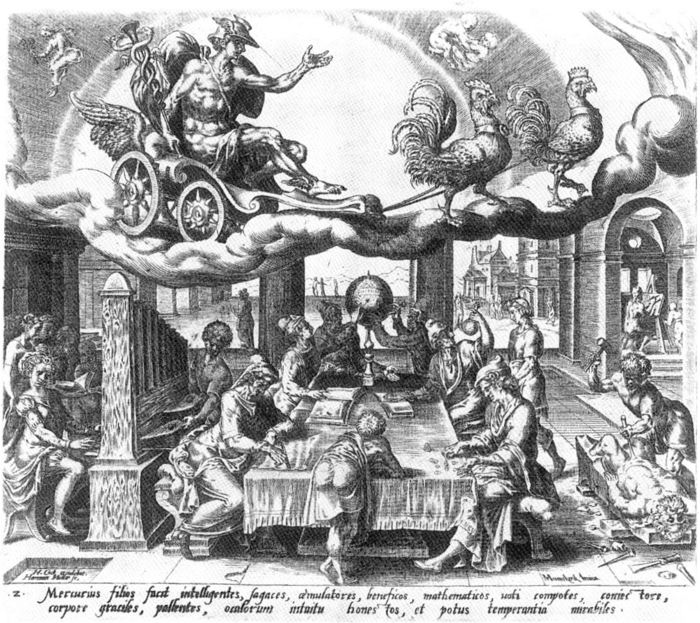

66 Marten van Heemskerck, *Children of Mercury*, 1568, engraving, 211 × 246 mm.

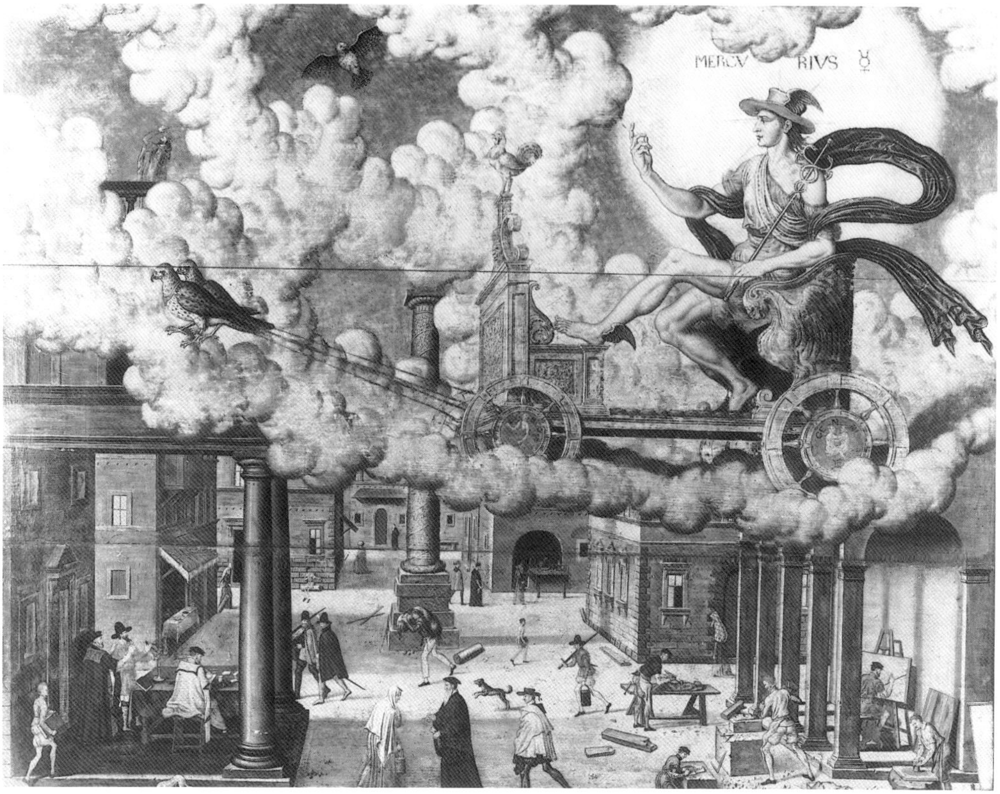

67 *Children of Mercury*, *c.*1550, panel, 30″ × 41″, Collection Kenneth Clark.

singers around her suggests muses remote from everyday life. The Latin inscription mentions only mathematicians, musicians and astronomers: 'Mercury makes children who are intelligent, sagacious, emulous, generous, mathematicians, astrologers, musicians, slender in body, pale in the lips, honest in appearance and marvellously abstemious in drinking.'[48]

The subject matter was not confined to the medium of books and prints. Four painted panels survive from a set of the Children of the Planets, by a Netherlandish artist, which have been dated about 1550 (Plate 67).[49] The panel for the Children of Mercury presents a grand vision of a classicising townscape, possibly evoking Florentine palace architecture and Rome, as it features a version of the column of Trajan or Marcus Aurelius in the centre. Pride of place is given to the doctor of medicine in the centre, to whom a woman brings her urine in a rush basket. The sculptors, masons and painters are given a foreground position on the right. As so often, the artist is associated with the city. One man carries a sword, recalling the presence of the armourer in the Milanese manuscript. Scribes and accountants are busy under a portico to the left, where a well-dressed man seems to be giving orders. He might be undertaking new business enterprises or artistic commissions, and there may also be a reference to how auspicious Mercury is, for those introducing themselves to powerful patrons. The astrologer has climbed up to the roof of the palace on the left, above them, to view the heavens. At only about a third of a metre high the panels were presumably made for close up, one-to-one viewing, possibly in a domestic setting. Painting, sculpture and building are linked with wealth, learning and healing. Although a cock sits on the rail of the classicising chariot of Mercury, the steeds are hawks and a hawk flies in the sky.

The continuing currency of these beliefs in the Netherlands is underlined in the issue of an engraved series of Children of the Planets, dated 1596, by Jan Saenredam after original designs by Hendrik Goltzius (Plate 68).[50] Goltzius was a painter and printmaker whose father and grandfather were painters, and was born in Mülbracht, but died in Haarlem. In 1590 he set out to visit Italy and spent time in Rome, where he met Federico Zuccari. Saenredam (1565–1607) was born at Zaandan and died at Assendelft, working in Golztius's studio in Haarlem from 1589 onwards. The setting is the usual marketplace, and actors are captivating a huge audience from an open-air stage, whilst opposite them a preacher is standing on an outdoor pulpit. The emphasis, then, is on rival forms of rhetoric. Stall holders are setting up to catch the crowd; the painter and sculptor are at work, with scholars in the foreground. Goltzius has returned to the tradition of evoking the bustle of a contemporary city. Yet he also publicised his knowledge of classicising styles, by representing all the planetary deities as if they were ancient Roman statues, around which their children clustered. Mercury presides on his plinth in the market. A Latin inscription explains 'Me Dys commendat facundiae gratia linguae, Et varias rudibus monstro mortalibus artes' ('The deity granted me fine eloquence and I show various arts to unskilled humans').

An anonymous treatise on the Seven Planets, published in Leipzig in 1598, emphasises the continuity in Mercury's astrological connotations. Mercury's children are described as eager for fame (*Ruhmhasstig*), and inclined to rhetoric, geometry and philosophy and 'all natural arts whether written, spoken, pictorial or all the other similar skills'.[51] Those under his influence are still keen on travel and good at winning friends, and his hour is auspicious for 'sending children to school, learning new things, marrying, tree planting, travelling and buying and selling'.[52]

However, it is interesting that Goltzius also seems to have transgressed the genre to introduce viewers to the new ideas about the status of *disegno*, because he edged in a draughtsman, along with rulers, among the Children of Jupiter in the same series (Plate 69). It was no accident presumably that Goltzius had the chance to meet Zuccari, on a trip to Italy between 1590 and 1591, since Zuccari led in attempting to raise the status of *disegno* at this period. The Latin inscription

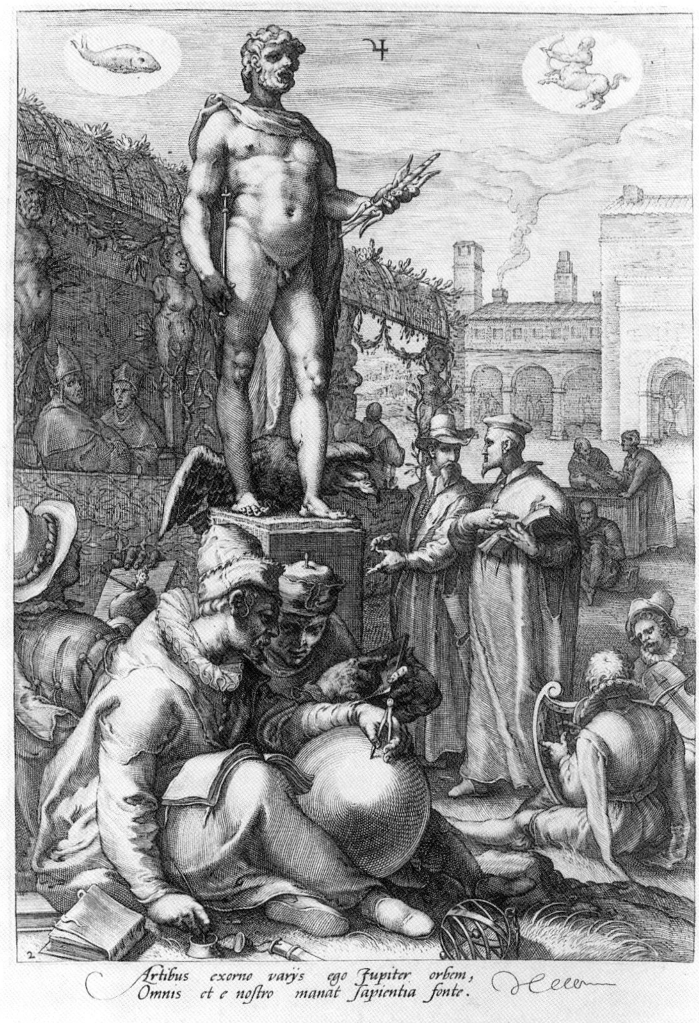

68 Hendrik Goltzius, *Children of Jupiter*, 1596, engraved by Jan Saenredam.

explained: 'With various arts, I, Jupiter, adorn the world, and all wisdom emanates from our fountainhead' (*Artibus exorno variis ego Jupiter orbem, /Omnis et nostro manat sapientia fonte*). A bishop and other dignitaries converse under a pergola, while scholars walk about consulting a book, two musicians are seated to the right, and an astronomer measures a terrestrial globe in the foreground. Behind them the artist is seated, drawing the statue of Jupiter, as if he were studying an ancient sculpture of the god. In the distance is what appears to be a civic loggia.[53]

It therefore seems that the prestigious connections between the Liberal Arts and artists, which were often pursued in the personification of painting, sculpture, architecture and *disegno*, and also in representations of Luke as scholar and doctor, could be exhibited in astrological illustrations. In addition to offering imagery to match the ambitions of aspirant artists, the notion of a mercurial personality presented a cluster of characteristics which accorded, to some extent, with the traits required for success. For the mercurial child was inventive, emulous, gregarious, good at business, manually skilled yet conversant with the higher arts, ready for travel, teaching or learning new things, and good at approaching lords and rulers: a Cellini or a Frans Floris fitted that sort of personality model rather well. In some cases, the potential psychological 'fit' was even accompanied by institutional regulations, since some guilds included activities corresponding to astrological categories. For

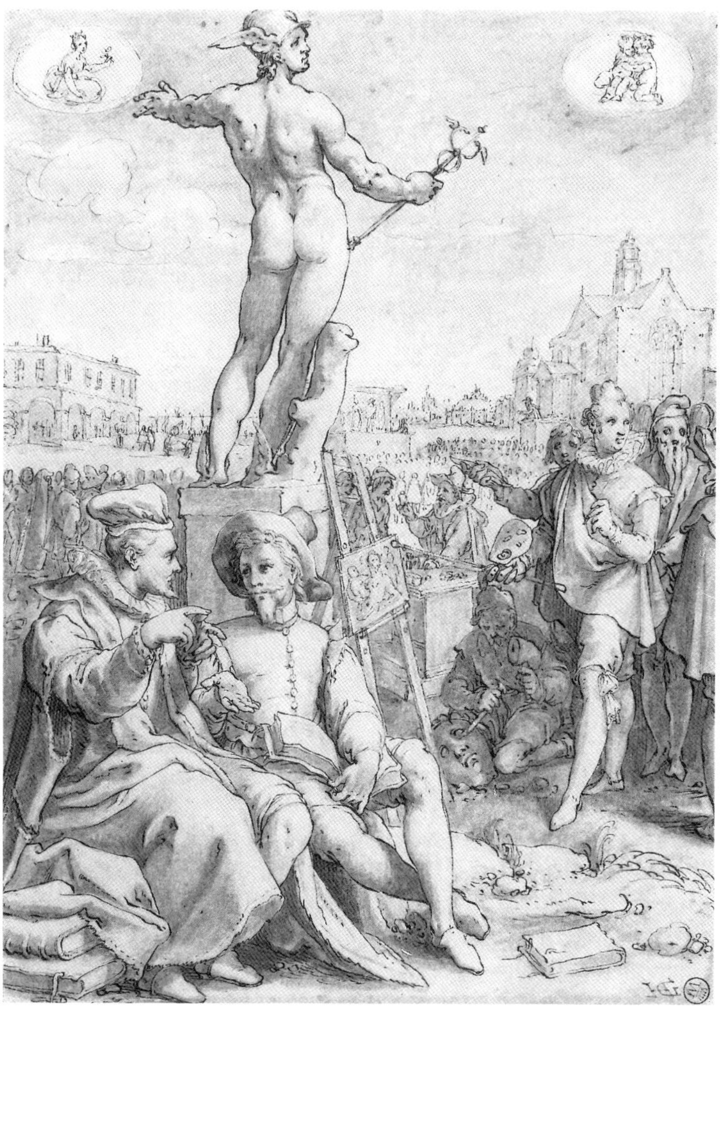

69 Hendrik Goltzius, *Children of Mercury*, 1596, drawing, 235 × 175 cm, Prentenkabinett, Leiden.

example, at Antwerp the Guild of Saint Luke included painters with gold- and silversmiths, organ makers and bookbinders, whilst at Haarlem the Guild of Saint Luke regulated painters as well as clock makers and organ makers.

Mercury as mythological helper of artists

Resting in part on this astrological tradition, some artists, beginning in 1540, represented the mythological god Mercury as their protector. This in itself registered quite an ambitious shift, because figures from mythology were customarily reserved to allegorise the trials and triumphs of leaders in thought and society. For example, Apollo adorned the funerary urn of the King of France (Plate 12), and Mercury accompanied other Gods in the celebration of the virtues of Francesco Maria I Duke of Urbino (Plate 8).

According to literary traditions, Mercury had sometimes been linked with stealing, while in Roman religious practice he had been associated with success in business dealing. However, artists represented his 'best' side for their purposes, and chose him as a companion, rather, because of his legendary invention of speech, music and writing, as well as his guidance of souls to heaven. Mercury's high standing had been expressed most influentially in the *De nuptiis philologiae* or *Marriage of Mercury with Philology* by Martianus Capella, composed in the fifth century CE. This was well known throughout the medieval period and printed for example in Basel in 1532 and in Lyons in 1592. Capella related how Mercury was the brother of learned Minerva, and fell in love with Philology, or the personification of the study of languages, who was herself the leader of the Liberal Arts. Martianus Capella added that Mercury 'has a wonderful magic in painting and, as a sculptor in bronze or marble, he brings life into the features'.[54] This positive view of Mercury was continued in sixteenth-century mythological texts. For example, Lilio Gregorio Giraldi, in *De deis gentium*, 1548 dwelled mostly on Mercury's good qualities.

> To have taught everyone not only how to read but also how to instruct is certainly a precious work. Added to this he is also said to have invented the art of deception, and also to have laid down the names of things, to have reduced words to order, and to have founded the sacred cult of the gods. He observed the course of the stars and planets and discovered numbers, medicine and the lyre.[55]

The visual representations which linked art with the qualities of Mercury (sometimes paired with Minerva) belonged to traditions of interpreting the stories of pagan deities as fables of the earliest deeds of mankind. This could entail the invention of speech by Mercury or weaving by Minerva. Such interpretation had become intertwined with moralising reading, in order to render pagan stories understandable to a society which wished to find divine messages in all of creation, including the pre-Christian past. In this way, Mercury might signify love of learning, and Minerva could indicate wisdom or chastity. During the sixteenth century therefore, allegories involving Mercury in a leading role were developed, to boost the prestige of artists themselves, first in Italy, and then, from 1563 onwards, both by Italian speaking artists and also by Netherlandish sculptors, painters and printmakers.

Italy 1521–62

The earliest illustration of Mercury as protector of artists, outside the general astrological market of the Children of Mercury, was made by the Milanese painter and architect Cesare Cesariano, and published in the first Italian translation of Vitruvius' *Ten Books on Architecture* (Como, 1521).[56] Although this still stressed Mercury's planetary powers, it was aimed at artists and those interested in art (Plate 70). Cesare gave plenty of space to his allegory, awarding it a full page, and entitling it 'The choices of the world represented by Cesare Cesariano' (*mundi electiva Caesaris Caesariani configurata*). This was an allegory of attainment, through Learning, Prudence and Audacity, with the help of Mercury despite a crowd of vices led by Poverty. Mercury points up to a providential God beside the inscription 'Thus the Fates decree', (*sic fata volunt*) and is placed in the centre right, where he is able to dominate Fortune (*Sors*). This permits a female personification with wings on her head, labelled Audacity (*Audacia*), to assist a young man to take Fortune (*Sors*) by the forelock (referring to the traditional adage that one must take opportunity by the forelock). The hero is crowned with the laurel wreath of victory, and holds the attributes of architecture: a ruler and compasses. Behind him Prudence or *Prudentia* pushes away 'Dire Poverty, daughter of Ignorance' (*Dira paupertas filia ignoranciae*) accompanied by Calumny. Beyond them to the left, Hardwork with a spade (*Labor*) Patience with her yoke, and Hope looking upwards (*Spes*) are outnumbered by Desperation or *Desperatio* tearing her hair, Fraud (*Fraus*), Hypocrisy (*Hippocrasia*) and Sloth (*Inertia*) in 'the train of Poverty' (*Paupertatis coetus*). The 'hero' is labelled on his back 'the learned man is led away at last from poverty' (*Exigitur tandem a paupertate doctus*). The role of Mercury as a teacher, and his reputation for loving learning, could be relevant here. Above them an inscription reads *In mundi nubibus stat paupertatis status* ('In the clouds of the world poverty reigns'). Above, preside Constant Envy (*Invidia consta*[*ntia*]) and a donkey-eared 'Lady Ignorance' (*D*[*omin*]*a Ignorantia*), who are accompanied by a woman releasing insects, labelled Persuasion or *Persuasio*. These personifications are surrounded by monstrous clouds.

To the right are divine, ecclesiastical and temporal powers. At the top is divine power, labelled 'The serenity of the commanders'

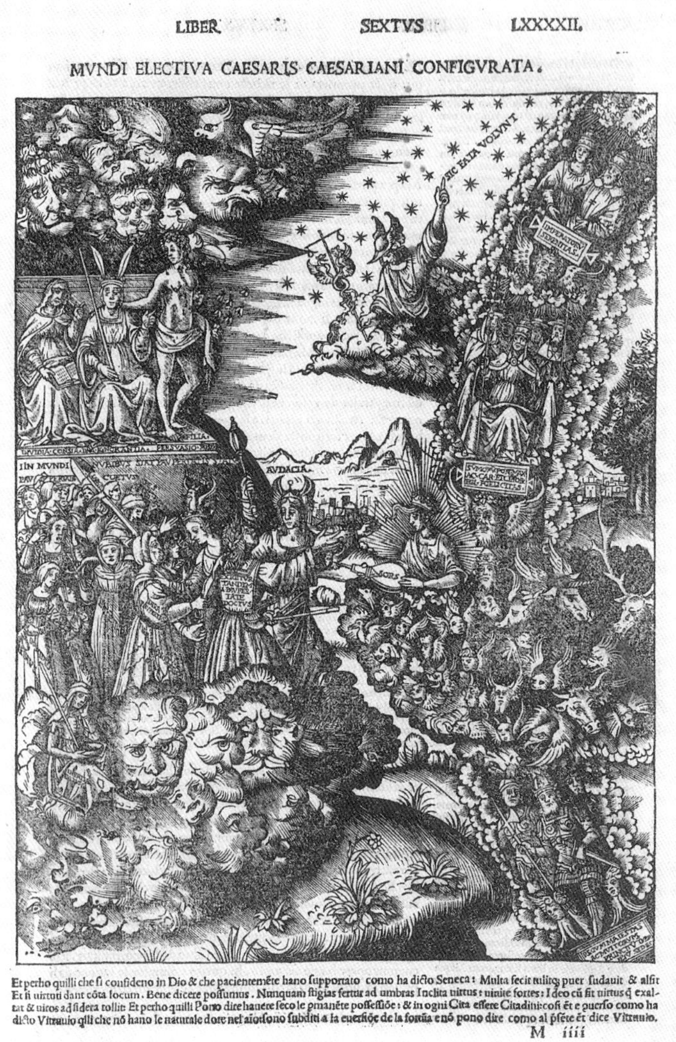

70 Cesare Cesariano, *Mercury watches over the learned architect escaping Poverty*, 1521, British Museum.

(*Imperator*[*or*]*um serenitas*). Below is the spiritual rule of the world: 'The felicity of the most lofty popes, cardinals and the whole church' (*Sum*[*m*]*oru*[*m*] *pont*[*ificorum*] *max*[*imorum*] *ac car*[*dinalorum*] *et chor*[*um*] *ec*[*c*]*l*[*esiae*] *foelicitas*). Beneath them is temporal power, which is inscribed 'The majesty of the king and the thrones of many immortal princes' (*regum maiestas ac multorum principium immortalium sedes*). Does the allegory suggest that the artist is succeeding in attracting worldly preferment from the loftiest rulers? Or, given the presence of divine powers, is there a suggestion that artists ultimately seek more abstract rewards in some heavenly sphere? According to the accompanying commentary, Cesare presented this allegory as expressing his gratitude for achieving the publication of his book against the odds.

Cesare was the son of Lorenzo Cesariano or Ciserani, and was born in Milan in 1483. According to his autobiography, he had been disappointed of his inheritance following his father's early death in 1488, through the schemes of the woman he called his stepmother and her notary husband. In spite of being what Cesare described as educated in law and the humanities, Lorenzo had died intestate. Thrust from his stepmother's house at his majority, aged fifteen, Cesare had sought his living as a painter and architect in Reggio Emilia, Parma and Ferrara. True to his father's high educational status, he had begun to translate Vitruvius about 1500, but did not achieve financial backing to print his work until two decades later, from two Milanese citizens. It was this eventual success that he celebrated in 'the allegory of choices'. In the life story which Cesare inserted beside the allegory, he narrated the difficulties with which his wicked stepmother and poverty beset him, as if they were the personifications he drew: 'the murky world of the evil forces of the stepmother and of poverty, and the obscene envies and blandishments of the daughters of the dire stepmother and all her calumnies and hidden falsehoods.'[57] At his lowest ebb, when he prayed at the grave of his father at Santo Stefano in Milan, 'Mercury sent by divine clemency and called upon for good reason (not in a beastly or monstrous form but as a good spirit) appeared so that helpful Fortune could blow through me'.[58] Indeed, Fortune is puffing her bellows at the hero in the facing illustration.

Cesare used the design to illustrate his own personal story of triumph, despite losing his paternal inheritance, and his success in obtaining patronage, which he had related on pages adjacent to this allegory. However, it was sufficiently abstract to appeal to others. This was an influential work which circulated in an edition of 1,500 copies and is of large format.[59] Significantly, Cesare chose to label his erudite allegory in Latin, although the commentary accompanying it was in Italian.

The next allegory featuring Mercury as artist's helper was made by Giulio Romano, for the front of his house in Mantua, in around 1540. This time the stress was more on the god's mythological role (Plate 71). This scheme was ostentatiously erudite, for it provided no helpful labels, and referred to an abstruse Greek dialogue known only to scholars. Whereas Cesare's allegory had included the attributes of the architect, this façade focused on Mercury as the god of rhetoric. Arguably, the intention was to suggest links between this Liberal Art and Giulio's profession as painter and architect. Born in Rome in 1499, Giulio had arrived in Mantua as a painter who had been trained in the prestigious workshop of Raphael, with some experience as an architect. Over the

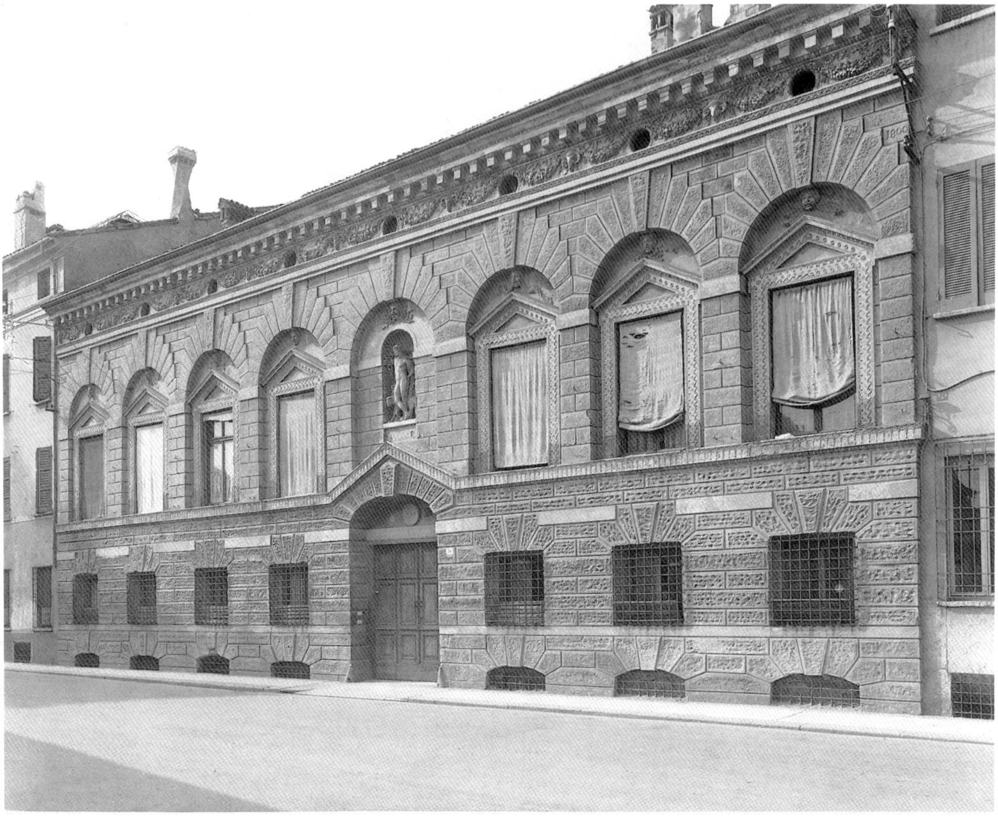

71 Mercury on the façade of Giulio Romano's house, Mantua, 1540–44.

next decade he achieved a controlling position over architectural and pictorial designs for the Marquis of Mantua, Federigo Gonzaga. Having bought a house in 1538, Giulio transformed it between 1540 and 1544. The original building consisted of the six bays situated on the left of the present building, with the main portal then positioned in the third bay from the left (the façade was expanded in 1800).[60] It seems likely that Giulio knew Cesare's allegory, as architects had eagerly awaited a printed vernacular Vitruvius.

Giulio placed Mercury life size in a niche over the original door, in the form of an ancient Roman statue. He had had the statue adapted, by making stucco additions to a torso from a Roman sculpture, and adding a caduceus as well as a ram, which may refer to Mercury's attribute as a shepherd.[61] In masks, moulded in relief from stucco, over the five windows and the central niche, he made allusion to Lucian's dialogue *On Hercules*, which had been composed in Greek in the second century CE, and was first printed in 1496. It described a painting of the Celtic god of eloquence (their equivalent of Mercury). Lucian explained that

Celts gave the attributes of Mercury to the god they called Ogmios, whom they depicted with his tongue connected by golden chains to people's ears, and it was this bizarre symbol which was placed over the head of Giulio Romano's statue of Mercury.[62] It seems possible that Giulio knew the precedent for this imagery, which had been drawn by Dürer and publicised after his death, on an illustrated title page, printed for a work by Appian (Ingolstadt, 1534). Wilfully abstruse as it was when Giulio made the façade, the legend of Mercury's golden hold on people's ears was reiterated during the sixteenth century. For example, the manual of Natale Conti *Mythologiae sive explanationis fabulae*, which was reissued several times between 1567 and 1605, explained that the ancients had shown Mercury attached by golden chains to everyone's ears because of the power of his tongue: 'Mercury was a man of singular inventiveness and wisdom for it is agreed that he was most intelligent in oratory both when explaining things and in his innate talent for rapidly producing new ideas.'[63] On Giulio's façade, two other masks appear to illustrate further attributes of eloquence, as retailed by Lucian in the same passage. There is a mask from whose mouth issues flowers, and another which seems to breathe out bees, to indicate Lucian's references to 'flowery' language, 'honeyed' oratory and words as 'flying'. Two masks are associated with more conventional attributes of Mercury, in the form of the snakes from his caduceus, and his cloak or chlamys. One mask may represent the Gorgon's head from the shield of Minerva. Giulio's scheme as a whole, therefore, made no direct reference to art, dwelling instead on the enviable place of rhetoric as a Liberal Art, and inviting the deduction that the owner of the house saw architecture and painting as equal to rhetoric.

Inside his house Giulio continued the theme of the patronage of Mercury, only this time he paired Mercury with Minerva, by painting these deities on either side of the door to his reception room (Plates 72a and b).[64] The image of Mercury and Minerva together was connected with philosophical and literary academies in antiquity. Most famously, Cicero's *Letters to Atticus* described his own academy in Rome as being adorned with an image of Hermes (Mercury) with Athena (Minerva) to signify that it was an intellectual centre. Cicero had written: 'It is an appropriate ornament of my academy, since Hermes is the common emblem of such places and Minerva is special to the gymnasium.'[65] For this reason printers sometimes used figures of Minerva with Mercury as devices for scholarly imprints in the sixteenth century.[66] In Giulio's reception room, however, Mercury and Minerva were paired up to guard the doorway, but were not alone since they were accompanied on the remaining three walls by other pagan deities.

The prestige of Cesare's book and Giulio's house may help to explain why mercurial attributes were regarded as protecting an artist, and introducing him to Fortune, in a portrait medal for Lomazzo, dating

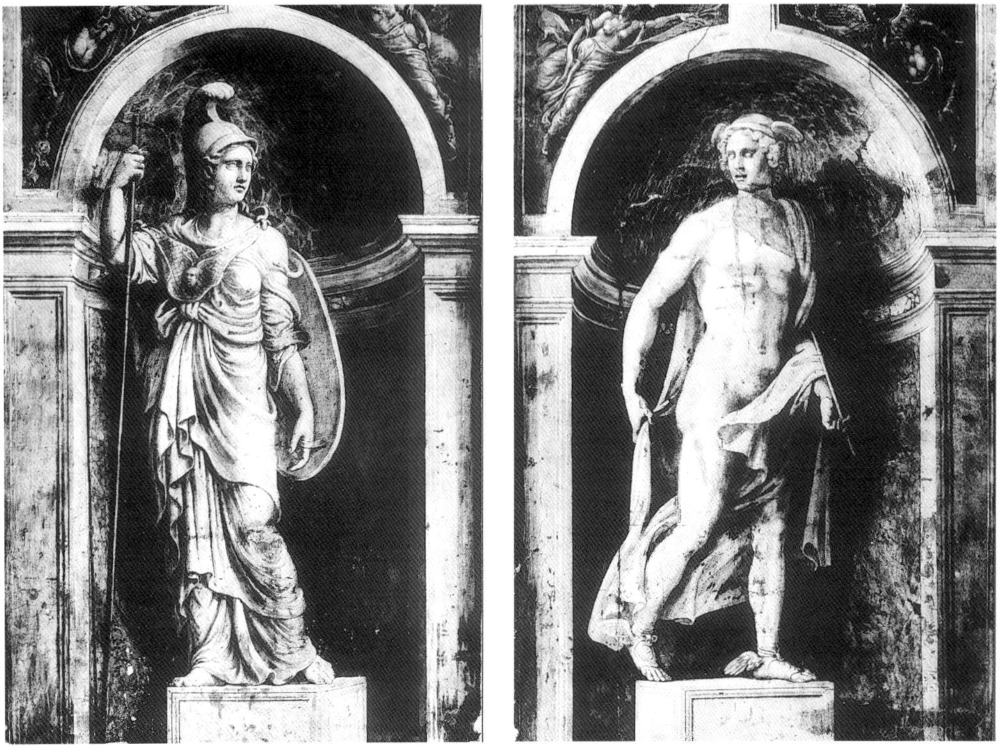

72 a and b Giulio Romano, *Mercury and Minerva*, Sala grande, House of Giulio Romano, Mantua, 1540–44.

from 1562 or a little later (Plate 73). Lomazzo (1538–1600) was a Milanese painter who later wrote two treatises on art following the onset of blindness in 1571. This medal showed a portrait of Lomazzo as if he were an ancient artist, nude with a robe knotted on his shoulder, on the obverse. On the reverse was a relief of a figure wearing the winged hat of Mercury and holding his caduceus, with a young man and Fortune. This medal was made by Annibale Fontana (1540–87) in a collegial spirit, since Lomazzo painted Annibale's portrait in exchange. As the motto for the reverse was *Utriusque* ('Of both sorts'), it seems likely that Lomazzo and Fontana were thinking of good and bad luck.[67] Fortune to the left is poised on a sphere to show her inconstancy, and holds a veil blowing in the wind to suggest the wind of change. A poem published by Lomazzo in 1587 stated that the youth to the right was Lomazzo himself, bowing to Fortune and also that: 'I had Prudence together with Fortune, before whom I am bowing, placed on the reverse of the medal'. It may be relevant that the original Milanese allegory by Cesariano had shown a personification of Prudence, wearing a winged hat and protecting the youth, so that he might reach Fortune under the watchful eye of Mercury. Both the medallist and the painter prided themselves in their learning. Fontana was a medallist and sculptor of

Milan, who along with Lomazzo belonged to the literary academy called the Accademia della Val di Blenio, which had been founded in 1560 to promote the dialect spoken in the eponymous valley. Lomazzo was elected as its head or 'Abbot'.

Netherlands and Italy 1563–77

During the next two decades, the imagery of Mercury as one who protects artistic life was further developed in Italy, this time by members of the Accademia del Disegno in Florence, and was also appropriated by painters and sculptors in the Netherlands.

Only a year after Lomazzo's medal was made, on a house façade in Antwerp dated 1563, the painter Cornelis van Dalem had a relief made representing Painting as a woman reclining with her easel and brushes over the door way labelled *Pictura* (Plate 15). She was flanked in the spandrels of the doorway by sculptures of Minerva and Mercury. *Pictura* was framed by portraits of Dürer and van Eyck (Plate 37), which have been attributed to the work of the local sculptor Willem van den Broucke (*c.*1530–79) . Cornelis van Dalem was a painter of landscapes, a linen merchant, a landowner and had a fine library. According to van Mander, Bartolomaeus Spranger, who was apprenticed to him between 1560 and 1562, remembered reading ancient literature and history, more than

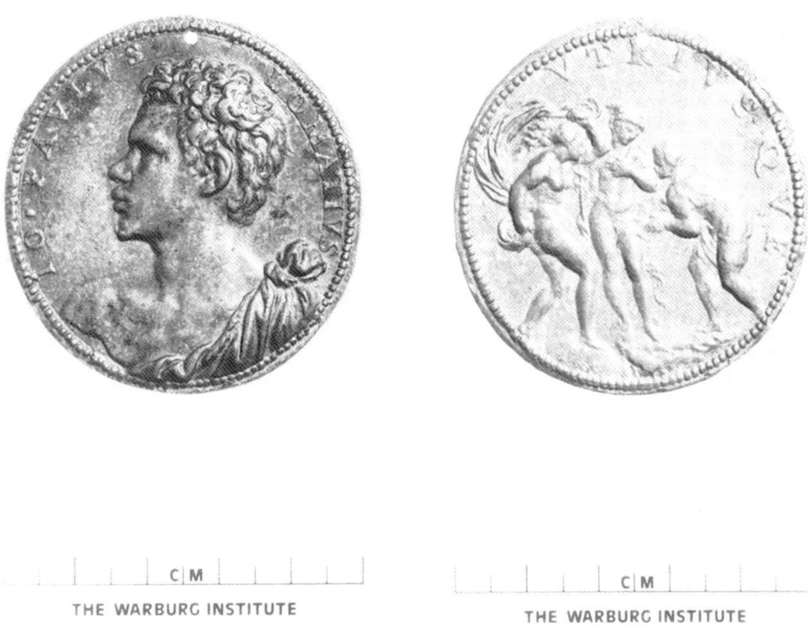

73 Annibale Fontana, Portrait medal of Giovanni Paolo Lomazzo, ?1562, bronze, 50 mm diameter, British Museum, George III illustrious persons 551.

painting, in his house.[68] Unlike Cornelis, Willem is known to have undertaken a study journey to Italy.[69] Willem was born in Mechelen and died in Antwerp, and had three brothers who were sculptors and architects. He entered the Guild of Saint Luke in Antwerp in 1557 and had travelled to Italy for some time before 1557. He worked with his brother Crispijn on the most prestigious building in Antwerp, the *Stadthuis*, with Cornelis Floris.

In myth, Minerva was the sister of Mercury, since both were the offspring of Jupiter, and she was associated with learning and wisdom, since she had been born from her father's head. As a virgin she was linked with virtue; as a martial goddess she could be portrayed as defender of artists. Virtue here probably indicated both Christian moral goodness and worthy, skilled art. According to the discussion by Hyginus, for example, in his *De imaginibus deorum*, published in Basel in 1549, and written in the second century CE, 'Minerva signifies the supreme theoretical state devoted to the contemplation of wisdom, for it is said that she was born from the head of Jove because personal inventiveness [*ingenium*] is placed in the brain'.[70] Hyginus went on to explain that her armour, including the breastplate with the head of the Gorgon whom she had slain, denoted the use of wisdom to protect against attack. The long spear indicated the long words employed by the wise to vanquish opponents, and the Gorgon head terrified her enemies, while her purity stood for the incorruptibility of wisdom.

It was a bold move for Cornelis to place Mercury and Minerva alone together on the exterior of an artist's house, since the only precedent, in Giulio Romano's house, was on the interior. The contemporary German scholar Georg Pictor, writing in Latin, had advised in 1548 that 'we link Minerva goddess of wisdom together with Mercury on the same footing rightly, since we know he was the god of eloquence most subtle in inventiveness out of all the gods'.[71] It seems possible that Cornelis knew of the literary and philosophical academy which had been designed by Vignola for the scholar Achille Bocchi, in Bologna, in emulation of Cicero's academy. This was built from 1545 onwards, and was decorated with statues of Mercury and Minerva. It could have been known to him from Achille's own book entitled *Of Symbols* or *Symbolicarum* (Bologna, 1555), which was engraved by Giulio Bonasone. Bonasone also represented Mercury and Minerva together, as they were intended to appear in relief on one exterior corner of the academy. The inscriptions read: 'Thus are monsters subdued' and, below, 'With me leading, you may achieve some progress'.[72] It is not certain that Vignola was able to install this sculpture when he completed the building in 1550. Cornelis might have seen the separate engravings published by Bonasone in 1550, which illustrated the house-cum-academy of Bocchi. According to these, the main façade represented freestanding statues of Mercury (left) and Minerva (right) above the entablature.[73] Since Cornelis completed his façade decoration in 1563, in the same year that the Florentine Academy of Design was founded, the idea of academic references on his house front in Antwerp might well have appealed.

A year later Mercury and Minerva also appeared side by side on the catafalque of Michelangelo in 1564 (Plate 16). Although this was a short-lived display, it reached a larger audience in the account given by Vasari in his *Lives*. According to Vasari, Mercury denoted Michelangelo's personal inventiveness or *ingenium*, and this time Minerva stood for his Skill. These personifications were sculpted in stucco and the catafalque had been topped with a figure of Fame, whilst below were Poetry, Painting, Sculpture and Architecture. Beneath these in turn were Religion and Virtue along with *Ingegno* and Art herself. *Ingegno*, sculpted by the Perugian sculptor Vincenzo Danti (1530–76), was represented on one corner of the catafalque, as 'all spirit' combating the vice of Ignorance. It was characterised, by Vasari, as 'a young man slender and in appearance all spirit [*spirito*] and of the most vivacious beauty, representing personal talent [*Ingegno*] with two little wings over the temples, in the guise in which at times Mercury is painted'.[74] Clearly the astrologers had attributed the talent of *ingegno* to the planet and his children. The *Calendrier des bergers* 1499 had written of Mercury's 'subtle invention' (*subtil engin*), while the Milanese *De sphaera* described his children as full of inventiveness (*ingegnioso*) in 1490. The mythological treatises had told the same story with Conti accounting Mercury as 'most astute in speaking and in *ingenium*' in 1567.[75] What Vasari meant by *spirito* is not clear. In the earliest Italian–English dictionary, entitled *The World of Wordes* (London, 1598), by John Florio, the word is translated as 'breath', 'soul' or 'courage'. On the next corner Minerva was sculpted by Lazzaro Calamec, to show Art vanquishing Envy. Vasari explained that it indicated how the supreme skill of Michelangelo had earned him glory, and had placed him beyond detractors. Conti explained that Minerva was the inventrix of skills in his *Mythologiae*, of the arts of war, house building, painting, weaving and growing olives.[76]

In either Antwerp or Bruges a few years later, Mercury was represented by Marcus Gheeraerts (1521–87) as the inspirer and helper of the painter in another allegory. This time, however, the design did not celebrate success, but rather harked back to the image by Cesariano in bewailing the poverty of the artist (Plates 70, 74). Whereas Cesare Cesariano had shown Mercury presiding over the artist's escape from want, Gheeraerts represents a struggle whose outcome is in doubt. Nevertheless, the allegory does link Mercury with that learning which may provide the pathway to attainment. Gheeraerts was a painter from Bruges who dated this highly polished drawing 1577, when he was 56 years old. At this point he was working with engravers in Antwerp, and it may well have been intended to become a print, since the inscription 'IN. B.', which may stand for 'invented in Bruges', is placed on one of

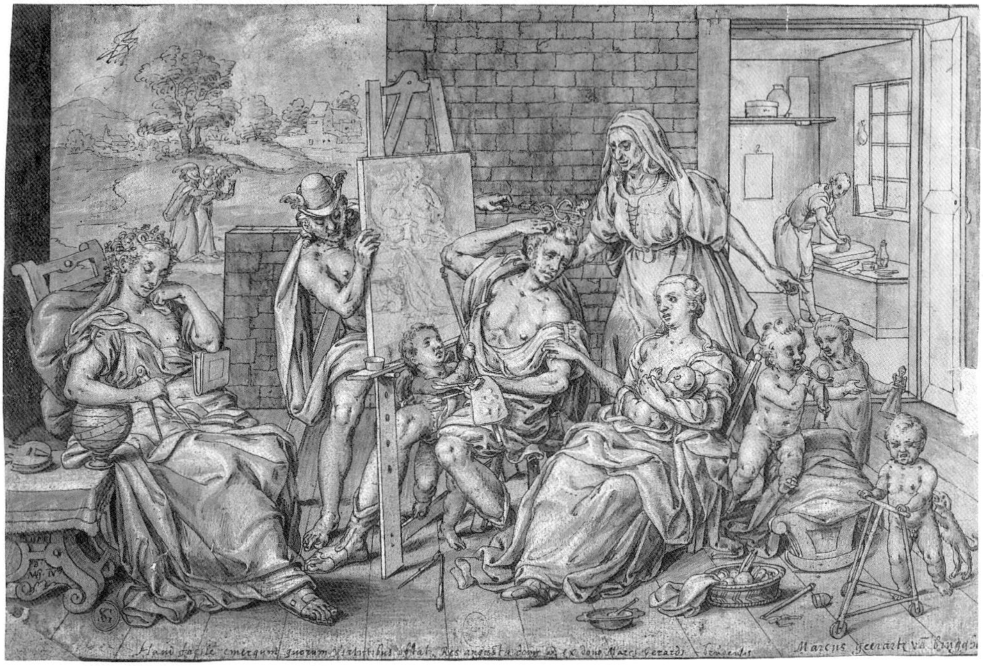

74 Marcus Gheeraerts, *Mercury attempts to help the painter in poverty*, 1577, ink and wash on paper, 239 × 376 mm, Bibliothèque Nationale de France, Paris.

the books held by the female personification, on the left. The base of the drawing bears the explanatory Latin inscription, derived from Juvenal's *Satires*, 'Not at all easily do those succeed whose worthiness is hampered by the condition of poverty in the home'.[77] Gheeraerts inscribed the drawing as a gift to someone – perhaps a rich patron whom he wished to attract: *ex dono Marci Gerardi brugensis* ('the gift of Marcus Gheeraerts of Bruges'). Appropriately, the *Satire* he illustrated bewails the difficulties of those seeking patronage in Rome. Gheeraerts was in contact with the scholars Johannes Vivianus and Abraham Ortelius, who could have advised him in choosing the text from Juvenal.[78]

The allegorical nature of the image is emphasised by the use of classicising dress for everyone, except the colour grinder. The enemy of the painter, in the inscription, is represented as 'Poverty', but in the drawing it is the family which is shown as exacerbating the problem. The painter's wife clutches at his arm, and another woman taps his shoulder and points to the toddlers. The left-hand side of the drawing contains gods and personifications who may assist the artist. Mercury pats the painter on the head with his caduceus, perhaps to help him develop his personal talent. Below, Cupid as 'Love of Art', pulls at his mahl stick, as if to remind him to keep painting. To the left is seated what appears to be a personification of some of the Liberal Arts, or possibly one of the Muses associated with the Liberal Arts. She rests her elbows on a globe (for astronomy) and a book, and she holds compasses (which signify geometry). She reads another book on her lap. With her bared breast, she seems to be designed as the counterpart of the needy wife. This 'abstract woman' is perhaps the model for the one the artist is painting on his easel. In the background, as if outside the room, can be identified Saturn, holding his hourglass to signify the passing of Time. Saturn is accompanied by another figure, who wears a blindfold. If the painter does not hurry, it seems that Time may overtake him. In producing such a learned allegory, of course, Gheeraerts could claim to have acquired a considerable level of intellectual attainment already.

Prague, Italy and the Netherlands 1585–1603

The final sixteenth-century phase of experimentation took the imagery of mythological Mercury to the capital of the Holy Roman Emperor Rudolf II. During the 1580s and 1590s Spranger used the image of Mercury as protector of painters, sculptors and architects in three influential designs which presented the latest ideas about the high status of art to the city of Prague. It is no coincidence that Spranger was the pupil of van Dalem, who had introduced the mythological Mercury to transalpine audiences, and that Spranger had then travelled and worked in Italy. Spranger painted Mercury flying above Fame at the apex of his own house façade, which was located in the centre of Prague in 1585. In 1592 Spranger invented an allegory of art education for his son Georg, which showed Mercury leading the youth to success, in the form of a drawing, which was quite soon engraved for other artists. Finally, in 1595, Spranger redesigned the insignia of the Guild of Saint Luke in Prague on the orders of Emperor Rudolf II. Although retaining the traditional heraldry of the guild, with its silver shields on an azure ground, he now placed Mercury and Fame supporting the blason on either side, whilst Minerva was put at the apex.[79] The imagery on the guild insignia was significantly elevated, because the Emperor had conceded that his court artists should belong to the local Guild of Saint Luke. In all three designs Spranger linked Mercury in some way with Fame: the connection which had been made on the catafalque of Michelangelo.

In 1585 Spranger set out to educate the citizens of Prague as to the high status of painting and sculpture by inventing a façade decoration for his house which showed Mercury in the dominant position controlling Fame.[80] This house decoration seems also to mark his achievement of the assured position of court painter in 1584. Spranger had worked in Italy between 1565 and 1575 (where he painted with Federico Zuccari), and had then worked in Vienna for Maximilian II. His high attainment at the imperial court may explain the way he represented Mercury as a guide who guarantees success, in contrast to the tentative interpretation of Gheeraerts. Van Mander described the house front as painted in yellow to resemble bronze relief:

> At the top, there are little children as large as life: on the right hand side they are painting and drawing, and on the left they are sculpting and drawing. In the middle [is] a flying Mercury life sized. Beneath are lunettes. Beneath this vaulting you see Fame.[81]

By association the mural seems to suggest that Mercury presides as teacher over the education of young pupils in painting and sculpting.

These educational references may be confirmed by the fact that, a little over a decade later, Spranger invented a pedagogic allegory for his own son Georg, which showed Mercury confidently leading the young artist up to the temple of Minerva (Plate 75). This was made initially as a familial allegory of attainment, in the form of a drawing, but was later shown by his grandson Matthaeus to the engraver Jan Harmensz. Muller, and printed for public consumption in 1628 in Amsterdam.[82] Such a history suggests some continuity in attitudes during the end of the sixteenth and the beginning of the seventeenth centuries. Spranger probably intended the allegory to apply to architecture and sculpture, as well as painting, since the personification of Abundance with her cornucopia, is climbing the hill in the background, with women holding a statuette, a palette and mahl stick, and a set square for building. At the top of the hill the young artist is kneeling before the throne of Minerva. He is cloaked with the skin of the hard-working ox, which signified Labour in the abstract, but also held resonances of the attribute of Saint Luke. Minerva hands to him a laurel wreath of victory, and a palm which indicates immortality. Fame flies overhead with two trumpets. Chained to Minerva's throne are Ignorance, Sloth and Envy. According to the Latin and Flemish inscriptions,

> Minerva adorns the head of the youth with laurel, palm and the beautiful skin of the indefatigable ox. With Mercury as his guide he is showered abundantly with riches, whom Labour and Study lead to the noble arts, and Fame raises him above the heavens and Mortality.[83]

In using the term 'noble arts' (*ingenuas artes*), the inscription makes clear that painting, sculpture and architecture are regarded as Liberal Arts. Mercury to the left taps the young man on the shoulder with his caduceus. A pen is in the youth's hand, and his ink bottle is on the ground, as if to suggest attainment in writing, as much as in drawing. It seems likely that Minerva stands for virtue here since the imagery appears to fit the traditions of depicting the way of virtue or *via virtutis* for artists (see Chapter 6). However, it is important to note the fluidity of interpretations, where Minerva had stood for supreme skill on the catafalque of Michelangelo, and was also regarded as signifying wisdom by some of the mythological handbooks.

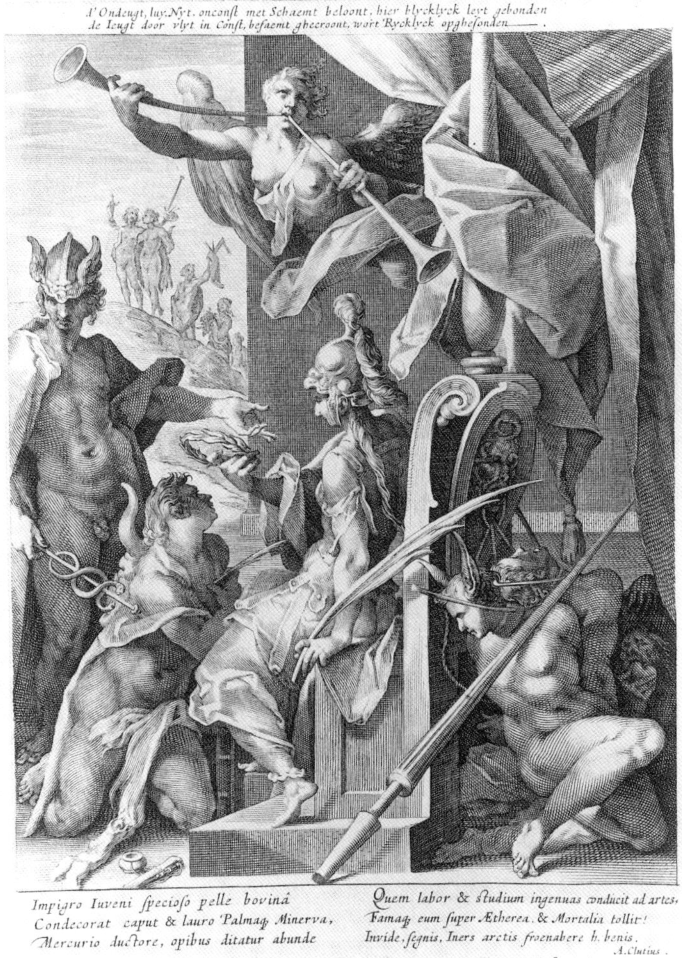

75 Bartholomaeus Spranger, *Mercury leads the learned and hardworking artist to Minerva*, 1592, engraved 1628 by Jan Muller.

The prestige of Mercury's allegorical protection was therefore advertised by Spranger to a large civic audience in the capital of Holy Roman Empire both on his house and on the guild insignia of the Guild of Saint Luke at Prague. It was embedded in his teaching of his son and, through the later engraving, formed part of general advice to young artists.

At the same time as Spranger drew this lesson for his son, the imagery of Mercury as mythological helper of artists was also being pursued in Rome by his former colleague Federico Zuccari, for didactic purposes. Federico employed the image of Mercury twice in the pictorial biography which he made of his brother the painter Taddeo.

This narrative was available to visitors to Rome, from the 1590s onwards, on the vault of one the rooms in his palace in Rome. The scheme survives in two sequences of drawings and one pictorial series, although the decoration was dismantled.[84] Mercury here appears as one who assists in the early studies of artists, recalling the theme of the façade of Spranger's house. In this role Federico represented Minerva holding the caduceus of Mercury, on left of the shield of the Zuccari family, and labelled her *Intelligenzia*. Opposite, he placed a figure of Study or *Studio*. In another scene, Federico gave the mercurial attributes of little wings on the temples to a figure he labelled as *Spirito* on the hem of its robe, which he showed as assisting the young Taddeo as he entered the city of Rome to begin his studies. *Spirito* is assisted by a personification of *Disegno* (Plate 76). Federico Zuccari had emulated Vasari, while he was working alongside him in Florence, so that it is not surprising to find him recalling the mercurial figure from the catafalque of Michelangelo, which Vasari had described as, 'all spirit [*spirito*] and of the most vivacious beauty representing personal talent [*ingegno*] with two little wings at the temples'. Federico's palace was the site of his studio and appears to have been designed to be something of a showcase of new attitudes to artists for practitioners staying in Rome from the rest of Italy and Northern Europe.[85]

That a mythological reference to Mercury was regarded as a signal of academic standing is suggested by the fact that when the Bolognese academy of painters designed the funeral decorations for the painter Agostino Carracci, in 1603, they included a scene which depicted Mercury showing a personification of the City of Bologna how Agostino's initials had now been traced in the sky with stars.[86] This academy had been established by the Carracci brothers in 1582 and the funerary apparatus was recorded in the engravings by Guido Reni, which illustrated the account published of the obsequies.

Drawings, engravings and sculpture made in the early seventeenth century, display the extent to which the employment of Mercury as mythological helper of artists was also established in the Netherlands. He appeared on the title page of a new edition of Cock's collection of the portraits of Netherlandish painters (1610), in the funerary commemoration of Goltzius (1620) and on the most impressive artist's house built north of the Alps to that date, by Rubens (1618). These were all images reaching a large audience of artists and art lovers.

Mercury's caduceus might be placed as an attribute of Painting herself, as it was on the frontispiece for the edition of the *Pictorum aliquot celebrium* (*Portraits of the celebrated Painters of the Netherlands*), published by Hendrik Hondius at The Hague in 1610. This was the earliest reprint of the first collection of portraits of Netherlandish artists originally printed by Volxken Dircks in Antwerp in 1572. Hendrik Hondius (1573–1650) was a printmaker and publisher, who trained with the

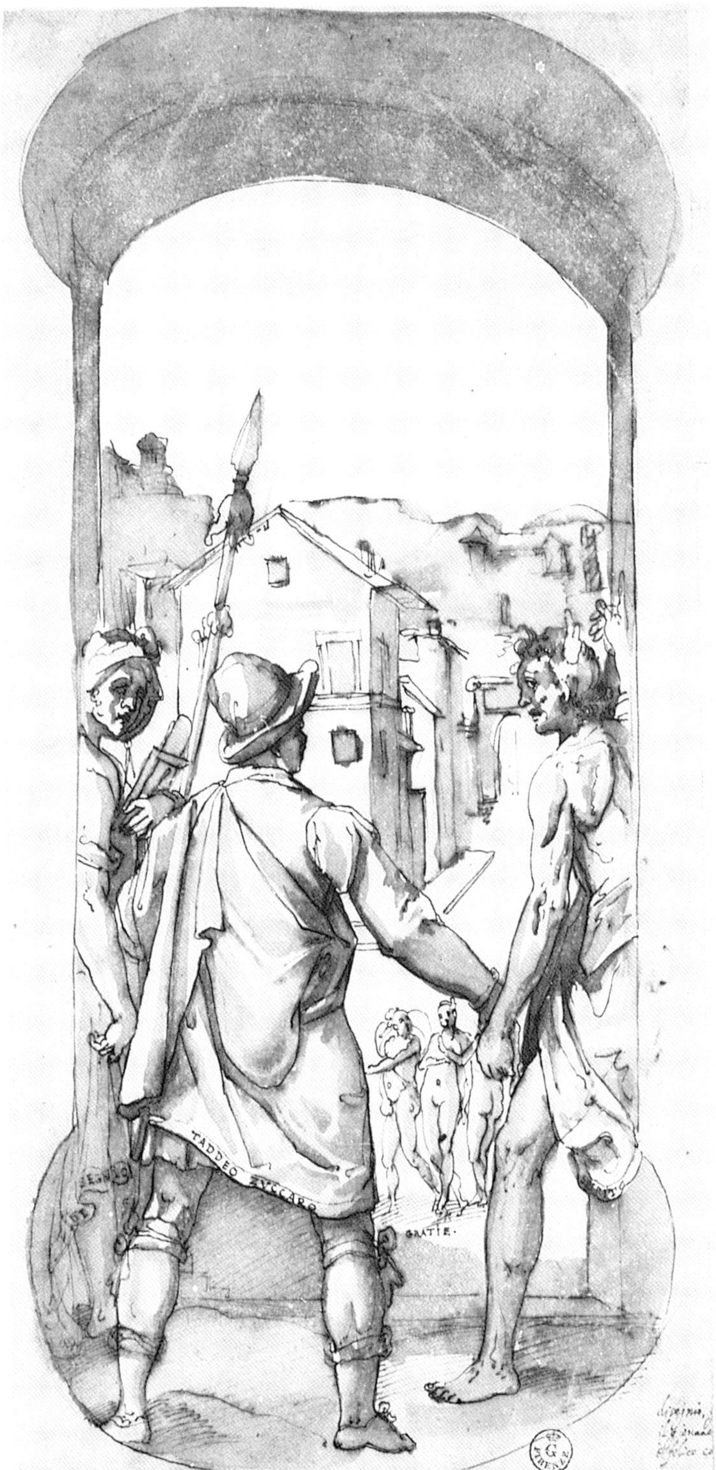

76 Federico Zuccari, *The young Taddeo with Spirito and Disegno*, *c.*1590, Galleria degli Uffizi, Gabinetto Disegni e Stampe, 11018F, Florence.

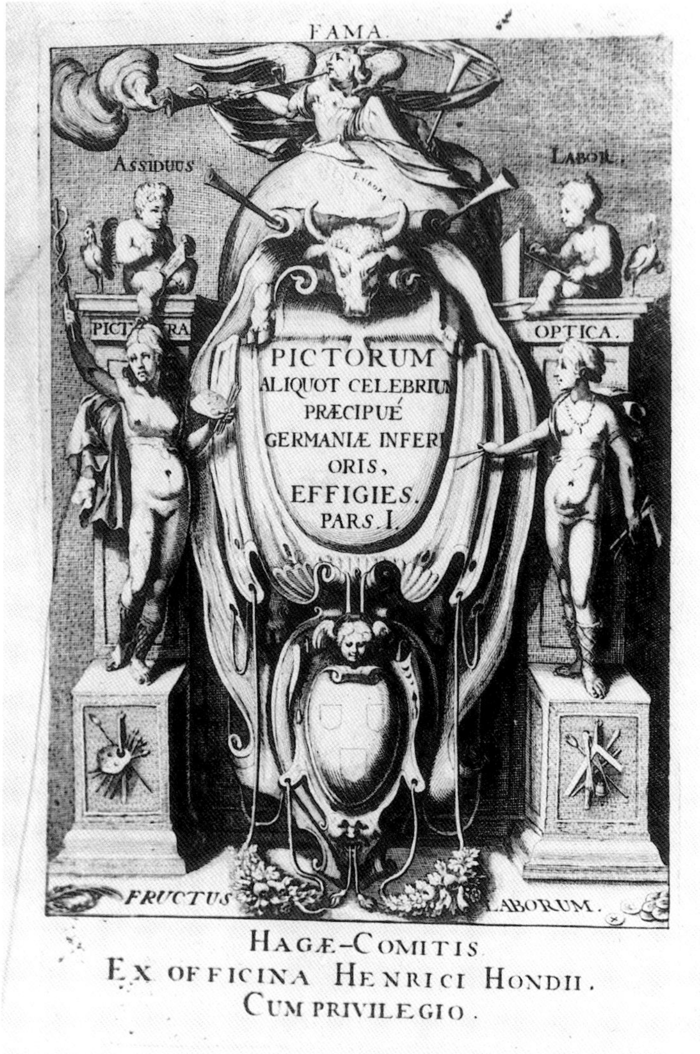

77 Frontispiece to *Pictorum aliquot celebrium*, The Hague, 1610, published by Hendrik Hondius.

goldsmith Godefry van Gelder in Brussels and with printmaker Jan Wierix in Antwerp, as well as travelling to Cologne, Paris and London, before settling in The Hague in 1605.[87] The frontispiece showed Painting flourishing a caduceus whilst Optics (*Optica*) held the compasses opposite her (Plate 77). Suitably for an encomium of painters, the title of the book is supported by the bull of Saint Luke and the shield of Saint Luke is placed below. Above, Fame trumpets her praise across a segment of the globe labelled *Europa*, and two children at work are labelled Assiduity and Labour. The children are accompanied by Mercury's attributes, of the cock and the crane. At the base are the *Fructus laborum*

('Fruits of Labours') in the form of, on the left hand, the laurel and palm of honour and, on the right hand, the worldly riches of a pile of coins.

The currency of these new ideas is suggested by an anonymous drawing dated 1613 which presents Mercury and Minerva assisting painters and sculptors to attain renown in a manner somewhat reminiscent of the Gheeraaerts drawing (Plate 78). This may well have been for the frontispiece of a book on art. It is in the Musée Fabre Montpellier and is listed as 'German school'. It presents a life-size statue of Hercules, standing on a tall plinth in a classicising townscape – presumably as a symbol of virtue. Hercules was the object for Christian moralisation because of his Twelve Labours, in which he was seen as battling against the odds to achieve immortality in heaven. To the left, a female personification of Painting is portraying the statue of Hercules on her easel.

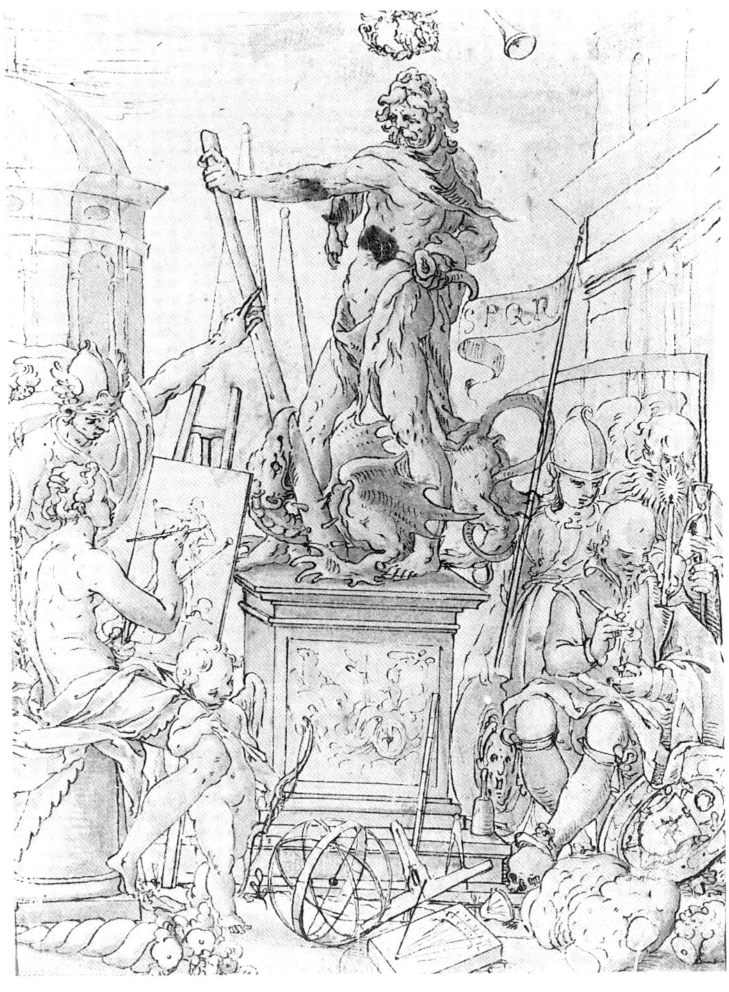

78 Anonymous, *Mercury and Minerva assist Painting and Sculpture to attain Virtue*, 1613, Musée Fabre, Number 1145, Montpellier.

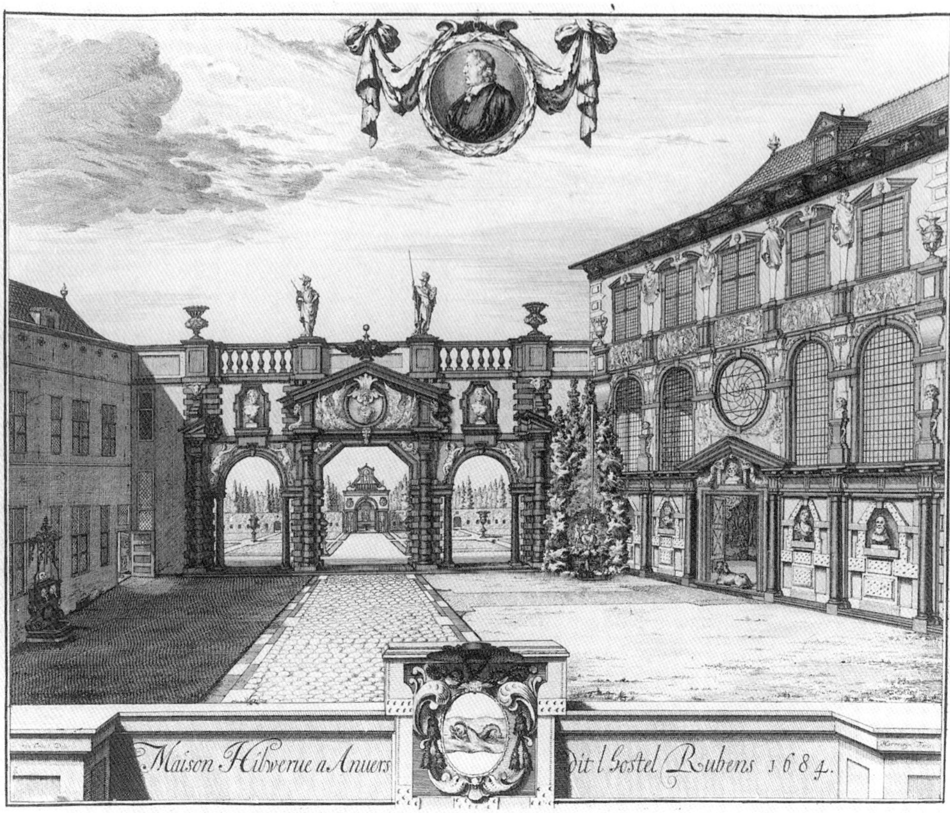

79 Rubens's house to left and studio to right, Antwerp, 1618, engraved by Jacob Harrewijn, 1684.

Behind her, Mercury points up to the example she emulates. At her knee, Love of Art, in the form of *Amor* with an arrow, urges Painting to love of her art or possibly love of virtue. To the right, a sculptor is working at a statue. Minerva leans over him, holding a candle to light his work; to her spear is attached a pennant marked SPQR. In the background Father Time urges viewers to work hard, lest they be overtaken by time. The sculptor reassures the spectator, by placing his foot firmly on a skull. The symbols of attainment which are the proper reward of the emulous artist appear above, in the form of a hand holding a wreath of honour, and of the tip of the trumpet of Fame. At their feet are placed attributes of the Liberal Arts related to painting and sculpture: the armillary sphere, the architect's ruler with plumb line, and instruments for measuring angles. The message appears to be that the artist should emulate the unremitting labours and virtue of Hercules, with the help of Minerva and Mercury.[88]

A related idea seems to have been pursued by Rubens five years later in 1618, when he designed his house in the centre of Antwerp, so that the open portal to the garden was decorated with figures of Mercury and Minerva. Through this gateway one saw (and still sees) a statue of Hercules at the end of the walk sheltered by a pavilion (Plate 79).[89] Rubens had been a pupil of Otto van Veen, who had been taught by Federico Zuccari.

The extent to which Mercury had come to be thought of as mythological helper of artists is confirmed by the imagery selected by the Haarlem printmaker Goltzius to indicate his own identity. Goltzius was the engraver who had advertised the astrological affinities of painting and sculpture with Mercury as well as the ambitions of *Disegno* to seek the protection of Jupiter in his series of the Children of the Planets (Plates 68, 69). He was in touch with Spranger – whose designs he was engraving from 1585 onwards, and had also met Federico Zuccari on his trip to Italy (1590–91).[90] Goltzius employed mercurial imagery in two drawings dated 1600 and 1612, which illustrated his initials, of 'H' placed above 'G'. This, according to his inscription, stood for *Eer boven Golt* ('Honour before wealth') (Plate 80). A laurel-wreathed cherub's head is supported by a caduceus, which is propped on top of golden vessels and ornaments. It seems that Mercury's caduceus might signify the achievement of laurels, through learning and inventiveness, regardless of profit.[91] That his identification with mercurial attainments was well known is suggested by the way his stepson and heir Jacob Matham (1571–1631) engraved a funerary commemoration for him in 1620, which affirmed that Mercury was sustaining his fame (Plate 81). The Latin inscription below the portrait of Goltzius, who had died in 1617, was composed by the Leyden historian Theodore Schrevelius:

> This is the true image of Goltzius and conveys the idea of a great spirit [*spiritus*] and a great personal talent [*ingeni*] . . . In this theatre of praise and glory he deserves to be seen, and, as witness to this, here are both Mercury and the learned Minerva with the honourable Graces, who all ensure that his name will be remembered.[92]

Matham translated these ideas by placing the Graces at the apex of the frame enclosing the portrait, and putting a figure labelled *Spirito* to the left, who holds the caduceus of Mercury and has wings at his temples. The personification labelled *Disegno* is shown on the right, holding drawing implements and a set square. The Italianate references are confirmed by the use of Italian for these two inscriptions, and the coupling of *spirito* and *disegno* which recalls the personifications paired up on Federico Zuccari's tribute to Taddeo. The notion of *spirito* seems to have included both the idea of inspiration, and that of the personal soul and courage. Matham was the pupil of Goltzius and worked in Rome too, before returning to Haarlem, and registering in the Guild of Saint Luke in 1600.

During the sixteenth century the traditional visual discourse of Mercury as planetary protector of artists was therefore sustained, in

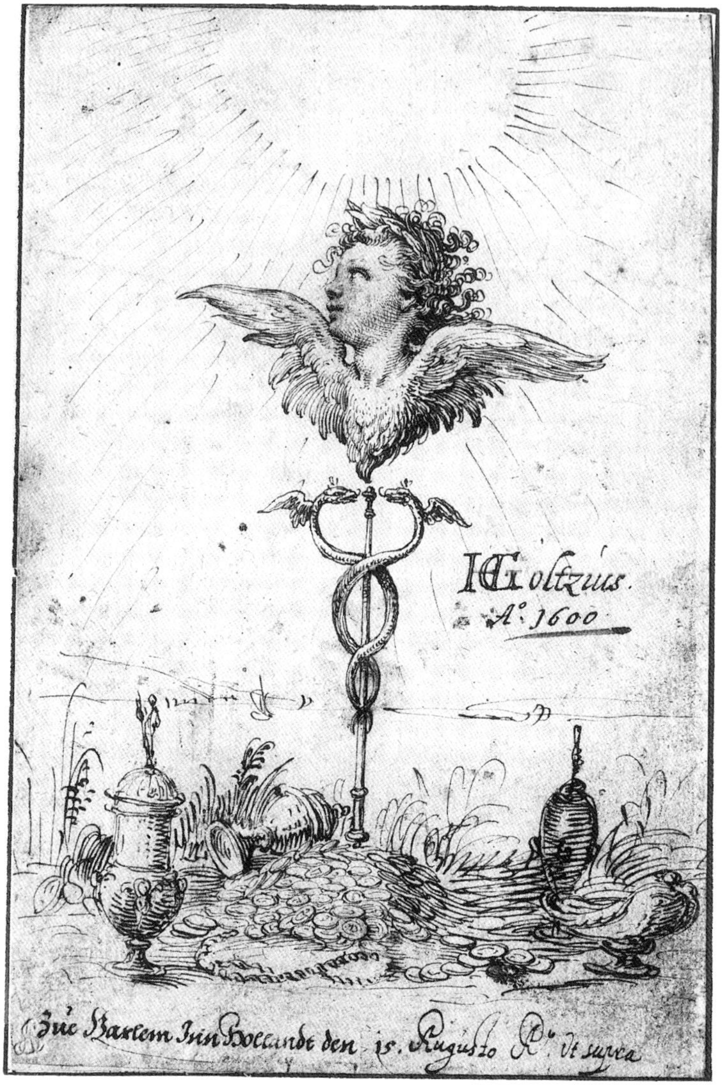

80 Hendrik Goltzius, *Eer boven Golt* ('Honour before wealth'), 1600, drawing, 150 × 100 mm, Graphische Sammlung, Albertina, Vienna.

German-speaking and Netherlandish locations, and provided chances to represent painters and sculptors in the company of a range of occupations, from organ makers to astronomers. From the 1540s onwards, new allegories connecting artists with Mercury in mythological terms were explored by Italian and Netherlandish artists. These stressed the affinities between the visual arts and Rhetoric, and associated artists with personal talent, originality and spirited inventiveness, rather than mere skill. Mercury or his attributes were employed in representations which applauded the past attainment of individuals (Michelangelo), or proposed ways to obtain success, fame and honour, through prudence (Lomazzo), hard work (Spranger) or intelligence (Zuccari). Arguably, the representation of Mercury as mythological assistant was facilitated by the pre-existing astrological concepts which had led Francesco di Giorgio Martini in the 1490s to describe the planetary Mercury as 'the lord of those who strenuously seek excellence' in the arts of geometry, arithmetic, perspective and drawing. It also seems possible that the new mythologising tradition was making some impact on the way astrologers defined the influence of the planet, since one reads in an astrological

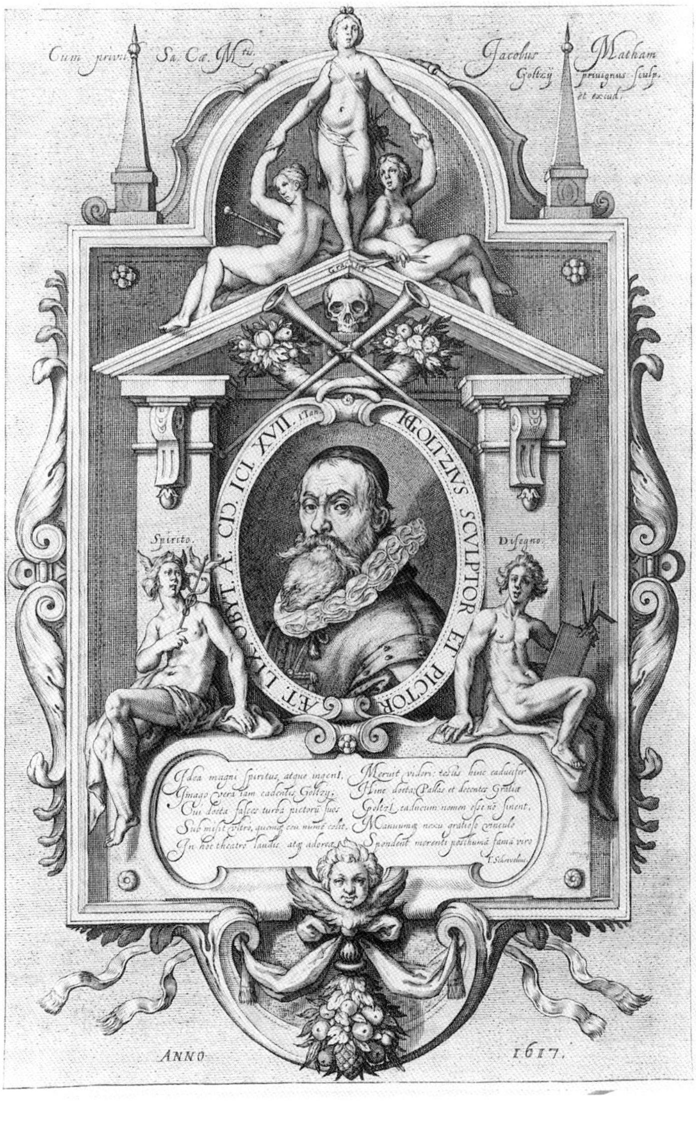

81 Jacob Matham, funerary portrait of Hendrik Goltzius, 1620, engraving.

handbook published in Leipzig, in 1598, that the Children of Mercury are in a hurry for fame – *ruhm hasstig*.[93]

The representation of allegories of artistic success, with Mercury (and often Minerva) taking key roles, seems to date from 1521 with the illustration by Cesariano on his edition of Vitruvius. The use of this genre to dramatise the struggles of the artist registered something of a shift, because allegory of personal success was associated with praising the attainments of political and intellectual leaders. During the sixteenth century artists also began to employ allegory in other, equally professionally specific, ways.

Notes

1 Jeffrey Muller, *Children of Mercury: The Education of Artists in the Sixteenth Century*, Providence, RI, 1984.

2 Jane Martineau and Charles Hope, eds, *The Genius of Venice*, London, 1983, pp. 306–10.

3 Albrecht Dürer, *The Writings of Albrecht Dürer*, ed. and trans. W.M. Conway, London, 1958, p. 121; André de Hevesy, *Jacopo de'Barbari: le maître au caducée*, Paris, 1925.

4 Von Schlosser, *Letteratura artistica*, p. 248; Paul Kirn, 'Friedrich der Weise und Jacopo de'Barbari', *Jahrbuch der preussischen Kunstsammlungen*, XLVI, 1925, pp. 130–4.

5 Albricus, *Allegoriae poeticae*, Paris, 1520, facsimile, ed. Stefan Orgel, New York, 1976, fol. xxxiii verso: 'Virgam ideo (secundum Remigio) fert quod sermo facundiae recto rationis tramite promptissimo pronunciatur.'

6 Horace, *Odes*, trans. C.E. Bennett, London, 1914, Book II, xvii, p. 154: 'mercurialium . . . virorum'.

7 Erwin Panofsky and Fritz Saxl, *Dürer's Melancholia I*, Hamburg, 1923; Margaret and Rudolf Wittkower, *Born under Saturn*, London, 1963, pp. 104–5.

8 Albricus, *Allegoriae poeticae*, fol. xxxv recto: 'sole spiritu[m] sortiri, a luna corpus, a marte sanguinem, a mercurio ingeniu[m], a jove horum desiderium, a venere cupiditates, a saturno humore[m].'

9 Saint Thomas Aquinas, *Summa theologiae*, ed. P. Faucher, 4 vols, Rome, 1948, II, p. 488: 'Unde corpora caelestia non possunt esse per se causa operum liberi arbitrii. Possunt tamen ad hoc dispositive inclinare: in quantum imprimunt in corpus humanum . . . sed contra inclinationem caelestium corporum homo potest per rationem operari.'

10 Battista de' Ruberti, *Osservazioni de astrologia, et altre appartenenze, circa la medecina, e mutazione de' tempi*, Florence, 1567, p. 9: 'Nelle azioni dell'uomo, si à da considerare le hore, che coronano delli pianeti se saranno prospere è accomodate alla qualità conveniente al tuo effetto, ma tutto depende dalla volontà del signore iddio benedetto.'

11 *Francesco di Giorgio architetto*, pp. 358–79.

12 Francesco di Giorgio Martini, *Trattati di architettura, ingegnierà e arte militare*, ed. Corrado Maltese and Livia Maltese Degrassi, 2 vols, Milan, 1967, II, pp. 293–4: 'Questa medesima cagione me longo tempo ha tenuto

dubbio e sospeso: massimo cognoscendo essere conforme alla prima [delli influssi celesti] cioè alla influenzia di Mercurio, signore di quelli che nelle arti prenominate sono atti a venire eccellenti, peroché [essendo] così non mi determinavo a quello che la natura me inclinava, ma più volte mosso da la ragione, non sottoposto alle inclinazioni corporee.'

13 *La piacevol astrologia di Ravanello nel qual si dichiara à tutti gli'uomini quello à che sono inclinati*, Siena, 1578, no pagination.

14 Bialstocki, *Dürer and his Critics*, p. 27.

15 Ascanio Condivi, *Vita di Michelangelo*, ed. Antonio Mariani, Florence, 1927, pp. 9–10.

16 Fritz Saxl, 'The literary sources of the "Finiguerra Planets"', *Journal of the Warburg and Courtauld Institutes*, II, 1938, pp. 72–4.

17 Arthur M. Hind, *Early Italian Engraving: A Critical Catalogue*, 7 vols, London, 1938–48, I, p. 82, number 6, British Museum, AIII, 6: inscribed 'Eloquente e ingegnioso ama le scienzie matematica e stiudia nelle divinazione [h]a il corpo gracile c[i]oe schietto e l[a]bri sottili istatura chonpiuta.'

18 A. Hauber, *Planetenkinderbilder und Sternbilder*, Strasburg, 1916.

19 Vincent of Beauvais, *Speculum naturale*, Strasburg, 1472, *De propriis effectibus ceterarum planetarum*, Book 16, Chapter XLV, no pagination no foliation numbers.

20 Georg Pictor, *Theologia mythologica*, Antwerp, 1532, facsimile ed. Stefan Orgel, New York, 1976, p. 39: 'alas mercatorum adscribamus agilitati'.

21 S. Samek-Ludovici, *Il 'De sphaera' estense e l'iconografia astrologica*, Milan, 1958, pp. 46–5, 54.

22 Samek-Ludovici, *Il 'De sphaera' estense*, p. 46: 'Mercurio di Ragion lucida/ Stella, Produce d'eloquenza gran Fontana,/Subtili ingegni et ciaschuna arte bella,/et é nemico d'ogni cosa vana.'

23 Ptolemy, *Tetrabiblos*, ed. and trans. F.E. Robbins, Cambridge, MA, 1980.

24 It was translated by Plato of Tivoli at Barcelona in 1138: see Lynn Thorndike, *A History of Magic and Experimental Science*, 8 vols, London, 1923, II, p. 82.

25 *Das gross Planetenbuch, Alles auss Platone, Ptolomeo, Hali, Albumaser unnd J. Königsberger gezogen*, Strasburg, 1546.

26 Ptolemy, *Tetrabiblos*, pp. 353–7.

27 Ptolemy, *Tetrabiblos*, p. 259.

28 Ptolemy, *Tetrabiblos*, p. 383.

29 Ptolemy, *Tetrabiblos*, p. 387.

30 Ptolemy, *Tetrabiblos*, p. 387.

31 Abu Ma'shar, *Flores Albumazaris*, Augsburg, 1488, fol. b1 verso: 'Mercurius est significator scriptorum, arismetricorum, negociatorum, puerorum, ac magistrorum operum.'

32 Abu Ma'shar, *Introductorium in astronomiam*, Augsbourg, 1489, fol. h 5 verso: 'Mercurius cum discipulis ingenium; eloquentia, plena sapientia: sana doctrina: salubris exhortatio, arguta deceptio; probabiles inductiones necesarii silogismi: philosophiae ac poetriae stadium plurimisque in mathematica: arismetrica: geometria et astronomia . . . Tum divinationum sortilege quoque, cum auguriis at auspiciis praeterea grata et fructuosa facundia . . . aptitudo in omne artificium.'

33 Abraham ben Ezra *The Beginning of Wisdom*, ed. and trans. R Levy and F. Cantera, Baltimore, MD, 1939.

34 Abraham ben Ezra, trans. Pietro d'Abano, *Abrahe[m] Avenaris judei astrologi peritissimi in re iudiciali opera*, Venice, 1507.

35 Abraham ben Ezra, *The Beginning of Wisdom*, p. 200.

36 Abraham ben Ezra, *Abrahe[m] Avenaris*, fol. 95 verso: 'Hora Mercurii bonum est emere omnes res pictas: scriptas:frumentum:milium:panicum et omnes vestes varii coloris que pertinent ad usum hominum species omnes:bonum est emere:bombace:setum sive sericum:et omnia opera quae sunt de serico;et incipere placitum facere: uxorem quoque ducere ac societatam facere: medicinam etiam accipere: sanguinem minuere optimum est: iter quoque causa negociationis facere.'

37 Leonhardt Thurneisser zum Thurn, *Archidoxa dorin der Recht war Motus Lauff und Gang der Planeten*, Munster, 1569, fol. S iv verso: 'Stecher, Moler, Keysser, Bildhouer, Possierer, Buchstab Giesser, Buchtrucker, Steinschneider und Pallierer'.

38 *Le Calendrier des bergers*, Paris, 1499, fol. g3 recto–verso; *Le Grand Kalendrier des bergers*, Paris, 1569, fol. Q3 verso–Q4 recto; *Le Grand Calendrier des bergers*, Paris, 1589, fol. Q3 verso–Q4 recto.

39 *Le Calendrier des bergers*, Paris, 1499, British Library, Call mark IB39718.

40 *Le Grand Kalendrier des bergers*, Paris, 1569, fol. Q3 verso–Q4 recto: 'de subtil engin est trouve/bon religieux . . . homme d'eglise aussi marchant . . . aymera point aller a guerre/De l'argent grosse chevance/Armassera par sa prudence/On pourra estre bon ouvrier/D'aucun mecanique mestier/Grand prescheur rhetoricen/Philosophe geometrien/Bien aymera ses escritures/Nombres et metrificatures/l'art de musique et mesurer/Draps toilles scaura composer/Procureur d'aucun grant seigneur/ou de leurs derniers receveur.'

41 F.W.H. Hollstein, *Hollstein's German Engravings, Etchings and Woodcuts, 1400–1700, XXXI*, ed. Tilman Falk and Robert Zijlma, Roosendaal, 1991, pp. 121, and 196, number 94, 298 × 206 mm.

42 This reads on the print 'Mercurius ist ein Planet der kunst und maysterschafft heysz und trucken verkerlicher nature, gut bey den guten und boss bey den bosen, ein bezeychner, der schreyber, Rechner, Kaufflewt, Rentmayster, Vers und Lieder dichter, der Astronomie, Loyci, Poetria und aller juptiller kunstner und Poete. Seine kunst sind Astronomi, Arithmetica Loyca, Poetria . . . In der stund Mercurii ist gut brieff schreyben, potten senden, kauffen, wandern, artzneyen, reytten, baum pflanzen, mit Kunigen reden, kinder lernen, brunnen graben.'

43 Walter L. Strauss, *The German Single Leaf Woodcut 1550–1600*, New York, 1975, pp. 175–8.

44 Elfried Bock, *Die Zeichnungen älter Meister im Kupferstichkabinett Staatliche Museen in Berlin, Die deutschen Meister*, Berlin, 1921, p. 16, number 4326. For the related Saturn roundel see Hermann Schmitz, 'Eine neuerworbene Rundscheibe von Jörg Breu D. Ä im Schlossmuseum', *Berliner Museen Berichte aus den Preussischen Kunstsammlungen*, XLV, 1924, pp. 8–81.

45 *Die Chroniker der deutschen Städte*, xxix, ed. F. Roth, Leipzig, 1906.

46 Thomas Kerrich, *A Catalogue of Prints after Marten van Heemskerck*, London 1829, p. 96; F.W.H. Hollstein, *Hollstein's Dutch and Flemish Etchings,*

Engravings and Woodcuts, c.1450–1700, The Muller Dynasty, compiled by Jan Piet Filedt Kok, ed. by Ger Luijten and Christiaan Schuckman, 3 vols, Rotterdam, 1999, I, number 106, pp. 27–213.

47 Caius Julius Hyginus, *De imaginibus deorum*, Basel, 1549, p. 131: 'pennata vero talaria, quod negociantium pedes ubique pergendo quasi pennati sunt'.

48 The inscription on the engraving reads: 'Mercurius filios facit intelligentes, sagaces, aemulatores, beneficos, mathematicos, voti compotes, conies tore, corpore graciles, pallentes osculorum, intuitu honestos, et potus temperantia mirabilis.' The engraver seems to have misread, or possibly misheard, 'carnes torrere' as 'conies tore': see, for example, the former phrase used in describing Mercury's skill in 'plucking the guts', i.e. lyre strings, in Apollodorus of Athens, *Bibliotheces*, Antwerp, 1565, fol. 68 recto.

49 *Christie's Catalogue* (*London*) Sale on 9 May 1930, Lot 144, Lord Clark Collection (panel, 30″ × 41″).

50 F.W.H. Hollstein, *Hollstein's Dutch and Flemish Etchings, Engravings and Woodcuts, c.1450–1700, XXIII*, ed. G.S. Keyes, Amsterdam, 1980, numbers 51 Jupiter and 55 Mercury, pp. 41–4.

51 *Warsager Kunst aus den sieben Planeten*. Leipzig, 1598, fol. e iii recto: 'Und in somma zu allen naturlichen Kunsten es sen [sic] in schreiben, dichten, mahlen oder was der gleichen kunste sind.'

52 *Warsager Kunst aus den sieben Planeten*, fol. a viii recto–bi recto: 'er gewinnet viel Freunde . . . ist gut Kinder zur Schule thun, Erknen nemen, Ehemachen, Bäume pflanzen, wandern, kauffen und verkauffen'.

53 E.K.J. Reznicek, *Die Zeichnungen von Hendrik Goltzius*, 2 vols, Utrecht, 1961, I pp. 296–8, II, Plates 282, 284.

54 Martianus Capella, trans. W.H. Stahl, R. Johnson and E.L. Burge, *Martianus Capella and the Seven Liberal Arts*, 2 vols, New York, 1977, II, pp. 18–19.

55 Lilio Gregorio Giraldi, *De deis gentium*, Basel, 1548, facsimile New York, 1976, p. 61: 'quem totum non modo legere, sed etiam ediscere, valde est precium operae. Sunt et qui addunt, eundem praestigiatorum artem excogitasse, sed et rebus nomina imposuise, et verba in ordinem redegisse, et deorum cultum et sacra instituisse, astrorum et siderum cursus observasse, numeros excogitasse, et medicinam, testitudinem id est chelym.'

56 Paolo Verzone, 'Cesare Cesariano', *Arte Lombarda*, XVI, 1971, pp. 203–10.

57 Vitruvius, *De architettura, Vitruvio*, ed. and trans. Cesare Cesariano, Como, 1521, fol. LXXXXI verso: 'il tenebroso orbe delle malitie de la noverca e de paupertate da le obscaenie invidie et persuasione de li filii de la Dira Noverca et fraudolente insidie.'

58 Vitruvius, *De architettura, Vitruvio*, fol. LXXXXI verso: 'certamente ivi ex insperato a fortuita apparentia uti Mercurius missus a divina clementia et bonis satis evocatus, non deli ferini et monstruosi, ma del uno bono spirito pare, che me perflasse la auxiliante Fortuna.'

59 Vitruvius, *De architettura, Vitruvio*, facsimile ed. A. Bruschi, A. Carugo and P.F. Fiore, Milan, 1981, fol. LXXXXII recto, entitled 'Mundi electiva Caesaris Caesarii configurata'.

60 *Giulio Romano 1499–1546*, ed. Manfredo Tafuri, trans. Fabio Barry, Cambridge, 1998, pp. 150–4; 202–8. See also Stefano Maggi, 'Un paride ritrovato: il "Mercurio"della casa di Giulio Romano', *Quaderni di Palazzo*

Te, anno IV, numero 8, January–June, 1988, pp. 37–41; Kurt W. Forster and Richard J. Tuttle, 'The Casa Pippi. Giulio Romano's House in Mantua', *Architectura, Zeitschrift für Geschichte der Architektur*, 1973, pp. 104–30. Tuttle argued that Giulio saw himself as Mercury to his patron's Jupiter.

61 Georg Pictor, *Theologiae mythologica*, Antwerp, 1532, facsimile New York, 1976, p. 40.

62 Lucian of Samosata, *Lucian*, 8 vols, trans. A.M. Harmon, London and New York, 1913–67, I, pp. 63–71: dialogue on Hercules.

63 Natale Conti, *Mythologiae sive explicationis fabularum*, 1567, fol. 134 recto–137 recto and Natale Conti, *Mythologiae sive explicationis fabularum*, 1605, Lyons, pp. 433–41: 'Hunc finxerat antiqui aurea cathena auribus hominum annexa, mortales quocunque collibuisset trahere solitum, sicuti de Hercule dicitur . . . nam acutissimum et oratione et ingenio ad res celerrime inveniendas et explicandas orationem esse convenit.'

64 *Giulio Romano 1499–1546*, pp. 202–5.

65 Cicero, *Letters to Atticus*, ed. and trans. D.R. Shackleton Bailey, 4 vols, Cambridge, MA, 1999, I, p. 49, Letter 1, 4, 3.

66 For example, Francesco Barozzo, *Procli diadochi lycii philosophi platonici ac mathematici probatissimi in primum Euclidis elementorum librum commentariorum*, Padua, 1560.

67 Hill, *Portrait Medals*, p. 62; Philip Atwood, *Italian Medals c.1530–1600 in British Public Collections*, 2 vols, London, 2003, I, Catalogue number 123, pp. 139–40, I, Plate 33.

68 Van Mander, *Lives*, I, pp. 333–4 and V, p. 89.

69 Josef Duverger and M.J. Onghena, 'Beeldhouwer Willem van den Broecke alias Guglielmus Paludanus 1530–1578/9', *Gentsche Bijdragen tot de Geschiedenis* V, 1938, pp. 75–140; Anna Jolly, 'Netherlandish sculptors in sixteenth-century Northern Germany and their Patrons', *Simiolus*, 1999, XXVII, pp. 119–43, especially p. 125.

70 Caius Julius Hyginus, *De imaginibus deorum*, Basel, 1549, p. 134: 'Primam vitam theoreticam, quam nos in contemplandae sapientiae honore dicimus. Ideo de Iovis vertice natam dicunt, quia ingenium in cerebro positum.'

71 Georg Pictor, *Apotheoseos*, Basel, 1548, facsimile New York, 1976, p. 41: 'Minerva sapientiae deam, ordine servato, recte Mercurio iungimus, dum eloquentiae subtilissim[um] q[ue] ingenii deum, omniumq[ue] deoru[m] hunc fuisse novimus.'

72 Stefania Massari, *Giulio Bonasone*, 2 vols, Rome, 1983, II, p. 124: 'Sic monstra domantur', and 'Me duce perficies tum[m]odo progredere'.

73 King, 'Artists' houses', pp. 178–9.

74 Vasari, *Le opere di Giorgio Vasari*, VII, pp. 300–2: 'un giovane svelto e nel sembiante tutto spirito, e di bellissima vivacità, figurato per l'Ingegno, con due aliette sopra le tempie, nella guisa che si dipinge alcuna volta Mercurio.'

75 Conti, *Mythologiae* [1567], fol. 137 recto: 'acutissimum in oratione et ingenio'.

76 Conti, *Mythologiae* [1567], fol. 95.

77 Susanna Morton Braund, ed. and trans., *Juvenal and Persius*, Cambridge, MA, 2004, pp. 180–1, Satire III, 164–5: 'Haud facile emergunt quorum virtutibus obstat res angusta domi'. An edition of the poem was published

in Antwerp in 1566: Juvenal, *Satyrarum Libri V*, ed. Theodore Pulmann, Antwerp, 1566.

78 Maximiliaan P.J. Martens, ed., *Bruges et la Renaissance*, Bruges, 1998, pp. 158–9.

79 Michael Šroněk, 'Painters in Prague between the Guild and the Court, 1595–1650', pp. 216–19 in Lubomír Konecný, ed., *Rudolf II: Prague and their World*, Prague, 1998.

80 Thomas DaCosta Kaufmann, *The School of Prague: Painting at the Court of Rudolf II*, Chicago, 1988, pp. 249–79, especially pp. 249 and 260. Parts of the house survive as Nové Zamacké Schody, numbers 196 and 193.

81 Van Mander, *Lives*, V, pp. 105–6.

82 Adam Bartsch, *The Illustrated Bartsch IV: Netherlandish Artists: Matham, Saenredam, Muller*, ed. Walter L. Strauss, New York, 1980, p. 500, Number 67 (285); Lubomír Konecný, 'Climbing the rocky path: or, the Rudolphine artist in quest of Fame' pp. 192–200 in Lubomír Konecný, ed., *Rudolf II: Prague and their World*, Prague, 1998.

83 Inscribed on the engraving: 'Impigro iuveni specioso pelle bovina condecorat caput et lauro palmaque Minerva. Mercurio ductore, opibus ditatur abunde, Quem labor et studium ingenuas conducit ad artes. Famaque eum super Atherea et Mortalis tollit.'

84 Cristina Acidini-Luchinat, *Taddeo e Federico Zuccari fratelli pittori del Cinquecento*, 2 vols, Milan, 1998, I, pp. 9–17 and II, pp. 224–7.

85 Hans-Joachim Raupp, 'Allegorische Selbstporträts und selbstdarstellungen in der Graphik um 1600', pp. 177–92 in Gunther Schweikhart, ed., *Autobiographie und Selbst Portrait in der Renaissance*, Cologne, 1998, pp. 186–7: amongst these visitors was the German painter Adam Elsheimer, who participated in the Accademia di San Luca and made a drawing honouring the powers of Mercury to inspire, in a manner reminiscent of the composition by Gheeraerts, as well as Italian traditions for representing 'spirit'.

86 Benedetto Morello, *Il funerale d'Agostino Carraccio in Bologna sua patria dagli incaminati academici del disegno*, Bologna, 1603, p. 21 (engraved by Guido Reni).

87 Nadine M. Orenstein, *Hendrik Hondius and the Business of Print in Seventeenth-century Holland*, Rotterdam, 1996, pp. 50–1, 132–3.

88 King, 'Late sixteenth-century careers' advice', pp. 87–90: Musée Fabre, Montpellier, dated 1613 German School, number 1145, Gernsheim 5896.

89 Elizabeth McGrath, 'The painted secoration of Rubens's house', *Journal of the Warburg and Courtauld Institutes*, XLI, 1978, pp. 245–77.

90 E.K.J. Reznicek, *Die Zeichnungen von Hendrik Goltzius*, 2 vols, Utrecht, 1961, I, pp. 6, 84.

91 The more complex version was sold by Sotheby Parke Bernet, 22 October 1970, signed HG and dated 1612, while for the two simpler versions dated 1600, see Reznicek, *Zeichnungen*, I, pp. 315–17, II, Plates 428 and 439.

92 F.W.H. Hollstein, *Dutch and Flemish Engravings, Etchings and Woodcuts, XI*, Amsterdam, 1955, p. 238, number 379: 'Idea magni spiritus atque ingeni/Imago vera iam cadentis Goltzii/ . . . In hoc theatro laudis atque adorea/ Meruit videri testis hinc caducifer/Hinc docta; Pallas et decentes Gratia/Goltzi caducum nomen esse non sinent.'

93 *Warsager Kunst aus den sieben Planeten*, fol. a viii recto.

Allegories

6

In Italian treatises, compositions which expressed some improving message through the representation of mythological figures, personifications or symbolic devices were accorded prestige, since scholarship and inventiveness were considered necessary for devising them. Leon Battista Alberti, who used the term *istoria* to denote such a symbolic narrative, had, for instance, recommended painting the Three Graces described by Hesiod as an *istoria*. They might be shown, 'laughing, and taking each other by the hand, with their clothes girdled and very clean. This symbolises liberality, since one of these sisters gives, the other receives, the third returns the benefit.'[1] Alberti advised that, to compose new inventions of this sort, painters should 'make themselves familiar with poets, rhetoricians and others equally well learned in letters'.[2] The term *allegoria* was a literary term in the sixteenth century, which was used to describe the way writers signified one thing by means of another, as when the Three Graces holding hands stood for *Amicitia* or 'mutually beneficial friendship'. It has since been appropriated, as 'allegory', to denote the production of symbolic visual images in the visual arts.

Artists had traditionally employed allegorical forms to show personifications of Painting, Sculpture and Architecture as Practical Arts. However, it was not until the sixteenth century that they began to apply such modes to a number of other themes relating to artistic matters. In the sixteenth century, the figurative arts and architecture were compared with Liberal Arts (Chapter 1). A little later, devices and personifications were invented to signify the concept of *Disegno*, and Mercury was symbolised as mythological assistant of artists (Chapters 2, 4). The importance of the sixteenth century in establishing a rich iconography of art is, however, is signalled by the fact that it was also at this time that artists appropriated for their own use allegories of fame, virtue, fortune, calumny, truth and envy, which had previously been dedicated to scholars, poets and leaders.[3] As indicated by Alberti, these sorts of inventions required contact with learned men to achieve, either in terms of being given instructions on what to represent and why, or being able to consult and discuss, what it would be fitting to produce.

The Calumny of Apelles as a model

The allegory entitled *The Calumny of Apelles* had been invented by the ancient Greek painter himself, and so was an important precedent for sixteenth-century artists. It allowed Leonardo, for example, in his *paragone* to argue 'if a poet should say I will write a story which will signify great things, the painter can do likewise, for even so Apelles painted the Calumny'.[4] The *Calumny* had been described by Lucian of Samosata, and had been a response by the artist to defend his own innocence. The Greek text had been translated into Latin by Guarino da Verona by 1416, and subsequently Alberti in *Della pittura* (1436) and Filarete in his *Trattato* (*c.*1460) had recommended it as a subject for artists.[5] The allegory was indeed illustrated from the 1470s onwards, but was used by non-artists, who saw its relevance to their own vulnerability to slander and to judicial proceedings.[6] Only twice was it retrieved for the defence of artists: firstly by Lorenzo Leonbruno in a painting made about 1530 or a little earlier and, secondly, in a painting by Federico Zuccari, which was engraved by Cornelis Cort and published in 1572.

As explained by Lucian, Apelles had been falsely accused of plotting against King Ptolemy IV of Egypt. His accuser was a fellow painter, and Apelles had escaped death only because another prisoner attested his innocence, and the King was willing to listen. In relief and anger, Apelles then painted his *Calumny*. In it a young man was depicted as standing for the innocent artist:

> On the right hand, sits a man with such a respectable length of ears that they might be taken for those of Midas, reaching out his hand towards Calumny, yet at a distance, coming to him. Near him on either side, stands a female figure which I take to represent Ignorance and Suspicion. From the other side advances Calumny in the form of a beautiful maiden, but in her countenance expressing hate, anger and rooted malice. She bears in her left hand a burning torch, while in her right she drags a young man along by the hair, who stretches forth his hands to heaven calling upon the gods to attest his innocence. Before her walks an ugly, pale-faced, hollow-eyed man, looking emaciated, as if undermined by some slow disease, and whom without trouble we discover to be Envy. Behind Calumny walk two other females, who seem to be irritating, supporting and adorning her, of whom one, as my guide and interpreter informed me, was Artifice, and the other Deceit. At a greater distance behind her followed Repentance in a black tattered mourning habit; she wept, and turned away a face for shame before Truth.[7]

Lucian sets the scene of the King being influenced by Ignorance and Suspicion, so that he is ready to listen to Calumny, accompanied by Artifice and Deceit and led by Envy. The eventual willingness of the King to listen to the defence of the innocent Apelles is suggested by the appearance of Truth and the idea that the accusers will accept the Repentance of their misdeeds.

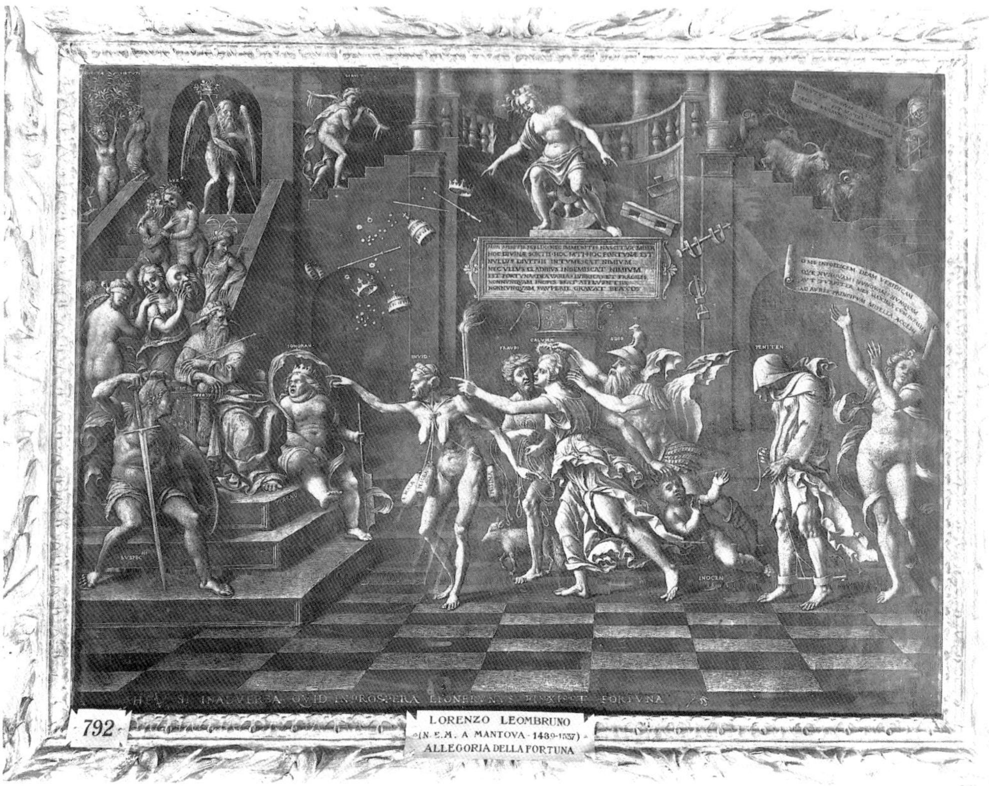

82 Lorenzo Leonbruno, *Calumny of Apelles and Fortune*, *c.*1530, oil on wood, 76 × 100 cm, Pinacoteca di Brera, Milan.

The earliest *Calumny* made for an artist is a pessimistic variant on the theme. It was executed in monochrome and inscribed by the Mantuan painter Lorenzo Leonbruno (1489–1537), who had been ousted from his position as court painter to the Gonzaga (Plate 82). Raphael's pupil Giulio Romano had gained favour on his arrival in Mantua in 1524, and Leonbruno had had to leave his native city, where he had been trained by Andrea Mantegna, to work in Milan during the period 1531–32.[8] Leonbruno was, however, received back at the Mantuan court from 1533 to 1537. In his version, the accused has not yet obtained justice, if he ever will, and Truth is represented as imprisoned. On the lower border is inscribed the question 'If Leonbruno painted this in bad fortune, what would he have painted in good fortune?'[9] Instead of showing the moment when the figure of Innocence is about to be given fair hearing, Leonbruno's interpretation stresses the baleful forces sustained against Apelles. Truth has been placed behind bars, and Fortune has been added, showering down both rewards and slights indiscriminately. Over Truth is a further inscription bewailing the artist's lack of a fair hearing: 'Oh unhappy I, the truth-speaking goddess have I never, never approached, nor ever, it is disgraceful to add, have I reached the ears of the Prince concerning my most wretched Calumny.'[10] It seems possible that the allegory was painted while Leonbruno was in voluntary exile in Milan and that it might have played a part in his return to his native city.

The second example is the painting by Zuccari which was published as an engraved version in Rome in 1572 (Plate 83).[11] It is intriguing that Zuccari added the figures of Mercury and Minerva to the well-known iconography detailed by Lucian – presumably to stress that this really was about the problems of artists (see Chapter 5). In Zuccari's design Mercury assisted the innocent artist as he walked away (presumably with a favourable outcome from the judgement) accompanied by Truth. Minerva was introduced to stand beside the judge, and perhaps counsel him wisely against accepting Calumny at face value. Zuccari added the attribute to the innocent figure representing Apelles himself, of a cloak made from an ox skin, signifying Hard work. He also inserted a scene, as if viewed through a window in the back wall of the king's audience chamber, which showed peasants trying to collect their harvest in a thunder storm. This was labelled in the painting *Impavidum ferient* ('They may smite him undismayed'), which was a quotation from

83 Federico Zuccari, *Calumny of Apelles*, engraved by Cornelis Cort, Rome, 1572, 518 × 557 mm, Prints and Drawings, British Museum.

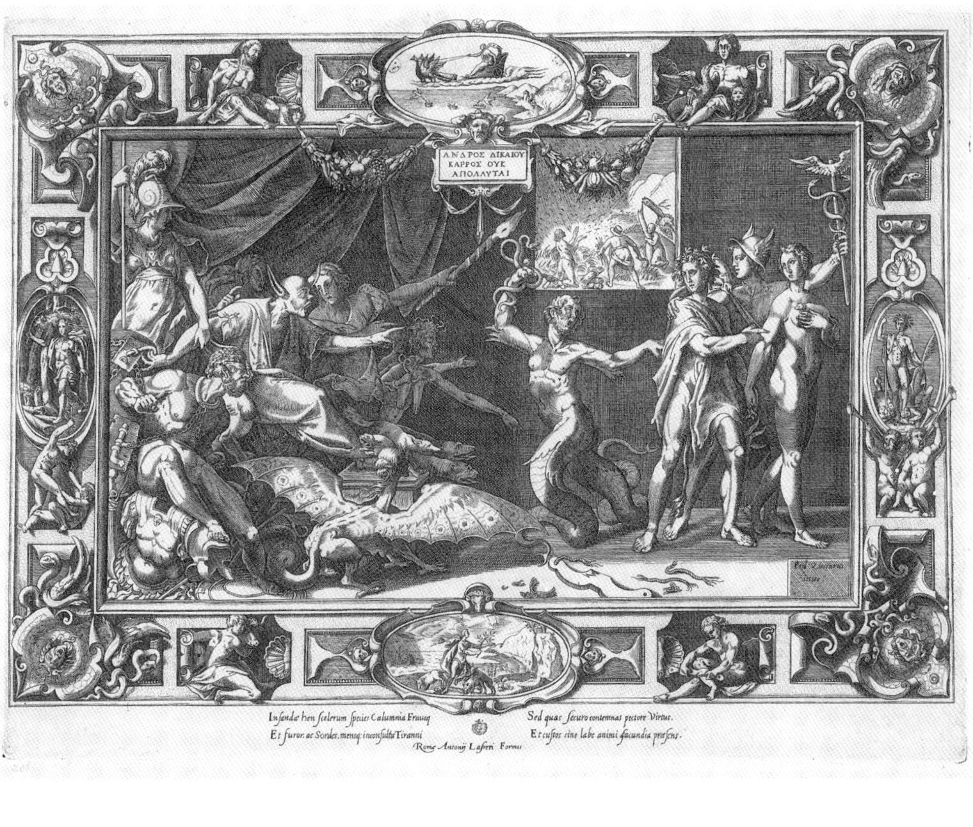

Horace's *Odes* III, III, 1–10.[12] Zuccari's son Ottaviano wrote an explanation of the allegory, which was published in 1628. Peasants, he stated, like artists, should not lose the 'fruit of their labours' through ill fortune.[13] The *Ode* had claimed that, 'the man tenacious of his purpose in a righteous cause, is not shaken from his firm resolve . . . were the vault of heaven to break full upon him, its ruins would smite him undismayed.'[14] In the engraving Zuccari further displayed his contact with scholarship by quoting from a Greek adage, attributed to the poet Menander, stating that the just should not be deprived of the harvest of their toil. It is evident that the *Calumny* reached a wide audience, since three paintings of it survive, and ten issues (one with a written key to the main scene) rapidly followed the first imprint.[15] It was reported in a letter by the agent of the Duke of Urbino in Rome, Baldo Falducci, in 1581, and in print by van Mander in 1604, that Zuccari had made this *Calumny* as a protest, against his own ill treatment by his patron Alessandro Farnese at Caprarola in 1569.[16] Cort was a Netherlandish engraver trained in the workshop of Hieronymous Cock in Antwerp who had engraved after Frans Floris before moving to Italy in 1565. The right to complain in this manner, taking the precedent of Apelles, against powerful patrons, if they were not deemed fair judges, was an important assertion. At the same time the print could sell well to non-painters as relevant to them. Yet in whatever form *The Calumny of Apelles* appeared, it always alluded to artists' competence to invent their own subject-matter.

Medallic allegories

During the second half of the fifteenth century, painters, sculptors and architects had begun to make small-scale personal allegories suggesting their aspirations on medals. Cryptic statements and images, termed *imprese*, were placed on medallic reverses, relating to the ambitions of the person portrayed. The genre of cast medal, usually in bronze, had been invented by Antonio Pisanello (*c.*1395–*c.*1455) in the late 1430s as a conscious renovation of an antique form, and was associated with the celebration of the elite. In appropriating such a prestigious art form however, artists tended to obey social decorum in selecting a relatively modest diameter. The Florentine scholar and architect Leon Battista Alberti had had a portrait medal made, about 1440, attributed to Matteo de'Pasti (*c.*1420–*c.*1467) of Verona. It had an ambiguous reverse inscribed *Quid tum* ('What then') and a winged eye, which has been variously interpreted: for instance as referring to his optical expertise or as standing for divine justice.[17] The Venetian painter Giovanni Boldù made two self portraits, dated 1458, with reverses which seem to allude to his hopes for a pious life. One showed a sorrowing young man beside a winged *putto*, who leans on a skull and has a fire behind it. The other displayed a weeping youth, seated above a skull, being chastised by another, and offered a chalice beneath the rays of the sun.[18] When copied in 1530, the former reverse was labelled *Innocentia et memoria mortis* ('Innocence and the memory of death'). Horst Janson argued that these reverses indicated death and the hope of immortality. With some pious parallel, Pisanello made a self-portrait medal in about 1450, which stated his desire for moral virtue in the form of a reverse showing the first letters of the three theological virtues (faith, hope and charity), and the four cardinal virtues (fortitude, justice, temperance and prudence) surrounded by a laurel wreath.[19]

In the sixteenth century artists continued sometimes to choose *imprese* for their medals which referred to hopes for a virtuous life or for their continuing piety, but began also to allude to desires for good fortune, to status in their profession, and to the limited span of life.

Medallic allegories were ambiguous. For instance, it seems possible that the Nuremberg sculptor Hermann Vischer chose the reverse of Hercules standing between the pillars of Gades to signify the virtuous labours of the demi-god. Dated 1507, the medal celebrated the young man when he was aged twenty-one, perhaps at his emancipation. Alternatively, the reverse could denote the claim to unlimited scope, by analogy with the limits of the classically known world, at the so-called pillars of Hercules by the straits of Gibraltar, soon to be the device of Charles V.[20] Virtue was specified as the theme of a medal for the Venetian painter Giovanni Bellini (*c.*1430–1516), made by Vittorio Gambello, engraver to the Venetian mint in 1484–1523. His reverse showed a relief of an owl, which was the attribute of Minerva. However, the virtue celebrated was the skill of Gambello himself: 'Vettor Gambello of virtue and personal talent made this' (*Virtutis et ingenii Victor Camelius faciebat*).[21] This is assumed to date some time before Giovanni Bellini's death in 1516. Possibly around 1562, Lomazzo had identified the virtue of Prudence with Mercury on the reverse of the portrait medal made for him by Fontana (see Chapter 5). On another portrait medal for Lomazzo, inscribed '1562' and signed by Pier Paolo Galeotti, a reverse which also embraced virtue had been chosen. Here virtue is pitted against avarice, and the *impresa* showed a column withstanding waves, and the motto *Virtus fulmina avaritiae contemnit* ('Virtue spurns the fulminations of avarice').[22] Galeotti (*c.*1520–84) was a Roman sculptor trained by Cellini who worked in Florence and Milan. In about 1560 the Cremonese painter Bernardino Campi (1522–91) picked a reverse which encourages modesty as a route to fame. The medal is unattributed. His medal showed Fame with two trumpets, who stands on crocodiles. One interpretation may be found in Achille Bocchi's *Symbolicorum quaestionum*, engraved by Giulio Bonasone in 1545, in Bologna, with the explanation that scholars should imitate Cato, who achieved greatness by walking away from Fame. The accompanying illustration showed Cato being chased by a crocodile, and the text stated that Fame is like a crocodile – it only follows those who flee from it.[23]

Artists were happy to advertise yearning for Good Fortune. Thus Vettor Gambello made his own medallic portrait, in 1507, with a reverse showing a pagan sacrifice and the inscription begging Fortune to favour one who makes sacrifices.[24] Across the Alps the sculptor Matthes Gebel (*c.*1500–74) provided a portrait medal for the Nuremberg engraver Augustin Hirschvogel, with the sphere of Fortune on the reverse. Dated 1543, the medal was inscribed *spero fortunae regressum* ('I hope for the return of Fortune').[25] In Italy the painter Alessandro Ardenti (flourished 1537–95), who worked in Lucca around 1537 and died in Turin in 1595, selected the *impresa* of Fortune in about 1565.[26] The reverse represented a sphere with figures ascending and descending, and the motto *et me* ('I too'), and the medal was signed by Alfonso Ruspagiari (1521–76).

One Netherlandish and one Italian painter selected obverses with images of the classical legend of Fate. Some time before 1572, the Cremonese painter Giulio Campi (*c.*1508–73), brother of Bernardino Campi, selected a reverse with a vase in which the lots of Fate were placed, with the inscription *Atropos* denoting the Fate that snips the thread of life with her shears.[27] This medal is unattributed. A little earlier, Anthonis Mor had also referred to classical myth, quoting the words of the Roman hero Aeneas. Dating from about 1560, his portrait medal presented a reverse of one of the Fates, who is shown spinning. The inscription suggested God's providence: 'God will give to them also their end' (*Dabit his deus quoque finem*). This medal has been attributed to Stephanus Hollandus.[28] Significantly, the inscription was similar to that chosen for the medal by Leone Leoni (1509–90) of the ruler Don Gonsalvo Ferdinando II of Cordoba, in around 1560, with a variant word order: *Dabit deus his quoque finem*. Gonsalvo, who was Governor of Milan, had chosen an image of Hercules for his reverse.[29] Both reverses quoted the words of Aeneas to his companions, from Virgil's *Aeneid*, Book I, when the hero had given thanks, following perils that he and they had survived.

Some artists were commemorated with portrait medals bearing allegories which referred to their personal powers. The Paduan bronze sculptor Andrea Riccio (1470–1532) was complimented with a medal reverse representing the stump of a tree, which had had one branch broken, but was sprouting from a new shoot. Above the tree is a star. The inscription read *obstante genio* ('with personal talent withstanding').[30] The obverse provided the date of Riccio's death in 1532 and mentioned his famous bronze candelabrum for Sant'Antonio in Padua. On the one hand, the allegory may praise the strength of Riccio's personal talent or *genius*, or, it has been suggested, the valedictory meaning may be that his pupils carry on his talent now that he is dead ('through talent enduring'). Less ambiguously the Cremonese artist

Giovanni Battista Caselli boasted his own strength, in a self-portrait medal dated 1551. This presented, unusually, a vernacular inscription: *E null'astringo et tutto il mondo abraccio* ('I hold onto nothing and embrace the whole world'). The motto accompanied a relief of Atlas, sustaining the globe.[31] A little later a monastic artist called Timoteo Refato, working in Mantua, had a more modest portrait medal made for him, which had the engaging obverse of a camel lying by its burden. The motto wryly observed 'Know your strength' (*non ultra vires*).[32]

Portrait medals occasionally referred to the professions of artists in an allegorical manner. For example, the portrait medal for the architect and painter Donato Bramante (*c.*1443–1514) celebrated him as an architect, who worked hard and was a man of faith, by means of an obverse showing a personification of Architecture and the words *Fidelitas Labor* ('Faith, Labour'). Dated some time before his death in 1516, the obverse shows the new Saint Peter's in the background, which Bramante was beginning to erect in Rome in 1506. Architecture is displayed as a woman seated, with a diadem, holding compasses in one hand, but the spade for digging in the other.[33] Some obverses made more secular claims concerning art. For instance, the medal for a pupil of Lomazzo, the Milanese sculptor Girolamo Figino (1548–1608), probably dated 1562, and made by Annibale Fontana, showed Minerva as protector of the Liberal Arts including sculpture (see Chapter 1).[34] Similarly, the obverse of the medal celebrating the Bolognese painter Lavinia Fontana, signed by the Bolognese medallist Felice Antonio Casoni (flourished 1592–1634) and dated 1611, stressed that painting was an intellectual and imaginative activity.[35]

Allegorical statements about the value of Christian piety were relatively rare, although this may be the import of Bramante's medal. It was certainly the interpretation for the self-portrait medal made by Hans Rosenberger, medallist of Dresden (*c.*1495–1570) and dated 1551. His obverse showed a man kneeling at prayer with the vernacular asseveration *Bit Got danck Got gib Gott* ('Pray God, Thank God and Give to God').[36] Religiosity was also the theme of the portrait medal, which was made of Michelangelo by Leone Leoni. According to Vasari, this dated from 1560. It had an obverse which presented a relief of a blind man with a pilgrim's staff and a water bottle, who is led by a dog. The inscription derived from *Psalm* 51, 13 and read *Docebo iniquos vias tuas et impii ad te convertetur* ('I shall teach the wicked and the impious shall be converted to thee'). Michelangelo was then aged eighty-eight.[37] Philip Attwood suggested that the allegory might refer to Michelangelo himself, as a blind man who is led by faith. The allusion may gain poignancy in the sense that Michelangelo's supreme skills had to do with seeing. The dog was a traditional attribute of the theological virtue of Faith.

These miniature allegories were largely on Italian medals, and most of the obverses used classicising rather than biblical imagery and Latin rather than vernacular inscriptions. However, the *imprese* on medals were circulated in a number of copies so that quite numerous influential spectators might see them, whether colleagues or patrons. Nevertheless, the allegories which were made on a larger scale (whether attached to artists' houses, or as part of artists' obsequies, or published as prints) provided larger design spaces for experiment. Nor were these larger allegories so confined to Italian producers.

One of the earliest large-scale artistic allegories was produced by Vasari in 1542 for a vault in his Aretine house and showed Painting, Sculpture, Architecture and Poetry beneath Fame (Plates 9, 40). However, in a Christian society, the enjoyment of fame was represented as taking place in the context of seeking virtue, whether in terms of moral goodness, or of worthy skill and the industry, practice and toil, which were supposed to enable one to acquire virtuosity. The associated idea that the best artists love their art, and put the exploration of inventiveness and skill ahead of the desire for money and worldly honours, is a notion which was an important element in the new discourses of art: one which would form one of the key premises of artists in western Europe during the next four centuries.

The way of virtue and the struggle of virtue and vice

The pursuit of virtue and its rewards drew on medieval and classical traditions, such as the convention of comparing the choices of human life with the selection of a virtuous, rather than a vicious, path in life's journey, and the image of a struggle between vice and virtue in motivating people to success or failures.[38] During the sixteenth century, first Italian and then Netherlandish artists explored these concepts, and added new imagery to the tradition, such as the climb to the 'tree of art'. The whole topos had been part of the written discourses of art, composed by Florentine artists, from the beginning of the fifteenth century. Cennini, Ghiberti, Alberti and Leonardo represented their profession as best pursued for motives beyond those of money: indeed Cennini advised 'for love of art'.[39] Alberti warned that:

> Avarice is always the enemy of virtue. A mind intent on gain will rarely obtain the reward of fame with posterity. I have seen many in the very flower of learning descend to gain and thereafter obtain neither riches nor distinction, who if they had improved their talent with study [*ingegnio con studio*], would early have risen to fame and there received both wealth and the satisfaction of renown.[40]

Leonardo had counselled artists not to allow 'the greed for gain to prove a stronger incentive, than renown in art'.[41] The earliest illustrations of the artist's struggle to achieve virtue, other than on medallic obverses, were produced by three artists working in Milan: Filarete, Leonardo and Cesariano.

The theme of the *via virtutis* ('the way of virtue') was first appropriated for the architect by Filarete in his *Treatise on Architecture* (1461–64), which was written in Italian for Duke Francesco Sforza of Milan. A copy was dedicated to Piero de' Medici, de facto ruler of Florence, as was a further one for Duke Alfonso of Calabria, heir to the throne of the Kingdom of Naples, in the late fifteenth century. It was translated into Latin in 1484 for King Matthaeus Corvinus of Hungary by Antonio Bonfini d'Ascoli. Five Latin copies were made from the Latin manuscript. Consequently, Filarete's allegory was quite widely circulated. Filarete wished so much to be identified with the pursuit of virtue that he adopted a name which was the transliteration of the Greek for 'lover of virtue'. In his treatise he described the ideal city of Sforzinda which his patron might build, and included the House of Virtue – which was the house of the architect himself. This had a façade decorated with a self-portrait, and a carved representation of the paradoxical advice, that the easy path leads to perdition and the hard path takes one to virtue, fame and ease. Filarete described how this image would show Virtue at the apex of a mountain, to which only one narrow path led, while Vice skulked below in a cave. Over Virtue was to be inscribed *Questo è la via ad andare acquistare la virtù con fatica* ('This is the way to achieve virtue with hard work'). Over Vice was to be written *Qui entrate, brigata, che goderete e poi con dispiacere il piagnerete* ('Whoever enters will be in good company and enjoy themselves, yet soon will lament in misery'). In the drawings accompanying his descriptions, Filarete suggested that Virtue should be armoured, and accompanied by the winged facial features of Fame floating around its head as disembodied eyes, ears, nose and mouth.[42]

The theme of the pursuit of the virtuous path had been discussed in ancient literature with reference to the Choice of Hercules, and also the careers of the Roman leaders Scipio and Marcellus. Xenophon had used the legend of Hercules' labours to explain that lasting achievement and fame could only be attained by turning one's back on transient pleasures. As a demi-god, Hercules had been raised to heaven for his achievements, following his twelve labours. Almost as well known as this legend was the transposition of the story by Silius Italicus to fit the Roman warrior Scipio. In a dream, Scipio saw Pleasure attended by vices, while by contrast Virtue was accompanied by honour and renown. Scipio vowed to ascend to the temple of Jupiter and earn the wreath of victory through hardship. The choices of vice and virtue were also encapsulated in the legend that Pythagoras had taken the manuscript letter 'Y' as image of human life, arguing that the branch on the right was the virtuous one, for it was steep and narrow but lead to a comfortable flat summit, while the branch to the left resembled vice, since it was gently sloping, yet ended in a defile. Another version was retailed by Valerius Maximus, as the moralisation of the fact that in ancient Rome the temple of Virtue was the porch to the temple of Honour. According to him, Marcellus had built the temples so that the one dedicated to Honour could only be entered by way of that of Virtue. This account had been repeated in Boccaccio's well-known text the *Genealogia deorum*.[43] The temples were described by Vitruvius, but as having been built by Marius.[44]

A quarter of a century after the Filarete treatise was circulated, and also in the Milanese court, Leonardo invented several allegories of virtues struggling with vices. While some designs have been connected with plans for court festivities, other drawings, which represent the paradoxical relationships between pain and pleasure in the tradition of the *via virtutis*, have been related to Leonardo's personal meditations on the choices of life. These drawings, and their written commentaries, date from about 1485, soon after the artist had arrived in Milan from Florence. On one of them, in which two torsos are supported on one pair of legs, Leonardo explained, 'They are made growing out of the same trunk because they have one and the same foundation. For the foundation of pleasure is labour with pain, while the foundation of pain is vain and lascivious pleasure.'[45] The idea then is that immediate pleasure brings long-term pain, while initial pain can earn the rewards of eventual pleasure (Plate 84). Colin Eisler, amongst others, has analysed these allegories in terms of the artist's subconscious desires.[46] At the same time, they may also be interpreted as belonging to the moralising tradition explored by Filarete for the artist.[47] Leonardo may have known Filarete's illustrations, since the manuscript had originally been intended for the Sforza, for whom Leonardo was working. Carlo Pedretti demonstrated that, later, in his *Trattato* (Milan, 1584), Lomazzo, who had seen these drawings and their inscriptions, recommended them as models, along with the *Calumny*.[48]

The image of struggle between virtues and vices was then adapted for the architect by the Milanese architect and painter Cesariano in his *Choices of Human Life* (Plate 70). The allegory dramatised the battle between the virtues of prudence, audacity, hard work and hope, and the vices of despair and sloth, as a psychodrama of the young architect's fight for success. In addition, it pitted these virtues against the external vices of other people's ignorance, envy, fraud, hypocrisy, slander and blandishments, as well as the threat of poverty. This type of moral allegory in which the virtues battled the vices rested on a long tradition although it had not yet been appropriated for the artist.[49] Allegories of this sort had been the privilege of leaders – as for example on the tomb of Sigismondo Malatesta of Rimini around 1460, which had been adorned with reliefs of the Triumph of Scipio and of warriors welcomed at the Temple of Minerva.[50] For instance, the portrait of Cardinal Bernardino Rossi, Bishop of Treviso, celebrating his career success had been painted by Lorenzo Lotto (*c.*1480–1556) with a pendant panel, showing the difficult ascent of the mountain of virtue in 1505.[51] On

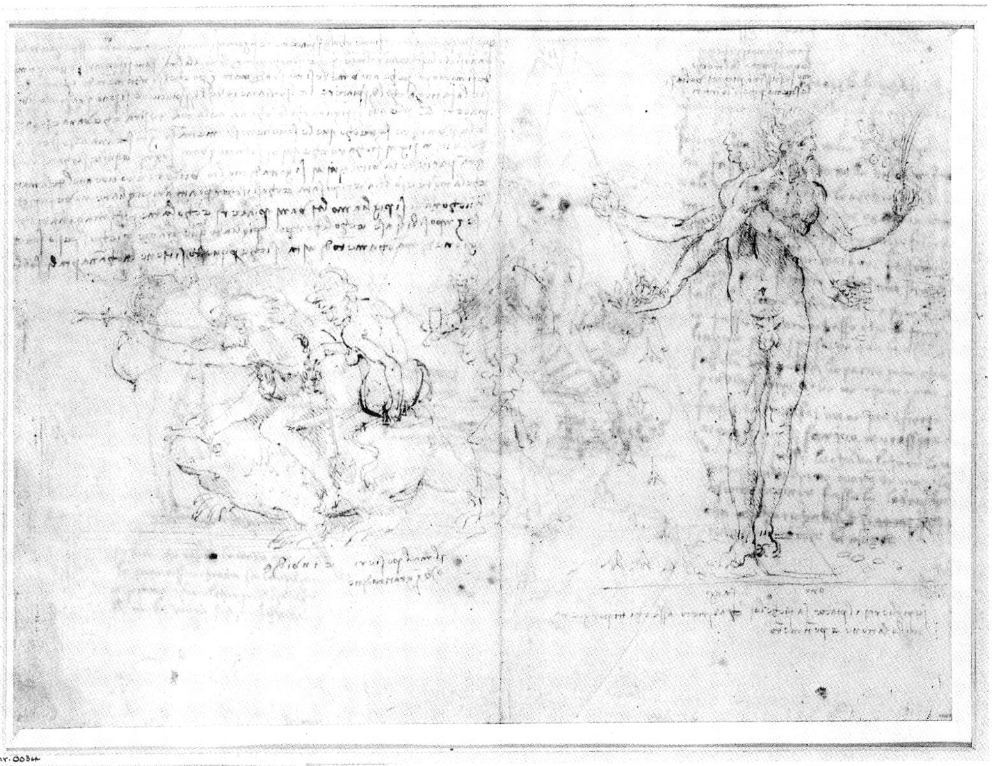

84 Leonardo da Vinci, *Pleasure is inseparable from Pain*, *c.*1485, drawing, Christchurch Art Gallery, Oxford.

another example, which seems to focus on the role of the noble lady as moral educator, the Virtues were depicted by Mantegna for the Marchioness Isabella d'Este of Mantua for her *studiolo* in 1502.[52] In this canvas Minerva accompanied by Prudence chased the vices, who had imprisoned the mother of Virtue, out of the Garden of Virtue.

Following these initiatives, allegories of the pursuit, or the struggles, of virtue in the context of architecture and the visual arts were explored, from 1548 onwards, in Arezzo, Antwerp, Florence, Rome, Venice and Prague during the sixteenth century. The 1548 room decoration by Vasari at his Arezzo house offered a tentative exploration. Here, in the largest reception room, on the flat ceiling, a personification of Virtue grabs Good Fortune by the forelock, and treads down Envy, while the mural scheme on the walls below presents virtues which theoretically assist attainment (Fortitude, Liberality, Wisdom, Prudence, Hard Work). These are accompanied by personifications of Honour and Felicity, which may suggest the artist's reward (Plates 85, 100).[53]

A decisive shift occurred in the 1560s, when the *via virtutis* imagery for artists was placed on public show in Antwerp on the house façade of the painter Frans Floris in about 1563.[54] Frans Floris placed

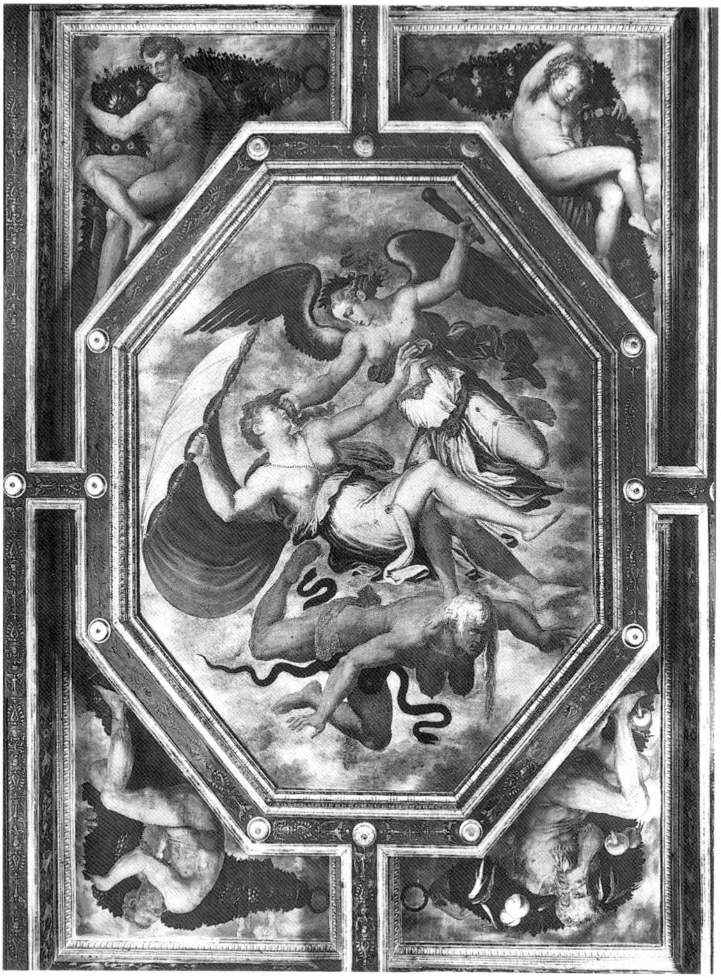

85 Giorgio Vasari, *Virtue grasps Opportunity by the forelock and vanquishes Envy*, 1548, fresco, Sala della Virtù, oil on wood, ceiling, Casa del Vasari, Arezzo.

Painting, Sculpture and Architecture along with Poetry in this pictorial scheme (Plates 14, 20). With more ponderous didacticism than Vasari, Floris had accompanied these figures with four others signifying Labour, Diligence, Experience and Practice, in such a way as to suggest the kinds of qualities which were necessary for success in the figurative arts and architecture (Plate 86). Floris had undertaken a study visit to Italy in 1541, but returning in 1545, before Vasari completed the whole of his Aretine house decoration.

In Italy, at the 1564 funeral of Michelangelo, the imagery of attainment through virtue was institutionalised when the Florentine academicians placed Fame at the apex of pyramid over Michelangelo's catafalque. Here again Vasari's contribution was of considerable importance. Below were personifications of Poetry, Sculpture, Architecture

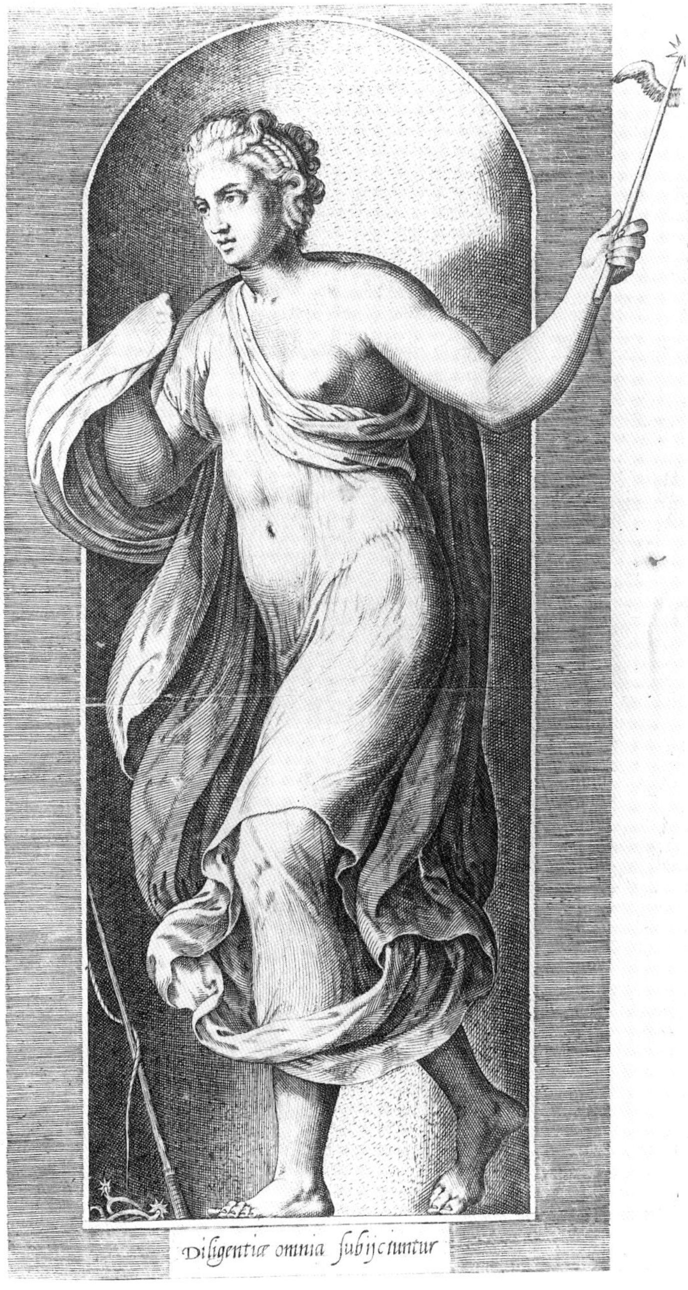

86 After Frans Floris, *Diligence*, engraved by 'T.G.' 1576, Antwerp, Albertina Vienna.

and Painting to explain his fields of prowess (Plate 16). As if to support his claim to fame in these arts, four groups of Virtues vanquishing Vices were put at the corners of the base. These represented Personal Talent (*Ingenium*) as Mercury versus Ignorance who was shown with the ears of a donkey, and Virtue as Minerva versus Envy. Envy was modelled as 'an old woman dried up and ruined with the eyes of a viper, in all ways with features that breathed venom and poison'.[55] The third sculpture represented Religion as an aggregate of the theological Virtues vanquishing Vice, and was sculpted by Valerio Cioli (*c.*1529–99). On the fourth corner stood Study, which was imagined as:

> a strong and bold young man with two wings just above his wrists to indicate speed and frequency of work. He stood above Sloth or Idleness, who seemed his prisoner, and was a lean and tired woman sleepy and ponderous in every act.[56]

This was modelled by Andrea Calamec (1524–89), a pupil of Ammanati. The message seems to be that through *Ars* (Minerva), *Ingenium* (Mercury), piety and study, Michelangelo had attained fame. This scheme, while temporary, was publicised in the 1568 edition of the *Lives* by Vasari.

The imagery of the 'way to virtue' was further displayed, in the 1570s, in Rome, by means of the allegorical frame designed by Zuccari for the border of his painted and engraved *Calumny*, and on the façade mural painted by Raffaellino da Reggio for Diana Scultori and Francesco da Volterra. While one design was for a commercially successfully print, the other was on open view in the street. The artists involved knew one another's work well, and the precedents for their designs, for Zuccari had been made a member of the Florentine academy in 1565, and had worked with Vasari on the wedding festival decorations for Joanna of Austria in that same year. Raffaellino worked with Zuccari from 1572 onwards, and Diana Scultori made engravings after Raffaellino.

In the frame he designed for the painting, and the engraving, of the *Calumny* during the period between 1569 and 1572, Zuccari developed the heroic story of Aeneas seeking and using the Golden Bough, as told by Virgil, to exemplify the struggles of the artist to find the true path (Plate 83). He also alluded to the themes of the Temples of Virtue and Honour, and the Labours of Hercules. The description by Zuccari's son Ottaviano emphasised the importance of every little detail. Aeneas is depicted in the oval cartouche, centre base, holding the bough, and being led to climb the rocky path to Virtue and Honour by Mercury. He is menaced by a wolf, an ass and a boar. He appears on one cartouche, ornamenting the left border, as cutting down trees in search of the Golden Bough, which Ottaviano asserted meant 'the desire for virtue', so as to pass safely through Hades, as described in the *Aeneid*, Book VI. In the oval cartouche on the other vertical border, he stands holding the shield and spear of Minerva as well as the palm of victory, and treading on Vices, having reached the temple of Honour. At the top centre, the cartouche showed Juno led by peacocks, above the calm sea of success, resting, after the struggles against Sloth, Vice and Slander. Here kingfishers were building their nests on the waves. Bracketing the lower cartouche are youths personifying Hard Work, who embrace an ox and break a yoke. The upper border stressed the 'generous soul' (*animo generoso*) of the artist, by means of a youth who embraces an eagle, and has a lion at his feet, as well as the figure of Hercules.[57] The corners of the frame were adorned with the shield of Minerva, the goddess sometimes signifying virtue itself. The engraving represented a landmark in the way a Netherlandish and an Italian artist, together, publicised an ambitious design concerning art.

Not surprisingly, the themes of the Roman engraving were rapidly emulated: first by Raffaellino da Reggio, who was from Reggio Emilia and became Zuccari's assistant in Rome from 1572. In 1575 the Tuscan architect Francesco da Volterra and the Mantuan engraver Diana Scultori commissioned an impressive house façade from Raffaellino for their dwelling in Rome.[58] This showed the artist in the guise of a soldier being assisted to climb the path to virtue by Minerva and Hercules (Plate 87). It also referred to the story that one could only get into the Temple of Honour through the Temple of Virtue. Their façade had on it the Latin inscription *Evexit ad aethera virtus* ('Virtue ascends to the heavens'). Since the young man was shown in armour, there may be a reference to the Roman warrior Scipio. Francesco da Volterra was a Tuscan architect, seeking commissions in Rome, and his wife Diana was from a family of Mantuan engravers, now working in Rome as an engraver; she engraved designs by Raffaellino.[59] As described by Giovanni Baglione, the mural was still visible in the middle of the seventeenth century, and represented 'Virtue who takes Hercules and Genius [*Genio*] by the hand and they all go up to the Temple of Eternity'.[60]

Venetian artists had been permitted to become members of the Florentine Academy, and the plans for Titian's funeral in Venice in 1576, perhaps not surprisingly, emulated Michelangelo's obsequies in including *via virtutis* imagery. As described by Ridolfi, one of the images to have adorned the dado area on the walls of the church was to have been 'a steep mountain with a lofty summit piercing the heavens like a pyramid' and this was to have been inscribed *per ardua virtus* ('virtue through arduousness').[61] Painting was given pride of place and then Ridolfi listed Apollo as Poetry, History probably as Mnemosyne, Design, Sculpture and Architecture. Ridolfi's source explained that this was because Poetry and History provided painting with its subject matter whether legendary or true. These five figures were to have been accompanied by Symmetry (*Simmetria*), Hard work (*Fatica*) and Honour. The personifications elaborated on the theme of the *via virtutis* topos,

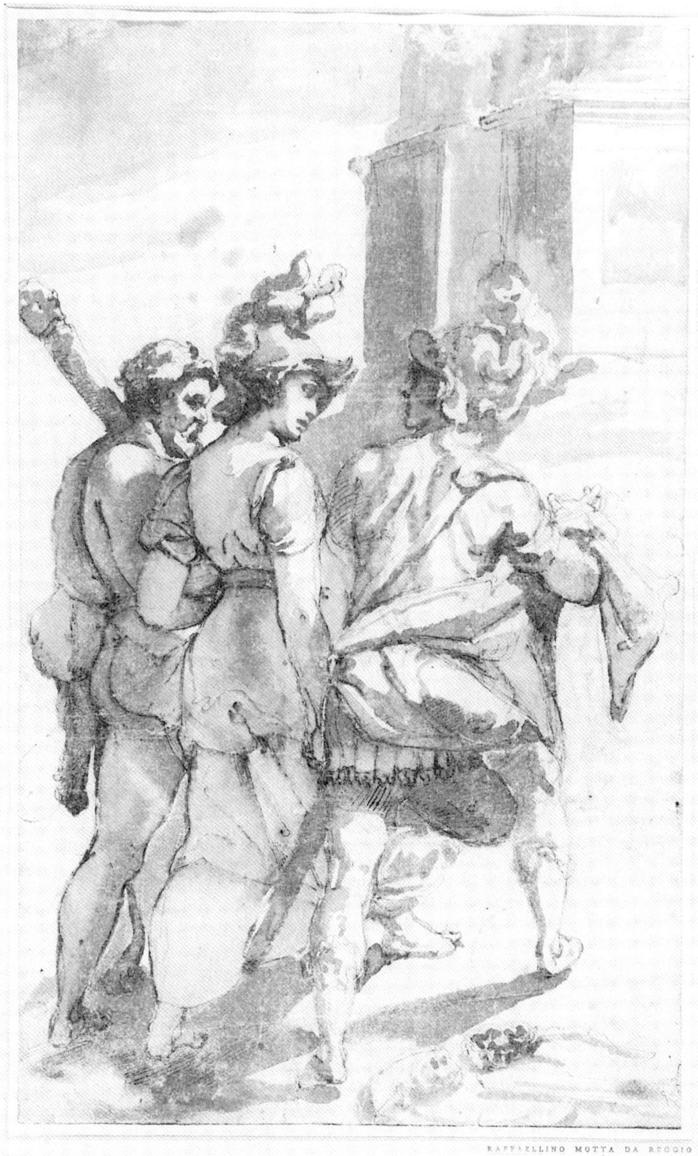

87 Raffaellino da Reggio, The house of Francesco da Volterra and Diana Scultori, drawing, *c.*1575, British Museum.

since Hard Work was regarded as the way to achieve acclaim. She was represented as a strong young woman poorly dressed 'because she cannot produce the fruits of virtue unless she is poor and strong, since she must stand up to the continuous application to study'.[62] She was labelled *sic itum ad gloriam* ('thus one may attain glory'). Ridolfi next described a figure whom he did not name but which has the attributes of Honour, according to Cesare Ripa.[63] 'Honour' was to have been shown as crowned with palms and holding a spear accompanied by the motto *certaminis trophea* ('the trophies of struggle'). He was crowned with palms, wore a royal mantle and he held a shield, on which was a depiction of 'the temple of Marco Marcello', inscribed with the words *virtute praevia* ('with virtue leading the way'). He also held crowns, bracelets, and necklaces, inferring the honours which are the dues of virtue.[64] *Simmetria* was a term which had been used by Pliny the Elder and may be translated as proportionality. She was described by Ridolfi as one 'who regulates everything with measure and proportion', and was to have held compasses in her hand and have had the word *perfectiora* ('the more perfect') written beneath her.[65] (Proportionality was regarded as fundamental, like *disegno*, to painting, sculpture and architecture.) The entire scheme sought to praise Titian, comparing him to a star, with the exhortation *micat inter omnes* ('let him shine amongst them all'), and it seems that the theme of the *via virtutis* played an important role in justifying such exaltation.[66]

The study trip by Frans Floris to Italy seems likely to have contributed to his interest in making his own version of the way of virtue for artists in Antwerp. Similarly, the period when Spranger (also trained in Antwerp) was working in Italy between 1565 and 1575 is likely to have prepared him, a generation later, to explore the theme too. Spranger knew of the mural by Raffaellino da Reggio in Rome since he made a version of it, for engraving in 1591, and had worked in Italy, part of the time with Zuccari.[67] Spranger's versions were made, however, in the cultural milieu of the Imperial court at Prague where, in 1592, he had translated the theme to a drawing for the instruction of his son Georg featuring Mercury and Minerva in leading roles (Plate 75). The fact that Spranger's house façade in Prague had depicted small children working at drawing, painting and sculpture on either side of Mercury and Fame (Chapter 5) suggests that here too he may also have been thinking about the way application earns fame.

Having explored the theme of the *via virtutis* on the small scale of the *Calumny* frame, Zuccari took up the imagery again, two decades later, close to the time when he was appointed first President of the Accademia di San Luca. This time Zuccari painted it on a grand scale for the entrance to his new house, the Palazzo Zuccari, in Rome. Soon after 1590, Zuccari decorated his hall vault with the legend of Hercules choosing the steep path of virtue rather than the easy path of vice, as originally told by Xenophon (Plate 88). According to the description of the scheme by his son, the vault scheme also referred to the legend that Pythagoras had taken the manuscript letter 'Y' as image of human life. Viewers were shown Aeneas holding the Golden Bough, ascending the mountain of virtue, to enter the temple of Honour through that of Virtue. At the base, Hercules, with his lion skin and club, leant on the Erymanthian boar he had slain, and was being urged to follow Aeneas by a winged

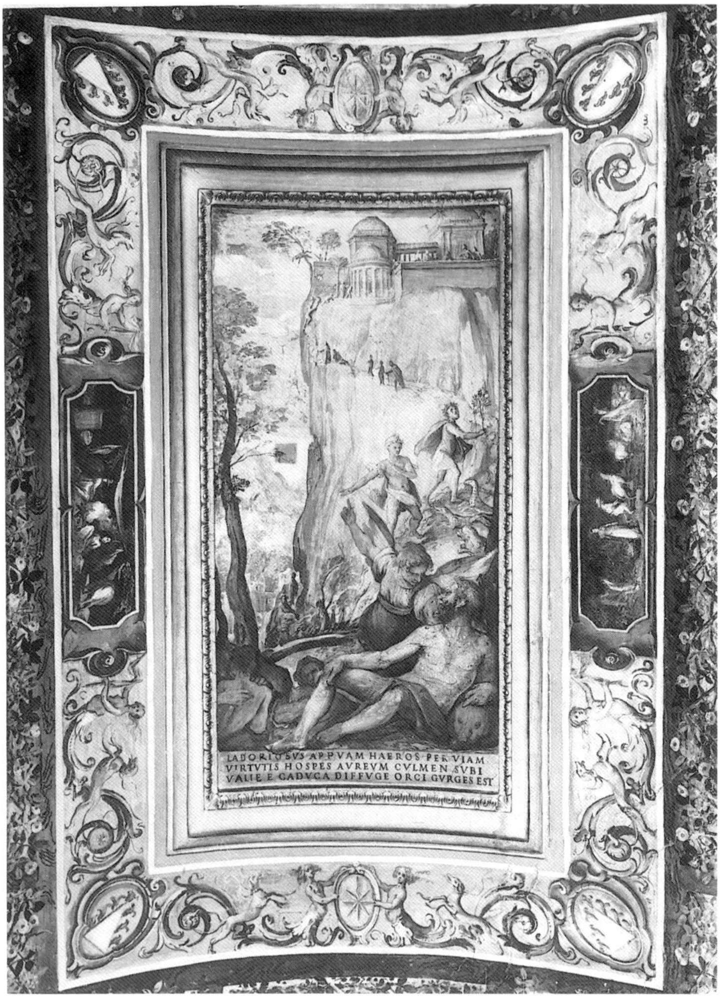

88 Federico Zuccari, *The Choice of Hercules*, *c.*1595, vestibule, fresco, Palazzo Zuccari, Rome.

woman, who may personify Virtue. Beside him is a path leading down into a valley containing musicians and amorous couples: the way of vice. Above him a youth is climbing the precipitous path and being threatened by the three beasts, described by Dante in the *Divina commedia* as having menaced him in Hell: the leopard standing for lust, the lion for pride and the wolf for arrogance. Some of the small figures appear to scramble and fall. The twelve labours of Hercules were depicted in the friezes.[68] The whole scene was inscribed as if exhorting visitors to imitate Hercules: 'Climb up stranger, to the golden summit by the arduous path of virtue. Shun the transient valley, which is the raging torrent of hell' (*Laboriosus arduam haeros per viam virtutis hospes aureum culmen subi valle e caduca diffuge orci gurges est*).[69] A further inscription in Italian clarified the exhortation: 'You may realise that you can never hope for honour, riches or virtue without hardwork' (*Intendere potrai che non giamai senza fatica si possi sperare Honore richezza nè virtù*).[70]

Zuccari continued the theme in the vestibule that follows the entrance hall, with a vault depicting labelled personifications of the qualities which an artist should cultivate so as to achieve Fame and Honour (Plate 98). These were Wisdom (*Sapientia*), who was given the implements of the seven Liberal Arts and brushes, along with Perseverance (who was depicted teaching children and with a crane); then there was Diligence, who holds a spade and a cornucopia and has a crane beside it, and is paired with Hard Work (embracing an ox). The crane, used twice, was associated with Mercury and it signified application and vigilance, since it was thought to hold a stone in one claw, so that it would awake as soon it dozed.[71] Accompanying them were Frankness (*Animi candor*), who holds her heart in her hand and has the attributes of a spotless ermine and a white dove, coupled with *Spirito* – the quality that Vasari had allied with originality and personal talent when he had described the obsequies of Michelangelo. Zuccari's *Spirito*, however, possessed the wings at his wrists and temples which had been given to Study in the catafalque design for Michelangelo. In the same palace, Zuccari painted a series of canvases narrating the biography of his brother Taddeo, and included allegorical figures signifying the Intelligence and Study which had gone to make him such a successful painter before his early death (see Chapter 4). Zuccari also depicted his brother's Faith and Hope, Wisdom and Diligence, as well as his Patience and Fortitude.[72] The house was much visited by the artistic community.

Zuccari made a finished drawing, possibly intended for an engraving, in which he developed the imagery of climbing a tree to pick the fruits of one's labours (Plate 89). The drawing provided a close-up view of the scene on the hall vault of his Roman house, with the rewards awaiting diligent artists at the summit of the mountain of virtue.[73] To the left, Zuccari shows some scaling the wall of the temples of Virtue and Honour rather than going in the right way, through the entrance labelled 'virtue' (*virtus*), where Minerva is standing. These artists grasp at what he labelled 'pestiferous fruit' (*fruto pestifero*), which is hanging on trees by the wall. Some of the impatient artists tumble down. His inscription warned that they 'no longer know what carries knowledge' (*non piu sapere quod porte sapere*). In contrast, the true seekers of knowledge and virtue reach the temple of Honour. There Zuccari shows a platform recalling the Pythagorean summit of the letter Y, where the seven Liberal Arts are conversing with Painting, Sculpture and Architecture, whilst Apollo, the Muses and Mercury accompany them. Figures of Fame fly down, and a youth inscribed *Spirito* greets the arrivals. The fine drawing therefore, shows in detail what the hall vault could only suggest.

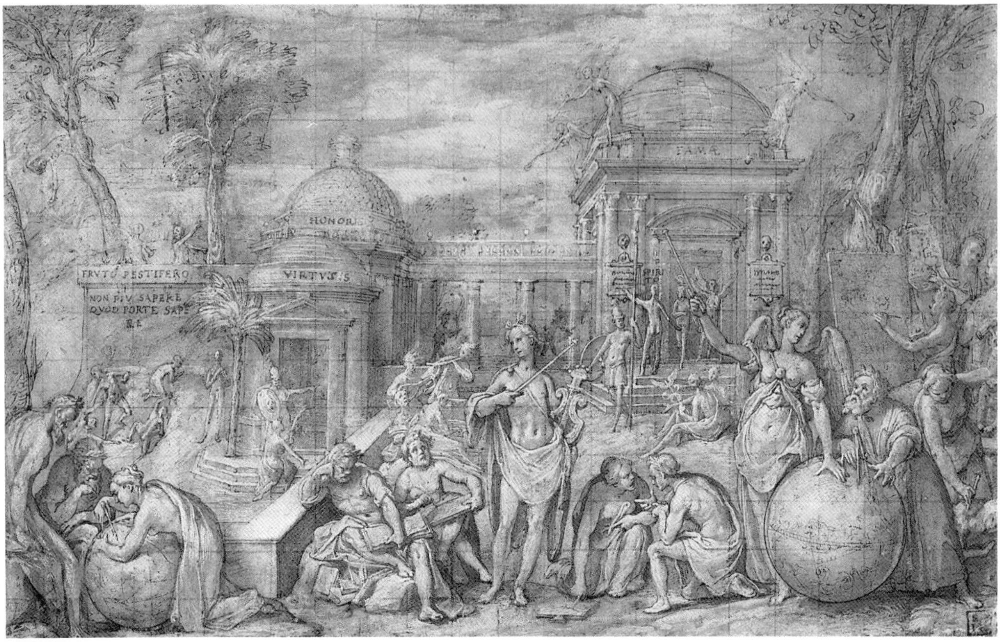

89 Federico Zuccari, virtuous artists reach the summit of the mountain of virtue, *c.*1590, Pierpont Morgan Library, New York.

This intensely moralising elevation of the importance of artists' search for a good life was also being pursued by Vasari's colleague, Jan van der Straet, in Florence, in designing the frame for his own portrait. Possibly in 1587, or a little later, Jan Wiericx (1549–*c.*1618) reprinted the portrait which van der Straet had made about 1583. Van der Straet invented a new frame, complete with inscriptions extolling his own search for virtue (Plate 90),[74] which read *Sola manet virtus labuntur caetera quaeque divitiae vires, fama, iuventa, decus* ('Only virtue lasts when all else in strength, riches, honour, fame and youth have been toppled'). The image was placed in a pious context, being, for example, used to preface a series of engravings of *The Passion of Christ* under the patronage of the Medici. Below the portrait of the author was the motto 'with assiduousness none may rival you' (*assiduitate nihil non adsequitur*). Small *imprese* were placed in the corners of the frame, including one showing the crane standing on one leg, holding a stone in the other claw, and inscribed *non fallitur* ('never failing'). The artist was also complimented as employing intellect, in the motto *ratione perfectius* ('more perfect through reason'), above the image of a mirror and a serpent. Serpents were linked with wisdom through the biblical adage 'wise as serpents' (*Matthew*, 10, 16) while the mirror could indicate self-knowledge.[75]

The *via virtutis* theme had been chosen by the Florentine academy for Michelangelo's funeral, and by Zuccari the president of the Roman academy, as well as the Venetian Fraglia dei Pittori for the funeral of

Titian. However, the academic connection was pursued more explicitly in an elaborate allegory by an unknown artist in the circle of Zuccari around 1590, which is now in the Graphische Sammlung, Albertina, Vienna (Plate 91).[76] This presented ideals of art education, with painters, sculptors and architects studying an academic curriculum, entailing anatomy, geometry and the antique. These activities are taking place in a barrel-vaulted building, through whose arches one sees outside, to a piazza and a loggia. At the base of the drawing was illustrated the struggle of young artists who are attempting to ascend the steps to learning and success. This may have been intended for an engraved frontispiece. The style suggests the circle of Zuccari, but the content is paralleled in aspects of a poem which the Amsterdam artist Cornelis Ketel (1548–1616) attached to a drawing of the 'Tree of Art'. His tree metaphor, in turn, reminds one of the imagery of collecting fruit from trees in the Zuccari's finished drawing, showing the close-up of his palace-hall decoration (Plate 89). Like the *Calumny* engraving, it suggests interchange between Netherlandish and Italian traditions at this period. Van Mander described the poem and drawing by Ketel in the part of Ketel's biography covering the period 1589 to 1595:

90 Jan van der Straet, self-portrait, engraved by Jan Wiericx, *c.*1587, Prints and Drawings, British Museum.

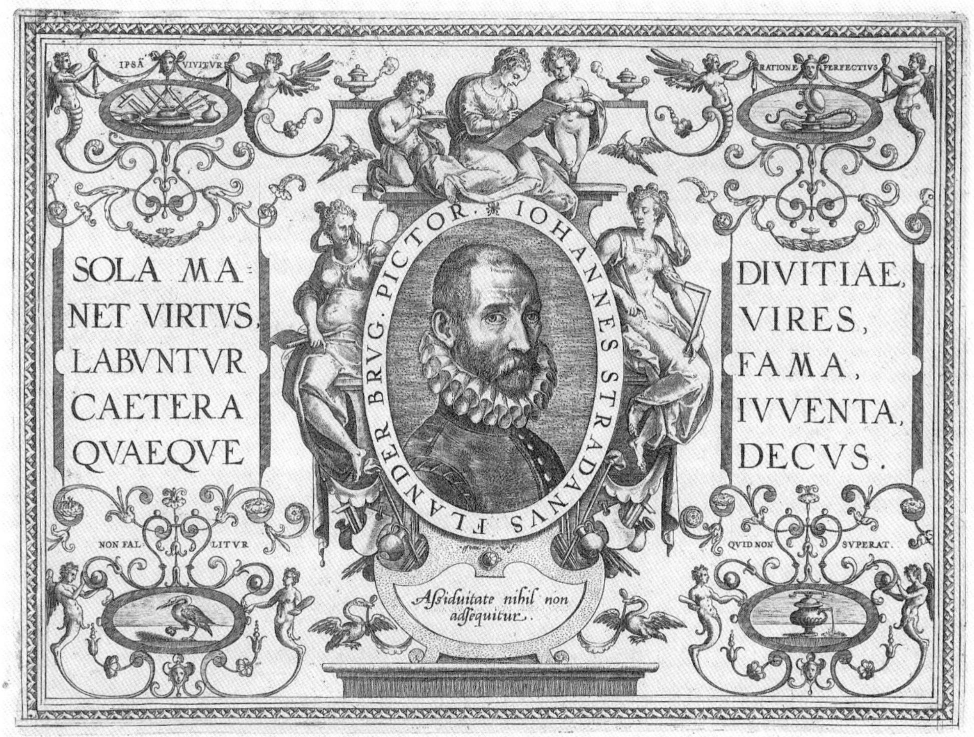

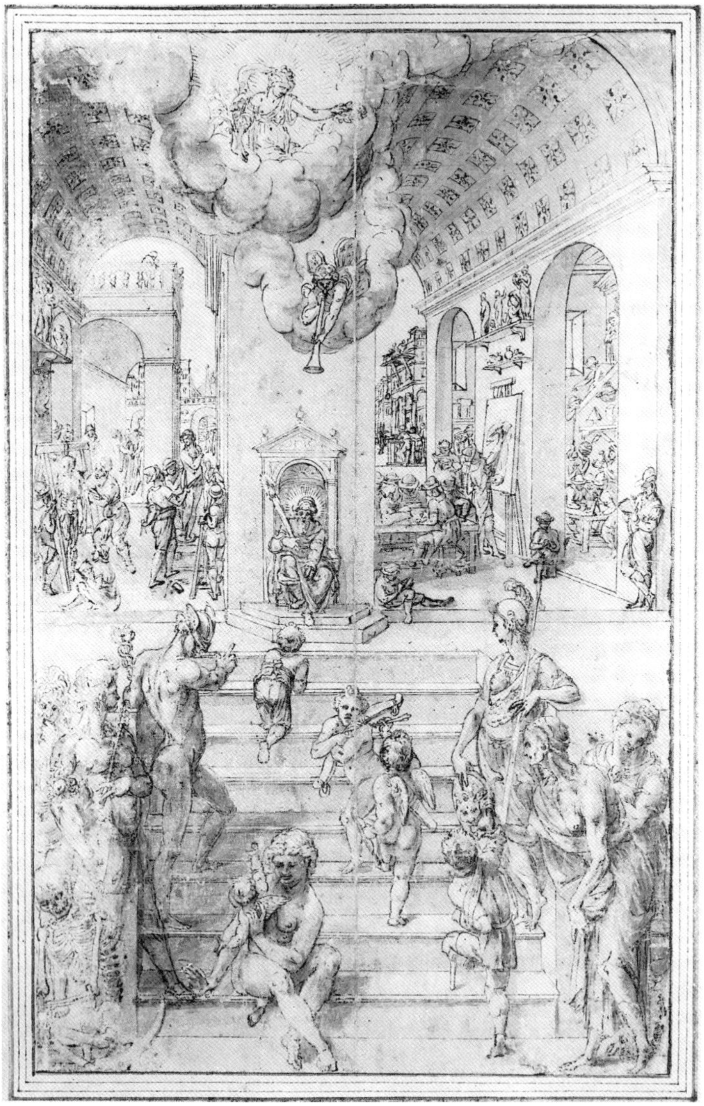

91 Anonymous, *The progress of the young artist*, *c.*1590, drawing, Graphische Sammlung Albertina, Vienna, Inventory number 2763.

A drawing which represented by means of a Tree of Art, the three major inducements through which all the arts are learnt – money, honour and love of art – and also the way success arouses envy, along with the following lines of verse which he attached to it. 'Three things there are that most spur the pupil: money, and love of art and noble science [*Wetenschap*]. He who seeks for money always meets avarice, who is a menace to him and trips him up at every step. He who seeks after renown or honour can certainly climb higher, for worldly ambition does lead to the tree of Arts. But since he is satisfied with the mere sight of the fruit, and too fearful or too sluggish to climb further himself, he only picks the unripe fruit at the base of the tree.

But one whom love urges up the noble path of art will certainly succeed at this work in the end. When he is supported by diligence and attains the summit, where money and honour await him, he will belittle all his toil because of the fruition of his efforts.'[77]

In the second verse Ketel explained how Fortune was attacked by hate, envy and calumny, though truth would win, given time.

At the bottom of the steps, in the anonymous Albertina drawing, sits a personification of many-breasted Nature, who is producing young talents, and is shown in the act of attaching wings to one of her hopefuls, who already stretches a hand out to the scene of learning above (Plate 91). Ahead of him one young boy has managed to get near to the top. Below him another boy is being pierced with the arrow of Love of Art (who is winged and who carries a bow and quiver) so as to climb higher, carrying a yoke – probably indicating Labour. These talents are being encouraged by Mercury to the left, and Minerva to the right, who guard the steep stairs. The base is filled with personifications denoting factors which may hold back a youthful talent. To the left is a woman gnawing her hand, who may indicate Pain. Pleasure holds a cornucopia and a Bacchic wand or thyrsus, and Death is a skeleton with a scythe. To the right is Envy wrapped with snakes, and a boy, hampered by a wooden leg, takes a money bag from Avarice.

At the centre of the design sits a bearded man with an aureole of light round his head, holding a torch. This is the person to whom the foremost talent kneels. It seems possible that he personifies *Disegno*, both because this is the most obvious figure to preside over the three arts, and also because Zuccari signified *Disegno* in his Sala del Disegno, in his palace, as a patriarch with a halo (Plate 30). Appearing in a heavenly cloud over the throne are Fame with her trumpet and, above her, Honour, who carries a bough and holds out a laurel wreath. The bough could refer to the Golden Bough granting Aeneas immortality, and more generally to Virtue, since Ripa described the attribute of an oak bough as an emblem of virtue, because it resists all weathers.[78]

The design draws further on Italian and Netherlandish imagery. For example, the representation of many-breasted *Natura* may owe something to a similar personification on Cellini's seal proposal for the Florentine academy who, he stated, 'suckled everything' (see Chapter 2). Yet it may also recall an engraving entitled the *Rewards of Labour and Diligence* after van Heemskerck, which was published by Philips Galle (Antwerp, 1572). There Nature suckles a naked child beside a globe, covered with the attributes of different arts. The Latin inscription suggests one explanation for the way Nature attaches wings to the young talents in the Albertina allegory:

Just as the parent bird brings forth her fledglings so insistently and repeatedly from the nest, and urges them to follow her, and fly out on their stubby wings, similarly so does Nature, the mother of all things, bring forth the human species from the soft cradle and the pregnant womb, and urges them out to toil and hard labour.[79]

Envy recalls the representation of envy entwined with snakes displayed on Vasari's Aretine scheme of 1548 and on Michelangelo's catafalque in 1564. The figure of Pleasure in the guise of Bacchus may echo the way that Filarete had described Bacchus, Venus and Priapus as standing by the door of Vice, in one of his allegories for his imaginary house.[80] Ketel was a learned painter, engraver and poet of Amsterdam, who could have met Zuccari when they were both in London in 1575. Although Ketel did not, apparently, travel to Italy, his poem and the lost drawing illustrating it might have been known in Italy. The Albertina allegory chimed with sentiments expressed by Zuccari in a letter written to the Florentine academy in 1575, asking for young artists to be taught anatomy, architecture, perspective and mathematics, so that they 'might travel by the good road and have their path made easier up the difficult ascent of the mountain of the knowledge of our Art'.[81] The stylistic and conceptual genealogy of the allegory indicates some cross fertilisation between Italian and Netherlandish traditions at the time.

At the end of the period the network of connections between the Netherlands and Prague was further in evidence, in the use of *via virtutis* imagery for the celebration of art. The trope of Hercules and Minerva assisting the artist, which had been used by Zuccari and by Raffaellino da Reggio, was employed by a pupil of Ketel. He was the painter and engraver Pieter Isaacsz. (1569–1625), who designed a framed portrait, in Amsterdam, as a tribute for his second master, Hans van Aachen (1552–1615), which was then engraved by Jan Saenredam in Haarlem in 1601 (Plate 92). Van Aachen is recorded as having sent the self-portrait from Prague to his former pupil by 1598. The engraving may represent a celebration of van Aachen's success: trained in Antwerp, he was from Cologne, and had worked in Venice, Florence and Rome, before taking up residence at Prague, where he had been appointed Imperial court painter in 1592. The frame displayed Hercules and Painting, standing on either side of the portrait, holding Fortuna steady, by tugging at her two long forelocks equally. Two winged children draw assiduously. To underline the idea that Hans had undertaken Herculean labours, there is a scene inset at the base of the frame, telling how Hercules and Minerva assist the young to climb the steep mountain of virtue.[82] The inscription pronounces *vivit post funera virtus* ('virtue survives death').[83] The re-issue, in 1605, may commemorate the conferment of a knighthood on van Aachen, by the Emperor in that year.

The transformation of the *via virtutis* imagery for the use of artists appears to have begun in Milanese circles, and have then been taken up by Vasari in the decoration for his house at Arezzo (1548), and by

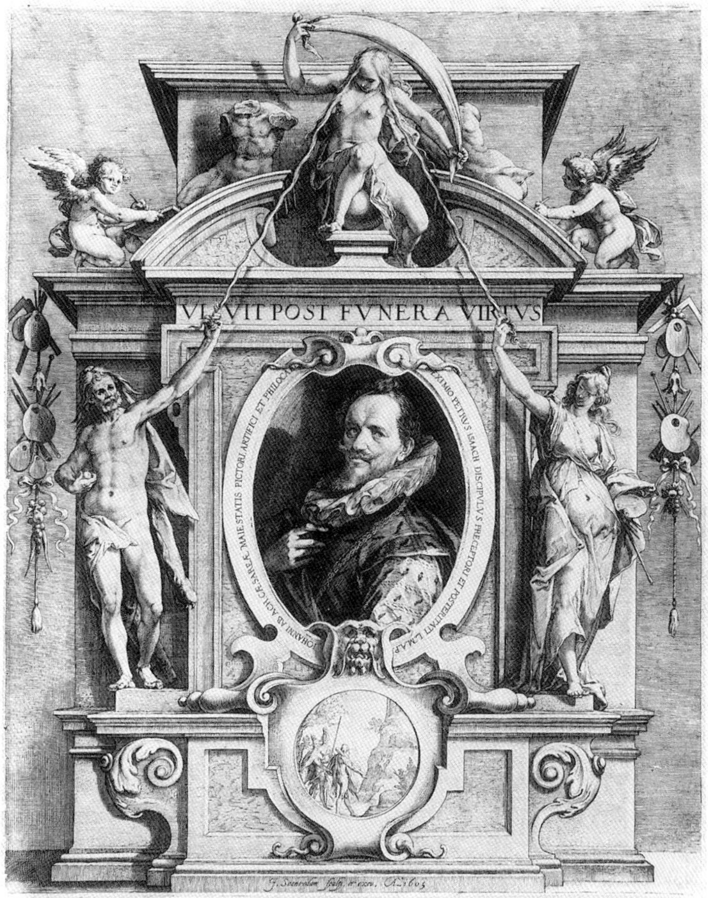

92 Pieter Isaacsz, portrait of Hans van Aachen, 1601, 401 × 324 mm, engraving by Jan Saenredam.

others in Florence for Michelangelo's funeral (1564). It seems likely that the version which Floris made for his house in Antwerp (1563) reflected his Italian journey. The imagery was then apparently furthered by networks of artists, related to one another through membership of the academies, as work colleagues or as pupils. Thus the topic was pursued in Rome in the 1570s by Zuccari (who had worked in Florence beside Vasari), in collaboration with Cort (who had trained in Antwerp) and also by Raffaellino da Reggio (Zuccari's colleague). At the same time, Venetian painters, some of whom belonged to the Florentine academy, set out to refer to the 'way of virtue' in their funerary commemoration of Titian. In the 1590s the imagery was translated to Prague by Spranger, who had worked with Zuccari and knew the Raffaellino mural well. As with Floris, Spranger was originally an Antwerp artist. Also in the 1590s, and in Rome, Zuccari made his second and perhaps equally influential intervention in his decoration of his palace vestibule, which was viewed by artists visiting Rome. The key roles of Vasari and Zuccari in the introduction of the *via virtutis* imagery could therefore be linked to their institutional importance for the academies of Florence and Rome. Van der Straet's engraved self-portrait underlines the role of Netherlandish artists working in Italy for the establishment of the theme. That the trope was also current in the Netherlands is shown both by Ketel's lost drawing and poem, and by the commemoration of van Aachen (who was working alongside Spranger at the Imperial court) to which Ketel's pupil contributed. Its currency is also apparent in the designs by Goltzius and Hondius made in the first decade of the sixteenth century, which pointedly rejected the pursuit of wealth for itself (Plates 77, 80). The survival of the Albertina allegory also suggests that, by the end of the period, the flow of ideas was no longer one way, and that Netherlandish inventions on this theme could attract an Italian draughtsman (Plate 91).

Artists rebut their detractors

From the 1540s onwards artists began, sporadically, to make images of malignant critics in an unflattering way. The theme has connections with the trope of the *Calumny* with its representation of the detractors of Apelles. However, the defence in the new allegories was against those criticising one's art, not slandering one's actions. What seems to be the earliest representation of malign critics occurred in two stucco reliefs which Daniele da Volterra placed at the bases of the pilasters framing the chapel he decorated for Elena Orsini at Santa Trinità de' Monti in Rome (Plate 93). This was begun soon after 1541, when the contract was

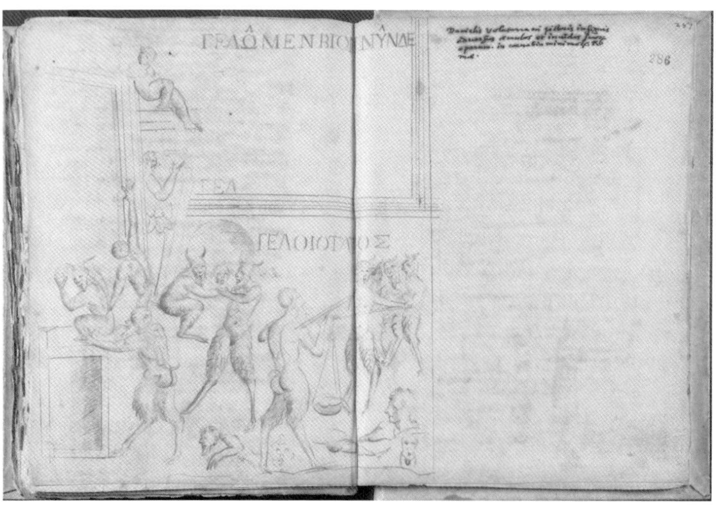

93 Alonso Chacon, drawing, *c.*1585, of the stucco by Daniele da Volterra showing satyrs weighing up his abilities, Bibliotheca Angelica, Rome, MS. 1564, fol. 288 recto.

signed, with the Prior of Santa Trinità, who was the executor of Elena's father's will, and was probably complete by 1550. Vasari described them in the *Lives* (1568), thus ensuring that Daniele's ideas had quite a wide audience. Vasari wrote that Daniele made the reliefs,

> out of caprice or as a sort of defence, as if to show that Michelangelo and Fra Sebastiano del Piombo, whose works he imitated, and whose principles he followed, were his friends, and his imitation of such friends should suffice to protect him from the envious and the malignant even if he was slow and laboured. In one of these scenes he represented a number of satyrs weighing legs, arms and other members, to pass the good ones of correct weight, and to give the bad to Michelangelo and Fra Sebastiano who are judging them: in the other Michelangelo is looking at himself in a mirror the meaning of which is apparent.[84]

Vasari implied that Michelangelo (who died in 1564) and Sebastiano (who died in 1547) were Daniele's live arbiters; Daniele (*c.*1509–66) worked in Rome from 1535 onwards.

Drawings were made of the reliefs, in about 1585, by the Dominican scholar Alonso Chacon. As explained by David Jaffé, the stucco on the right showed the very chapel itself, with critics, in the shape of satyrs, weighing and measuring Daniele's abilities at representing the nude;[85] satyrs are weighing limbs, from the painting, on scales. A Greek inscription as translated by Jaffe stated 'We laugh at life but now it is really laughable', which may invite derision of envious critics. The other inscriptions as deciphered by Jaffe were in Greek as well. The pendant stucco on the left showed a woman offering Michelangelo a mirror. Above was the statement 'My advice to artists is "nothing"', and halfway down the relief was the statement 'Know thyself'. This had been attributed to Socrates, who had told pupils to examine themselves as if in a mirror every day, to learn their weaknesses. This might explain the mirror being held out by the woman.[86] Below is the statement 'Beyond measure'. Daniele could have been advising artists to seek a personal style of grace beyond slavish attention to the regulations implied by the scales. This advice recalls the statement by Vasari, in his biography of Michelangelo, that all artists 'are perpetually indebted to Michelangelo for the example he showed of *licenzia*' – in advising artists to free themselves from exact adherence to the measurements and rules of classical architecture.[87] Chacon inscribed the drawing of the satyrs as 'against those vying with and envious of his work' (*adversus aemulos et invidos suorum operum*). These reliefs were visible during the sixteenth century, although by the mid-eighteenth century only the relief showing the satyrs was still extant. Chacon's drawings and Vasari's description demonstrate that the actual stucco altarpiece frame for the chapel also put forward Mannerist ideas. This was a game with the logic of the classical architectural orders, since the entablature seems to be held up by figures on either side who are still putting the columns and capitals into place. Both in the altarpiece frame and the stuccoes, then, Daniele drew attention to the business of making and viewing art. The church in which the stuccoes were situated was adjacent to the site of Zuccari's Roman palace.

The choice of satyrs (half-goat and half-human creatures, who live in the wild) was a telling one to represent carping critics. Because the subject of the satyrs Marsyas and Pan foolishly challenging Apollo as musician was well known, the notion of the satyr as a critic with poor judgement might have been considered plausible.[88] The satyr had also been used to signify hatred of truth, most influentially by the Venetian writer Pietro Aretino, who had employed it as the emblem on the title page of his publications from 1536 onwards, and for his medal. As analysed by Fritz Saxl, Aretino's design had shown naked Truth seated with her foot on a satyr armed with talons, and accompanied by the motto *Veritas odium parit* ('Truth gives birth to hatred').[89]

Daniele's initiative may have been known to the Aretine sculptor Leone Leoni, since he employed the image of a satyr prominently as an enemy for his house frontal in Milan in 1567.[90] However, as Leoni was the kinsman of Pietro Aretino, and lived under his protection in Venice from 1533 to 1537, it seems more likely that he derived the idea from Aretino. Leoni had worked in Rome between 1537 and 1540, but had then been banished. On his Milanese house Leoni placed a relief over the main entrance, which showed two lions signifying his own name – that is, 'lions' or *leoni* – who are eating a satyr, starting from its genitals (Plate 94a and b). Leoni had modelled a bronze statue of the ruler of Milan in 1560, usually entitled *Ferrante Gonzaga conquering Evil and Envy*, in which a satyr stood for Envy, while a harpy signified Evil. It seems likely that the satyr on Leoni's house front indicated those seeking, enviously, to harm the artist.

The association between satyrs and foolish or malign critics gained ground when Zuccari also employed satyrs for his design of the *Porta virtutis* ('portal of virtue'), in which they were shown attacking Zuccari's skill. This was the cartoon which he set up on the steps of San Luca, being the church of the confraternity and guild of painters in Rome, on the Feast day of Saint Luke in 1581 (Plate 95). The exhibition, while temporary, could be viewed by many and became notorious through Zuccari's resulting trial and exile. The composition is known through three preparatory drawings, one painting and Zuccari's deposition.[91] The metaphor is that of the fortress of Roman painting, with Minerva treading down a personification of Vice, to defend her territory. Her shield has the motto *Sic semper* ('Thus always') inscribed on it, and she is flanked by the Three Graces and a personification labelled *Spirito*. Minerva, or 'Virtue' as Zuccari called her, guards a portal which is adorned as if with soldierly figures in relief, labelled Diligence and

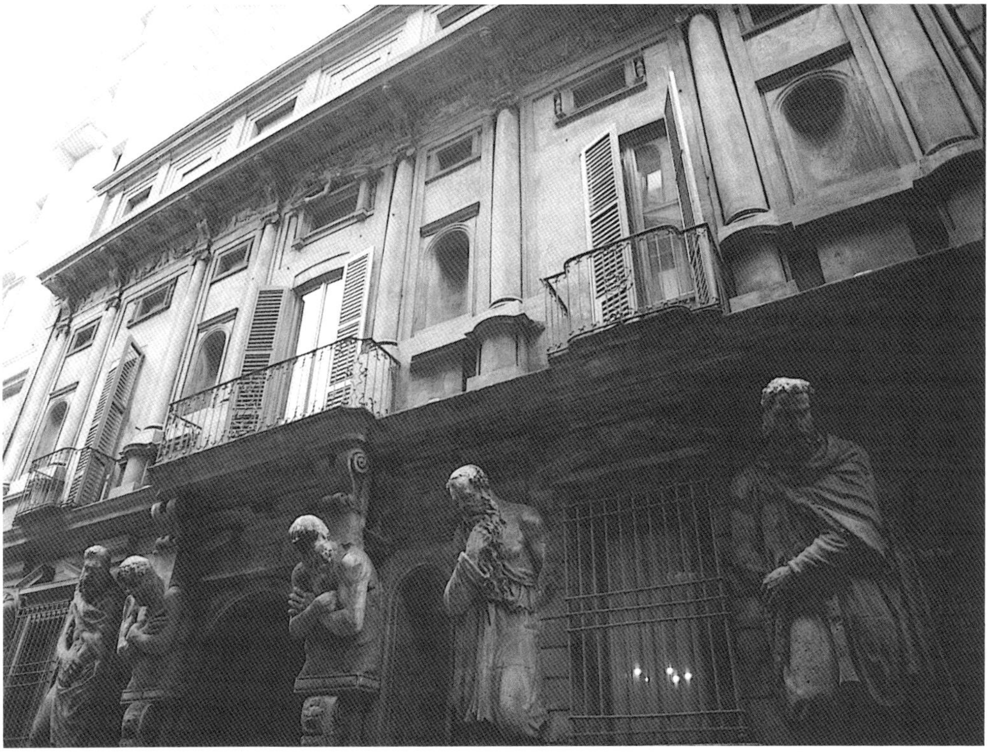

94 Antonio Abbondio, façade of the house of Leone Leoni, 1567, Milan.

Labour, each of whom holds a shield decorated with famous Roman monuments. On the inside walls of the archways are statues of Study and Intelligence, and on the cornices of the barrel vault sit figures inscribed as the four Cardinal Virtues, while others, who are blowing the trumpets of fame, fly overhead. Behind Minerva, is a building labelled 'palaces of Virtue' recalling Filarete's house in Sforzinda. Above Minerva floats an ideal painting inscribed with the terms 'invention', 'decorum', *disegno* and 'colouring'. Outside the gate, nearest the viewer, is to the left Crass Ignorance, holding compasses and a set square, into whose ears are whispering Adulation and Presumption, which thus recalls the *Calumny*. Ignorance sits on a pile of books, whose titles are 'Perspective' and 'Painting'. At his feet, Envy lies covered with snakes, while to our right are three satyrs, one tall and two shorter ones, holding scissors and knives, and described by Zuccari at the trial as 'evil speaking and his assistants, that is the little satyrs' (*maldicenzia et suoi parti cioè di satiri piccoli*). On one of the drawings, he inscribed the taller satyr, as 'servant of Envy'.

The allegory seems to have been occasioned by the rejection of an altarpiece which had been commissioned by Paolo Ghiselli, a member of the papal court, for his chapel in the Madonna del Baraccano,

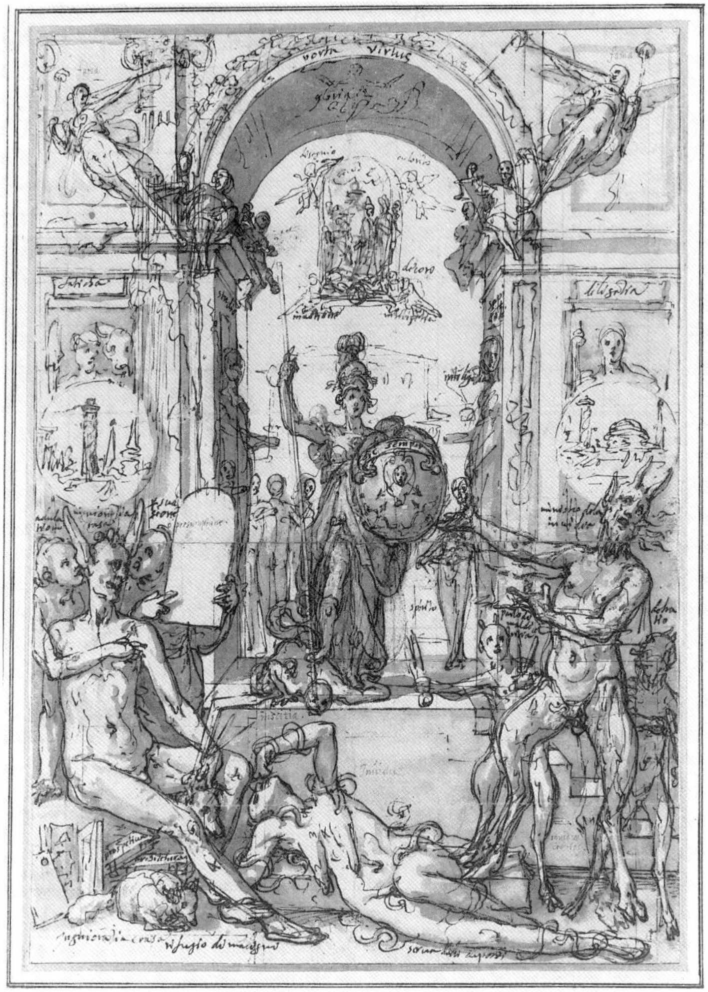

95 Federico Zuccari, *Porta virtutis*, 1581, drawing, Christchurch Gallery, Oxford.

Bologna. It had represented the *Procession of Saint Gregory* with the Bolognese Pope Gregory XIII portrayed in the lead role. After Zuccari responded with the cartoon, he was tried in the ecclesiastical court. According to Zuccari, the painters of Bologna had supported Ghiselli, and criticised his colouring, proportions and perspective.[92] At his trial, Zuccari stated that he was thinking of criticism levelled at him long before in Florence and that his allegory related in general to the struggles of the artist to attain virtue and to conquer envy and ignorance. The riposte allegorical turned out to be dangerous on the short term, since he was banished from 1581 to 1583, although he was received back in favour, and, following his return to Rome was eventually appointed as first president of the academy.[93]

Following what was now the beginnings of a tradition, Ketel in 1602 employed his house façade in Amsterdam to rebut his own critics, who had taken exception to him painting with a foot or his mouth holding the brush. However, Ketel chose different imagery to that employed by Daniele, Leoni and Zuccari, with reference to more traditional religious iconographies, for on his façade Ketel painted the personification of Patience withstanding the attack of Falsehood. As described by van Mander, in other elements of his design he drew from ancient philosophical history.[94] Thus Ketel selected figures of the ancient Greek philosophers Heraclitus and Democritus to demonstrate the 'philosophical' attitude that it was wise to take up in the face of criticism. It was the ancient adage that while the one philosopher, Democritus, had laughed all the time, the other, Heraclitus, had cried continuously. Renaissance scholars had pointed the moral for one another and for those in governing positions, that a wise moderation was the best course of action in the face of adversity.[95] Ketel had himself portrayed these philosophers for wealthy clients, but he was innovating in taking over their scholarly advice for himself.[96] To represent his critics, Ketel depicted Momus and Zoilus. Ovid had described the mythological critic Momus as finding fault with all the gods for no good reason, and ancient literary history recorded that Zoilus had never had a good word to say about Plato and Homer.[97] Although the irrationality of Momus had been mocked by van Heemskerck in an engraving, no one had illustrated Zoilus before.[98] The French architect Philibert de l'Orme had, however, addressed a Latin verse to Zoilus, in his architectural treatise entitled *Nouvelles inventions pour bien bastir* (Paris, 1561), challenging him to criticise only if he could do better.[99] This text could have been known to Ketel, who had spent time working in Paris. Ketel therefore drew on mythology, on ancient literary and philosophical history, and also on Christian traditions for inventing a virtuous response to critics.

The geographical spread of the themes of the way of virtue and the struggle against envy is confirmed in two drawings by the Frankfurt artist Adam Elsheimer (1578–?1606), produced before he reached Italy. One was made in about 1596, when Elsheimer was eighteen, and displayed Fame winged and blowing her own trumpet, holding painter's implements. Beneath her are containers for money. Elsheimer inscribed a poem below which suggests the importance of the *via virtutis* imagery for aspiring artists: 'Who strives after art and honour, than after all the riches of this world, his praise will at all times be widely disseminated by Fame'.[100] The other was dated 1598 and signed by Elsheimer for an *Album amicorum* (that is, a form of autograph book) probably as he travelled from Frankfurt to Venice.[101] Here Mercury is seen holding palette, mahl stick and brushes beside a painting, which shows satyrs dragging down a woman who points upwards with her left hand to which two wings are attached at the wrists. In the foreground a winged child, perhaps Love of Art, points to the painting, while a young man kneels to the left, supported by a person wearing a classicising robe. Hans-Joachim Raupp identified this figure as Nature and he and Keith Andrew linked Mercury's painting to contemporary emblems demonstrating how talent (*ingenium*) can conquer impediments.

Truth will out given Time and Patience

Time had been seen as a threat, in some artists' allegories (Plates 74, 91). However, it could also be represented as an ally. As argued by Saxl, the theme of Time revealing Truth was used as a prestigious topos by scholars and rulers from 1536 onwards in visual form, so that, like the path to virtue, it could hold positive associations for artists. Rather than Time being represented as 'the grim reaper', it could be seen as a benevolent force, promising recognition. Saxl pointed out that it had first been used on a work published by Marcolino da Forlì in 1536, in the form of Father Time swooping down to snatch naked Truth away from a person, who was brandishing handfuls of snakes and who had a serpent's tail. This had had the motto *Veritas filia temporis* or 'Truth the daughter of Time'. Marcolino had continued to use the design on a series of books issued by his publishing house in Venice, including Serlio's architectural treatises.[102] Saxl demonstrated that the adage relied on a long literary tradition, including for instance Seneca, who had written that 'given time the day of truth will dawn'.[103] Saxl related that the authorities for this saying had been summarised by Vincenzo Cartari in the *Imagini degli dei* (Venice, 1556), citing the authority of Democritus, Plutarch and Sophocles amongst others. Saxl showed that the saying was repeated by early sixteenth-century writers, who were quite widely read, such as Erasmus in his *Adages* (Basel, 1526): 'when the ancient poets spoke of Time being the Daughter of Truth, they meant that whatever is hidden may emerge into the light with the progress of time'.[104]

Time in the shape of the Four Ages of Man and the Four Seasons had been introduced as framing the activities of Virtue, in the decoration made by Vasari in 1548 for his house at Arezzo.[105] In his drawings for the border of the *Calumny* about 1570, Zuccari had experimented with the idea of a flying Father Time, who snatches Truth from the grasp of Envy.[106] Shortly afterwards in 1578, in his house in Florence, Zuccari had expanded the proposal that Time could be an ally in the career of the artist (Plate 96). Here Zuccari painted Father Time on the vault of his main reception room, and crowned him optimistically with the harvest of flowers and seed heads. Zuccari depicted Time as if seated on the band of the Zodiac, looking down at an open book covered in writing – presumably the book of history. On one side sat the Past (a feeble figure), and on the other was the robust personification of the Future. In the surrounding picture fields on the vault, Zuccari had

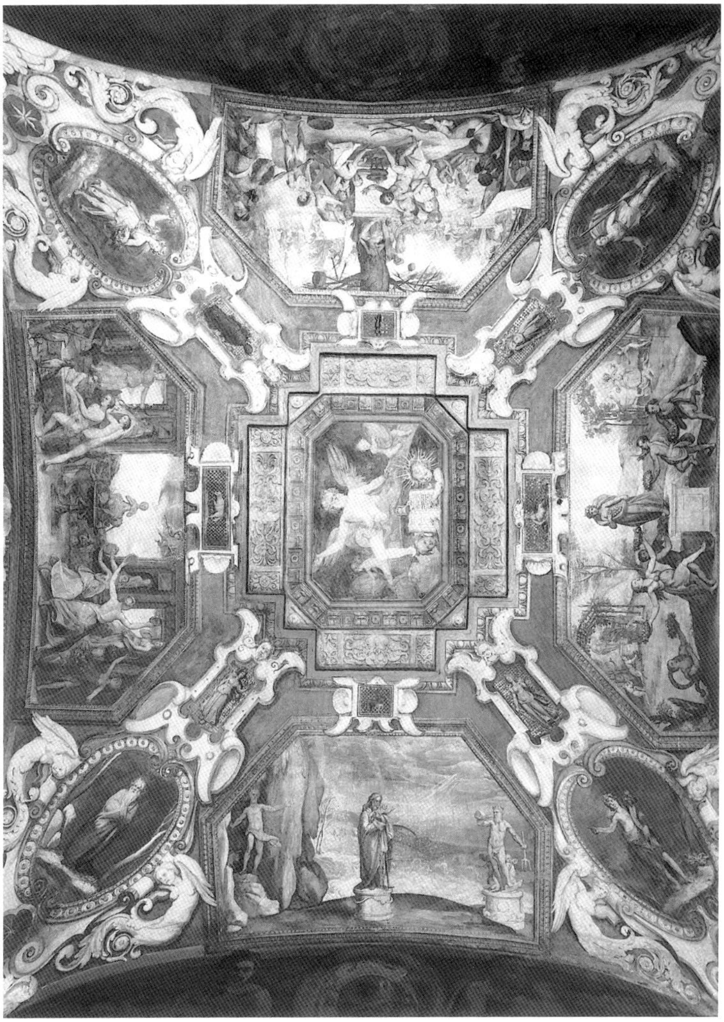

96 Federico Zuccari, *Time reveals Truth*, Casa del Federico Zuccari, 1578, Florence.

demonstrated further ways of signifying time, in terms of the personifications of the Four Times of Day, and of the Four Seasons.[107]

The scholarly tradition had enjoined those who felt misunderstood or maligned, that given time and patience, truth and worth would finally be recognised.[108] It was this idea which Zuccari pursued in the narrative cycle he provided in four scenes, painted as if they were gilded reliefs, on the soffits of the arches supporting the vault. Heikamp showed how these illustrated the misfortunes of the ancient writer and philosopher Aesop (Plate 97). They had hitherto been interpreted as a story of innocence and virtue.[109] However, it seems possible that Zuccari was also thinking of Aesop as an exemplar of patience, following the advice of

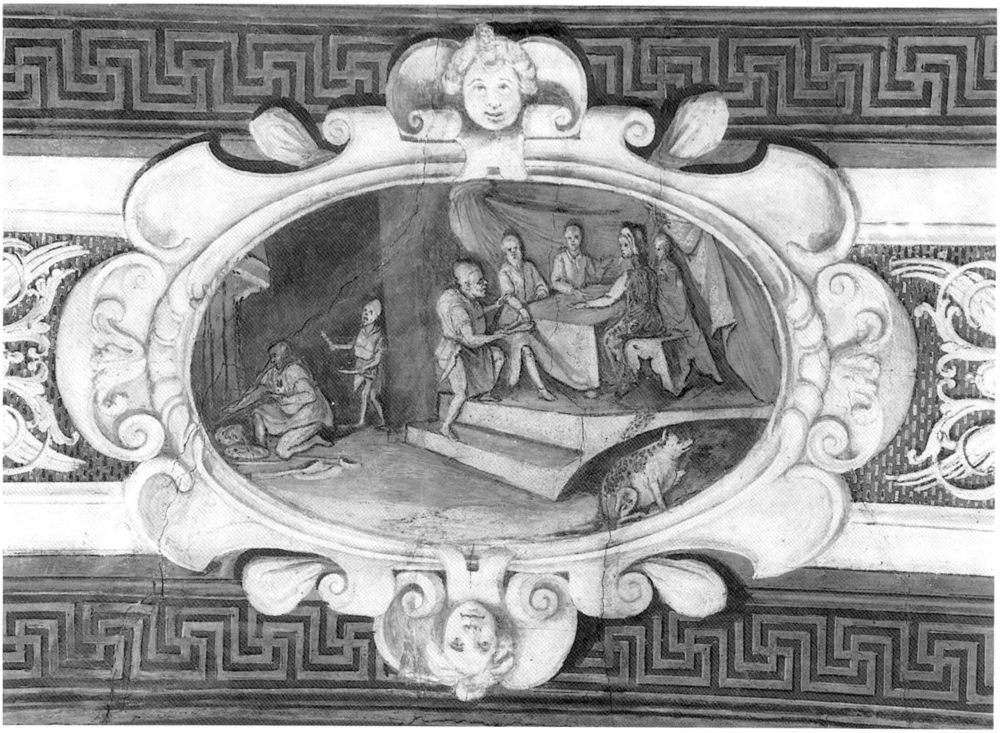

97 Federico Zuccari, *Aesop is made to cook pigs' trotters*, Casa del Federico Zuccari, 1578, Florence.

Cesariano, who retailed his emulation of Aesop's patience in the commentary provided beside his allegory on *The Choices of Human Life* (Plate 70). Following his father's death and disinheritance, Cesariano wrote that,

> hoping to get myself benefits beyond the paternal and impatient to acquire the most distinguished sciences and doctrines, I recalled the life of Aesop the Greek philosopher and with patience started to praise God concerning all my relatives and the protection of my Milanese compatriots.[110]

The comparison between the artist and Aesop was a modest one, since Aesop was described as deformed in stature, treated as a menial and a slave. Aesop's *Fables* were issued in translation from 1474 onwards, including a biography of Aesop, which employed one of Zuccari's favoured themes, that is the image of the *via virtutis*, averring that 'Fortune has shown mortal men two pathways in this life'.[111]

Zuccari explored the power of Time again in the vestibule of his house in Rome in the 1590s. There Time is seated over an open book, presumably of history, and is flanked by Minerva to the left, who is treading on a figure which resembles the coiled tail given to Hatred in Aretino's *impresa*, and to the right by Apollo, who is standing on Envy with the attribute of snakes (Plate 98). Above Time is a serpent eating its tail which signified Eternity. The scene is labelled 'Lead by Virtue' (*Virtute duce*). (The identity of the central bearded figure who holds an pen and brush and is helped to ascend further by Minerva as Virtue is uncertain.[112])

Ketel included an allegory on his house front which depicted Time protecting Intelligence and Spirit, and which van Mander described thus:

In the middle directly above the door of the house stands fast flying Time, crowned with roses, in the one hand [holding] a scythe or sickle, in the other an hourglass accompanied by two flying children, the one representing Intelligence and the other Spirit [*een Verstandt, t'ander den Gheest*], because all arts emerge in due course from spirit and insight.[113]

The presence of 'Intelligence' and 'Spirit' indicates Netherlandish knowledge of the visual traditions initiated in the designs for Michelangelo's funeral. In addition, Ketel could have had access to an engraving of a composition by Zuccari, which was the first to display Time crowned with roses. This design showed Time rescuing Truth from Envy. It had been engraved by Pieter Valck in Antwerp, and then published in Venice, in 1575, as well as being issued later by Philips Galle.[114] As already pointed out, Ketel may have met Zuccari in London in 1575.

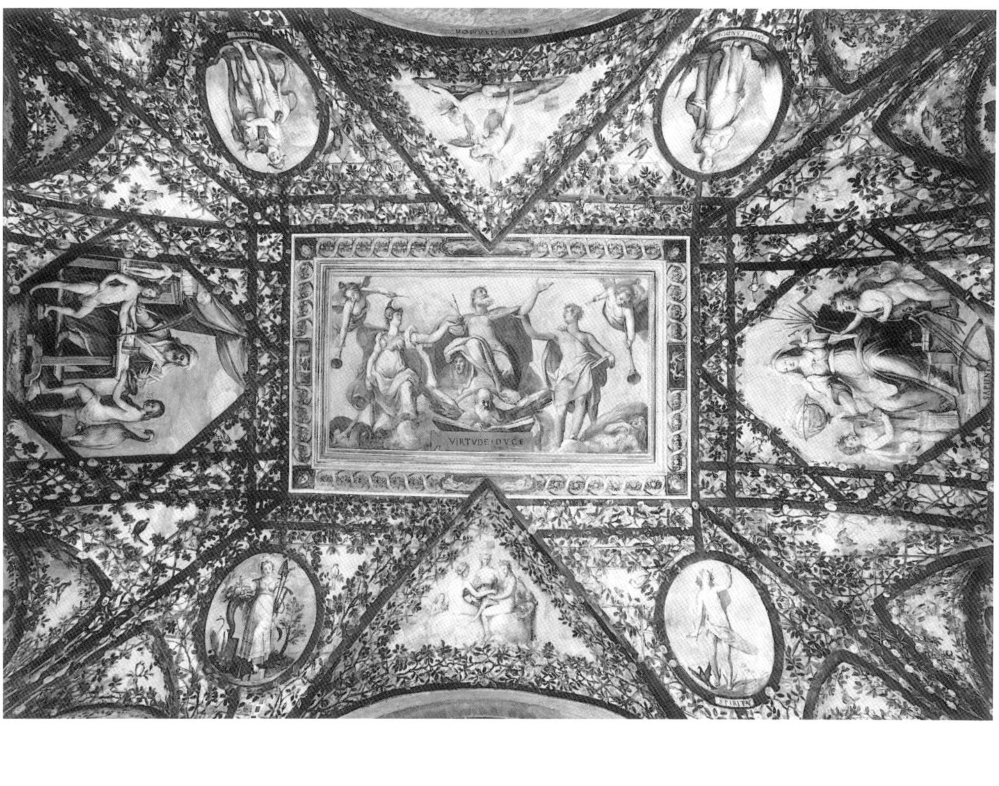

98 Federico Zuccari, *Time below Minerva and Apollo, with Perseverance (left) and Wisdom (right)*, hall vault, *c.*1595, Palazzo Zuccari, Rome.

Like Zuccari, Ketel had emphasised that Patience was required to await the revelations of Time. Van Mander had described this element:

On the left hand side, is laughing Patience seated upon an anvil, under attack from Falsehood who shoots three arrows simultaneously, that is: envy, gossip and slander. Envy spitefully pulls her backwards by the braids of her hair; vicious Hate sets a dog on her to devour her; Mortal Violence, a man with a skull, from whose eyes shoot flames of fire, represents the great plague in Amsterdam in the year 1602, the year in which this was made. These grisly monsters seem to want to destroy Patience which she endures with laughter, holding a little lamb in her arm and a cross in her hand, her face turned towards heaven as if to her Maker.[115]

Saxl showed that the tradition was sufficiently established to be adopted by Gian Lorenzo Bernini (1598–1680), who sculpted a large group of *Time unveiling Truth*, which he displayed in his house in Rome. It had been made to rebut accusations of his incompetence in 1646.[116]

The continuing importance of allegorical modes, in general, is evident in the funerary tribute to Agostino Carracci by the Bolognese academy in Bologna in 1603. The artists concerned seem to have been determined to equal previous valedictions. Guido Reni's engraved record displayed a variety of mythologies painted by Bolognese artists: 'Apollo and the Muses honour the tomb of Agostino', 'Ceres laments to Jupiter over the death of Agostino', 'Mars is represented as so jealous of the painting of Adonis that he takes Agostino to the skies', and 'The Fates lead Agostino to the throne of Jupiter'.[117] Such a splendid display confirms the trend for artists to be awarded the accolade of 'mythological company'.

During the sixteenth century the production of allegories of art accelerated, from the decade beginning in 1540 onwards, and branched out to include not only the favoured tradition of the way of virtue, but also the satiric rebuttal of envious critics (from 1541) and the counsel that Patience and Time were allies (from 1578). These representations offered artists classical models, in historical figures such as Scipio and Aesop, or legendary exemplars in Hercules, Minerva and Aeneas. Artists were also able to refer to the precedent of Apelles, who had made his *Calumny* to record the slander he had suffered.

Artists were making ambitious statements of their status in transposing imagery otherwise associated with rulers and scholars. In addition, the adaptation, and sometimes invention, of devices and complex compositions to signify ideas was a prestigious activity since it usually drew on a wealth of learning. The knowledge of classical texts, and the use of Latin and Greek inscriptions, points to the importance during the sixteenth century of some artists' contact with scholars.

These artistic allegories were represented on portable paintings and drawings, in portrait medals of artists, and prints on artistic concerns, to illustrate art treatises, on many artists' houses, and on three funerary decorations for artists. In most cases, therefore, this was imagery particular to the profession, rather than being part of the celebration of a ruler, as was the case of some allegories of the Liberal status of art. One message of these professional allegories was that the best art required love of art itself, rather than desire for wealth or honours. Warnke associated these claims with the ambition of court artists to distance them selves from trade.[118] Another message was that artists had the right to answer their critics in permanent (Daniele's stuccoes) or transient forms (Zuccari's cartoon). Finally, the interest in Time as defender may be associated with assertions about the historical importance of good art for posterity. There were therefore several notions in common between these visual traditions and other iconographies of art produced at this period.

Notes

1 Leon Battista Alberti, *On Painting*, *Della pittura*, ed. and trans. John R. Spencer, New Haven, CT, 1966, p. 91.
2 Alberti, *Della pittura*, p. 91.
3 Hermann Fiore, 'Die Fresken Federico Zuccaris', pp. 35–112; Kristina Hermann Fiore, 'Il tema "Labor" nella creazione artistica del Rinascimento', pp. 245–92 in Matthias Winner, ed., *Die Künstler übersich in seinem Werk internationales Symposium der Bibliotheca Hertziana Rom*, Weinheim, 1992.
4 Edward MacCurdy, *The Notebooks of Leonardo da Vinci*, 2 vols, London, 1954, II, p. 212.
5 Jean-Michel Massing, *Du texte à l'image. La Calomnie d'Apelle et son iconographie*, Strasburg, 1999, p. 30; Alberti, *Della pittura*, p. 90; Filarete, *Trattato di architettura*, II, pp. 268–9.
6 For the whole theme see David Cast, *The Calumny of Apelles*, New Haven, CT, and London, 1981; and Massing, *Du texte à l'image*.
7 Cast, *Calumny of Apelles*, pp. 3–4.
8 Cast, *Calumny of Apelles*, pp. 15–51; Massing, *Du texte à l'image*, pp. 171–96 and 321–2.
9 Cast, *Calumny of Apelles*, p. 150: 'H[a]ec si in adversa quid in prospera Leonbrunus pinxisset Fortuna?'
10 Cast, *Calumny of Apelles*, p. 150: 'O me infelicem deam veridicam/quam nunquam nunquam/nunquam aut turpiter mea maxima cum infamia/ad aures principum misella accessi.'
11 Cast, *Calumny of Apelles*, pp. 121–33; and Massing, *Du texte à l'image*, pp. 197–217, 360.
12 Massing, *Du texte à l'image*, p. 203.
13 Detlef Heikamp, 'Vicende di Federico Zuccari', *Rivista d'arte*, XXXII, 1957, pp. 175–232, especially pp. 219–21 (p. 220: *frutto delle sue fatighe*); and Cast, *Calumny of Apelles*, pp. 132–3.
14 Horace, *The Odes and Epodes*, ed. and trans. C.E. Bennett, London, 1914, p. 179.

15 Massing, *Du texte à l'image*, pp. 360–70; Manfred Sellink and Jurgen Leeflang, eds, *The New Hollstein: Dutch and Flemish Etchings, Engravings and Woodcuts 1450–1700, Cornelis Cort*, 3 vols, Rotterdam, 2000, Volume III, p. 253, number 148.
16 Cast, *Calumny of Apelles*, p. 133; and Massing, *Du texte à l'image*, p. 356.
17 Hill, *Portrait Medals*, pp. 29–31.
18 Horst W. Janson, 'The putto with the death's head', *Art Bulletin*, XIX, 1937, pp. 425–49; and Jean Seznec, 'Youth, Innocence and Death', *Journal of the Warburg and Courtauld Institutes*, I, 1937–38, pp. 293–303.
19 Catherine King, 'Italian self-portraits and the Rewards of Virtue', pp. 69–91 in Gunther Schweikhart, ed., *Autobiographie und Selbst Portrait in der Renaissance*, Cologne, 1998, p. 82.
20 G. Habich, *Die deutschen Medailleure des XVI Jahrhunderts*, Halle a. d. Saale, 1916, p. 3; Arthur Henkel and Albrecht Schöne, *Emblemata: Handbuch zur Sinnbildkunst des XVI und XVII Jahrhunderts*, Stuttgart, 1967, column 1198, for Emperor Charles V.
21 Hill, *Portrait Medals*, pp. 38–40.
22 Hill, *Portrait Medals*, pp. 62–3.
23 King, 'Italian self-portraits', pp. 77–8.
24 Hill, *Portrait Medals*, pp. 43–4, 'Fave For. sacrif.'
25 Gerhard Bott, ed., *Wenzel Jamnitzer und die Nüremburger Goldschmiedekunst 1500–1700*, Munich, 1985, p. 446. Hirschvogel was thirty-nine years old, and made engravings of his portrait also with the same motto.
26 Hill, *Portrait Medals*, pp. 65–6.
27 Hill, *Portrait Medals*, pp. 55–6.
28 H. Hymans, *Antonio Moro: son oeuvre et son temps*, Brussels, 1910, pp. 108–9, signed Ste. [ephanus]. H. [ollandus].
29 Philip Attwood, *Italian Medals c.1530–1600 in British Public Collections*, 2 vols, London, 2003, I, p. 110 giving the reference *to Aeneid* I, 199.
30 Hill, *Portrait Medals*, pp. 49–50; Attwood, *Italian Medals*, I, p. 183.
31 Hill, *Portrait Medals*, pp. 58–9.
32 Hill, *Portrait Medals*, pp. 67–8; and for Gonsalvo's version see Atwood, *Italian Medals*, I, pp. 145–6.
33 Hill, *Portrait Medals*, pp. 41–2.
34 Hill, *Portrait Medals*, pp. 63–4; Attwood, *Italian Medals*, I, p. 140. By Annibale Fontana (1540–87).
35 Catherine King 'Looking a sight: sixteenth-century portraits of women artists', *Zeitschrift für Kunstgeschichte*, LVIII, 1995, pp. 404–5; Attwood, *Italian Medals*, I, p. 418: signed by Felice Antonio Casoni (1559–1634), who studied in Bologna and was from Ancona.
36 *Wenzel Jamnitzer*, p. 447, Catalogue number 625; Hans Rosenberger was aged forty-one.
37 Hill, *Portrait Medals*, pp. 60–1; Attwood, *Italian Medals*, I, pp. 111–12.
38 Samuel S. Chew, *The Pilgrimage of Life*, New Haven, CT, 1962, pp. 175–8; Erwin Panofsky, *Hercules am Scheidewege und andere Bildstoffe in der neueren Kunst*, Lepzig, 1930; Andor Pigler, 'Neid und Unwissenheit als Widersacher der Kunst', *Acta Historiae Artium*, I, Budapest, 1954, pp. 215–35.

39 King, 'Late sixteenth-century careers' advice', p. 77.
40 King, 'Late sixteenth-century careers' advice', p. 78.
41 King, 'Late sixteenth-century careers' advice', p. 78.
42 King, 'Late sixteenth-century careers' advice', pp. 80–2.
43 Giovanni Boccaccio, *Genealogiae deorum*, Venice, 1494, fol. 25 recto: 'ut apparere neminem nisi per virtutem honorem consequi posse' ('so that it would be clear that no one can attain honour without virtue').
44 Vitruvius, *Vitruvio De architectura*, trans. Cesare Cesariano, Libri II–IV, ed. Alessandro Rovetta, Milan, 2002, pp. 172–3. Cesare attributed the temples to 'Mario', while *Vitruvius on Architecture*, ed. and trans. Frank Granger, 2 vols, London, 1931, attributed the joint temple to 'Mucius' or 'Marius': see I, p. 169; II, p. 79.
45 MacCurdy, *Notebooks of Leonardo*, London, 1954, II, p. 444.
46 Bradley I. Collins, *Leonardo, Psychoanalysis and Art History: Critical Study of Psychobiographical Approaches to Leonardo da Vinci*, Evanston, 1997, pp. 140–2.
47 King, 'Italian self-portraits', pp. 76–7.
48 Carlo Pedretti, 'Leonardo's Allegories at Oxford explained by Lomazzo', *Burlington Magazine*, IVC, 1954, pp. 175–7.
49 A. Katzenellenbogen, *Allegories of the Virtues and the Vices in Medieval Art*, London, 1939.
50 Corrado Ricci, *Il Tempio Malatestiana in Rimini*, Milan, 1924, Plates 94–6.
51 *European Paintings: An Illustrated Summary Catalogue, National Gallery of Art Washington*, Washington, 1975, p. 22, number 267.
52 E. Verheyen, *The Paintings of the Studiolo of Isabella d'Este*, New York, 1971, p. 35.
53 Cecchi, 'Le case di Giorgio Vasari', pp. 30–56.
54 King, 'Artists' houses', pp. 182–9.
55 Vasari, *Le opere di Giorgio Vasari*, VII, p. 302: 'l'Invidia; la quale era una vecchia, secca e distrutta, con occhi viperini, ed in somma con viso e fattezze che tutte spiravano tossico e veleno.'
56 Vasari, *Le opere di Giorgio Vasari*, VII, p. 303: 'un giovane fiero e gagliardo il quale alla fine del braccio poco sopra la giuntura della mano aveva due aliette, significanti la Velocità e spessezza dell'operare. Si avea sotto, come prigione, cacciata la Pigrizia, ovvero Ociosità, la quale era una donna lenta e stanca ed in tutti i suoi atti grave e dormigliosa.'
57 Massing, *Du texte à l'image*, pp. 204–5; Heikamp, 'Vicende di Federico Zuccari', pp. 220–1 (for 'il desiderio della virtù' see p. 220).
58 John Gere, P. Pouncey and R. Wood, *Italian Drawing in the British Museum: Artists Working in Rome c. 1550–1640*, London, 1983, pp. 147–8; King, 'Late sixteenth-century careers' advice', p. 83.
59 Massari, *Incisori Mantovani*, pp. 100–16.
60 Giovanni Baglione, *Le vite dei pittori, scultori, architetti*, Rome, 1649, p. 26: 'la Virtù che tien per mano Hercole, e'l Genio, e vanno verso il Tempio dell'Eternità.'
61 For this and the whole description see Ridolfi, *Le meraviglie dell'arte*, I, pp. 201–18, especially 201–3.

62 Ridolfi, *Le meraviglie dell'arte*, I, p. 203: 'poiche non produce frutti di virtù, che povera e robusta, dovendo resistere alle continue applicationi degli studi.'
63 King, 'Late sixteenth-century careers' advice', p. 84 for the identification of Honour and the way the programme relates to the *via virtutis* imagery.
64 Ridolfi, *Le meraviglie dell'arte*, I, p. 205.
65 Ridolfi, *Le meraviglie dell'arte*, I, p. 204.
66 Ridolfi, *Le meraviglie dell'arte*, I, p. 217.
67 Catherine King, 'An etching and Lelio Orsi's house', *Print Quarterly*, XXIII, June 2006, pp. 181–2.
68 Hermann Fiore, 'Die Fresken Federico Zuccaris', pp. 72–81; King, 'Late sixteenth-century careers' advice', p. 86; Acidini-Luchinat, *Taddeo e Federico Zuccari*, II, pp. 208–11.
69 King, 'Late sixteenth-century careers' advice', p. 86.
70 King, 'Late sixteenth-century careers' advice', p. 86; King, 'Italian self-portraits', pp. 87–8.
71 Cesare Ripa, *Iconologia*, Padua, 1611, pp. 57–8; Henkel and Schöne, *Emblemata*, column 820.
72 Heikamp, 'Vicende di Federico Zuccari', pp. 200–15; *The Life of Taddeo Zuccaro by Federico Zuccari from the Collection of the British Rail Pensions Fund*, Sotheby's New York, 1990, pp. 18–19, 28–9, 38–9, 56–7.
73 King, 'Late sixteenth-century careers' advice', p. 85.
74 Alessandra Baroni Vannucci, ed., *Jan van der Straet detto Stradano*, Milan 1997, p. 389; Boon, *Netherlandish and German Drawings*, I, pp. 345–56, Plate 85 and II, Figures 107–8.
75 King, 'Italian self-portraits', pp. 82–5.
76 King, 'Late sixteenth-century careers' advice', passim, and King, 'Italian self-portraits', pp. 78–80.
77 For text and translation see King, 'Late sixteenth-century careers' advice', p. 80.
78 Ripa, *Iconologia*, p. 542.
79 King, 'Late sixteenth-century careers' advice', p. 89; Grosshans, *Marten van Heemskerck*, Figure 245 and p. 247; F.W.H. Hollstein, *The New Hollstein: Dutch and Flemish Etchings, Engravings and Woodcuts, 1450–1700*, 2 vols, Roosendaal, 1994, II, compiled by Ilya M. Veldman, pp. 181–3.
80 King, 'Italian self-portraits', p. 79.
81 Nikolaus Pevsner, *Academies Past and Present*, Cambridge, 1940, p. 52; King, 'Italian self-portraits', p. 96.
82 Hans-Joachim Raupp, 'Allegorische Selbstporträts und Selbstdarstellungen in der Graphik um 1600', pp. 177–92 in Gunther Schweikhart, ed., *Autobiographie und Selbst Portrait in der Renaissance*, Cologne, 1998, pp. 176–7.
83 F.W.H. Hollstein, *Hollstein's Dutch and Flemish Etchings, Engravings and Woodcuts, c.1450–1700*, XXIII, ed. G.S. Keyes, Amsterdam, 1980, p. 98.
84 Vasari, *Le opere di Giorgio Vasari*, VII, pp. 55–6.
85 David Jaffé, 'Daniele da Volterra's satirical defence of his art', *Journal of the Warburg and Courtaud Institutes*, LIV, 1991, pp. 247–52.
86 King, 'Italian self-portraits', p. 83.

87 Vasari, *Le opere di Giorgio Vasari*, VII, p. 193.
88 Edith Wyas, *The Myth of Apollo and Marysas in the Art of the Renaissance*, Newark, NJ, and London, 1996.
89 Fritz Saxl, 'Veritas Filia temporis', pp. 197–216 in Raymond Klibansky and Herbert J. Paton, eds, *Philosophy and History: Essays Presented to Ernst Cassirer*, Oxford, 1936, pp. 198–9.
90 Michael P. Mezzatesta, *Imperial Themes in the Sculpture of Leone Leoni* (PhD, New York, 1980), Ann Arbor, 1991, pp. 172–80.
91 Heikamp, 'Vicende di Federico Zuccari', pp. 185–94; J. Byam Shaw, *Drawings by Old Masters at Christchurch Oxford*, Oxford, 1976, p. 255, number 544.
92 Cast, *Calumny of Apelles*, pp. 134–8.
93 Acidini-Luchinat, *Taddeo e Federico Zuccari*, II, pp. 128–9.
94 Van Mander, *Lives*, I, p. 373.
95 Veldman, *Marten van Heemskerck*, pp. 76–80; van Mander, *Lives*, V, pp. 150–3.
96 *Dawn of the Golden Age: Northern Netherlandish Art 1580–1620*, ed. Ger Luijten. Amsterdam, 1996, see p. 70, Figure 111 for Cornelis Ketel, *Heraclitus the weeping philosopher*; van Mander, *Lives*, I, p. 370.
97 Van Mander, *Lives*, V, p. 153.
98 David Cast, 'Marten van Heemskeck's Momus criticising the works of the gods: a problem in Erasmian iconography', *Simiolus*, VII, 1974, pp. 22–34; Veldman, *Marten van Heemskerck*, pp. 101–3.
99 Philibert de l'Orme, *Traités d'architectures*, ed. Jean-Marie Pérouse de Montclos, Paris, 1988, *Nouvelles inventions pour bien bastir*, fol. 58.
100 Keith Andrews, *The Paintings, Drawings and Prints of Adam Elsheimer*, London, 1977, p. 56, Plate 2 (trans. Andrews).
101 Andrews, *Paintings, Drawings and Prints*, p. 157, Plate 3; Raupp, 'Allegorische Selbstporträts', pp. 184–5 and pp. 186–7 for a drawing following Gheerearts' allegory of poverty.
102 Saxl, 'Veritas filia temporis', pp. 198–202; Chew, *Pilgrimage of Life*, pp. 17–22.
103 Saxl, 'Veritas filia temporis', p. 200, note 1: 'dandum est tempus; veritatem dies aperit.'
104 Saxl, 'Veritas filia temporis', p. 200: 'quendam veterum poetarum Veritatem Temporis Filiam vocasse, quod licet aliquando lateat, temporis progressu in lucem emergat.'
105 Vasari, *Le opere di Giorgio Vasari*, VII, pp. 685–6; A. Paolucci and A.M. Maetzke, *La casa del Vasari in Arezzo*, Florence, 1988, pp. 45–88.
106 King, 'Late sixteenth-century careers' advice', p. 84, n. 36, Hamburg, Kunsthalle, number 21516.
107 Acidini-Luchinat, *Taddeo e Federico Zuccari*, I, pp. 105–14.
108 Chew, *Pilgrimage of Life*, pp. 119–21.
109 D. Heikamp, 'Federico Zuccari a Firenze 1575–1579, II, Federico a casa sua', *Paragone*, XVIII, 1967, pp. 3–34, especially pp. 24–5.
110 Vitruvius, *De architettura, Vitruvio*, ed. Bruschi, Carugo and Fiore, fol. LXXXXI verso: 'Sperando farmi havere et[iam] altri beni piu che li paterni, et pho tu [sic] impaciente ad aquistare praeclarissime scientie et doctrine, ricordate de la vita de esopo graeco philosopho, et cosi di questa

mia Patientia quale ad laude[m] Dei et tuti li miei pare[n]ti et de alma Mediolane[n]se patria.'

111 *Aesop's Fables with a Life of Aesop*, trans. John E. Keller and L. Clark Feating, Kentucky, 1993, p. 39.

112 Acidini-Luchinat, *Taddeo e Federico Zuccari*, II, pp. 207–9.

113 Van Mander, *Lives*, I, pp. 372–3.

114 Acidini-Luchinat, *Taddeo e Federico Zuccari*, II, pp. 56–8; *The New Hollstein*, ed. Sellink and Leesberg, III, pp. 37–8.

115 Van Mander, *Lives*, I, pp. 372–3

116 Saxl, 'Veritas Filia temporis', pp. 216–18.

117 Morrello, *Il funerale d'Agostino Carraccio*.

118 Warnke, *Hofkünstler*, pp. 150–2.

7 Programmes of decoration for artists' houses

The subject matter which artists chose to display in decorating their houses played an important role in communicating new ambitions concerning artistic status and goals. Evidence survives with reference to the adornment of twenty-two such houses by nineteen artists, between about 1536 and 1618. Exteriors could be viewed by any passer-by, while interiors could be enjoyed by patrons and colleagues. The incidence of artists decorating houses seems quite often to have been associated with disciples, pupils or sons following their teachers. Eight artists' houses which impressed contemporaries appear to have been decorated, or lived in, by disciple-and-teacher pairings. Del Sarto, whose house displayed his heraldry, was revered by Vasari; Raphael, whose house had a richly articulated façade, taught Giulio Romano; Lelio Orsi probably taught Raffaellino da Reggio; and van Dalem taught Spranger. Two more houses seem to have been linked to a father (Ottaviano Zuccari) and son (Federico) relationship, while Rubens was taught by Otto van Veen, who had been a pupil of Federico Zuccari. Del Sarto had also impressed Federico Zuccari's father. Although Raphael's and del Sarto's houses did not include programmes of decoration overtly celebrating art, it seems possible that they provided some precedent for pupils to design more elaborate dwellings. Arguably, these displays helped to raise the status of artists in terms of asserting their intellectual and technical skills, their social standing and their abilities to publicise their views. These houses were concentrated in Italy, where eleven were made, and the Netherlands, in particular Antwerp, which contained three instances. The importance of Antwerp is underlined, when account is taken of the fact that two more houses, in Middelburg and Prague, were made by artists from Antwerp.

The apparent increase in the number of artists decorating their houses could be a matter of the increased survival of evidence about most aspects of artistic production. Alternatively, a variety of reasons can be considered to explain a change. Decorating one's house could demonstrate technical skills for patrons, as for instance in the case of Orsi's spectacular foreshortenings or Ketel's dexterity with his feet. This might be connected with the premium on virtuosity in performing difficult tasks, which has been charted in the literary texts associated with 'Mannerist' art. Decorative programmes also showed artists' powers to devise their own schemes of meaning (presumably relying on scholars to advise). The adornment of a house was sometimes quite an ostentatious piece of expenditure entailing the commissioning of experts, as for instance in the carved façades ordered by the painter van Dalem, and by the bronze sculptor Leoni. In other situations, however, artists could execute their own designs relatively cheaply, as when Vasari reported that he painted his house in Arezzo in his spare time. Either way, however, artists obtained houses which made claims to good social standing. Such respectable houses may be something of a counterpart to the way artists were increasingly gaining honours from pope and emperor. The search for wealth and dignity was also being expressed in literary texts that equated prospering artists with high standards. This is evident, for instance, in the letter written by Jacopo de' Barbari in about 1500 to Friedrich der Weise of Saxony, in which he argued that in the ancient world patrons had encouraged artistic excellence by paying their artists well.[1] Similarly, in 1507 the Sienese painter Bernardino Pinturicchio had acquired tax exemption from the Sienese government by asking them to imitate the ancient Romans and ensure the prosperity of artists.[2] In addition, the sixteenth century is a period when more and more literary texts were being produced about art by artists themselves. That some artists were increasingly aware of the ways that they could also use their own houses to represent their views is therefore perhaps not so surprising.

These decorative schemes offered platforms for exploring ideas about art and artists. Thus a succession of houses linked the visual arts and architecture with the Liberal Arts and their mythological protectors. They include, in chronological order, the houses of Giulio Romano at Mantua, of Vasari at Arezzo, of van Dalem at Antwerp, of Floris at Antwerp, of Leoni in Milan, of Vasari in Florence, of Zuccari in Rome, and of Rubens in Antwerp. Less frequently, artists' houses pronounced traditional allegiances to patron saints, whether in the statue of Saint Quentin on the house of Quinten Metsys in Antwerp, or the Crowned Martyrs represented by Valckenaere at Middelburg. Rather more frequently, references were made to the patronage of Mercury, as in the houses of Giulio Romano, van Dalem, Spranger and Rubens. Other themes, which may be regarded as professionally specific, included the commemoration of teachers and mentors: in personalised histories of art by Vasari at Arezzo and Florence; the narration of the career of his brother Taddeo by Federico Zuccari in Rome; and the selection of van Eyck and Dürer as the heroes of 'Belgian' and 'German' painting by van Dalem. A comparable interest in the history of ancient art characterised the celebrations of artists who had worked in Greece and Rome: by Stephan Ziegler in Sélestat, by Vasari both at Arezzo and Florence, by Rubens and possibly by Floris.

Artists were often interested in showing their family name and heraldry as part of their iconographic programmes, in emulation of the façades favoured by their wealthy patrons. In this way Orsi and Leoni devised schemes centring on patronyms, while Vasari, in his Florentine house, and Zuccari, in both his Florentine and Roman houses, featured family shields. With another type of emphasis on family values, Vasari at Arezzo and Zuccari in Rome included mural decorations which celebrated marital virtues and family obligations. Many houses used designs which acknowledged the help of the artist's major courtly patron. This was probably the case in the house of Giulio Romano, and overtly displayed in the examples of Leoni to the Emperor, of Vasari in Florence to the Medici, and Spranger to Rudolph II. The presence of the symbol of the eagle on the house of Valckenaere at Middelburg might be either a reference to the Empire or to the sculptor's family name as a falconer.

Artists also appropriated the iconographies of virtue, a tactic which aligned them with their social and intellectual superiors. The pursuit of virtue was a theme on many houses: in that of Ottaviano Zuccari at Sant'Angelo in Vado, of Vasari at Arezzo, of Diana Scultori and Francesco da Volterra in Rome, of Spranger in Prague, of Zuccari in Rome and Rubens in Antwerp. At Asolo and Middelburg, houses were designed which explored the pursuit of virtue too, but with more emphasis on following biblical teaching. Three schemes represented the triumph of Time: in the house of Vasari at Arezzo, that of Zuccari in Florence and that of Ketel in Amsterdam. Three houses alluded to the defence of virtue: including Orsi at Reggio Emilia and Novellara, Leoni in Milan and Ketel in Amsterdam.

From the middle of the fifteenth century onwards there is evidence that artists were acquiring substantial houses and that the styling and size of these buildings could represent claims to social standing. These houses acted as precedents for the later even more elaborate ones, carrying iconographic programmes. For example, Dieric Bouts (*c.*1415–75), according to van Mander, had a house in Haarlem with a façade adorned in the antique style.[3] For instance, in 1476 Andrea Mantegna began building his house in Mantua, on land acquired from Marquis Lodovico Gonzaga, and adopted a central plan, with an unprecedented cylindrical courtyard, which he seems to have adapted from the designs for noble houses cited in the treatise on architecture by Francesco di Giorgio.[4] In 1496 Biagio Rossetti in Ferrara was given permission by Ercole d'Este to build a house in the new area of city which he himself had designed. Both the latter houses were made from brick, with stone or terracotta detailing. In 1509 Dürer bought a house in Nuremberg which had belonged to a practitioner of the Liberal Arts, the mathematician Regiomontanus.[5] In 1517 Raphael acquired a palace in Rome which, Vasari reported, he built with reference to a design by Bramante. Although its cladding was only moulded in plaster (*getto*), the palace presented inventive classicising articulation, with a rusticated ground floor alluding to the Forum of Augustus, and an imposing upper order of paired Doric columns and tabernacle windows with balconies.[6] In 1520 Andrea del Sarto bought a large plot beside Santissima Annunziata in Florence and was resident in his new house by 1527, having placed the arms of himself and his wife over the portal.[7]

Such houses seem to be cultural representations of new social aspiration. However, those decorated in the sixteenth century moved one step further, by drawing on a range of subject matter to illustrate their owners' views. One theoretical precedent was provided by Filarete, in about 1460, who had described an architect's house when he outlined the ideal city of Sforzinda (see Chapter 6). His proposal contained two of the themes, the portraiture of ancient artists and the display of the way of virtue, which were to be actualised in the sixteenth century. The earliest record concerning the subject matter chosen to decorate an artist's house that survives refers to the residence of Piero della Francesca, at Borgo San Sepolcro, built in about 1465. This was described as a group of 'magnificent houses' by a contemporary.[8] Reconstructed soon after 1536, when it was damaged by war, the dwelling seems to have had some finely vaulted chambers, including a large salon on the *piano nobile*, where a life-size figure in fresco by Piero was discovered in *c.*1860–70, which represented Hercules cloaked with lion skin and holding his club – a hero often associated with the pursuit of virtue. The decision to take for himself the sort of mural decorations depicting mythological heroes which were commissioned by his social superiors was an important statement of social aspiration. Evidence also survives concerning the decoration of the house of Quinten Metsys in Antwerp. This had a polychrome iron statue of his name-saint, Quinten, over the door, carried the date 1528, and was reportedly decorated inside with grotesques, festoons and *putti* in grisaille, as well as columns carrying his heraldry, inscribed with the phrase *plus ultra*. The columns recall those of Hercules chosen by Vischer for his medal in 1507 (see Chapter 6), while the motto (with the columns of Hercules) was used by the Emperor Charles V to indicate power, 'yet further'. The painter inherited the house in 1521 and died in 1530.[9]

The production of programmes of decoration entailing subject-matter relating to artists' concerns appears to have accelerated from some time a little before 1536, when the architects' house at Asolo was built. This was followed by decorative schemes for houses in Sélestat, Mantua and Arezzo. Thence from the 1560s the practice spread to other areas in Italy (to Florence, Milan, Novellara and Reggio Emilia). At the same time the idea was taken up in Antwerp, and, then, from the 1570s, examples were also made in Rome, Prague, Middelburg and Amsterdam. The classicising articulation of some façades showed off artists' knowledge of the latest architectural trends, as well as making prestigious framing for their iconographical programmes. If the artists were architects, their house might take motifs which were already associated with their style of building (Vasari, Giulio Romano). If they were not, they still tended to ally themselves with new ideas (Floris engaged his brother Cornelis Floris, van Dalem emulated Vignola). The use of classicising forms, Latin inscriptions and often obscure or unfamiliar allegorical references on house fronts and interiors suggest that some artists were playing the interesting game of being simultaneously attention-seeking and elusive. It is as if artists were announcing that art was well worth knowing about, but knowing about it would require effort and privileged information. Viewers were being invited to form part of a rather exclusive audience.

The interpretations of the decorative schemes would have been varied depending on the class, gender, lay or religious calling of viewers. The fact that van Dalem's house was called 'The Hen Coop' when he bought it, but *Pictura* after he had redesigned it, or that Leone Leoni's house came to be called 'the house of the big men', with reference to the statuary on its front (Plate 94a), suggests something of the vagueness of meaning attached to these civic statements for most people. However, the way the Antwerp sculptors brought specific allegorical readings of the decoration of the house of Frans Floris into a lawsuit in 1607, when they were fighting for better guild treatment, emphasises that artists themselves might scrutinise these programmes. Patrons, by contrast, could have treated them as demonstrating new forms or techniques, versions of which they might wish to commission. House decorations were marked by notions of class in terms of the cultural capital required for interpreting allegorical signing or Latin inscriptions. They were also highly gendered. The places of the feminine in these stories were multiple – as wife, daughter, goddess, idea – but it was only the masculine which was presented overtly as the hero emulous of artistic virtue, whose story was so often the master narrative.

From the start the theme of the pursuit of virtue was an attractive topos. The house of the architect Francesco Grazioli at Asolo encouraged the general pursuit of virtue and fame, while the house of Ottaviano Zuccari at Sant'Angelo in Vado also seems to have favoured striving for artistic achievement.

Francesco and Bartolomeo Grazioli, Asolo, before 1536

The architects' house at Asolo, north-west of Treviso in the Veneto, is inscribed 'Master Francesco Grazioli and Bartolomeo his son, professional sculptors, built this, with skill' (Plate 99). Positioned on the outskirts of the town on the via Santa Caterina, this small house is assumed to have been completed by the death of Francesco in 1536. It exhibited the latest styles of Mannerist architecture, though in a crude form. A lower order of Doric pilasters was decorated with two male caryatids, while the upper order employed Ionic pilasters and a female caryatid.

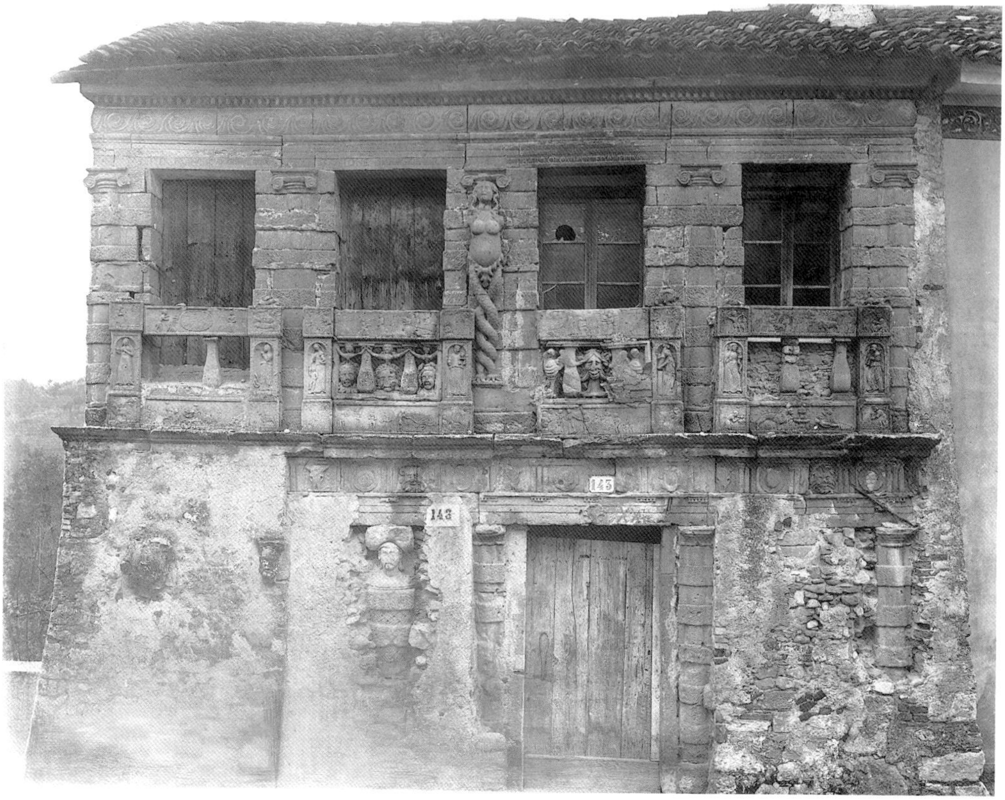

99 The house of Francesco and Bartolomeo Grazioli, before 1536, Asolo.

The cornering displayed the latest device of buried columns as if strapped in with strips of stone.[10] Decorating the balcony on the first floor were four panels representing, in relief, the seven Christian virtues with Fame. Reading left to right, Faith is paired with Justice, then Charity with Hope, while Temperance is accompanied by Fortitude. These three panels were adorned at their corners with the twelve signs of the Zodiac. In the panel furthest to the right, Prudence was given the pendant figure of Fame blowing two trumpets, and the corners displayed the Four Seasons. This association of Fame with Christian virtues suggests a bow in the direction of the *via virtutis* theme. Each panel contained two further scenes in relief, which, while weather worn, appear to counsel good conduct, employing biblical events such as the Justice of Solomon, mythological ones such as Hercules and Deianira, and scenes alluding to the medieval bestiary, in the maiden and the unicorn. It has been surmised that the Graziolis achieved some status, of a courtly nature, by playing a role in building the fortified villa of Queen Caterina Cornaro at Altivole, on the plain just below the hill town where their house is situated.

Ottaviano Zuccari, Sant'Angelo in Vado, *c.*1540

The house of the painter Ottaviano Zuccari in the town of Sant'Angelo in Vado was reported by Vincenzo Lanciarini in 1893 to contain a representation of the arts with the advice *Unica via parandi honoris* ('There is only one way of achieving honour') still visible on the vault of one of the rooms. This town lies in the Marche, between Borgo San Sepolcro, where Piero della Francesca's house could be seen, and Urbino. Lanciarini attributed the (now no longer visible) mural on grounds of style to Ottaviano, and dated it about 1540.[11] Ottaviano had studied in Florence, where he had learned from the work of Andrea del Sarto.[12] It was in this house on the present via Zuccari (then via Terrato) that Federico Zuccari was brought up.[13] At about the same time, in Mantua, Giulio Romano set out to complete a decoration which also showed off his access to classical learning, and claimed liberal status for his profession, as well as honouring his patron Federigo Gonzaga.

Giulio Romano Mantua, 1540–44

Giulio had arrived in Mantua as a painter, trained in the workshop of Raphael, with some experience as an architect. He had already planned to remodel the house he inherited from his father at the Macel de'Corvi in Rome in 1524. This small structure – known from sixteenth-century drawings – would have had a rusticated façade divided into two bays, adorned with narrative reliefs, and focusing on the portal with a robust window above.[14] However, during the same year, Giulio left for Mantua, where he achieved success at the court of the Gonzaga. Having bought quite a large house in 1538, Giulio transformed it between 1540 and 1544. It was situated in a sector which was being newly developed, on the present Via Poma, near the church of San Barnabà. The original building consisted of the six bays on the left of the present building, with the main portal then situated in the third bay from the left (the façade was expanded in 1800). Vasari reported that this was 'a fantastic façade worked with coloured stuccoes'.[15] It was relatively modest, since it avoided the classical orders and the articulation was made, like Raphael's house, from cheap clay. However, it was rich in Mannerist caprice. The rusticated façade divides the building into a ground floor and a *piano nobile*, although the fenestration reveals the existence of the attic and cellars. An entablature with a frieze decorated with rams' heads – referring to the statue of Mercury over the portal – and swags was provided, even though no pillars or columns were present to support it. Instead of using semi-circular arches throughout and a horizontal string course moulding, to suggest a classically correct trabeation, this moulding bends upward to make a shallow gable over the flattened arch of the doorway. The iconographical programme represented Mercury for the first time as a mythological deity associated with art (Plate 71). The message seems to be that the powers of the Liberal Art of rhetoric can stand for the powers of painting, following the traditional comparison between painting and poetry. The scheme had the prestige of drawing on an obscure text by the Greek writer Lucian.[16]

In the main reception room on the *piano nobile* Giulio painted the walls to suggest the illusion of fictive pilasters supporting an entablature, with ancient reliefs built into the bays between. The effect was of rich stone panelling painted red and green, to suggest expensive porphyry and serpentine insets. The chimney breast is decorated with a relief of local stone, representing the public acclamation of the statue of a Roman leader holding the baton of power. It may be relevant that Giulio was called 'Romano', so that a reference could be made to his name. (It was this relief that Rubens had copied and treasured in his house in 1618.) On either side, at this level, were painted scenes of *Securitas* and *Annona* – the corn supply – possibly indicating peace and prosperity. Below, flanking the fireplace, are represented Prometheus and Apollo. On the opposite wall is a fictive relief of Jupiter, leader of the Gods, bracketed by Neptune and Venus, and battle trophies. On the garden side of the room are fictive statues of Mercury and Minerva (Plate 72). The centrality of rulers, heavenly and temporal, in the scheme – and the references to security, food supply and battle – suggests that the decoration was a tribute to Giulio's employer, the Marquis, who had entrusted a collection of antique sculpture to Giulio to care for in this house. However, it is in this mural decoration that Minerva appears to have been coupled with Mercury for the first time in relation to an artist (see Chapter 5). Giulio seems to have set out to gentrify artists' traditional patron Mercury, by associating him with eloquence and learned allusions, and, inside, with the company of learned Minerva.

Giorgio Vasari, Arezzo, 1542–48

In the same decade Vasari outdid every other artist so far, with a series paintings for his house in Arezzo. Here he linked architecture for the first time with painting, sculpture and poetry, and, as the Graziolis had done, associated art with fame. In addition, he made his own elaborate version of the theme of virtue, he depicted the exploits of ancient artists, he planned portraits of modern artists, and he associated painting with the elevated realm of Apollo and the Muses. Vasari also imitated his betters by according himself a vault representing his pious hopes for producing his own family heirs, by means of a successful marriage, and by featuring his heraldry.

The lead taken by Vasari at this point could be seen as having parallels with the lead he was taking in composing the *Lives*. While Giulio 'spoke' as chief pupil of Raphael and as court artist, Vasari had developed a wealthy clientele in Florence and had worked in Venice and Rome. In 1540 he had bought an unfinished house in the Borgo di San Vito, in his home town of Arezzo, with *un sito per fare orti bellissimi* ('a site for making most beautiful gardens').[17] When completed, the building presented a plain façade adorned with sober stone window and portal frames. The first space which he recorded decorating, in August 1542, was the reception room on the *piano nobile* opposite the head of the main staircase.[18] Here he had built a grand cross-vaulted chamber supported on pendentives (Plate 9). At the centre of this vault he painted a figure of winged Fame seated on a globe. When he came to publish his account of his life, in 1568, he explained the unique symbolism which he invented: she blows a golden trumpet for Good Fame, and hurls away one of fire to represent Bad Fame or Calumny. Below, in the pendentives, Vasari depicted female personifications of Painting, Sculpture, Architecture and Poetry. While such personifications had been grouped for the panegyric of rulers (see Chapter 1) they had not been used in praise of art itself until this point. In the soffits of the windows Vasari painted further figures of Fame and his own heraldry. In his autobiography (1568) Vasari explained that he had intended to add a series of portraits of *primi* ('first') artists in the lunettes in this room. In fact, he only achieved the project in 1568 (Plate 40).[19] The artists whose fame was especially signalled then were ones who were associated with Arezzo and with his own career later in Florence (Chapter 3).

In the summer of 1548, having completed the manuscript of the *Lives*, Vasari recorded making designs to finish the decoration of his house.[20] He listed first the painting of a large room, looking over the street, to one's left, at the top of the stairway. Here he took, for the first time for an artist, the prestigious form of a carved and gilded wooden ceiling with painted panels (Plate 85). In the tradition of Filarete, Piero della Francesca, Francesco Grazioli and Ottaviano Zuccari, he connected the career of the artist with the pursuit of virtue (see Chapter 6). In the centre panel of the ceiling he painted a personification of Virtue who vanquishes Envy and takes control of Fortune. Virtue's head is wreathed with laurel and she has wings; she is surrounded with symbols of time, which may indicate the way time reveals worth. Time is indicated by the Four Seasons shown as a *putto*, a young man, a mature man and an older man, as well as by the ancient gods and goddesses associated with the signs of the Zodiac. (It may be recalled that the Graziolis had appended images of the Zodiac and the Seasons to their façade.) Vasari links the generalised statement about the power of virtue in the course of human life with his own career by placing his arms in the four corners of the ceiling.

The decoration of the walls below is devoted to celebrating the history of ancient Greek art (Plates 47, 100). As in Giulio Romano's house, the walls were painted to create the effect of marble panelling.

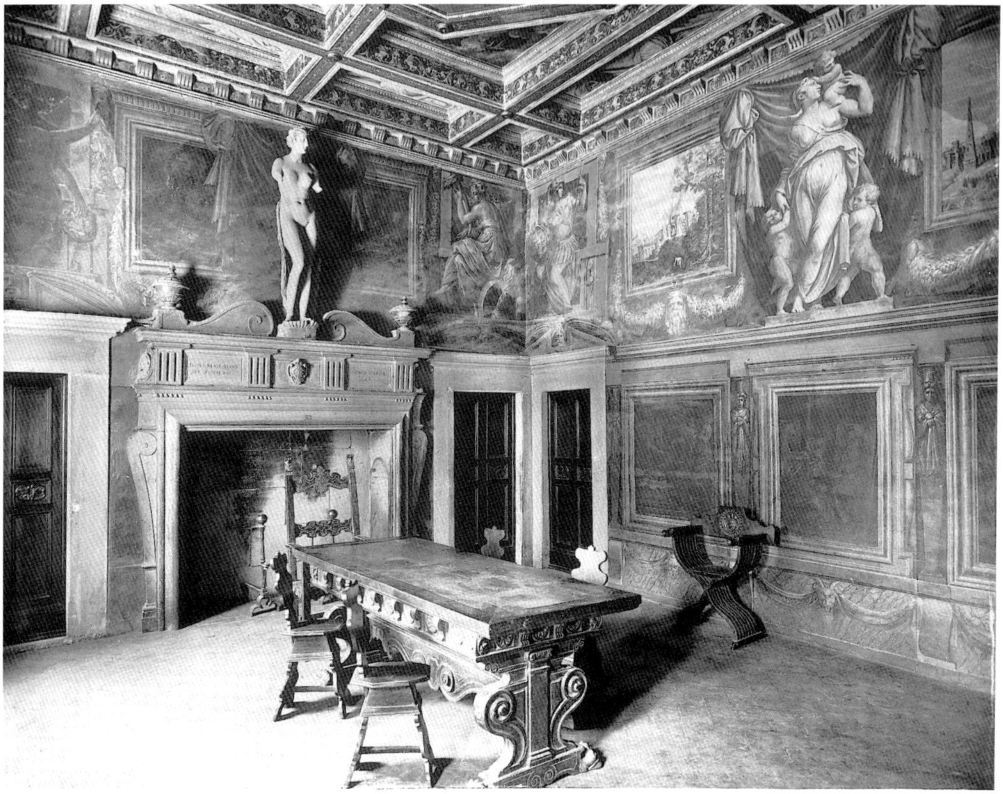

100 Giorgio Vasari, Sala della Virtù, with copy of Ammanati's Venus over the mantle, 1548, Casa del Vasari, Arezzo.

In the lower zone, between the windows and doors, he depicted key events from the history of ancient Greek art as told by Pliny the Elder (see Chapter 3); these are made to suggest the effect of gilded bronze reliefs. Vasari placed a statue of Venus over the fireplace on the south wall, and opposite her, also in the middle zone of the north wall, painted a fictive statue of Diana as Natura. This opposition may offer the two artistic models, of the antique and nature. The statue of Venus was a prized piece, in the form of the plaster cast, of the Venus which Bartolomeo Ammanati had made for Medici. This presentation of a sequence of scenes from the history of ancient art on a monumental scale was unprecedented.

In the centres of the corresponding middle zones of the west and east walls he placed fictive statues of the virtues of Charity and Abundance. Above, in the upper zone, he represented fictive statues personifying virtues, which are related by implication to good art and good life as depicted overhead. They are Fortitude, Liberality, Wisdom, Prudence, Hard Work, Justice, Honour and Felicity. Vasari created a rich illusionistic effect by adding fictive polychrome paintings, of views of ancient ruins, between the reliefs of ancient artists, and *trompe l'oeil* doorways. Vasari made himself a seigneurial fireplace here, complete with Latin inscriptions *Ignem gladio ne fodite* ('Do not poke the fire with a sword') and *Homo vapor est* ('Man is but a spark flying upwards') (*Psalms* 144, 4).

At one exit he painted an image which stressed the power of the master of the house:

As it were in jest, I painted a bride holding a rake, with which she seems to have raked up and carried away with her from her father's house everything that she has been able, and in the hand that is stretched in front of her, entering into the house of her husband, she has a lighted torch, signifying that where she goes she carries a fire that consumes and destroys everything.[21]

This personification of the feminine as simultaneously taking from and giving to the masculine suggests that one of the motives for the 1548 session of decoration was preparation of the house for his marriage. It underlines yet again the way artists could invent personal allegories.

In the room beside the Sala della Virtù, prefaced by the figure of the bride, Vasari again used the grand form of a carved and gilded wooden ceiling with painted panels. In the centre of this ceiling he painted Abraham holding his child Isaac, and having his progeny blessed by God (*Genesis* 22, 17). Vasari described the surrounding personifications (which are also marked by features unique to his invention) as Virtue, Peace, Concord and Modesty (Plate 101).[22] The scheme, which was painted in the spring of 1548, may relate to his forthcoming marriage in 1550. The personifications indicate wifely qualities: Virtue signifies feminine virtue as chastity, rather than the manly virtue of worthiness and expertise in some skill, and Modesty wears a veil, keeps her eyes downcast, and holds open a book stating *modestia vestra nota sit omnibus hominibus* ('Our modesty may be well known to all men'). It is as if Vasari were making for himself a version of auspicious decorations of nuptial apartments which patrons commonly commissioned for their sons' marriages. The theme of auspiciousness is reiterated in the ceiling painting of Ceres, in the corridor leading from this room to the kitchen, and the chapel. Vasari used the invention he would re-use, for Pope Julius III in 1553 at the Villa Giulia in Rome, to present a golden goddess holding a cornucopia full of grain, driving a chariot pulled by golden serpents.[23]

The next room which one enters from the Sala della Fama was also provided with an impressive cross vault. Although Vasari did not describe this chamber, he probably painted it at about the same time. Here Apollo appears as if seated on Mount Parnassus, at the summit of the vault, with his lyre at his side, while two *putti* fly down to place the victorious wreath of laurel on his head. In the pendentives are depicted

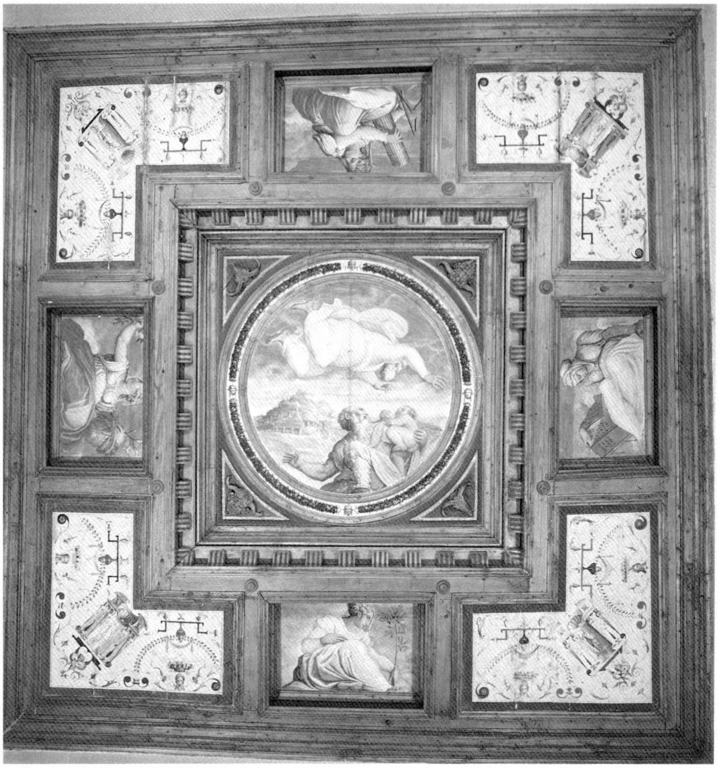

101 Giorgio Vasari, *Abraham, with Virtue, Peace, Concord and Modesty*, 1548, Casa del Vasari, Arezzo.

all nine Muses (Plate 102). Given their mythological associations with dance, writing, speaking and music, this legendary grouping was fit company for artists who drew parallels between their own activities and those of poets and musicians.

Stephan Ziegler, Sélestat, 1545

While Vasari was completing the most ambitious artist's house to date, Stephan Ziegler, municipal architect in Schlettstadt or Sélestat in Alsace, was finishing a spectacular house which is dated 1545 (Plate 46). The house occupied a corner site in the centre of town (presently 18, Rue de Verdun). It represented all the architects whom Vitruvius had listed in the *Ten Books*, as well as portraying Vitruvius himself with each bust being inscribed with their name (see Chapter 3).[24] The existence of this important tribute to ancient architects stresses diversity in the ways in which building was organised in different areas of Christendom. Ziegler was one of the official civic architects appointed in German-speaking locations to oversee the municipal erection which was actually undertaken by professional masons and builders, trained in the lodges attached to important buildings.[25] Evidently, Ziegler could see Vitruvius as an exemplar for one who was the scholarly planner of building and city design. As the example of the house of Giovanni Battista Bertano in Mantua shows, a house façade could also be used by an architect for a didactic demonstration.

Giovanni Battista Bertano, Mantua, 1556

Giovanni Battista Bertano's house in Mantua was, like Ziegler's, a celebration of Vitruvius. As in the case of Vasari, it was the counterpart to a book. Bertano, who took over the post from Giulio Romano as Prefetto delle Fabbriche Ducali in Mantua, in 1549, bought his house in 1554. His book set out to resolve the problem of the imprecise description by Vitruvius of the way one should model the Ionic order. Bertano published his resolution in 1558, in Mantua, entitled *Gli oscuri e difficili passi dell'opera ionica di Vitruvio*, but he had already demonstrated his discovery on his house portal, which was completed in 1556. One semi-column flanking the doorway represented the perfect Ionic column, whereas its pendant was shown in vertical section, so that diagrams and measurements could be clearly inscribed (Plate 103).

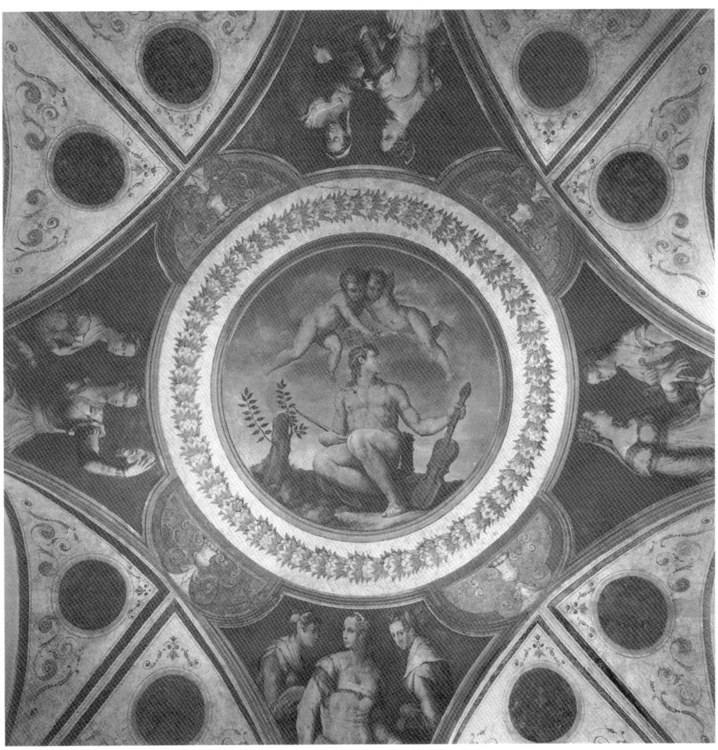

102 Giorgio Vasari, *Apollo and the Muses*, 1548, Casa del Vasari, Arezzo.

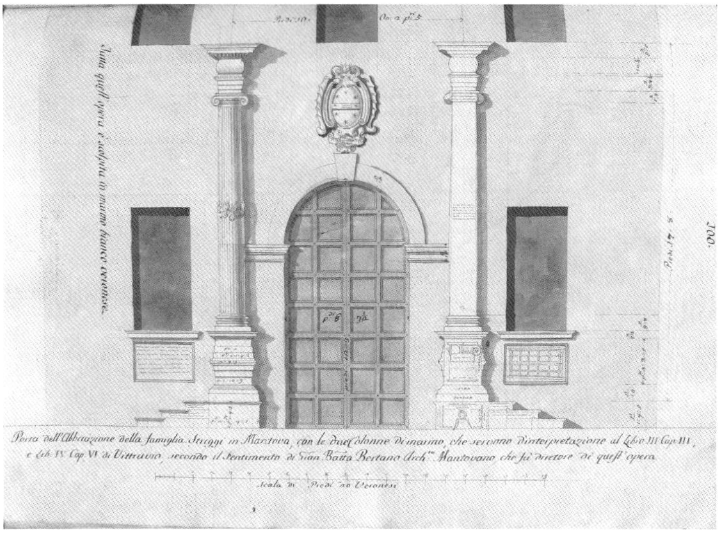

103 Luigi Trezza, drawing of the portal of the house of Giovanni Battista Bertano (1556, Mantua) Biblioteca Civica, Verona, MS1010 *c*.100.

Bertano referred to his house front as providing 'the theory and practice' for replicating his solution. Here the façade is being used to claim the theoretical powers of the architect, and the learning required to elucidate Vitruvius' text. Bertano described how he had made 'the doorway of my palace of bronzo' (that is, of the sought-after stone from Verona, which was so called because it made a ringing noise when it was struck). Two inscriptions, using the text of Bertani's book, were placed beside the columns.[26] The house was placed in a newly settled area, on the road leading to the Porta Cerese (presently 8 via Trieste).

If Bertano's house claimed him as scholarly authority on classical architecture, the houses of Lelio Orsi at Novellara and Reggio Emilia showed off his virtuosity in handling foreshortening, and, arguably, defended his personal reputation and the honour of his family.

Lelio Orsi, Novellara and Reggio-Emilia, *c*.1546–*c*.1578

Some time between 1546 and 1563 or a little later, the painter and architect Lelio Orsi designed an impressive façade decoration in fresco for his house in the town of his birth at Novellara (Plate 104). Then, or at least by 1579, when someone made an engraving of it *in situ*, he made a version of the Novellara composition for a house in nearby Reggio Emilia (probably the one his brother was inhabiting on the present via Corradini).[27] Orsi, whose style suggests admiration for the work of Correggio and Giulio Romano, worked for the branch of the Gonzaga family who ruled Novellara. He also worked in Reggio, but took voluntary exile when implicated in a murder in 1546, and returned there, only briefly, in the period 1579–81. The date of 1563 for the Novellara mural has been proposed in relation to a decree issued by the Gonzaga, ordering the painting of all houses in the town. However, the fact that the design refers to the defence of the Orsi family suggests that it might date from closer to his flight from Reggio. As reconstructed by Gaetano Gaddi, the mural was painted probably in grisaille on the façade of his house beside the church of the Carmine, where he was buried. The design did not make statements about art theory or history, but rather about the skills of Orsi himself, in demonstrating feats of foreshortening and knowledge of anatomy, and showing his high status in presenting the arms of the house of Orsi: that is of two bears. In a cluster of drawings Orsi developed the bold idea of an heroic defence of his heraldic shield, to be painted above the central window, as if in a heavenly cloud, being guarded from assault by naked men and women. Strenuous attempts are being made by other nude figures to pull down, and set on fire, the columns of the building. The illusion of the entablature they supported was presumably to appear as if above the three real windows

104 Anonymous, the house of Lelio Orsi, Novellara, mid sixteenth-century, ink and brown wash on paper, 270 × 340 mm, Chatsworth, Duke of Devonshire, number 351.

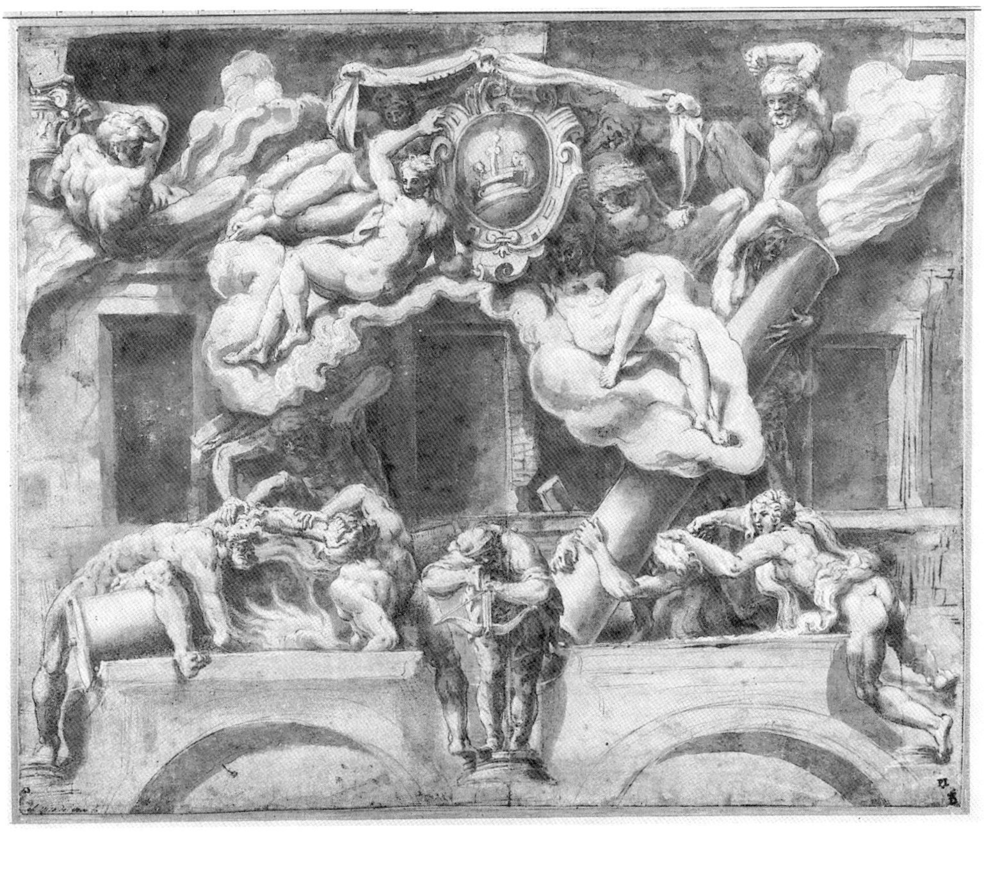

of the *piano nobile*. Poised, probably over the actual door, was an archer in contemporary dress, depicted in steep foreshortening, as if ready to shoot at attackers.[28] Arguably, Orsi paraded his mastery of Mannerist games here, in ways which recall the *Fall of the Giants* painted by Giulio Romano for the Gonzaga in Mantua. Perhaps he also put forward metaphors of rank, strength and practiced accuracy, as analogues of the power of art.[29] The house was pulled down in 1950.

During the 1560s two painters decorated their house façades in Antwerp. In some ways they respond to Italian precedents but there are new emphases, both in showing the worth of Northern painters and in the praise for educating artists according to a common curriculum. Some viewers would have been aware of the foundation in Florence of the first Academy in 1563, with its proposal of core training in *disegno* for painters, sculptors and architects.

Cornelis van Dalem, Antwerp, 1563

In 1563 Cornelis van Dalem completed the decoration of his house façade on the Lange Nieuwstraat in Antwerp (Plates 15, 37). This was one of the busiest thoroughfares in the city, so that he was reaching a large audience. Van Dalem was registered as a free master in 1556 and was a painter of landscapes, some of which referred to the fables of Lucretius and Ovid. Van Mander reported that he was a learned artist with a house full of books, and from other sources we know that he was a noble holding land in fief and acted as linen merchant. He bought the house, then known as *de Cagie* ('the bird cage' or 'hen coop') from his teacher, Jan Adriaensens, in 1559. The appearance of the house was recorded in the 1830s, before it was demolished in 1852. In the frieze over the door, van Dalem placed a sculpted personification of Painting working at her easel, labelled *Pictura*, with reliefs of Mercury to the right and Minerva to the left in the door spandrels below. Flanking *Pictura* he placed busts of van Eyck and Dürer inscribed as 'splendour of Belgians' and 'worthy of Germans'. He put the date 1563 at the apex of the façade.[30] According to Jan van Damme, when his widow came to sell this house in 1606 the legal documents now called the house the '*Cagie* or *Pictura*'. The change of name marks what appears to be the first large-scale permanent public announcement of the high status of Northern European painting. The articulation of the façade announced classicising Italianate aspirations, for the house looked like one narrow central bay of a large *palazzo*. A grand portal edged with rough blocks of stone suggests rustication. There are round headed arches here, and on the second and third stories, while a triangular pediment was placed at the apex. At the ground and the top floor, heavy volutes are used in a manner associated with the contemporary Bolognese architect Jacopo Barocci, called Il Vignola. Sad to relate, van Dalem was forced to leave

Antwerp for the Northern Netherlands in 1565 because of his Protestant beliefs; he had lived in his house for only six years. In the late eighteenth century, van der Sanden attributed the sculpture on this building to Willem van den Broecke. As he was an accomplished local sculptor, who had travelled to Italy and was known to Vasari this is a possibility.

This was an innovating statement in every way. The personification of Painting seems to have been her first monumental showing in the Netherlands (see Chapter 1). The coupling of Mercury and Minerva (previously only present in Giulio Romano's house) had prestigious connections with philosophical and literary academies (see Chapter 5).[31] Van Dalem may have seen the engravings published by Giulio Bonasone in 1550, which showed plans for the academy-cum-house of Achille Bocchi at Bologna, which was designed by Vignola. It too presented a rusticated ground floor, the lavish use of heavy volutes and an attic over the portal with a triangular pediment. In addition, the main façade represented freestanding statues of Mercury (left) and Minerva above the entablature.[32] Since it was in 1563 that the Florentine Accademia del Disegno was founded, the idea of academic references on his house front might have appealed to a scholarly Netherlandish artist. It may be noteworthy, too, that Vignola had planned to adorn his façade with pairs of busts on the lower storey, and had used pairs of volutes with heads of lions and *bucrania* to create a heavy entablature. The engravings of Vignola's plans may have inspired van Dalem to have busts of van Eyck and of Dürer placed between volutes on either side of *Pictura*, to form his ground-floor entablature. Perhaps, then, for the artists of Antwerp, van Dalem's house announced that the painting of the south Netherlands and German-speaking areas was of high merit.

Frans Floris, Antwerp, *c.*1563

At about the same time as van Dalem made his house front, Frans Floris was completing the decoration of his house nearby, only in this case it was painted in monochrome to create the effect of bronze statuary. Its appearance was recorded by Jan van Croes in about 1700 (Plates 14, 22, 86).[33] As shown by van de Velde the house had been built for Frans in 1562 in a less frequented area in the Arenbergstraat. Frans was, according to van Mander, someone who liked talking of poetry and philosophy. He had completed his studies with Lambert Lombard in 1540, and then went to Italy in 1541, where he visited Mantua, the site of Giulio Romano's house. There, a portrait attributed to the Bolognese engraver Giulio Bonasone was made of him; the Latin inscription praises him as 'holding a high place among Belgian Painters'. He was back in Antwerp by 1545 and died there in 1570. The architect of Floris' house was his brother Cornelis Floris. Since he was the builder of the city hall, Cornelis was one of the most prestigious designers in Antwerp and employed the latest classicising style. Given that the articulation seems to have been designed with the paintings in mind, it seems likely that the mural was completed soon after this. The Doric order was chosen for the ground floor of the house, and adorned with roundels, swags and masks. The *piano nobile* employed a version of Ionic, which concealed the window apertures with wide pilasters, and provided space for seven painted niches in the bays between, and a fictive relief over the portal. The house was demolished in 1816.

Van de Velde showed that a series of engravings signed with the initials 'TG', dated 1576 and made in Antwerp represented the central composition and the niche figures. They rendered everything in reverse. Foreground left, in the over door, appears a personification of Painting, seated at her easel, while, on the right, Sculpture carves a statue (Plate 14). 'TG' added or replicated the inscription 'Necessities for human society'. In the sky are two flying figures, whose meaning was suggested by van de Velde. The one on the left, with a bow holding seven arrows, could, he thought, be Apollo, leader of the Muses of Arts and Sciences; perhaps the arrows signified the seven Liberal Arts. The figure on the right, who has wings and points to heaven, might indicate Eternal Reward or Fame. In the centre is a woman seated on a globe with a large compass. The Netherlandish scholar Jochen Becker pointed out that these are attributes of the Liberal Art of geometry, as represented in contemporary engravings.[34] A man background right is writing Arabic numerals on a panel, and other men seem to be watching over the learning of small boys. A child near Painting is drawing or writing, and another near Sculpture is carrying a mallet and a set-square, which may allude to the activities of the architect.

The peroration for the biography of Lombard published by Lampsonius in 1565 might explain these references to education. Both Lampsonius and Floris were pupils of Lombard. Lampsonius stated he had written the life,

> so that having placed his [Lambert's] example (as if it were a painting of someone illustrious) before the eyes of young men dedicated to the arts, not only might I inflame them to pursue the acquisition of the most complete knowledge from all talented men, but that also I might lead them to believe most truly that they cannot aspire to the great praiseworthiness which he has attained, unless they unite scholarly learning with study of art, following the precepts of Pamphilos, teacher of the greatest painter, and of Leone Battista Alberti, the Florentine, of Albrecht Dürer, and of Pomponius Gauricus.[35]

Pliny the Elder had described Pamphilos as the tutor of Apelles and Melanthios, and as:

> the first painter who was thoroughly trained in every branch of learning, more particularly in arithmetic and geometry without which, so he held, art

could not be present. He taught no-one for less than a talent – that is five hundred denarii – a year, the fee paid him by both Apelles and Melanthios. It was owing to his influence that drawing on tablets of boxwood was the earliest subject taught to free born boys and accepted as the first step to a liberal education.[36]

Frans could be showing how ancient artists like Apelles and Melanthios had followed Phamphilos in instructing young artists, in all branches of the liberal arts, especially geometry and arithmetic. The man background right, who is writing Arabic numerals on a panel, could indicate the teaching of arithmetic while the central figure on the globe would represent geometry. The idea that this is an allegory of education would explain the way it shows men watching over the learning of small boys. The men with draped heads could represent ancient scholars – 'all branches of learning'. The flying figure might then be signalling the fame of Phamphilos – or perhaps his pupil, Apelles. The allegory could be one which celebrates pioneers in ancient art education, who provide exemplars for modern artists to follow.

The inscriptions under the niches show that five of the figures represented qualities needed for the education of artists. They are: Diligence, Practice, Hard Work, Experience and Industry. Frans used the figures on either side of the main scene to show Poetry and Architecture. The engraver included an inscription beneath Poetry, which states: 'Let the worthy man be prevented from dying by the praise of the Muse' (*Dignum laude virum musae vetat mori*). The choice of the swan as attribute may relate to the *Odes* of Horace, in which the poet had compared poetry to a swan who could lift the poet himself to heaven and fame. The swan was also a bird sacred to Apollo. Architecture was given a crown of trowels and a plumb line, compasses, set-square, chisels and mallet, and the inscription 'Architecture, ornament of cities' (*Architectura urbium ornamentum*).

Floris seems to have been demonstrating something of the new ideas represented in the founding of the Accademia del Disegno in Florence: that Painting, Sculpture and Architecture were allied to the Liberal Arts of poetry, arithmetic and geometry, and that the three arts should be taught together rather than in separate guild enclaves. That his message was appreciated, is proved by the way his façade was cited by Antwerp sculptors fighting through the courts between 1593 and 1607 to be allowed solely to join the Guild of Saint Luke as designers, like the painters, and not be forced to belong to the guild of the stone cutters as well. To prove the dignity of sculpture they claimed that Frans Floris had shown sculpture as a Liberal Art on his house.

Four years later Leone Leoni completed his house in Milan. Like the houses of Orsi, this house set out to defend Leoni's virtue against attack. Unlike any of its predecessors, it was a large palace adorned with costly marble carvings. Like Vasari, Leoni claimed to control Fortune, and compared his skills with those of poetry and music. As with Giulio Romano's house, Leoni honoured his patron.

Leone Leoni, Milan, 1567

In 1548 the sculptor and goldsmith Leone Leoni travelled to Brussels to discuss the making of an equestrian portrait of Charles V, the Holy Roman Emperor, following the battle of Mühlberg. Although he did not achieve this project, he was awarded other large-scale bronze commissions, and in token of this trust was given a knighthood and a house by the Emperor in 1549. The house was in Milan, then under Hapsburg rule, where Leoni had been Master of the Mint since 1542. Here Leoni set up his studio in 1550, and completed the promised imperial commissions. Charles V died in 1558 and the sculptor set out to cultivate Milanese patrons. In 1565 he bought another site next to his dwelling, in the Contrada de Morono near the church of Santo Stefano, and petitioned the Milanese Senate to have permission to build. The renovated and enlarged palace was completed in 1567, after his own design, with stone sculpture commissioned from Antonio Abbondio. Leoni had been born and brought up in the region of Como, but also identified with Arezzo, the site of Vasari's house, which was the home town of his family.

The façade may have been a demonstration of budding architectural skills. The ground floor is adorned with massive doric pilasters to which are attached six giant captives, in the manner of herms, labelled with the names of men, representing the peoples conquered by the Emperor Marcus Aurelius: Svevus, Quadus, Adiabenus, Parthus, Sarmata, Marcomanus. Rustication is employed to give a sense of strength and the central portal is flanked by two further caryatids, with arms crossed as if in homage. The second order is ionic and uses the buried columns made fashionable by Michelangelo. It supports a rich entablature carrying a frieze, which is decorated with lions for the Leoni family, placing their paws firmly on the wheel of fortune to stop it turning. These alternate with eagles (referring to his status as Imperial Knight or to the Emperor himself) holding laudatory garlands. In the centre, over the portal, one relief seems to spill over from the frieze, and shows two lions eating a satyr, signifying a malicious or ignorant critic (see Chapter 6). Vasari had visited the house in 1566 and wrote: 'As for the prisoners, his idea may be variously interpreted.'[37]

The reference to Marcus Aurelius was confirmed when the visitor entered the courtyard to find a replica, in the centre, of the horse from the antique Roman statue of this emperor, raised on a platform supported by four columns. This was a copy in *gesso* taken from the gilded bronze equestrian portrait in Rome, by permission of Pope Pius IV, in 1560. The placement in Leoni's *cortile* might have alluded to the way

Michelangelo's design for the Capitol had placed the original statue as its centrepiece. Vasari stated that the house was dedicated to Marcus Aurelius, and the allusion would have been a suitable one to make, in relation to Leoni's most powerful patron, since Marcus Aurelius was regarded as one of the few model Emperors of ancient Rome. Leoni might also have been encouraging respect for his own potential skills, since the equestrian bronze was regarded as one of the most challenging tasks for any sculptor. Since there were also casts of Michelangelo's *Risen Christ* and the *Pietà* in the courtyard, Leoni could also have been paying tribute to the prowess of modern art.[38]

Leoni's name and skills were further advertised in the columns opposite the entrance in the courtyard, which were decorated with bronze lions' heads, and in the frieze round the courtyard, which contained reliefs showing 'the instruments of art' according to Vasari. Now badly damaged, these reliefs represented, reading clockwise from the entrance, according to Michael Mezzatesta: the instruments of sculpture, of the goldsmith, and architecture and a scenographic or theatrical prospect; a group of musical instruments; Pegasus over the caduceus of Mercury and two cornucopias, possibly as a symbol of poetry; a lion holding the wheel of fortune as personal *impresa* of the artist himself; more instruments of drawing and sculpture; and finally an image of the city of Milan.[39] Leoni could here have been registering his expertise in working for the Milanese in arranging festival and theatrical performances, as well his skills in modelling. Originally the niches in the upper storey of the courtyard held exemplars of ancient and modern sculptures belonging to Leoni. Inside he housed an enviable collection of ancient and modern works in an octagonal gallery. This was a house which impressed the most erudite viewers, such as the local scholar Cicereio, who praised it in a Latin dialogue in 1596 as 'magnificently built, most elegant and most learned'. It was also impressive for ordinary citizens, who came to call it the *casa Omenoni* ('house of the huge men').

Giorgio Vasari, Florence, 1573

The decoration of Vasari's Florentine house – which he acquired, like Leoni, from his patron, in 1570 – soon followed. In it Vasari repeated themes used in his Aretine house such as the Liberal status of painting, sculpture and architecture, the commemorative portraits of ancient artists and the display of his heraldry. Yet having published the second edition of the *Lives* and secured his position as artist to the Medici court, he now included portraits of the founders of Florentine art as part of his own personal heritage, and painted the Medici shield in his frieze.

Seven years after praising Leoni's house, Vasari completed the decoration of his Florentine house. Vasari had entered the employment of Cosimo de' Medici in 1554. He had been lodged in a tall narrow house, in the centre of town, on the Borgo Santa Croce, from 1557 onwards, but the Grand Duke did not give him the house until 1570. In 1573 Vasari set about decorating the large room on the *piano nobile* with three windows opening onto the Borgo (Plates 17, 29). This room was provided with a wooden ceiling painted with stars on a blue background, and with a scheme selected from the programme he had developed for his house in Arezzo. Again the celebration of art was deflected back onto the ancient Greeks, and the portraits of great moderns were small and placed high up. Again there were grand personifications of Architecture, Painting, Sculpture and Poetry but this time they were joined by Music (see Chapter 1).[40]

Paint is used to create the illusion of a rich stone panelling. The effect is of jutting brackets which sustain bronze caryatids that appear to be holding up swags of fruit and flowers. These swags form the frieze and carry thirteen small portraits of modern artists and the arms of Cosimo de' Medici. Relying on his second edition of the *Lives*, Vasari boldly selected artists who summed up the history of Tuscan art from Cimabue to Michelangelo and added some recent artists with special reference to his own career (Chapter 3). Vasari added his own portrait and placed his arms on the chimney breast.

In the large middle zone of three of the walls, Vasari portrayed three scenes, as if they were framed polychrome paintings set into the panelling. As at Arezzo he depicted Zeuxis taking the best features from the five young women of Croton to make a perfect image of a goddess, and his own version of the invention of Painting. The ancient inventor kneels as if to the left of the real fireplace, and outlines his own shadow as if thrown by Vasari's fire. Unlike the Aretine scheme, Vasari now represented Apelles hiding behind his painting of Diana, while he listened to a cobbler judging his composition. Vasari had meditated long on the process of artistic idealisation, as his section on *disegno* in the *Lives* of 1568 demonstrated. In his own house he presented the Zeuxian story as the allegory of the transformation by the skilled painter of the imperfect data of observed 'nature' into an ideal beauty (see Chapter 2). Cecchi noted the presence of four fragments of a ceiling decoration by Vasari formerly in this house, for which Vincenzo Borghini apparently wrote the programme, honouring the achievements of theologians, jurists, soldiers and poets of Arezzo. This scheme points up the way elements in the original appearance of the Florentine house promoted Vasari's Aretine, as well as his adoptive Florentine, identity.

Francesco da Volterra and Diana Scultori, Rome, 1575

At the same time as Vasari was decorating the interior of his second house, Francesco da Volterra and his wife Diana Scultori leased a house in the centre of Rome in the Campo Marzio, near the Via Scrofa. As the condition of rental entailed repainting, they commissioned Raffaellino da Reggio to decorate the façade (Plate 87). Francesco was a sculptor and architect trying to launch his career in Rome, and the arresting façade may have been part of his campaign to obtain patronage.[41] On his arrival in Rome in 1572 Raffaellino, probably a pupil of Orsi, had painted with Federico Zuccari, and his relationship with Diana was also a working one, since she inscribed engravings after his designs between 1575 and 1581. This was the earliest programmatic façade for artists in the city. Following in the tradition of Filarete, Piero, and Ottaviano Zuccari they chose the theme of the 'one path to virtue'.[42] Drawings display Hercules with his club, and a helmeted Minerva, goddess of Virtue and Wisdom, flanking a soldierly figure who may be identified as Scipio. A drawing at Lulworth Manor shows a section of the façade of the house with a *piano nobile* of windows with segmental and triangular pediments.[43] These pediments are broken, demonstrating Mannerist styling, and are adorned with *putti* and a portrait bust in the breaks. The Lulworth drawing suggests that the allegory was presented in two parts: in the upper picture are represented the two temples of Honour and Virtue at the summit of the hill towards which figures are scrambling; below this scene are three figures as if in close-up climbing up to the temple of Virtue. Indeed, the Lulworth drawing recorded the inscription 'Virtue climbs to the heavens', which may have been inscribed not too far from eye level. It is noteworthy that all the figures turn their backs to viewers, in a rare narrative ploy. This may mark the allegory as aimed at a knowing professional spectatorship which did not require 'actors' to 'face front'. The façade was the subject of artistic interest. Bartholomaeus Spranger (who designed his own house façade twelve years later) supplied the 'front view' of this Roman design, in an engraving published about 1591 with a Latin caption suggesting that the engraver understood it to signify Hercules and Scipio striving for virtue.[44] Within a few years Federico Zuccari was to take the theme of the pursuit of virtue for his house in Florence, only this time with the motif of Time revealing Truth.

Federico Zuccari, Florence, 1577–79

During the period 1576–79 Federico Zuccari was in Florence working on the prestigious task of completing the mural on the cathedral dome, begun by Vasari. In this prominent position he acquired the house of Andrea del Sarto on a corner site (presently 22 via Gino Capponi) in 1577. Federico reshaped the house, applying *pietra serena* cornices on the first-floor windows carrying his name and the date 1578, which was the year he married Francesca Genga, daughter of the architect Girolamao Genga. While he left the arms of Andrea's widow on the portal (after all, his father Ottaviano had revered Andrea), he designed a distinctive cornering for the house, which used a buried column recalling the style of Michelangelo, and supporting his family shield, flanked by cornucopias, and topped with the Medici arms of his patron. Federico had the entrance hall enlarged, and provided a *loggia* opening onto the garden. Originally from Sant'Angelo in Vado, Federico had worked in Rome with Raffaellino da Reggio, and had visited Antwerp in 1574–75, where he could have seen the houses of Floris and van Dalem.[45]

Zuccari decorated a vaulted room on the ground floor beside the garden with an elaborate series of allegories and narratives declaring his ambitions (Plates 96–7). The centrepiece of the cross vault was a depiction of Benevolent Time (see Chapter 6), accompanied by the Past, the Present, the Times of Day, and the Seasons. In order to underline Zuccari's erudition, the Seasons were indicated by the festivals of ancient Roman religion, and also in more homely vein by typical occupations of the year, including scenes which seem to refer to the painter's own domestic routine. In four scenes, depicted as if in gilded bronze relief, he represented episodes from the life of the philosopher Aesop. Aesop is shown accused of stealing, stupidity and inability to obey instructions, but is repeatedly exonerated. As with the figures which walk away from the viewer on the mural of Raffaellino da Reggio, the choice of the deformed Aesop as a kind of hero would presumably have been unacceptable to a patron.

The way Time is depicted has been related to the recommendation written by Antonio Francesco Doni, which Federico had already used at the Villa d'Este. Doni advised in *Le pitture* (1584) that Time should be shown 'crowned with roses, corn, fruits and dried branches as King of the Seasons' and should be 'seated on the Zodiac'. A 'thin and wasted *putto*' was to depict 'Time Past destroying wherever it goes and ending in nothing', while 'a fine fat *putto*' would denote 'the Future'. In addition,

> at his [Time's] feet shall be a great big book in which two babies are writing continuously and above them to signify Day the baby boy shall have the sun at his head, while to denote Night the baby girl shall have the moon at her head. So Time triumphs over temporal powers and the world.[46]

At the bottom of the garden Federico built a tall studio with an arresting Mannerist façade facing onto the street (presently via Giuseppe Giusti). It was treated as if it were one bay of a larger building. The first order was heavily rusticated, with rough hewn piers flanking a tall portal and giant benches either side. Federico's arms were placed over the door and the ground-floor windows. Reliefs showed the instruments of architects, sculptors and painters. The upper order was brick, but continued the articulation of the floor below, with niches for statuary and a central field, as if awaiting a mural. In 1608 Zuccari sold this house to devote funds to his Roman palace.[47]

Following this spate of Italian houses, Spranger the pupil of van Dalem followed his master's example and painted an elaborate programme on the front of his house at Prague, which seems to honour the Emperor Rudolph II and celebrate the fame of painting and sculpture under the aegis of Mercury.

Bartholomaeus Spranger, Prague, 1585

Around 1585 Bartholomaeus Spranger decorated a house front in Prague with murals imitating the effects of metalwork, which set out to educate the citizens of Prague as to the dignity of painting and sculpture. Spranger had been impressed by the house of Francesco da Volterra and Diana Scultori, and had been a colleague of Federico Zuccari at Caprarola. The Prague house decoration seems to mark his achievement of an assured position. From 1565 onwards Spranger had worked in Paris, Milan, Parma and then Rome. In 1577 he had entered the service of Maximilian II at Vienna. He had travelled to Prague in the service of Rudolf II, the heir of Maximilian, in 1580, had been made painter by royal appointment in 1584 and had bought the house the next year.[48] Van Mander described the design:

> At the top, upright, there are little children as large as life: on the right hand side they are painting and drawing, and on the left they are sculpting and drawing. In the middle [is] a flying Mercury life sized. Beneath are lunettes. Beneath this vaulting you see Fame. In the middle and underneath, a female figure: Rome, who stands on a sphere being carried by an eagle. The lower part of the eagle ends in the frieze. The frieze is further filled with captives, trophies and spoils. On each side of the frieze are two large figures, eight feet high, the one a Hercules and the other Justice. In the middle, below the frieze, there is a little child, larger than life-size, in colour, holding an epitaph.[49]

It seems possible that Spranger was demonstrating how the arts of sculpting and painting were to be regarded as allied skills. As in Vasari's house at Arezzo, the Fame of the arts of design was extolled, and as on van Dalem's and Giulio Romano's houses Mercury was given pride of place (see Chapter 5). A drawing shows part of the façade, in the form of a helmeted personification of Rome, holding a small figure of Victory and a sword, while standing on a globe supported by an Imperial eagle (Plate 105). The frieze at her feet is clearly indicated.[50] It seems possible that the lower part of the house front represented the way the patronage of the Holy Roman Emperor supported the arts of design. The frieze of trophies and the eagle might indicate the power of his reign, while Hercules could indicate Fortitude or Virtue as pendant to Justice. Spranger had worked in Milan, so he would have seen the façade adorned with giant figures and Imperial eagles belonging to Leoni. Situated on the approach to the castle, on the New Castle Stairs

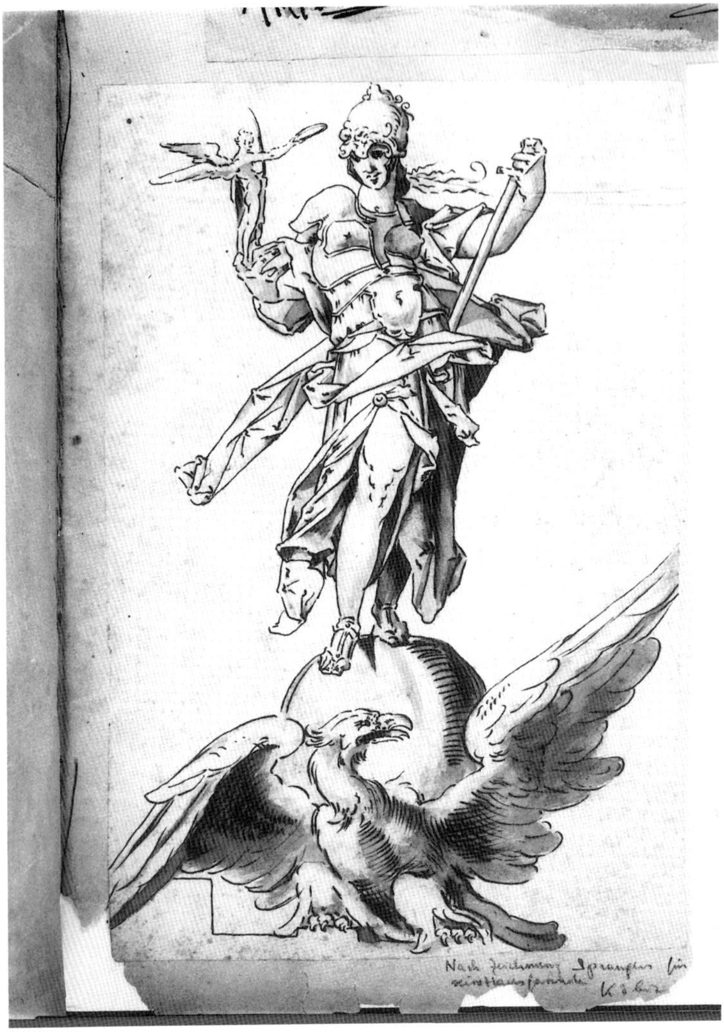

105 After Bartholomeus Spranger, *Rome triumphant*, *c.*1585, Rensi Collection, Museum der Bildenden Künste, Leipzig.

(currently 193–6 Nové Zámecké Schody) the house was visible to many. Another transalpine house stresses, however, that artists might choose religious themes to enhance the dignity of their profession.

Andries de Valckenaere, Middelburg, Zeeland, 1590

In 1590 Andries de Valckenaere, a sculptor from Antwerp, completed the house, inscribed over the portal *In de Steenrotse* ('On the rock of stone'), in the town of Middelburg, in the province of Zeeland just north of Antwerp.[51] The façade, clad in expensive cut stone, survived until 1940, and celebrated the hagiographical and biblical exemplars of those who hammer stone. Photographs record the richly classicising articulation, which seems to have been designed to introduce new Antwerp styles of decoration to the town (Plate 106). Roundels in the scrolls of the gable held two busts of Roman Emperors. In between were figures of the Four Crowned Martyrs. They were carved as herms on the pilasters, which were used to divide the three windows, shaped in a Serlian format, on the uppermost floor of the building. The façade seems to have proclaimed Andries's piety as member of the Guild of the Four Crowned Martyrs (see Chapter 4). There were five windows on the *piano nobile* below, which were divided by classicising pilasters supporting a frieze of narrative reliefs. They told the story of Moses finding

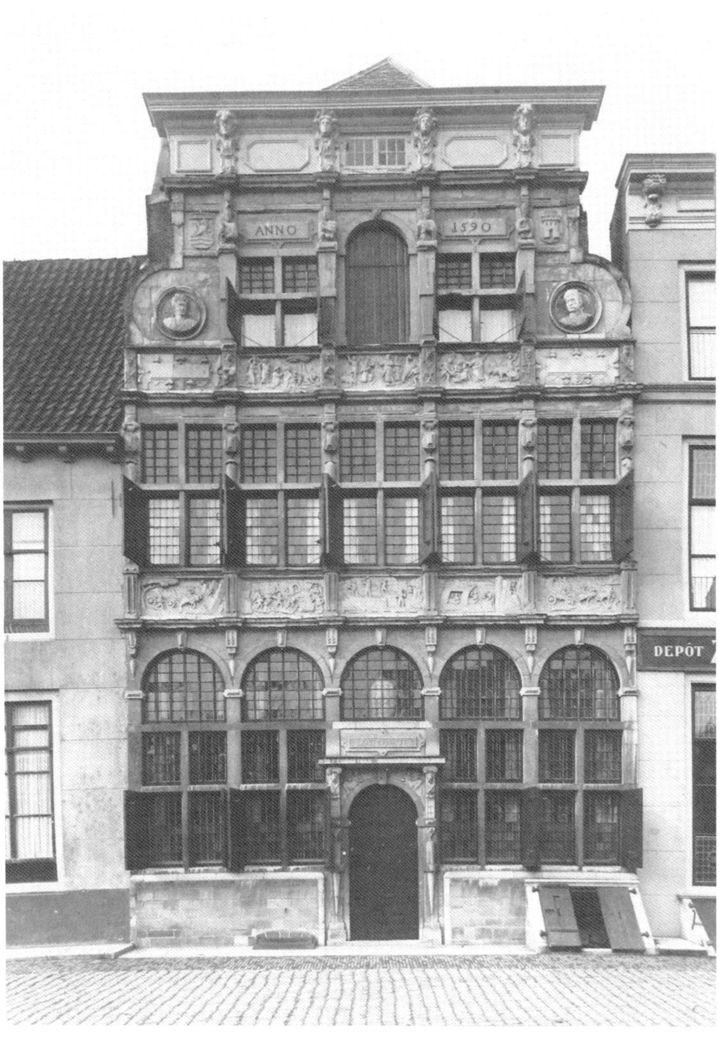

106 The house of Andries de Valckenaere, 1590, Middelburg (destroyed 1940).

water for his people in the desert by instructing Aaron to strike a rock. Moses' action was often seen as a 'type' of the New Testament, presaging the coming of salvation through the water of baptism (*Numbers* 20, 10). Into the spandrels of the central portal Valckenaere fitted personifications of Sculpture, while he represented the work of contemporary sculptors in reliefs, filling the frieze of the ground-floor entablature. In the overdoor he presented an eagle. Traditional statements of religious faith and innovating imagery for signifying the powers of sculpture were here united, in a classicising architectural scheme. The house possessed a fine site, on a quay (presently 24 Dwarskaai) convenient for loading stone.

Federico Zuccari, Rome, 1590–99

The last house to be decorated in the sixteenth century was situated in Rome and was owned by Federico Zuccari. It was probably the most elaborate to date. As with Vasari's houses, it was produced by someone who was an academic leader and an author of a treatise, entitled *L'idea de' pittori, scultori ed architetti* (Turin, 1607). He was also active in lecturing his colleagues on art theory. Like Vasari, he decorated two houses. Like him, Zuccari employed print to communicate his ideas to a wide audience, and his house was in a centre for artistic activity. Federico explored themes which had become part of the tradition for artists' houses (the *via virtutis*, the role of painting, sculpture and architecture, the celebration of his family, and a tribute to the sanctity of marriage) but he pursued them with lavish inventiveness and added new tropes with the celebration of the career of his brother Taddeo and his magisterial survey of the role of *disegno* amongst all the human arts.

In the year that Valckenaere completed his house, Federico had bought the site of the Palazzo Zuccari in Rome.[52] He had made a name for himself in the city, in 1581, when he vindicated his skill in the *Porta virtutis* cartoon (see Chapter 6), then, following papal pardon in 1583, he had worked in Spain as well as Rome. Federico considered this house not only as a personal statement of status, but also, in part, as a location for the Accademia di San Luca, of which he was appointed the first president in 1593. In his will in 1603 he designated his studio as a meeting place for the academy, and a section of the palace as lodging for young academicians.

The main, west, façade, containing the studio looking onto the *piazza* of Santa Trinità de' Monti and a superb view of Rome, was a version of his Florentine studio frontage. On the south side of his wedge-shaped palace, he provided a bizarre door to the garden resembling a gaping mouth such as those at the Villa Bomarzo. The garden entrance held portrait busts of himself and Francesca above the door. The annoyance with which this project was received may be gauged by the response of

Grazioso Graziosi, ambassador of the Duke of Urbino, who wrote to his master in 1593 that Federico had 'embarked on his poetic caprice, which will easily be the ruin of his children'.[53]

Within his palace Federico designed a grand barrel-vaulted hall, which he painted in about 1598 (Plate 88).[54] The vault is frescoed with the Labours of Hercules, and a central allegory depicting the difficult climb to the Temple of Honour seems to explain in detail the adage concerning the way of virtue, which his father had painted on the family house in Sant'Angelo in Vado, half a century earlier. This hall led to a vaulted room giving access to the garden. Here the imagery of the Florentine house was reworked, and a figure of Father Time was now actually seen writing deeds in a large book with the serpent of eternity over his head (Plate 96). Below is inscribed the advice *Virtude duce*, which students of Cicero knew continued: *comite Fortuna* ('With Virtue leading, Fortune is one's companion').[55] Two figures blowing trumpets of Fame fly overhead. To the left is Minerva, with the Moon over her head, who is treading down a vice – possibly Calumny. To the right is a young man (perhaps Apollo) with the Sun above him, who vanquishes Envy. Minerva and Apollo would be suitable given their roles as leaders of the arts. At the apex is standing a mature bearded man, who looks upward. Some kind of apotheosis of artistic talent seems to be indicated, since he is holding a quill and a brush in his right hand. The message appears to be a variation on the allegory Federico had devised for his Florentine house, with Time revealing the talent of the artist, as long as he adheres to the way of virtue. This allegory is surrounded by labelled personifications detailing the qualities talent requires to achieve the loftiest reward (Diligence, Hard work, Frankness, Spirit, Perseverance and Wisdom) (Plate 98). In the two triangular fields in the vault, created by the doorways, appear labelled representations of the approved kinds of love. These are 'friendship' (*amicitia*) symbolised by the Three Graces (recalling Alberti's advice) and the charitable love which combats sensual pleasure, in a scene depicting Anteros subduing Eros.

Below this aspirational vault are eight lunettes, presenting engaging portraits of his family as if they were leaning over the top of the walls. The series includes his grandfather and great-uncle, his mother, father and sister, and himself and his brother when young. He dwells on himself in maturity, wearing the order of Philip II of Spain round his neck, beside his wife Francesca (Plate 107). He includes his four sons, and his three daughters. These intimate portraits take Vasari's idea of including portraits relating to one's career one step further. In both the hall and this room Zuccari invented attractive framing devices which suggest bowers of red and white roses.

Three more finely decorated and vaulted rooms were made. They include the so-called Sala del Disegno, which may have been a study.

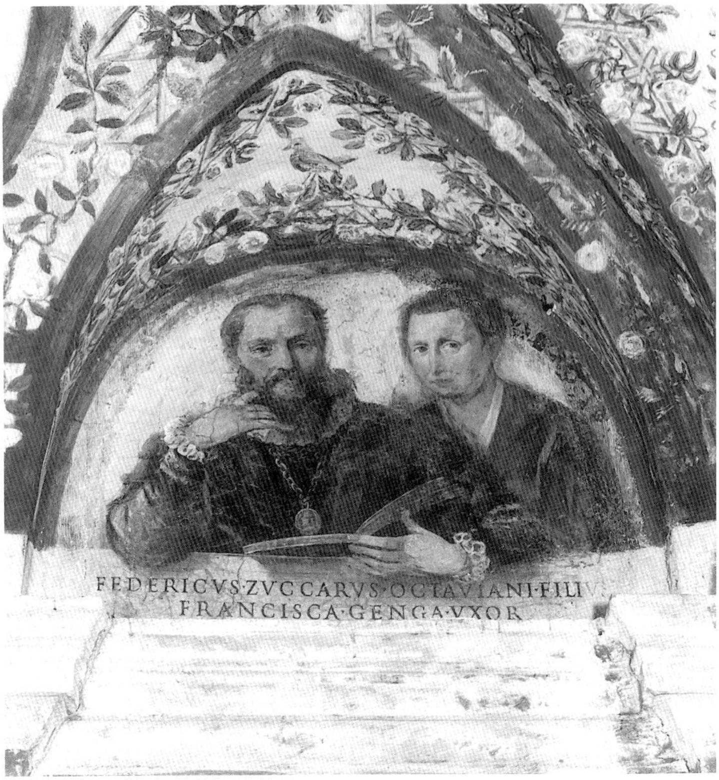

107 Federico Zuccari, portraits of Federico Zuccari and Francesca Genga, *c.*1595, hall, Palazzo Zuccari, Rome.

This seems to have been painted about 1599 (Plate 30). The decoration summed up the revolution which Zuccari proposed in his treatise *Idea*, as to the executive place of *disegno* in the scheme of human knowledge. Rather than considering it an adjunct of servile Practical Arts, Zuccari placed it as the controlling theoretical principle from which stemmed all branches of knowledge to enable the smooth running of human society (see Chapter 2). In addition, Zuccari decorated a vaulted room with a virtuoso display of foreshortening depicting Ganymede being taken up to heaven by Jupiter's eagle. Kristina Hermann Fiore has connected this subject matter with a scene illustrated by the painter from Dante's *Inferno*,[56] which had been glossed by Cristoforo Landino as signifying the way heavenly grace lifted up the human soul to celestial heights; Zuccari had recently transcribed and illustrated Dante's poem, in 1586–88. In addition, Zuccari made his version of the kind of seigneurial decoration which Vasari had created for his house in Arezzo in a marriage chamber (Plate 108). On the vault he depicted himself and his wife Francesca Genga kneeling for their marriage vows. Whereas Francesca was painted holding her mirror, Federico was accompanied by armour and weapons: presumably being an allusion to the honour given him by Philip II. The four roundels framing this scene depicted personifications of the virtues associated with successful union. Over the heads of the couple was Chastity, and beneath their feet was Concord, while on either side were Continence and Felicity. The vault was inscribed with the hope that 'In all your ways the angel of the Lord may look after you'.[57] The painter's identification with these virtues was underlined by depicting the personifications of Concord, as two people semi-nude, with the faces of himself and Francesca embracing. Again, one wonders if a patron would have relished so intimate a device. In a further room Federico inset a sequence of canvases in a panelled ceiling, which narrated the life of his brother Taddeo. Echoing the narrative for Michelangelo's funeral, this was the

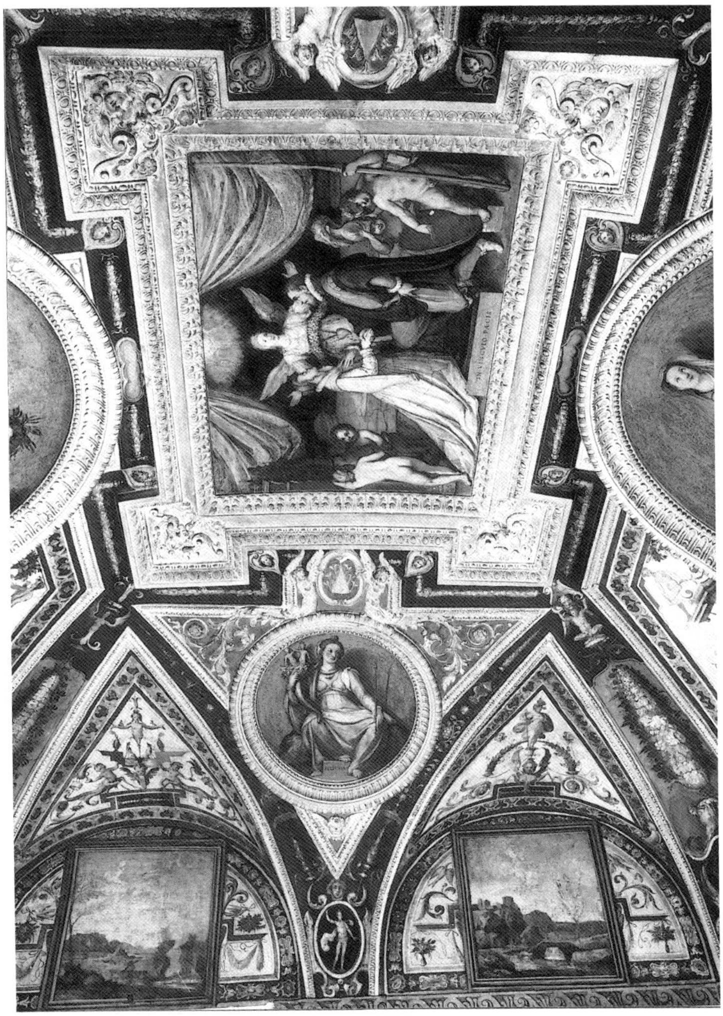

108 Federico Zuccari, Federico and Francesca Genga with Chastity, Concord, Felicity and Continence, *c.*1595, Palazzo Zuccari, Rome.

earliest permanent memorial to an artist in the form of a pictorial biography (Plate 76).

Since Federico's palace was situated in Rome, at a time when increasing numbers of artists were travelling to the city to study, both from the peninsula and outside, it was in a position to impress many visitors. It was followed by a house decoration which was more modest in dimensions but which made equal claims for the ingenuity and learning of the painter.

Cornelis Ketel, Amsterdam, 1602

The façade designed by Cornelis Ketel in Amsterdam, in 1602, took up the familiar themes of the defence of the artist against his critics, the assertion that painting is not a manual art, and that Time would vindicate virtue. Ketel was a painter and a poet who had been born in Gouda in 1548, and was trained there by his uncle. He went to Delft in 1565 to be taught by Anthonie Blocklandt, and then worked in Paris and Fontainebleau. He travelled to London in 1573, where he may have met Federico Zuccari in 1575. Having returned to the Netherlands in 1581, Ketel eventually bought a house on the old Zijds Voorburgwal in Amsterdam, opposite the Oude Kerk in 1593. Van Mander knew Ketel well, transcribing his poetry, and describing his paintings, including his house front:[58]

> On the right hand of the façade [are] Democritus and Heraclitus with a globe between them, these he painted with his right foot. On the left hand side [he painted] Momus and Zoilus with the left foot. In the middle directly above the door of the house stands fast flying Time, crowned with roses, in the one hand [holding] a scythe or sickle, in the other an hourglass accompanied by two flying children, the one representing Intelligence and the other Spirit, because all arts emerge in due course from spirit and insight. This was done without brush painted with the left hand.
>
> In these aforementioned pieces the figures are life-sized, and in paint, that is in colour. Between them are two pieces in copper coloured grisaille: that which stands on the right hand side of Time is a representation of Pictura painting with hand and foot; the other, on the left hand side, is laughing Patience seated upon an anvil, under attack from Falsehood who shoots three arrows simultaneously, that is: envy, gossip and slander. Envy spitefully pulls her backwards by the braids of her hair; vicious Hate sets a dog on her to devour her; Mortal Violence, a man with a skull, from whose eyes shoot flames of fire, represents the great plague in Amsterdam in the year 1602, the year in which this was made. These grisly monsters seem to want to destroy Patience which she endures with laughter, holding a little lamb in her arm and a cross in her hand, her face turned towards heaven as if to her Maker.[59]

The façade seems to have been intended to show off the powers of Ketel to paint without relying on his right hand, and on occasion without using brushes. Although the façade does not survive we can get some idea of it through his other works. For example, he had painted the theme of Democritus and Heraclitus several times and had also drawn a version of the allegory of Patience.[60]

To a significant extent Ketel drew on philosophical and literary references, not artistic ones, in rebutting his critics. For example, his employment of the theme of the ancient Greek philosophers Heraclitus and Democritus on either side of a globe had prestigious scholarly precedent in the form of the decoration selected by Marsilio Ficino for his villa, inscribed 'shun excess, shun business, rejoice in the present'.[61] Representations of the two philosophers had been produced in the Netherlands, from Sebastian Brant's *Navis stultifera* of 1497 onwards; while Heraclitus had wept at everything, Democritus had laughed at everything. Ficino had stressed the wisdom of detachment, but other moralists pointed to the need for endurance rather than extreme responses, or advised that responses should be appropriate to an event.[62] As a poet, Ketel could have been aware of the references to Momus and Zoilus in mid-sixteenth-century French and English poetry to stand for unreasonable criticism (see Chapter 6).

The theme which Ketel had selected for his centrepiece was that of the power of Time, with reference to an engraving designed by Federico Zuccari.[63] In the engraving Benevolent Time protects Truth from Envy, who pulls her back by the hair. Time is wreathed with flowers and grain, and accompanied by a winged *putto* holding an hourglass, and a bat-winged figure carrying a scythe. Ketel's representation of 'intelligence' and 'spirit' tied into new imagery initiated on the decoration of Michelangelo's catafalque in 1564 and published through Vasari's account in the *Lives* (see Chapter 5). Ketel's Patience referred to older traditions of depicting Christian moral values. An idea of some of its components can be gauged with reference to Johannes Sadeler's engraving after Ketel, which showed Patience standing on an anvil, turning her face up to heaven, with a lamb at her feet, being attacked by Falsehood, shooting three arrows.[64]

At first sight, Ketel's complex allegories may seem eccentric. Nevertheless, the scheme drew on themes which earlier artists had used for their houses. There were the references to time revealing the artist's worth, and to defence against calumny, envy and unjust criticism. Finally, the allegories showed learning and ingenuity to express the artist's personal views.

Peter Paul Rubens, Antwerp, 1618

With something of the splendour achieved otherwise only by Vasari, by Leoni and by Federico Zuccari, Rubens returned from Italy to Antwerp, and completed his house in 1618. Following tradition he celebrated ancient artists, demonstrated virtuoso skills, showed off his erudition, displayed the latest architectural trends, featured Mercury and Minerva as protectors, and Hercules as exemplar, and, arguably, alluded to the way of virtue.

In 1618, Peter Paul Rubens decorated *his* studio, in the centre of Antwerp on de Wapper, with a programme of paintings celebrating the achievements of ancient Greek artists in the tradition initiated by Vasari. Rubens had travelled widely in Italy (in Mantua, for example, acquiring a copy of the relief from Guilio Romano's house) and was able to create a dwelling of grandeur and exquisite classicising taste. The living quarters were placed to the left, as one entered from the street, and the large studio was on the right. The building was grander than the house of any previous Netherlandish artist, and Rubens' claims to scholarly distinction were considerable. Indeed, Otto Sparling found Rubens seated in this studio in 1621, painting, whilst reading Tacitus, and dictating a letter. Rubens' studio was extensively re-shaped in the late eighteenth century, and the twentieth-century reconstruction was based on the existence of engravings by Jacob Harrewijn of its condition in 1684 (Plate 79). The house was modelled after the designs of Giovanni Alessi for palaces in Genoa, and included a museum for his collection of ancient art.

Elizabeth McGrath has deduced the subjects of many of the scenes originally placed on the frieze, above the large studio windows. She has pointed out that they are described as having been painted, not carved. (The twentieth-century reconstruction of the studio at present provides sculpted reliefs in this frieze area.)[65] Some of these painted scenes refer to Pliny the Elder's accounts. Reading left to right, McGrath identified Rubens' scenes of the famous painting made by Timanthes showing the sacrifice of Iphigenia, of the portrait of Alexander which Apelles had made showing him as if he were a God with a thunderbolt in his hand, of the Calumny of Apelles, and of the painting of Juno by Zeuxis. Rubens also seems to have invented a *Drunken Hercules*, a *Chariot Race* and *The Sacrifice of an Ox*, perhaps to suggest the repertoire of ancient painting. Beside the door to his studio Rubens placed a giant *trompe l'oeil* mural, a *tour de force* described by Filippo Baldinucci in 1681. According to him, Rubens had created the illusion that one of his own large canvasses was hanging in front of the frieze, to dry in the sun. Below this canvas, representing Perseus and Andromeda, he gave the impression of a balcony and a loggia, beyond which one sees a palatial interior. Rubens demonstrated his scholarly knowledge of the history of ancient art and he also showed that he could rival ancient painters like Parrhasius, whose illusionistic feats in *trompe l'oeil* were well known.

Rubens placed a bust of Seneca over the door to his studio, thereby advertising his adherence to the values of Stoic philosophy. He quoted from the Latin poet Juvenal on the portico – the only part of the house which was relatively untouched by the re-building. Over this portico, as Harrewijn recorded, Rubens placed statues of Mercury and Minerva, which the visitor now sees in modern copies. In placing Mercury to the left and Minerva to the right of the doorway, there was perhaps an echo of the house of van Dalem close by. Latin inscriptions were put over the side arches which were adorned with busts of a satyr and a satyress. They quoted passages from Juvenal's *Tenth Satire*. On the left was 'Leave the Gods themselves to decide what is appropriate and useful for us. Man is dearer to them than he is to himself'. On the right it continued 'Ask only for a sound mind in a healthy body, a brave spirit, fearless of death and ignorant of anger or incontrollable desire'.[66] It may be relevant that this *Satire* goes on to offer advice on what readers should ask for in their prayers, and suggests emulating Hercules: 'Esteem the Labours of Hercules. I point to nothing but what you yourself may give yourself. The only road to Peace lies through virtue.[67] The main arch framed a distant view of a statue of Hercules in the garden, which was sheltered by a pavilion originally accompanied by statues of Bacchus, Ceres and Abundance. The idea could be a variation on the traditional references to the 'way of virtue'.

Conclusion

During the period from about 1536 to 1618, evidence survives of twenty-two houses with programmes of decoration addressing matters concerning artists. Six of the artists who adorned their houses were painters, and four were architects, while two were sculptors and six were artists practising as painters and architects. These houses asserted professional concerns and exhibited comfortable or sometimes elevated social position. They drew on all the iconographies of art which were being invented during the period. Eight houses made reference to the Liberal status of the visual arts and architecture. Two houses explored the nature of *disegno*. One decoration focused on an artist's patron saints, while four referred to the protection of Mercury. Eleven houses showed the pursuit, or the defence, of virtue. Four houses displayed portraits of modern artists. Finally four (or possibly five, counting the house of Frans Floris) celebrated the artists of ancient Greece. Only six of these twenty-two houses were made by artists who wrote on artistic matters (Vasari, Bertano, Federico Zuccari and Ketel). The large majority therefore represent unique insights into the views of artists concerning their professions. While artists certainly needed to consider what was acceptable to their random or invited audiences on these exteriors and interiors, they were still able to do what they wished to an unusual degree.

Notes

1 Von Schlosser, *La letteratura artistica*, p. 248; Paul Kirn, 'Friedrich der Weise und Jacopo de'Barbari, '*Jahrbuch der preussischen Kunstsammlungen*', XLVI, 1925, pp. 130–4.

2 Gaetano Milanesi, *Documenti per la storia dell'arte senese*, 3 vols, reprint of 1854–56 edition, Holland, 1969, III, p. 33.
3 Van Mander, *Lives*, II, pp. 272–3.
4 Marie Kraitrová, 'La casa di Andrea Mantegna a Mantova e quella di Piero della Francesca a Borgo San Sepolcro', pp. 43–5 in Eduard Hüttinger, ed., *Case d'artista: dal Rinascimento ad oggi.* Turin, 1992.
5 Ames-Lewis, *Intellectual Life of the Renaissance Artist*, p. 70.
6 Franco and Stefano Borsi, *Bramante*, Milan, 1989, pp. 322–3.
7 John Shearman, *Andrea del Sarto*, 2 vols. Oxford, 1965, I, p. 5.
8 Kraitrová, 'La casa di Andrea Mantegna, pp. 46–8.
9 Larry Silver, *The Paintings of Quinten Massys*, Oxford, 1984, pp. 4, 27.
10 J. Anderson, 'The Casa Langobarda in Asolo: a sixteenth-century architect's house', *Burlington Magazine*, CXVI, 1974, pp. 296–302: 'Magister Franciscus Graziolus Longobardus et Bartolomeus eius filius arte sculptores professores extruxerunt.'
11 Detlef Heikamp, 'Le case di Federico Zuccari a Firenze', pp. 80–137 in R.P. Ciardi, ed., *Case di artisti in Toscana.* Florence, 1998, p. 137.
12 Vasari, *Le opere di Giorgio Vasari*, VII, p. 73
13 King, 'Late sixteenth-century careers' advice', pp. 77–96, 193–8.
14 For this and all that follows see *Giulio Romano*, ed. Manfredo Tafuri, trans. Fabio Barry, Cambridge, 1998, pp. 150–4, 202–8.
15 Vasari, *Le opere di Giorgio Vasari*, V, p. 549.
16 *Lucian*, I, pp. 63–71.
17 Vasari, *Le opere di Giorgio Vasari*, VII, pp. 667–8; Vasari, *Lives*, X, p. 185; for all that follows see Cecchi, 'Le case di Giorgio Vasari', pp. 30–56.
18 Vasari, *Le opere di Giorgio Vasari*, p. 671; Vasari, *Lives*, X, p. 188.
19 Vasari, *Le opere di Giorgio Vasari*, VII, p. 671.
20 Vasari, *Le opere di Giorgio Vasari*, VII, pp. 685–6; Vasari, *Lives*, X, p. 200.
21 Vasari, *Lives*, X, p. 200.
22 Vasari, *Le opere di Giorgio Vasari*, VII, pp. 686; Vasari, *Lives*, X, p. 200.
23 Cecchi, 'Le case di Giorgio Vasari', pp. 54–5. Alessandro Cecchi noted in addition the presence in inventories of a room on the floor above this one of a decoration consisting of the twelve signs of the Zodiac on canvases one *braccia* square in a wooden ceiling presumably dispersed at the sale of the house in 1678.
24 D. Metzler, 'Renaissance Bildnisse antiker Architekten am Haus eines Stadtbaumeisters in Sélestat', *Antike und Abendland*, XIX, 1973, pp. 146–62; Hans Peter Schwarz, *Das Künstlerhaus Anmerkungen zur Sozialgeschichte des Genies*, Braunschweig, 1990, pp. 150–60.
25 Coldstream, *Medieval Craftsmen*, p. 10.
26 Paolo Carpeggiani, *Il libro di pietra: G.B. Bertani architetto del Cinquecento*, Milan, 1992, pp. 70–3, Plates 20–3.
27 Catherine King, 'An etching and Lelio Orsi's house', *Print Quarterly*, XXIII, June 2006, pp. 176–82.
28 *Lelio Orsi 1511–1587: Dipinti e disegni*, Reggio Emilia, 1987, pp. 210–11.
29 Maria Rita Bentini, 'Il progetto decorativo per la casa dell'artista', pp. 123–38, and Gaetano Gaddi, 'La casa di Lelio Orsi', pp. 275–9 in Jadranka Bentini, ed., *Lelio Orsi e la cultura del suo tempo.* Reggio Emilia, 1988.
30 King, 'Artists' Houses', pp. 173–82.

31 Massari, *Giulio Bonasone*, II, p. 124: 'Sic monstra domantur' and 'Me duce perficies tumodo progredere'.
32 King, 'Artists' Houses', pp. 178–9.
33 King, 'Artists' Houses', pp. 182–9.
34 Jochen Becker, 'Zur niederländischen Kunstliteratur des 16. Jahrhunderts: Lucas de Heere', *Simiolus*, 6 (1972–73), p. 126, n. 86.
35 Lampsonius, *Lamberti Lombardi*, p. 37: 'ut eius [that of Lombard] exemplo tanquam illustri pictura ante oculos posito adolescentes iisdem artibus deditos non solum ab absolutissimam earum scientiam omnibus ingenii viribus consectandam inflammarem, sed etiam in verissima illam persuasionem adducerem ut statuant se ad hanc tanta laudem adspirare non posse, nisi ex Pamphili illius, qui optimi pictoris magister fuit, Leonis Baptistae Alberti Florentini, Alberti Dureri, et Pomponii Gaurici praeceptis litterarum studia cum his artibus coniunxerint.'
36 Pliny the Elder, *Chapters on the History of Art*, p. 119.
37 Mezzatesta, *Imperial Themes*, pp. 172–80.
38 Bruce Boucher, 'Leone Leoni and Primaticcio's moulds of antique sculpture', *Burlington Magazine*, CXXIII, 1981, pp. 23–6.
39 Marco Rossi 'La casa di Leone Leoni a Milano', pp. 21–30 in Maria Luisa Gatti Perer, ed., *Leone Leoni tra Lombardia e Spagna: atti del Convegno Internazionale 1993*. Milan, 1995.
40 Cecchi, 'Le case di Giorgio Vasari', pp. 56–77.
41 Luisa Marcucci, *Francesco da Volterra: Un protagonista dell'architectura post tridentina*, Rome, 1991; Paolo Bellini, ed., *L'opera incisa di Adamo e Diana Scultori*, Vicenza, 1991.
42 King, 'Late sixteenth-century careers' advice', p. 83.
43 King, 'Late sixteenth-century careers' advice', pp. 83–4.
44 Hollstein, *The New Hollstein* ed. Kok, II, pp. 189–9: 'Quod petit Alcides [another term for Hercules], Scipio quodq[ue] petit' ('What Hercules sought, so too did Scipio').
45 Detlef Heikamp, 'Le case di Federico Zuccari a Firenze', pp. 80–137 in R.P. Ciardi, ed., *Case di artisti in Toscana*. Florence, 1998.
46 Heikamp, 'Le case di Federico Zuccari a Firenze', p. 93: 'corona di rose, di spighe, di frutti, et di tronchi secchi, come Re delle quattro stagioni. Farenlo a sedere, se ben si posa in terra fra noi sopra il zodiaco . . . uno ne terrà un putto secco come la notomia, un ombra quasi da una parte, per il Tempo passato che struggendo si vado e risolvendo in nulla: et dall'altro putto bello grassotto ne havrà altro, che vorrà dinotare l'avvenire. A piedi sarà un librone grande dove due putti scriveranno sopravi, significato uno per giorno con un Sole in testa, et l'altra che sarà femina in capo la Luna per la notte. Così il Tempo trionfa i nomi e'l mondo.'
47 Bonita Cleri, ed., *Per Taddeo e Federico nelle Marche*, Sant'Angelo in Vado, 1993, p. 118.
48 DaCosta Kaufmann, *The School of Prague*, pp. 219, 260–1.
49 Van Mander, *Lives*, I, pp. 349–50.
50 Van Mander, *Lives*, V, pp. 105–6, Fig. 57, Leipzig Museum der Bildenden Künste, Rensi Collection.
51 W. Kuyper, *The Triumphant Entry of Renaissance Architecture into the Netherlands*, 2 vols. Leyden, 1994, I, pp. 255–6; II, Figs 448–51.

52 Acidini-Luchinat, *Taddeo e Federico Zuccari*, II, pp. 199–220; Hermann Fiore, 'Die Fresken Federico Zuccaris', pp. 37–112 ; King, 'Late sixteenth-century careers' advice', pp. 85–6.
53 Acidini-Luchinat, *Taddeo e Federico Zuccari*, II, p. 199: 's'è imbarcato in un suo capriccio poetico, il quale sara facilmente la rovina de suoi figlioli.'
54 *Per Taddeo e Federico nelle Marche*, ed. Cleri, p. 118.
55 Hermann Fiore, 'Die Fresken Federico Zuccaris', p. 59.
56 Hermann Fiore, 'Die Fresken Federico Zuccaris', p. 48.
57 Hermann Fiore, 'Die Fresken Federico Zuccaris', p. 91: 'In omnibus viis tuis angelus domini custodiat te.'
58 Van Mander, *Lives*, V, pp. 116–60.
59 Van Mander, *Lives*, I, p. 373.
60 For Ketel's *Weeping Heraclitus*, see *Dawn of the Golden Age*, pp. 70–1, Fig. 111.
61 Arnaldo della Torre, *Storia dell Accademia Platonica*. Florence, 1902, pp. 539–40: 'fuge excessum, fuge negotia, laetus in praesens'.
62 Veldman, *Marten van Heemskerck*, pp. 76–9. Heemskerck published an engraving of the two philosophers in 1557 as an 'Allegory of the Vanity of human Passions'.
63 F.W.H. Hollstein, *Hollstein's Dutch and Flemish Etchings, Engravings and Woodcuts, c.1450–1700, XXXII*, ed. Dieuwke De Hoop Scheffer, Rosendaal, 1988, p. 9, no. 2.
64 Johannes Sadeler I, engraving after Ketel (identified as Hope because of the anchor at her feet): see F.W.H. Hollstein, *Dutch and Flemish Engravings, Etchings and Woodcuts, c.1450–1700, XXI–XXII*, ed. K.G. Boon, compiled by Dieuwke De Hoop Scheffer, Amsterdam, 1980, XXI, p. 162, no. 487; XXII, p. 147, no. 487. Patience stands on a triangular anvil looking up to heaven with the lamb at her feet. Falsehood shoots three arrows from the left.
65 Elizabeth McGrath, 'The Painted Decoration of Rubens's House', *Journal of the Warburg and Courtauld Institutes*, XLI, 1978, pp. 245–77.
66 G.G. Ramsay, ed., *Juvenal and Persius*, London 1918, pp. 219–21: 'permittes ipsis expendere numinibus quid/conueniat nobis rebusque sit utile nostris;/nam pro iucundis aptissima quaeque dabunt di./carior est illis homo quam sibi', lines 347–50; 'orandum est ut sit mens sana in corpore sano./fortem posce animum mortis terrore carentem,/qui spatium uitae extremum inter munera ponat/naturae, qui ferre queat quoscumque labores,/nesciat irasci', lines 356–60.
67 Ramsay, *Juvenal and Persius*, pp. 219–21: 'Herculis aerumnas credit saevosque labores/ . . . monstro quod ipse tibi possis dare; semita certe/ tranquillae per virtutem patet unica vitae', lines 361–4.

Conclusion

Most of the visual traditions invented and maintained during the sixteenth century could be interpreted as proposing some improvement in the position of visual art in the hierarchy of the arts. Images implied, in a great variety of ways, that art required innate personal talent, intellect and imagination, and could therefore be regarded as equal to noble arts such as astronomy, rhetoric, mathematics and logic. Like these Liberal Arts, it was argued, the figurative arts and architecture therefore merited written histories and written theories. Since the Liberal Arts were associated with noble status and education in Latin and Greek, the claims made for the worth of the figurative arts and architecture were bound up with expectations, however unrealised, of higher education and social rank for artists. Whether or not this related to the realities of many artists' lives, these visual images publicised new ambitions for the intellectual and social position of their authors. Furthermore, when artists produced erudite designs they were offering substantive proof of access to learning, and when they decorated their own houses they were actually displaying considerable social status.

The imagery which represented painting, sculpture and architecture in the company of Liberal Arts overtly supported the idea that art was a theoretical and imaginative skill comparable with music and poetry, and employing geometry and arithmetic. The cerebral nature of art was perhaps even more evident in the iconographies produced for *disegno*, since the emphasis was on the ability to discern terrestrial forms of celestial beauties, whether in buildings or figures. The association with Liberal Arts held social expectations, however unmet, concerning educational levels, while the philosophical debates concerning *disegno* implied that those who sought the goal of beauty in the microcosm were likely to be special sorts of people.

Most of the new sorts of commemorative portraiture produced during the sixteenth century proclaimed that artists were worthy of a visual history, and drew attention to the importance of their unique personal talents: that is to say, the inborn quality or *ingenium* which had been regarded as qualifying the most eminent men – such as saints, philosophers, poets, statesmen and generals – to be celebrated for posterity. These visual representations could be regarded as the counterparts to the literary texts which claimed that art was a theoretical enterprise and merited historical accounts. The portrayal of the artists of the ancient world offered prestigious models for modern artists, since ancient artists were considered to be of superlative worth and, erroneously, thought to have enjoyed lofty status. It also allowed comparisons of considerable cultural grandeur to be drawn between the standards of the past and the present.

Nevertheless, other representations of art and architecture, which presented them as Practical Arts, continued to reiterate their lowly manual status, and the celebration of artists' historical importance did include the commemoration of artistic invention alongside innovations in other craft skills. Even commemorative portraiture which did draw attention to personal talent or intellectual attainment often chose to obey social decorum, with respect to the portrait modes favoured by wealthy patrons – by means, for instance, of taking a smaller size, a cheaper medium, or a head or head-and-shoulders format. In addition, the genre of portraits praising great patrons underlined the dependent positions of artists.

The representation of saints as the devout exemplars of artists presented members of the profession as worthy of respect for their piety throughout the period. Changes in the way they were represented also drew attention to their professional attainments. The trend, evident from the second decade of the sixteenth century onwards, to display them in dress or setting as Imperial Roman masters could add to their prestige. The depiction of Saint Luke as artist, scholar and doctor, from the 1520s onwards, and of the interpretation of the Crowned Martyrs, which showed them handling tools of measurement and calculation more than hammers, might be seen as relating to debates about the liberal skills of artists. Nevertheless, some representations of the Crowned Martyrs went on emphasising their proficiency across the full range of tasks that were undertaken by guild members, including the heavy work.

Astrological representations of artists were highly flexible, since they could be interpreted as promoting ideas either of the more liberal or the more mechanical nature of art. Illustrations of the Children of Mercury showed painters and sculptors in the company of those practising the Liberal Arts of astronomy, mathematics and geometry. Adjacent textual commentaries could describe them as eloquent people, possessing *ingenium*, intelligence and sagacity. Such illustrations placed sculpture and painting together as having common figurative skills (which the academies favoured) rather than separating them according to their media, in the manner laid down by many guilds. The Children of Mercury included physicians, and this could be compared with the depictions of Luke as doctor, and potentially related to discussion of the kinds of learning shared by medicine and art. However, astrological representations could also show artists in the company of armourers and swordsmiths, and normally placed them in the marketplace, if not at work in their shops.

The new ambitions of artists to be treated as members of elevated professions were, however, unambiguously served by showing them as being protected by the mythological god of the Liberal Art of rhetoric, Mercury, and as watched over by his sister Minerva, goddess of wisdom, in the manner associated with scholarly and philosophical academies. Arguably, the existence of the astrological tradition licensed this appropriation of mythological protectors, previously exclusive to the praise of great men in government and learning. Mercury in this visual discourse was described directly as signifying *ingegno* (at Michelangelo's funeral) or labelled precisely as symbolising *intelligenzia* (by Federico Zuccari in his pictorial history of his brother). As mythological helper, Mercury was shown as assisting artists to success, through vanquishing ignorance and enjoining study. He also appeared in some images overtly calling for better treatment of artists, by pointing to the actual poverty, and want of proper art education in the workshop system, being endured by some contemporaries.

The employment of the mythological Mercury in allegories of personal attainment was linked with the way artists took over visual traditions of struggle and success (the *Calumny of Apelles*, the way of virtue, and the battle of virtue against its enemies) which had been, and were, used, to praise leaders in action or thought. The very act of translating these modes to the lives of artists implied some, if decorous, comparison with these leaders. In the case of the *Calumny*, it entailed following in the footsteps of the best-known ancient painter Apelles. It also tended to involve mythological figures and reference to Greek and Roman literary sources, which proved the learning, or contact with the learned, which the artist had achieved. The theme of the 'way of virtue' had implications for social standing, in the sense that it suggested a heroic struggle to reach high standards, quite outside the notion of craft attainment. In addition, where the message was that the best artists do not regard money as their prime reward, artists were allying themselves with the way scholars were treated at court. Significantly, the allegories combating ignorant critics, and trusting in Time as one's defence, had also been taken over from scholarly traditions.

The use of representations to 'signify great things', to quote Leonardo, was entailed in much of the imagery representing art and artists. Allegorical ways of interpreting narratives had been assumed in the scenes celebrating the life of Saint Luke, most obviously in the presence of the bull. In a different type of signification, men working at their tasks had symbolised different occupations, in the illustrations of the Children of Mercury. From the 1440s onwards, artists had made, or bought, portrait medals – decorated with symbolic objects, personifications, mythological figures and events on their reverses – to signify their views on life and art. From the early sixteenth century, personifications had been produced to represent Painting, Sculpture and Architecture as

Liberal Arts. From the 1550s onwards, personifications, scenes, objects and mythological figures had been used to symbolise the concept of *Disegno*. From the 1540s onwards, artists had adapted from cognate traditions, ways of signifying the attainment of the best standards in art, their protection and their defence, employing personifications and mythological figures. During this period, artists had therefore acquired a wide range of representations of an allegorical sort for their own professional use. Arguably the ones which drew most on ancient literary sources pointed to the scholarship of artists or their aspirations to education.

All the visual themes which dealt with artists or matters of art related in some way to literary discourses. However, artists had differential access to, and ownership of, these textual traditions. It is of considerable interest to note that in one case, that of the iconographies of *disegno*, the majority of the written texts on which the visual traditions rested had been produced by artists themselves. In the written debates about the liberal status of art, as well, artists had played an important role, although texts by scholars were still influential. However, artists were publishing increasing numbers of treatises, which provided evidence that theory was important to art and architecture. In the case of the written histories, which may be seen as the counterparts to commemorative portraiture, artists took a lead with the biography of Condivi, and the large-scale histories of Vasari and of van Mander. In contrast, the other main visual themes drew on literary traditions which belonged to scholars. Representations of artist-saints relied on a body of hagiographical texts by theologians, although the poem prefacing the Ghent guild regulations which told the story of Luke in the vernacular may not have been exceptional. Scholars also dominated the astrological traditions, although many texts were available in the vernacular. In addition, they published the literature that related the legends of the ancient gods, which artists drew on to produce the imagery of Mercury and Minerva as helpers of artists, and of the pursuit and defence of virtue.

What was the geographical and chronological scope of these different iconographies? The figurative arts and architecture continued to be represented during the period, if sporadically, as Practical Arts, largely in the medium of print, in Italian-, French- and German-speaking areas, as well as in the Netherlands. In contrast, the representation of the visual arts and architecture as Liberal Arts was initiated in the Veneto, and remained exclusive to Italy until 1550. In the middle decades of the century, the theme was transposed to France and the Netherlands, appearing in three public locations (the urn of François I, and the two Antwerp houses). Between 1542 and 1576, the new iconography was used in Italy on works acclaiming artists, especially in Florence by members of the new academy, but also in Milan and Venice, and was further confirmed in the decoration of palaces and villas. From the

1570s onwards the Liberal status of these three arts was publicised in a few prints issued in the Netherlands, in Italy and in German-speaking areas, and, finally, in the decoration of the Stadthuis in Bruges, but was less established than it had become in Italy. By comparison, the visual discourse related to the concept of *disegno*, was confined to Italy, until the very end of time-span (with the exception of the urn of François I). Italian dominance maybe related to the way Italian writers had produced the body of written texts debating the dignity of art and justifying the term *disegno*. In conjunction with these developments, Italian ruling elites seem to have regarded cultural leadership, which included the re-evaluation of the visual arts and architecture, as an extension of their political powers. The support for the institution of the academies, whose members played key roles in producing the new imagery in the second half of the century, appears to have expressed this politico-cultural strategy on behalf of the papacy and the Medici.

The pattern is different for the production of new genres of commemorative portraiture, since the lead was taken from the beginning of the period, by German-speaking artists making prints. Their example was followed in the 1540s by Italian printmakers. The use of portraits of artists in civic contexts was initiated in 1549 in Antwerp, and followed in 1565 in Florence. Portraits of artists were included in galleries, printed and actual, of great men, from the time of the collection of Giovio, and his collection achieved publication in Basel in 1589. Portraits were used to preface a biography first in Rome in 1553, and this precedent was next followed in Bruges in 1565. Vasari printed the earliest series of portraits of Italian artists in 1568, and Lampsonius produced the earliest Netherlandish sequence designed by Cock in Antwerp in 1572. The inclusion of portraits in pictorial histories of patronage was begun in Rome in 1546, and continued in the Medici cycles painted by Vasari. The portrayal of artists in personal autobiographical gatherings was essayed by Vasari between 1568 and 1573. Between 1564 and 1590 or so, three Italian schemes set out to narrate the biography of an artist pictorially. The representation of ancient artists, in artistic contexts, dated from about 1507 in Italy, and was continued in examples made in Sélestat in 1545, at Arezzo in 1547, in Antwerp in 1549 (possibly in 1563 by Floris), in Florence for Michelangelo's funeral, and in Vasari's house in 1573. Although Italian interest in the production of written histories of art and Italian rulers' interest in cultural investment were probably of some importance, it seems that German-speaking and Netherlandish artists took key initiatives, or quickly followed some Italian ventures. The early production of independent painted and drawn portraits of artists, in German-speaking and Netherlandish areas, and the invention of printing may be salient factors here.

The traditional celebration of artists' patron-saints continued throughout Christendom until the 1520s, when the spread of

Protestantism meant that only those areas which adhered to Roman observances continued to produce such images. It referred to ecclesiastical teaching, and pious practice, concerning the use of devotional images in worship. The traditional illustration of artists as Children of Mercury was, however, current in Italy only at the beginning of the period and otherwise confined to French- and German-speaking areas and the Netherlands. These popular images related to widespread beliefs in the influence of the stars, to medicinal practices, and to vernacular texts on astrology.

The innovating representation of Mercury as the mythological helper of artists was initiated in Italy in 1542, then taken up in designs made in Italy between 1562 and the 1590s, in the Netherlands between 1563 and 1618, and, at the end of the period, in Prague. The representation of the pursuit of virtue and its defence with respect to artists was begun in Italy, and (with the exception of the house of Floris in Antwerp and the role of Cort in engraving Zuccari's *Calumny*), it was explored by Italian artists until the 1590s. In the late sixteenth century Spranger transposed the theme to Prague, and the Amsterdam painter Ketel made a drawing (now lost) relating to the *via virtutis* theme. The other related themes, of the rebuttal of unjust criticism and the reliance on Time revealing Truth, were also Italian initiatives, in which Ketel showed an interest (1602). The dominance of Italian artists here and in other fields may be related to Italian leadership in the literature of art, and the more widespread acceptance and encouragement of new attitudes, by Italian viewers and buyers, who increasingly regarded the ability to discuss artistic issues (on the model of *The Courtier*) as a proof of their own social status.

Printed images were of considerable importance in spreading ideas about the nature of art. Print was employed to represent the three arts as Practical Arts, and, in the series of the Children of the Planets, displayed the ambiguous status of artists between scholars and craftsmen. Printed single-leaf portraits in German- and Italian-speaking areas praised the attainment of artists during the first half of the century, with special reference to Dürer and Michelangelo. Printed portraits decorated a succession of histories of art from 1553 to 1572 in Italy and the Netherlands, and prints of the *Calumny* and the *Lament* by Federico Zuccari and Cornelis Cort were issued from 1572 onwards. The house front of Frans Floris was engraved in 1576, and Zuccari's *Lament* was emulated in Nuremberg in 1587. Engraved tributes to van der Straet, van Aachen and Goltzius followed (1583–1620). Hondius provided an elaborate frontispiece to his edition of Cock's portraits in 1610, and Spranger's advice to his son was printed in 1628. The imagery for the guilds and confraternities was not part of print culture, though representations of Saint Luke as artist were published for public consumption. Many prints, such as the *Calumny* or the portraits in Vasari's *Lives*, contained references to more than one of the discourses dealing with matters of art.

Whether ideas travelled in prints or through people travelling (as artists were increasingly doing from the north to the south, and as some had continued to do in search of work from south to north), those concepts and forms were always being adapted to new artistic and cultural contexts. Traditions and expectations were distinct in each city and region, and the range of interpretations which various kinds of spectators brought to viewing, say, the representation of an ancient Greek artist in Sélestat or in Arezzo in the 1540s was likely to differ considerably, and then to change during the period. Artists took over motifs and ideas selectively, and might well add new forms and concepts to what they had appropriated from another artist and another set of traditions. The transformations which occur in translation are most obvious when Netherlandish-, French- or German-speaking artists drew on some tradition originating in Italy, as for instance when the Haarlem engraver Matham represented *Disegno* in tribute to his stepfather Goltzius. Yet within Italy, too, the frames of reference could be diverse, and the interpretations of that same personification of *Disegno* would differ depending on whether, for example, it was being viewed in Venice or in Florence.

To what extent were these traditions furthered by artists themselves? In some situations artists were working at the behest of powerful patrons, whether in decorating their palaces and villas (in one case a *Stadthuis*), in contributing to temporary schemes for dynastic or civic festivities, or in undertaking a funerary commission. Nevertheless, in an unusually large number of instances, as far as the normal working habits of artists were concerned, the iconographies of art were being produced by artists for themselves or for other artists.

Prints, such as the funerary tributes to van Aachen and Goltzius, could be initiated by artists, though it is important to stress that they were usually geared also to meet some perceived tastes in buyers, as commercial ventures. Illustrations on books about art were likely to require backers as in the case of Cesariano and Vasari, but might otherwise be published by one's own printing house, as in the example of the collection of portraits made by Hieronymous Cock, which were issued by his widow Volcxken. Medals, either commissioned or made by artists for themselves, could be regarded as representing artists' own aspirations, if in succinct form. Some portable paintings and drawings appear to have been made by artists to represent their own views. This seems to have been the case with Leonbruno's *Calumny*, and it was certainly so with the cartoon by Zuccari of the *Porta virtutis*. The decoration of houses by artists provided larger opportunities for exhibiting new ideas with a degree of autonomy. The distinctive programmes selected for display on the houses of artists started, or pursued, aspects of all the iconographical traditions which referred to art. Houses which had particular significance in this respect were those of Giulio Romano,

by this approach are those of Floris and van Dalem (for the production of their house decorations in Antwerp), and that of Spranger (whose drawing of Mercury introducing the artist to Minerva was engraved in 1628). Attention is also to be drawn to Philibert de L'Orme, with respect to the urn commissioned by Henri II, and to the Venetian painters who planned Titian's funeral.

The evidence of the iconographies for representing art and artists in this period suggests that Italian artists tended to dominate in displaying new ambitions, although Netherlandish artists played an increasing role. The data confirms the link one would perhaps anticipate between writing histories or treatises, participating in new institutions, enjoying court patronage and inventing new visual imagery. However, the way that the evidence also includes representations made by many artists, who did not publish nor join academies, nor obtain court preferment, enables one to build up a new picture of the quite high level of participation in debates about the status of art taking place in several different traditions. By the end of the sixteenth century, through a combination of continuity and innovation, to which large numbers of practitioners contributed, there existed the most varied visual repertoire yet available for representing art and artists in Christendom.

Note

1 Warnke, *Hofkünstler*, pp. 168–71.

Bibliography

Abraham ben Ezra, *The Beginning of Wisdom*, ed. and trans. R. Levy and F. Cantera, Baltimore, 1939.

Abu Ma'shar, *Flores Albumazaris*, Augsburg, 1488.

Abu Ma'shar, *Introductorium in astronomiam*, Augsburg, 1489.

Acidini-Luchinat, Cristina, *Taddeo e Federico Zuccari fratelli pittori del Cinquecento*, 2 vols, Milan, 1999.

Acta sanctorum novembris, LXVI, eds J. Bollandus and G. Henschenius 5–8 November, Brussels, 1910.

Alberti, Leandro, *Cronichetta della Gloriosa Madonna di San Luca del Monte della Guardia di Bologna e de'suoi miracoli*, Venice, 1579.

Alberti, Leon Battista, *L'architettura, De re aedificatoria*, ed. and trans. Giovanni Orlandi, 2 vols, Milan, 1966.

Alberti, Leon Battista, *Della pittura*, ed. Luigi Mallè, Florence, 1950.

Alberti, Leon Battista, *L'architettura: De re aedificatoria*, ed. and trans. Giovanni Orlandi, Milan, 1966.

Alberti, Leon Battista, *On Painting, Della pittura*, ed. and trans. John R. Spencer, New Haven, CT, 1966.

Alberti, Romano, *Accademia del Dissegno de' Pittori, Scultori e Architetti di Roma*, Pavia, 1604.

Albricus, *Allegoriae poeticae*, Paris, 1520, facsimile ed. Stefan Orgel, New York, 1976.

Ames-Lewis, Francis, *The Intellectual Life of the Early Renaissance Artist*, New Haven, CT, 2000.

Anderson, J., 'The Casa Langobarda in Asolo: a sixteenth-century architect's house', *Burlington Magazine*, CXVI, 1974, pp. 296–302.

Andreas of Crete, 'De sanctarum imaginum veneratione' in *Patrologiae graecae*, 97, ed. J.P. Migne, Paris, 1865, cols 1303–10.

Andrews, Keith, *The Paintings, Drawings and Prints of Adam Elsheimer*, London, 1977.

Anzelewsky, F., *Albrecht Dürer: das malerische Werk*, Berlin, 1971.

Apollodorus of Athens, *Bibliotheces*, Antwerp, 1565.

Aquinas, Saint Thomas, *Summa theologicae*, ed. J.F.B.M. de Rubeis and C.R. Billuart, Turin, 1922.

Aquinas, Saint Thomas, *Summa theologiae*, ed. P. Faucher, 4 vols, Rome, 1948.

Armstrong, Lilian, 'The illustration of Pliny's *Historia naturalis*: manuscripts before 1430', *Journal of the Warburg and Courtauld Institutes*, XLVI, 1983, pp. 19–39.

Attwood, Philip, *Italian Medals c.1530–1600 in British Public Collections*, 2 vols, London, 2003.

Aureli, A. Bessone, *I marmorari romani*, Rome, 1935.

Baglione, Giovanni, *Le vite dei pittori, scultori, architetti*, Rome, 1649.

Baldini, Umberto, *The Complete Sculptures of Michelangelo*, London, 1982.

Barocchi, Paola, *Mostra di disegni del Vasari e della sua cerchia*, Florence, 1964.

Barocchi, Paola, *Scritti d'arte del Cinquecento*, 3 vols, Milan and Naples, 1971–77.

Baroni Vannucci, Alessandra, ed. *Jan van der Straet detto Stradano*, Milan, 1997.

Baronius, C., *Annales ecclesiastici*, 12 vols, Antwerp, 1610.

Barozzo, Francesco, *Procli diadochi lycii philosophi platonici ac mathematici probatissimi in primum Euclidis elementorum librum commentariorum*, Padua, 1560.

Barthélémy, de Chasseneux, *Catalogus gloriae mundi*, Lyons, 1546.

Barthélémy de Chasseneux, *Catalogus gloriae mundi*, Venice, 1571.

Bartrum, Giulia and Leesberg, Marjolein, eds, *The New Hollstein: German Engravings, Etchings and Woodcuts1400–1700, Jost Amman 1539–91*, compiled by Gero Seelig, 11 vols, Rotterdam, 2001–03.

Bartrum, Giulia, *Albrecht Dürer and his Legacy: The Graphic Work of a Renaissance Artist*, London, 2002.

Bartsch, Adam, *The Illustrated Bartsch IV: Netherlandish Artists: Matham, Saenredam, Muller*, ed. Walter L. Strauss, New York, 1980.

Bartsch, Adam, *The Illustrated Bartsch XIII: German Masters of the Sixteenth Century, Erhard Schoen and Niklaus Stier*, ed. W.L. Strauss, New York, 1984.

Bartsch, Adam, *The Illustrated Bartsch XVI: Early German Masters, Jacob Bink, Geog Pencz and Heinrich Aldegrever*, ed. Robert A. Koch, New York, 1980.

Bartsch, Adam, *The Illustrated Bartsch, XVIII: German Masters of the Sixteenth Century*, ed. Jane S. Peters, New York, 1982.

Bartsch, Adam, *The Illustrated Bartsch, XXVII: The Works of Marcantonio Raimondi and his School*, ed. K. Oberhuber, New York, 1978.

Baxandall, Michael D.K., *Painting and Social Experience in Fifteenth-century Italy*, Oxford, 1971.

Becherucci, Luisa and Brunetti, Giulia, *Il Museo dell' Opera del Duomo a Firenze*, 2 vols, Milan, 1969–71.

Becker, Jochen, 'Zur niederländischen Kunstliteratur des 16. Jahrhunderts: Lucas de Heere', *Simiolus*, 6 (1972–73), pp. 118–30.

Bellini, Paolo, ed., *L'opera incisa di Adamo e Diana Scultori*, Vicenza, 1991.

Bentini, Maria Rita, 'Il progetto decorativo per la casa dell'artista' pp. 123–38 in Jadranka Bentini, ed., *Lelio Orsi e la cultura del suo tempo*, Reggio Emilia, 1988.

Bergamo, Jacopo da, *Supplemento delle chroniche del Reverendo Padre Frate Jacopo Philippo da Bergamo*, Venice, 1539.

Bialstocki, Jan, *Dürer and his Critics: 1500–1971*, Baden-Baden, 1986.

Bibliotheca sanctorum, 10 vols, Rome.

Biscaro, G., 'La scuola dei Quattro Martiri Coronati presso il duomo di Milano', *Archivio storico lombardo*, XX, 1913, pp. 214–27.

Blunt, Anthony, *Philibert de l'Orme*, London, 1958.

Bober, Phyllis Pray and Ruth Rubenstein, *Renaissance Artists and Antique Sculpture*, Oxford, 1986.

Boccaccio, Giovanni, *Von etlichen Frowen*, Ulm, 1473.

Boccaccio, Giovanni, *Genealogiae dei dei*, Venice, 1494.

Bock, E., *Die Zeichnungen älter Meister im Kupferstichkabinett Staatliche Museen in Berlin, Die deutschen Meister*, Berlin, 1921.

Bombe, W., *Urkunden zur Geschichte der Peruginer Malerei*, Leipzig, 1929.

Boon, Karel G., *The Netherlandish and German drawings of the XVth and XVIth centuries of the Frits Lugt Collection*, 3 vols , Paris, 1992.

Borsi, Franco and Stefano, *Bramante*, Milan, 1989.

Borsi, Franco and Stefano, *Paolo Uccello*, Milan, 1992.

Bottari, Giovanni and Ticozzi, Stefano, *Raccolta di lettere sulla pittura, scultura, ed architettura*, 8 vols, Milan, 1822.

Boucher, Bruce, 'Leone Leoni and Primaticcio's moulds of antique sculpture', *Burlington Magazine*, CXXIII, 1981, pp. 23–6.

Braund, Susanna Morton, ed. and trans., *Juvenal and Persius*, Cambridge, MA, 2004.

Bresc-Bautier, Geneviéve, *Primatice, Maître de Fontainebleau*, Paris, 2005.

Brivio, Ernesto, *Le vetrate del Duomo*, Milan, 1998.

Buchner, E., Die Werke Friedrich Herlin', *Münchner Jahrbuch der bildenden Kunst*, XIII, 1923, pp. 1–51.

Byam Shaw, J., *Drawings by Old Masters at Christchurch Oxford*, Oxford, 1976.

Calamandrei, Piero, *Scritti e inediti celliniani*, Florence, 1971.

Calendar mit Underrichtung astronomischer Wirckungen für Artznei und Medicin, Frankfurt am Main, 1543.

Cantaro, Maria Teresa, *Lavinia Fontana Bolognese 1552–1614*, Milan, 1989.

Capella, Martianus, *Martianus Capella and the Seven Liberal Arts*, trans. W.H. Stahl, R. Johnson, and E.L. Burge, 2 vols, New York, 1977.

Carpeggiani, Paolo, *Il libro di pietra: G.B. Bertani architetto del Cinquecento*, Milan, 1992.

Casier, J. and Bergmans, P., *L'Art ancien dans les Flandres*, Brussels and Paris, 1922.

Cast, David, 'Marten van Heemskeck's Momus criticising the works of the gods: a problem in Erasmian iconography', *Simiolus*, VII, 1974, pp. 22–34.

Cast, David, *The Calumny of Apelles*, New Haven, CT and London, 1981.

Castiglione, Baldassare, *Il libro del cortegiano*, ed. Vittorio Cian, Florence, 1947.

Castiglione, Baldassare, *The Book of the Courtier*, trans. George Bull, Harmondsworth, 1967.

Cecchi, Alessandro and Allegri, Ettore, *Guida storica del Palazzo Vecchio*, Florence, 1980.

Cecchi, Alessandro, *Giorgio Vasari: La Toscana nel '500, principi, letterati, e artisti nelle corte di Giorgio Vasari*, Florence, 1981.

Cecchi, Alessandro, 'Le case di Giorgio Vasari ad Arezzo e Firenze', pp. 30–56, in R.P. Ciardi, ed., *Case di artisti in Toscana*, Florence, 1998.

Cecchini, G., *La Galleria Nazionale dell'Umbria in Perugia*, Rome, 1932.

Cellini, Benvenuto, *Vita di Benvenuto Cellini*, ed. Orazio Bacci, Florence, 1901.

Cellini, Benvenuto, *The Treatises of Benvenuto Cellini on Goldsmithing and Sculpture*, trans. C.R. Ashbee, New York, 1967.

Cellini, Benvenuto, *L'opera completa*, ed. S. Barbaglia, Milan, 1981.

Cennini, Cennino, *The Craftsman's Handbook: The Italian* Il libro dell'arte, trans. D.V. Thompson, New York, 1960.

Cennini, Cennino, *Il libro dell'arte*, ed. Franco Brunello, Vicenza, 1971.

Cesariano, Cesare, *Cesare Cesariano e il classicismo di primo Cinquecento*, ed. Alessandro Rovetta, Milan, 1996.

Chew, Samuel S., *The Pilgrimage of Life*, New Haven, CT, 1962.

Christie's Catalogue (London), Sale on 9 May 1930.

Chroniker der deutschen Städte, xxix, ed. F. Roth, Leipzig, 1906.

Cicero, *Letters to Atticus*, ed. and trans. D.R. Shackleton Bailey, 4 vols, Cambridge, MA, 1999.

Cicero, Marcus Tullius, *Officia*, Augsburg, 1531.

Cicero, Marcus Tullius, *Vonn Gebüre und Billicheit*, Frankfurt am Main, 1550.

Cicero, Marcus Tullius, *Tusculan Disputations*, trans. J.E. King, London, 1927.

Cleri, Bonita, ed., *Per Taddeo e Federico nelle Marche*, Sant'Angelo in Vado, 1993.

Coldstream, Nicola, *Medieval Craftsmen: Masons and Sculptors*, London, 1991.

Coliva, Anna and Schütze, Sebastian, eds, *Bernini scultore: La nascità del Barocco*, Rome, 1998.

Collins, Bradley I., *Leonardo, Psychoanalysis and Art History: Critical Study of Psychobiographical Approaches to Leonardo da Vinci*, Evanston, 1997.

Condivi, Ascanio, *Vita di Michelangelo*, ed. Antonio Maraini, Florence, 1927.

Conti, Natale, *Mythologiae sive explicationis fabularum*, Lyons, 1605.

Cott, P.B., 'The Ellis Collection, continental European paintings', *Worcester Art Museum Annual*, IV, 1941, pp. 7–33.

d'Hulst, R.A., *Jacob Jordaens*, trans. P.S. Falla, London, 1982.

d'Hulst, R.A., De Poorter, Nora, and Vandenven, Marc, eds, *Jacob Jordaens 1593–1678*, Antwerp, 1993.

Damascene, John, 'De sanctis venerandis imaginibus ad Theophilum Imperatorem', in *Patrologiae graecae*, 95, ed. J.P. Migne, Paris, 1864.

Das gross Planetenbuch, Alles auss Platone, Ptolomeo, Hali, Albumaser unnd [sic] *J. Königsberger gezogen*, Strasburg, 1546.

Dawn of the Golden Age: Northern Netherlandish Art 1580–1620, Amsterdam, 1996.

De Holanda, Francisco, *Da pintura antigua*, ed. Joaquim de Vasconcellos, Porto, 1918.

De Holanda, Francisco, *Four Dialogues on Painting*, trans. A.E.G. Bell, London, 1928.

Debergh, Nadine, *Koorgestoelten in West-Vlanderen*, Lannoo, 1982.

Delen, A.J.J., *Musée Royale des Beaux Arts Anvers*, Antwerp, 1948.

Derolez, A., *Inventaris van de Handschriften in de Universiteitsbibliotheek te Ghent*, Ghent, 1977.

Desiderius, Erasmus, *Collected Works*, volume 26, ed. J.K. Sowards, *Literary and Educational Writings*, 4, *De recta pronuntiatione*, Toronto, 1985.

Desiderius, Erasmus, *The Collected Works of Erasmus*, 33, *Adages, II, i, 1 to II, vi 100*, trans. R.A.B. Mynors, Toronto, 1991.

Destombes, C.J., *Histoire de l'église de Cambrai*, 2 vols, Lille, 1890.

Dhanens, Elisabeth, *De Iconografie der Van Eycks*, Bruges, 1982.

Dionigi, R., *SS. Quattuor Coronati: Bibliography and Iconography, An Essay*, Milan, 1998.

Dobschütz, E. Von, *Christusbilder: Untersuchnungen zur christlichen Legende*, Leipzig, 1899.

Dolce, Lodovico, *Aretino: A Dialogue on Painting*, trans. W. Brown, London, 1770.

Du Colombier, P., 'Les Quatre-Couronnées patrons des tailleurs de pierre', *La Revue des arts*, IV, 1952, pp. 216–17.

Durand, Georges, *Monographie de l'église Notre-Dame Cathédrale d'Amiens*, 2 vols, Amiens, 1901–03.

Dürer, Albrecht, *The Writings of Albrecht Dürer*, ed. and trans. W.M. Conway, London, 1958.

Duverger, E., *Antwerpse Kunstinventorissen uit de Zeventiende eeuw*, Brussels, 1984.

Duverger, Josef and M.J. Onghena, 'Beeldhouwer Willem van den Broecke alias Guglielmus Paludanus 1530–1578/9', *Gentsche Bijdragen tot de Geschiedenis*, V, 1938, pp. 75–140.

Ebengreuth, Arnold Luschin von, 'Das Admonter Hüttenbuch und die Regensberger Steinmetz-ordnung vom jahre 1459', *Mitteilungen der Kaiserliche, Königliche Central-Commission zur Erforschung und Erhaltung der Kunst und Historischen Denkmale*, new series, XIX, 1893, pp. 227–41.

Eck, J., *De non tollendis Christi et sanctorum imaginibus contra haeresim Faelicianum*, Ingolstadt, 1522.

Edis-Barzman, Karen, *The Florentine Academy and the Early Modern State: The Discipline of Disegno*, Cambridge, 2000.

Dhanens, Elisabeth, *De Iconografie der Van Eycks*, Bruges, 1982.

Enlart, C., *Rouen*, Paris, 1928.

European Paintings: An Illustrated Summary Catalogue, National Gallery of Art, Washington, 1975.

Evans, Michael, 'Allegorical women and practical men: the iconography of the artes reconsidered', pp. 305–29, in Derek Baker, ed., *Medieval Women*, Oxford, 1978.

Faggin, G.T., 'Nuove opere di Lanceloot Blondeel', *Critica d'Arte*, XV, 1968, pp. 37–54.

Faldi, Italo, 'Contributi a Raffaellino da Reggio', *Bollettino d'arte*, XXXVI, 1951, pp. 324–33.

Falk, T., *Lucas Cranach: Gemälde, Zeichnungen, Druchgraphik*, 2 vols, Basel, 1974.

Fanti, Sigismondo, *Trionpho della fortuna*, Venice, 1527.

Ferguson, W.K., *Renaissance Studies*, Humanities Departments University of Western Ontario, Studies in Humanities 3, London, Ont., 1963.

Filarete, Antonio di Piero Averlino, called Filarete, *Filarete's Treatise on Architecture*, ed. and trans. J.R. Spencer, 2 vols, New Haven, CT and London, 1965.

Filarete, Antonio Averlino, *Trattato di architettura*, ed. Liliana Grassi and Anna Maria Finoli, 2 vols, Milan, 1972.

Fiore, F.P. and Tafuri, M., eds, *Francesco di Giorgio architetto*, Siena, 1993.

Forster, Kurt W. and Tuttle, Richard J., 'The Casa Pippi. Giulio Romano's house in Mantua', *Architectura*, 1973, pp. 114–19.

Francesco di Giorgio Martini, *Trattati di architettura, ingegniera e arte militare*, ed. Corrado Maltese and Livia Maltese Degrassi, Milan, 2 vols, 1967.

Frangi, Francesco and Morandotti, Alessandro, *Il ritratto in Lombardia da Moroni a Ceruti*, Milan, 2002.

Freedberg, D., *Iconoclasm and Painting in the Revolt of the Netherlands, 1566–1609* New York and London, 1988.

Friedländer, M.J., *Early Netherlandish Painting, XII, Jan van Scorel and Pieter Coeck van Aelst*, trans H. Norden, ed. H. Pauwels, G. Lemmers, Monique Gierts, and Anne-Marie Hess, Leiden, 1975.

Friedman, Luba, 'Britto's portrait after Titian's earliest self-portrait', pp. 123–44 in *Autobiographie und Selbstportrait*, 1998.

Gaddi, Gaetano, 'La casa di Lelio Orsi', pp. 275–79 in Jadranka Bentini, ed., *Lelio Orsi e la cultura del suo tempo*, Reggio Emilia, 1988.

Gage, John, 'The *locus classicus* of colour theory: the fortunes of Apelles', *Journal of the Warburg and Courtauld Institutes*, XLIV, 1981, pp. 10–11.

Garrard, Mary D., 'The Liberal Arts and Michelangelo's first project for the tomb of Julius II (with a coda on Raphael's "School of Athens")', *Viator*, XV, 1984, pp. 335–404.

Gaurico, Pomponio, *De sculptura*, Florence, 1504, ed. and trans. André Chastel and Robert Klein, 1969.

Gaurico, Pomponio, *De sculptura*, ed. Paolo Cutolo, Naples, 1999.

Gere, John, Pouncey, P. and Wood, R., *Italian Drawing in the British Museum: Artists Working in Rome c. 1550–1640*, London, 1983.

Germanorum rerum scriptores varii, 3 vols, Frankfurt am Main, 1602.

Gerstenberg, Kurt, *Die Deutschen Baumeisterbildnisse des Mittelalters*, Berlin, 1966.

Ghiberti, Lorenzo, *Ghibertis Denkwürdigkeiten (I commentari)*, ed. Julius von Schlosser, Berlin, 1912.

Giraldi, Lilio Gregorio, *De deis gentium*, Basel, 1548; facsimile, New York, 1976.

Giulio Romano, 1499–1546, ed. Manfredo Tafuri, trans. Fabio Barry, Cambridge, 1998.

Gnoli, U., *Pittore e miniatori nell'Umbria*, Spoleto, 1923.

Goddard, S.G., *The Master of Frankfurt and his Shop*, Brussels, 1984.

Goldberg, Victoria, 'Graces, Muses and Arts: the urns of Henri II and François I', *Journal of the Warburg and Courtauld Institutes*, XXIX, 1966, pp. 206–18.

Goldscheider, Ludwig, *Five Hundred Self-Portraits*, Vienna and London, 1937.

Grandjean, M., *Die Kunstdenkmäler der Schweiz, Monuments d'art et d'histoire de la Suisse: du Canton de Vaud, Ville de Lausanne*, Basel, 1965.

Grosshans, R., *Marten van Heemskerck: die Gemälde*, Berlin, 1980.

Grotemeyer, P., *'Da ich het die gestalt': deutsche Bildnismedaillen des 16 Jahrhunderts*, Munich, 1957.

Guillhermy, R.E.F., *Inscriptions de la France du Ve au XVIIIe siècle*, 5 vols, Paris, 1873–83.

Habich, G., *Die deutschen Medailleure des XVI Jahrhunderts*, Halle a. d. Saale, 1916.

Hauber, Anton, *Planetenkinderbilder und Sternbilder*, Strasburg, 1916.

Heikamp, Detlef, 'Vicende di Federico Zuccari', *Rivista d'arte*, 32, 1957, pp. 175– 232, especially pp. 219–21.

Heikamp, Detlef, 'Federico Zuccari a Firenze 1575–1579, II, Federico a casa sua', *Paragone*, XVIII, 1967, pp. 3–34.

Heikamp, Detlef, 'Le case di Federico Zuccari a Firenze', pp. 80–137 in R.P. Ciardi, ed., *Case di artisti in Toscana*, Florence, 1998.

Henkel, Arthur and Schöne, Albrecht, *Emblemata: Handbuch zur Sinnbildkunst des XVI und XVII Jahrhunderts*, Stuttgart, 1967.

Henne, A. and Wauters, A., *Histoire de la ville de Bruxelles*, 3 vols, Brussels, 1845.

Hermann Fiore, Kristina, 'Der Palazzo Zuccari als Haus eines römischen Patriziers, Künstlers und Akademikers', *Römisches Jahrbuch der Bibliotheca Hertziana*, XVIII, 1979, pp. 35–112.

Hermann Fiore, Kristina, 'Il tema "Labor" nella creazione artistica del Rinascimento', pp. 245–92 in Matthias Winner, ed., *Die Künstler übersich in seinem Werk internationales Symposium der Bibliotheca Hertziana Rom*, Weinheim, 1992.

Hevesy, André de, *Jacopo de'Barbari: le maître au caducée*, Paris, 1925.

Hill, G.F., *Portrait Medals of Italian Artist in the Renaissance*, London, 1912.

Hind, Arthur M., *Early Italian Engraving: A Critical Catalogue*, 7 vols, London, 1938–48.

Hochmann, Michael, *Peintres et commanditaires à Venise 1540–1628*, Rome, 1992.

Hoffmann, W., *Köpfe der Lutherzeit*, Munich, 1983.

Hollstein, F.W.H., *Dutch and Flemish Etchings, Engravings and Woodcuts c. 1450–1700*, IX, ed. Menno Herzberger, Amsterdam, 1953.

Hollstein, F.W.H., *German Engravings, Etchings and Woodcuts, 1400–1700*, XII, ed. Fedja Anzelewsky, Amsterdam, 1965.

Hollstein, F.W.H., *Hollstein's Dutch and Flemish Etchings, Engravings and Woodcuts, c.1450–1700*, XXI–XXII, ed. K.G. Boon and compiled by Dieuwke De Hoop Scheffer, Rosendaal, 1980.

Hollstein, F.W.H., *Hollstein's Dutch and Flemish Etchings, Engravings and Woodcuts, c.1450–1700*, XXIII, ed. G.S. Keyes, Amsterdam, 1980.

Hollstein, F.W.H., *Hollstein's German Engravings, Etchings and Woodcuts 1400–1700*, XXIV, *Israhel van Meckenem*, ed. Tilman Falk and compiled by Fritz Koreny, 2 vols, Roosendaal, 1986.

Hollstein, F.W.H., *German Engravings, Etchings and Woodcuts, 1400–1700*, XXXI, ed. Tilman Falk, compiled by Robert Zijlma, Roosendaal, 1991.

Hollstein, F.W.H., *Hollstein's Dutch and Flemish Etchings, Engravings and Woodcuts 1450–1700, The Muller Dynasty*, Part II, ed. Jan Piet Filedt Kok, Rotterdam, 1999.

Holt, Elizabeth G., *A Documentary History of Art*, 2 vols, New York, 1957.

Hope, Charles, 'Historical Portraits in the *Lives* and in the frescoes of Giorgio Vasari', pp. 321–38 in *Giorgio Vasari tra decorazione ambientale e storiografica artistica*, ed. Gian Carlo Garfagnini, Florence, 1985.

Horace, *Odes and Epodes*, ed. and trans. C.E. Bennett, London, 1914.

Hubaux, J. and Puraye, J., 'Dominique Lampson Lamberti Lombardi vita: traduction et notes', *Revue belge d'archeologie et d'histoire de l'art*, XVIII, 1949, pp. 53–77.

Hughes, A., 'An Academy for doing', *Oxford Art Journal*, IX, 1986, pp. 3–10.

Hülsen, C. and Egger, H., *Die römischen Skizzenbücher von Marten van Heemskerck*, 2 vols, Berlin, 1913–16.

Huth, Hans, *Künstler und Werkstatt der Spätgotik*, Darmstadt, 1967.

Hyginus, Caius Julius, *De imaginibus deorum*, Basel, 1549.

Hymans, H., *Antonio Moro: son oeuvre et son temps*, Brussels, 1910.

Isidore of Seville, 'Allegoriae quaedam scripturae sacrae', in *Patrologiae latinae*, 83, ed. J.P. Migne, Paris, 1862.

Jacopo da Voragine, *The Golden Legend or Lives of the Saints*, trans. William Caxton, ed. F.S. Ellis, 7 vols, London, 1900.

Jacopo da Voragine, *Leggenda aurea*, ed. A. Levasti, Florence, 1924.

Jaffé, David, 'Daniele da Volterra's satirical defence of his art', *Journal of the Warburg and Courtaud Institutes*, LIV, 1991, pp. 247–52.

Jan van der Straet detto Stradano, ed. Alessandra Baroni Vannucci, Milan, 1997.

Jan van Scorel d'Utrecht: retables et tableaux de son atelier vers 1540, Utrecht, 1977.

Janson, Horst W., 'The putto with the death's head', *Art Bulletin*, 19, 1937, pp. 425–49.

Janson, Horst W., *Apes and Ape-lore in the Middle Ages and Renaissance*, London, 1952.

Jerome, Saint, 'Commentariorum in Evangelium Matthaei', in *Patrologiae latinae*, 86, ed. J.P. Migne, Paris, 1884.

Johannes de Sacrobosco, *Sphaera mundi*, Venice, 1488.

Jolly, Anna, 'Netherlandish sculptors in sixteenth-century Northern Germany and their Patrons', *Simiolus*, XXVII, 1999, pp. 119–43.

Jürg, Meyer zur Capellen, *Andrea Previtali*, Lüneburg, 1972.

Katzenellenbogen, A., *Allegories of the Virtues and the Vices in Medieval Art*, London, 1939.

Kaufmann, Thomas DaCosta, *The School of Prague: Painting at the Court of Rudolph II*, Chicago, 1988.

Keller, John E. and Feating, L. Clark, trans., *Aesop's Fables with a Life of Aesop*, Kentucky, 1993.

Kemp, Martin, 'The super-artist as genius: the sixteenth-century view', pp. 32–53 in Penelope Murray, ed., *Genius*, Oxford, 1989.

Kemp, Wolfgang, 'Beiträge zur Geschichte des Begriffs zwischen 1547 und 1607', *Marburger Jahrbuch für Kunstwissenschaft*, XIX, 1974, pp. 219–40.

Kempers, Bram, *Painting, Power and Patronage: The Rise of the Professional Artist in Renaissance Italy*, Harmondsworth, 1992.

Kerrich, Thomas, *A Catalogue of Prints after Marten van Heemskerck*, London, 1829.

King, Catherine, 'National Gallery 3902 and the theme of Luke the Evangelist as artist and physician', *Zeitschrift für Kunstgeschichte*, XLVIII, 1985, pp. 249–55.

King, Catherine, 'Late sixteenth-century careers' advice: a new allegory of artists' training – Albertina, inv. No. 2763', *Wiener Jahrbuch für Kunstgeschichte*, XLI, 1988, pp. 77–96.

King, Catherine, 'Mnemosyne and Calliope in the Chapel of the Muses, San Francesco Rimini', *Journal of the Warburg and Courtauld Institutes*, LI, 1988, pp. 186–7.

King, Catherine, 'Filarete's portrait-signature on the bronze doors of Saint Peter's and the dance of Bathykles and his Magnesian assistants', *Journal of the Warburg and Courtauld Institutes*, LIII, 1990, pp. 296–99.

King, Catherine, 'Looking a sight: sixteenth-century portraits of women artists', *Zeitschrift für Kunstgeschichte*, LVIII, 1995, pp. 381–406.

King, Catherine, 'Italian self-portraits and the Rewards of Virtue', pp. 69–91 in Gunther Schweikhart, ed., *Autobiographie und Selbst Portrait in der Renaissance*, Cologne, 1998.

King, Catherine, 'Italian artists in search of Virtue, Fame and Honour', pp. 56–87 in Emma Barker, Nick Webb, and Kim Woods, eds, *The Changing Status of the Artist*, New Haven, CT, 1999.

King, Catherine, 'Portrait of the artist as a woman', pp. 37–60 in Gill Perry, ed., *Gender and Art*, New Haven, CT, 1999.

King, Catherine, 'Artists' houses: mass-advertising artistic status in Antwerp *c.*1565', pp. 173–89, Michèle Caroline Heck, Frédérique Lemerle and Yves Pauwels, eds, in *Théorie des arts et création artistique dans l'Europe du Nord du XVIe au début du XVIIIe siècle*, Lille, 2002.

King, Catherine, 'An etching and Lelio Orsi's house', *Print Quarterly*, XXIII, 2006, pp. 176–82.

King, Catherine, 'Making Histories, Publishing Theories', 250–80, in *Making Renaissance Art*, ed. Kim Woods, New Haven, CT, 2007.

Kirn, Paul, 'Friedrich der Weise und Jacopo de'Barbari', *Jahrbuch der preussischen Kunstsammlungen*, XLVI, 1925, pp. 130–4.

Klein, Dorothy, *Lukas als Maler der Maria*, Berlin, 1933.

Kleiner, Diane E., *Roman Sculpture*, New Haven, CT, 1992.

Klinger, Linda Susan, *The Portrait Collection of Paolo Giovio*, 2 vols Princeton University PhD, Ann Arbor, 1991.

Koerner, Joseph Leo, *The Moment of Self-Portraiture in German Renaissance Art*, Chicago, 1993.

Konecný, Lubomir, *Kunst und Kultur am Hofe Rudolfs II*, 2 vols, Essen, 1988.

Kraitrová, Marie, 'La casa di Andrea Mantegna a Mantova e quella di Piero della Francesca a Borgo San Sepolcro', pp. 46–8 in Eduard Hüttinger, ed., *Case d'artista: dal Rinascimento ad oggi*, Turin, 1992.

Kuyper, W., *The Triumphant Entry of Renaissance Architecture into the Netherlands*, 2 vols, Leyden, 1994.

La piacevol astrologia di Ravanello nel qual si dichiara à tutti gli'uomini quello à che sono inclinati, Siena, 1578.

Lambert Lombard et son temps, Liège, 1966.

Lampsonius, Dominic, *Lamberti Lombardi, apud Eburones pictoris celeberrimi, vita*, Bruges, 1565.

Lampsonius, Dominique, *Les Effigies des peintres célèbres des Pays-Bas*, 1572, ed. J. Puraye, Bruges, 1956.

Landucci, A., *Origine dal tempio dedicato in Roma alla Vergine Madre di Dio Maria detto hoggi del popolo*, Rome, 1646.

Laschke, Birgit, 'Montorsolis Entwürfe für das Siegel der Accademia del Disegno in Florenz', *Mitteilungen des Kunsthistorischen Instituts in Florenz*, XXXI, 1987, pp. 392–402.

Le Calendrier des bergers, Paris, 1499.

Le cose maravigliose de l'alma città di Roma, Venice, 1565.

Le Grand Calendrier des bergers, Paris, 1589.

Le Grand Kalendrier des bergers, Paris, 1569.

Legrand, Francine C. and Sluys, Felix, *Arcimboldo et les Arcimboldesques*, Aalter, 1955.

Lemaire, Jean, *La Plainte du desiré*, Lyons, 1509.

Lemaire, Jean, *Les Illustrations de Gaule*, Lyons, 1549.

Leonardo da Vinci, *The Literary Works of Leonardo da Vinci*, trans. Jean Paul Richter, 2 vols, London, 1970.

The Life of Taddeo Zuccaro by Federico Zuccari from the Collection of the British Rail Pensions Fund, Sotheby's New York, 1990.

Lightbown, Ronald, *Mantegna*, Oxford, 1986.

Lomazzo, Giovanni Paolo, *Idea del tempio della pittura* (1590), ed. Robert Klein, 2 vols, Florence, 1974.

Lombard Lambert, et son temps, Liège, 1966.

Lorenzoni, A., *Carteggio artistico inedito di Vincenzo Borghini*, 2 vols, Florence, 1912.

Lorris de, G. and de Meung, J., *Romance of the Rose*, ed. C. Dahlberg, Princeton, 1971.

Lucian, 8 vols, trans. A.M. Harmon, I, London, 1961.
Luijten, Ger, ed. *Dawn of the Golden Age: Northern Netherlandish Art 1580–1620*, Amsterdam, 1996.
Mabillon, J. and Germain, M., *Museum italici*, Paris, 1689.
MacCurdy, Edward, *The Notebooks of Leonardo da Vinci*, London, 1954.
Maggi, Stefano, 'Un paride ritrovato: il "Mercurio" della casa di Giulio Romano', *Quaderni di Palazzo del del Te*, IV (8), January–June 1988, pp. 37–41.
Maillard, E., de Montremy, F. and Harancourt, E., *Catalogue des bois sculptés et meubles: Museé des Thermes et de l'Hôtel de Cluny*, Paris, 1925.
Manni, D.M., *Dell'errore che persiste di attribuirsi le pitture al Santo Evangelista*, Florence, 1766.
Marcucci, Luisa, *Francesco da Volterra: un protagonista dell'architectura post tridentina*, Rome, 1991.
Maroni Lumbroso, M. and Martini, A., *Le confraternite romane nelle loro chiese*, Rome, 1963.
Martens, Maximilian P.J., ed., *Bruges et la Renaissance*, Bruges, 1998.
Martindale, Andrew, *The Rise of the Artist*, London, 1972.
Martineau, Jane and Hope, Charles, eds, *The Genius of Venice*, London, 1983.
Martini, A., *Arti, mestieri e fede nella Roma dei papi*, Bologna, 1965.
Martone, Thomas, 'Piero della Francesca's "Triumphs of the Duke and Duchess of Urbino"', pp. 211–22 in Konrad Eisenbichler and Amilcare Iannucci, eds, *Petrarch's Triumphs: Allegory and Spectacle*, Toronto, 1990.
Massari, Stefania, *Incisori Mantovani del '500: Giovan Battista, Adamo, Diana Scultori, e Giorgio Ghisi*, Rome, 1980.
Massari, Stefania, *Giulio Bonasone*, 2 vols, Rome, 1983.
Massing, Jean-Michel, *Du texte à l'image. La Calomnie d'Apelle et son iconographie*, Strasburg, 1999.
McGrath, Elizabeth, 'The painted decoration of Rubens's house', *Journal of the Warburg and Courtauld Institutes*, XLI, 1978, pp. 245–77.
Melion, W.S., *Shaping the Netherlandish Canon: Karel van Mander's Schilder-boek*, Chicago and London, 1991.
Meloncelli, Katia Brugnolo, *Battista Zelotti*, Milan, 1992.
Mende, M., *Dürer Medaillen*, Nuremberg, 1983.
Metzler, D., 'Renaissance Bildnisse antiker Architekten am Haus eines Stadtbaumeisters in Sélestat', *Antike und Abendland*, XIX, 1973, pp. 146–62.
Mezzatesta, Michael P., *Imperial Themes in the Sculpture of Leone Leoni* (PhD, New York, 1980), Ann Arbor, 1991.
Michaelis, A., 'Römische Skizzenbücher Marten van Heemskerck und anderer nördischen Künstler des XVI Jahrhunderts', *Jahrbuch des Deutschen Archaeologischen Institutes*, VI, 1891, pp. 125–72.

Michiel, Marcantonio, *The Anonimo: Notes on Pictures and Works of Art in Italy*, trans. Paolo Mussi, London, 1903.

Middeldorf, Ulrich, 'On the Dilettante sculptor', *Apollo*, CVII, 1978, pp. 310–12.

Molanus, Johannes, *De historia sanctorum imaginum et picturam*, Louvain, 1570 and Ingolstadt, 1594, ed. and trans. François Boespflug, Olivier Christian and Benoît Tassel, 2 vols, Paris, 1996.

Monneret de Villard, U., *Le vetrate del duomo di Milano*, Milan, 1918–20.

Montballieu, A., 'Bij de interpretatie en de datering van Jan Gossaerts Lucas en de Madonna vit Mechelen', pp. 125–38 in *Miscellanea Jozef Duverger: Bijdragen tot de Kunstgeschiedenis der Nederladen*, 2 vols, I, Ghent, 1968.

Montias, J.M., *Artists and Artisans of Delft*, Princeton, 1982.

Morrello, Benedetto, *Il funerale d'Agostin Carracci*, Bologna, 1603.

Muller, Jeffrey, *Children of Mercury: The Education of Artists in the Sixteenth Century*, Providence, RI, 1984.

Murray, Peter, 'Art historians and art critics IV: uomini singhularii', *Burlington Magazine*, XCIV, 1957, pp. 330–6.

Neefs, E., 'La peinture et la sculpture à Malines', pp. 364–473 in *Messager des sciences historiques des archives des arts et de la bibliographie de Belgique*, Ghent, 1871.

Nelson, Robert S. and Shiff, Richard, *Critical Terms for Art History*, Chicago, 1992.

Niklaus Manuel Deutsch: Maler, Dichter, Staatsmann, Katalog der Ausstellung, Bern, 1979.

Orange, Hans P.C., *Die spätantike Bildschmuck des Konstantinsbogens*, Berlin, 1939.

Orsi, Lelio, 1511–1587: Dipinti e disegni, Reggio Emilia, 1987.

Paatz, E. and W., *Die Kirchen von Florenz*, 6 vols, Frankfurt am Main, 1940–54.

Pacioli, Luca, *De divina proportione*, ed. G. Masolti Biggiogero, Milan, 1956.

Panofsky, Erwin and Saxl, Fritz, *Dürer's Melancholia I*, Hamburg, 1923.

Panofsky, Erwin, *Hercules am Scheidewege und andere Bildstoffe in der neueren Kunst*, Lepzig, 1930.

Panofsky, Erwin, *Renaissance and Renascences in Western Art*, London, 1960.

Panofsky, Erwin, *Early Netherlandish Painting*, 2 vols, New York, 1971.

Paolucci, A. and Maetzke, A.M., *La casa del Vasari in Arezzo*, Florence, 1988.

Parma, Elena, *Il cinquecento: la pittura in Liguria*, Genoa, 2000.

Partridge, Loren, 'The Room of the Maps at Caprarola 1573–75', *Art Bulletin*, LXXVII (3), 1995, pp. 413–44.

Passavant, J.D., *Le Peintre-Graveur*, 6 vols, Leipzig, 1860–64.

Pauwels, H., *Jan Gossaert genaamd Mabuse*, Rotterdam and Bruges, 1965.

Pedretti, Carlo, 'Leonardo's allegories at Oxford explained by Lomazzo', *Burlington Magazine*, XCVI, 1954, pp. 175–7.

Pevsner, Nikolaus, *Academies Past and Present*, Cambridge, 1940.

Philibert de l'Orme, *Traités d'architectures*, ed. Jean-Marie Pérouse de Montclos, Paris, 1988.

Pictor, Georg, *Apotheoseos*, Basel, 1548; facsimile, ed. Stefan Orgel, New York, 1976.

Pictor, Georg, *Theologia mythologica*, Antwerp, 1532; facsimile, ed. Stefan Orgel, New York, 1976.

Pietrangeli, C., *L'Accademia Nazionale di San Luca*, Rome, 1974.

Pigler, Andor, 'Neid und Unwissenheit als Widersacher der Kunst', *Acta Historiae Artium*, I, 1954, pp. 215–35.

Pignatti, Teresio, *Giorgione*, Venice, 1969.

Pinchart, Alexandre J., *Archives des arts, sciences et lettres: documents inédits publiés et annotés*, 2 vols, Ghent, 1860.

Pirro, Roccho, *Notitiae Siciliensum ecclesiarum*, Palermo, 1733.

Pliny the Elder, *Chapters on the History of Art*, ed. Eugenie Sellars and trans. Katharine Jex-Blake, London, 1968.

Pliny the Elder, *Historia naturalis*, ed. H. Rackham, 8 vols, London, 1938.

Poggetto, Paolo dal, 'La Villa Imperiale: l'attività di Rafaellino dal Colle', in *Pesaro nell'età dei Della Rovere*, ed. Guido Arbizzoni, Antonio Brancati, Maria Rosaria Valazzi and Maria Letizia Brancati, Venice, 2001.

Poirier, Maurice, 'The role and concept of *disegno* in mid sixteenth-century Florence', pp. 53–68, in *The Age of Vasari*, New York, 1970.

Pope-Hennessy, John, *Paolo Uccello*, London, 1969.

Pope-Hennessy, J., *Cellini*, London, 1985.

Popham, A.E., *The Drawings of Leonardo da Vinci*, London, 1971.

Primatice Maître de Fontainebleau, Paris, 2004.

Prinz, Wulfram, 'Vasari's Sammlung von Künstlerbildnissen', Beiheft zu Band XII der *Mitteilungen des Kunsthistorischen Instituts in Florenz*, Florence, 1966.

Prinz, Wulfram, *Die Sammlung der Selbstbildnisse in den Uffizien: Geschichte der Sammlung*, Berlin, 1971.

Ptolemy, *Tetrabiblos*, ed. and trans. F.E. Robbins, Cambridge, MA, 1980.

Quednau, R., *Die Sala di Constantino im Vatikanischen Palast*, Hildesheim, 1979.

Ramsay, G.G., ed., *Juvenal and Persius*, London, 1918.

Raupp, Hans-Joachim, 'Allegorische Selbstporträts und selbstdarstellungen in der Graphik um 1600', pp. 177–92 in Gunther

Schweikhart, ed., *Autobiographie und Selbst Portrait in der Renaissance*, Cologne, 1998.

Reusner, Nicolaus, *Icones sive imagines*, Basel, 1589.

Reznicek, E.K.J., 'De reconstructie van t'Altaer van S. Lucas van Marten van Heemskerck', *Oud Holland*, LXX, 1955, pp. 233–46.

Reznicek, E.K.J., *Die Zeichnungen von Hendrik Goltzius*, 2 vols, Utrecht, 1961.

Rhiza, Franz von, 'Die Siegel der ehemaligen Bauhutte von St Stefan in Wien', *Mitteilungen der Kaiserliche, Königliche Central-Commission zur Erforschung und Erhaltung der Kunst und Historischen Denkmale*, new series, XVI, 1890, pp. 151–6.

Ricci, Corrado, *Il Tempio Malatestiana in Rimini*, Milan, 1924.

Ridolfi, Carlo, *Le meraviglie dell'arte*, ed. D.F. von Hadeln, 2 vols, Berlin, 1914.

Ripa, Cesare, *Iconologia*, Rome, 1603.

Ripa, Cesare, *Iconologia*, Padua, 1611; ed. Erna Mandowsky, Hildesheim, 1970.

Rombouts, P. and van Lerius, T., *De Liggeren en andere historische Archieven der Antwerpische Sint Lucasgilde*, 2 vols Gravenhage, 1864–76.

Rossi, Marco, 'La casa di Leone Leoni a Milano', pp. 21–30 in Maria Luisa Gatti Perer, ed., *Leone Leoni tra Lombardia e Spagna: atti del Convegno Internazionale 1993*, Milan, 1995.

Röttinger, Heinrich, 'Burgkmair in Hochzeitskleide', *Münchner Jahrbuch der bildenden Kunst*, II, 1908, pp. 48–52.

Roy, M., *Artistes et monuments de la renaissance en France*, Paris, 1929.

Ruberti, Battista de', *Osservazioni de astrologia, et altre appartenenze, circa la medecina, e mutazione de' tempi*, Florence, 1567.

Rupprich, H., ed., *Dürer schriftlicher Nachlass*, 3 vols, Berlin 1956–69.

Samek-Ludovici, S., *Il 'De sphaera' estense e l'iconografia astrologica*, Milan, 1958.

Santi, Giovanni, *La vita e le gesta di Federico di Montefeltro*, ed. Luigi Michelini Tocci, 2 vols, Vatican City, 1985.

Saxl, Fritz, 'Veritas filia temporis', pp. 197–216 in Raymond Klibansky and Herbert J. Paton, eds, *Philosophy and History: Essays Presented to Ernst Cassirer*, Oxford, 1936.

Saxl, Fritz, 'The literary sources of the "Finiguerra Planets"', *Journal of the Warburg and Courtauld Institutes*, II, 1938, pp. 72–4.

Schmitz, Hermann, 'Eine neuerworbene Rundscheibe von Jörg Breu D. Ä im Schlossmuseum', *Berliner Museen Berichte aus den preussischen Kunstsammlungen*, XLV, 1924, pp. 8–81.

Schreiber, W.L., *Manuel de l'amateur de la gravure sur bois et sur métal au XVe siècle*, 8 vols, Berlin, 1891–1900.

Schultz, Alwin, ed., 'Johannes Butzbach's "Libellus de praeclaris picture professoribus" aus der Bonnenser Handschrift veröffentlich',

Jahrbücher für Kunstwissenschaft herausgegeben von A. von Zahn, Leipzig, II, 1869, pp. 60–72.
Schütz Rautenberg, Gesa, *Künstlergrabmäler des 15 und 16 Jahrhunderts in Italien*, PhD thesis, Cologne, 1978.
Schwarz, Hans Peter, *Das Künstlerhaus Anmerkungen zur Sozialgeschichte des Genies*, Braunschweig, 1990.
Schweikhart, Gunther, ed., *Autobiographie und Selbst Portrait in der Renaissance*, Cologne, 1998.
Scorza, R.A., 'Vincenzo Borghini and *invenzione*: the Florentine Apparato of 1565', *Journal of the Warburg and Courtauld Institutes*, XLIV, 1981, pp. 57–75.
Sellink, Manfred and Leeflang, Huigen, *The New Hollstein: Dutch and Flemish Etchings, Engravings and Woodcuts 1450–1700, Cornelis Cort*, 3 vols, Rotterdam, 2000.
Severin, Ingrid, *Baumeister und Architekten: Studien zur Darstellung eines Berufstandes in Porträt und Bildnis*, Berlin, 1992.
Seznec, Jean, 'Youth, Innocence and Death', *Journal of the Warburg and Courtauld Institutes*, I, 1937–38, pp. 293–303.
Shapley, Fern Rusk, *Catalogue of the Italian Paintings, National Gallery of Art, Washington*, 2 vols, Washington, 1979.
Shearman, John, *Andrea del Sarto*, 2 vols, Oxford, 1965.
Shorr, D.C., *The Christchild in Devotional Images*, New York, 1954.
Silver, Larry, *The Paintings of Quinten Massys*, Oxford, 1984.
Siverio, R., *Accademia delle Arti del Disegno*, Florence, 1982.
Smeyers, M. and van der Stock, Jan, eds, *French Illuminated Manuscripts 1475–1550*, Ghent, 1996.
Sotheby's Catalogue, London Lord Mostyn Sale: Manuscripts, 13 July 1920.
Šroněk, Michal, 'Rudolf II and the Guild of Saint Luke', pp. 216–21 in R. Konecny, ed., *Rudolf II, Prague and the World*, Prague, 1998.
Steinmann, E., *Die Portraitdarstellungen des Michelangelo*, Leipzig, 1913.
Sternagel, P., *Die Artes Mechanicae im Mittelalter*, Munich, 1966.
Strauss, W.L., *The German Single Leaf Woodcut, 1550–1600*, New York, 1975.
Strieder, P., 'Hans Holbein der Älter und die deutschenWiederholungen des Gnadensbildes von Santa Maria del Popolo', *Zeitschrift für Kunstgeschichte*, XX, 1959, pp. 252–67.
Summers, David, 'The sculptural programme of the Cappella di San Luca', *Mitteilungen des Kunsthistorischen Instituts in Florenz*, XIV, 1969, pp. 67–90.
Thöne, F., *Daniel Lindtmayer 1552–1606/07*, Zürich, 1975.
Thorndike, Lyn, A., *History of Magic and Experimental Science*, London, 1923.
Thurneisser zum Thurn, Leonhardt, *Archidoxa dorin der Recht war Motus Lauff und Gang der Planeten*, Munster, 1569.

Tolnay, Charles de, *The Drawings of Pieter Brueghel*, London, 1952.
Torre, Arnaldo della *Storia dell Accademia Platonica*, Florence, 1902.
Trombelli, G.C., *De cultu sanctorum*, Bologna, 1743.
Valla, Lorenzo, *Libri sex elegantiarum latinae linguae*, Lyons, 1544.
Van de Casteele, D., 'Documents divers de la société de s. Luc à Bruges', *Annales de la Société d'Émulation pour l'Étude de l'Histoire et des Antiquités de la Flandre*, Bruges, 1866, I, pp. 1–43.
Van de Velde, Carl, *Frans Floris 1519/20–1570, Leven en Werken*, 2 vols, Brussels, 1975.
Van der Haeghen, V., *La Corporation des peintres et des sculpteurs de Gand*, Ghent, 1905.
Van der Willigen, A., *Les Artistes de Harlem: notices historiques avec un préçis sur la gilde de St Luc*, Haarlem and The Hague, 1870.
Van Mander, Karel, *The Lives of the Illustrious Netherlandish and German Painters Het Schilderboek*, ed. Hessel Miedema, trans. Derry Cook Radmore, 6 vols, Doornspijk, 1994–99.
Vasari, Giorgio, *Le opere di Giorgio Vasari con nuove annotazioni e commenti*, ed. Gaetano Milanesi, 9 vols, Florence, 1906.
Vasari, Giorgio, *Lives of the Most Eminent Painters, Sculptors and Architects*, trans. Gaston du C. de Vere, 10 vols, London, 1910–15.
Vasari, Giorgio, *La vita di Michelangelo*, ed. Paola Barocchi, 5 vols, Milan, 1962.
Veldman, Ilya M., *Marten van Heemskerck and Dutch Humanism in the Sixteenth century*, trans. M. Hoyle, Maarsen, 1977.
Vergerio, Pier Paolo, *Della camera et statua della Madonna chiamata di Loretto*, Tübingen, 1554.
Verheyen, E., *The Paintings of the Studiolo of Isabella d'Este*, New York, 1971.
Verzone, Paolo, 'Cesare Cesariano', *Arte Lombarda*, XVI, 1971, pp. 203–10.
Victor, Hugh of, Saint, *Didascalicon opera omnia*, Rouen, 1648.
Villani, Filippo, *De origine civitatis Florentiae et de eiusdem famosis civibus*, ed. G. Tanturli, Padua, 1997.
Vincent of Beauvais, *Speculum naturale*, Strasburg, 1472.
Vitruvius, *De architettura, Vitruvio*, ed. and trans. Cesare Cesariano, Como, 1521; facsimile ed. A. Bruschi, A. Carugo and P.F. Fiore, Milan, 1981.
Vitruvius Pollio, *De architettura*, trans. and ed. Gianbattista Caporali, Perugia, 1536.
Vitruvius Pollio, *De architectura*, ed. Guillaume Philandrier, Strasburg, 1543.
Vitruvius Pollio, *I dieci libri dell'architettura*, trans. and ed. Daniele Barbaro, Venice, 1556.
Vitruvius, *On Architecture*, ed. Frank Granger, 2 vols, London, 1931.
Vitruvius Pollio, *De architectura*, ed. Laura Cherubini, Pisa, 1975.

Vitruvius, *Vitruvio De architectura*, trans. Cesare Cesariano, Libri II–IV, ed. Alessandro Rovetta, Milan, 2002.

Von Schlosser, Julius, *Quellenbuch zur Kunstgeschichte des abendländischen Mittelalters*, Vienna, 1896.

Von Schlosser, Julius, 'Geschichte der Portraitbilderei in Wachs: ein Versuch', *Jahrbuch der Kunsthistorisches Sammlungen des allerhöchsten Kaiserhauses*, XXIX, 1910–11, pp. 171–258.

Von Schlosser, Julius, *La letteratura artistica*, ed. Otto Kurz, Florence, 1954.

Vos, Dirk de, *Groeninge Museum, Catalogus Schilderijen 15de en 16de Eeuw*, Bruges, 1979.

Walters Art Gallery Illuminated Books of the Middle Ages and Renaissance, Baltimore, 1949.

Warnke, Martin, *Hofkünstler, Zur Vorgeschichte des modernen Künstlers*, Cologne, 1985; trans. David McLintock, as *The Court Artist: On the Ancestry of the Modern Artist*, Cambridge, 1993.

Warsager Kunst aus den sieben Planeten, Leipzig, 1598.

Wethey, H., *El Greco and his School*, 2 vols, Princeton, 1962.

Wenzel Jamnitzer und die Nürnberger Goldschmiedekunst 1500–1700, Munich, 1985.

Whitney, Elspeth, 'Paradise restored: the mechanical arts from antiquity through the thirteenth century', *Transactions of the American Philosophical Society*, LXXX (1), 1990, pp. 1–169.

Wilkinson, Catherine, 'Renaissance treatises on military architecture', pp. 467–74 in *Les Traités d'architecture de la Renaissance*, ed. J. Guillaume, Paris, 1988.

Wingert, P., 'The funerary urn of Francis I', *Art Bulletin*, XXI, 1939, pp. 383–96.

Wittkower, Margaret and Rudolf, *Born under Saturn*, London, 1963.

Wittkower, Margaret and Rudolf, *The Divine Michelangelo*, London, 1964.

Wittkower, Rudolf, *Architectural Principles in the Age of Humanism*, London, 1949.

Woods Marsden, Joanna, *Renaissance Self-portraiture: The Visual Construction of Identity and the Social Status of the Artist*, New Haven, CT and London, 1998.

Woodward, William H., *Studies in Education during the Renaissance 1400–1600*, New York, 1965.

Wyas, Edith, *The Myth of Apollo and Marysas in the Art of the Renaissance*, Newark, NJ and London, 1996.

Zampetti, P. and Chiappini, I., 'Andrea Previtali', pp. 87–167 in G.A. dell'Acqua and P. Zampetti, *Il cinquecento*, Bergamo 1975 (Part 1, of volume 3, in the series *I pittori bergameschi dal XIII al XIX secolo*, in 5 volumes), especially pp. 151–3.

Zaremba Filipczak, Zirka, *Picturing Art in Antwerp, 1550–1700*, Princeton, 1987.

Zuccari, Federico, *Scritti d'arte di Federico Zuccaro*, ed. Detlef Heikamp, Florence, 1961.

Zweite, A., *Studien zu Marten de Vos*, Göttingen, 1974.

Index

Abbondio, Antonio, 265, 298
Abraham ben Ezra, 198
Abu Ma'shar, 197–8
Accademia del Disegno, 7, 75–9, 82, 124, 168, 215, 295, 297
Adriaensen, Jan, 119, 294
Aesculapius, 172, 179
Aesop, 269–72, 302
Agostino di Duccio, 75
Alamanni, Luigi, 131
Alberti, Leandro, 147
Alberti, Leon Battista, 8, 13, 27, 32, 62–4, 67, 105, 120–1, 133, 236–7, 240, 244, 307
Alberti, Romano, 87, 92
Albricus, 192–4
Aldegrever, Heinrich, 113
Aldrovandi, Ulisse, 164
Alessi, Giovanni, 312
Alexander the Great, 134, 138
Alfonso, Duke of Calabria, 245
Alfonso, Duke of Ferrara, 127
allegories of art history, 124–5, 230, 236–73, 297, 302, 319
Allori, Alessandro, 81, 137, 169
Altissimo, Cristofano, 123
Ames-Lewis, Francis, 15, 105
Amman, Jost, 24–6
Ammanati, Bartolomeo, 43, 75, 122
Andrea del Castagno, 122
Andrea del Sarto, 106, 109, 125–6, 130–1, 279, 282, 285, 301
Andrea del Verrocchio, 82
Andreani, Andrea, 111
Andrew, Keith, 268
Androuet du Cerceau, Jacques, 9
Angelico, Fra, 122
Anne, St, 159
Antoninus, St, 21
Antonio da Faenza, 92
Antonio da Sangallo, 109, 130–1
Apelles, 103, 113, 118, 120, 127, 133–4, 137–9, 237–40, 262, 296–7, 300, 319
Apollodorus, 127
apprenticeship system, 5–7
Aquinas, Thomas, 147, 194
Arcimboldo, Giuseppe, 52–3, 325
Ardenti, Alessandro, 242
Aretino, Pietro, 15, 264, 270
Aretino, Spinello, 125
Ariosto, Lodovico, 115
Aristotle, 192
Armenini, Giovanni Battista, 87–8, 91
Ascoli, Antonio Bonfini d', 245
astrology, 191–5, 199, 206–7, 229–30, 318
Attwood, Philip, 243
autobiographies of artists, 12–13
Avernier, Antoine, 23

Baglione, Giovanni, 182, 251
Baldung, Hans, 113
Bandinelli, Baccio, 70, 105, 109, 114, 117, 122, 130–1, 325
Barbari, Jacopo de', 3–4, 27, 64, 71, 192, 280
Barbaro, Daniele, 66
Barocci, Jacopo, 294
Baronius, Cesar, 148
Barozzi detto il Vignola, Jacopo, 9
Barthélémy de Chasseneux, 3
Bartolomeo della Gatta, 125
Becker, Jochen, 296
Behaim, Lorenz, 195
Belli, Valerio, 106, 109, 130–1
Bellini, Giovanni, 241
Bembo, Pietro, 36, 122
Bernini, Gian Lorenzo, 272, 325

Bertano, Giovanni Battista, 291–2, 313
Bink, Jacob, 113
biographies of artists, 12–13
Biscaro, Gerolamo, 181
Blocklandt, Anthonie, 310
Blondeel, Lanceloot, 154–5, 165
Boccaccio, Giovanni, 133, 149, 246
Bocchi, Achille, 216, 241, 295
Boldù, Giovanni, 44, 240–1
Bonasone, Giulio, 114–17, 216, 241, 295
Bonaventure, St, 147
Bontemps, Pierre de, 38–9, 74
Borgherini, Giovanni, 30
Borghini, Raffaele, 37, 87, 92–3
Borghini, Vincenzo, 43, 77, 81–2, 124, 300
Borromeo, Carlo, 181
Bosch, Hieronymus, 129
Boulin, Arnould, 23
Bouts, Dieric, 281
Bouts, Thierry, 129
Bramante, Donato, 158, 165, 243, 281
Brant, Sebastian, 311
Bresc-Bautier, Geneviève, 74–5
Breu, Georg the Elder, 201–2
Britto, Giovanni, 116–17
Bronzino, Agnolo, 32, 75, 77, 168
Brunelleschi, Filippo, 10, 105, 122–7, 138
Burgkmair, Hans, 108
Butzbach, Johannes, 149, 162
bystander portraits, 105, 107

Calamandrei, Piero, 79–80
Calamec, Andrea, 250
Calamec, Lazzaro, 217
Camerarius, Joachim, 12, 110
Campaspe, 134
Campi, Bernardino, 241–2
Campi, Giulio, 242
Capella, Martianus, 208
Caporali, Giambattisa, 66
Carracci, Agostino, 14, 192, 222, 272, 324
Carracci, Ludovico, 7
Cartari, Vincenzo, 268
Caselli, Giovanni Battista, 242–3
Casoni, Felice Antonio, 243
Casotti de Mazzolenis family, 22
Castiglione, Baldasarre, 31, 69–70
Cato, 241–2
Cavalcanti, Andrea, 105–6
Cecchi, Alessandro, 84–5, 300
Cellini, Benvenuto, 17, 43, 71–80, 91–2, 122, 207, 241, 259
Cennini, Cennino, 8, 32, 62, 134, 244
Cesariano, Cesare, 65–6, 115, 209–14, 217, 230, 244, 246, 269–70, 323
Cesariano, Lorenzo, 211
Chacon, Alonso, 129, 262–3
chapels, 156–70; decoration of, 178–83
Charles V, Emperor, 33–4, 103, 114, 118, 127, 241, 282, 298
Chasseneux, Barthélémy, 21–6
Children of Mercury, 2–3, 183, 193–208, 230, 318–19, 322
Christian II of Denmark, 14–15
Cicereio, 299
Cicero, 41, 65, 133, 136, 192, 213, 216, 307
Cimabue, 10, 124–6, 300
Cioli, Valerio, 250
civic display, 118–20
Claeissens, Anton, 52, 54
Clement VII, Pope, 31, 54, 73, 77, 325
Cock, Hieronymous, 15, 113, 127–8, 202–3, 222, 240, 321, 323
Colijn de Coter, 156
Columbus, Christopher, 48–9
commemorative portraits of artists, 103–10, 132–3
Condivi, Ascanio, 12–13, 27–8, 114, 116, 120, 132, 195
Constantine, Emperor, 31–2
Conti, Natale, 213, 217
Corrado de Mochis, 181
Correggio, Antonio, 292
Cort, Cornelis, 49, 51, 127–8, 237, 239, 261, 322
Cortez, Hernando, 48–9

court culture and patronage, 6, 14–15, 20, 54
Cranach, Lucas the Elder, 14–15, 113–14, 325
Cranach, Lucas the Younger, 14
Cyrene, 133

Daniele da Volterra, 262–4, 267, 273
Dante, 105, 308
Danti, Vincenzo, 217
Democritus, 267–8, 311
Deutsch, Niklaus Manuel, 159–60
Diaconus, Johannes, 147
Diercx, Volcxken, 113, 127–9, 222, 323
Diocletian, Emperor, 146, 171–2, 176, 179–82
disegno concept, 1–4, 7, 55, 61–93, 138, 183, 205, 222, 227, 236, 259, 313, 317, 320–4
Dolce, Lodovico, 87
Donatello, Donato di Niccolo, 11, 65, 122–7, 138
Doni, Antonio Francesco, 15, 70–1, 75, 80, 87–8, 302
Dossi, Battista, 32
Dossi, Dosso, 32
Drechsel, Wolf, 51–2
Dürer, Albrecht, 5, 9, 12–14, 41, 69, 103, 110–13, 118–22, 132, 192–5, 201, 213, 215, 280–1, 294–5, 322

Egmont, Count of, 15
Eisler, Colin, 246
Eligius, St, 146, 154–5, 159
Elsheimer, Adam, 267
Emo, Leonardo, 48
enoblement of artists, 14, 325
Erasmus, 69, 115, 136
Este, Ercole d', 281
Este, Isabella d', 247
Eudoxia, Empress, 150
Eugenius IV, Pope, 105
Eusebius, 150
Eyck, Johann von, 149–50

Facio, Bartolomeo, 118
Falducci, Baldo, 240
Fanti, Sigismondo, 109
Farnese, Alessandro, 35, 48, 122, 240
Ferdinand, Archduke of Austria, 129
Ferrari, Gaudenzio, 69
Ferrero, Bernardo, 46
Ficino, Marsilio, 91, 311
Figino, Girolamo, 44, 243
Filarete, Antonio Averlino, 8, 62–3, 105, 133, 237, 244–6, 265, 282
Finiguerra, Maso, 195–6
Fiorentino, Rosso, 72, 126
Florio, John, 217
Floris, Cornelis, 5, 295–6
Floris, Frans, 3, 5, 14–17, 21, 38–41, 49–50, 114, 117–18, 152–4, 166, 169, 207, 240, 247–9, 253, 261, 295–8, 280, 283, 322–6
Fontana, Annibale, 214–15, 243
Fontana, Lavinia, 129–30, 243
The Four Crowned Martyrs, 146, 170–83, 280, 305, 318; Guild of, 179–80
Francesco di Giorgio, 63–4, 67, 194, 229, 281
Francesco Maria I della Rovere, Duke of Urbino, 32–4, 54, 73, 208
Francesco da Volterra, 17, 250–2, 281, 300–3, 323–4
François I of France, 21, 38, 54, 71–8, 92, 134, 320–1
Freedberg, David, 150
Freedman, Luba, 117
Friedrich der Weise, 64, 280
funerary commemoration, 13–14, 20–1, 28, 45, 105–8, 120, 124, 173–6, 227
Furtenagel, Lucas, 108

Gaddi, Gaetano, 293
Gaddi, Taddeo, 124, 138
Gage, John, 134
Galen, 90, 165

Galeotti, Paolo, 44, 241
Galle, Philips, 131, 259, 271
Gambello, Vittorio, 241–2
Garrard, Mary, 28
Gassel, Lucas, 113
Gaurico, Pomponio, 8–10, 27, 32, 63–5, 72, 80, 85, 93, 120–1
Gebel, Matthes, 107, 110–11, 242
Geldenhauer, Gerard, 158
Gelli, Giovanni Battista, 10
Genga, Francesca, 301, 308
Genga, Girolamo, 32, 301
Gerard de Jode, 23–4
Gertrud von Nonnenwurth, 149
Gheeraerts, Marcus, 217–20, 225, 325
Ghiberti, Lorenzo, 8–11, 62, 64, 87, 122, 133
Ghiselli, Paolo, 244, 265–6
Ghisi, Giorgio, 114–17, 129
Giannicola di Paolo di Giovanni Manni, 178–9
Giorgi, Francesco, 68
Giorgione, 21, 30, 38
Giotto, 10, 21, 82, 84, 103, 105, 118, 124–7, 133, 138
Giovanni Andrea dei Giraldoni, 175–6, 179
Giovio, Paolo, 32, 36, 103, 109–10, 115, 122–5, 129–32, 321, 325
Giraldi, Lilio Gregorio, 208
Giuliano da Sangallo, 126–7
Giusti, Giuseppe, 302
Goltzius, Hendrik, 17, 82, 205–7, 222, 227–9, 262, 322–3
Gonsalvo Ferdinando II of Cordoba, 242
Gonzaga, Federigo, 212, 285
Gonzaga, Lodovico, 281
Gossaert, Jan, 17, 157–8, 161, 165, 179
Grazioli, Bartolomeo, 283–4
Grazioli, Francesco, 283–4
Graziosi, Grazioso, 306–7
Gregory the Great, Pope, 147, 149
Gregory XIII, Pope, 266
Gretser, Jacob, 148
Grimani, Cardinal, 109
Grosshans, Rainuld, 162–3
Guarino da Verona, 237
guild system, 5–7, 16–17, 146, 151–8, 163, 166, 170, 173, 191–2, 207–8, 219, 324

Hagan le Juif, 198
Harrewijn, Jacob, 226, 312
Heere, Lucas de, 5, 13, 120, 129
Heikamp, Detlef, 269
Henri II of France, 28, 38, 73–4, 92, 325–6
Heraclitus, 267, 311
Herlin, Friedrich, 107
Hermann Fiore, Kristina, 308
Hermann of Dalmatia, 198
Hesiod, 236
Hippocrates, 90
Hirschvogel, Augustin, 107, 114, 242
histories of art, 9–13, 16, 37, 103–4, 127, 131, 183, 320
Hoecsster, Joachim, 113
Holanda, Francisco de, 68, 70, 77, 116
Holbein, Hans the Elder, 108, 113, 148
Hollandus, Stephanus, 242
Homer, 267
Hondius, Hendrik, 129, 222–3, 262, 322
Hope, Charles, 125
Horace, 8, 162, 192, 240, 297
Horn, Count of, 15
Huet, Alexandre, 23
Hugh of St Victor, 21
Hughes, Anthony, 7
Hyginus, Caius Julius, 203, 216

ingenium, 194, 217, 317
Isaacsz, Pieter, 260–1

Jacopo da Bergamo, 150, 158
Jacopo da Voragine, 147, 150, 172
Jaffé, David, 263
Janson, Horst, 28, 241
Jerome, St, 151
Joanna, Queen of Anjou, 28

Joanna of Austria, 81, 88, 124, 250
Johannes of Liège, 106–7
Johannes of Troppau, 147, 163
Jongelinck, Nicolaas, 38
Julius II, Pope, 20, 27–9, 32, 124, 170
Juvenal, 218, 312–13

Kemp, Wolfgang, 61, 91
Ketel, Cornelis, 4, 17, 257–62, 267, 271–2, 279, 281, 310–13, 322–4
knighting of artists, 14, 325

Lampadius, 179
Lampsonius, Dominique, 12–15, 120–1, 128–9, 132, 296, 321
Lanciarini, Vincenzo, 285
Landino, Cristoforo, 10, 133, 308
Landucci, Ambrogio, 147
Lautensack, Hans, 113–14
Lautensack, Paul, 113–14
Lemaire, Jean, 118
Leonardo da Vinci, 11–12, 15, 32, 44, 63–4, 67, 71–2, 80, 82, 109–10, 122, 125–7, 130–1, 237, 244–7, 319
Leonbruno, Lorenzo, 237–9, 323
Leoni, Leone, 15, 242–3, 264–7, 280–3, 297–9, 303, 311, 323–4
Liberal Arts, iconography of, 8, 20–1, 27–39, 43–9, 52, 55, 61–6, 72–5, 86, 90–3, 183, 206–7, 218, 220, 226, 236, 280, 286, 297, 317–21, 324
Libergier, Hugues, 107
Linard le Clerc, 23
Lindtmayer, Daniel, 148–9
Lippi, Filippo, 122, 124, 134, 138
Lomazzo, Giovanni Paolo, 9, 12, 17, 44, 47, 68–9, 87, 213–15, 229, 241
Lombard, Lambert, 12–15, 120–1, 295–6
Lorch, Melchior, 112, 120
Lotto, Lorenzo, 246
Lucas, Jan, 163
Lucian of Samosata, 212–13, 237, 239, 286
Lucio, Francesco, 65
Luke, St, 146–71, 183, 201–2, 206–7, 220, 224, 318

McGrath, Elizabeth, 312
Malatesta, Sigismondo, 28, 246
Manetti, Antonio di Tuccio, 10–11, 126
Mannerism, 263, 279, 283–5, 294, 301–2
Mantegna, Andrea, 146, 238, 247, 281
Mantovano, Camillo, 32
Marcellus, 245–6
Marcia, 133
Marcolino da Forli, 268
Marcus Aurelius, Emperor, 298–9
Margaret of Austria, 109, 177, 192
Marten de Vos, 17, 166–7
Martindale, Andrew, 3
Masaccio, 124–7, 138
Matham, Jacob, 4, 227, 229, 323
Matteo de'Pasti, 240
Matthaeus Corvinus, King of Hungary, 245
Maximilian II, Emperor, 69, 219, 303
medallic allegories, 240–4
Medici, Catherine de', 38, 325
Medici, Cosimo de', 43–6, 75–9, 83, 92, 122–3, 299–300, 325
Medici, Francesco de', 81, 134
Medici, Giovanni de', 122
Medici, Giulio de', 124
Medici, Lorenzo de', 124
Medici, Piero de', 245
Medici family and court, 37–8, 43, 122–3, 127, 129, 256, 281, 288, 299, 302, 321, 325
Melanthios, 296–7
Melzi, Francesco, 44
Memling, Hans, 109
Menander, 240
Mercury: imagery of, 192–3, 198–9, 209–30, 239, 267–8,

285–6; as mythological helper of artists, 207–9, 222, 227–9, 236, 280, 319–20, 325; *see also* Children of Mercury
Metsys, Quentin, 163, 280, 282
Meurisse, Pierre, 23
Mezzatesta, Michael, 299
Michelangelo, 11–14, 20–1, 27–9, 36, 43, 45, 68–72, 76, 81, 92, 103–5, 109, 114, 118–32, 137, 192, 195, 217–22, 228, 243, 248–51, 255–6, 260–3, 271, 298–302, 319, 322–5
Michiel, Marcantonio, 109
Miltiades, Pope, 172
Molanus, Johannes, 150, 157, 181–2
Montefeltro, Federico da, Duke, 34, 122
Montorsoli, Giovanni Angelo, 15, 70, 75, 80–1, 124, 138, 168, 325
Mor, Anthonis, 14, 108, 242
Morandini, Francesco, 134
Muller, Hartman Jansz, 202–3
Mylius, Georg, 14

Nicephores, 150
Nicholas of Cusa, 107
Nicoletto da Modena, 134–5

Orange, Prince of, 15
Orsi, Lelio, 279, 281, 292–4, 297, 301
Orsini, Elena, 262–3
Ortelius, Abraham, 218
Ottavio Semino dal Soprani, 46–7
Ovid, 267, 294

Pacioli, Luca, 15, 30, 67–8
Paggi, Giovanni Battista, 7–8
Palladio, Andrea, 9, 48
Pamphilos, 69, 120, 296–7
Panofsky, Erwin, 91–2, 162, 193
Parrhasius, 113, 137–8
Paul, St, 146, 150, 166
Paul III, Pope, 35–6, 77, 122, 124, 127
Pedretti, Carlo, 246
Pedro di Toledo, 36
Pélerin, Jean, 9
Pencz, Georg, 199–201
Penni, Giovanni Francesco, 31
Pepijn, Marten, 166
Perino del Vaga, 126
Perna, Waldkirch, 130
Petrarch, 33, 195
Philandrier, Guillaume, 72, 109, 137
Philibert de L'Orme, 9, 38–9, 73–5, 87, 267, 326
Philip II of Spain, 307–9
Pictor, Georg, 216
Piero della Francesca, 15, 34, 282
Pietro d'Abano, 198–9
Pinturicchio, Bernardino, 280
Pirckheimer, Wilibald, 13–15, 119–20
Pisanello, Antonio, 240–1
Pisano, Andrea, 21
Pisano, Niccolò, 175–6
Pisano, Nicola, 10
Pittori, Fraglia de', 45
Pius IV, Pope, 298
planetary influences, 193–4, 197–9, 229–30
Plato, 91, 197–8, 267
Plato of Tivoli, 197
Pliny the Elder, 10–11, 30, 65, 69, 113, 119–21, 133–7, 149, 192, 253, 288, 296–7, 312
Plutarch, 268
Poggini, Domenico, 76, 80
Poirier, Maurice, 61
Pole, Cardinal, 122
Polo, Marco, 48–9
Pontormo, Jacopo, 75, 124, 138
Porphyrius, 172
portrait medals, 213–14, 240–3
portrait signatures, 104–5, 110
Practical Arts, iconography of, 20–7, 32, 93, 183, 308, 318, 320
Praxiteles, 138
Previtali, Andrea, 22–4
Primaticcio, Francesco, 72, 134
Prinz, Wulfram, 125

Protogenes, 137
Ptolemy, Claudius, 197–8
Ptolemy IV of Egypt, 237
Pythagoras, 67, 253

Quentin, Guillaume, 23

Raffaellino dal Colle, 32–3
Raffaellino da Reggio, 17, 182, 250–3, 260–1, 279, 301–2
Raphael, 11, 14, 21, 34, 38, 67, 72, 103, 106, 114–18, 126–7, 132, 170, 211, 279, 281, 285–6
Raupp, Hans-Joachim, 268
Rauscher, Johann, 14
Rayscop, Adelheid, 149
Refato, Timoteo, 243
Regiomontanus, 281
Remigius, 192
Reni, Guido, 14, 222, 272
Reusner, Nikolaus, 130
Rhenanus, Beatus, 113, 137
Riccio, Andrea, 242
Ridolfi, Carlo, 45–6, 86, 251, 253
Ripa, Cesare, 86, 252, 259
Rivius, Walther, 115
Robbia, Luca della, 122
Robert, King of Anjou, 28
Romano, Giulio, 31, 126, 211–16, 238, 279–87, 291–5, 298, 303, 323, 325
Romerini, Anna, 136
Roriczer, Matthes, 108
Rosenberger, Hans, 243
Rossetti, Biagio, 281
Rossi, Bernardino, 246
Rossi, Stefano Pieri, 76–7, 80
Rubens, Peter Paul, 14, 222, 226–7, 279–81, 286, 311–13, 323–5
Ruberti, Battista de', 194
Rudolph II, Emperor, 6, 52, 219, 281, 303, 324
Ruspagiari, Alfonso, 242

Sachs, Hans, 24–5
Sadeler, Johannes, 311
Saenredam, Jan, 205, 260
saints, artists as, 146–83, 320
Salviati, Francesco, 124, 126, 138
Sangiorgio, Teodoro, 15
Santi, Giovanni, 118, 122
Santi di Tito, 168–9
Saxl, Fritz, 193, 264, 268
Scheurl, Christoph, 111, 113
Schön, Erhard, 111, 113
Schopper, Hartmann, 24–5
Schrevelius, Theodore, 227
Schütz Rautenberg, Gesa, 105
Schwartz, Hans, 110–12, 120
Scipio, 245, 251, 272, 301
Scultori, Diana, 17, 105, 250–2, 281, 300–3
Sebastian, St, 172
Sebastiano del Piombo, 263
self-portraits, 110, 114, 241, 243
Seneca, 268, 312
Serlio, Sebastiano, 9
Sforza, Francesco, 245
Sforza, Lodovico, 67, 196
Signorelli, Luca, 125
Silius Italicus, 34, 245
Simplicius, 175–6, 181
Sixtus IV, Pope, 28
Sophocles, 268
Sparling, Otto, 312
Spranger, Batholomaeus, 4, 14, 17, 215–16, 219–22, 227–9, 253, 261–2, 279–81, 301–4, 322–6
Spranger, Georg, 219–21, 253
Stimmer, Tobias, 130
Strozzi, Roberto, 28
Summers, David, 81

Tenck, Wolfgang, 173–5
'T.G.' of Antwerp, 41, 49–50, 296
Thamar, 133
Theodorus Lector, 150
The Three Graces, 82, 92, 236, 264, 307
Thurneisser zum Thurn, Leonhardt, 199
Tibaldi, Pellegrino, 181
Timanthes, 137
Tintoretto, Jacopo, 15

Titian, 14, 45, 86–7, 92, 104, 109, 114–17, 122, 127, 130–1, 251, 253, 256–7, 324–6
treatises, 8–9
Trezza, Luigi, 292
Tribolo, Niccolò, 122
Turpin, Jehan, 23

Uccello, Paolo, 11, 122–7, 138

Valck, Pieter, 271, 323–4
Valckenaere, Andries de, 178, 280–1, 304–6
Valerius Maximus, 65, 245–6
Valla, Lorenzo, 24, 27
van Aachen, Hans, 14, 260–2, 323, 325
van Boghem, Lodewijk, 176–7
van den Brouck, Willem, 41, 119, 215
van Croes, Jan, 295
van Dalem, Cornelis, 3, 17, 41–2, 118–20, 129, 215–19, 279–80, 283, 294–5, 303, 313, 323–6
van Damme, Jan, 294
van Eyck, Jan, 41, 103, 108, 118–20, 128–31, 215, 280, 294–5
van Gelder, Godefry, 222–4
van Heemskerck, Marten, 17, 107, 160–6, 176, 179, 202–3, 259, 267, 324
van Mander, Karel, 6–7, 13, 15, 128, 162, 168, 215–16, 220, 240, 257, 271–2, 281, 294–5, 303, 310, 320
van Meckenem, Israel, 108, 113
van Oostsanen, Dirck Cornelisz, 108
van Opstal, L., 42
van Scorel, Jan, 107–8
van der Straet, Jan, 3, 17, 46, 82, 92, 122, 131, 256–7, 262
van Veen, Otto, 166, 227, 279
van de Velde, Carl, 39–40, 295–6
van der Weyden, Rogier, 107, 109, 129, 158
Varchi, Benedetto, 14, 72–3
Vasari, Giorgio, 11–14, 17, 21, 28, 30, 34–8, 43–7, 51, 54, 75–7, 81–9, 92–3, 105, 116, 122–9, 132–3, 137–9, 169, 217, 222, 243–4, 247–50, 255, 260–3, 268, 279–81, 283, 286–91, 295–300, 303, 306–13, 320–5
Vecchi, Giovanni de', 48
Veldman, Ilja, 165
Venusti, Antonio Maria, 44
Vergerio, Pier Paolo, 148
Veronica, St, 149
Vesalius, Andreas, 165
Vignola, Giacomo da, 216, 283, 295
Villani, Filippo, 10–11, 27, 105
Vincent de Beauvais, 195
Virgil, 250
Vischer, Hermann, 107, 241, 282
Vitruvius, 62, 65–7, 72–5, 115, 33–7, 209, 211, 230, 290–1
Vivianus, Johannes, 217
von Schlosser, Julius, 8

Warnke, Martin, 6, 14, 20, 325
Weiditz, Hans, 133–4
Wellenberg, Apollonia Lang von, 107
Wiericx, Jan, 3, 127, 222–4, 256
Wimpfeling, Jakob, 113
Wittkower, Margaret and Rudolph, 193

Xenophon, 245, 253

Zacharias, 151
Zaremba, Zirka Filipczak, 153
Zelotti, Giovanni Battista, 47–8
Zeuxis, 103, 118, 127, 137–8, 300
Ziegler, Stephan, 135–7, 280, 290–1, 323–4
Zuccari, Federico, 3–4, 17, 49–51, 76, 88–92, 104, 127, 205, 219–23, 227–9, 237–40, 250–73, 279–81, 285, 301–13, 319, 322–5
Zuccari, Ottaviano, 240, 250, 279, 281, 283, 285
Zuccari, Taddeo, 104, 127, 221–2, 227, 255, 280